British History
for AS Level

1783 - 1850

Derek Peaple & Tony Lancaster
Edited by Steve Eddy

CPL

Causeway Press

Contents

Unit 1 Political developments under Pitt the Younger   5-29

Part 1   **Pitt's rise to power**   **6**
Section 1   Why was Pitt appointed Prime Minister in December 1783?   6
Section 2   How did the 1784 general election consolidate Pitt's power base?   12
Section 3   Why did Pitt stay in power for so long?   13

Part 2   **Pitt and reform**   **17**
Section 1   What were the main features of Pitt's reforms?   17
Section 2   Was Pitt a pragmatist or a principled reformer?   21
Section 3   Did Pitt bring about a 'national revival'?   21

Part 3   **Pitt and reaction**   **25**
Section 1   How successfully did Pitt contain the Jacobin threat?   25
Section 2   Was Pitt an effective wartime leader?   25

Unit 2 The impact of the French Revolution   30-55

Part 1   **The development of popular protest after 1789**   **31**
Section 1   What was radical protest in Britain like before the French Revolution?   31
Section 2   How have different historians interpreted the impact of the French Revolution on British politics and society?   36
Section 3   What impact did the French Revolution make on radical protest in Britain?   37

Part 2   **Government repression and popular loyalism**   **42**
Section 1   What were the main features of Pitt's 'Reign of Terror'?   42
Section 2   How effective were these measures?   44
Section 3   What was the role of popular loyalist organisations in the suppression of radicalism?   44

Part 3   **The 'revolutionary underground' and the radical threat 1795-1815**   **48**
Section 1   What was the 'revolutionary underground'?   48
Section 2   Britain and revolution, 1790-1815   51

Unit 3 Political developments under Lord Liverpool   56-78

Part 1   **'Reactionary Toryism'**   **57**
Section 1   What problems did the Liverpool administration face in its early years?   57
Section 2   Is it appropriate to describe the policies of the Liverpool government between 1812 and 1822 as 'Reactionary Toryism'?   58

Part 2   **Can Liverpool's premiership be divided into two phases?**   **62**
Section 1   Was 1822 a turning point in the Liverpool administration?   62
Section 2   Government reforms in the 1820s   64

Part 3   **Liverpool's achievements and failures**   **71**
Section 1   What did Liverpool achieve?   71
Section 2   What were Liverpool's failings?   73
Section 3   Why did Liverpool manage to stay in power for so long?   74

Unit 4 Protest 1810-31   79-111

Part 1   **Luddism**   **80**

Section 1   What was 'Luddism'?   80
Section 2   Was Luddism ever revolutionary?   80
Section 3   How did the authorities respond to Luddism?   83

Part 2   **Protest and unrest 1815-21**   **86**
Section 1   Why did popular protest revive and intensify after 1815?   86
Section 2   What were the main forms of protest in this period?   93

Part 3   **Unrest 1822-32**   **103**
Section 1   Radicalism in the 1820s   103
Section 2   What was the nature of the 'Swing Riots' of 1830-31?   104

Unit 5   The 'Great' Reform Act   112-38

Part 1   **The unreformed system: 'Old Corruption'**   **113**
Section 1   The unreformed electoral system   113
Section 2   Why did the unreformed system last so long?   114
Section 3   Political parties and reform   115

Part 2   **The development of the reform crisis 1828-32**   **119**
Section 1   Key factors in the development of pressure for change   119
Section 2   The passage of the Reform Act 1831-32   122
Section 3   Interpreting the Whigs' motives   123

Part 3   **Extra-parliamentary pressure and threats of revolution**   **126**
Section 1   Extra-parliamentary protest   126
Section 2   The threat of revolution reconsidered   128

Part 4   **The consequences of the Great Reform Act**   **133**
Section 1   The terms of the Reform Act 1832   133
Section 2   What changes resulted from the passing of the Reform Act?   133
Section 3   Different interpretations of the 1832 Reform Act's impact   134

Unit 6   Chartism   139-77

Part 1   **The origins and nature of Chartism**   **140**
Section 1   What was 'Chartism'?   140
Section 2   What led to the growth of the movement?   142

Part 2   **Tactics, supporters and leaders**   **146**
Section 1   Chartist tactics - the first phase   146
Section 2   Chartist tactics - the later phases   151
Section 3   The role of Feargus O'Connor in the development of Chartism   158
Section 4   Who were the Chartists?   163

Part 3   **Chartism's achievements and failures**   **170**
Section 1   What reasons have historians put forward for Chartism's failure?   170
Section 2   What, if anything, did Chartism achieve?   173

Unit 7   Political developments under Peel   178-213

Part 1   **Peel's early political career and the development of the Conservative Party**   **179**
Section 1   Peel's early career   179
Section 2   Peel and the Conservative Party   185

Part 2	**Peel in power 1841-46**	**192**
Section 1	What were the aims of Peel's second administration?	192
Section 2	Economic policy	194
Section 3	Peel and social reform	197

Part 3	**Peel and the repeal of the Corn Laws**	**200**
Section 1	Peel, Ireland and the Corn Laws	200
Section 2	Why did Peel decide to repeal the Corn Laws?	202
Section 3	Peel's downfall	207
Section 4	Was Peel the 'greatest statesman of his age'?	210

Unit 8 Poverty and reform   214-52

Part 1	**Children and the Factory Acts**	**215**
Section 1	How the 1833-53 Factory Acts affected children and the family	215
Section 2	The importance of child labour in the factory reform movement	219
Section 3	What education was provided for the children of the poor?	221

Part 2	**The unreformed Poor Law**	**224**
Section 1	The origins of the Old Poor Law	224
Section 2	How did the Old Poor Law operate in the early 19th century?	225
Section 3	Why did opposition to the unreformed Poor Law grow after 1815?	226
Section 4	The role of the Poor Law Commission of 1832-34	229

Part 3	**The 1834 Poor Law Amendment Act**	**233**
Section 1	What were the main features of the 'New' Poor Law?	233
Section 2	Opposition to the operation of the New Poor Law	233?
Section 3	How far were the 'principles of 1834' actually put into effect?	237
Section 4	How effectively did the New Poor Law tackle poverty?	238

Part 4	**Public health**	**241**
Section 1	The impact of industrialisation on public health	241
Section 2	The main obstacles to progress on the public health issue	242
Section 3	What were the main pressures for reform?	246

Unit 9 Ireland to the mid 19th century   253-90

Part 1	**What led to the Act of Union?**	**254**
Section 1	Early ties between Britain and Ireland	254
Section 2	Ireland in the 18th century	258

Part 2	**The consequences of the Act of Union**	**264**
Section 1	Did the Act of Union lead to significant change?	264
Section 2	Why was the Roman Catholic Emancipation Act passed in 1829?	267
Section 3	What were the lessons of the campaign?	270
Section 4	The origins of the Repeal movement 1829-35	274
Section 5	The revival of the Repeal campaign after 1840	275

Part 3	**The Great Famine**	**280**
Section 1	What factors led to the Great Famine?	280
Section 2	What measures did the government take to relieve the Famine?	281

Part 4	**The writing of Irish history**	**287**
Section 1	What are the main trends in recent historical research?	287

Index		**291**

Political developments under Pitt the Younger

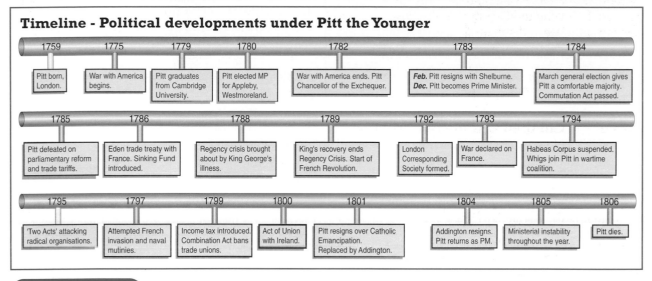

Timeline - Political developments under Pitt the Younger

1759	1775	1779	1780	1782	1783	1784
Pitt born, London.	War with America begins.	Pitt graduates from Cambridge University.	Pitt elected MP for Appleby, Westmoreland.	War with America ends. Pitt Chancellor of the Exchequer.	**Feb.** Pitt resigns with Shelburne. **Dec.** Pitt becomes Prime Minister.	March general election gives Pitt a comfortable majority. Commutation Act passed.

1785	1786	1788	1789	1792	1793	1794
Pitt defeated on parliamentary reform and trade tariffs.	Eden trade treaty with France. Sinking Fund introduced.	Regency crisis brought about by King George's illness.	King's recovery ends Regency Crisis. Start of French Revolution.	London Corresponding Society formed.	War declared on France.	Habeas Corpus suspended. Whigs join Pitt in wartime coalition.

1795	1797	1799	1800	1801	1804	1805	1806
'Two Acts' attacking radical organisations.	Attempted French invasion and naval mutinies.	Income tax introduced. Combination Act bans trade unions.	Act of Union with Ireland.	Pitt resigns over Catholic Emancipation. Replaced by Addington.	Addington resigns. Pitt returns as PM.	Ministerial instability throughout the year.	Pitt dies.

Introduction

On 19 December 1783 William Pitt became Britain's youngest ever Prime Minister at the age of 24. Pitt the Younger ('Younger', because his father, also a William Pitt, had already himself been Prime Minister in the 1750s and 1760s) remained in office for the next 18 years, resigning over the issue of the Act of Union and Catholic Emancipation in 1801, but returning for a further two years in office from 1804 until his death in 1806. Historians have examined the reasons for both his initially unexpected appointment by King George III and his subsequent political longevity. Some have argued that Pitt can be described as a 'lucky beneficiary of circumstance'. However, the question arises, to what extent did Pitt make his own luck? One must consider Pitt's own political skill in dealing with both his opposition and the wide-ranging problems which confronted him as Prime Minister. This assessment feeds into a further debate over the extent to which

his first administration can be divided into two distinct and contrasting 'phases'. The first, from his appointment to the early 1790s, is seen as being characterised by reformism. His financial and administrative reforms, spearheaded, it is argued, a period of 'national revival' after the economic problems and political instability of the later 1770s and early 1780s. The second, from the early 1790s to his resignation in 1801 when Britain was at war with France, is linked to reaction and the so-called 'reign of terror' designed to crush an emerging radical threat. There is less controversy over his premiership of 1804-6, an administration described by one historian as an 'impaired ministry' (Erhman) and characterised by domestic instability and foreign defeat. Despite this 'unworthy coda to what had gone before' (Evans 1999, p.75), historians have identified the notion of a 'Pittite tradition' in 19th-century British politics.

UNIT SUMMARY

Part 1 examines the reasons for Pitt's appointment as Prime Minister, setting it in the context of both the structure of late 18th-century politics and the mounting, shorter-term constitutional crisis of 1782-83. It then goes on to account for Pitt's subsequent retention of power until 1801, focusing on the controversial general election of 1784.

Part 2 analyses the first phase of Pitt's

premiership from 1783 to the early 1790s, considering the extent to which his administrative and financial reforms can be said to have stimulated a 'national revival'.

Part 3 deals with Pitt's response to the radical threat of the 1790s. It concludes with a consideration of his administration of 1804-6 and his longer-term influence on the direction of British politics in the 19th century.

1 Pitt's rise to power

Key issues

1. Why was Pitt appointed Prime Minister in December 1783?

2. How did the 1784 general election consolidate Pitt's power-base?

3. Why did Pitt stay in power for so long?

1.1 Why was Pitt appointed Prime Minister in December 1783?

Explaining Pitt's appointment as Prime Minister requires an understanding of:

- the structure of late 18th-century politics in Britain, and particularly the power of the monarch
- the period of political crisis and instability from 1782 to 1783 following Britain's defeat in the American War of Independence
- George III's support for Pitt as a long-term solution to what he saw as a political threat from a grouping known as the Rockingham Whigs during the period 1782-83
- Pitt's own political skill and luck.

Politics in the late 18th century

In order to understand the reasons for Pitt's appointment as Prime Minister it is necessary to suspend any understanding of the workings of the modern political system in Britain and transport yourself back to a very different constitutional world. In 1783 the political system in Britain differed from that of today in a number of highly significant ways. The most notable contrasts were:

- the power of the monarchy to make key political decisions (see Box 1.1)
- the relative power of the House of Lords compared to the House of Commons
- the role and character of political 'parties'
- the extremely restricted franchise.

Cabinets and prime ministers

In 18th-century British politics, the idea of cabinet solidarity was still in its infancy. Ministers were responsible individually to the King, not to each other, and not to a party. Cabinets existed to deal with the King's business, and their members were appointed with that objective in mind. They were normally not appointed as a group and they did not come to office to carry out an agreed programme of measures. Indeed, much routine business was done by individual ministers conferring with the King in his closet, the small chamber in which he gave audiences to his ministers. In theory, the cabinet could not have a leader or leading ('prime') minister because every minister was appointed by the King and was responsible individually to the King. However, the term was used to describe ministers who found favour with the King and who sat in the Commons as First Lord of the Treasury and 'Minister for the King in the House of Commons'. Such ministers could be called 'prime' ministers in the

---

BOX 1.1 Parliament and the monarchy

Britain in the 18th century was a parliamentary monarchy. The structures, ideologies and conventions of parliamentary government lay in the future. As yet, Parliament did not regard itself as being in competition with the Crown. Indeed, for much of the 18th century it adopted the role of junior partner in politics and administration. Parliament had the right to protest against ministers and their policies. It retained the right to impeach them, and ultimately it could refuse to support their continuation in office, but these were measures to be used only as a last resort. For the most part, it was assumed that Parliament would cooperate with the monarch. Indeed, efficient and stable government depended on this. Standing at the centre of the political stage, the monarch was the dominant figure in the nation's political life. Responsible for policy and for appointments, he initiated executive action and appointed the ministers who would carry it out.

This power to appoint ministers was unquestionably the most important single power enjoyed by the monarch. By appointing the ministers the King could at least influence, and even control, both policy and patronage, although the realities of carrying business through Parliament meant that he needed to exercise his royal powers with care. The King retained the right to appoint to a host of lesser offices, in the royal household, in government departments, in the Church and, most of all, in the armed services. In practice, the monarch's freedom to make such appointments was limited by a number of factors: life grants, reversions, the freehold rights of office and the traditional rights of office-holders to appoint their own assistants. Moreover, the huge increase in routine government business after 1689 made it impossible for the monarch to exercise personal control. It required a cabinet of leading ministers to transmit it and to advise the monarch accordingly. However, the composition of the cabinet and its functions were nowhere laid down. Everything depended on personality and circumstance.

Adapted from O'Gorman 1997.

sense that they carried responsibility for the performance of the government as a whole and defended it in the House of Commons. Their achievements were largely personal ones, not those of a party. Indeed, their constitutional position was very different from the prime ministers of the later 19th century, who owed their position to electoral victory and their leadership of a united cabinet and party.

Achieving a government majority

Eighteenth-century governments, lacking reliable party support, had to create their own majorities. These were composed principally of the solid body of 'placemen' or office-holders, numbering about 180. A secure ministerial majority required leadership and direction of the placemen by the professional politicians, about 100-120 of whom sat in the Commons. These ambitious men competed for, and occupied, the top posts. In pursuing the rewards of office, they provided energy and leadership both to government and opposition. They included the great Whig political families of the 18th century, with their dependants and their retainers, including the Walpoles and Pelhams, the Pitts, Foxes and Devonshires. The remaining 250 or so MPs have usually been described as 'Independents'. In the sense that they were 'backbenchers', mostly uninterested in carving out high-profile political careers, the description is appropriate. But many of them were prepared to use their positions to procure favours for family and friends. Many of them were active in parliamentary committees, advancing the interests of their towns and counties. They were suspicious of political connections and their political behaviour was therefore unpredictable. Most independents prided themselves on the fact that their vote could not be relied upon, and it was for this reason that the leading politicians often directed their powers of persuasion at them.

Ministerial survival depended not only on majorities in the House of Commons but on control of the House of Lords, in which most Cabinet ministers sat. The peers controlled extensive estates, influenced numerous constituencies and filled the senior posts in the armed services, the Church, the civil service and local government. Thus the function of the House of Lords was to incorporate this wealthy and influential class within the political order and to guarantee its continued indispensability.

The American War of Independence

Britain after 1763 was a much wealthier and more self-confident nation, but one facing a new set of problems, notably of imperial government and finance. American affairs were politically charged, not least because of the large number of British emigrants in North America and the close links with the British economy. The discontent and divisions of the 1760s over the determination of George III to pick ministers of his own choice and other issues paled into insignificance beside the collapse of the imperial relationship with America. The determination to make colonies shoulder a portion of their defence burden, despite their lack of representation in Parliament, was crucial to the conflict. So too was the increasing democratisation in American society, a rejection of British authority, concern about British policy in Canada, and the borrowing of British conspiracy theories about the supposed autocratic aims of George III. The increasingly serious social, economic and political crises in the American colonies were crucial. However, the immediate catalyst that turned discontent and conflict into open war was the Boston Tea Party (see Box 1.2). The Americans declared independence in 1776 and the British were driven from most of the Thirteen Colonies in that year. However, they regained New York and continued to hold Canada. The British seizure of Philadelphia was matched by defeat at Saratoga in 1777. After the French entered the war on the revolutionary side in 1778, the British lacked the resources with which to sustain their earlier level of operations in America and were pushed onto the defensive in a world war. Spain joined France in 1779, to be joined at the end of 1780 by the Dutch. Though the Franco-Spanish attempt to invade England in 1779 failed, and the British held on to Gibraltar, India and Jamaica, defeat at Yorktown in 1781 led to British acceptance of American independence and to the fall of the North government.

Political developments and crisis 1782-83
The impact of the American War of Independence in Britain

Pitt's appointment as Prime Minister in December 1783 followed a period of political crisis which developed out of Britain's defeat in the American War of Independence. Following a period of ministerial upheaval during the first years of George III's reign, Lord North's appointment as Prime Minister in 1770 initially appeared to have restored political stability in Britain. However, during the course of the 1770s and early 1780s, North's administration was gradually undermined by problems in Ireland and America.

Political opposition to North increasingly focused on his handling of the developing crisis in America (see Box 1.2), and reached its peak with news of the defeat of British forces at Yorktown in October 1781. Criticism of George III also intensified as he exercised his political patronage to continue to keep the unpopular North in office for a further six months. North's resignation in March 1782 was the trigger for a further period of acute political instability - a situation which had all the characteristics of a major constitutional crisis in the making, and which provided the background to Pitt's initially unlikely emergence as Prime Minister.

George III, the Rockingham Whigs and the Fox-North Coalition

The subsequent political crisis of 1782-83 (see below) can be seen as emerging from a combination of three factors - George III's own character and political views, the ideas of the Rockingham Whig grouping and their criticisms of George III and the formation of the Fox-North coalition government, to which George III was bitterly opposed.

The character and political ideas of George III

For some historians, Pitt's appointment represents the culmination of George III's political interference during the period of instability. Indeed, some historians have regarded George III's behaviour as unconstitutional and it has traditionally been argued that the power and influence of the monarchy further increased after 1760 during the reign of George III. This interpretation is based on two contentions:

- the view that the first Hanoverians - George I and George II - 'lost' elements of royal power between 1714 and 1760 which George III consciously set out to regain
- an assessment of George III's character which emphasises personal ambition and a tendency towards authoritarianism.

George III was, Evans has argued, 'determined to reassert the powers of the monarchy and, in doing so, to reduce those of the great Whig landowners who had effectively ruled Britain for two

---

BOX 1.2 The Boston Tea Party

After the controversy caused by the Stamp Act of 1765, the Revenue Act of 1767 drawn up by Charles Townshend imposed American customs duties on a variety of goods including tea, which was brought from India by the East India Company. It led to a serious deterioration in relations between the British government and its American critics. The latter responded with a trade boycott and action against customs officials, leading the British ministry to send troops to Boston in 1768. In 1769 the government decided to abandon all the Townshend duties save that on tea, whose retention was seen as a necessary demonstration that it would not yield to colonial agitation. Relations remained poor, with serious constitutional disputes of varied cause in a number of colonies, particular tension in Massachusetts and a growing hostility towards parliamentary claims to authority over American affairs. The Boston Tea Party of 16 December 1773 arose from American fears that the authorities would seize boycotted tea and force its sale. About 60 men boarded three ships in Boston Harbour and dumped the contents of 342 chests of tea into the sea. This forced the government to confront the growing problems of law and order and the maintenance of authority. They believed these arose from the actions of a small number in America, rather than from widespread disaffection, and thus mistakenly hoped that action against Massachusetts, the so-called Coercive or Intolerable Acts of early 1774, would lead to the restoration of order. The Boston Port Act was designed to protect trade and

American rebels, disguised as Native Americans, dump imported tea into the sea.

customs officials from harassment, the Administration of Justice and Quartering Acts to make it easier to enforce order. These measures were criticised by the opposition in Britain as oppressive, but passed by overwhelming majorities. Parliamentary sovereignty over the Thirteen Colonies was generally supported and there was widespread backing for a policy of firmness. More troops were sent to Massachusetts. Fighting broke out near Boston in April 1775 as the result of the British government's determination to secure its authority, and the willingness of sufficient Americans to resist it.

Adapted from Black 1993.

generations' (Evans 1984, p.4).

The recent work of historians such as Derry and Christie has challenged both the notion of the decline and recovery of royal power and George III's supposed desire to subvert the constitution. However, it is still important to set Pitt's appointment in the context of George III's character, ideas and aims. Most historians would therefore now reject the argument that the King set out to establish a 'new absolutism', and instead stress his 'resilience and resourcefulness' (Derry 1990, p.16) in dealing with the constitutional crisis of 1782-83. It is in these aspects of George III's character and role that, according to historians such as Derry, the genesis of Pitt's appointment is to be found. In understanding this appointment, it is certainly crucial to grasp the extent of George III's opposition to the Fox-North Coalition government of March-December 1783, and the Rockingham Whig group which constituted the majority of its parliamentary support. Speaking of the Fox-North Coalition, the historian Eric Evans states:

'[It] outraged the King on at least three grounds. First, he was by no means convinced that Shelburne had to go; in his view, the Prime Minister could have fought on to test the durability of his new grouping. Second, he hated Fox and most of his supporters with a passion. Third, he had reposed absolute faith in North as Prime Minister for almost 12 years. A combination of interests between Foxites and Northites he thought of as virtual treason. It was, to him, proof of the view he had held when he came to the throne in 1760: that established politicians were motivated by greed and personal ambition, rather than by any desire to provide good government.' (Evans 1999, p.7)

The Rockingham Whigs

Opposition to George III was strongest amongst the political grouping known as the Rockingham Whigs. These were initially the 100 or so followers of the Marquess of Rockingham, who first became Prime Minister in 1765. This group believed that they represented the spirit and tradition of the Glorious Revolution and that they were the natural defenders of the constitution against absolutism and potential tyranny. They believed that, whilst the monarch was entitled to respect, government should be in the hands of responsible ministers rather than royal favourites and they remained suspicious of what they saw as the potentially malevolent influence of the Crown. In the late 1760s and early 1770s, this set of beliefs was increasingly refined by the Whig politician and writer Edmund Burke into a specific critique of George III's reign. This focused in particular on the way in which a new and

---

BOX 1.3 The character and political ideas of George III - historians' views

In 1760, after a reign lasting 33 years, George II died. He was succeeded in October by his grandson, a stubborn and rather dull 21-year-old, who had inherited but not absorbed his father's prejudices. The first Hanoverian king to consider himself British, he had declared in 1761: 'Born and educated in this country, I glory in the name of Britain.' Contrary to his historical reputation, he was neither stupid nor ill educated, but it is generally agreed that he was bluntly honest, courageous, tactless, often inept, and, in his early years as King, disastrously advised. It is now accepted that he was not, at least until the last few years of his life, insane. Rather, he suffered from porphyria, a genetic illness which on a number of occasions racked his body, and later disturbed his mind. This illness can have a devastating effect on the nervous system, causing great physical suffering and, in the most severe stages, producing delirium and a loss of self-awareness and self-control.

George III had looked on his grandfather as a 'king in chains', and on the ministers who surrounded him as evil men who had 'captured' the King in order to exploit his authority for their own gain. Well grounded in the British system of government, George believed that it

George III

represented the summit of human political wisdom. But he saw it menaced on every side by human treachery, and he was terrified by his responsibility for making it work and preserving it. His mistrust and contempt for all politicians was hardly the best foundation for a harmonious reign.

His inexperience and lack of judgement were obvious early on in his reign, but he quickly came to grasp the realities of political life. By 1770 he was one of the shrewdest politicians in Britain, using his substantial political influence in zealous defence of royal authority. He also remained opposed to the very idea of political parties, which he regarded as a threat to his own influence. In particular, he believed that the Whigs wanted to hack away at the royal prerogative, and he was determined to resist. He also hoped to balance and neutralise the impact of party. However, he generally avoided direct interference in policy-making, placing great store on having people he trusted in both his court and his cabinet. Once they were there, he relied on their judgement.

Adapted from Reilly 1978, Christie 1982, Derry 1990, and Evans 1999.

BOX 1.4 Charles James Fox - a historian's view

Born in January 1749, Charles James Fox was the younger son of Henry Fox, Lord Holland, who had made a fortune from his dealings as Paymaster of the Forces between 1757 and 1765. As a child, Charles was grossly spoilt, and when he was 14 he was taken to Paris, where his father is said to have acted as his 'pimp and bookmaker'. A year later he went up to Hertford College, Oxford, where he managed to combine serious study with heavy gambling and the satisfaction of his huge appetites. He had been elected, in his absence, Member of Parliament for Midhurst in Sussex, and took his seat in November 1768 while only 19. On his return from his travels in France and Italy, he made his appearance as a man of fashion, in red-heeled shoes and with his hair powdered blue. Later he wore the blue coat and buff waistcoat worn by American troops in the revolutionary war, as did many of his followers. Fox's private life was squalidly public. He was debauched and lazy, drinking, gambling and whoring all night and then stumbling, hung over and unshaven into the House of Commons to make a brilliant speech of two hours or more. George III loathed him, not only for his violent attacks on the royal prerogative but also because he held him responsible for the bad behaviour of the Prince of Wales. Fox's hatred of Pitt sprang from the mistaken belief that it was Pitt who had robbed him of the highest office. In reality, at no time after 1783 would George III have accepted Fox as his Chief Minister.

James Gillray's satirical view of Fox – with his mistress

Fox possessed all the qualities of a great politician, and he was one of the greatest parliamentarians of his century, but he lacked self-discipline. His natural spontaneity and lack of moderation led him to take up battle positions that he later found he had to abandon. His early speeches declaring the inviolability of the constitution later contrasted oddly with his arguments for the sacrosanctity of Parliament, and his disastrous defence of the hereditary rights of the Prince of Wales. Fox's disorderly genius was the complete opposite of Pitt's icy control.

Adapted from Reilly 1978.

---

unconstitutional system of government based on the secret influence and interference of the Crown had developed since the early 1760s. On Rockingham's death in July 1782, leadership of the group passed to Charles James Fox (see Box 1.4). The antipathy between the Rockingham group and George III was therefore a major catalyst for the political instability that developed after North's resignation in March 1782. The King was initially resentful at having to turn to Rockingham himself on North's resignation, and this anger was intensified a year later with the formation of the Fox-North Coalition when the formerly trusted North entered into an alliance with Rockingham's political heir, Charles James Fox.

The development of the political crisis 1782-83

The political crisis of 1782-83 developed in three phases:

1. An initial period of ministerial instability from March 1782 to February 1783 when the Rockingham and Shelburne administrations followed each other in rapid succession.
2. An interim period between March and November 1783 when George III schemed against the Fox-North coalition government, which he both hated and regarded as a threat to his powers as monarch.
3. The final period of direct constitutional confrontation from November to December 1783 when George III controversially dismissed the Fox-North coalition following Fox's India Bill and replaced it with an administration headed by Pitt as Prime Minister.

The details of the development of the crisis are as follows.

March 1782 Resignation of Lord North as Prime Minister. The administration was replaced by a coalition of anti-North Whigs led by the Marquess of

Rockingham as Prime Minister, with the Earl of Shelburne as Home Secretary and Charles James Fox as Foreign Secretary. The ministry was internally divided due to rivalries between Fox and Shelburne and disliked by George III because of its support for administrative reforms which would have reduced the powers of royal patronage.

July 1782 Rockingham's death led to the end of the administration. Shelburne became Prime Minister, triggering Fox's resignation. Pitt was appointed Chancellor of the Exchequer in the new administration. The administration was largely concerned with peace-making with the American colonies and unsuccessful attempts at cost-cutting administrative reforms. In the meantime, Fox assumed the leadership of the Rockingham group of reformist Whigs in Parliament following Rockingham's death.

Early 1783 Former political opponents Fox and North began scheming together to bring the Shelburne administration down through an alliance of their supporters in Parliament.

24 February 1783 Shelburne resigned as Prime Minister following two motions criticising the administration brought by Fox and North.

March 1783 Formation of Fox-North coalition government, nominally headed by the Duke of Portland as Prime Minister. This was very reluctantly accepted by George III after a five-week delay due to a combination of his intense dislike of Fox and feeling of betrayal by the formerly trusted North. The formation of the Fox-North Coalition was at the centre of the short-term political crisis leading to Pitt's appointment the following December.

March-November 1783 George III schemed against the Fox-North Coalition, which he saw as a threat to royal power, exerting pressure and influence in the House of Lords to shape the pattern of voting.

November-December 1783 Fox introduced his India Bill designed to reform the government of India by transferring power from the East India Company to a Board of Commissioners in London. As the seven proposed commissioners were all Fox supporters, this was used by George III as the opportunity to dismiss the Fox-North Coalition on the basis that they were undermining the constitution through an

BOX 1.5 Pitt's background and character - a historian's view

Pitt was the youngest Prime Minister in British history. He was also one of the few to die in office. While his great political opponent Fox was fat, emotional and good with people, Pitt was lean, disciplined and good at figures. Pitt was Prime Minister for longer than anyone else except Sir Robert Walpole, and his period of office spanned what were perhaps the two most significant changes of modern history – the French Revolution and the Industrial Revolution. He exercised a dominance over both Parliament and his monarch which very few Prime Ministers have equalled. Pitt may also be considered as the first leader of the modern Conservative Party – although he would have disclaimed this title.

No major leader was so steeped in politics from his earliest years. His father, 'Pitt the Elder', also a William, was Prime Minister when young William was born on 28 May 1759. Pitt's mother was a member of an even more established Whig family, the Grenvilles. His uncle, George Grenville, was Prime Minister from 1763 to 1765. Pitt possessed extraordinary intellectual gifts. At the age of 7, on hearing that his father had been made the Earl of Chatham, he announced that 'he was glad he was not the eldest son, but that he could serve the country in the House of

William Pitt

Commons like his papa'. He was educated at home before going to Cambridge University at the age of 14.

Pitt failed to win the parliamentary seat of Cambridge University in 1779 but did not have to wait long to enter Parliament. A Cambridge friend, the Marquess of Granby, was politically linked to Sir James Lowther, who controlled a number of parliamentary boroughs. He put one of them, Appleby in Westmoreland, at the disposal of the younger Pitt, all expenses paid. Pitt was nominated in November 1780, 'elected' the following month and took his seat in the Commons in January 1781. He was just short of 22 years old. Such rapid progress was not uncommon in the 18th century. 'Rotten' boroughs were a recognised route for able, well-connected young politicians to reach Parliament. What was unusual was Pitt's rapid progress once in Parliament. In less than two years he was Chancellor of the Exchequer, and within three years, Prime Minister. This was owing to two factors: his own abilities and the political instability resulting from Britain's war with America.

Adapted from Evans 1999.

unscrupulous attempt to increase their power and influence. His actions in doing so were at the time seen as very controversial and have subsequently been interpreted by some historians as constitutionally questionable. When the bill, having passed through the Commons, reached the Lords, the King controversially intervened in the process - probably unofficially advised by Pitt. Earl Temple, Pitt's cousin, was given a letter from the King which he was instructed to show to any members of the House of Lords considering supporting Fox's Bill in the lead-up to its consideration. This letter made it clear that any lord voting for the bill would be regarded as an enemy of the King, and therefore was a means of coercing them into opposition to the government.

17 December 1783 The pressure applied on the Lords by the King's actions worked as intended. The government was defeated for a second time in the Lords on the India Bill and this was used by George III as the pretext for the Coalition's dismissal on the dubious grounds that this indicated that it had lost public confidence.

19 December 1783 George III invited Pitt to become Prime Minister and form a new administration. As the historian Eric Evans puts it, 'the younger Pitt's promotion was, therefore, a clear exercise of independent royal power' (Evans 1985, p.6). Fox and his supporters certainly attacked George III's actions as being unconstitutional and compared his abuse of power to that of Charles I.

1.2 How did the 1784 general election consolidate Pitt's power base?

Pitt's initial position

Pitt's new government did not have a majority in the House of Commons. Calculations suggest that Pitt could rely on only 149 votes and he was opposed by a grouping of ex-ministers and their supporters, led by Fox and North, numbering about 230 in total. Even allowing for the support of some independent MPs, this probably left Pitt about 60 short of a majority on his assumption of office. Moreover, his position in the Commons also appeared to be weakened by the fact that he was the only member of his cabinet to sit in the lower house and that he deliberately chose not to include 'heavyweights' (Evans 1999, p.12) such as Shelburne and Jenkinson in the government. In light of the apparent weaknesses of Pitt's position and the contrasting strength of their own, the opposition was convinced that they could quickly defeat Pitt's government and that it would be no more than a short-lived stopgap - a view most famously expressed by Frances Anne Crewe, the wife of John Crewe, one of the leading

Rockingham Whigs, who described it as 'mince pie administration', to be devoured by the opposition and therefore gone by the end of the Christmas holidays. That Fox and his supporters were unable to 'devour' Pitt, and that George was not in fact forced to turn back to the coalition can be explained by two factors: Pitt's own political skill and the powers still available to the Crown. These are both demonstrated in the lead-up to the election of March 1784. This was a tactical manoeuvre which crushed the opposition and which was to consolidate Pitt's hold on power for the next 17 years. It can therefore be seen as the sequel to the events of November-December 1783 which led to Pitt's appointment.

Pitt's strategy

Pitt rapidly and consciously set out to secure his position as Prime Minister. His initial strategy involved presenting himself positively both inside and outside of Parliament.

Raising support within the Commons

First, Pitt wanted to delay an immediate election, which the King appeared to favour, in order to give himself time to tackle the opposition head-on in the House of Commons. This he believed would demonstrate his ability to independent MPs who might go on to support him on a longer-term basis as a non-partisan, 'national' leader of promise, and at the same time sow seeds of division and doubt within the coalition: a general election could then be held in more favourable circumstances. The historian Derry writes:

'Pitt did not want an immediate general election...Pitt was determined to face his critics in the Commons, and events showed that his judgement was sound. It needed considerable courage and immense nerve to defy the coalitionists in the Commons. Pitt calculated that if he could impress the House he would set in train a shift of opinion away from the opposition and towards himself. This would mean that when the general election took place the morale of the opposition would already be low. He knew that many of North's followers had been reconciled to the coalition with Fox only because it held out the prospect of a stable ministry. Now that this expectation had been dashed, many Northites were less than happy to continue the alliance with Fox, especially when this had earned the implacable disapprobation [hardened disapproval] of the King.' (Derry 1990, p.49)

Moreover, the fact that Pitt's government did not contain any of those leading politicians so tainted in the eyes of the independents by the rather tawdry events of the previous 18 months, and that he did appear so impressively alone in the Commons, appeared to accelerate his acceptance. Evans, for instance, suggests:

> 'Unfortunately for Fox, what he saw as weaknesses, Pitt rapidly turned to strengths. The absence of Shelburne strongly implied that Pitt intended to be his own man, while the exclusion of Jenkinson made the point to independent MPs that the new Prime Minister was no royal cipher...his authority in the face of adversity was certainly impressive.'

During the first months of 1784, Pitt's strategy succeeded in reducing the opposition's majority so that by March it was in single figures. As Evans concludes, 'for Fox...it was clear that the tide was flowing uncontrollably against him' (Evans 1999, p.13).

Raising support outside the Commons

However, Pitt's work in the Commons had not taken place in isolation. The second strand of Pitt's strategy was, as Derry goes on to explain, based on an appeal to opinion outside the House of Commons:

> 'If he could show that his command of financial issues was assured, that he was willing to cultivate key interests rather than offend them, and that he was nevertheless interested in certain types of reform, he would rally both conservative and reformist support, both of which had been antagonised by the coalition.' (Derry 1990, p.50)

The results of the 1784 election (see below), suggest that this strand of his strategy was also successful. Although the ability of the Crown to manage elections was still apparent, Pitt appears to have been genuinely popular in many of the larger constituencies where 'it was almost impossible to bribe one's way to victory' (Evans 1999, p.14).

The election

On 2 March 1784, Pitt asked the King to dissolve Parliament, believing that the time was now right for a general election which would cement his hold on power, and George willingly agreed. It is in relation to the tactical timing and organisation of the election that the importance of the royal powers in helping to secure Pitt's position can clearly be seen. The Septennial Act of 1716 had limited the life of a parliament to a maximum of seven years. Since then, the constitutional convention had been that they should run as close as possible to this maximum, with only one since 1715 lasting less than five and a half years (a general election being automatically called on the death of George I in 1727). The existing Parliament, having assembled in 1780, was less than three and a half years old in March 1784. By breaking with what had become established practice and dissolving it so early, George was blatantly exercising his powers in such a way as to benefit Pitt and disadvantage Fox. This tactical ploy certainly worked as intended. Pitt's performance in

his first months in office and his support in larger constituencies such as Middlesex and Yorkshire suggest that he was genuinely regarded as a 'new broom', whilst at the same time the King's electoral agents went to work in smaller constituencies to ensure his victory by offering sinecures (positions requiring little or no work but conferring profit or honour) in return for a pledge of support for the government. The result was a crushing blow for the opposition, with about 160 of Fox's supporters going down to defeat. (These were the so-called 'Fox's martyrs' because their loyalty to their leader cost them their seats.) This gave Pitt the support of somewhere in the region of 31 MPs - certainly a sufficient majority for effective government.

The 1784 election therefore also confirms the recurrent theme in Pitt's appointment and subsequent retention of power (see Section 1.3 below): the combination of Pitt's own skills in winning over parliamentary and popular opinion and the Crown's powers of political influence and electoral management.

1.3 Why did Pitt stay in power for so long?

The reasons for Pitt's subsequent political longevity - he was to remain Prime Minister for all but three years of the rest of his life - has been debated by historians. There are of course obvious connections with the factors that explain his initial rise to power, in particular the significance of the support of the King and his own political acumen. Three major factors can be identified in the interpretations offered by historians for the length of Pitt's hold on power.

1. Pitt was a 'lucky beneficiary of circumstance' in that he had the support of George III and many independent MPs and could increasingly exploit both the underlying strength of a growing industrial economy in the 1780s and threat of revolution in the 1790s.
2. Pitt was an astute and skilful politician in his own right.
3. Pitt established a new 'Tory' Party in 1794 as the basis for support.

Factor 1: Pitt was a 'lucky beneficiary of circumstance'

There are four strands to the argument that Pitt was simply the right politician in the right place at the right time:

1. The King wanted him to be Prime Minister and, in the context of late 18th-century politics, this alone was sufficient to guarantee Pitt's political longevity. George III saw Pitt as an antidote to the threat he believed to be posed by Fox and Rockingham Whigs and he was therefore prepared to give him a virtually free hand to get

on with the job. Indeed it is significant in this respect that Pitt's resignation in 1801 followed the one issue over which the two men had disagreed in principle during Pitt's premiership - that of Catholic Emancipation. It is this factor and from this perspective - looking backwards from Pitt's resignation to explain the reasons for his longevity - that many historians have seen the relationship between Pitt and George III (see Activity 1.1) as being so crucial to the former's survival: had the two not disagreed on this issue, Pitt would have stayed in power beyond 1801.

2. Pitt - a fresh political face apparently untarnished by any long-term connection with previous administrations, corruption or failures - appealed to many independent MPs who had grown increasingly tired of the instability and in-fighting which had characterised political life in Britain over the previous two years. As the historian Eric Evans puts it, 'the independent country gentlemen were willing to throw their support behind any minister who represented a clean break with the constitutional affronts of 1782-83' (Evans 1996, p.29).

3. It is suggested that Pitt was increasingly able to build a reputation as an effective financial reformer on the back of the underlying, if initially masked, strength of the British economy. Pitt was, in other words, arguably the first Prime Minister of the industrial age and, as Evans goes on to point out, 'the young minister therefore came into a more powerful inheritance than was apparent in December 1783.' (Evans 1996, p.29)

4. Finally the circumstances of the 1790s, when the fears of revolution dominated political life in Britain, further undermined Fox's credibility as an alternative to Pitt as Prime Minister.

Factor 2: Pitt was an astute and skilful politician in his own right

Most historians now reject the view that Pitt's political longevity can be explained exclusively in terms of luck and, in particular, his relationship with George III. Whilst acknowledging the obvious importance of this relationship, they point out that this must be seen in combination with his own political acumen. Eric Evans writes of Pitt:

'Almost the lucky beneficiary...but not quite. Pitt's gifts exactly matched the needs of the first decade of his premiership. His amazingly - and to opponents alarmingly - professional grasp of the complex administrative and financial issues of the day enabled him to harness the energy and dynamism of the British economy...That same grasp of detail, allied to clear-headed, even glacial, delivery made him a formidable

opponent in debate.' (Evans 1996, p.30)

There is much evidence for an interpretation of Pitt's political longevity which stresses his own skill and ability to adapt to changing circumstances. For example:

- His actions during his first three months in office when a wide cross-section of MPs were won over by his ability to 'command events, to defy criticism and to outwit his opponents' (Derry 1990, p.50).

- His skills in holding onto the support of the Commons, particularly when responding to defeats on issues to which he was personally committed. The historian Erhman has argued that defeats on matters such as parliamentary reform and economic union with Ireland (see Section 2.2) 'are significant not because they threatened his position, but rather because they suggested how he might buttress his strengths' (Ehrman 1969, p.236). Pitt, in other words, learnt from his mistakes and had the political judgement to identify what was crucial to his long-term strategy and what could be sacrificed in order to secure political survival. As Derry puts it, 'when defeated...he took stock of the situation, tried to see where his judgement had faltered, and sought to regain his political balance as quickly as possible. He recognised that he had to attune everything to the mind of the House of Commons, even though he was fully conscious of the limited perception of the typical backbencher' (Derry 1990, p.56). However, this has led some historians to argue that his political survival was a 'negative achievement': Pitt stayed in power for so long because he dropped controversial and potentially damaging measures.

- His financial measures (see Section 2.1 below), which directly appealed to politicians and a public who were conscious of the need for a policy of reconstruction and regeneration after the traumatic experiences of the American War. Measures such as the Sinking Fund, gradual diminution of sinecure offices, consolidation of customs duties and the Commutation Act and development of bonded warehouses had varying degrees of success, but were broadly supported by MPs as being appropriate to the needs of the moment. These measures therefore helped to consolidate and strengthen his hold on power. Many of these measures, which stimulated economic recovery and overseas trade, were particularly popular with the increasingly influential merchant lobby.

- His astute handling of the Regency Crisis of 1788-89, when George III was incapacitated by an attack of 'madness' (see Box 1.3 above). The call from Fox and his supporters for an unrestricted Regency was countered by a bill closely restricting the powers of the Regent. This enabled Pitt to further discredit the opposition and label them as hypocrites - critical of Pitt for relying on George III but attempting to manufacture their own route to power through the elevation of the Prince of Wales, with whom they had close connections. Although 'lucky' in so far as the King did rapidly recover from the attack of porphyria, Pitt exploited the situation to pose as a champion of constitutional tradition.
- His pragmatic and flexible response to the threat of revolution during the so-called 'Reign of Terror' in the 1790s (see also Section 3.1 below).

Factor 3: Pitt established a new Tory Party in 1794 as the basis for support

Most historians reject the view that Pitt's political longevity was based on the support of a 'party' - certainly in the modern sense of a cohesive grouping united around a common set of policies. Indeed, a key element of the so-called 'Pittite tradition' (see Activity 1.3) is his reputation as a 'national' leader above party politics. Eric Evans argues:

'[Pitt] professed a distaste for party [and] did less than many 18th-century prime ministers to build up a personal following among MPs. He preferred to rely on royal support, his own mastery of administrative detail which enabled him to control most debates and, increasingly, on financial achievements. These sufficed to keep the independents happy' (Evans 1985, p.11). However, there has been a great deal of debate between historians over whether the specific political realignment which occurred in 1794 marked the birth of a new Tory Party, and the extent to which this was a conscious action by Pitt to bolster his power and position. By 1794 the strains associated with the domestic impact of the French Revolution and war with France had stretched the opposition to breaking point. Fox became increasingly isolated and in July 1794 his former ally, the Duke of Portland, joined the Cabinet as Home Secretary in a coalition with Pitt. Four other leading Whigs also joined Pitt at this point. The Prime Minister was able to benefit from the disintegration of the opposition and from this point used conservative popular sentiment to launch an assault on domestic radicalism. However, most historians now agree that the coalition is probably best seen as no more than an expedient wartime government. In other words, it reflected Pitt's desire for national unity rather than any change in his political ideology.

MAIN POINTS - Part 1

- Britain in the 18th century was a parliamentary monarchy, with the King at the centre of politics. Parliament usually cooperated with the King.
- The King influenced policy by his power to appoint ministers.
- Political parties were in their infancy, most MPs were independents, and Cabinet ministers were responsible to the King.
- The House of Lords had a great deal of influence.
- American resentment towards British taxes, and other grievances, led to the War of Independence, sparked by the Boston Tea Party.
- North was criticised over the war but was kept in power by George III, resigning only in 1782. This led to the Fox-North coalition government, backed by the Rockingham Whigs but resented by the King.
- Pitt came to power in the wake of the 1782-83 crisis. George III used his influence to defeat Fox's India Bill, then took the defeat as an excuse to dismiss the Coalition. He then invited Pitt to form a government.
- Pitt initially had no majority in the Commons and was opposed by supporters of Fox and North. He resolved to delay an election and win the House round by his oratory. The King helped him by dissolving Parliament at a time which favoured Pitt, and by offering sinecures in return for supporting Pitt. The 1784 election was a victory for Pitt.
- Historians explain Pitt's hold on power in three main ways: (1) he was 'lucky', having the support of George III and of indpendent MPs wanting a break with the recent past, and benefiting from a growing economy; (2) he was a skilful politician; (3) he established a new 'Tory' Party as the basis for support.
- Pitt was skilful in his oratory and handling of the Commons, fairly successful with economic measures such as the Sinking Fund and taxation, handled the Regency Crisis well, and took a pragmatic approach to the threat of revolution.
- Most historians agree that Pitt did not form a Tory Party in the modern sense. However, it has been suggested that the modern Conservative Party had its beginnings with his use of conservative popular sentiment to counter radicalism.

Activity 1.1 Pitt and George III

ITEM 1 A contemporary cartoon

This 1783 Gillray cartoon is entitled 'A connoisseur examining'. It shows King George III examining a cameo portrait of Oliver Cromwell, whom some regard as having ruled England virtually as a dictator in the 1650s.

ITEM 2 A historian's view (i)

At first, Pitt owed much to George III. Quite apart from the King's electoral influence, the royal household officers formed the core of a government party in the Lords which usually outvoted the opposition by about two to one. Pitt's majority was also strengthened by the King's willingness to create new peers, an advantage which he had denied the Rockinghams in 1783. These new peers were mostly strong government supporters, landowners becoming steadily wealthier with rising agricultural prosperity. Many also had control of rotten boroughs and could therefore consolidate Pitt's position in the Lords and Commons alike. The King's ability to grant honours enabled Pitt to reward service and demand loyalty. Relations between Pitt and the King were correct and reserved. The minutes of Cabinet meetings reached the King punctually and he responded courteously, seldom proposing new initiatives or questioning decisions. By the mid-1780s, George III was a dutiful and competent king, albeit a limited and obstinate one. Pitt knew on what matters the King was not to be challenged and usually managed to avoid compromising either his policies or his principles by doing so. For his part, the King recognised a good ministry when he saw it and was wise enough not to interfere. He saw in Pitt a long-term salvation from the constitutional ambitions of the Rockinghams. As for Pitt, he knew well enough that he still needed royal support and was grateful that securing it did not significantly restrict his actions. The occasional conflicts between the two men were more over personality than policy. It is ironic that Pitt's resignation in 1801 was on one of the few issues of principle - the religious question in Ireland - on which the two disagreed.

Adapted from Evans 1996.

ITEM 3 A historian's view (ii)

His rise to power was an astonishing feat. He had persuaded powerful and widely differing political forces to associate his name with the achievement of their hopes or the allaying of their fears. For the King, he meant release from dependence on Fox and North; for the financial Establishment, the right to enjoy and dispose their own patronage; for the reformers, a more just electoral system. All these were in suspense until they could be sure of his survival. With the King's help he recreated the House of Lords, swamping the old Whig aristocracy under a flood of new peerages, many of which went to the nouveaux riches, to men of great wealth, connected with the City, upon whose support Pitt increasing relied.

Adapted from Plumb 1963.

ITEM 4 A historian's view (iii)

Unity of purpose between monarch and ministers characterised politics after the formation of the Pitt ministry, and played an important role in stabilising government. There were of course difficulties between Pitt and George III. The King disapproved of Pitt's support for parliamentary reform in 1785, even though the reform proposed was hardly radical and would not have led to any major increase in the size of the electorate or the House of Commons. However, George III was opposed to constitutional change. The proposed reforms were defeated by 248 to 174 on 18 April 1785. Pitt was careful not to pursue this divisive issue after its defeat, and this caution helped to align his ministry with conservative opinion and to alienate political and religious reformers.

Adapted from Seldon 1996.

ITEM 5 George III's view

I had flattered myself that, on the strong assurance I gave Mr Pitt of keeping perfectly silent on the subject [of Catholic Emancipation] whereon we entirely differ, provided on his part he kept off any **disquisition** on it for the present...we both understood our present line of conduct; but as I unfortunately find Mr Pitt does not draw the same conclusion, I must come to an unpleasant conclusion, as it will deprive me of his political service, of acquainting him that, rather than forgo what I look on as my duty, I will without unnecessary delay attempt to make **the most creditable arrangement**.

Glossary

- **disquisition** - lengthy statement
- **the most creditable arrangement** - the best possible arrangements for a new government

A note from George III written on 5 February 1801 regarding the issue of Catholic Emancipation and Pitt's resignation.

ITEM 6 George III's illness and the Regency Crisis

This contemporary cartoon alludes to the breakdown of George III's health in 1788 and the ensuing Regency Crisis. The debauched Prince Regent looks forward to becoming King. A shocked priest has been reading a prayer for the King's health. The picture on the wall is of 'The Prodigal Son'.

Questions

1. Study Item 1. In what ways might this interpretation of the character and political aims of George III explain the nature of his relationship with Pitt?
2. Study Items 2 and 3. Explain in your own words (a) the different ways in which George III supported Pitt in power and (b) the reasons for this support.
3. Study Items 4 and 5. Explain why the issue identified in Item 4 did not lead to a breakdown in the relationship between Pitt and George III, whereas that in Item 5 did.
4. Explain how the situation shown in Item 6 posed a threat to Pitt and how he tackled it.
5. In view of the evidence provided by Items 1-6 and your own knowledge, how important is the relationship between George III and Pitt in explaining why Pitt stayed in power for so long? Refer to Items 1-6 in your answer.

2 Pitt and reform

Key issues

1. What were the main features of Pitt's financial and administrative reforms?
2. Was Pitt a pragmatist or a principled reformer?
3. Did Pitt bring about a 'national revival'?

2.1 What were the main features of Pitt's reforms?

Most analyses of Pitt's first administration split the period 1783-1801 into two distinct phases, characterised by his contrasting priorities and policies:

- the period 1783 to the early 1790s, which focused on cautious financial and administrative reforms designed to stimulate what has been described as a 'national revival' following the economic problems of the 1770s and early 1780s, and
- the early 1790s to his resignation in 1801, which was dominated by his response to the domestic and international threat posed by the French Revolution - a period of repression and reaction generally termed the 'reign of terror'.

The following section explores Pitt's reputation as 'a

cautious reformer' (Evans 1996, p.26) during the 1780s and early 1790s, while Section 3.1 below and Unit 2, Part 2 consider his handling of both the threat of revolution at home and international crisis abroad.

Pitt's economic inheritance

Pitt's financial and administrative reforms of the 1780s were introduced at a time of economic dislocation and crisis caused by the American War. Following sustained and substantial long-term growth in Gross National Product from the start of the century, the 1770s witnessed a fall in the real value of Britain's industrial and commercial production. At the same time, the value of exports fell by 12% and the national debt rose by 91% to just under £250 million by 1783. The annual interest on this debt amounted to just under £9 million. In the year in which Pitt assumed office, government expenditure exceeded income by £10.8 million.

In this sense, an agenda for 'national revival' was already set for Pitt. Arguably, his methods for restoring financial stability and confidence, whilst not fixed, were based on efficiency and rationalisation rather than radical new thinking, and in some areas he borrowed directly from earlier policies. In essence, Pitt introduced measures to raise more revenue while reducing expenditure by increasing administrative efficiency. He supplemented this with an enlightened, if pragmatic, commercial policy designed to stimulate trade.

Pitt's financial, administrative and commercial policies

The key elements of Pitt's approach to 'national revival' combined a series of financial, administrative and commercial policies which operated both simultaneously and on a number of different levels. At times they merged, and it is quite difficult to distinguish between them. Historian Robin Reilly writes:

> 'There were three methods by which Pitt could hope to master the situation: by increasing taxes; by cutting government expenditure; and by stimulating trade. It was clear from the outset that he would be obliged to employ them not as alternatives but as complementary parts of a single policy.' (Reilly 1978, p.108)

These 'parts' included:

- the specific targeting of smuggling in order to reduce the attractiveness of the 'black economy', increase legitimate trade and hence ultimately expand the customs revenue
- the introduction of a range of new taxes
- the increasingly efficient collection of existing taxes
- the extension of the 'Sinking Fund' to tackle the problem of the massively increased national debt

- a reduction in government expenditure through increased administrative efficiency achieved, essentially, through a process of rationalisation
- a commercial policy designed to stimulate increased overseas trade, in turn contributing to the growth in customs revenue and an overall climate of economic confidence.

Pitt's first objective was the restoration of national finances. As political and economic stability are so closely related, Pitt also had the broader aim of restoring confidence in the British government and political system. Within this framework for recovery, his first priority was to raise revenue. He began with an attack on smuggling, which, Evans estimates, may have accounted for up to one-fifth of all Britain's imports.

Combating smuggling

Pitt's intention was to reduce the attractiveness and profitability of smuggling through a reduction in the duties on those goods which were most subject to illicit transportation into Britain, thereby stimulating the volume of legitimate trade and, in the long term, expanding the customs revenue. In the short term, this policy necessitated the reduction of duties on those goods which most attracted the smugglers. The Commutation Act of 1784 therefore reduced the import duty on tea - it has been estimated that 3 to 4.5 million tons were smuggled into Britain each year - from 119% to 25%. This was followed between 1785 and 1787 by reductions on wine, spirits and tobacco.

At the same time as this financial strategy for dealing with the issue of smuggling, Pitt also increased the threat of detection by amending the earlier Hovering Act of 1780 so that officials could now search ships with suspicious cargoes 12 miles out of port.

Bonded warehouses

Both strands of this anti-smuggling scheme were also supported by Pitt's extension of the system of bonded warehouses, first proposed by Sir Robert Walpole in 1733, as a means of increasing the volume of legitimate trade. Before the establishment of this system the importer had to pay import duties immediately on their landing at port - even where those goods were not for sale in Britain itself but were only being held for re-export to Europe. With the setting up of bonded warehouses the importer put his goods into official storage where they would be guarded, free of tax, by customs officials. If the goods were then taken out of the bonded warehouse for re-export, the importer was exempted from paying any import tax at all. If the goods were required for sale in Britain, the importer paid the duty only when he took out the goods and only on the quantity taken out at any one time.

Long-term success

This strategy proved to be a long-term success, with the value of food and raw material imports rising from £13 to £27 million between 1783 and the mid-1790s and government yields increasing by 29% on spirits, 63% on wines and 39% on tobacco. In the interim, Pitt further offset the immediate loss of revenue resulting from the reduction of customs duties by the introduction of new taxes and more efficient collection of those already in place.

Taxation policy

There were two strands to Pitt's approach to taxation: introducing new taxes and ensuring greater efficiency in the collection of those which already existed.

New taxes

Evans describes the first strand of Pitt's approach to taxation as 'little more than a shuffling of the Hanoverian pack' (Evans 1996, p.27). In other words, he was not primarily a financial innovator, but simply varied the range of luxury goods which were subject to tax within the framework accepted by previous 18th-century governments. This framework was based on the principle that government should raise most of its revenue through indirect taxation on items of consumption rather than by income tax - direct taxation on income at source. By ensuring that the goods taxed were those consumed in larger quantities by the wealthier classes, governments were likely to avoid the popular disturbances which accompanied sudden rises in the price of basic foodstuffs such as bread. As the historian Christie puts it, Pitt therefore concentrated on 'ringing the changes on luxuries ranging from hair-powder to servants and horses' (Christie 1982, p.185).

While attempting to meet the immediate need to raise revenue, Pitt tried to avoid the dangers of overtaxing expanding areas of commercial activity. He explored new sources of income - but often with limited success and even in the face of direct opposition. For example, the impact of his graduated window tax - an attempt to capitalise on the increasing trend for private wealth to be converted into housing property - was limited by the tendency of the owners of large properties to respond by simply bricking up their windows. Although Evans believes that, in his approach to taxation, 'Pitt probably got the balance about right' (Evans 1999, p.19), Christie concludes:

> '...the final impression is one of rather desperate and unsuccessful improvisation. In 1784 increases in excise duties on calicos, muslins and other cotton textile products brought down a storm from the manufacturers which led to rapid repeal. Another Act of 1784 compelled bleachers,

printers, and dyers to take out licences at a charge of £2 per annum, and a tax was laid on all printed and bleached textiles. This was represented as so injurious to the industry that it had to be abandoned the following year. Likewise a tax on coals had to be given up the following year under pressure from the mining and metal-working interests. The most novel of his experiments, the shop tax, was also highly unpopular and was eventually brought to an end in 1789.' (Christie 1982, p.185)

Increased efficiency

In this sense innovation really lay in the new efficiency with which sources of government revenue were collected and subsequently managed - essentially the administrative reforms described in detail below. However, with respect to revenue collection and management, the most significant of these reforms was the Consolidated Fund Act of 1787, whereby the previous 103 separate Exchequer accounts were replaced by a single fund account at the Treasury, into which most revenues collected were paid, and from which most outgoing payments were subsequently made. This considerably streamlined the Treasury's financial management and for the first time made some form of national accounting possible.

National debt - the Sinking Fund 1786

Pitt's mechanism for dealing with the problem of the national debt was the Sinking Fund - another area of policy where he 'borrowed' and then modified the ideas of others.

Walpole's precedent

The concept of a sinking fund, whereby money would be set aside from surplus revenue each year and accumulated for the purpose of running down the national debt, had first been introduced by Walpole in 1716. This device had been partially successful in reducing the national debt in the 1720s and 1730s but its potential had been limited because ministers tended to raid the fund for immediate purposes during short-term crises rather than letting it accumulate as intended. In 1772, the idea of the Sinking Fund was revived by the Nonconformist minister Richard Price. In a pamphlet on methods for reducing the national debt, published in 1772, he advocated a fund which would be regularly topped up and not drawn on to meet short-term needs. By earning compound interest, it would eventually extinguish the debt.

How the fund worked

Price's ideas greatly influenced Pitt's thinking on the issue of debt reduction, and the sinking fund which he introduced in 1786 clearly reflected the modifications to Walpole's original mechanism as suggested in the 1772 pamphlet. Every year, a fixed sum was set aside from surplus revenue for the repayment of part of the debt. The interest which would have been paid on that part of the debt was also collected in following years to repay even more of what was owed, with the aim of eventually paying off the debt in full. In order to protect the fund from the kind of 'crisis-raiding' which had occurred in the past, it was managed not exclusively by ministers but by a statutory board of six commissioners, who included the governor and deputy governor of the Bank of England.

To work most effectively, the Sinking Fund required low government expenditure, an annual surplus of income over expenditure, and a non-aggressive foreign policy to prevent the additional spending associated with war. As these conditions characterised the period from the fund's introduction in 1786 to 1793, it initially worked well and the debt was reduced by almost £11 million. Moreover, the implied commitment to the achievement of regular government surpluses associated with the operation of the fund had an important psychological dimension. It boosted business confidence and therefore indirectly stimulated the volume of investment, which was to underpin much of the expansion of overseas trade in this period. In this way it could be argued that the Sinking Fund made a wider contribution to the 'National Revival' associated with the first phase of Pitt's premiership.

A qualified success

Pitt's decision to continue with the scheme after 1793, when Britain was again at war, has been severely criticised. The war with France undermined the rationale for the Sinking Fund and it became a liability. Rather than paying off the debt, the increased economic demands of war (see Section 3.2 below) meant that it was impossible to maintain the payments of £1 million surplus to the commissioners and the government had to borrow money at higher rates of interest than the original debt in order to sustain its operation! It is in this context that Christie once again qualifies the extent of Pitt's success as a reformer:

> 'Pitt's reformed sinking fund of 1786 was perhaps more important as a step towards recreating national confidence than producing financial improvement.' (Christie 1982, p.187)

Administrative reforms

If Pitt's financial reforms were essentially concerned with raising revenue, his administrative reforms aimed to contribute to the restoration of financial stability by reducing expenditure. This meant running the government and associated administrative machinery with maximum efficiency and minimum

waste. This is seen by many as the essence of Pitt's approach to reform. As Evans puts it, 'Pitt's restrained reformism is nowhere better in evidence than in the sphere of administration' (Evans 1996, p.28).

The rationalisation of government

Pitt engaged in a process of cautious rationalisation - cautious because any attempt to prune the administrative 'system', based as it was historically on the operation of patronage, was potentially sensitive, and even politically dangerous. His basic problem was that the 'system' was neither systematic nor structured in such a way as to encourage efficiency. Instead it had evolved in a ramshackle fashion and for essentially political purposes as government offices were created and filled with the nominations of influential aristocratic patrons aiming to develop their own spheres of influence. Pitt's solution was to avoid confrontation with established and powerful vested interests by simply allowing 'offices of profit' to lapse on the holder's death. With regard to the tightening of financial management and accountability, the importance of the 1787

BOX 1.6 **The nature of Pitt's administrative reforms - a historian's view**

The existing system of government had developed to meet political rather than administrative needs. Offices, whether sinecures or not, were rewards given in return for political support, a consequence of the needs of patronage. In order to create financial stability Pitt had to rationalise this system. Radical reform would have provoked the opposition of the patronage-mongers, and Pitt operated in a more cautious and indirect manner. Sinecures were simply allowed to lapse on the death of their holders. Most of the 180 posts which the public accounts commissioners recommended should be abolished in 1786 disappeared over the next 20 years. Departmental management was gradually made more efficient and brought under Treasury control. A Treasury Commission of Audit was created in 1785 to oversee public expenditure. The Board of Taxes was reinforced by transfers from the Treasury and the Excise Board. Talented people, like Richard Frewin at Customs, were promoted and encouraged to develop administrative policies on their own initiative. The creation of a central Stationery Office in 1787 reduced the cost of supplying stationery to the departments. Management of naval funding by the Treasurers of the Navy was brought under control by requiring that any moneys issued should be kept in a Bank of England account and withdrawn only when needed. This all greatly increased administrative efficiency, reducing the amount of labour required and the level of confusion.
Adapted from Evans 1995.

Consolidated Fund Act has already been referred to above. As Christie concludes, 'it is hardly exaggerating to say that his tenure of the financial departments signified the watershed between medieval and modern financial administration' (Christie 1982, p.185).

The paradox of Pitt's reforms
Bearing in mind the circumstances of Pitt's appointment and consolidation of power (see Part 1 above), it is possible to point to a fascinating paradox in relation to the impact of his administrative reforms. Pitt's own accession to and maintenance of political power owed much to the exercise of royal patronage, and George III had himself wanted Pitt as Prime Minister as a means of protection from what the saw as the Rockingham Whigs' assault on his position. However, Pitt's subsequent administrative reforms were designed to dismantle much of the old patronage network, albeit in the interests of efficiency. In the long run, this would permanently deprive the monarchy of much of its political influence. As Evans therefore concludes:

'It may seem bizarre, and it is certainly too simple, to argue that Pitt the Younger destroyed the powers of the monarchy, but the observation contains more than a grain of truth.' (Evans 1996, p.25)

Commercial policy
Pitt also recognised the importance of the relationship between financial stability and commercial confidence. Hence his financial and administrative reforms were supported by a commercial policy designed to stimulate international trade. Pitt was well aware that Britain's prosperity depended on overseas trade, and was therefore linked to its diplomatic and foreign policy. Equally, however, Britain was more diplomatically isolated in 1783 than at almost any other time in the 18th century. Therefore, during the period 1783-92, Pitt sought to open trade negotiations with the major European states to secure reciprocally lowered tariffs. The so-called Eden Treaty signed with France in September 1786 was, however, the only major, if temporary, result of this policy. Named after William Eden, whom Pitt used as his chief negotiator, the treaty meant that manufactured goods from both countries would be allowed in on easier terms than before, and that duties on other types of goods (such as wine and silk) would be lowered. This, Christie suggests, 'is generally hailed as one of Pitt's great successes...British rather than French businessmen gained the lion's share of advantage out of the general lowering of tariffs on both sides of the Channel' (Christie 1982, p.194).

The treaty certainly enabled Britain to gain the benefit of lower prices for French goods imported into Britain, whilst simultaneously opening up French markets to the increasing productivity of British manufacturers. However, in this sense it should not be seen as necessarily marking the first step in an intellectual conversion to free trade. Pitt is sometimes portrayed by historians as the 'father' of 19th-century free trade and a disciple of the writings of Adam Smith. Although Pitt had certainly read Smith's *Wealth of Nations*, written in 1776, and agreed with the argument that wider national interests were best served by trade wars between countries, the Eden Treaty was a product of more pragmatic politics. As Evans puts it, Pitt was simply 'backing a horse which could not lose' (Evans 1996, p.33) - exploiting Britain's growing competitive advantage as the world's first industrial nation and France's economic miscalculation in not recognising it (see also Box 1.7 below). The outbreak of war in 1793 (see Part 3) brought the arrangement to an end and led to a return to protectionism.

2.2 Was Pitt a pragmatist or a principled reformer?

Most historians now regard Pitt as a highly capable, practical and pragmatic reformer rather than as a political visionary or innovator. Politics has been described as the art of the possible, and Pitt was a particularly acute judge of what could be realistically tackled and achieved and what, in the context of the opposition, had to be left alone or even, despite personal conviction, abandoned altogether. This pragmatic approach to reform is perhaps most clearly seen in his approach to parliamentary reform, his plans for freer trade with Ireland and economic union with the United States, and free trade (see Box 1.7).

2.3 Did Pitt bring about a national revival?

Enquiry into the nature of Pitt's reforms also prompts a further key question: how far was Pitt responsible for the economic recovery which occurred in the 1780s, and to what extent was it based on the longer-term and underlying strengths of the British economy - strengths which were only temporarily masked by the disruptive effects of war with America? Pitt did benefit from Britain's gradual rise to the position of foremost industrial power, and from France's failure to acknowledge it. Free trade benefits the most efficient producer, and Pitt's most successful move in the direction of free trade, the Eden trade treaty with France (see Section 2.1), favoured Britain because it opened up a market for Britain's increasingly efficient manufacturers, particularly in textiles. Here, Britain benefited from having control of India - a source of raw materials, and from technological advances such as

BOX 1.7 **Pitt - pragmatist or principled reformer: a historian's view**

Given Pitt's reputation as a defender of the constitution and social order in the 1790s, it is important to recognise that he was known as a cautious reformer in the early 1780s, though he never allowed this to interfere with the practical necessities of administration. In 1785 he unsuccessfully attempted to abolish 36 rotten boroughs and transfer their seats to London and the counties, failed to achieve economic union with Ireland, and had already dropped the notion of economic union with America, which he had considered when Shelburne was Chancellor of the Exchequer. These failures confirmed that Pitt was unable to lead the country in his own reforming terms because of the extent of the opposition. Parliamentary reform was lost by 248 votes to 174 and he abandoned economic union following opposition from British manufacturing and commercial interests.

The framework of Pitt's government was overwhelmingly 'administrative', reacting to problems when they arose rather than initiating programmes of a fundamentally reforming nature. Pitt can best be seen in the first part of his ministry as an individual concentrating on streamlining the machinery of government. He was primarily a pragmatic administrative reformer, an efficient minister rather than an innovative one. He rationalised the existing systems of government and taxation rather than embark on a radical programme of reform. His approach was cautious, following rather than leading opinion, and responsive to the influence of opposition.

Historians frequently argue that Pitt has a reputation as an individual committed to free trade. This may be true but it did not divert him from the practicalities of politics. Diplomatic and commercial realities meant that Pitt's commitment to free trade was always limited. The year 1786 saw both a Navigation Act and the Anglo-French Treaty. Britain's commercial successes had been built on protectionism, and the move to freer trade was a result of British industries no longer needing protection as much as the intellectual attraction of the new system. The outbreak of war in 1793 drove the British government back to protectionism.

Adapted from Brown 1991.

Crompton's spinning mule. Britain also had a ready market for cotton and luxury goods in its West Indian colonies. Pitt can be given credit for taking control of trading activities in India, through the India Act of 1784, which created a Board of Control to superintend the political and military affairs of the powerful but inefficient East India Company and increased the powers of the Governor-General.

Despite this, many historians believe that Pitt, rather than single-handedly bringing about a revival, simply made the most of Britain's already increasing advantages. Evans, for example, notes that, during the 20 years following 1784, exports tripled and imports doubled. However, he concludes:

'The Industrial Revolution is much more responsible for this than any grand design of the Pitt administration. Government initiatives were more consolidatory than innovatory.' (Evans 1996, p.38)

MAIN POINTS - Part 2

- Pitt's first administration can be divided into two periods: (1) 1783 to the early 1790s, focusing on financial and administrative reforms; (2) early 1790s to 1801, dominated by the the French Revolution.
- Britain was weakened by war with America. Government expenditure far exceeded income, and the national debt was high. Pitt combined measures to increase revenue with a drive for administrative efficiency. His commercial policy stimulated trade and encouraged economic confidence.
- He cut import duties and introduced bonded warehouses, which reduced incentives for smuggling and actually increased revenue. He taxed luxury goods and made tax collection more efficient.
- He rationalised the Treasury and introduced a Sinking Fund which reduced the national debt by £11 million – though it became a liability once Britain was at war with France.
- He cautiously reformed the administrative system, while avoiding clashes with those who benefited from patronage.
- He made moves towards free trade, but the Eden Treaty (1786) was the only significant success.
- Most historians now see Pitt as a capable, pragmatic reformer, not a great innovator. He was prepared to drop reforms (such as economic union with Ireland and America) rather than risk his position by coninuing to campaign for them. His main reforms were administrative rather than matters of principle.
- Some historians have argued that Pitt was a champion of free trade. Others say that he was flexible on this issue, merely taking advantage of Britain's manufacturing strength, and reverting to protectionism with the outbreak of war in 1793.
- Historians debate whether Pitt was responsible for a 'national revival'. Some argue that to some extent he simply benefited from the underlying strength of the British economy and by Britain's growth as the foremost industrial nation of the period.

Activity 1.2 Did Pitt bring about a 'national revival'?

ITEM 1 A statistical overview

Table (a): trade - annual averages (£ millions)

	Imports	Exports	Re-exports
1750-59	8.3	8.8	3.5
1760-69	10.7	10.0	4.8
1770-79	12.1	9.3	5.1
1780-89	13.8	10.2	4.3
1790-99	21.8	17.5	9.4

Adapted from Cook & Stevenson 1983.

Note: re-exports are colonial goods passing through Britain on their way to other markets.

Table (b): government income and expenditure (£000s)

	Income	Expenditure
1781-85	13,693	25,726
1786-90	16,468	16,323
1791-95	18,606	24,455
1796-99	24,875	48,716

Adapted from Evans 1996.

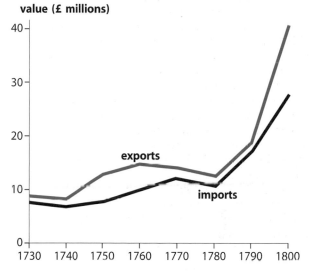

ITEM 2 Pitt: some interpretations

A financial genius
Holland Rose 1911, p.187

An able administrator and a first class financier.
Derry 1963, p.6

Pitt was an outstanding finance minister. In a series of judicious budgets he restored the economy, reduced and simplified customs and excise duties, and stimulated trade... All this restored the credibility of the political system.
Derry 1990, p.53

His achievement was, by any standards remarkable... The instruments he chose were not original... but he made use of them, in combination, to create a practicable pattern of retrenchment and recovery that was his own.
Reilly 1978, p.113

William Pitt

He was the parent of more practical reforms in administration and political economy than almost any other English statesman.
Bryant 2002

In the years 1783-93 Pitt did much to restore the economy by promoting sound national finance and presiding over a veritable explosion in commercial activity.
O'Gorman 1997, p.218

ITEM 3 A contemporary view

'John Bull baited by the Dogs of Excise', Gillray, 1790. Pitt encourages his ministers and excise officers, a shopping list, of taxes in his pocket including the butcher and baker. John Bull calls for 'Liberty and no excise'; the barrel is labelled 'Tobacco', the dog chews a bone labelled 'Ministry' and 'Opposition'. A painter replaces the name 'Treasury' with 'Excise Office'.

ITEM 4 A historian's view

How much credit should Pitt claim for the so-called 'National Revival'? Historians in the second half of the 20th century have been less inclined to hero worship. It is important to put the contribution of any individual - even one as able and dedicated as Pitt - into a wider context. There is much about a nation's economic performance which cannot be commanded by the policies of its governments. Britain's economic growth, based to a large extent on the massive increases in overseas trade during the 18th century, had only been temporarily checked by the American War. With the return of peace, trade - not least with the newly independent United States - boomed once more. The value of British imports almost doubled overall between the mid-1780s and mid-1790s. In the early stages of Britain's industrial revolution, moreover, manufactured goods contributed more than 80% of the value of exports. Concern about the state of the nation in 1783 rapidly came to be seen as alarmist. Pitt's inheritance was far less sickly than it appeared at the end of 1783. Also, he inherited and adapted the ideas and policies of others. Any basic assessment must take account both of the basic strength of the British economy in the 1780s and of Pitt's indebtedness to others. This still leaves substantial scope for recognising Pitt's own merits. Throughout his peacetime administrations, he showed remarkable sure-footedness. He directed taxation policy and debt reduction with skill and perseverance, while his contribution to the reform of the governmental machine was massive.

Adapted from Evans 1999.

Questions

1. What evidence is there in Item 1 to support the interpretations of Pitt's role in achieving a 'national revival' expressed in Item 2?
2. Using your knowledge, comment on how accurately Item 3 reflects (a) the extent of Pitt's customs and excise reforms, and (b) their effect on the nation.
3. Study Item 4. In what ways does Evans qualify Pitt's contribution to the 'national revival'?
4. Using the evidence of Items 1-4, and your own knowledge, produce arguments for and against the view that Pitt was the architect of a remarkable 'national revival' between 1783 and the early 1790s.

3 Pitt and reaction

Key issues

1. How successfully did Pitt contain the Jacobin threat?
2. Was Pitt an effective wartime leader?

3.1 How successfully did Pitt contain the Jacobin threat?

As suggested above, the second phase of Pitt's first administration was dominated by his response to the internal and international threat posed by the French Revolution of 1789. The main features of Pitt's policy for containing the domestic threat of revolution posed by a range of British radical groups in the wake of the French Revolution are developed in Unit 2, Section 2.1. An assessment of the effectiveness of Pitt's measures is also offered, reflecting two schools of thought. The first is that, through the combination of selective repression and skilful exploitation of a rising trend of popular loyalism and xenophobia, the Jacobin threat had, to all intents and purposes, been effectively contained by 1795–96. This in turn meant that the repressive legislation that was introduced was temporary and expedient in nature. On the other hand, it has been argued by historians such as Thomis and Holt (1977) and E.P. Thompson (1980) that the measures were counterproductive. The heavy-handed over-reaction to what were essentially reformist organisations drove more extremist groups and individuals 'underground'. After 1795, they continued to survive and function in secret, in what were arguably more dangerous and potentially revolutionary 'cells'.

However, in relation to the wider assessment of Pitt's effectiveness as Prime Minister two key points seem to emerge from his handling of the Jacobin threat during the second 'phase' of his administration in the 1790s.

1. Short-term preservation of the constitution

First, it is important to note that whilst Pitt has been criticised for his reactionary response to what were, for the most part, reformist groups, the so-called 'Reign of Terror', the term now generally used to describe the government's methods of controlling radical activity after 1793, was not just a blunt instrument of repression but in fact operated at several different levels. There can of course be no doubt that there was harassment, blatant use of the law for political and ideological purposes and, at times, the atmosphere of a witch-hunt. However, historians have increasingly emphasised the importance of an essentially empathetic explanation of the government's methods and thought processes. They point out that Pitt and his ministers saw themselves not as acting tyrannically, but as taking desperate short-term measures to protect the benefits of the constitution at a time of national emergency and crisis. It is also stressed that none of the measures taken were ever intended to form the basis of a permanent change to the constitution. Pitt himself emphasised that repressive legislation was a regrettable but ultimately temporary expedient. When set in the context of both contemporary repression on the Continent and subsequent wartime standards during the 'total' wars of the 20th century, Pitt's methods appear less severe. Moreover, they build upon a strong vein of fiercely loyalist public opinion.

2. Pitt's ability to cope with varied challenges

Second, if one assumes an interpretation of the 'Reign of Terror' which emphasises its success in containing the Jacobin threat, Pitt deserves credit for his equally effective role in political circumstances so different from the period of peace and recovery in the 1780s, and historians have used this as evidence of his ability. During his period in office Pitt was simultaneously confronted by a range of problems not faced by any other British leader either before or since - recovery from one major war, a further war, political intrigue, the threat of revolution, and a process of profound social and economic change. Pitt developed strategies to meet each of these challenges, and his effectiveness in the 1790s should therefore be seen in this context as a further reason for his political longevity (see also Section 1.3 above).

3.2 Was Pitt an effective wartime leader?

The other dimension to an assessment of Pitt's performance during the second 'phase' of his administration during the 1790s is a more specific consideration of his effectiveness as a wartime leader.

Pitt's government was at war with Revolutionary France by February 1793. There were three strands to his strategy for conducting the conflict:

1. Financial and military support to European allies in their direct attacks on France. During his period in office Pitt supplied £9 million in subsidies to Austria and Prussia.
2. The so-called 'blue water' strategy of deploying Britain's navy to threaten and capture French

colonies, thereby weakening France's commercial strength and undermining its economic capability to wage long-term war.
3. The provision of support to counter-revolutionary groups within France, particularly in the west of the country, where the population was felt to be strongly opposed to ideological change.

Support to allies and counter-revolutionaries

The first and third of Pitt's strategies in fact yielded disappointing returns. For a number of reasons the anti-French coalition was far more fragile that Pitt had initially hoped. Austria and Prussia's principal strategic interests were, unlike Britain's, in Central and Eastern Europe, whilst these two powers also remained suspicious of both Britain's growing industrial wealth and the wider colonial ambitions associated with the 'blue water' strategy. Moreover, although troops were landed at the important port of Toulon in August 1793 at the invitation of counter-revolutionary forces who held the area, these were rapidly defeated and the Revolutionary government was back in control of the region by December. A similar plan to land counter-revolutionary forces in southern Brittany in July 1795 also failed. This suggests that Pitt had seriously miscalculated the strength of national consciousness and patriotism in France at this time. As Evans puts it:

> 'The French revolutionary forces were better prepared and had higher morale born of early success than had been expected...Many in France preferred a Bourbon to a Jacobin government. They were all French, however, and most preferred a French government - almost any French government - to the restoration of monarchy engineered by the national enemy.'
> (Evans 1999, p.47)

This is a view also supported by the historian O'Gorman, who points to Pitt's initial strategic miscalculations:

> 'Believing France to be in ruinous chaos, Pitt did not anticipate a long military campaign. He underestimated the strength and stamina of France's new ideological convictions.'
> (O'Gorman 1997, p.234)

On mainland Europe the period 1793-96 therefore saw a succession of French victories set against the backdrop of a rapidly disintegrating international coalition. By January 1795 Holland had fallen under French control and much of Italy was occupied. In April 1795 the Prussians sued for peace with France, to be followed in July by the Spanish – who negotiated an alliance with their former enemies in August 1796 and declared war on Britain two months later. Following major defeats in 1796 and 1797, the Austrians were forced to negotiate the disadvantageous Treaty of Campo Formio, thus leaving Britain temporarily alone in the war against Revolutionary France. Although a second coalition comprised of Britain, Austria, Russia, Turkey, Portugal and Naples was formed late in 1798, this also quickly fell apart.

Naval successes

The success of the British navy during this period in part offset the potentially disastrous impact of military and diplomatic failures, particularly on 'the Glorious First of June' in 1794 when Admiral Howe defeated the French fleet and in the period 1798-1801 when Nelson played a major role in containing Napoleon's progress through Italy and North Africa. However, even the success of the 'blue water' strategy in relation to its primary objective of capturing French colonial possessions in the Caribbean came at a price. It has been calculated that up to 70% of the 89,000 troops sent to the region at this time were lost - largely to tropical diseases.

Financing the war

Historians' balance sheets of the successes and failures of Pitt's conduct of war in the period 1783-1801 also tend to include a consideration of the financial dimension to the war - a dimension which initially 'blew all Pitt's peacetime financial calculations to smithereens' (Evans 1999, p.50). Until 1797 Pitt funded the war through increased borrowing, with the national debt rising by 80% in the first five years of the conflict. This decision was based on his basic, and ultimately unfounded, assumption that the war would be short. By early 1798, debt repayment was accounting for almost a third of total government expenditure. Pitt's solution was to take the key step of introducing a graduated income tax - initially levied at 10% on all incomes over £200 per annum, with lower rates for annual incomes between £60 and £200. The new tax came into effect in 1799. Remaining in force until 1816, it had a major impact on wartime finance, eventually accounting for 28% of all the additional funding raised to wage war between 1793 and 1815. Pitt's successful introduction of income tax is usually regarded as indicating two things, although neither directly relate to the quality of his wartime leadership:

1. the increased efficiency of the tax collection system due to his reforms in the 1780s
2. the underlying wealth of British society in the early industrial age.

BOX 1.8 Pitt's effectiveness as a wartime leader - a historian's interpretation

Pitt left office before a lull in Anglo-French hostilities was agreed at the Treaty of Amiens in 1802. The best that can be said about matters in 1802 was that Britain had not been defeated. Pitt was not a victorious war leader. How much blame does he deserve for the failures of the 1790s?

Britain's tenacity after 1797 when all the old allies had fallen by the wayside is worthy of the highest praise, and Pitt's determined leadership was important to this. Loyalist opinion rallied and a sense of national purpose was evoked. After a period in the early 1790s when government finance depended dangerously on loans (a policy Pitt himself regretted) Pitt put national finances on a new, taxation-based, footing which just about carried Britain through the remainder of a very long war.

It would, however, be foolish to assert that Pitt was a good wartime leader. A number of basic errors were made which it is easy to identify, albeit with hindsight. First, Britain entered the war unprepared and undermanned. Second, it took Pitt and his ministers too long to realise that that their strategic concern with the situation in north-west Europe was not shared by Britain's main allies. This basic misconception was an error of judgement which helped France to retain an advantage in the early stages of the war. Third, Pitt believed for too long that the war would be short. His financial policies from 1793 to 1796 operated on this assumption. Much national wealth was wasted by inadequate early financing of a war which turned out to be very different from the one first envisaged. Closely linked to this, Pitt was slow to react to the frequently rapid changes in 1793-94 and he seems not to have appreciated the need for more military and naval training. It seems that it was 1795 before the government realised that the nation was in for a long haul, with fewer advantages than it had originally calculated. Pitt underestimated both the French fighting capability and France's sense of patriotic identity.

Although Pitt acquitted himself well enough as Britain's war leader, the experience brought him face to face if not with defeat, then at least with the realisation that events were not his to command.

Adapted from Evans 1999.

The GIANT-FACTOTUM amusing himself

Pitt in a 1797 Gillray cartoon, 'The Giant Factotum amusing himself'. He stands astride the Speaker's box and plays cup and ball with the world. He has 'Resources for supporting the War' in one pocket, and numbers of troops in the the other. His left foot stands on Fox.

MAIN POINTS - Part 3

- From the early 1790s, Pitt was preoccupied with the war with Revolutionary France and with the threat of domestic revolution. There are two main views of his handling of the latter: (1) by selective repression and exploitation of popular sentiment he succeeded in averting the threat; (2) by over-reacting to groups which were reformist rather than revolutionary, he drove them underground, where they were more dangerous.
- Historians have increasingly argued that Pitt's repressive measures were a short-term attempt to protect the constitution, and were never intended to be permanent. Moreover, some historians have praised him for operating effectively in a political situation presenting very different challenges from those of the pre-war years.

- Pitt's strategy for tackling France was threefold: (1) he gave financial and military support to Britain's allies; (2) he used the navy to threaten and seize French colonies; (3) he backed French counter-revolutionary groups. Only the second of these was effective – athough huge numbers of British troops were lost to disease in the Caribbean.
- While the British had naval successes under Howe and Nelson, the French had major land victories in Europe and the first coalition against them fell apart in 1797, leaving Britain isolated. A second coalition collapsed in 1798.
- Pitt had expected the war to be short. Therefore he initially funded it by increased borrowing. The rise in the national debt led him to introduce income tax in 1799.

Activity 1.3 Pitt's legacy

ITEM 1 The Pittite tradition

A number of historians have argued that Pitt's approach to government set the tone for three of the major premierships of the 19th century – those of Liverpool (see Unit 3), Peel (see Unit 7) and Gladstone (see *British History for AS Level 1867-1918*, Unit 1). These continuities have been referred to as the 'Pittite tradition' and are shown in this diagram.

William Pitt (1783-1801, 1804-6)
- Administrative efficiency to cut costs
- Executive professionalism
- National above party interests
- Cautious reform
- Consideration of commercial interests

Liverpool (1812-27)
- 'Liberal Tory' reforms to preserve the constitution
- Consideration of commercial interests

Peel (1834-35, 1841-46)
- Administrative efficiency to cut costs
- Professionalism
- National above party interests (split party over repeal of Corn Laws, 1846)

Gladstone (1868-74, 1880-86, 1892-94)
- Administrative efficiency to cut costs
- Professionalism
- National above party interests (split party over Home Rule for Ireland)

1832 Reform Act: 'Conservative' reform to avoid revolution

ITEM 2 A historian's view (i)

For almost a generation after Pitt's death, many eagerly claimed the title 'Pittite'. This partly reflected admiration for a great man. Almost all of those he promoted to high office, especially from the early 1790s onwards, held him in high esteem. Liverpool, for example, who had served Pitt faithfully since 1793, was generous in his praise. He wrote in 1814 that he always 'endeavoured to make the principles of Mr Pitt the chief guide of our political conduct'. Others called themselves Pittites not because of any particular policies but because Pitt had come to symbolise steadfast opposition to France and 'French principles' and also support for the old order. A Pittite, therefore, was a patriotic anti-reformer. By extension, a Pittite was a supporter of orthodox religion as a shield against 'Jacobinism and Atheism' – although Pitt himself was not especially religious. In fact, many 'Pittites' held views which ran counter to Pitt's own.

Part of Pitt's legacy was his concern for efficient administration and executive expertise. Under him, government became more professional. He did not mount a direct attack on the patronage system, which gave undeserved advancement to those who were inefficient but loyal, but he starved it of oxygen by promoting on merit where possible and by not replacing mere sinecurists. In doing so he paved the way for Peel and Gladstone, whose governments both earned a justified reputation for professionalism. Pitt also avoided one of the main traps of 'party government' in the 1780s. His parliamentary majorities were usually founded on the support of fellow ministers and the votes of backbenchers and independents who favoured cheap government and debt reduction - again, anticipating Peel and Gladstone.

Sir Robert Peel did not enter Parliament until 1809, but he certainly copied Pitt's ministerial style. Like Pitt, Peel developed a group of ministers he could trust to do an efficient job and aimed to win over Parliament by masterful debate. He was also prepared to put national interests above party concerns. This explains the collapse of the Conservatives over the repeal of the Corn Laws in 1846. For Gladstone, Ireland became the great moral cause to which, if necessary, the unity of his own party might be sacrificed. Presented in this light, it is very easy to see how Peel and Gladstone, like more immediate successors such as Liverpool, could be considered 'Pittites'.

Adapted from Evans 1999.

ITEM 3 A historian's view (ii)

For half a century, British politics were dominated by two men, the Younger Pitt and Lord Liverpool. Their values were derived from the 18th century but their political skills ensured that the country's institutions survived war and domestic change, and that the nation underwent transformation without experiencing revolution or long-term social conflict. Pitt established a particular style of political behaviour, which Liverpool reactivated. Both looked back to traditions of a balanced constitution. Nevertheless, they recognised the need for making adjustments to the political system. Their defence of familiar institutions led to innovation. Although Catholic Emancipation and parliamentary reform marked the end of an era, the Old Order in England ended on a note of achievement. The system established by Pitt and refined by Liverpool showed considerable resilience and a capacity for meeting new challenges. Reform was eventually accomplished, but through constitutional means and on the basis of traditional values. Both Pitt and Liverpool understood the need to consider merchants and manufacturers, whose confidence was necessary for the success of the government, even though it was taken for granted that they would be junior partners, not the equals of the landed gentry. Pitt and Liverpool were aware of the latest economic thinking, but they grafted elements of it onto an approach to politics which was essentially traditional.

Judged by the standards of the time both Pitt and Liverpool were superb politicians. They showed that the traditional system could survive challenges. Yet they had an openness to new developments which enabled change to take place within a framework of continuity. They enabled change to be accomplished in a fashion which preserved all that was best in the old while cautiously opening the door to the new. Thus they laid the foundations of the 1832 Reform Act. Throughout the era of Pitt and Liverpool, the three essentials of good government were seen as being the protection of personal liberty, the security of private property, and a modest level of taxation. These aims were less visionary than the rights of man, but they were a more reliable guide through the confusion of war and change.

Adapted from Derry 1990.

Questions

1. Using Items 1-3, summarise in your own words the notion of a 'Pittite tradition'.
2. Why, according to Item 2, did the notion of a 'Pittite tradition' initially develop?
3. Study Item 2. In what ways can the Pittite tradition be described as (a) progressive and (b) reactionary?
4. Using your knowledge of 19th-century administrations, what are the possible shortcomings of the notion of a Pittite tradition as outlined in Items 1-3?

References

- **Black (1993)** Black, J., *The Politics of Britain*, 1688-1700, Manchester University Press, 1993.

- **Brown (1991)** Brown, R., *Church and State in Modern Britain 1700-1850*, Routledge, 1991.

- **Bryant (2002)** Bryant, A., *The Years of Endurance*, Stratus, 2002.

- **Christie (1982)** Christie, I.R., *Wars and Revolutions Britain 1760-1815*, Arnold, 1982.

- **Cook & Stevenson (1983)** Cook, C., and Stevenson, J., *The Longman Handbook of Modern British History 1714-1980*, Longman, 1983.

- **Derry (1963)** Derry, J.W., *Reaction and Reform*, Blandford Press, 1963.

- **Derry (1990)** Derry, J.W., *Politics in the Age of Fox, Pitt and Liverpool: Continuity and Transformation*, Palgrave, 1990.

- **Erhman (1969)** Ehrman, J., *The Younger Pitt: The Years of Acclaim*, Constable, 1969.

- **Evans (1985)** Evans, E.J., *Political Parties in Britain 1763-1867*, Methuen, 1985.

- **Evans (1996)** Evans, E.J., *The Forging of the Modern State: Early Industrial Britain 1783-1850*, Longman, 1996.

- **Evans (1999)** Evans, E.J., *William Pitt the Younger*, Routledge, 1999.

- **Holland Rose (1911)** Holland Rose, J., *William Pitt and National Revival*, Bell, 1911.

- **O'Gorman (1997)** O'Gorman, F., *The Long Eighteenth Century: British Political and Social History 1688-1832*, Arnold, 1997.

- **Plumb (1963)** Plumb, J.H., *England in the Eighteenth Century*, Penguin, 1963.

- **Reilly (1978)** Reilly, R., *Pitt the Younger*, Cassell Ltd, 1978.

- **Seldon (1996)** Seldon, A. (ed.), *How Tory Governments Fall: The Tory Party in Power since 1783*, Fontana Press, 1996.

- **Thomis & Holt (1977)** Thomis, M.I., and Holt, P., *Threats of Revolution in Britain 1789-1848*, Macmillan, 1977.

- **Thompson (1980)** Thompson, E.P., *The Making of the English Working Class*, Penguin, 1980.

UNIT 2 | Britain and the impact of the French Revolution

Timeline - Britain and the impact of the French Revolution

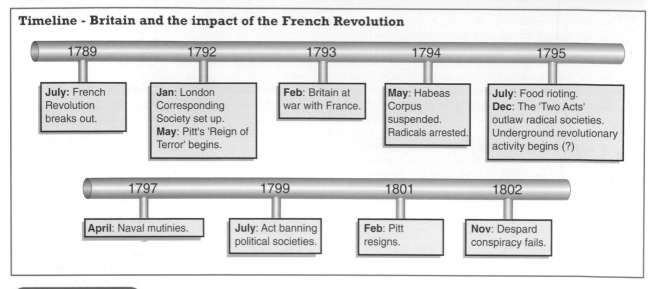

1789 — **July:** French Revolution breaks out.

1792 — **Jan:** London Corresponding Society set up. **May:** Pitt's 'Reign of Terror' begins.

1793 — **Feb:** Britain at war with France.

1794 — **May:** Habeas Corpus suspended. Radicals arrested.

1795 — **July:** Food rioting. **Dec:** The 'Two Acts' outlaw radical societies. Underground revolutionary activity begins (?)

1797 — **April:** Naval mutinies.

1799 — **July:** Act banning political societies.

1801 — **Feb:** Pitt resigns.

1802 — **Nov:** Despard conspiracy fails.

Introduction

The 1790s have sometimes been seen as a turning point in the development of protest in Britain. The French Revolution of 1789, it has been argued, stimulated genuinely popular, radical organisations (see Box 2.1 for an explanation of the term 'radical') to such an extent that, in the words of one historian, 'the people entered politics' (Williams 1968, p.4).

Some historians, however, question the strength of the new radical organisations and deny the existence of a genuinely revolutionary threat, seeing the 1790s as a fascinating but ultimately false dawn in the development of popular politics in Britain. Although contemporary opponents of the French Revolution certainly viewed radical groups like the London Corresponding Society in the same light as the extreme Jacobins who seized power in France in 1792, today most historians agree that the majority of British radicals had very little in common with them. Moreover, even if the British 'Jacobins' had

ever developed the structure and tactics necessary to pose a revolutionary threat, it is often claimed that they would still have stood very little chance of success in the face of determined government oppression and a counter-revolutionary explosion of popular loyalism.

For many historians, then, the impact of the French Revolution on British politics and society in the 1790s is the opposite to that which might be initially expected. The French Revolution ultimately strengthened rather than weakened the position of the ruling elite. An alternative view, however, has been advanced by the historian E.P. Thompson, who claimed that the 'revolutionary underground' which developed between c.1795 and 1815 exercised a profound influence on the growth of working-class consciousness and organisation. This unit explores the debate that has raged since Thompson first put forward his case in the 1960s.

UNIT SUMMARY

Part 1 considers two ways of interpreting the development of radical protest in the 1790s and examines the aims, organisation and tactics of British 'Jacobin' societies in the light of these interpretations and the character of constitutional protest in Britain before 1789.

Part 2 examines the government's response to the perceived radical threat and assesses the role

of loyalist organisations and propaganda.

Part 3 explores the argument that suppression of constitutional forms of radicalism by the mid-1790s was followed by the development of a more subversive revolutionary 'underground'. It also assesses why Britain avoided revolution in the period 1795-1810.

1 The development of popular protest after 1789

Key issues

1. What was radical protest in Britain like before the French Revolution?

2. How have different historians interpreted the impact of the French Revolution on British politics and society?

3. What impact did the French Revolution make upon radical protest in Britain after 1789?

1.1 What was radical protest in Britain like before the French Revolution?

Protest - a long tradition

A starting point for any assessment of the impact made by the French Revolution is a consideration of the extent and character of protest in Britain before 1789. How much of a catalyst to change was the French Revolution? There certainly was a significant growth of radical activity in the 1790s with events in France producing a range of responses - from the revitalisation of old constitutional reform societies to

BOX 2.1 The term 'radical'

The term 'radical' came into use in English as a political label in the years around 1820. Although it was later used much more broadly to describe any kind of reformer who wanted change 'from the roots', it originally had a fairly specific meaning. It referred to a supporter of the programme of radical parliamentary reform which was the goal of protest around the time of Peterloo in 1819 (see Unit 4 for details on Peterloo). The central item in this programme was manhood suffrage (often loosely described at the time as 'universal suffrage'), though it also included demands for annually elected Parliaments and the secret ballot. Radical reformers were frequently contrasted with moderate reformers who campaigned for less sweeping measures such as household suffrage and triennial Parliaments (Parliaments elected every three years). The radical programme of the 1820s was not new. It was promoted in the 1770s by Major John Cartwright (who was still active in the 1820s) and it was adopted in the 1790s by the first groups set up by working-class reformers - such as the London Corresponding Society.

Adapted from Dinwiddy 1994 (in this book, 'radical' is used in the broad sense to describe people who supported a programme of change 'from the roots' - whether or not the term was applied at the time).

subversive revolutionary activity. However, most historians now agree that British radicalism was not created by the French Revolution - the events of 1789 were simply one of many factors feeding into the aims and tactics of the groups which emerged in the 1790s. Rather than stimulating fundamental change, events in France intensified and broadened existing trends.

Urbanisation and radicalism

The British radicals of the 1790s drew on a tradition of political protest whose origins can be located in the developing urban centres of the second half of the 18th century:

'By the later 18th century, major social and economic developments within Britain were combining to create a growing body of opinion critical of the power and policies of the aristocratic elite. These changes had their greatest impact on the political consciousness of the middling orders, especially those who lived in urban areas...Many of the middling orders resented their dependence upon the landed elite whose policies could have a profound effect on their economic welfare...Government policies could result in wars which dislocated trade or in legislative restrictions on the activities of traders and manufacturers.' (Dickinson 1985, pp.1-2)

For most of the 18th century, therefore, opposition to government was rather exclusive:

'The language of opposition in the 18th century was that of independent country gentlemen, opposed to expensive continental wars which threatened to increase government indebtedness and taxation; and against ministerial corruption exercised through royal patronage, placemen,* pensions and seven year Parliaments. Rarely did the mass of the people have any say in affairs, except as vocal, riotous and ultimately ineffective bystanders at election time. The Houses of Parliament were regarded as private gentlemen's clubs, the proceedings of which were not for discussion or even scrutiny by the public at large.' (Royle 1997, p.119)

* 'Placemen' were people who owed their well-paid jobs and influential position to the contacts they had with members of the ruling elite.

Clubs, discussion groups and societies

This urban, essentially middle-class, culture which had developed by the mid-18th century spawned a number of clubs, discussion groups and societies which, although initially social in their character, rapidly became politicised. This was largely due to the expansion of the press since, especially after John Wilkes' campaign for press freedom in the 1760s (see

BOX 2.2 | John Wilkes

John Wilkes was a journalist, MP and outspoken critic of both government and monarch. In June 1762, a week after the Prime Minister, the Earl of Bute, began publishing a newspaper promoting his policies (the *Briton*), Wilkes published his own newspaper, the *North Briton*, which provided satirical attacks on ministers and policies on the grounds that 'a free press is the terror of all bad ministers'. In April 1763, on the publication of Number 45 of the *North Briton*, the government issued a 'general warrant' permitting the arrest of any of those involved in the publication of the paper. Number 45 had directly criticised King George III. Wilkes and 48 others were arrested on the grounds that they had published a seditious and treasonable paper. The resulting storm of protest, in and out of Parliament, startled the government. Large crowds of people marched in Wilkes' support and Number 45 became the symbol of liberty. It should be noted, however, that general warrants had a shaky legal basis since their authority came, ultimately, from the Licensing Act of Charles II, which had lapsed in 1695. In due course, the courts were to declare them illegal. In May, Wilkes was released after pleading parliamentary privilege as an MP. In December, however, his fortunes changed. The discovery of an obscene and blasphemous 'Essay on Woman' he had written made him vulnerable to renewed prosecution. He went into exile in France, was given a suspended sentence in his absence and was expelled from Parliament. In 1768, Wilkes returned from exile and successfully stood for Parliament in Middlesex. Middlesex's electorate was untypically made up of small traders and artisans, voters who liked Wilkes' talk of liberty. Wilkes was then charged with outlawry (he was cleared) and libel (he was sentenced to 22 months in jail and a fine). Supporters paid his fine and mobs roamed the streets shouting 'Damn the king, damn the government, and damn the justices'. Troops were called in to restore order. In 1769, Wilkes was again expelled from Parliament, but in 1774 he was elected Lord Mayor of London and re-elected MP for Middlesex. He died in 1797.

Adapted from Langford 1999.

Box 2.2), the press began reporting on political affairs: 'By the late 18th century, London alone was served by 13 daily and ten tri-weekly newspapers, while in the provinces there were over 50 weekly newspapers...Most of the more successful publications were anti-ministerial in their politics...Long before the French Revolution, the opponents of the political elite had waged a propaganda campaign in the press against the growing power of the executive...Long before the radicals began demanding a major extension of the franchise there were constant references in the press to the rights and liberties of Englishmen.' (Dickinson 1985, p.3)

Opposition groups and the Glorious Revolution

The clubs, discussion groups and societies which grew up in the late 1780s became places where people publicly criticised the abuse of aristocratic and royal power. Their arguments commonly drew on ideas which had been established as a result of the Glorious Revolution of 1688 (see Box 2.3) - such as the idea that ministers should not be above the law and that arbitrary government should be resisted.

John Wilkes - a pivotal figure

As Box 2.2 suggests, John Wilkes was an important figure in the development of radicalism for a number of reasons. First, he championed causes which challenged the status quo. He raised the question of the freedom of the press (by publishing the *North Briton*). He asserted the right of voters to choose an MP without interference from Parliament (by standing

BOX 2.3 | The Glorious Revolution

In 1688, after attempting to reassert the power of the monarch, James II was deposed and forced into exile. He was replaced by William of Orange, who was offered the throne on condition that he accepted a Bill of Rights limiting the monarch's powers. This 'Glorious Revolution', as it became known, effectively ended the monarch's claim to absolute power and established that government should be based on the rule of law.

Adapted from Cannon & Griffiths 1988.

for Parliament against the wishes of the Commons - which had expelled him). He supported the reporting of parliamentary debates (by giving sanctuary to reporters in his capacity as a City magistrate in 1771). And, in 1776, he put the case for universal male suffrage in Parliament, arguing that:

'The meanest mechanic, the poorest peasant and day labourer...has important rights respecting his personal liberty, that of his wife and children, his property however inconsiderable...Some share, therefore, in the power of making those laws which deeply interest them...should be reserved even to this inferior but most useful set of men...Without a true representation of the Commons, our constitution is essentially defective.'

By fighting these causes and linking them under the heading of 'liberty', he paved the way for more coherent radical programmes later. Second, from the time of his imprisonment over Number 45, Wilkes gained and maintained a great deal of popular support. Rudé (1962) notes that supporters roamed the streets shouting, or chalking up, 'Wilkes and Liberty'. They attacked those who tried to burn copies of Number 45, they smashed the windows of leading politicians and burned them in effigy. Thompson (1980), on the other hand, points out that Wilkes' great strength was his ability to call out a crowd of protesters whenever his key supporters (wealthy traders, merchants and manufacturers) needed support. In other words, whilst Wilkes certainly did have popular appeal, he used this to further his own interests. So, whilst Wilkes' career does involve the participation of the working classes (which looks forward to later radical campaigns), it does so on his terms. Third, Wilkes used a variety of tactics to further his causes. He used the press to promote his views, he spoke in the Commons (when allowed to), he used the courts and he drummed up popular support by using fiery rhetoric. The tactics used by Wilkes were the sort of tactics used by radicals who campaigned after him. And fourth, the Society of Supporters of the Bill of Rights was formed in February 1769 to raise money to pay off Wilkes' fine, but it evolved into a campaigning organisation, gathering petitions in the hope of extending the agitation in Middlesex to the rest of the country. This was the first radical political society to campaign in the 18th century.

Wilkes' impact
In all the ways described above, therefore, Wilkes' career looks forward to later radical campaigns. But it should be noted that the impact that he made at the time was limited. First, support for radical reform did not spread despite the raising of substantial petitions. Second, after the struggle over Middlesex (1768-74), Wilkes himself established himself in the City and no longer engaged in populist politics. And third, the political system remained intact. Perhaps Wilkes' most important legacy was the fact that, as a result of his efforts, reporting of proceedings in Parliament became established practice. By the late 1770s, major parliamentary debates were being summarised in almost every newspaper, a practice which has continued ever since.

Key political developments
By the early 1780s, a series of political developments had combined to further undermine the credibility of the ruling elite. These developments included:
- the disastrous and economically crippling American War (1776-83)
- fears that George III was abusing his powers of royal patronage to keep in power the unpopular administration of Lord North
- the exploitation of rotten boroughs to secure pro-government majorities.

These developments ensured that the terms of the debate put forward by those opposed to the government began to change:
> 'The seeds of radicalism sown in the 1760s germinated in the late 1770s as merchants and taxpayers in the American colonies rose in defence of their "liberties" against the heavy-handed exactions of George III's ministers, and elevated their struggle into one for the natural rights of man (excluding women and slaves).' (Royle 1997, pp.120-21)

Groups in the 1780s
Groups which responded to these events and became active in the 1780s include, on the one hand, the Reverend Christopher Wyvill's Yorkshire Association and, on the other hand, the Society for Constitutional Information. Both groups were set up in 1780. They had significantly different aims, but a similar make-up in terms of the sort of people who joined them:
> 'Those who challenged the political system in the 1780s were still largely drawn from the "respectable classes" - professional men, merchants and gentry - and they even enjoyed some aristocratic support. The radical message had not yet become identified as the ideology of an emerging political class. This began to change in the 1790s as the Revolution in France inspired reformers to hope for an extension of civil and religious liberties in Britain also.' (Royle 1997, p.121)

The Yorkshire Association was set up as a forum through which country gentlemen could petition Parliament against corruption and call for greater accountability for government actions. It was, in other words, a body which supported moderate reform. The Society for Constitutional Information, on the other hand, had a more radical programme. Its aim was to educate people in all classes about the need for reform. It supported universal male suffrage and annual Parliaments. Although the society aimed to reach all classes, this did not mean that its members came from all classes. Rather, members from the middle or upper classes wrote pamphlets which explained why reform was necessary and then distributed them in the hope that the message would spread. One of the most active members of the Society for Constitutional Information was Major John Cartwright, brother of Edmund Cartwright, the man who invented the power loom. Born in 1740, Cartwright remained an active radical from the 1760s until 1824, the year in which he died.

Popular support for the status quo
Whilst there were some signs that a new phase of radicalism was developing in the period before the French Revolution, there was, equally, plenty of evidence of popular support for the status quo. This can be demonstrated in two ways. First, it should be clear from the discussion above that, although there was support for radical views in some areas, this was

not true of Britain as a whole. Although the Wilkesites undoubtedly found support for their cause outside London when they collected petitions in the summer of 1769, even they did not claim to have won the support of more than 25% of the voters. In other words, 75% of the voters did not support them and there is little evidence of popular support from non-voters (the majority of the population) outside London. Similarly, although the Yorkshire Association grew rapidly for two years, enthusiasm soon drained away. By 1783, the group had little support outside Yorkshire. And second, there is evidence both of popular support for the Establishment and for the status quo. As for support for the Establishment and, in particular, the monarchy, Langford notes:

'Students of history were well aware that no nation could rely on hereditary monarchy to produce the ruler it needed. There was a growing belief by the 1780s that Britain was, for the moment at least, blessed in this respect as it had not been more than briefly since the reign of Elizabeth. George III was truly regarded by many as "The Father of his People", as the antiquarian John Nichols expressed it in a dedication.' (Langford 1999, p.724)

As well as support for the Establishment, there were other signs that the popular mood in the 1780s was not suited to radicalism. The Gordon Riots in 1780, for example, were an open display of religious intolerance. In 1778, the Roman Catholic Relief Bill was passed. In 1779, a similar measure was proposed for Scotland. This was opposed by Lord George Gordon's Protestant Association. This organisation campaigned long and hard against the proposals and, in June 1780, organised a march to petition Parliament. That march turned into a full-scale riot which included attacks on prominent Catholics and their property. Whilst the riot was finally put down by the army, it revealed that, far from supporting the radical cause, many ordinary people harboured reactionary prejudices.

MAIN POINTS - Section 1.1

- Most historians now agree that British radicalism was not created by the French Revolution. Rather, the French Revolution provided momentum to a process already underway.
- For most of the 18th century, opposition to government was rather exclusive. Rarely did the mass of the people have any say in affairs.
- Opposition to government came from clubs and societies and was fuelled by the press.
- John Wilkes' career was important because - (1) he championed causes which challenged the status quo, (2) he relied on popular support, (3) he used a variety of tactics, and (4) his actions resulted in the Society of Supporters of the Bill of Rights being set up - the first radical group of the 18th century.
- Political events encouraged the growth of opposition groups - like the Yorkshire Association and the Society for Constitutional Information which were set up in 1780 - but they made a limited impact. There is evidence of popular support for the status quo.

Activity 2.1 The reform movement of the early 1780s

ITEM 1 John Wilkes

The political system worked well and it was not until the third quarter of the 18th century that anyone suggested that it was in any way in need of revision. The idea that revision might be desirable arose as a result of the notorious career of an outright rogue and demagogue, John Wilkes. Although Wilkes had become an MP through the support of the aristocracy, he found his path to advancement blocked and attacked George III's minister, Lord Bute, so violently that he was put in prison. By getting his friends to apply for a writ of habeas corpus, which implied he had been illegally arrested, the equation Wilkes and 'Liberty' was born. Later, in 1768, Wilkes was to get himself elected MP for Middlesex on a tide of public outrage on his behalf and, although he was repeatedly expelled from the House, he was always re-elected. The fact that he was utterly pernicious (destructive) was neither here nor there. Looked at from the outside, it seemed that the will of the electorate had been over-ruled by a corrupt elite and that something about Parliament was in need of reform. As a result, a parliamentary reform movement came into being.

John Wilkes

Adapted from Strong 1996.

ITEM 2 The Society for Constitutional Information

The design of this society is to diffuse throughout the kingdom, as universally as possible, a knowledge of the great principles of Constitutional Freedom, particularly knowledge on such matters as the election and duration of the **representative body**. With this in view, **Constitutional Tracts**, intended for the extension of this knowledge and to communicate it to persons of all ranks, are printed and distributed **gratis**, at the expense of the society. To procure short parliaments, and a more equal representation of the people, are the primary objects of the attention of this society. The society wishes to **disseminate** that knowledge among its countrymen which may lead them to a general sense of the importance of these objects, and which may **induce them to contend** for their rights, as men and as citizens, with ardour and firmness. Gentlemen desirous of becoming members are to be admitted by ballot and to subscribe from **one to five guineas per annum**.

A statement printed in 1780 by the newly formed Society for Constitutional Information.

Glossary

- **representative body** - Parliament
- **constitutional Tracts** - pamphlets
- **gratis** - free
- **disseminate** - spread
- **induce them to contend** - encourage them to fight
- **one to five guineas** - a guinea was one pound and one shilling (there were 12 pence in a shilling and 20 shillings in a pound)
- **per annum** - each year

Questions

1. a) Compare the account in Item 1 and Box 2.2. What is different and what is the same?
   b) Describe the tone of the historian in Item 1. What did the historian think of John Wilkes and what does this tell us about the views of the historian?
   c) Using Item 1 and Box 2.2 explain why John Wilkes' career was an important step in the development of radicalism in Britain.
2. a) What do Items 2 and 3 tell us about the nature of radicalism in Britain before the French Revolution?
   b) Suggest reasons (i) why radical groups began growing up at this time and (ii) why they stood little chance of success.
3. Using Item 4, explain why the reform movement failed to gain momentum in the 1780s.

ITEM 3 A letter to Major John Cartwright

Newington Green, 2 April 1776

Dear Sir,

...I am, however, afraid that it will not be easy to get any number of great men, though favourable in their opinions, to such a scheme as yours, to be active and zealous in carrying it to execution; nor have I much hope that any great reformation will take place in this country until some calamity comes that shall make us feel more, and awaken us more to reflection.

I am, dear Sir,
Your most obedient and humble servant,

Richard Price

ITEM 4 A historian's view

The aims of the extra-parliamentary movement which emerged in the 1770s were strictly limited. Christopher Wyvill, for example, was a leading reformer. His chief aim was 'economical reform'- he wanted to eliminate placemen from the Commons and, by this means, reduce royal influence. Wyvill, however, was no modern democrat. It was still land and property that were significant, not the number of people without the vote. Universal suffrage was best left to the realms of theory. In any case, the movement's influence did not last long. Many of the discontented country gentlemen were alienated by the extreme radical proposals of groups like the Society for Constitutional Information which included universal manhood suffrage, annual elections, equal electoral districts, the introduction of a secret ballot and the payment of MPs. After 1781 the movement declined rapidly. Outside London and Yorkshire, there was very little support for parliamentary reform. The American crisis, which had stimulated the agitation in the first place, came to an end. Reformers began to quarrel amongst themselves. It needed the writings of the French Revolution to root the reform movement in deeper soil.

Adapted from Wright 1970.

1.2 How have different historians interpreted the impact of the French Revolution on British politics and society?

The terms of the debate

Although it would be logical to assume that the French Revolution (which began in 1789) would have stimulated radical protest in Britain, most historians argue that its impact is not so simple or straightforward. Indeed, many would now agree with the view of Asa Briggs, who claimed that

'The main effect of the French Revolution was not to revitalise English politics at the base of society but to encourage repression from above.' (Briggs 1959, p.133)

On the other hand, there are those, such as the historian E.P. Thompson, who argue that something very new and significant happened in Britain during the 1790s and that this decade witnessed the start of a long-term process which resulted in the formation of working-class political consciousness.

These two different viewpoints are summarised below. Interpretation One represents a synthesis of the views of historians such as Briggs (1959), Dickinson (1985), Emsley (1979) and Thomis & Holt (1977). Interpretation Two is derived from the work of E.P. Thompson (1968) and Williams (1968).

Interpretation One

The groups were limited tactically and ideologically

There never was any real revolutionary threat in Britain during the 1790s. The French Revolution undoubtedly broadened the social basis of political debate and activity in Britain, but the objectives of the majority of radical groups which emerged in its wake retained the largely moderate characteristics of their predecessors in the 1770s and 1780s. They were, in short, reformist rather than revolutionary. One reason for this was the nature of the leadership of the groups. Most leaders came from the middle or upper classes and imposed their values on the groups. Those who came from the working class were skilled workers with middle-class aspirations. As a result, groups rejected violence or conspiracy as methods of achieving their aim of constitutional reform. Also, the radicals failed to politicise the masses and they were unable to harness what the historian Eric Hobsbawm (1968, p.89) has described as 'collective bargaining by riot' - namely, food rioting (a long popular tradition) and early trade union activity (see Unit 4).

The government played its hand skilfully

Tactical limitations and a lack of ideological direction on the part of the radical societies is only a partial explanation of the absence of any revolutionary threat in Britain during this period. William Pitt's government (see also Unit 1) remained in control of the situation throughout and was able to suppress the radical societies through a successfully coordinated policy of ruthless legal repression and propaganda. This propaganda tapped effectively into what were in fact more deep-seated and stronger popular sentiments - namely, loyalism, and (after the outbreak of war with revolutionary France in 1793) patriotism and xenophobia. To put it in simple terms, despite the economic dislocation and social tensions associated with a major war, there was very little real danger of a revolution in Britain during the 1790s because there was very little support for one. What contemporaries perceived as a threat of revolution in the 1790s is, therefore, best seen as a panic reaction amongst some of the propertied classes as a result of the intensification and growing violence of events across the Channel. Genuine revolutionaries in Britain only ever made up a small and largely impotent minority. They resorted to revolution only when their peaceful campaigns for reform were suppressed. Their activities were then effectively tracked through the growing intelligence network and, where necessary, ringleaders were easily picked off.

Interpretation Two

The French Revolution - a stimulus

The French Revolution acted as a major stimulus to popular radicalism in Britain. The activities of the newly formed Corresponding Societies, for example, stimulated the creation of a political consciousness amongst working men and women which, by 1815, had spread beyond the traditional centres of established craft industries to the new and rapidly expanding manufacturing towns of the North and Midlands. This growing radicalism created a genuinely revolutionary impulse which, although defeated in the short term by heavy-handed government repression, was nevertheless to make an important long-term impact on the development of British society in the 19th century.

The middle class betrayed the workers

Before the British radicals were able to mount a sustained challenge on the governing elite, they were betrayed by Whig politicians and members of the middle class who initially welcomed the French Revolution but then lost their nerve and retreated into a panic-stricken defence of the status quo. This 'desertion' produced a decisive and long-term split in British politics and society because it broke the 'natural' alliance between the politically unrepresented classes in Britain (before 1832, few members of the middle class and no members of the working class had the vote and many urban areas were unrepresented in Parliament - see Unit 5, Part 1).

The desertion of the middle class from the revolutionary cause deprived the masses of the sort of leadership essential in any concerted and successful attack on the existing political system. Instead of producing a progressive popular alliance between the middle class and the working class, therefore, the French Revolution resulted in Britain in a consolidation of 'Old Corruption' with the old aristocratic elite and the new manufacturing and commercial elite uniting in a common defence of property.

The radicals made an impact

Whilst it is certainly the case that the British radicals were not strong enough to challenge the existing political order during the 1790s, their impact should not be underestimated. Their struggle in the 1790s created a permanent legacy of dissent which was sustained during the war years of 1793-1815 and re-emerged more forcefully in the periods 1815-20, 1830-32 and the later 1830s (see Units 4-6). The radical movement did not collapse in the mid-1790s under the pressure of repressive legislation. Rather, it went underground, with the United Societies and later Luddism (see Unit 4, Part 1) forming part of a continuous attempt by committed working-class radicals to secure change to their lives. This struggle was of profound importance in the long-term development of working-class political identity.

> **1.3 What impact did the French Revolution make on radical protest in Britain?**

Reaction within Parliament

Within Parliament, the early stages of the French Revolution produced a positive reaction from some of the more liberal members of the Whig opposition. Indeed, the Whig leader, Charles James Fox, even commented that the fall of the Bastille (the infamous Parisian prison) on 14 July 1789 was 'the greatest event that ever happened in the world'. This initial enthusiasm was based upon the belief that the French were about to develop a constitutional monarchy based upon the English model - an idea which led a small group of opposition Whigs to develop plans for moderate parliamentary reform in Britain and, in July 1792, to form the Society of the Friends of the People.

Edmund Burke

It was in response to what he saw as the dangers of his party's flirtation with potentially revolutionary ideas that the young Whig politician Edmund Burke wrote *Reflections on the Revolution in France* (1790). In this essay, which has come to be seen as an early statement of conservative ideology, Burke attacked the idea of natural rights and defended Britain's existing constitution on the grounds that it had grown organically out of Britain's unique history. Moderate reform, Burke warned, would lead to violent revolution; it should therefore be resisted.

The Revolution develops

As events in France took a more extreme and republican turn, so the initial enthusiasm for the early stages of the Revolution amongst the British political elite was replaced by hostility and anxiety. In September 1792, the French National Convention abolished the monarchy and declared a Republic. On 23 January 1793, Louis XVI was executed. His execution was followed by 'the Terror'- the rounding up and execution of alleged opponents of the Revolution. By July 1794, the Revolutionary Tribunal had ordered the execution of 2,400 people in Paris and 30,000 people across France. These developments, together with the expansionist tendencies of the French Republican government, ensured a change in the climate of opinion in Parliament in Britain - opposition Whigs supporting the French Republic became a very small, isolated minority.

Developments outside Parliament

It is developments outside Parliament in the early 1790s, however, which have most excited historians. From about 1792 it is possible to identify the emergence of new radicals - the British 'Jacobins'. By the mid-1790s, it has been estimated that at least 80 new political clubs and societies had been set up across Britain - largely in the major urban centres such as London, Norwich, Sheffield, Manchester, Leeds and Nottingham. By far the largest of these organisations was the London Corresponding Society (LCS), set up by the shoemaker Thomas Hardy in January 1792.

The new radical societies

An analysis of the organisation, membership, tactics and ideas of the new radical societies is fundamental to any understanding of both their nature and the extent of the threat which they posed to the ruling elite. If an extra-parliamentary protest group were to pose a significant - perhaps even a revolutionary - threat to the Establishment in this period, it might be assumed that such a group would be:
- well organised
- widely supported (especially by members of the working class)
- effectively led
- inspired by a clear set of aims and ideas about change
- capable of using a variety of tactics to achieve their aims.

But, although it is clear that many new organisations did spring up in response to the French Revolution, and although membership of these organisations was open to a wider membership than was the case with previous groups, most historians now agree that the new groups lacked many of the criteria listed above. As a result, they never posed a serious threat to the ruling elite in this period.

Organisation and membership

The idea that the membership of the new groups was wider than that of previous groups is supported by three main pieces of evidence. First, there are records which show that tradesmen were members and officers of the new groups. Second, most of the groups were run on a subscription of a penny a week - which can be contrasted with the 'one to five guineas per annum' requested by the Society for Constitutional Information in Activity 2.1, Item 2 (one guinea was 252 pennies or more than four times a penny a week whilst five guineas was 1,260 pennies or more than 24 times a penny a week). And third, as the historian E.P. Thompson points out, groups like the LCS made it explicit that they were 'open to all'.

Typically, groups were organised in a way that clearly reflected the traditions of contemporary craft societies. A Treasurer, Secretary and Executive Committee would be appointed. The officers and Executive Committee would, in turn, be answerable to a General Committee made up of delegates from each branch. Meetings of the General Committee would usually take place in a local tavern on a weekly basis.

The structure of the LCS

The structure of the largest of these groups, the London Corresponding Society (LCS), followed this relatively sophisticated pattern. Smaller branches and divisions were rapidly established across the metropolitan areas in an attempt to evade the growing restrictions placed upon large popular organisations in this period (see Part 2 below). Each of these divisions then elected a delegate to represent it on the LCS's general committee which met once a week to discuss issues. The general committee, in turn, elected an executive committee which planned the Society's policy and coordinated the activities of the individual branches. The founder of the LCS, Thomas Hardy, claimed an active membership of 5,000 in the early 1790s, but a closer analysis of LCS membership suggests that it was both considerably smaller and a far from exclusively working-class organisation. Although the LCS's most famous activists were tradesmen, many other leading figures in the organisation - and indeed also a proportion of the rank and file - were drawn from higher social groupings:

'The London Corresponding Society had an active membership of less than 1,000 for most of its existence, composed in the main of artisans, tradesmen and various members of the "uneasy"

middle class - booksellers, printers, publishers, authors and insecure members of the legal and medical professions.' (Belchem 1996, p.17)

It is important to remember that the LCS was the largest of the radical societies in this period. Many of the other societies were composed of only a handful of active members and often folded under pressure from local loyalist associations (see Part 2 below). It is also important to remember, however, that an organisation's success cannot always be judged by the size of its membership. Regardless of the number of formal members, the LCS was able to attract many thousands of supporters to the open air meetings it organised in the period 1793-95.

Geographical distribution

Just as the extent of mass support for the new radical societies has been questioned, so too has their geographical distribution:

'Some substantial provincial towns, including Bristol, Hull, Liverpool, Plymouth and Portsmouth could not sustain radical societies...Clearly the cause of radical parliamentary reform had more support than ever before in the 1790s, and it made impressive advances among urban artisans and tradesmen in some areas, but it failed to rally support across the whole country or within all social groups in the nation.' (Dickinson 1985, p.13)

Aims and ideology

By definition, a coherent radical movement has clear aims and an ideology - a vision of a better society or political system which inspires and motivates the rank-and-file during periods of difficulty or setback. Groups like the LCS certainly had a political agenda. The organisation adopted a reform programme which called for:

● universal manhood suffrage
● annual elections
● the redistribution of parliamentary seats following the abolition of rotten boroughs (see Unit 5, Part 1 for a definition).

Most historians now agree, however, that this programme went no further than calling for reform of the existing system - it did not aim for the complete replacement of the existing system with an alternative, republican structure. Indeed, it appears that leaders of both the LCS and the other major provincial organisation, the Sheffield Society for Constitutional Information, were anxious to distance themselves from the more extreme ideas published in Thomas Paine's two-volume *Rights of Man* (1791-92) - see Box 2.4.

Tactics and leadership

The tactics chosen by the radical societies in the early 1790s also appear to emphasise moderation and the general absence of revolutionary intent.

BOX 2.4 | Thomas Paine (1737-1809)

Thomas Paine was the son of a textile manufacturer based in Norfolk. He worked as an apprentice in his father's firm and then became an excise officer, before being sacked for leading a strike for higher pay. In 1774 he emigrated to the USA and worked as a journalist. He fought on the colonists' side against Britain and, when his pamphlet *Common Sense* was published in 1776, it influenced the terms of the American Declaration of Independence. Paine returned to Britain in 1787 and in 1791-92 wrote *The Rights of Man* in two volumes. This was a reply to, and a rejection of, Edmund Burke's *Reflections on the Revolution in France*. In the first volume, Paine laid out an ideological basis for republican reform by rejecting the notion that societies develop organically from their past and asserting instead that each age has the right to establish a new political system if that is what best fits its needs. In the second volume, he went on to demonstrate how a reformed government would subsequently go on to relieve the poor by

Thomas Paine

raising a property tax to finance a remarkable range of state welfare benefits. Paine's writings were very popular (by 1793, 200,000 copies of *The Rights of Man* had been sold in cheap editions) and their revolutionary implications certainly alarmed wide sections of the propertied classes, but they were never fully incorporated into the programme of the major radical societies in Britain. Paine questioned the legitimacy of the monarchy, nobility and established Church and promoted the idea of republican democracy. None of the radical societies ever went this far, with the LCS consistently denying any connection with republicanism or broader schemes for the redistribution of wealth. In September 1792, Paine was charged with treason over *The Rights of Man* and went into exile in France. In France he became a member of the National Assembly, but was imprisoned during the Terror. He returned to the USA in 1802.

Adapted from Cole & Filson 1965.

Historians (such as Thomis & Holt 1977, Dickinson 1985 and Evans 1996) emphasise that:

- the LCS, in particular, distanced itself from unconstitutional methods and violence, favouring meetings and the use of pamphlets and periodicals to spread ideas about reform
- radical publications emphasised the importance of the peaceful petitioning of Parliament, together with the broader political education of the people and appeals to reason as the best means of achieving change
- there was an absence of national leaders to provide a focus for the different local organisations
- the radical groups failed to capitalise on a tradition of direct popular action and of trade union activity, and, as a result, they were unable to harness the labouring poor to their demands for political change.

For most historians, this last point represents the greatest tactical failing by the radical societies. Despite the tradition of food rioting and labour disputes, the leaders of the radical groups in the 1790s made little or no attempt to 'politicise' this type of essentially economic protest and, as a result, failed to rally the mass of the population behind their call for constitutional reforms.

Why did radical groups fail to gain popular support?

Any explanation of why radical groups failed to rally the mass of the population must consider the social composition of the leadership of these groups. Since the majority of radical leaders were drawn from what can be described (to use the 18th-century term) as the 'middling orders' of society, they had little direct contact with workers and were, as a result, fearful of unleashing forces they might not then be able to control. Besides, economic and social reforms were not their priority. Their goal of political equality was simply not linked to a programme designed to alleviate the economic suffering of the masses:

'The most extensive popular movements of those years were not concerned with politics, except indirectly, and these were the food riots of 1795...Yet this potentially dangerous situation for the government never assumed real political menace because the food rioters remained men apart, quite separate from the movement of political protest, and never recruited on behalf of any political movement. They had the force of a revolutionary mob, but they employed it in a cause and manner that were traditional and almost legitimate within English life. The food rioter was a familiar animal whose aid was neither obtained nor sought by the political reformer.' (Thomis & Holt, 1977, p.25)

The National Convention

The one area of controversy surrounding the tactics of the radical societies is the plan of some (predominantly Scottish) leading reformers to establish a National Convention (an assembly made up of delegates elected from all parts of Britain) in Edinburgh during November and December 1793. The term 'National Convention' was a provocative reference to the French body which had proclaimed the establishment of the French Republic in September 1792, and it does appear that some figures (such as the republican Thomas Muir) hoped that it could form an alternative 'popular Parliament' composed of delegates representing radical societies from around the country. Muir and other leading delegates were quickly convicted for sedition, however, and the National Convention was closed down in what was to be the first in a series of decisive moves by the governing elite against the further development of radical activity (see Section 2.1 below).

The tactical dilemma

In practice, it seems that the new radical societies were unable to overcome a tactical dilemma - namely, how is it possible to reform an unwilling Parliament by peaceful means? If Paine was read literally, his message was revolutionary, but he did not openly support revolution or offer any strategic plan for obtaining change. In any case, his ideas were not (as noted above) widely accepted as a basis for action by the radical leaders. As the government's response to the radical societies became increasingly repressive (see Section 2.1 below), so the societies found themselves increasingly starved of the oxygen of publicity they required for survival in their existing constitutional and essentially moderate forms. This resulted, after 1795, in the disappearance of some societies, or, in a small number of more extreme cases, a shift towards more subversive underground activity (see Section 3.1 below).

MAIN POINTS - Sections 1.2 - 1.3

- Historians have interpreted the impact of the French Revolution on British radicalism in two main ways - (1) rather than stimulating radical protest, the French Revolution encouraged its suppression, and (2) although there was no chance of revolution in the 1790s, the French Revolution made an important contribution to the growth of class consciousness.
- Within a short time, the vast majority of those in Parliament strongly opposed the course of the French Revolution.
- In the short term, the French Revolution stimulated extra-parliamentary activity - many new radical groups were set up and, for the first time, these groups encouraged the participation of artisans and tradesmen.
- The organisation, membership, tactics and ideas of the new radical societies were such that there was never any real likelihood of revolution in the 1790s. The groups were run by moderate, mainly middle-class leaders who had limited aims and were fearful of unleashing forces they might not be able to control.

Activity 2.2 The new radical societies

ITEM 1 An address from the LCS

An LCS medal

Confident in the purity of our motives, and in the justice of our cause, let us meet falsehood with proofs, and hypocrisy with plainness. Let us persevere in declaring our principles, and misrepresentation will meet its due reward - contempt. In this view, the comments of the late Aristocratic Association call for a few remarks, on account of the declaration they have published relative to other Clubs and Societies formed in this nation. They take it on themselves to assert that bodies of their countrymen have been associated, professing opinions favourable to the 'rights of man, to liberty and equality' and, moreover, that those opinions are conveyed in the terms 'No King!' and 'No Parliament!' So much for their assertions. If this be intended to include the Societies to which we respectively belong, we here, in the most solemn manner, deny the latter part of the charge; while, in admitting the former, we claim the privilege and glory in the character of Britons. Whoever shall attribute to us (who wish only the restoration of the lost liberties of our country) the expressions 'No King!' 'No Parliament!' or any design of invading the property of other men, is guilty of a wilful, an impudent and a malicious falsehood. We know and are sensible that the wages of every man are his right; that differences of strength, of talents and of industry do and ought to afford proportional distinctions of property which, when acquired and confirmed by the laws, is sacred and inviolable. We defy the most slavish and malevolent man to bring the remotest proof to the contrary.

Adapted from a pamphlet produced by the LCS in 1792.

ITEM 2 A historian's view (i)

The British 'Jacobins' of the late 18th century derived their name from revolutionary France but their political role had little in common with their French counterparts. The name 'Jacobin' was a blanket term of abuse (like the term 'Red' in the West during the Cold War) of a kind that many societies find it convenient to employ to cover all those who disturb their complacency and settled ways of thought. Just as contemporaries found it convenient to label as 'Jacobins' all reformers of various kinds (however remote from the power and fury of the French) so have historians been content to use this easily accessible if misleading name for British reformers who never came close to leading a revolution in their own country.

Adapted from Thomis & Holt 1977.

ITEM 3 A historian's view (ii)

'That the number of our members be unlimited' was the first rule of the LCS as cited by its Secretary, Thomas Hardy, when he wrote to a similar society in Sheffield in March 1792. In his memoirs, Hardy recalled that the first meeting of the LCS (a meeting at which nine were present) went as follows: 'After having had their bread and cheese and porter for supper, as usual, and their pipes afterwards, with some conversation on the hardness of the times and the dearness of all the necessities of life...the business for which they had met was brought forward - Parliamentary Reform - an important subject to be deliberated upon and dealt with by such a class of men.' There are features in even this brief description of the LCS's first meeting which indicate that a new kind of organisation had come into being. There is the working man as Secretary (Hardy was a shoemaker who had once worked as a bricklayer). There is the low weekly subscription. There is the intermingling of economic and political themes - 'the hardness of the times' and Parliamentary Reform. There is the function of the meeting - both as a social occasion and as a centre for political activity. Above all, there is the determination to air opinions and to organise the converted, embodied in the leading rule 'that the number of members be unlimited'. Today, we might pass over such a rule as a commonplace; and yet it is one of the hinges on which history turns. It signified the end to any notion of exclusiveness, of politics as the preserve of an elite. It meant the LCS was turning its back on the age-old identification of political with property rights and also turning its back on the days of 'Wilkes and Liberty' when the 'mob' did not organise itself but was called into action. In other words, it implied a new notion of democracy. Such a revolutionary challenge was bound to lead to a charge of high treason.

Adapted from Thompson 1980.

ITEM 4 A cartoon from 1795

The wave of radical activity which developed in response to the French Revolution reached its peak in 1795. This cartoon by Gillray shows one of the many open-air meetings held in London in 1795.

Questions

1. a) Describe the ideological stance of the LCS as outlined in Item 1.
   b) Why do you think the LCS chose to respond to the charges made by the Aristocratic Association?
   c) Using Item 3, explain why the authorities might feel that the LCS was threatening revolution.
2. Look at Item 2.
   a) How useful is the term 'British Jacobins'?

b) How does the interpretation in Item 2 differ from that in Item 3?
3. a) Describe what is happening in Item 4.
   b) What is the attitude of the cartoonist? How do you know?
   c) 'After the French Revolution, protest in Britain was never the same again'. Explain this statement using Items 2-4.

2 Government repression and popular loyalism

Key issues

1. What were the main features of Pitt's 'Reign of Terror'?

2. How effective were these measures?

3. What part did popular loyalist organisations play in the suppression of radicalism?

2.1 What were the main features of Pitt's 'Reign of Terror'

A revolutionary equation

One way of explaining British radicalism in the 1790s is to use what could be described as a 'revolutionary equation'. On one side of the equation is the radicals' failure - or unwillingness - to develop the organisational structure and tactics necessary to mount a sustained challenge to the governing classes. On the other side is the government's ability to use its executive, judicial and legislative powers - together with an effective propaganda campaign - to undermine the position of the radical movement.

Pitt's 'Reign of Terror'

In the 1790s, the government was headed by William Pitt (Prime Minister from 1783 to 1801 and again from 1804 to 1806 - see Unit 1). The phrase which is usually used to describe the Pitt government's strategy for dealing with the radical threat from 1793 is 'Reign of Terror' - an ironic term first developed by the radicals themselves in an attempt to equate the Pitt government's policies with the 'Terror' in France (the period of extremism and violence in France from 1793 to 1794 - see Section 1.3 above). Although the repressive policies pursued by Pitt's government were far less violent than those pursued by the Jacobin regime

in France, it is clear that, by May 1792, the British government genuinely believed that the nation was, or could be, threatened by a revolutionary conspiracy, if the radical societies were not rapidly checked, and that steps must be taken to ensure that this did not happen. It is also important to bear in mind that, after February 1793, Britain was a country at war with Revolutionary France and that, in such circumstances, the control of 'alien' and 'treacherous' ideas (however vaguely associated with the events of 1789) was justified as a patriotic and necessary defence of national security:

'In government eyes, open-air meetings demanding parliamentary reform were both a threat to the established political order and the precursors of revolutionary mobs demanding blood, whatever the protestations of the reformers about the limits of their aims and the means which they would employ to achieve them. The events which occurred in France from 1789, the coming of war in 1793 and the subsequent invasion scares all combined to ensure that the British government would act in a less than rational manner when confronted with reform demands.' (Thomis & Holt 1977, pp.12-13)

Whilst Pitt's government has been criticised for its heavy-handed approach, it is important to note that the policy of controlling radical activity took various forms and operated at several levels.

Intimidation

On one level, the government used intimidation. It did this in three ways. First, between 1790 and 1793, the government relied on magistrates to monitor and discourage radical action in the localities - the tactic which had operated for most of the 18th century. Since, for example, magistrates were responsible for issuing licences to pubs, they could threaten to take away licences from publicans who allowed radical meetings to take place on their premises (see Box 2.5).

BOX 2.5 | Magistrates clamp down

The Magistrates having received information that certain persons are in the habit of frequently assembling at several public houses within this borough and there forming clubs and associations and reading libelous publications and holding **seditious discourses**, tending to deceive and **render the unwary discontented in their stations** and to disturb the

Glossary
- **seditious discourses** – treasonable discussions
- **render the unwary discontented in their stations** - encourage the unwary to become dissatisfied with their place in society

public peace, think it proper to give notice to all publicans and ale-house-keepers in this borough that it is expected from them strictly to observe the several rules and conditions contained in their licences; and that if any such illegal meetings are held at their houses, their licences will not in future be renewed.

Judgement issued by Mayor Edmund Lacon at the Court of Mayoralty held in the Borough of Great Yarmouth on 8 December 1792.

Second, by 1793, the use of purely localised agencies of law and order was no longer regarded as sufficient and, as a result, the Home Office was expanded. An Alien Section and a small Secret Service Section were set up. The Home Secretary also made extensive use of spies and informers who successfully infiltrated the LCS and other leading radical societies. And third, the government mobilised the judicial system by bringing prosecutions against prominent radicals. Two sets of trials became particularly notorious. The first took place in Scotland in 1793-94. The Scottish

BOX 2.6 | The trial of Thomas Muir

The question, then, gentlemen, for your consideration is simply this...do you think the panel guilty of sedition or not? Now, in examining this question, there are two things which you should attend to which require no proof. The first is that the British constitution is the best in the world - for the truth of this, gentlemen, I need only appeal to your own feelings. Is not every man secure in his life, liberty and property?...The other circumstance, gentlemen, which you have to attend to is the state of this country during last winter. There was a spirit of sedition and revolt going abroad which made every good subject seriously uneasy. I observed the reflection of the master of the Grammar School of Glasgow who told Mr Muir he conceived that proposing reform then was very ill timed. I coincide in that opinion and leave it to you to judge whether it was perfectly innocent or not in Mr Muir, at such a time, to go about among ignorant country people and among the lower classes of the people making them leave off their work and inducing them to believe that a reform was absolutely necessary to preserve their safety and their liberty, which had it not been for him, they never would have suspected to have been in danger. You will keep this in remembrance and judge whether it appears to you, as to me, to be sedition.

Part of the speech made by the judge to the jury at the end of the trial of Thomas Muir in August 1793.

radical, Thomas Muir (who, with others, had tried to set up a National Convention - see Section 1.4 above), was charged with sedition (inciting revolution) and sentenced to 14 years' transportation after a trial in which the judge displayed great bias (see Box 2.6). And then, the Reverend Thomas Palmer was charged with encouraging others to read the works of Thomas Paine and other subversive literature. He was sentenced to seven years' transportation.

The second set of trials - the 'treason trials' - took place in England in 1794 when leaders of the LCS and Constitutional Society were arrested and charged with treasonable conspiracy. Although, following a skilful presentation of the defence by lawyer Thomas Erskine, Thomas Hardy and John Horne Tooke were acquitted by the jury and the other charges dropped in London, this did not prevent the government from proceeding against many radicals in other parts of England. Even in London, fears aroused by the trials and government action led to the break-up of the Constitutional Society and many other local groups.

Legislation

As well as intimidation, the government passed a number of laws designed to curb the activities of radicals. First, in 1794, the Act of Habeas Corpus was suspended. Habeas Corpus had been seen as an essential principle of the justice system in Britain, guaranteeing those who were arrested the right to a trial within a stated period. Its suspension meant that the government could hold what were, in effect, political prisoners for an indefinite length of time.

Second, in December 1795, after an attack on the King's coach, the government rushed the so-called 'Two Acts' through Parliament. The first, the Treasonable and Seditious Practices Act, broadened the law of treason. The second, the Seditious Meetings Act, banned meetings of more than 50 people whose object was to petition Parliament or discuss any reform of the Church or state. And third, in 1799 and 1800, restrictions were also extended to the labour market, with the Combination Laws effectively banning the development of early trade unions.

Propaganda

There was more to the government's policy than repressive legislation. The 'Reign of Terror' was underpinned by a propaganda campaign designed to tap into and mobilise conservative sentiment throughout British society. The 1790s saw a flood of conservative publications such as *The Oracle*, *The Sun* and *The True Briton*, all of which advanced the virtues of the existing system and banded together all radicals, claiming that they were dangerous traitors and anarchists. The effectiveness of such propaganda was reflected at two different levels. First, parliamentary support for Pitt's government steadily increased during the 1790s as the more conservative Whigs broke away from Charles James Fox and joined the coalition (see Unit 1). And second, conservative propaganda appears to have been particularly effective in exploiting deep-seated feelings of popular patriotism, which were further stimulated by invasion fears and the ongoing war with first Revolutionary and then Napoleonic France. This has led some historians to argue that popular loyalism was actually a far more widespread and potent force than popular radicalism (see Section 2.3 below).

2.2 How effective were these measures?

The 'Reign of Terror' was effective

Historians have long debated both the nature and the effectiveness of Pitt's 'Reign of Terror'. Most now accept that government policy was essentially an expedient emergency response to a perceived domestic crisis which was intensified by the onset of war. They point out that there was little opposition to Pitt's approach within Parliament and that this consensus was reflected across the country as a whole in the growth of popular loyalist organisations. It is emphasised that most of the measures introduced were of a temporary nature - the suspension of Habeas Corpus was initially limited to six months and the Seditious Meetings Act was designed to remain in force for three years. The temporary nature of these measures, together with a reluctance to use the legislation to clamp down on any large scale, have led to the broad conclusion that Pitt was not planning any permanent change to the constitution. Rather, the government exploited the opportunity created by fears of a French invasion both to build up broad parliamentary backing for the administration and to strike a major blow against the radicals. By 1795-96, most historians would agree, Pitt's combination of repression and propaganda had eliminated the threat of popular radicalism:

'The pressure on radicals was remorseless. It matters little that the legislation was not much used. The Two Acts set an example and alerted the propertied classes to the potential danger in which the country stood. They increased the pressure on the radical societies which, by the summer of 1796, were in serious decline.' (O'Gorman 1997, p.246)

The 'Reign of Terror' was ineffective

Thomis & Holt (1977), on the other hand, have argued that the 'Reign of Terror' was counterproductive. They admit that, on one level it was effective because it suppressed radicalism and, as a result, ended the overt threat. But on another level, they argue, it was not so effective since it drove the more extreme elements in the movement 'underground', where they continued to function in conspiratorial and, arguably, more dangerous and potentially revolutionary 'cells' (see Section 3.1 below).

2.3 What was the role of popular loyalist organisations in the suppression of radicalism?

Loyalism

As already indicated in Section 2.1 above, conservative propaganda tapped into a rich vein of popular loyalist feeling across the country. The historian Ian Christie (1982) argues that this support is sometimes underestimated. Support for the traditional institutions of monarchy, aristocracy and the Church of England, he claims, was based on:

- a general recognition of the country's increasing prosperity
- improvements in the Poor Law
- relative freedom to take part in trade union activity (until the 1790s).

For the lower classes in Britain, Christie argues, everyday life in Britain was perceived as being preferable to that experienced on the Continent and especially to that experienced in Revolutionary France.

Crowds in the late 18th century

This point of view fits with the results of research into 18th-century crowds and riots carried out by George Rudé (see Rudé 1964) and others. Rudé's research shows that:

- crowds in the 18th century were not irrational or aimless (as many historians had previously assumed); their actions should instead be interpreted in the context of the political climate of the time
- the stereotypical view that the majority of participants were drawn from the ranks of the criminal or unemployed population

should be rejected - larger disturbances often contained a fairly typical cross-section of the whole working population

- disturbances were often highly disciplined and ritualised forms of protest in which the populace acted in accordance with a coherent set of values.

Historians used to assume that rioting crowds were primarily a problem of law and order. The lower classes, it was assumed, were fickle and prone to respond to rumours and agitation. Once a few ringleaders had been arrested, peace was normally restored. This view is now generally regarded as an oversimplification. An examination of what rioters actually said and did reveals that:

'The common people had certain strongly held notions of justice and when these were grossly offended direct action followed.' (Harrison 1984, p.244)

A term now often used to describe the deep-rooted patterns of behaviour and belief exhibited by 18th-century crowds is 'moral economy' of the poor:

'Underlying the demands and actions of the rioters was a traditional view of society in which everyone, rich and poor alike, had a proper function to perform in the community.' (Harrison 1984, p.244)

As this suggests, the 18th-century tradition of rioting was essentially conservative rather than progressive. Indeed, for the most part it was stimulated by popular opposition to changes in local customs and practices. It is, therefore, perhaps not surprising that the threat to the traditional view of society posed by the radicals should have sparked a backlash amongst the lower classes.

Loyalist associations

In the 1790s, anti radical feelings were increasingly formalised by the emergence of a large number of popular loyalist associations. Although these organisations were often financially backed and encouraged by the local propertied elite, magistrates and clergymen, it seems that these counter-revolutionary organisations were genuine reflections of popular feeling and were not directly established as part of any government initiative. On the whole, the membership (like that of the radical groups) was confined to men of property, though, when action was taken, support from the lower classes was encouraged.

The development of this movement had powerful results:

'The propaganda victory of the loyalists over the godless republican levellers [ie the radicals] should not be attributed to superior argument. Much of the loyalist case...relied on evasiveness, misrepresentation and transparent special pleading. Where loyalists triumphed was in

quantity not quality, through their supremacy in what sociologists call "resource mobilisation". Untroubled by the authorities or by lack of funds, loyalists deployed every medium and resource from parish pulpit to national organisation (Reeves' Association for the Preservation of Liberty and Property against Republicans and Levellers was the largest political organisation in the country) to spread the patriotic conservative message in popular...form among the lower orders. Many of the new "corresponding" societies fell victim to this conservative onslaught.' (Belchem 1996, p.19)

Church and King clubs

'Church and King' clubs grew up in many parts of the country during the early 1790s. These staunchly Anglican and loyalist organisations used violence and intimidation to crush the threat which they believed was posed to the Church and the state by political reformers and dissenters (members of Christian sects which had broken away from the Church of England - such as Baptists and Unitarians). The most serious disturbances occurred in Birmingham in July 1791 and in Manchester in 1792

BOX 2.7 A historian's account

Birmingham, 1791
Dissenters played so large a part in the economic, intellectual and corporate life of Birmingham that the 'Church and King' party had long felt bitterness. What sparked the riot was a dinner held by middle-class reformers (many of them dissenters) on 14 July to celebrate the fall of the Bastille. That night and for the next three days a mob ran amuck in the city sacking two Unitarian and one Baptist meeting houses, burning a score of houses and many shops of wealthy dissenters and releasing prisoners from the Town Prison. There can be no doubt about popular resentment against some of the wealthy dissenters. But there are a number of suspicious circumstances. First, there is the undoubted complicity of several prominent Tory magistrates and clergy who encouraged the rioters, directed them at the meeting houses, intervened half-heartedly, refused to prosecute offenders and may have pointed out targets. Second, there is the small number of rioters. Apart from miners and others who joined at the weekend, the mob was rarely above 250 and accounts repeatedly identify a hard core of about 30 who did most of the serious damage. And third, there is evidence that this hard core (some or all of whom may not have been locals) worked to a definite plan and was exceptionally well-briefed as to the religious and political beliefs of prominent Birmingham citizens.
Adapted from Thompson 1980.

when Church and King members attacked the property of leading dissenters and reformers. In both cases, there is evidence to suggest that the attacks may initially have been encouraged by local magistrates (see Box 2.7).

Reeves Associations

Throughout 1792-93, the number of loyalist organisations grew rapidly, with historians estimating that several thousand groups were in existence by the end of 1793. Most modelled themselves on the largest and most influential of these groups - the Association for Preserving Liberty and Property against Republicans and Levellers (APLP). This group was set up in November 1792 by John Reeves, a lawyer. Reeves did have connections with the government, but it appears that he established the APLP without any official prompting. The APLP rapidly grew to become the largest of all political organisations in the country at this time with nearly 2,000 branches nationwide. Local APLP activists were usually men of property and these 'Reeves Associations' as they became commonly known mirrored the membership and organisational structure of their radical opponents.

A changing role

At first, loyalist groups concentrated on the (often violent) intimidation of known radicals in their local area. Increasingly, however, they also became a vehicle for the production and distribution of loyalist propaganda. After their success in preventing the spread of radical activity, their role changed again. In response to the growing demands of the war, many groups shifted their focus to supporting the war effort against France, raising funds to aid recruitment and to provide relief for the dependants of the dead or injured, and even, in some places, transforming themselves into a paramilitary internal defence force - the Volunteers - which, by 1804, was 450,000 strong. In this way, the Reeves Associations continued to act as agents of political stability in Britain, ensuring that the various pressures and strains of war did not stimulate a revival of radical activity:

'In March 1794, the government...authorised the raising of the Volunteers...Though never called upon to meet the French, the Volunteers did become a major police force for the preservation of internal order. In many ways, however, its primary significance was as an instrument of propaganda. It demonstrated the willingness of the propertied classes to fight to preserve their privileged position. Only the totally reliable poor were allowed to join as private soldiers and even then they were commanded by their landlords and employers. The willingness to serve at any level became a political test of loyalty to the existing regime. The parades, the military exercises and the patriotic speeches at celebration dinners were all designed to demonstrate the strength and commitment of the propertied class. The Volunteers not only sought to intimidate their radical opponents, they also succeeded in encouraging loyalty and patriotism among the public at large.' (Dickinson 1985, p.36)

MAIN POINTS - Part 2

- Pitt's 'Reign of Terror' was a response to the belief that the nation was, or could be, threatened by a revolutionary conspiracy and to the fact that, from February 1793, Britain was at war with France.
- Pitt's 'Reign of Terror' had three main strands - (1) intimidation (encouraging magistrates to take action against radicals and putting prominent radicals on trial), (2) legislation (passing laws to curb radical activity) and (3) propaganda.
- Most historians accept that the 'Reign of Terror' was essentially an emergency response to a perceived domestic crisis which was intensified by the onset of war. Most also agree that, by 1795-96, the combination of repression and propaganda had eliminated the threat of popular radicalism.
- The extent of popular loyalism should not be underestimated. Even many riots had a conservative rather than a radical goal.
- In the 1790s, anti-radical feelings were increasingly formalised by the emergence of a large number of popular loyalist associations - notably, Church and King clubs and Reeves' associations. The role of these groups changed as the radical threat receded and the war against France continued.

Activity 2.3 The impact of popular loyalism

ITEM 1 Contemporary loyalist propaganda

THE CONTRAST
1792

BRITISH LIBERTY.   FRENCH LIBERTY.

RELIGION.   MORALITY.   ATHEISM   PERJURY.
LOYALTY OBEDIENCE TO THE LAWS   REBELLION TREASON ANARCHY MURDER
INDEPENDANCE PERSONAL SECURITY   EQUALITY MADNESS CRUELTY INJUSTICE
JUSTICE INHERITANCE PROTECTION   TREACHERY INGRATITUDE IDLENESS
PROPERTY INDUSTRY NATIONAL PROSPERITY   FAMINE NATIONAL & PRIVATE RUIN.
HAPPINESS   MISERY
            WHICH IS BEST

'The Contrast', a cartoon by Thomas Rowlandson produced in 1793. This was commissioned and published by the Crown and Anchor (Anti-levelling) Society.

ITEM 3 Loyalist activity in 1792-93

Guy Fawkes-type demonstrations against Tom Paine were promoted throughout the country. In the small Pennine weaving town of Ripponden, a prosperous lawyer noted in his diary for 7 January 1793 that he paid certain people 'who carried about Tom Payne's effigy and shot at it, 10s 6d'. A Heckmondwike mill owner himself impersonated Paine and had himself 'discovered' reading Rights of Man among the coal pits. His mask was transferred to a straw effigy which was dragged around the village and 'executed'. At nearby Littletown, a wooden image of Paine was pounded to bits with a sledge-hammer with such vigour that the executioner's hands 'ran with blood'. In December 1792, 'the effigy of Tom Paine was, with great solemnity, drawn on a sledge from Lincoln Castle to the gallows and then hanged, amidst a great multitude of spectators. After being suspended the usual time, it was taken to the castle hill and there hung on a gibbet post erected for the purpose. In the evening a large fire was made under the effigy which...was consumed with ashes, amidst the acclamation of many hundreds of people accompanied with a grand band of music playing "God Save the King".' Even in small market towns like Brigg and Caistor, branches of Reeves' associations were formed among whose purposes (to quote the Caistor Society) was 'vigilance and activity in discovering and bringing to justice all persons who shall, either by publishing or distributing seditious papers or writings or by engaging in any illegal associations or conspiracies endeavour to disturb the public peace'. If the distribution of *Rights of Man* was nationwide, so also was the promotion of anti-Jacobin societies. In England, the revolutionary impulse had scarcely begun to gather force before it was exposed to counter-revolutionary assault backed by the resources of established authority.

Adapted from Thompson 1980.

ITEM 2 A Church and King club statement

Declaration
This society beholds with infinite concern the many dangerous plots and associations that are forming in the different parts of this kingdom for the **avowed** purpose of **disseminating discord** and for subverting one of the most beautiful systems of government that the combined efforts of human wisdom has ever yet been able to accomplish. When we see such deadly wounds aimed at our glorious constitution, we consider it the duty of all good citizens publicly to step forward and express their **abhorrence** of the most wicked of those disappointed men who are **audaciously clamorous** for a reform in Parliament but whose real object is to excite civil commotion in this our happy and well-governed state...

Principles
It is a principle of this society to revere the constitution and obey the King, according to the laws of that constitution. It is a principle of this society to **reprobate** the wild theories and seditious doctrines respecting the rights of man which have lately been **promulgated** by the enemies of our most excellent constitution in church and state, as they are subversive of all civil authority; and that, if they were put into practice, would tend to nothing but anarchy and confusion - which is contrary to all order...It is a principle of this society that the legislature of this country ought ever to consist of King, Lords and Commons. It is a principle of this society that it is **requisite** in every good governed state that there must exist **an established church** and that no one is to bear any office, either in church or in state, but such as will conform, and be in communion, with that church.

Part of the document laying out the declaration and principles of the Church and King Club set up in June 1792 at the Weaver's Arms on Cockpit Hill, Manchester.

Glossary
- **avowed** - express
- **disseminating discord** - spreading trouble
- **abhorrence** - hatred
- **audaciously clamorous** - shamelessly loud in their appeals
- **reprobate** - reject
- **promulgated** - made public
- **requisite** - a requirement
- **an established church** - ie the Church of England

ITEM 4 A Church and King riot

A mob of several hundred people led by an atrocious ruffian came in front of the house and with shouts of 'Church and King for ever! Down with t'Jacobins!' began to smash the windows and break open the doors. Every article of furniture was broken. The glasses, jugs, and other vessels were dashed on the floor and trampled under foot. The bar was gutted. Others again were beating and kicking and maltreating in various ways the persons found in the house. Several of these were lamed. Others were seriously crushed and injured in their persons. The parson of the place, whose name was Berry, standing on an elevated situation, pointed them out to the mob, saying -'There goes one; and there goes one! That's a Jacobin; that's another!'

This extract describes a Church and King riot near Manchester in April 1794. It was written by Samuel Bamford, a literate weaver.

Questions

1. 'The extent and impact of loyalism in the early 1790s should not be underestimated'. Explain this statement using Items 1-4.

2. a) What point is being made by the cartoon in Item 1?
   b) Explain how you know it is a loyalist cartoon.
   c) Explain why it would be accurate to describe Item 1 as a piece of propaganda.

3. Look at Items 2-4.
   a) Why were loyalist organisations set up and what tactics did they use?
   b) How did the demands of loyalist organisations differ from those of radical organisations?
   c) How do Items 2-4 help to explain the failure of radicalism in the early 1790s?

3 The 'revolutionary underground' and the radical threat 1795-1815

Key issues

1. What was the 'revolutionary underground'?
2. Why did Britain avoid revolution in this period?

3.1 What was the 'revolutionary underground'?

E.P. Thompson's thesis

Before the publication of E.P. Thompson's groundbreaking work *The Making of the English Working Class* (Thompson 1980), the traditional argument was that popular radicalism in the 1790s ended with the apparently conclusive defeat of the Jacobin societies in 1795-96. Today, however, most historians agree with Thompson that radicalism went 'underground' between 1795 and 1815 - although few would agree with his conclusion that this activity formed part of a coherent movement which continued to pose a serious and genuinely revolutionary threat. Thompson's argument has often been challenged on the grounds that his claims about the existence of a conspiratorial revolutionary underground were founded almost exclusively on reports by spies, informers and agent provocateurs

whose payment and continued employment was essentially based on results - in other words, the more 'conspiracy' they successfully 'unearthed' the more and longer they were paid! Nevertheless, historians as diverse as Dickinson (1997), Thomis & Holt (1977) and O'Gorman (1997) have all agreed that underground activity can be identified in the period 1795-1815. Where they differ from Thompson is in their assessment of the significance and extent of this activity:

'When more evidence becomes available, the historian still has to decide whether these revolutionary plots were in any sense practical projects or merely the over-optimistic fantasies of deluded men.' (Dickinson 1997, p.6)

The question of the extent and significance of this 'revolutionary underground' is usually considered in relation to:

- the involvement of the more militant and determined survivors of the LCS and other provincial societies with Irish revolutionaries, as reflected in the formation of United Societies in mainland Britain
- the naval mutinies of 1797
- food rioting and the 'Black Lamp conspiracy' 1800-1802
- the Despard conspiracy of 1802
- Luddite disturbances after 1810.

The United Irishmen and United Societies in Britain

Developments in Ireland were a concern to the British government throughout the 1790s (see Unit 9). The 'Society of United Irishmen', a radical organisation similar in social composition to those established on the mainland, was set up in 1791. Its aim was to unite both Catholics and Protestants in an attempt to gain an independent Irish republic. To achieve this, the Society of United Irishmen was prepared to use force. Despite attempts to develop a military organisation and to secure aid from France, the group suffered from internal divisions and from the infiltration of spies and informers. Also, the formation of rival sectarian organisations, especially the Protestant Orange Order, led to violence and a loss of clear political direction. The strongly nationalistic element in early Irish radicalism did much to separate it initially from the emerging reform movement in England and Scotland. It was not until the activity of radicals in mainland Britain was suppressed that the United Irishmen formed any real contact with the underground groups that had survived Pitt's 'Reign of Terror'.

Links after 1795

After 1795, there is evidence of growing links between the United Irishmen and the remnants of the radical movement in Britain. Supporters of the United Irishmen who had settled as immigrants in parts of Lancashire, central Scotland and the poorer districts of London made contact with members of local radical groups. Some of these Irish exiles set up Societies of United Irishmen and encouraged the more militant and increasingly discontented British radicals to form similar groups. Having already attempted to secure French support for an Irish rebellion, it seems that the United Irishmen increasingly recognised the benefit of a simultaneous uprising in Britain. This would help to tie down forces on the mainland, giving an uprising in Ireland a greater chance of success and, perhaps, forcing concessions from the British government.

United Societies in Britain

Contact between United Irishmen and British radicals led to the growth of 'United Societies' on the mainland. In 1797, George Mealmaker formed a Society of United Scotsmen in Dundee, while in Lancashire and North-West England a similar organisation was set up, with both groups adopting the structure and constitution of the United Irishmen. By the end of 1797, there were said to be up to 80 United Englishmen societies in the North and Midlands - though their leaders were arrested before planning for an armed uprising had developed beyond a preparatory stage. There is also evidence of attempts to coordinate the activities of Irish and English revolutionary groups in London where militant survivors of the LCS such as John and Benjamin Binns, John Bone and Thomas Evans set up a series of conspiratorial cells, including one called the 'United Britons'. The authorities were just as successful in infiltrating these groups as they were in infiltrating the United Irishmen and, in February 1798, most of these potentially revolutionary leaders were arrested.

Whatever the extent of the connections with Ireland, a number of historians seriously doubt whether this revolutionary underground stood any chance of success. Thomis and Holt (1977), for example, point out fundamental differences between the protest in Ireland and on mainland Britain:

'In Ireland there was a mass base for rebellion and that was the peasant revolt, an element totally absent from the Scottish and English situation, and the Irish masses and their leaders were already part of a long tradition of insurrection against the foreign occupier. Theirs was an independence struggle that adopted republicanism as a direct alternative to the monarchy of the occupying power...In England and Scotland there were no such grounds for an independence struggle, no widespread counter-ideology such as Ireland's Catholicism to underpin revolt.' (Thomis & Holt 1977, p.21)

The naval mutinies of 1797

Whilst no historian denies that the naval mutinies which occurred in April and May 1797 at Spithead and the Nore were a serious blow to a government engaged in a war against France, a debate has developed over their significance. On the one hand, Thompson (1980) argues that there was more to the mutinies than discontent with pay and conditions:

'The greatest revolutionary portents [signs] for England were the naval mutinies at Spithead and the Nore in April and May 1797. There is no doubt that appalling conditions of food, pay and discipline precipitated the mutinies, but there is also some evidence of direct Jacobin instigation. There were Corresponding Society members among the mutineers...who brought into the fleet the language of the *Rights of Man* and some experience of committee organisation. The presence of 11,500 Irish sailors and 4,000 Irish marines added another revolutionary ingredient...It is foolish to argue that, because the majority of sailors had few clear political notions, this was a parochial affair of ship's biscuits and arrears of pay, and not a revolutionary movement. This is to mistake the nature of popular revolutionary crises, which arise from exactly this kind of conjunction between the grievances of the majority and the aspirations articulated by the politically conscious minority.' (Thompson 1980, pp.183-84)

On the other hand, Thompson's view has been challenged by historians who see the mutinies simply as the product of the appalling conditions experienced by seamen at this time, and not as an expression of revolutionary consciousness:

'Their grievances concerned wages, living conditions and impressment, however tempting it might be to link their emergence to political campaigns of the time. On 18 April 1797, delegates from Royal Navy vessels at Spithead petitioned Parliament for better conditions after the failure of their appeals to commanders, the petitioners professing their loyalty to the king and readiness to defend their country. Within a month, disputes were settled and the fleet left for war duties...And this remained the pattern of popular grievances that were ventilated during these years: they arose from precise and readily identifiable causes, food shortages, militia conscription or conditions of service.' (Thomis & Holt 1977, pp.25-26)

It should be noted that, to many contemporaries, the mutinies seemed to be proof that the French and their allies, the British Jacobins, were plotting to ruin Britain. At this time, the government was aware that the United Irishmen were planning an uprising and there were fears of a French attack through Ireland and of British Jacobins joining the attack.

Food riots

The debate over the naval mutinies of 1797 raises the question of how far a small number of militant radicals might be able to exploit economic distress as a means of politicising the masses. This is a question which has also been raised in relation to the wave of food riots which spread across the country in 1800-1.

Just as the naval mutinies can be interpreted as a traditional form of wage-bargaining, so most of the disturbances of 1800-1 can be explained as a demonstration of the traditional features of the 'classic' 18th-century food riot. There was, however, undoubtedly a geographical shift. More food disturbances took place in manufacturing areas than had been the case previously. Also, there is evidence that literature designed to spark political agitation was produced and distributed (see Box 2.8).

Belchem argues that the food riots of 1800-1 were significantly different from previous disturbances:

'Certainly, there were important changes in the pattern of collective behaviour. Previously, the North-West had witnessed considerable Church and King rioting, for the most part spontaneous effusions of public loyalty, triggered by the excitement of a public gathering or holiday...As wages fell and prices rose - by 1799 wartime inflation had reduced weavers' wages to half their

BOX 2.8 Leaflet printed in September 1800

Fellow countrymen

How long will ye quietly and cowardly suffer yourselves to be imposed upon, and half-starved by a set of mercenary slaves and government hirelings? Can you still suffer them to proceed in their extensive monopolies while your children are crying for bread? No! Let them exist not a day longer. We are the sovereignty, rise then from your lethargy. Be at the Corn Market on Monday.

Following the publication of this leaflet, there were six days of demonstrations in the Corn Market in London (this leaflet is cited in Thompson 1980).

real value in 1792 - textile workers rallied behind a new set of slogans: "No war", "Damn Pitt" and "A free constitution". Organised by "underground" radical and trade union groups, the food riots of 1799-1801 were characterised by careful planning and an extended demonology...the magistrates, clergy and local paternalists stood condemned as members of the repressive propertied class.' (Belchem 1996, p.26)

The 'Black Lamp conspiracy'

According to Thompson (1980), there is evidence that secret societies in Lancashire and West Yorkshire actively prepared for an armed uprising in the period 1800-2 - the so-called 'Black Lamp conspiracy'. Although the details are hazy, it seems that secret meetings were held at night in many parts of northern England. There were rumours of secret depots of buried weapons and of meetings being used to provide protestors with military training. There is some evidence to suggest that this activity was organised by the remnants of the United Englishmen and it is possible that plans for an armed rising were linked to the Despard conspiracy in London (see below).

Some critics have dismissed Thompson's suggestion that serious preparations were being made for an armed uprising. They argue that Thompson's account is based on the reports of a government spy later dismissed for fabricating alarmist reports. The extent and significance of the 'movement', critics argue, remain obscure, with much of the evidence for secret oaths, nocturnal meetings and drilling being based on conjecture. Against this, however, Thompson argues:

'There is too much evidence and from too many independent sources, for it to be possible to uphold the accepted historical fiction that "sedition" had no existence except in the imaginations of Ministers, magistrates and spies.' (Thompson 1980, p.522)

The Despard conspiracy 1802

Most historians agree that the Despard conspiracy of November 1802 represents the last significant example of underground activity bubbling to the surface in this period. Colonel Despard (a former member of the United Englishmen who was arrested in April 1798 and again in November 1802) appears to have been planning a coup d'état in the capital. The exact details of the conspiracy are still unclear, with some historians - notably Thompson - claiming that it was merely the London end of a much wider plan for a simultaneous armed uprising in the North (see above), rebellion in Ireland and a French invasion. Whatever Despard's intentions - and it appears that he was attempting military subversion in London as a prelude to the seizure of key buildings - it is certain that the government was kept fully informed of his movements by the spies who had successfully infiltrated the conspiracy at an early stage. As a result, Despard and 35 co-conspirators (including five soldiers) were arrested in November 1802 on charges of treason. Despard, together with five others, was subsequently executed in February 1803.

Luddism

The failure and subsequent execution of Despard is regarded by most historians as marking the end of significant conspiratorial activity in the period up to 1815. As O'Gorman puts it:

'Thereafter underground radical activity continued, but without much coordination or confidence, and for almost a decade the cause of extra-parliamentary reform is almost entirely lost to the historian.' (O'Gorman 1997, p.247)

Thompson, on the other hand, regards the Luddite disturbances of 1811-12 (see Unit 4, Part 1) as an ongoing part of this insurrectionary tradition. Belchem agrees with him that there was a degree of continuity:

'Despard was arrested in November 1802 as there was sufficient evidence to secure his conviction. His execution, followed by the failure of Robert Emmet's rising in Ireland, was a severe reverse. Thereafter, the underground was in decline, but local studies have uncovered

some remarkable continuities. Many of "Despard's men" were to the fore in Luddism and the risings of 1817 and 1820, proud veterans who bequeathed a commitment to physical force in the Chartist movement.' (Belchem 1996, p.27)

3.2 Britain and revolution, 1790-1815

A serious threat?

Despite the existence of underground activity in the period following the suppression of more overt and essentially moderate forms of protest in 1793-96, there is a broad consensus amongst historians that neither type of popular unrest posed a serious threat to the governing elite. A number of points can be made in support of this view.

First, there is little evidence that the moderate reform societies aimed to exploit economic dislocation and the grievances of the labouring poor. This can be seen as a major tactical failing given the growing burden of the French wars after 1793 and the accompanying social strains associated with a prolonged international conflict.

Second, while incidents such as the Black Lamp conspiracy suggest that there were members of the underground who did recognise the potential of exploiting localised, economic discontent, they were too isolated and marginalised from the majority of the working population to make any significant impact.

Third, despite the twin pressures of population growth and the demands of resourcing a major war, it appears that the British economy survived a unique test of simultaneous industrialisation and mobilisation for war. There were, of course, a number of violent short-term fluctuations, with particularly serious falls in purchasing power when food prices were very high in 1799 and 1800. On the other hand, real wages remained relatively stable during the war years. This was due in part to the fact that mobilisation withdrew a significant proportion of the male labour force from the market, reducing the pressure of population growth on wages. As a result, widespread and generalised economic discontent - a powerful 'trigger' of revolutionary activity on other occasions on the Continent - was largely missing from Britain in this period.

MAIN POINTS - Part 3

- Most historians agree that radicalism went 'underground' between 1795 and 1815, though few agree that this activity formed part of a coherent movement which continued to pose a serious and genuinely revolutionary threat.
- After 1795, there is evidence of growing links between the United Irishmen and the remnants of the radical movement in Britain. Some groups adopted the structure and constitution of the United Irishmen and aimed at an armed uprising.
- A debate has developed over the significance of the naval mutinies which broke out in 1797. Some historians argue that they reveal the growth of revolutionary consciousness. Others argue that they were simply the result of discontent at pay and conditions.
- There is also a debate over the significance of the food riots which broke out in 1800-1. Whilst some historians argue they are no different from earlier riots, others claim that they were different in important ways.
- Although the evidence is hazy, it does appear that secret societies plotted armed uprising, although the arrest and execution of Colonel Despard brought such plotting to an end.

Activity 2.4 The revolutionary threat 1795-1802

ITEM 1 The mutineers' manifesto, 1797

(i) The mutineers and the government

This cartoon shows the leaders of the naval mutiny at the Nore putting their case whilst members of the government hide under the table.

(ii) The mutineers' manifesto, 1797

Countrymen,

It is to you particularly that we owe an explanation of our conduct. His Majesty's ministers too well know our intentions which are founded on the laws of humanity, honour and national safety - long since trampled underfoot by those who ought to have been friends to us - the sole protectors of your laws and property. The public prints teem with falsehoods and misrepresentations to induce you to credit things as far from our design as the conduct of those at the helm of national affairs if from honesty or common decorum. Shall we who have endured the toils of a tedious, disgraceful war, be the victims of tyranny and oppression which vile, gilded, pampered knaves, wallowing in the lap of luxury, choose to load us with?...No the Age of Reason has at length revolved. Long have we been endeavouring to find ourselves men. We now find ourselves so. We will be treated as such. Far, very far, from us is the idea of subverting the government of our beloved country. We have the highest opinion of our Most Gracious Sovereign and we hope that none of the measures taken to deprive us of the common rights of men have been instigated by him...Hitherto we have laboured for our sovereign and you. We are now obliged to to think for ourselves for there are many (nay, most of us) in the Fleet who have been prisoners since the commencement of the war, without receiving a single farthing. Have we not a right to complain? Let his Majesty but order us to be paid and the little grievances we have made known redressed, we shall enter with alacrity upon any employment for the defence of our country.

This manifesto was produced by the naval mutineers at the Nore in June 1797.

ITEM 2 The Black Lamp conspiracy

With respect to the nocturnal meetings, they continue, though the place is never known to others till they take place. On Friday evening at or near midnight a meeting was held in a hollow way or narrow valley about six miles from Leeds and two from Birstall, at some distance from any public road. A man of perfect veracity assures me that he attempted to form one of the party, but found that scouts were stationed on all sides at some distance, the outermost of whom accosted him and aimed at drawing him off in a different direction. On his persevering, he found another irregular and moving line of scouts who asked his business and upon his continuing to proceed towards the 'Black Lamp' of men, a whistling was made and he heard expressions and tones of voice that quite deterred him from his purpose. That some particular persons whom they called gentlemen were expected and were not then arrived, he could easily recollect from what he overheard on the way...From another quarter on which I can depend, I learn that the committee forming the 'Black Lamp' and which on Friday night might be composed of about 200 men consists of those who have discoursed on the subject with nine others and have sworn them in, each of which again, ad infinitum, becomes a committee man on the same grounds. 'Abolition of all taxes and the full employment of their rights' are the subjects on which the leaders hold forth and the cement which holds them together. By Christmas they should be able to carry their points and on one night the rise was to take place in every quarter.

Part of a letter from the Mayor of Leeds to Earl Fitzwilliam in August 1802.

ITEM 3 Prices 1788-1823

The blue line shows prices of consumer goods. The black line shows the price of wheat in shillings by calendar year. It should be noted that there was relative long-term economic stability in the late 18th century. Despite being at war and despite the occasional bad harvest, the creation of wealth which resulted from industrialisation ensured that, on the whole, workers retained their buying power. Some historians argue that this relative stability over the long term helps to explain why Britain lacked the revolutionary impulse of other European countries.

Adapted from Cook & Stevenson 1996.

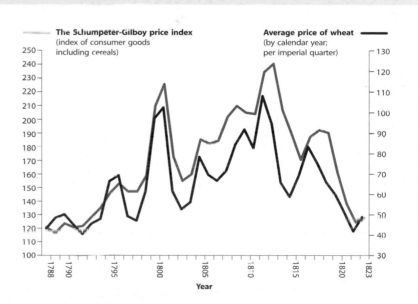

The Schumpeter-Gilboy price index (index of consumer goods including cereals)

Average price of wheat (by calendar year; per imperial quarter)

Year

ITEM 4 A historian's view

Radical activity after 1795 turned increasingly to the possibility of a coup d'état. It is beyond dispute that many radical activities in this period were inherently bizarre and self-destructive. Additionally, an effective government spy system ensured that most cadres were penetrated almost as soon as they were set up. Yet, the government was right to treat the threat seriously. The years 1797-98 and 1801-2 were ones of real crisis. Harvests failed again and, against a background of economic discontent and widespread unemployment, the country was nearer military defeat in 1797 than at any time during the wars. A demoralised and underpaid navy mutinied twice and the second mutiny at the Nore showed much evidence of radical sympathy. Its leader, Richard Parker, was a member of the LCS and sought to bring the *Rights of Man* onto the lower deck. Had the French mounted an invasion in the spring or early summer, as they threatened to do, it is difficult to see how it could have been repelled. After 1795, Manchester became a focus for disaffection, rumours of arms caches and the administration of secret oaths. Spies' reports pointed to a close correlation between economic hardship and political disturbance. The spate of large meetings which followed the expiry of the Two Acts and the return of Habeas Corpus in April-May 1801 strengthens the argument that there had been much underground preparation earlier. An alarmed government rapidly put the Acts back into operation and removed Habeas Corpus again. One should naturally be wary of evidence accumulated by spies, but some historians have too readily discounted it. Much information about secret meetings and plotting can be independently corroborated. So, a transformed radical movement survived the repression of 1795 and offered a real threat at times when hunger and high prices provided receptive ears. Then lower prices brought respite in 1802 and the Peace of Amiens (a peace deal concluded between Britain and France) further removed the most potent radical propaganda thrust - war causes distress.

Adapted from Evans 1996.

Questions

1. a) What does Item 1 tell us about the nature of the naval mutiny at the Nore and the threat it posed?
b) Does the information in Item 1 add strength to the argument that Britain was on the verge of revolution in the period 1795-1802? Explain your answer.

2. a) What does Item 2 tell us about the nature of the 'revolutionary underground'?

b) What are the problems with using source material of this kind?

3. How might a historian use the figures in Item 3 to explain political developments in the period 1795-1802?

4. 'The idea that Britain was on the verge of revolution in the period 1795-1802 is a great exaggeration'. Using Items 1-4 give arguments for and against this view.

References

- **Belchem (1996)** Belchem, J., *Popular Radicalism in Nineteenth Century Britain*, Macmillan, 1996.

- **Briggs (1959)** Briggs, A., *The Age of Improvement*, Longman, 1959.

- **Cannon & Griffiths (1988)** Cannon, J. & Griffiths, R., *The Oxford History of the British Monarchy*, Oxford University Press, 1988.

- **Catterall (1994)** Catterall, P. (ed.), *Britain 1815-1867*, Heinemann, 1994.

- **Christie (1982)** Christie, I., *Wars and Revolutions, 1760-1815*, Arnold, 1982.

- **Cole & Filson (1965)** Cole, G.D.H. & Filson, A.W. (eds.), *British Working Class Movements: Select Documents 1789-1875*, Macmillan, 1965.

- **Cook & Stevenson (1996)** Cook, C. & Stevenson, J., *The Longman Handbook of Modern British History 1714-1995*, Longman, 1996.

- **Dickinson (1985)** Dickinson, H.T., *British Radicalism and the French Revolution*, Blackwell, 1985.

- **Dickinson (1997)** Dickinson, H.T., 'The radical reaction in Britain to the French Revolution', *New Perspective*, Vol.3.2, December 1997.

- **Dinwiddy (1994)** Dinwiddy, J.R., 'English radicalism before the Chartists' in *Catterall (1994)*.

- **Emsley (1979)** Emsley, C., *British Society and the French Wars*, Blackwell, 1979.

- **Evans (1996)** Evans, E., *The Forging of the Modern State: Early Industrial Britain 1783-1870*, Longman, 1996.

- **Harrison (1984)** Harrison, J.F.C., *The Common People: a History from the Norman Conquest to the Present*, Flamingo, 1984.

- **Hobsbawm (1968)** Hobsbawm, E., *Industry and Empire*, Pelican, 1968.

- **Langford (1999)** Langford, P., *A Polite and Commercial People: England 1727-1783*, Oxford University Press, 1999.

- **O'Gorman (1997)** O'Gorman, F., *The Long Eighteenth Century: British Political and Social History 1688-1832*, Arnold, 1997.

- **Royle (1997)** Royle, E., *Modern Britain: a Social History 1750-1997*, Arnold, 1997.

- **Rudé (1962)** Rudé, G., *Wilkes and Liberty*, Oxford University Press, 1962.

- **Rudé (1964)** Rudé, G., *The Crowd in History: A Study of Popular Disturbances in France and England, 1730-1848*, Serif, 1964.

- **Strong (1996)** Strong, R., *The Story of Britain*, Hutchinson, 1996.

- **Thomis & Holt (1977)** Thomis, M.I. & Holt, P., *Threats of Revolution in Britain 1789-1848*, Macmillan, 1977.

- **Thompson (1980)** Thompson, E.P., *The Making of the English Working Class*, Penguin, 1980 (first published in 1963).

- **Williams (1968)** Williams, G.A., *Artisans and Sans Culottes: Popular Movements in France and Britain During the French Revolution*, Edward Arnold, 1968.

- **Wright (1970)** Wright, D.G., *Democracy and Reform, 1815-1885*, Longman, 1970.

UNIT 3 Political developments under Lord Liverpool

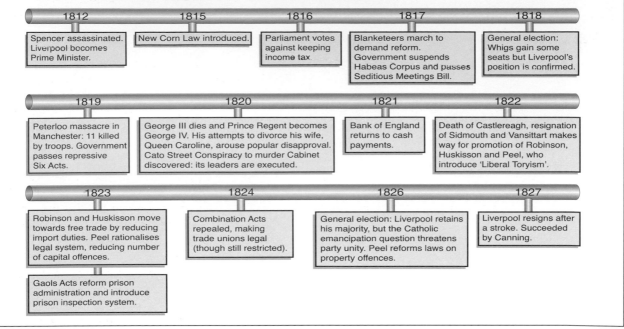

Timeline - Political developments under Lord Liverpool

1812 Spencer assassinated. Liverpool becomes Prime Minister.

1815 New Corn Law introduced.

1816 Parliament votes against keeping income tax.

1817 Blanketeers march to demand reform. Government suspends Habeas Corpus and passes Seditious Meetings Bill.

1818 General election: Whigs gain some seats but Liverpool's position is confirmed.

1819 Peterloo massacre in Manchester: 11 killed by troops. Government passes repressive Six Acts.

1820 George III dies and Prince Regent becomes George IV. His attempts to divorce his wife, Queen Caroline, arouse popular disapproval. Cato Street Conspiracy to murder Cabinet discovered: its leaders are executed.

1821 Bank of England returns to cash payments.

1822 Death of Castlereagh, resignation of Sidmouth and Vansittart makes way for promotion of Robinson, Huskisson and Peel, who introduce 'Liberal Toryism'.

1823 Robinson and Huskisson move towards free trade by reducing import duties. Peel rationalises legal system, reducing number of capital offences. Gaols Acts reform prison administration and introduce prison inspection system.

1824 Combination Acts repealed, making trade unions legal (though still restricted).

1826 General election: Liverpool retains his majority, but the Catholic emancipation question threatens party unity. Peel reforms laws on property offences.

1827 Liverpool resigns after a stroke. Succeeded by Canning.

Introduction

According to Benjamin Disraeli (writing in 1841), Lord Liverpool was an 'arch-mediocrity'. He had little talent, few ideas and no charisma. This judgement stuck and it was not until 1941 that a serious attempt was made to resurrect Liverpool's reputation. In that year, the historian W.R. Brock published a book which claimed that Liverpool had been misunderstood and underrated. According to Brock, the turning point in Liverpool's premiership was the Cabinet reshuffle of 1822-23. The result of this reshuffle was a change in direction and the development of a new approach - what Brock called 'Liberal Toryism'. Brock's defence of Liverpool, however, soon came under attack. In the 1960s, a number of historians began to argue that Disraeli's criticism of Liverpool did not go far enough. Liverpool, they claimed, was a reactionary who used undue severity to crush the popular unrest which developed in the post-war years. In recent years, however, this interpretation has, in turn, been challenged, with several historians (notably Norman Gash and John Plowright) coming to Liverpool's defence. Liverpool, they point out, remains Britain's longest-serving Prime Minister (he was Prime Minister from 1812-27). During his premiership, he led Britain to victory in the French wars and then managed to overcome the many difficulties that arose in the post-war period. Not only was he a skilled politician, he also introduced important reforms. His qualities, therefore, outweighed his failings. This chapter explores the historical debates surrounding Liverpool's long premiership.

UNIT SUMMARY

Part 1 examines the problems faced by the Liverpool government in its early years and considers whether it is appropriate to describe the government as 'reactionary'.

Part 2 looks at the arguments for and against the view that 1822 was a turning point in Liverpool's premiership and that a new 'Liberal Toryism' emerged between 1822 and 1827.

Part 3 assesses the achievements and failings of Liverpool and his administration. It also analyses the reasons for Liverpool being able to stay in power for so long.

1 'Reactionary Toryism'

Key issues

1. What problems did the government face between 1812 and 1822 and how did it deal with them?

2. Why did the government survive the period 1812-22?

3. Is it appropriate to describe the policies of the Liverpool government between 1812 and 1822 as 'Reactionary Toryism'?

1.1 What problems did the Liverpool administration face in its early years?

The birth of the Liverpool government

The Liverpool government came into office at a most volatile moment. In May 1812, Spencer Perceval, the Prime Minister, was shot dead as he walked through the lobby of the House of Commons (Perceval is the only British Prime Minister to have been assassinated in office). His death released a flood of political squabbling and bad feeling and, for over a year after Lord Liverpool became Prime Minister (in June 1812), the government remained in a state of flux:

'For over a year the administration had been deprived of real political strength by the widely held conviction that it was only a temporary arrangement. After Perceval's death, his post was hawked round among five other independent or opposition politicians. When, in the end, the Prince Regent turned to Liverpool, it seemed that, far from being the first choice, he was a last resort.' (Gash 1984, p.100)

Despite this, Liverpool began his premiership with a number of advantages. First, he was an experienced politician. He had entered Parliament in 1790 at the age of 20, had served as Pitt's Commissioner at the Board of Control (1793) and as Master of the Mint (1796), and had then served in Cabinet from 1801, holding all three senior secretaryships - Foreign Secretary (1801-3), Home Secretary (1804-9, with a break in 1806-7) and Secretary for War and the Colonies (1809-12). Second, he represented continuity (his administration was essentially a continuation of Perceval's) - which endeared him to the Prince Regent. And third:

'He had been the choice of his colleagues and presented by them to the Prince Regent as their preferred leader.' (Gash 1984, p.101)

Problems facing the Liverpool government

It was important that Liverpool did begin his premiership with these advantages since the government encountered a number of thorny problems in its early years.

The war against Napoleon

First, Liverpool became Prime Minister at a crucial period in the war against Napoleon. As Derry points out:

'In the summer of 1812, the war situation was more complex than ever. Napoleon's invasion of Russia eventually transformed the military and diplomatic outlook but no one could be certain that the Emperor's ambitious adventure would end in disaster...In 1812, most Europeans were in awe of Napoleon. He seemed invincible.' (Derry 1994, p.20)

As Secretary for War and the Colonies in the years 1809-12, Liverpool had wholeheartedly supported the war against Napoleon in Portugal and Spain, despite a reluctance amongst some opposition MPs, and he continued to back the war effort as Prime Minister:

'He believed that there was no alternative policy but to wage it until victory was achieved.' (Derry 1994, p.23)

The war against Napoleon was, therefore, the foremost concern of the first three years of the Liverpool administration.

Economic depression

Second, the economic position of Britain was being severely eroded by the war with France. At the end of the 18th century, Britain had been the richest country in the world, with that wealth being largely based on commerce. But Napoleon's economic blockade began in November 1806. Then, at the end of 1807, Britain passed the 'Orders in Council', which attempted to break the blockade by preventing neutrals trading with Napoleonic Europe. These developments disrupted British trade and encouraged the British economy to over-specialise in the ordnance (war) industries (iron, cotton and chemicals). The result was rising inflation and rising prices. The crisis point came in the winter of 1811-12 (a particularly severe winter). According to Cook and Stevenson (1996, p.258), wheat prices averaged 126 shillings a bushel in 1812 (the average price in 1793, the year the war began, was 49 shillings), yet, at the same time, the wages of many workers actually fell. In Sussex, for example, farm labourers suffered a wage cut from 13 to 12 shillings a week and in Bolton handloom weavers watched their wages fall from 25 to 15 shillings a week. It is no coincidence, therefore, that 1812 was the year of Luddite machine-breaking (see Unit 4, Part 1).

Plowright notes two further long-term economic problems facing the new Liverpool government (see Box 3.1).

BOX 3.1 Long-term economic problems

There were two long-term economic problems facing the new Liverpool government. First, the move towards a more capitalist system of farming was socially destabilising in that it encouraged both rural depopulation and massive population growth. The population of Britain rose from 10.5 million in 1801 to 14.1 million in 1821. And second, popular unrest was also fuelled by industrialisation. The increasing concentration of potential rebels was particularly alarming for those in authority. Moreover, the industrial revolution also brought unemployment, as new machinery made traditional skills - and skilled workers - redundant.

Adapted from Plowright 1996.

By 1815, Britain had an £861 million national debt on which the interest payments alone were 30 million annually. Britain had also acted as the paymaster to the allied powers and was owed £57 million by 1815. On top of this, the war had forced the government to impose a highly unpopular income tax in 1799, set at two pence per pound. By 1815, this was producing £15 million per year - 30% of government revenue.

War against the USA

In addition to (and adding to) this economic burden, Britain went to war with the USA in June 1812. Tension had been increasing ever since Britain began enforcing the Orders of Council and intercepted all American ships bound for Europe. Enterprising American sailors (supported by their government) made fortunes by running the blockade, but, in the process, severely undermined the British war effort. American opinion against Britain hardened and President Madison endorsed the hawks' view that British control over the Caribbean, the northern fisheries and Canada should be broken. United States forces went into action against British fishermen off Newfoundland and against the tobacco and sugar traders in the Caribbean and in Canada. Peace was negotiated in December 1814, but the war carried on into 1815 as it took time for news of peace to reach the troops.

The parliamentary system

A fourth major problem facing Liverpool in the early years was the parliamentary system within which his government functioned:

'Liverpool could only govern the country if he retained the confidence and goodwill not only of the Prince Regent, but also of the large number of MPs who were not committed to one of the political parties.' (Plowright 1996, p.100)

This job was not made any easier by the fact that the Prince Regent could not be relied on to support ministers, by the fact that Liverpool was himself a member of the House of Lords (as were eight other members of the Cabinet in 1812), and by the fact that party organisation in the Commons was by no means as tight as it became later in the 19th century:

'Lacking the patronage resources of an 18th century minister, he was denied the party organisation available to a late-Victorian one.' (Derry 1994, p.24)

It is, therefore, no surprise that the government was sometimes forced to move in a direction that it did not want to take. Two occasions were particularly important. First, in 1815, to win backing for the Corn Law, the government was forced to agree that it should be absolutely forbidden to import foreign corn until the price reached 80 shillings (the government's preference was for a sliding scale of imports as prices rose). And second, in March 1816, the government's proposal to retain income tax was defeated by 37 votes and so income tax was abolished.

The end of the war

The end of the war against Napoleon in 1815 brought two further problems. First, the transition from a wartime to a peacetime economy was traumatic - a mini-boom was followed quickly by recession. And second (and linked to the economic climate), there was a revival of radicalism and extra-parliamentary protest (see Unit 4) on a larger scale than that which had so worried the Pitt government in the early 1790s (see Unit 2).

1.2 Is it appropriate to describe the policies of the Liverpool government between 1812 and 1822 as 'Reactionary Toryism'?

The term 'Reactionary Tory'

The traditional view is that the Liverpool government's first ten years were characterised by 'Reactionary Toryism'. Before the validity of this view can be assessed, it is necessary to be clear about what the term means.

The term 'Tory' was only just gaining currency in the early 19th century. Box 3.2 explains what the term meant.

The addition of the term 'reactionary' by modern historians is significant. At face value a reactionary is:

'a person tending to oppose change or seeking to return to a former system.' (COED 1982, p.861)

In practice today, the word is usually used as an insult. A reactionary is an arch-conservative, somebody who:

- is predisposed to oppose any sort of democratic or liberal reform
- clings onto tradition and privilege

The term 'Tory'

Lord Liverpool believed in:
- the monarchy
- the Protestant succession (ie that no Catholic should inherit the British throne)
- the established Church of England
- the parliamentary system as it had evolved down the years.

From the early 1800s, the term 'Tory' was coming to denote this standpoint. After the end of the war in 1815, the anxieties often expressed about the danger of revolution added another strain to what was commonly understood as 'Toryism'. Tories were opposed to revolution and to any radical change.

Adapted from Derry 1994.

- favours repressive policies to keep the peace.

Whether or not the first ten years of the Liverpool regime can be labelled 'reactionary' has become a matter for debate.

The Liverpool government was reactionary

Historians have used the following arguments to support the view that the Liverpool government was reactionary during its first ten years in power.

Repressive policies

First, it is argued that the Liverpool administration used repressive policies to keep the peace:

'It is commonly alleged that Liverpool's government pursued repressive policies between 1815 and 1820. That is to say, the government acted in an unnecessarily harsh manner in crushing popular protest by, for example, suspending Habeas Corpus, passing the Seditious Meetings Act and breaking up the march of the Blanketeers in 1817, massacring those at "Peterloo" and passing the Six Acts in 1819.' (Plowright 1997, p.14)

These repressive policies (which are examined in detail in Unit 4) were, it is argued, designed to resist change and to maintain the status quo. By opposing reform, clinging to the existing system and using repression, the Liverpool government showed itself to be reactionary:

'One is left with the dominant impression of a ruling class convinced that the lower orders must be kept in their place, and that any attempt on their part to leave it must be treated as dangerous insubordination.' (Hunt 1972, pp.66-67)

Elitism

Second, the Liverpool government initiated and supported measures which were reactionary since they were designed to benefit a small elite and were detrimental to the mass of the people. The two obvious examples are:

- the Corn Law of 1815, which benefited large landowners but was harmful to the mass of ordinary people since it kept the price of bread artificially high
- the abolition of income tax in 1816 - a measure which benefited the rich but, because it led to large increases in indirect taxes on tea, sugar, tobacco, beer and salt, was harmful to the poor.

Refusal to make concessions

Third, Liverpool never departed from an aristocratic view of government. Despite the radical nature of extra-parliamentary protest and the demands for parliamentary reform, the Liverpool administration refused to make any concessions. Gash, for example, notes that:

'Even respectable opinion was tempted to ascribe many of the country's difficulties to [ie blame them on] extravagance in government and to see a remedy in parliamentary reform...The Cabinet's conclusion in 1816 was as guardians of the public purse to meet the legitimate demands of the public for further retrenchment [ie for cut-backs in public spending] but as guardians of law and order to seek stronger powers to deal with sedition and agitation.' (Gash 1984, p.129)

In other words, far from them considering the possibility of concession or reform, the Liverpool government decided to clamp down on those who publicly demanded it. It should be noted that the government did not have to take any notice of public opinion. After all, MPs were elected by a small elite of propertied voters whilst members of the House of Lords (who made up a large part of the Cabinet) were unelected. Given that the interests of the opposition (as well as the government) were generally the interests of the landed gentry, there was little incentive to rock the boat. In other words, the system itself encouraged a reactionary rather than a reforming outlook.

The Peterloo Massacre

Further evidence of a reactionary attitude can be found in the remarks made by senior ministers after Peterloo (see Unit 4, Section 2.2). Far from condemning the local authorities for losing control and using excessive force, members of the government praised them:

'If the government was unprepared for the news of Peterloo, no authorities have ever acted so vigorously to make themselves accomplices after the fact. Within a fortnight, the congratulations of Sidmouth (Home Secretary)...were communicated to the magistrates and military "for their prompt, decisive and efficient measures for the preservation of the public peace". Demands for a parliamentary enquiry were resolutely rejected. Attorney and

Solicitor-Generals were "fully satisfied" as to the legality of the magistrates' actions. The Lord Chancellor (Eldon) was of the "clear opinion" that the meeting was "an overt act of treason"...Lord Liverpool declared that the action of the Manchester magistrates was "substantially right".' (Thompson 1980, p.750)

The Liverpool government was not reactionary

Historians have used the following arguments to oppose the view that the Liverpool government was reactionary during its first ten years in power.

A mild and tolerant government

A number of historians have argued that, far from being 'unnecessarily harsh', the Liverpool government was surprisingly mild and tolerant in its reaction to the growth of popular discontent after the end of the Napoleonic war:

'It can be seen that studied restraint and considered moderation rather than needless severity and reckless repression characterised the response of Liverpool's government.' (Plowright 1996, p.38)

Evidence of 'studied restraint and considered moderation' is usually presented as follows. First, it is pointed out that the suspension of Habeas Corpus and the Seditious Meetings Act of 1817 were both temporary measures which were allowed to lapse in 1818. In other words, they were a short-term response to a crisis and, because they were temporary measures, they cannot be interpreted as being symptomatic of reactionary tendencies. A truly reactionary government would not have allowed them to lapse. Second, despite the outward severity of some of the legislation, in practice, it was not really enforced. Plowright points out that:

'Only 44 were arrested on suspicion of treason, of whom 37 were detained when Habeas Corpus was partially suspended in February 1817. One of these was released soon after, whilst a second was discharged on compassionate grounds and a third died in custody. The remaining 34 had all been released by the time Habeas Corpus was fully restored in January 1918. As Gash has stated, "It was not exactly a reign of terror".' (Plowright 1997, p.16)

And third, it is pointed out that Peterloo was not the work of the government but, once the incident had taken place, the government had no real choice but to support those in positions of authority:

'Liverpool, like several members of his government, was uneasy over the conduct of magistrates at Manchester in 1819 over the famous "Peterloo" incident...But whatever his misgivings in private, he knew that he had to support the magistrates in public, otherwise there would be the risk of a collapse in confidence among the magistrates, the body of men above any other which seemed to stand between the country and chaos.' (Derry 1994, p.25)

Far from being a reactionary government, therefore, (according to this line of argument), the Liverpool administration aimed at the minimal use of force and its outwardly repressive measures were intended more as deterrents than as genuine attempts to force protestors into submission.

Further arguments

There are two further arguments against the view that Liverpool's government was reactionary in its early years:

- First, there is the view that the Liverpool government had little or no room for manoeuvre. Derry (1994) and Plowright (1997) both point out, for example, that the government was beset by unprecedented and complex problems and had limited resources with which to keep the peace - it did not have a large standing army or civilian police force and was forced to rely heavily on spies and informants. As a result, whilst the government could not afford to ignore extra-parliamentary protests and rumours of insurrection, it aimed, wherever possible, to avoid confrontation. In other words, maintenance of law and order was the aim, not repression.

- And second, there is the view that the Liverpool government was open to new ideas. It was during the period 1815-20 that the foundations of the more 'liberal' policies of the 1820s were laid. It is wrong, therefore, to see the period 1815-20 as a period of reactionary government since a number of progressive measures were passed (see next section).

MAIN POINTS - Part 1

- The main problems Liverpool faced in the early years of his premiership were: (1) the war against Napoleon; (2) economic difficulties; (3) the war against the USA; (4) maintaining relations with the monarch; (5) maintaining a majority in Parliament; and (6) dealing with the post-war economic and political crisis.

- Arguments in support of the view that the Liverpool regime was reactionary include: (1) the government used repression to block demands for reform; (2) policies benefited an elite but harmed the masses; (3) the government supported the aristocratic view of government; (4) the government supported the authorities not the victims after Peterloo.

- Arguments against the view that the Liverpool regime was reactionary include: (1) the government was surprisingly moderate and restrained in the face of mass protest; (2) the government had little room for manoeuvre; and (3) the government was open to new ideas and initiated liberal reforms.

Activity 3.1 How reactionary was Liverpool's government 1812-20?

ITEM 1 A historian's view (i)

There is no reason to suppose that members of the Liverpool administration were squeamish - or indeed felt any guilt - about shedding blood. 'One can never feel that the King is secure upon his throne till he has dared to spill traitors' blood,' Lord Liverpool himself had written when refusing to intercede for the life of Napoleon's general, Marshal Ney. Castlereagh (the Foreign Secretary) has served his apprenticeship in the suppression of the Irish rebellion. The Lord Chancellor (Eldon) was fighting a rearguard action against the penal reformers, in defence of capital penalties. The government was, in June 1817, preparing to try for high treason not only Dr Watson and his colleagues (the radicals arrested for their part in the Spa Fields affair- see Unit 4), but also groups of Sheffield and Glasgow reformers. The government wanted blood - not a holocaust, but enough to make an example.

Adapted from Thompson 1980.

ITEM 2 A historian's view (ii)

Before the Napoleonic wars, George III had a key role in appointing ministers. When Pitt resigned as Prime Minister in 1801, for example, several ministers stayed in office showing that they were the King's appointment rather than Parliament's. During Liverpool's period in office, however, Cabinet ministers came to accept as a necessary convention of Cabinet government the principle that, if Liverpool was forced out of office, either because he had lost the confidence of the King or because he had been defeated in the Commons, they would all resign with him. The principle of collective resignation enabled Liverpool to put pressure on George IV which Pitt had been unable to put on George III. Liverpool was often weary of George IV's moods, but he could rely on the support of his colleagues in a way that Pitt could not. Although the conventions of collective responsibility for policy were still limited to foreign policy, finance, public order and war and peace, the growth of the Cabinet as a collective entity was noteworthy. True, the question of Catholic emancipation revealed there were areas of disagreement (in 1812 Liverpool ruled that it should remain an 'open question' which was not to be discussed in Cabinet since the Cabinet was split on the issue). Nevertheless, Liverpool was a more powerful Prime Minister in some respects than Pitt had been.

Adapted from Derry 1994.

ITEM 3 A cartoon

This cartoon was drawn by George Cruikshank in August 1819, days after news of the Peterloo massacre reached London. Cruikshank gives the yeomanry cavalry butcher's cleavers. Cartoons like this one were displayed in magazines, in the front windows of printshops and on tavern walls throughout the country.

Questions

1. Judging from your own knowledge and Items 1-3 would you say that 'Reactionary Toryism' is an accurate description of the Liverpool government in its early years? Give reasons for your answer.
2. Explain how Item 2 could be used to support the case that the Liverpool government was not reactionary.
3. How might Item 3 be used in support of the case

that the Liverpool government was reactionary?
4. Look at Item 1.
   a) Does the author support the view that the Liverpool government was reactionary? Explain how you know.
   b) How could you argue against the case being put in Item 1?

2 Can Liverpool's premiership be divided into two phases?

Key issues

1. Was 1822 a turning point in the Liverpool administration?
2. What reforms were implemented between 1820 and 1827?
3. Did a new 'Liberal Toryism' emerge in the 1820s?

2.1 Was 1822 a turning point in the Liverpool administration?

A key debate

One of the key debates surrounding the Liverpool government concerns the extent to which the administration can be divided into two clearly distinct phases. The traditional view (see, for example, Brock 1941, Wood 1960, Beales 1969) is that the first ten years of Liverpool's premiership (1812-22) were years of 'Reactionary Toryism' dominated by figures such as Castlereagh, Sidmouth, Eldon and Vansittart (see Box 3.3) and associated with protectionism and the suppression of popular protest. This phase ended in 1822 and a new phase began. The last five years of the premiership (1822-27), were years of 'Liberal Toryism', dominated by figures such as Canning, Peel, Huskisson and Robinson and associated with a range of commercial and legal reforms. The term 'Liberal Tory' was first used by the historian W.R. Brock in 1941. He argued that a new and distinct version of Toryism emerged during the 1820s.

Box 3.3 shows that there was an important reshuffle in 1822. It is important to note, however, that there was continuity as well as change after the reshuffle. Key figures remained in government after 1822 - for example, Lord Liverpool remained Prime Minister, Sidmouth remained as Minister without Portfolio and Eldon remained Lord Chancellor. Of Liverpool's Cabinet of 14 in 1812, only four sat in the House of Commons (Vansittart, Bragge-Bathurst and Robinson).

BOX 3.3 Lord Liverpool's Cabinet

Chancellor of the Exchequer	Nicholas Vansittart 1812-23
	Frederick Robinson 1823-27
Lord President of the Council	Earl of Harrowby
Lord Privy Seal	Earl of Westmorland
Lord Chancellor	Lord Eldon
Home Secretary	Viscount Sidmouth 1812-22
	Robert Peel 1822-27
Foreign Secretary	Robert Stewart (Castlereagh) 1812-22*
	George Canning 1822-27
Secretary for War and Colonies	Earl Bathurst
First Lord of the Admiralty	Viscount Melville
President of the Board of Control	Earl of Buckingham 1812-16
	George Canning 1816-21
	C. Bragge-Bathurst 1821-22
	Charles Wynn 1822-27
Master-General of the Ordnance	Lord Mulgrave 1812-19
	Duke of Wellington 1819-27
Chancellor of the Duchy of Lancaster	C. Bragge-Bathurst 1812-21
	Nicholas Vansittart 1823-27
President of the Board of Trade	Frederick Robinson 1818-23
	William Huskisson 1823-27
Ministers without Portfolio	Earl Camden 1812
	Earl Mulgrave 1819-20
	Viscount Sidmouth 1822-24

*Robert Stewart is better known as 'Viscount Castlereagh' (since he was the second son of the Marquess of Londonderry, he did not automatically inherit the title and was given a courtesy title). He became an MP in 1794. As well as serving as Foreign Secretary, he also held the position of Leader of the House of Commons in the period 1812-22. In 1821 he inherited the title Marquess of Londonderry.

What was 'Liberal Toryism'?

Before it is possible to judge whether a new 'Liberal Toryism' developed it is necessary to be clear about what is meant by the term 'liberal'. The political roots of liberalism lie in the upheavals of the 17th century, when new forces challenged the concentration of political power. The philosopher John Locke (1632-1704) argued that all people have 'natural rights' (the right to life, liberty and property) which cannot be removed except by their consent. The economic roots of liberalism, on the other hand, arose in response to industrialisation. Liberal economists such as Adam Smith (1723-90) criticised constraints on trade, arguing that prosperity depended on a willingness to accept the forces of the market based on freedom and competition. The key elements of liberalism are summarised in Box 3.4.

BOX 3.4 What is liberalism?

Liberalism is concerned with three key concepts: freedom, equality and toleration. Freedom is important because liberalism is concerned to allow the greatest possible freedom to the individual. Equality is closely linked to freedom. For example, by agreeing that all people should have equality before the law and equal political rights, liberals suggest that each individual should have an equal (though restricted) amount of freedom. Linked to the desire for freedom and equality is the liberal's ability to tolerate opposing viewpoints. The essence of toleration is for people to accept the people and ideas which they dislike. By believing in the existence of natural rights, such as the freedom of worship, liberals are bound to apply such rights to everyone.

Adapted from Roberts 1999.

It is clear from the definition of liberalism in Box 3.4 that a crucial element is the notion of political equality. Indeed, in the context of the early 19th century, it could be argued that support for parliamentary reform (broadening the franchise, if not supporting universal franchise) is an essential ingredient of any political programme which is to be labelled as 'liberal' - and yet, such support was distinctly lacking in the Liverpool Cabinet of the 1820s. Peel, in particular, would later prove to be an arch-opponent of parliamentary reform.

Brock, who coined the phrase 'Liberal Toryism', admitted that:

'The name is artificial - that is to say it is not found in the mouths of contemporaries...It is, however, of value because the High Tories accused the government of "liberalism"...because the "liberals" who dominated the Cabinet felt acutely their estrangement from the "ultras", and because the meaning of the phrase is readily

intelligible to a later age.' (Brock 1941, p.2)

According to this view, 'Liberal Toryism' is not used as a precise term to describe a political ideology. Rather, it is used rather loosely to mean 'more progressive and less authoritarian'. It is also used in this way by some historians who support Brock's idea that a distinct new phase began after 1822:

'By comparison with what had gone before, the measures of the administration between 1822 and 1827 seem notably liberal and reformist. By comparison with what followed they seem merely trivial tinkering...But the respectable public was temporarily satisfied that reform could proceed without constitutional change.' (Beales 1969, p.23)

The revisionist view

Most recent interpretations (for example, Gash 1984 and Plowright 1996) reject the reactionary/liberal view as misleading and simplistic. Historians now tend to emphasise a series of important continuities. 'Reactionary Toryism', it is argued, was less reactionary than once supposed and 'Liberal Toryism' was less liberal. Also, historians question the idea that the year 1822 was a turning point, arguing that there was no conscious or ideological transition from one set of policies to another. Rather, they argue, the development of more favourable economic and political circumstances allowed a shift of emphasis. Some historians (for example, Evans 1996) argue that 1819 is more of a turning point than 1822.

The Liverpool administration in 1822

The economy

By 1822, the economy had stabilised and, although the historical record is incomplete, it is clear that there was economic growth during the period 1822-27 (see Box 3.5).

The reshuffle of 1822-23

In the House of Commons, the government was under increasing pressure from the Whigs (who had made some gains in the general election of 1818). It was severely embarrassed over its handling of Peterloo, the spy system and the Queen Caroline Affair (see Unit 4). Matters were made worse by Castlereagh's weak defence (as Leader of the House of Commons) of the government position. The political crisis reached a new low when Castlereagh committed suicide in 1822.

Liverpool responded by reshuffling his Cabinet. The appointment of George Canning as Foreign Secretary was highly significant (see Box 3.6). Canning's popular image with the public contrasted markedly with the unpopularity of his predecessor. The appointment was sufficiently controversial to prompt several resignations and, therefore, further

BOX 3.5 Prosperity in the 1820s

Prosperity was the keynote of the 1820s, but it was neither universal nor continuous. Remarkably little is known about key economic indicators such as unemployment because no official records were kept until the 1890s. As a result, historians have to rely on contemporary judgements on the 'state of trade'. The national statistics which do survive assume the existence of a national economy, which is highly dubious. Movements within different sectors of the economy often contrast markedly and regional differences may be much more significant than national trends. Nevertheless some obvious statements may be made with confidence. The economy grew much more rapidly in the 1820s than in the 1810s. The gross national product (the measure of the amount of income generated as a result of a country's economic activity) is estimated to have fallen by 3.5% in the 1810s before rising by 16.8% in the 1820s. All the conventional indicators used by economists to demonstrate growth are firmly in place. However, while manufactures, mining, building, trade and transport grew at an overall rate of 26% in the 1820s, agriculture, having declined sharply as food prices plummeted at the end of the French wars, increased by only 4.6%.

Adapted from Evans 1989.

BOX 3.6 George Canning

There are significant parallels between Canning and Disraeli. Like Disraeli, Canning had a father who was a writer, in this case, of Irish origin. The elder Canning died young and poor and his widow, born in Ireland as Mary Anne Costello, was forced to become an actress. She had several illegitimate children by two lovers. A more improbable Tory Prime Minister (as Canning became in 1827) was not seen before Disraeli came along. Canning was, however, rescued from poverty by a rich uncle, Stratford Canning, who paid for his aristocratic education at Eton and Oxford. There Canning developed his brilliance at phrase making and his Tory political views. Canning married an heiress, may have had an affair with Princess Caroline and held a variety of government positions while retaining the well-deserved reputation for both flippancy and brilliance. He became an MP in 1793 (Pitt found him a pocket borough) and a junior minister in 1796. In 1807 he entered the Cabinet as Foreign Secretary, but had to resign in 1809 after quarrelling with and then fighting a duel with Lord Castlereagh, the War Secretary. He returned to the Cabinet in 1816 as president of the Board of Control. In 1822, he was about to go out to India in the lucrative position as Governor-General when, on Castlereagh's suicide, he was offered the Foreign Office. George IV, who knew that Canning might have been Caroline's lover, at first refused to agree to the appointment, but gave way after pressure from the Duke of Wellington.

Adapted from Rubinstein 1998.

Cabinet changes (see Box 3.3).

The changes of personnel in the Cabinet provided the impression of change, but, in a sense, this is illusory. The men promoted to senior Cabinet posts had already served in Liverpool's government (Canning had served in the Cabinet from 1816 to 1821, Robinson had been President of the Board of Trade from 1818 to 1823, Peel had served as Chief Secretary for Ireland between 1812 and 1818, and Huskisson had served as a junior minister since 1814) and they had all supported the government during its (supposedly) reactionary phase. There is no evidence to suggest that the promotions had a distinct ideological aim.

2.2 Government reforms in the 1820s

Those historians who argue that the Liverpool government had a new, liberal agenda after 1822 detect changing attitudes in four main areas.

1. Legal reforms

Between 1823 and 1827, Robert Peel, the Home Secretary, introduced a number of measures designed to modernise the legal system and prevent crime.

Capital offences

By 1820, juries were becoming increasingly reluctant to condemn petty criminals to death (around 200 offences carried the death penalty, including offences such as impersonating a Chelsea Pensioner, stealing five shillings from a shop, and forgery). Peel's reform of the criminal code in 1823 and his streamlining of the criminal law between 1825 and 1828 resulted in the abolition of 180 capital offences, though coining (making counterfeit coins), livestock theft, housebreaking and forgery still remained capital offences and people could still be jailed for debt or transported. Evans points out that:

'These relaxations of the penal code were possible partly because of thorough preparation within the Home Office. Peel relied much on the work of Henry Hobhouse, the diligent and experienced under-secretary he had inherited from Sidmouth. The political acceptability of this "liberalisation", however, owed much to MPs' realisation that transportation was an ostensibly more humane but equally permanent way of ridding the state of its major transgressors.' (Evans 1989, p.58)

Gatrell (1994) goes further and argues that the reforms were not liberal at all - see Box 3.7 below.

Prison reform

The traditional view is that Peel's reforms of the prison system provide evidence that Peel was a liberal reformer (see, for example, Trevelyan 1952). The key reform was the 1823 Gaols Act which, for the first time, gave central government a direct interest in local prisons. This made the following provisions:

- local rate-paid gaols were to be set up in every county and major town
- prisons were to be inspected by magistrates on an annual basis
- magistrates who undertook inspections were to submit reports to the Home Office
- prison discipline, medical and educational facilities were to be standardised
- women prisoners were to be, for the first time, guarded by female warders
- gaolers were to be paid
- prison chaplains were to be able to visit prisoners on a frequent basis.

Also, the following year, the classification of prisoners into petty offenders and serious offenders was introduced.

Recently, however, the traditional view has been questioned. Gatrell, for example, argues:

'[Peel] did little about the shortcomings in penal provision...The [1823 Gaols] Act's limitations are sometimes excused on the grounds that this was not an age when government could direct limited administrative and financial resources to prison building and that the 1823 Gaols Act at least moved tentatively towards national prison reform. But administrative bureaucracies were no less rudimentary and resistance to central expenditure no less inhibiting in the 1830s when the Whigs got to work more effectively. What was lacking in Peel was the political will or the inspirational drive to do more. God's retributions operated adequately as things were.' (Gatrell 1994, pp.578-79)

Gatrell and Jenkins (1999) point out that Peel believed that evil should be punished and he supported the use of corporal punishments such as the whip and the treadmill (where prisoners would spend hours stepping on a cylinder in much the same way that a hamster walks on its wheel). In other words, his aim was not to liberalise the prison regime. Rather, his aim was to make it work in a more uniform manner:

'Peel's concern was less with making prison life in general more comfortable, than it was with ensuring that standards did not vary arbitrarily according to the attitudes of the officials in each locality.' (Jenkins 1999, p.29)

Other legal reforms

Peel was also responsible, in 1825, for changes in the rules governing the selection of juries and, in 1825-28, for measures designed to streamline the criminal law:

'In 1826 and 1827, a total of seven Acts were passed, some dealing with the procedure in criminal justice cases and others disentangling and pruning the statutes [Acts of Parliament] in specific areas such as theft...As a result of Peel's labours, between 1825 and 1828 no less than 278 statutes were repealed and eight consolidated statutes put in their place. By the time he left the Home Office, in November 1830, more than three-quarters of all criminal offences were covered by legislation introduced since 1825.' (Jenkins 1999, p.27)

As early as March 1822, Peel set up a select committee to look into policing in London. Although the committee argued against setting up a police force, Peel continued to make plans and a letter written to junior minister Henry Hobhouse at the end of 1826 outlines a plan for a police force very similar to that which was put into practice when the Metropolitan Police Force was set up in 1829. So, although Peel's plan to set up a permanent police force was not realised under Liverpool, the groundwork was done in the period 1822-27. Whether or not the setting up of a police force is evidence of a 'liberal' attitude, however, is debatable. There is the argument that it was profoundly illiberal in that the presence of permanent law enforcers restricted individual liberty.

A new liberal approach?

The traditional view, therefore, was that, as Home Secretary, Peel was a great reformer. Certainly, that is the view taken by historians who argue in support of a new phase of 'Liberal Toryism' in the period 1822-27. Peel, they argue, was single-handedly responsible for reorganising and streamlining criminal law. He removed laws which were obsolete or rarely enforced and, as a result, gave credibility to the laws which remained. The fact that he drastically reduced the number of capital offences suggests that he had a liberal outlook, as did his reform of the prison system. This viewpoint does have some contemporary supporters. Rubinstein (1998), for example, describes the 1823 Gaols Act as a 'major reform'. He suggests that Peel's reforms led to a significant reduction in executions. He also argues that the idea that the punishment should fit the crime simply was not current in the early 19th century. Rather, the aim was that severe punishment would deter potential law breakers. By implication, therefore, he suggests that Peel cannot be held responsible for the limitations of his reforms.

BOX 3.7 | Peel as Home Secretary

(i) Peel's penal reforms

Peel's interest in criminal law reform had less to do with ending the barbarism of past times than with his interest first in restoring the law's credibility against public attack and, secondly, in making it more efficient, even more punitive - more of a terror not less. Far from dismantling the bloody code, or intending to begin to dismantle it, his reforms were intended to outflank the wholesale reform supported by the Whig radicals and to retain the legal values of the Establishment in their essentials. It was not without significance that his revisions were accepted by the Commons with scarcely a whisper of protest and were not even debated in the Lords. To give Peel his due, he was open about his motives. As early as May 1823, he acknowledged the need for change, but all he was ready to do was to abolish 'every part of the criminal statutes that could not with safety be acted on' or which 'could hardly ever be enforced'. What would be tidied away was the obvious drawback of sentencing people to death when it was public knowledge that they would not be hanged. Peel kept his word. The capital punishments he did abolish involved crimes for which the death sentence was never now carried out, either because few, if any, prosecutions took place (as in the case of impersonating a Chelsea Pensioner) or because conditional pardons had become routine. Peel was embarking on a holding operation - a tidying up. If Peel opened the way to the Whig reforms which reduced the number of capital crimes to a dozen by 1837, he did so unintentionally.

Adapted from Gatrell 1994.

(ii) Peel's record in context - executions 1817-40

Year	Convictions	Sentenced to death	Executed (all crimes)	Executed (murder)
1817	9,056	1,302	115	25
1818	8,958	1,254	97	13
1819	9,510	1,314	108	15
1820	9,318	1,236	107	10
1821	8,788	1,134	114	22
1822	8,209	1,016	97	18
1823	8,204	968	54	11
1824	9,425	1,066	49	15
1825	9,964	1,036	50	10
1826	11,107	1,203	57	10
1827	12,567	1,529	73	11
1828	111,723	1,165	58	17
1829	132,261	1,385	74	13
1830	12,805	1,397	46	14
1831	13,830	1,601	52	12
1832	14,947	1,449	54	15
1833	14,446	931	33	6
1834	15,995	480	34	12
1835	14,729	523	34	21
1836	14,771	494	17	8
1837	17,090	438	8	8
1838	16,785	116	6	5
1839	17,832	56	11	10
1840	19,927	77	9	9

This table makes it clear that the decline in the number of death sentences passed began only after Peel left the Home Office in 1830. The softening of the law with which he is so widely credited only amounted to repealing laws which were totally disused, and to a more generous policy of commutation (the legal process whereby a sentence may be changed to one which is less severe). The figures make it seem unsurprising that his reform of the forgery laws, in 1830, still left 42 capital offences in this category.

Noticeable change in the criminal law arrived only in the 1830s, under the Whig governments, first as a result of pressure from private members, then from Russell as Home Secretary from 1835 to 1839. Peel opposed some of these reforms, and he was not active in any of them. By the time Russell left the Home Office, the death penalty applied to only a handful of offences and, for practical purposes, only to murder. In ten years, the number of death sentences passed had been reduced to 7% of the number passed while Peel was Home Secretary, while the number carried out had been reduced to 10% of the number passed under Peel.

Adapted from Beales 1974.

Those who oppose the traditional view point out, first, that Peel's reforms were the response to the recommendations made by a report of a parliamentary committee of enquiry which sat in 1819. In other words, Peel was completing a process begun before his appointment and was not himself responsible for initiating the process. And second: 'The fact is that Peel may have succeeded in simplifying the criminal law, but the way in which it was applied was no more lenient than in the past. In the years between 1822 and 1828, the annual number of executions carried out in England and Wales averaged 63, remarkably similar to the figure of 67 executions per annum in the comparable period 1805-12. It is only through a misleading comparison with the exceptionally disturbed, economically depressed post-war years, 1815-21, when an average of 105 executions took place annually that Peel can be made to look like a humanitarian reformer.' (Jenkins 1999, p.27)

Gatrell (1994) and Hilton (1996) argue that Peel's aim in removing laws which were obsolete or rarely enforced was to ensure that lawbreakers would know exactly what to expect if they broke the law. Far from providing evidence of a liberal approach, Peel's reforms were conservative - they were designed to make the existing system work more efficiently, not to change it in any fundamental way. This case is summarised in Box 3.7.

2. Economic reforms

It has been noted above that there was economic growth during the period 1822-27. During this period, a number of economic reforms were introduced which suggested that the government was moving away from protection (the placing of tariffs - duties - on imports) and towards free trade. Since free trade is associated with liberalism, these reforms are often cited as evidence of the Liverpool government's liberalisation after 1822:

'It is commonly believed that economic liberalism and the drive to free trade and laissez faire began in earnest in this period, propelled especially by William Huskisson, President of the Board of Trade, although the role of F.J. Robinson (later Prime Minister, when known as Lord Goderich), the Chancellor of the Exchequer, was also very significant.' (Rubinstein 1998, p.18)

The key measures are outlined in Box 3.8.

Evidence of liberalisation?

On the one hand, it could be argued that there is overwhelming evidence of a liberalisation of economic policy after 1822. On the other hand, it should be pointed out that, whilst these measures were implemented by Huskisson (with the support of the Chancellor, Robinson), there is good evidence that their foundations were laid by Thomas Wallace (Vice President of the Board of Trade) between 1821 and 1823:

'Wallace began a process of rationalising and simplifying the complex legislation which weighed down trade with some 2,000 separate statutes.' (Evans 1989, p.52)

Wallace resigned in 1823, however, and, as a result, failed to receive credit for the initiatives implemented by Huskisson. The fact that the moves

BOX 3.8 Key economic reforms 1822-27

- **Reduction of duties** It was argued that lower tariffs on imported goods would mean lower prices for consumers and higher profits for manufacturers. The duties on rum, silk, wool, china, glass, books and paper were reduced, while the 50% tariff on manufactured goods was reduced to 20%. In 1825 the duties on coal were removed, as was window duty on small houses, helping the poor and cutting revenue bureaucracy. These measures helped to stimulate trade and employment
- **Reciprocity of Duties Act (1823)** This Act allowed the government to negotiate trading terms with individual nations. 'Reciprocity Acts' were made with many European states (for example, Prussia, Sweden and Denmark) as well as with some in South America. These agreements reduced tariffs and increased trade.
- **The Navigation Acts** The Navigations Acts (originally passed in 1650) were relaxed in 1823. The Acts laid down that British ships alone were to carry goods imported into Britain. As a result of their relaxation, trade to and from the colonies was permitted to use non-British shipping, charges made on port facilities were reduced and colonial trade restrictions were removed. The result was a freer flow of trade.
- **Corn Law relaxation** In 1828, a sliding scale of duty on imported corn was introduced to replace the 80 shilling fixed rate. So, as English wheat became dearer, the duty placed on foreign wheat was reduced until, at 72 shillings, entry was free.

towards a more liberal economic approach were being prepared before 1822 suggests that there was no decisive break in 1822. Rather, it could be argued, the government was simply responding to economic conditions - which, given the recovery after the end of the French wars - favoured a more liberal approach (Hilton 1977).

3. Trade union reform

The Combination Acts (1799 and 1800) made it illegal for workers to combine with others to improve working conditions or to press for higher wages. In other words, the Acts banned both trade unions and strike action. The Acts did not prevent strikes from taking place, however, and they did not prevent unions from being set up. In the 1820s, the veteran radical Francis Place (a master tailor based in London who had been involved in radical activity since the 1790s) launched a campaign to secure the abolition of the Combination Acts and he received support within Parliament from radical MPs such as Sir Francis Burdett and Joseph Hume.

Hume managed to persuade ministers to set up a select committee to look into the subject:

'Hume succeeded, in 1824, in the setting up of a parliamentary committee of inquiry, and Hume and Place so successfully stage-managed the workers who gave evidence that the Tory government, through Huskisson, agreed most remarkably to the repeal of the 1799 Act, a step literally inconceivable a few years earlier. As a result, the government passed the Combination Act of 1824, which repealed the 1799 and 1800 Acts. Under the new law, trade unions or strikes were no longer liable to prosecution, although threats of violence to persons or property by workers to coerce an agreement were made illegal.' (Rubinstein 1998, p.21)

The Amending Act

As soon as the Combination Act was passed, there was an immediate upsurge in union activity and strikes. The government responded by setting up a second committee which recommended the tightening of the law. The result was the Amending Act of 1825. This Act allowed trade unions to be formed, but made it illegal for them to use any form of force. The result of this was that:

'All combinations except those to fix hours and wages were made illegal and magistrates were given summary powers to punish any man using force to compel membership of an association or participation in a strike.' (Plowright 1996, p.50)

Evidence of liberalisation?

Although, at first sight, relaxation of the ban on trade unions might appear to be evidence of liberalisation, there are a number of counter-arguments. First, as noted above, the Combination Acts had not stopped strikes or the setting up of unions. Indeed, Place and Hume argued that the Combination Acts actually encouraged strikes - an argument which found favour with Huskisson. Second, although the 1824 Act accepted that unions should have legal status, it restricted unions' freedom of action. And third, as soon as it became clear that workers would take advantage of the new legislation, the government backtracked and passed the Amending Law. This suggests that the aim was to restrict rather than to encourage union activity. It was, in other words, an illiberal rather than a liberal measure.

4. Catholic emancipation

When Liverpool came to power in 1812, Catholics could not sit in Parliament or hold public office. Liverpool's Cabinet was divided over whether to support so-called Catholic 'emancipation' and Liverpool ruled that it should remain an 'open question' which was not to be discussed in Cabinet.

The issue, however, remained a nagging irritant to Liverpool throughout his premiership. Whilst Liverpool himself remained opposed to Catholic emancipation, some historians have argued that there are signs of a more liberal approach towards the issue after 1822. There are two main pieces of evidence for this.

First, reshuffling in 1822-23 meant that two pro-Catholics (Canning and Huskisson) were in the Cabinet after 1822. And second, between 1821 and 1827, three pro-Catholic Bills were presented to Parliament:

● Plunkett's Bill to relieve Catholic disabilities (1821)
● Canning's Bill for admitting Catholic peers to Parliament (1825)
● Burdett's Bill for Catholic relief (1825).

Each of the Bills was passed in the Commons, but each was decisively rejected in the fiercely Protestant House of Lords.

Counter-arguments

There are three main arguments against the view that the Liverpool administration became more liberal in its attitude towards Catholic emancipation. First, whilst it may be true that two pro-Catholics joined the Cabinet in 1822-23, the point has already been made that Liverpool's Cabinet was split over the issue in 1812. In other words, there were pro-Catholics in the Cabinet before 1822. Equally, there were anti-Catholics in the Cabinet after 1822 - notably Peel, who remained a leading opponent of the Emancipation Act until the Clare by-election of May 1828 convinced him that action must be taken to avoid civil war in Ireland (see Unit 9, Part 2). Second, one crucial reason why the issue gained in importance after 1822 was because of the formation of the Catholic Association under the leadership of Daniel O'Connell (see also Unit 9, Part 2). Evans claims:

'The emergence of Daniel O'Connell's pro-emancipation and anti-Union Catholic Association raised the political temperature in Ireland after 1823 and frustrated Liverpool's hopes. Only a strong "Protestant" majority in the House of Lords prevented both a measure of emancipation and government salaries for Irish Catholic clergy being accepted in the spring of 1825, following a campaign led by the radical MP Francis Burdett in the Commons. Both Liverpool and Peel came close to resignation.' (Evans 1989, p.47)

And third, it is significant that the issue of Catholic emancipation did not come to a head until after Liverpool's resignation (it was finally conceded in 1829 following the crisis provoked by the Clare by-election). Some historians argue that this was due to Liverpool's skill in making no concessions but keeping the two factions within his party together. In other words, far from moving towards a more liberal attitude towards Catholic emancipation, Liverpool can be said to have protected the interests of the reactionaries by ensuring that no action was taken.

Further debate over Liberal Toryism
Ideology or personality?
The Tory Party disintegrated after Liverpool's resignation in 1827, dividing into numerous factions. Those who accept the 'Liberal Toryism' model see these factions taking shape in the final years of the Liverpool administration. They then explain the disintegration of the party after 1827 by suggesting that, by then, it had split into Liberal and High Tory or 'Ultra' wings, divided in terms of their approach to Key issues. However, this suggests that there were ideological differences between the groups, when, in fact, clashes between personalities may have been more important:

'Cookson (1975) argues that the real gulf within the Liverpool Cabinet lay not between Liberals and High Tories, but between "those attracted to Canning and those repelled by him"...To the Canningites, Liverpool was the Foreign Secretary's indispensable patron; to Wellington and those who agreed with him, he was their only safeguard against Canning's conquest of supreme power. When the unthinkable happened in the spring of 1827, the refusal of Wellington, Peel, Eldon and three other senior ministers to serve under Canning signalled the break-up of the party which Liverpool had so patiently held together.' (Goodlad 1995, p.11)

It should be noted that, although Canning was often labelled as a 'liberal', it is by no means clear that he was a convinced 'liberal':

'Brock presents Canning as being perceived as being "liberal" not because his foreign policy objectives were actually liberal or were seen as liberal but rather because his means of conducting foreign policy were often condemned by contemporaries as being liberal.' (Plowright 1996, p.41)

Similarly, Hilton (1977) points out that Huskisson (and to a lesser extent Robinson) may have been the first experts in economics to enter a political system that had traditionally been dominated by amateurs. But whether their support for liberal economics was on ideological or pragmatic grounds is unclear.

Besides, it is by no means certain that the 'liberals' dominated the Cabinet. Even assuming that Canning, Robinson, Huskisson, Harrowby, Bexley and Wynn were liberals who voted together, their votes were counterbalanced by the votes of Wellington, Eldon, Sidmouth (until 1824), Bathurst, Westmorland and Melville who all supported the 'Ultra' or High Tory position. This left just Liverpool and Peel, neither of whom can easily be labelled as a 'liberal' (though Liverpool did tend to vote on the side favoured by Canning).

Revisiting the policies of Pitt
The historian Eric Evans argues that, rather than pursuing new policies after 1822, Liverpool was in fact revisiting the policies pursued by Pitt in the period 1784-93:

'Liverpool's notion of Toryism...incorporated from the very beginning a strong preference, implanted by Pitt, for free trade...Liberal Toryism was not...a new brand of reforming Toryism; its ideological basis reflected the influence of the Younger Pitt. There are close parallels between Pitt's peacetime policies of 1784-93 and Liverpool's between 1822 and 1827. Similarities also exist between Pitt's stress on public order between 1793 and 1801 and Liverpool's between 1815 and 1820.' (Evans 1989, pp.43-45)

If Evans is right, Liverpool's government can be seen as a truly conservative regime whose policies were determined by what had already been tried and tested by Pitt's peacetime administration. The term 'Liberal Toryism' is, therefore, misleading. Liverpool used repression to counter popular protest between 1815 and 1820, just as Pitt had done in the 1790s. Similarly, Liverpool followed Pitt in favouring freer trade and mild economic and administrative reform. Further, an ideological continuity between the two regimes has been identified:

'Throughout the era of Pitt and Liverpool the three essentials of good government were seen as residing in the protection of personal liberty, the security of personal property and a modest level of taxation. Such aims were less visionary that the rights of man, but...they constitute the best clues to an understanding of the men who won the war and enabled the nation to withstand the trials of peace.' (Derry 1990, p.197)

To understand Liverpool's administration, therefore, it may be necessary to move away from the idea that 1822 marked the beginning of a new, 'liberal' phase and to look instead at the way in which the Liverpool government looked back to Pitt's regime for inspiration.

MAIN POINTS - Part 2

- There is a debate about whether the Liverpool administration can be divided into two distinct phases - 1812-22 (Reactionary Toryism) and 1822-27 (Liberal Toryism). There appears to be change between 1821 and 1823 because Liverpool reshuffled the Cabinet.
- Since those promoted to the Cabinet had all served in the government before, their promotion may have been a matter of style rather than substance.
- Those who support the view that there was a shift to Liberal Toryism in the period 1822-27 point to reform in four main areas: (1) legal reform; (2) economic reform; (3) trade union reform; (4) relaxation of religious discrimination.
- Recently, historians have questioned whether there was genuine liberalisation after 1822. They point out that there were continuities and question whether the reforms actually were liberal.
- Evans (1989) argues that, rather than pursuing new policies after 1822, Liverpool was in fact revisiting the policies pursued by Pitt in the period 1784-93. If that is so, the term 'Liberal Toryism' is misleading since Liverpool's government was actually conservative. Its policies were based on what had already been tried and tested.

Activity 3.2 'Liberal Toryism'

ITEM 1 A historian's view (i)

It used to be argued that there was a transformation of the tone and practice of government in the early 1820s. But the liberalisation of the ministry was restricted. Two of the fastest-rising figures, Wellington and Peel, were Protestants and stood towards the tough and distinctly Tory end of the spectrum of opinion that supported Liverpool. Nor were the perceptions of the Tories transformed rapidly during the 1820s. Whigs still distrusted them and found little that was liberal in their continuing defence of the existing constitution. Radical opinion shared this view with an added bitterness after the experience of repression and prosecution. Nor did the ministry shed the image of Old Corruption. The early 1820s witnessed a change of style and presentation rather than of fundamental purpose. Nearly all those prominent in the reshuffled ministry had held office earlier. Liverpool, who had insisted on Canning's succession to Castlereagh and who encouraged the 'liberal' trend in economic policy, was himself an arch-survivor of administrations stretching back to the 1790s. There was no sharp change in his view of the purposes of government, though he had a keen appreciation of changing tactical possibilities. The real change was in circumstances as more settled and expansionary economic conditions arrived in the early 1820s. Discontent and agitation ebbed and pressures on government eased. Though it was scarcely the normalcy understood before 1789, it was nonetheless (except in Ireland) a return to a style of rational, responsive government after years of desperate survival. A reactive conservatism was replacing that of reaction.

Adapted from Coleman 1988.

ITEM 2 A historian's view (ii)

Liberal Toryism is usually associated with the name of Canning, and Canning certainly struck the public eye more than any other minister. Yet he was primarily a Foreign Secretary. He stuck fairly closely to his own department, and Liberal Toryism must mean a good deal more than Canning's foreign policy. Canning's peculiar contribution was his use of public opinion as a political weapon. But in that age politicians could not live by public opinion alone, and Canning himself could not have remained in power a day had he not had the unswerving support of the Prime Minister, Lord Liverpool. Liverpool as much as Canning was responsible for the experiment of Liberal Toryism. Within the Cabinet, Liverpool was the mainstay of 'liberal' opinion. He was perhaps the only man who could persuade the Tory Party as a whole to sanction such opinions, and he was certainly the only man who could hold the Cabinet together between 1822 and 1827. With the changes of

Lord Liverpool

George Canning

1821-23, Liverpool was able to gather round him a group of liberal-minded men ready to take whatever opportunities were offered for economic reform. Huskisson had been his confidential adviser since 1814 and was now President of the Board of Trade; Robinson became Chancellor of the Exchequer; Peel played a small part in the formulation of economic policy when he could spare time from the Home Office. As Prime Minister and as First Lord of the Treasury, Liverpool was the head and the coordinating agent in his 'economic Cabinet'. By inclination, he was not likely to shirk any of the duties and the responsibilities which belonged to such a situation. The next two years were of the greatest importance in the history of economic policy. They saw the applications of free trade, the consolidation of the Customs Laws, the repeal and subsequent re-enactment in a modified form of the Combination Laws, and the launching of a new colonial policy.

Adapted from Brock 1941.

ITEM 3 A historian's view (iii)

Lord Liverpool's long administration has traditionally been divided into two periods: a reactionary phase, 1812-22, and a liberal phase, 1822-27, which was associated with the economic policies and other reforms of Liverpools second-wave ministers, especially Huskisson, Robinson and Peel. Castlereagh's suicide in 1822 thus becomes the natural turning point. In fact, this division is misleading. The second-wave ministers associated with reform after 1822 were already serving their apprenticeships before then. Moreover, the groundwork for many of the reforms with which they are credited was laid by their supposedly reactionary predecessors. If turning points are sought, 1819 is a better candidate than 1822. However, the Liverpool government never underwent an ideological conversion. Liverpool, influenced by Huskisson, had always favoured free trade. As to reform of the franchise, Liverpool and his colleagues were no more in favour of it in 1827 than they had been in 1819.

Adapted from Evans 1996.

ITEM 4 Extract from the Annual Register

Fifty years ago, an economist who should have ventured to predict the present development of English commerce, capital, revenue or debt would have been laughed at as the most frantic of a visionary tribe; and it is by no means impossible that the next half century may work perhaps even a greater change than that which the preceding one has witnessed. A whole hemisphere of the globe has been, within the last ten years, been in a manner opened to our industry - an event of magnificent promise and which may ultimately change the aspect of the civilised world. All the relics of the commercial code, constructed with such perverse ingenuity by our barbarous ancestors - for such, in these matters, may we consider the statesmen of the 18th century - are fast being demolished under the new enlightened policy of their present successors; and we cannot but be assured that the wisdom of this change of system will yearly make itself more sensibly felt in the progressive expanding developments of the unrestricted energies of our trade.

From the Annual Register, *Vol.66, 1824, p.5.*

Questions

1. a) Judging from Item 2 and your own knowledge, what was 'Liberal Toryism'?
   b) Give arguments in support of the view that the period 1822-27 was characterised by 'Liberal Toryism'.
2. a) Compare the assessments of Liberal Toryism given in Items 1-3.
   b) Which view is most convincing? Explain your answer.
3. a) Make a list of the main points being made by Item 4.
   b) What was the 'new enlightened policy' referred to in Item 4?
   c) How might a historian use Item 4 as evidence to support the view that the 1820s were characterised by 'Liberal Toryism'? What counter-arguments might be made?
4. 'The term "Liberal Toryism" was invented by historians. It obscures the fact that Liverpool's ministry was simply benefiting from an economic revival.' Using Items 1-4, give arguments for and against this view.

3 Liverpool's achievements and failures

Key issues

1. What did Liverpool achieve?
2. What were Liverpool's failures?
3. Why did Liverpool manage to stay in power for so long?

3.1 What did Liverpool achieve?

The historical debate

The historical debate about the effectiveness or otherwise of the Liverpool administration has been raging since 1841 when the future Tory Prime Minister Benjamin Disraeli described Liverpool as:
   'The arch-mediocrity who presided rather than ruled over a "Cabinet of mediocrities"...In the conduct of public affairs, his disposition was exactly the reverse of that which is the characteristic of great men. He was pre-emptory [domineering] in little matters, and great ones he left open.' (quoted in Plowright 1996, p.53)
In recent years, two main schools of thought have developed - one keen to rehabilitate Liverpool's reputation and the other keen to go further than Disraeli in their criticism. As in the case with debates between historians, the approach taken reflects the ideological stance of the particular

historian. Those who praise Liverpool's achievements tend to approve of politicians whose primary aims are the preservation of order and defence of the status quo. Those who criticise Liverpool, on the other hand, tend to examine the Liverpool administration from the viewpoint of ordinary people rather than from that of the ruling elite and, therefore, have a very different perspective on government action.

Liverpool's achievements

Gash is one of a number of historians who argue that the Liverpool administration was both constructive and reforming. Indeed, he argues that within the context of the period it could have achieved little more:

'The reproach that his administration might have done more constructive work than it did must be balanced by a consideration of the narrow limits within which it exercised its authority. In the uneasy equilibrium which existed after the decline in the personal power of the Crown and before the rise of party rule, Liverpool's government had to supply from its own resources what it could not obtain from institutional strength.' (Gash 1984, p.6)

According to Gash and other historians who have formed a positive view of the administration, Liverpool's achievements were as follows.

The defeat of Napoleon

First, when Liverpool came to power in 1812, the key task was to defeat Napoleon. At the time, this seemed a long way off, with French troops marching towards Moscow and the sole British force on the Continent bogged down in the bloody and attritional Peninsular War. As pointed out in section 1.1 above, Liverpool (unlike the Whigs) always believed that the war had to be fought until the total defeat of Napoleon. He therefore gave Castlereagh complete support in his efforts to create a Grand Alliance. By 1815, Liverpool's belief had been vindicated and Napoleon defeated, leaving Liverpool's political position much strengthened. Liverpool, so the argument goes, can thus take some credit for the successful outcome of the war.

Economic prosperity

Second, some historians have argued that Liverpool coped well with the post-war crisis by guiding the country from debt and unemployment through social distress to economic prosperity by 1822. These historians tend to play down the measures taken against the radicals and to emphasise the government's 'moderation':

'The policy of so-called "repression" was more than simply a device of Liverpool's to curry favour with jittery backbenchers. The first duty of government is the maintenance of law and order and governments in the early 19th century acknowledged few additional duties...At a time when the penal code (largely as a consequence of the weakness of the agencies of law enforcement) was draconian [very severe], the basic moderation of the government's response is easily overlooked.' (Plowright 1996, p.58)

By acting with 'moderation', it is suggested, Liverpool cleverly ensured that the protest fizzled out without major loss of life or damage to property.

New governmental principles

Third, some historians have argued that Liverpool allowed some significant new governmental principles to be adopted during his period in office. Gash, for example, claims relations between monarch and government changed significantly during Liverpool's premiership:

'The 15 years of Liverpool's premiership marked an important stage in the development of the modern Cabinet. He was always a strong constitutionalist and his difficult parliamentary position between 1815 and 1822 was in itself an incentive for upholding the rights and powers of ministers of the Crown even against the Crown itself. The decline in the prestige of the monarchy which came with the Prince of Wales' accession to the regency in 1811 made it possible for Liverpool to press his views on his royal master more firmly than he would have been disposed to do in the previous reign.' (Gash 1984, p.5)

In addition, those who see the development of Liberal Toryism in the 1820s point to the adoption of liberal economic policies and penal reform as progressive innovations.

Maintaining a parliamentary coalition

Fourth, a number of historians praise Liverpool for his skill in building and maintaining a coalition in Parliament - a coalition which included Ultra Tories, conservatives and often Whigs. This, it is argued, was particularly impressive at a time when party ties were weak, the administrative machinery of government was poorly developed and the pressures which arose from a rapidly changing society were intense.

A 'middle way'

Fifth, there is the argument that Liverpool successfully followed a 'middle way'. His views, it is argued, were conservative, but he was not opposed to all change. He was flexible - even flexible enough to suppress his own views on occasion. For example, he allowed the issue of Catholic emancipation to become an 'open question' (the government remained officially neutral on the matter), even though he was personally opposed to emancipation. This 'middle way' (between the hardline Ultras on the one hand and the radicals on the other) ensured that he maintained support in Cabinet and in Parliament and, at the same time, it ensured that the existing system remained intact since issues like Catholic emancipation and parliamentary reform were effectively blocked.

Character and leadership skills
Sixth, several historians make a great deal of Liverpool's character and his leadership skills. These are outlined in Box 3.9.

BOX 3.9 Liverpool's character and leadership skills

(i) Brock's view
Liverpool was certainly the only man who could hold together the Cabinet between 1822 and 1827.
(Brock 1941, p.3)

(ii) Gash's view
The proof of Liverpool's ability was that, though he made mistakes and was more than once frustrated in his purpose, he never made a disastrous error and was always able to retrieve a damaged position.
(Gash 1984, p.6)

(iii) Plowright's view
Liverpool assembled a team of enormous talent, as suggested by the fact that it contained no fewer than four future Prime Ministers: Canning, Robinson, Wellington and Peel. Moreover, the fact that such highly talented but incompatible personalities managed to work together at all was due to Liverpool's diplomacy.
(Plowright 1996, p.58)

(iv) Evans' view
He may have lacked vision and originality but he possessed a gift which sustains many balanced, decent and considerate folk - and Liverpool, despite his fussiness, was all three. He inspired trust. That trust he used to his political advantage, since he was able to persuade intrinsically abler colleagues to work under him when they would have been reluctant to accept the authority of anyone else.
(Evans 1989, p.47)

Longevity
Finally, the longevity of Liverpool's premiership is often cited as an achievement in itself. One reason for this is that the Tories split and lost power so soon after his death. This suggests that it was Liverpool's skills (rather than circumstances) that prevented splits developing earlier. A second reason

is that Liverpool was the last Prime Minister to stay in power for 15 consecutive years (and he would have served longer if illness had not forced him to resign). With hindsight, therefore, the longevity of Liverpool's premiership seems particularly impressive.

3.2 What were Liverpool's failings?

Different interpretations
It should be clear from the section above that judgements about the Liverpool administration are related to key issues already discussed in this unit and in Unit 2 - for example:
- Can the government's response to radicalism 1815-20 be justified?
- Is 'reactionary' too strong a word to describe the Liverpool government in the years 1815-20?
- Did the Liverpool administration undertake a programme of liberal reforms in 1822-27?

Those historians who answer 'no' to all three questions are unlikely to agree with the assessment of the Liverpool administration's achievements outlined above. Indeed, what is interpreted as an achievement by one historian can be interpreted as a failure by another.

The Liverpool administration's failings have been described as follows.

Indifference to the poor
First, there is the argument that the government was indifferent to the suffering of the poor. Even Plowright, who praises Liverpool in other respects, admits:
'So harsh was the plight of the working class and so seemingly indifferent to that plight was Liverpool's administration, in adding to their burdens and responding to protest with repression, that the peaceful nature of much popular protest in this period can be regarded as remarkable.' (Plowright 1996, p.56)
The Liverpool government, in other words, failed a large part of the British population.

Handling the post-war disturbances
Second, historians such as Thompson (1980) have criticised the Liverpool administration for the way in which it handled the post-war disturbances (see Unit 4, Part 2, and Part 1 above):
'Those like Thompson who wish to argue that Liverpool unnecessarily pursued repressive policies claim that much disorder was actually provoked by the government - either indirectly through policies which placed intolerable burdens upon the poor (such as the 1815 Corn Law artificially inflating the price of bread), or

directly through the practice of employing agent provocateurs who encouraged law-breaking so that they could collect a reward by informing on the law breakers.' (Plowright 1997, pp.14-15)

Blocking reforms

Third, far from seeing the Liverpool administration as responsible for effective, progressive reforms, it is possible to argue that the policies pursued by the government were designed to block or avoid fundamental reforms:

'Liverpool's reputation in recent years has improved and deservedly so, but his undoubted political skills had simply postponed, not settled, a number of vital issues, including Catholic emancipation, parliamentary reform, and the question of a Corn Bill. These were, in the end, to destroy his Tory successors.' (O'Gorman 1997, p.354)

By making the issue of Catholic emancipation an 'open question'. Liverpool made sure that it was not discussed in Cabinet and, without government backing, there was little chance of an Emancipation Bill being passed by Parliament (even if there was a majority in favour of emancipation in the Commons, the House of Lords had a large majority against it). Similarly, despite extra-parliamentary pressure, the Liverpool government refused to introduce or support measures which would have resulted in parliamentary reform. When Lord John Russell introduced a Bill to disenfranchise 100 of the smallest boroughs in 1822, for example, the government refused to back it.

Political judgement

Fourth, Liverpool's political judgement can be challenged. The promotion of Canning, for example, can be seen as an act which was divisive and sowed the seeds for the later splits which so damaged the Tories:

'Although the reshuffle (of 1821-23) strengthened the administration in Parliament, it also brought to a position of power the controversial personality of Canning. The new Foreign Secretary aroused the distrust of older Tories as much for his flamboyant style and overt ambition as for the content of his policies.' (Goodlad 1995, p.11)

Although the promotion of Canning strengthened Liverpool's personal position (since Canningites were grateful for Canning's promotion whilst opponents of Canning saw Liverpool as the only safeguard against Canning), it ensured that there would be a power struggle after his resignation. Liverpool's judgement in promoting Canning can therefore be questioned.

Lack of imagination

Fifth, Liverpool has been accused of lack of imagination and clumsiness.

'A lack of imagination was compounded by clumsiness in the execution of policies, such as the demobilising of servicemen with such haste that they added to the already glutted market for labour and overreacting to popular unrest.' (Plowright 1996, p.55)

Longevity

And sixth, the longevity of Liverpool's premiership, it can be argued, was not such a great achievement bearing in mind that he was Prime Minister in an unreformed Parliament:

'Long tenure of power was anyway easier when general elections were infrequent and most parliamentary seats not actually contested. In such circumstances, public opinion, however hostile, was far less important than it was later to become. Before Liverpool, Walpole, Pitt and the formidably mediocre Lord North had all been Prime Minister continuously for more than ten years and all had successfully faced public hostility at least as great as anything encountered by Liverpool.' (Evans 1989, p.48)

3.3 Why did Liverpool manage to stay in power for so long?

The longevity of Liverpool's premiership

Historians who have considered why the Liverpool administration was able to survive for so long have come up with a number of reasons. It should be noted, however, that the longevity of Liverpool's premiership was the product of a combination of factors and had no single cause.

1. Experience

First, as was noted in Section 1.1 above, Liverpool was an experienced politician even before he became Prime Minister and he was able to use and develop his skills during his premiership.

2. Luck

Second, many historians are keen to emphasise that luck played a part in the longevity of Liverpool's premiership. Evans argues that luck was particularly important in the early years of Liverpool's administration:

'No one can hold supreme office for long periods in a country where mechanisms exist for the peaceful and orderly transfer of power without a good deal of luck. Luck undoubtedly helped Liverpool in the early years.' (Evans 1994, pp.9-10)

Gash, on the other hand, argues that Liverpool was lucky to become Prime Minister in an unreformed Parliament:

'Part of the explanation for Liverpool's unique place in British political history is the sheer accident that he lived in the unreformed parliamentary era when the choice of Prime Minister was decided by a very small number of people in a relatively small political society.' (Gash 1984, p.1)

3. The unreformed system

Third, as Gash suggests, the nature of the unreformed parliamentary system was such that Prime Ministers could retain power more easily than was later the case:

'The characteristic pattern of 18th-century government was an alternation of some long and many short administrations. Between the accession of George I in 1714 and the death of George IV in 1830, five Prime Ministers out of a total of 21 had ten or more years continuously in office.' (Gash 1984, p.1)

4. Personality and leadership skills

Fourth, those historians who argue that Liverpool's strengths were his ability to spot talent and to build a strong and disciplined Cabinet suggest that Liverpool's personality and leadership skills were an important factor in the longevity of his premiership:

'The ministry...had its full share of men of strong opinions, administrative capacity, political determination and personal resilience. But the personality of Liverpool was decisive for the ministry's longevity, harmony, and ability to function so effectively for so long.' (Derry 1990, p.152)

5. Ideology

Fifth, some historians argue that by pursuing a 'middle way', Liverpool brought stability and, at the same time, strengthened his own position. Liverpool's ideology, in other words, helps to explain the longevity of his premiership.

6. Divided opposition

Sixth, many historians note that the parliamentary opposition to the government was divided for much of Liverpool's premiership. The Whigs had split in 1794 and made little progress in the general elections of 1818 and 1826, while in 1822 the 'Grenville faction' (supporters of Lord Grenville, who had been a leading minister in Pitt's government in the 1790s and was Prime Minister in 1806-7) abandoned the Whigs in favour of the government. Evans suggests that this meant that opposition was ineffectual after 1822:

'The Whigs after 1822 were rarely able to raise more than a hundred supporters in any parliamentary division [vote]. The party battle in Parliament was less keenly fought in the mid-1820s than at any time since 1815.' (Evans 1989, p.46)

7. Royal support

Seventh, royal support (or at least indifference) was still important in the early 19th century. As noted in Item 2 in Activity 3.1 above, Liverpool had a stronger position in relation to the monarch than some previous Prime Ministers because of the development of the principle of collective resignation (if Liverpool resigned, all members of the Cabinet would also resign). Also, George IV was suspicious of the Whigs (especially since many of them favoured Catholic emancipation) and was, therefore, inclined to support the government (especially after Liverpool supported him during the 'Caroline affair' - see Unit 4). Further, as Gash (1984) points out, Liverpool also benefited from George's political apathy.

8. Momentum

And finally, there is the argument that Liverpool's premiership gained a momentum of its own. Historians who believe that Liverpool was skilful and successful would agree with Gash, who argues that:

'An administration with a record of efficiency over a number of years acquired an authority of its own. It could not easily be dismissed; it could not easily be replaced.' (Gash 1984, p.2)

MAIN POINTS - Part 3

- Disraeli described Liverpool as the 'arch-mediocrity'. Today some historians are keen to rehabilitate Liverpool, whilst others are keen to go further than Disraeli in their criticisms.
- Liverpool's achievements have been described as: (1) winning the war against Napoleon; (2) coping well with the post-war crisis; (3) encouraging significant reforms to be made; (4) building and maintaining a strong coalition in Parliament; (5) promoting a 'middle way'; (6) displaying excellent leadership qualities; (7) staying in power for so long.
- Liverpool's government has been criticised because: (1) it was indifferent to the suffering of the poor; (2) it handled the post-war crisis badly; (3) it blocked progressive reforms; (4) Liverpool's political judgement was not as sound as sometimes suggested; (5) Liverpool lacked imagination and made mistakes; and (6) it was not such an achievement to remain in power for a long period in the unreformed Parliament.
- Historians have suggested that Liverpool stayed in power for so long for the following reasons: (1) he used experience to consolidate his position; (2) he was lucky; (3) it was easier to retain power in an unreformed Parliament; (4) he had the right personality and leadership skills; (5) his ideology helped him to retain power; (6) opposition in Parliament was weak; (7) he had the support (or at least the indifference) of George IV; and (8) the government gained a momentum of its own.

Activity 3.3 Was Liverpool a good Prime Minister?

ITEM 1 A contemporary view

I went with Mr Arbuthnot to Sir Thomas Lawrence's to see a picture he had been painting of Lord Liverpool for the King. The picture was an excellent likeness. It has exactly his untidy look and slouching way of standing. It has, too, all the profound and penetrating facial expression which marks this distinguished statesman. Lord Liverpool has a disagreeable, cold manner and a most short, irritable temper which makes it a difficult and unpleasant task to act in public life with him. But he is a most upright, honest, excellent man, conscientiously devoted to the service and to the real good of his country. He has held the reigns of government in times of unequalled difficulty, but has done so excellently. If the King tried to force Liverpool out of office I have no doubt that every one of the Cabinet would support their Prime Minister and quit the King's service.

Adapted from the 'Journal of Mrs Arbuthnot' (a contemporary diary), 17 December 1821. Charles Arbuthnot was Liverpool's Treasury Secretary.

ITEM 2 Liverpool's changing reputation

Historical reputations often tell us more about the fashions of historical scholarship or the persistence of legend than about the truths of history. Certainly, in the case of Lord Liverpool, the past 40 years have seen a remarkable transformation in his standing among historians. For many years he was denounced as a reactionary or despised as a mediocrity. Those who sought to revive a romantic Toryism went back to Pitt and cast Canning in the role of the lost leader torn away by fate before he had the chance to fulfil himself in the highest office. Those who expected early 19th-century governments to act as 20th-century ones saw Liverpool as an unimaginative politician of limited ability who held back the cause of reform for too long. Those who longed for a British revolution criticised Liverpool for being an author of repression. Yet, many of these caricatures stemmed from a refusal to place Liverpool firmly in the context of his own times and to understand his political career in terms of the values and challenges of his era. Once we accept that the party system, the premiership, the structure of politics and the evolution of popular political activism were all at a distinctive stage of development in Liverpool's lifetime, it is easier to be just. To judge Liverpool by the criteria of late Hanoverian England is to bring out his virtues and to highlight his merits. He was a faithful servant of the Crown. He sought no higher praise than to be recognised as a minister of good judgement and integrity. With service as his watchword, he stamped his personality on the period just as surely as Pitt or Fox had done.

Adapted from Derry 1994.

ITEM 3 Historians' views

(i) Woodward's view

In some respects, and especially in his view on economic policy, Liverpool was in advance of the rank and file of his party, but he lacked originality and breadth of mind. A French critic once said of him that, if he had been present on the first day of creation, he would have called out in panic: 'My God, we must preserve the chaos!'. He had been a minister almost continuously since 1793 in the board

Liverpool - saint or sinner?

of control, the home, foreign, war and colonial offices without making any suggestions for the improvement of these departments. On the other hand, he had learned to deal with men. His tact and patience, his own modesty and common sense kept his party together. Liverpool looked at party divisions almost with the eye of a civil servant who can work loyally with chiefs of either party.

Adapted from Woodward 1962.

(ii) Gash's view

It is easy to forget that, having won the war, Liverpool also won the peace. The work of the 1820s laid the foundations of that great liberal free-trade revolution in financial and commercial policy which was carried on by Peel in the 1840s. There were other continuities of a wider political, even moral nature. The emphasis on trade and industry, on the interdependence of agriculture, manufacture and commerce, on the importance of pursuing national, not class or sectional interests are to be found in Liverpool's parliamentary speeches between 1820 and 1826. Liverpool clearly ranks as one of the great, though unacknowledged, architects of the liberal, free-trade Victorian state, second only to Peel in importance. For a man who had already led the country through the closing, victorious stages of the Napoleonic Wars and the equally strenuous post-war year of disorder and discontent, this was not a small achievement. In any analysis of his premiership three features are outstanding - his competence in every important branch of public business, his successful handling of an extraordinary variety of problems and his gift for getting the best out of his colleagues. It can be said of Lord Liverpool that he possessed ordinary virtues to a very extraordinary degree. He was one of the most professional British Prime Ministers ever to have served the country.

Adapted from Gash 1984.

(iii) Evans' view

Certainly, Liverpool was no intellectual giant. He had come into politics, like so many of his contemporaries, because of his family name (his father had been a leading adviser to George III and was rewarded with a hereditary title). Because of his privileged background, Liverpool was able to get into Parliament young and served a long political apprenticeship. As a young politician he was respected more than admired. Little about him marked him out as a future Prime Minister, let alone one who would stay in office for nearly 15 years. Beyond a certain point, however, brainpower is probably more of a handicap than an advantage for a successful politician. Consistency, dependability and the ability to compromise are more bankable assets, and Liverpool had all three. His ability to get the best out of colleagues, many of whom (like Canning and Peel) were abler than himself, was a priceless asset. His Cabinet colleagues trusted him - their private papers rarely, if ever, speak of their feeling let down by his leadership. Liverpool's long period as Prime Minister owes much to good fortune, both political and economic, and to weak opposition, but he was not just lucky; he was an experienced, knowledgeable and effective politician with a great talent for effective chairmanship and for getting ministers to work harmoniously under his leadership.

Adapted from Evans 1994.

Questions

1. a) What does Item 1 tell us about Liverpool's personality?
   b) How might the extract be used in an explanation of why Liverpool stayed in power for so long?
   c) What are the difficulties with using sources like this?

2. a) Using Items 2 and 3 and your own knowledge, draw up a table showing Liverpool's qualities and failings. Then write a profile of Liverpool's personality.

   b) How important was Liverpool's personality in determining (i) the nature of his premiership and (ii) the longevity of his premiership?
   c) 'Historical judgements based on assessments of personality are at best misleading and at worst simply inaccurate'. Comment on this statement using Items 2 and 3.

3. 'Liverpool was an outstanding Prime Minister'. Using Items 1-3 and your own knowledge, give arguments for and against this view.

References

- **Beales (1969)** Beales, D., *From Castlereagh to Gladstone 1815-1885*, Nelson, 1969.

- **Beales (1974)** Beales, D., 'Peel, Russell and reform', *Historical Journal*, Vol.17, 1974.

- **Blanning & Cannadine (1996)** Blanning, T. & Cannadine, D. (eds.), *History and Biography*, Cambridge University Press, 1996.

- **Brock (1941)** Brock, W.R., *Lord Liverpool and Liberal Toryism 1820-27* (2nd edn), Frank Cass, 1967.

- **Catterall (1994)** Catterall, P. (ed.), *Britain 1815-67*, Heinemann, 1994.

- **COED (1982)** *Concise Oxford English Dictionary*, Clarendon Press, 1982.

- **Coleman (1988)** Coleman, B., *Conservatism and the Conservative Party in the 19th Century*, Edward Arnold, 1988.

- **Cook & Stevenson (1996)** Cook, C. & Stevenson, J., *The Longman Handbook of British History, 1714-1995* (3rd edn), Longman, 1996.

- **Cookson (1975)** Cookson, J.E., *Lord Liverpool's Administration: the Crucial Years 1815-22*, Archon, 1975.

- **Derry (1990)** Derry, J., *Politics in the Age of Fox, Pitt and Liverpool*, Macmillan, 1990.

- **Derry (1994)** Derry, J., 'Lord Liverpool: the unobtrusive Prime Minister', *History Review*, No.20, December 1994.

- **Evans (1989)** Evans, E., *Britain before the Reform Act: Politics and Society 1815-1832*, Longman, 1989.

- **Evans (1994)** Evans, E., 'The premiership of Lord Liverpool' in *Catterall (1994)*.

- **Evans (1996)** Evans, E., *The Forging of the Modern State: Early Industrial Britain 1783-1870*, Longman, 1996.

- **Gash (1984)** Gash, N., *Lord Liverpool*, Weidenfeld, 1984.

- **Gatrell (1994)** Gatrell, V.A.C., *The Hanging Tree: Execution and the English People 1770-1868*, Oxford University Press, 1994.

- **Goodlad (1995)** Goodlad, G.D., '"Liberal" and "High" Tories in the age of Liverpool', *Modern History Review*, Vol.7.2, November 1995.

- **Hilton (1977)** Hilton, B., *Corn, Cash and Commerce: the Economic Policies of the Tory Governments 1815-30*, Oxford University Press, 1977.

- **Hilton (1996)** Hilton, B., 'The gallows and Mr Peel' in *Blanning & Cannadine (1996)*.

- **Hunt (1972)** Hunt, J.W., *Reaction and Reform*, Collins, 1972.

- **Jenkins (1999)** Jenkins, T.A., *Sir Robert Peel*, Macmillan, 1999.

- **O'Gorman (1997)** O'Gorman, F., *The Long Eighteenth Century: British Political and Social History 1688-1832*, Arnold, 1997.

- **Plowright (1996)** Plowright, J., *Regency England: the Age of Lord Liverpool, Lancaster Pamphlet*, Routledge, 1996.

- **Plowright (1997)** Plowright, J., 'Lord Liverpool and the alternatives to "repression" in Regency England', *History Review*, No.28, September 1997.

- **Roberts (1999)** Roberts, D. (ed.), *British Politics in Focus* (2nd edn), Causeway Press, 1999.

- **Rubinstein (1998)** Rubinstein, W.D., *Britain's Century: a Political and Social History 1815-1905*, Arnold, 1998.

- **Thompson (1980)** Thompson, E.P., *The Making of the Working Class*, Penguin, 1980 (first published in 1963).

- **Wood (1960)** Wood, A., *Nineteenth Century Britain, 1815-1914*, Longman, 1960.

- **Woodward (1962)** Woodward, L., *The Age of Reform, 1815-70* (2nd edn), Oxford University Press, 1962.

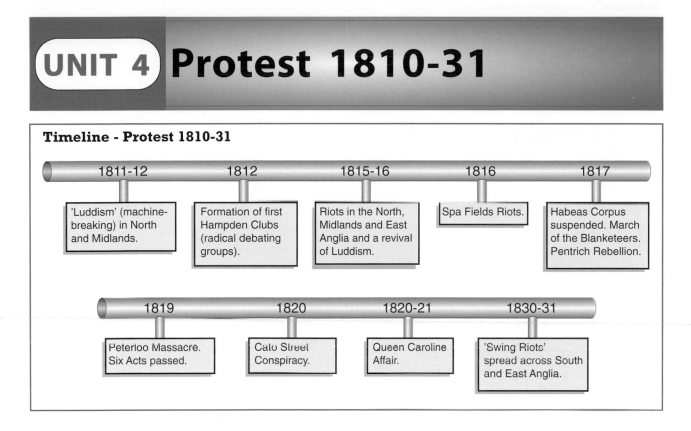

UNIT 4 Protest 1810-31

Timeline - Protest 1810-31

1811-12	1812	1815-16	1816	1817
'Luddism' (machine-breaking) in North and Midlands.	Formation of first Hampden Clubs (radical debating groups).	Riots in the North, Midlands and East Anglia and a revival of Luddism.	Spa Fields Riots.	Habeas Corpus suspended. March of the Blanketeers. Pentrich Rebellion.

1819	1820	1820-21	1830-31
Peterloo Massacre. Six Acts passed.	Cato Street Conspiracy.	Queen Caroline Affair.	'Swing Riots' spread across South and East Anglia.

Introduction

The period 1810-31 witnessed three different waves of popular protest. First, in the years between 1811 and 1816, there were sporadic outbreaks of 'Luddite' machine-breaking in the textile districts of the North and Midlands. Second, in the period 1815-21 there was a surge of radical protest with a series of riots, mass meetings, marches and uprisings occurring both in London and the industrial regions. And third, following a period of relative inactivity during the 1820s, the years 1830-31 saw a wave of agricultural protest - the so-called 'Swing Riots' - spread across the rural South of England, with incidents of machine-breaking, arson and animal maiming. Historians who have examined these waves of popular protest have focused on two main debates. First, there is a debate about the causes of the various outbreaks of popular protest. Some historians

argue that the intensity of activity in each phase is explained relatively easily in terms of levels of economic distress. Others, however, claim that economic distress alone is not a sufficient explanation. Rather, they claim, a number of factors contributed, including the policies of Lord Liverpool's Tory government and the development of working-class political consciousness. And second, there is a debate about the seriousness of the various outbreaks of popular protest. Some historians argue that Britain came to the brink of revolution in the period 1815-21 whilst others reject this idea. Since this unit focuses on the causes and seriousness of the outbreak of popular protest, many of its themes are similar to, and an extension of, the themes raised in Unit 2 (which examined popular protest in the 1790s).

UNIT SUMMARY

Part 1 considers the nature of Luddism, focusing on the key question of whether the activities of the machine breakers represented anything more than a primitive and essentially backward-looking form of economically motivated protest.

Part 2 examines the revival and intensification of organised forms of radical protest after 1815, assessing the reasons both for its re-emergence

and its failure to secure political change. It then goes on to assess the extent to which such activity posed a genuinely revolutionary threat to the ruling elite.

Part 3 explores the reasons for the relative lull in activity for most of the 1820s. It then goes on to assess the Swing Riots of 1830-31.

1 Luddism

Key issues

1. What was 'Luddism'?
2. Were the aims of Luddism ever revolutionary?
3. How did the authorities respond to Luddism?

1.1 What was 'Luddism'?

Machine-breakers

In 1811-12, a series of incidents occurred in which armed protesters stormed factories and broke up machinery (these machines were often described as 'frames'). This happened in the hosiery (underwear) and lacemaking districts of Nottinghamshire, Leicestershire and Derbyshire, in the woollen districts of Yorkshire and in the cotton industry of Lancashire and Cheshire. Those responsible for these acts of violence became known as 'Luddites' because letters sent to employers threatening to wreck machinery or, occasionally, to kill mill owners or even the Prime Minister were signed by 'Ned Ludd', 'King Ludd' or 'General Ludd' (see Box 4.1). The origins of the name are uncertain. It may have been derived from a framework knitter called Ludlam who smashed one of his father's machines in a fit of temper or it may have come from a wayward

BOX 4.1 Letter sent by Luddites in 1812

To Mr Smith of Huddersfield
March 1812

Sir

Information has just been given in that you are a holder of those detestable Shearing Frames, and I was desired by men to write to you, and give you fair warning to pull them down...You will take notice that if they are not taken down by the end of next week, I shall detach one of my lieutenants with at least 300 men to destroy them...And if you have impudence to fire upon any of my men, they have orders to murder you and burn all your housing. You will have the goodness to your neighbours to inform them that the same fate awaits them if their frames are not speedily taken down...

Signed by the General of the Army of Redressers
Ned Ludd['s] Clerk

This letter is quoted in full in Cole & Filson 1949.

Leicester apprentice called Ned Ludd. Whatever its origin, it was widely used and became closely linked with machine-breaking. It should be noted, however, that:

'Machine-breaking was not confined to Regency England. Indeed, there are well documented incidents of machine-breaking incidents in England from the Restoration to the Victorian era. Nor was it a uniquely English phenomenon. French silk workers attacked the jacquard loom after 1804 in Lyons as readily as Lancashire cotton workers had smashed Hargreaves' spinning jenny in 1768-69 or Arkwright's water frames and carding machines in 1779.' (Hargreaves 1995, p.9)

1.2 Was Luddism ever revolutionary?

The debate over Luddism

The nature of Luddite disturbances has been the subject of considerable debate between historians. The main lines of argument can be summarised as follows.

1. Industrial hooligans

The first view is that Luddites were no more than industrial hooligans who made a blind, spasmodic attempt to halt industrialisation. The term 'Luddite' is often used in this way in common speech today - to describe somebody as a 'Luddite' is to describe them as backward-looking and hostile to new technological developments. However, such a view now has few supporters amongst historians:

'The term "Luddite" is usually employed today in a pejorative [negative] sense to denote an attitude of stubborn resistance to change and innovation. Luddism as a historical concept is more complex and dynamic in its application than current usage of the term might suggest. Its meaning can only be properly understood by a careful investigation of the particular historical context from which the term is derived.' (Hargreaves 1995, p.9)

2. Proto-trade unionists

The second view (see, for example, Thomis 1970) is that Luddites shared what were basically trade union objectives, though Luddism differed from the trade unions in the methods used. This view has been expressed as follows:

'Luddism was industrial in its origins and industrial too in its aims...It remained devoid of any tendencies to develop into a political revolutionary movement, and even on the industrial front it was not demanding a new structure.' (Thomis & Holt 1977, p.33)

3. Revolutionaries

The third view (championed by E.P. Thompson) is that Luddism can be explained both as an economic phenomenon (ie as a response to great economic distress) and as a political phenomenon. It is his view that, following Pitt's repression of radicalism in the early 1790s, radical activity went 'underground' and developed into a coherent movement which continued to pose a serious and genuinely revolutionary threat (see Unit 2, Section 3.1). The economic distress of 1812 produced the conditions in which underground revolutionaries could attempt to fulfil their aims. Thompson describes Luddism as a 'quasi-revolutionary movement'. Luddites, he argues, had political as well as economic grievances and some Luddites worked actively and consciously to promote armed rebellion:

> 'One may suggest that by May 1812 Luddism in both Lancashire and Yorkshire had largely given way to revolutionary organisation, which was effecting contact, through the medium of Irish émigrés and old Jacobins, with many centres (Sheffield, Barnsley, Birmingham, the Potteries, Glasgow) where no Luddite outbreaks took place.' (Thompson 1980, p.654)

Difficulty with the evidence

One reason why historians are divided about the aims of the Luddites is because of the nature of the available evidence. There is little surviving evidence from the Luddites themselves and a great deal comes from government officials and spies who were, naturally, hostile towards the Luddites and had reason to talk up the threat posed by them:

> 'It is perhaps not surprising that contemporary reports by those responsible for the maintenance of law and order tended to take an alarmist view of the disturbances in light of the French Revolution and the continuing war with Napoleonic France...Luddite testimonies appear only through evidence collected at the time by the authorities and their agents who were inclined to emphasise the more sinister aspects of the movement or, more dimly through the oral tradition recorded in the late Victorian era...which makes it difficult to disentangle myth from reality.' (Hargreaves 1995, p.10)

Regional variations

Although historians differ about the Luddites' aims, they tend to agree that economic distress was a root cause. In all areas where Luddism broke out, economic distress resulting from unemployment, short-time working, wage cuts and price rises was acute. It is important, however, to be aware that there were highly complex, specific circumstances which influenced the character of the disturbances in each part of the country where Luddism sprang up:

> 'The grievances of the Nottingham stockingers were over wage reductions, frame rents [paying rent to hire a machine to make the stockings], truck payments [transport costs], the use of colts (unapprenticed workmen) and the production of cut-ups (inferior hose [ie cloth] made from broad pieces of knitwear). Frames were broken because they belonged to an employer who was held to be guilty of these practices, not because new machines were putting men out of work. But, in Yorkshire, Luddism was much more clearly a protest against machinery which caused unemployment...In Lancashire, the position was different again...It is unlikely that most of the low wages and unemployment among handloom weavers in the cotton industry in 1812 were caused directly by steam-power looms, which were not introduced widely until the 1820s. Nevertheless, factories using the new powerlooms were attacked, being held responsible or symbolical in some way for the distress.' (Harrison 1984, pp.245-46)

Given this diversity, it is important to examine the particular context in each area that gave rise to Luddism.

1. The East Midlands

The East Midlands (Nottinghamshire, Leicestershire and Derbyshire) specialised in the knitting of hosiery and lace. Traditionally, this had been done by hand, but technological developments led to the introduction of machines. The short-term factors leading to Luddism have been described (for example, by Stevenson 1992) as:

- the closure of the American market after the American Non-Intercourse Act was passed in February 1811 - exports worth £11 million in 1810 went down to £2 million by the end of 1811
- the rapid growth in unemployment and wage cuts suffered by workers
- the failure of the harvest which resulted in higher bread prices after August 1812.

Some of the long-term grievances were listed by Harrison in the passage cited above, namely:

- the introduction of frame rents
- high transport costs
- lower prices for finished goods
- the increasing use of unskilled labour
- the production of cheap 'cut ups'.

In addition, Napoleon had closed all Continental ports to British ships in May 1808, and by 1812 this economic blockade had begun to bite. Evans argues that:

> 'The period 1811-12 was a crisis point in the French Wars; many businesses were ruined by economic warfare which precipitated a sharp decline in European and American markets. The

peak of Luddite activity in 1812 exactly coincided with the highest point in the alarming rise in bread prices.' (Evans 1996, p.169)

The course of Luddism in the East Midlands is described in Box 4.2.

2. Yorkshire

Luddism spread to Yorkshire at the beginning of 1812. The first attack occurred on 19 January when a factory was burned down in Leeds. This factory contained gig-mills - machines for raising the nap on cloth. Gig-mills and shearing frames (machines which shaved the surface of wool after it had been woven) were a particular threat to 'croppers':

'[Croppers] were skilled men who trimmed or shaved the woollen cloth after it had been woven and fulled [cleaned]. The skills of these men acquired after several years of apprenticeship lay in neatly cutting off the nap of the cloth using giant iron shears...It was known that in cropping or dressing a piece of cloth well they could

double the value of the material. The croppers were highly paid workers.' (Downing 1988, p.19)

That croppers had good reason to be concerned about the introduction of the new machines is suggested by contemporary accounts. W. Dodds, writing in 1841, for example, noted that:

'In 1814 there were 1,733 croppers in Leeds, all in full employment; and now, since the introduction of machinery, the whole of the cloth...is dressed by a comparatively small number, chiefly boys...The old croppers have turned themselves to anything they can get to do; some acting as bailiffs, watercarriers, scavengers, or selling oranges, cakes, tapes and laces.'

The 'crisis' of Yorkshire Luddism

Croppers were at the centre of a series of attacks which culminated in what E.P. Thompson describes as the 'crisis' of Yorkshire Luddism in April 1812. On 11 April, Luddites attacked the mill belonging to William Cartwright at Rawfolds near Huddersfield. Cartwright had already suffered at the hands of the Luddites - the wagons transporting the frames to his mill had been ambushed and several of them broken. Presumably as a result of the ambush, Cartwright had taken steps to defend his mill. Five soldiers and four armed employees resisted the Luddite attack and shot two of the attackers, fatally wounding them. The remaining attackers left without managing to break any frames. A week later, there was an unsuccessful attempt to kill William Cartwright. Then, on 27 April, William Horsfall, a mill owner and outspoken critic of the Luddites, was shot as he rode home. Horsfall's assassination seems to have been a turning point. There were a number of raids on arms depots, but machine-breaking fizzled out after April:

'In the textile districts raids for arms, bullets and money marked the last phase of Yorkshire Luddism, but the precise motivation for the acquisition of arms is uncertain, at a time when the machine-breakers may have felt that they needed arms with which to carry out raids against increasingly well-defended targets or to leave people unprotected against future attacks. Thus on 25 July 1812, Earl Fitzwilliam [the Lord Lieutenant of Yorkshire] could report to Lord Sidmouth [the Home Secretary from June 1812] that while well-planned and perfectly executed arms raids had taken place... "the reports of nocturnal training and drilling...are the offspring of fear, quite imaginary and mere invention". By summer, even these raids petered out.' (Stevenson 1992, p.196)

3. Lancashire and Cheshire

Most historians agree that Luddism in Lancashire and Cheshire was of a more confused character than in the East Midlands or Yorkshire:

'Lancashire and Cheshire were the scenes of a particularly confused mixture of machine-breaking, food-rioting and political agitation. Rumours of delegates from Nottinghamshire making contact with Lancashire weavers began to circulate in the winter of 1811-12 and in February anonymous letters began to threaten attacks on power looms.' (Stevenson 1992, p.196)

The key events were as follows:

- 20 March - an attempt was made to burn down William Radcliffe's warehouse in Stockport (Radcliffe had invented an improved power loom)
- March-April - food riots broke out in several Lancashire and Cheshire towns
- 14 April - Luddites broke machines at a mill in Stockport
- 15 April - a crowd attacked a factory in Macclesfield
- 19 April - a crowd attacked a mill in Middleton.

The attack in Middleton

The attack on the mill in Middleton was the most serious incident. It took place a week after the attack on William Cartwright's mill in Yorkshire and had a similar outcome, initially:

'Following a food riot in Oldham on 19 April, an armed crowd marched on Middleton and attacked the steam loom factory of Mr Burton, but were beaten off by a heavy guard which killed five attackers and wounded 18 others.' (Stevenson 1992 p.197)

Unlike in Yorkshire, however, the attackers did not give up after the initial attack. The next day, a bigger crowd, reinforced with armed coal miners, attacked the mill again and succeeded in burning it down. Referring to this attack and to that on Cartwright's mill, Dinwoody argues:

'These incidents may have helped to give an insurrectionary turn to the agitation by bringing it home to the Luddites that they were in confrontation with the state as well as the masters. There is evidence from both Lancashire and Yorkshire that, in the summer of 1812, the administration of secret oaths became associated with talk of a "general rising" of the people and with the seizure of firearms from private houses. However the revolutionary impulse does not appear to have been very formidable or sustained.' (Dinwoody 1986, p.22)

With the exception of an attack of one further mill, there were no further machine-breaking incidents in Lancashire and Cheshire (as in Yorkshire) after the major confrontations in April 1812.

Thompson's thesis

E.P. Thompson argues that, although machine-breaking incidents had stopped by May 1812 in Lancashire and Yorkshire, serious preparations were being made by a well-organised underground movement. He claims that it is wrong to dismiss the evidence of spies simply on the assumption that they must have been exaggerating. On the contrary, he argues that such evidence adds substance to his case, especially in light of the disastrous decline in workers' living standards and the government's refusal to intervene and regulate the various trades. In such circumstances, Thompson asserts, it would be surprising if weavers had not started to plot revolution. Further, Thompson argues that Luddism was important because it was a key stage in the development of working-class consciousness. As Evans puts it:

'[Thompson] saw in Luddism a vital stage in the emergence of class consciousness by working men against a Parliament of landowners which deprived them of traditional controls on the organisation of their labour and against employers who used the freedom thus bestowed upon them to impose alien patterns of work constructed for the sole purpose of maximising profit to themselves. Against these assaults, workers armed themselves...fighting the might of industrial capitalism with their own weapons of secret oaths, drillings and revolutionary preparation.' (Evans 1996, p.170)

1.3 How did the authorities respond to Luddism?

The military presence

In the summer of 1812, the government stationed more than 12,000 troops in the areas affected by Luddism. This was a huge number of troops - a bigger force than the Duke of Wellington had at his disposal in the war against Napoleon in the Iberian Peninsular. Whether this huge military presence explains why machine-breaking incidents petered out is debatable. Evans argues:

'The 12,000 troops stationed in the North and Midlands had relatively little success in policing the seriously disturbed areas and machine-breakers remained well concealed.' (Evans 1996, p.170)

It should also be noted that machine-breaking had stopped before the summer. Indeed, the loss of life suffered by Luddites at Rawfolds (Cartwright's mill) and Middleton in April 1812 can be said to have been the turning point. The military presence, it could be argued, was as much a show of strength as a police force.

Infiltrating Luddite groups

As well as moving large numbers of troops into the Luddite areas, the government also employed spies to infiltrate the movement. After the attack on William Cartwright's mill, for example:

> 'The area was swamped with spies and informers and a reward of £2,000 (a fortune then) was offered for information which would lead to convictions.' (Downing 1988, p.20)

Although the Luddites responsible for the attack on Cartwright's mill and for the murder of William Horsfall remained undetected for several months, arrests were eventually made as the result of the confession of Benjamin Walker:

> 'Whether the man Benjamin Walker "grassed" on his friends or cracked under interrogation is not clear...[He] had been held for questioning for four days before he gave the authorities the information they wanted.' (Downing 1988, p.20)

Punishments

As noted above, in February 1812 the government passed a Bill making machine-breaking a capital offence. The severity of punishments then handed out to Luddites suggests that the authorities hoped that a tough approach would deter further Luddite attacks. In May-June 1812, eight Luddites were executed and 13 transported at the Lancaster assizes ('assizes' is another word for county court) whilst 15 were executed and eight transported at the Chester assizes. Similarly, when the trial of those arrested in connection with the attack on Cartwright's mill took place in January 1813, 14 men were executed and seven transported. Three others were executed for the assassination of William Horsfall. The attitude of the authorities to the Luddites is suggested by the remarks of a judge in York, Baron Thompson. He told prisoners:

> 'You have been guilty of one of the greatest outrages that ever was committed in a civilised country...It is of infinite importance...that no mercy should be shown to any of you...[and] that the sentence of the law...should be very speedily executed.' (Proceedings at the York Special Commission, January 1813, pp.209-10)

MAIN POINTS - Part 1

- In 1811-12, armed protesters made a series of attacks on mills, breaking machinery. These protesters became known as 'Luddites' because threatening letters sent to employers were signed by or on behalf of 'Ned Ludd'.
- The attacks began in Nottinghamshire and spread to Leicestershire, Derbyshire, Yorkshire, Lancashire and Cheshire.
- The nature of Luddite disturbances has been the subject of considerable debate between historians. There are three main viewpoints: (1) Luddites were industrial hooligans; (2) Luddism had purely economic origins and aims; and (3) Luddism had political as well as economic aims.
- Whilst historians agree that economic distress was a root cause of Luddism, specific circumstances influenced the character of the disturbances in each area.
- Two key attacks were those in Huddersfield and Middleton in April 1812. In both attacks, Luddites were killed by troops defending the mills.
- The authorities responded to the Luddite threat by making machine-breaking a capital offence, by posting over 12,000 troops to the Luddite areas, by using spies to infiltrate Luddite groups and by imposing severe penalties on convicted Luddites.

Activity 4.1 Luddism

ITEM 1 A contemporary view (i)

Oldham
22 May 1812

Dear Secretary of State...

...I am writing to inform you of the disturbances which have taken place in this county, of the peculiar political character and desperate cast of those wretches who have been the fomenters of them and of the object to which their diabolical efforts are directed. I have lately become acquainted with a member (and one of no uncommon activity) of the Secret Revolutionary Committee of Royton, a place in which every inhabitant (with the exception of not more than five or six) are the most determined and revolutionary Jacobins. I have had various interviews with him in which he expressed strong contrition for the participation he has had in exciting the people to these enormities and I have endeavoured to avail myself of the disposition he has manifested by inducing him to make a disclosure of their proceedings and to give information as would lead to the detection of their leading men and this complete frustration of their designs. I regret, however, to say that hitherto I have exerted all my address in vain. It is under this impression that I have taken liberty to trouble you upon this occasion and to suggest to your Excellency the propriety of trying him with a small sum of money by way of reward or proposing to engage him in a contrived service at certain wages.

Part of a letter written by William Chippendale (Captain of the militia in Oldham and a local magistrate) to Richard Ryder, the Home Secretary.

ITEM 2 A contemporary view (ii)

> Chester
> 23 May 1812
>
> Dear Secretary of State...
> ...It gives me great satisfaction on considering the whole of the situation of this district and, after weighing in my mind everything I have heard and everything that has actually occurred since I came here, to be able to state to you my decided conviction that those who may be concerned in any real revolutionary object are by no means so considerable in numbers as is generally credited by many; and believing, as I do, their numbers to be hitherto small, I am equally convinced that their plans and objects, such as they may be, are crude and indigested. I have not a doubt that their great supporter was fear, the operation of which induced many nominally to join them – who, the moment they saw themselves protected against them, deserted their cause. And though, undoubtedly, the present price of provision and labour must press upon the lower orders, I do not believe that dissatisfaction will get any head or that the real mischief will increase to any great extent, provided a vigilant eye be kept over them.

Part of a letter written by General Maitland (the general in charge of operations against the Luddites in Cheshire) to Richard Ryder, the Home Secretary.

ITEM 3 A contemporary image of the Luddites

The mythical 'Ned Ludd' leading his followers into battle. Although his pose is heroic in style, he wears a dress - some Luddites had been known to disguise themselves as women.

Glossary

- **conviction** - firm belief
- **indigested** - ill considered
- **induced** - encouraged
- **saw themselves protected against them** - ie as soon as they saw there was no reason to be frightened
- **provision and labour** - price of goods and level of wages
- **get any head** - make any progress

ITEM 4 A historian's account

No account of Luddism is satisfactory which is confined to a limited industrial interpretation or which dismisses the revolutionary undertones with talk of a few 'hotheads'. Even in Nottingham, where Luddism most obviously had industrial aims, the connection between frame-breaking and political rebellion was assumed by everybody. This was because the Luddites were supported not just by the framework knitters but by the 'lower orders' generally. In Lancashire, while most Luddites were weavers, coal miners, cotton spinners and tradespeople of every kind took part in the disturbances. In the West Riding of Yorkshire, although the targets were gig-mills and shearing frames, Luddites were not just croppers - weavers, tailors, shoemakers and other tradespeople also participated. The prisoners brought up for trial in York after the battle over Cartwright's mill and Horsfall's assassination included 28 croppers, 8 labourers, 4 weavers, 3 shoemakers, 3 coal miners, 3 cotton-spinners, 2 tailors, 2 clothiers and a butcher, cardmaker, carpenter, carpet weaver, hatter, hawker, shopkeeper, stonemason, waterman and woollen-spinner. It seems, therefore, that Luddism began in Nottingham in 1811 as a form of direct action in support of industrial ends and it immediately gained the support of the working community. Because of this, it was outlawed and this drove it in a more revolutionary direction. In the winter of 1811-12, delegates travelled to other parts of the North with the result that Yorkshire Luddism began with a more revolutionary temper.

Adapted from Thompson 1980.

ITEM 5 A historian's account

In order to support the view that Luddites had aims which extended beyond machine-breaking to changing government and society as a whole, it is necessary to find evidence of organisation beyond that needed to perform the limited local task of selective machine-breaking. The fears of revolution which were expressed at the time, however, tell us what people were afraid of, not what was actually happening. The accounts are rarely first-hand and when the sources are implicated themselves, they are supplying information for profit or to save themselves. The arms stores, the Jacobin cells, the secret armies were never found - perhaps because they never existed. The rumour, the gossip, the imagination and exaggeration of the panic-stricken and over-enthusiastic - all these, rather than the actual state of affairs, were the origins of the revolutionary scare that accompanied machine-breaking.

Adapted from Thomis 1970.

'Ned Ludd'

Questions

1. Look at Items 1 and 2.
   a) What do these passages tell us about the difficulties historians face when examining the nature of Luddism?
   b) 'Luddism brought (i) a real threat of revolution or (ii) no real threat of revolution'. Judging from these passages would you choose (i) or (ii)? Explain why.
   c) Which account would you expect the Home Secretary to take more notice of? Explain why.
2. a) Write a paragraph explaining the context in which Item 3 was drawn.
   b) Why do you think there are few contemporary images of Luddites?
   c) Would you say that the artist was sympathetic towards Luddism? Explain your answer.
3. Look at Items 4 and 5.
   a) Describe how the two passages differ.
   b) Assess the evidence in Items 1 and 2 from the point of view of each interpretation.
   c) Give arguments for and against the view that Luddism had political as well as economic aims.

2 Protest and unrest 1815-21

Key issues

1. Why did popular protest revive and intensify after 1815?

2. What were the main forms of protest in this period?

3. How did the Liverpool government respond to the radical threat?

4. How serious was the radical threat?

2.1 Why did popular protest revive and intensify after 1815?

Main reasons for the revival

Following the end of the first wave of Luddite disturbances, the period between 1812 and 1815 witnessed relatively little in the way of popular protest. The marked revival and intensification of radical activity which occurred in the period 1815 to 1821, however, has led E.P. Thompson to describe the period as 'the heroic age of popular radicalism' (Thompson 1980, p.660). Certainly, there was a marked change:

> 'During the five years following the end of the Revolutionary and Napoleonic Wars [ie 1815-20], popular radicalism gained the degree of mass support in both London and the industrial districts of the North and Midlands which had been lacking since the turn of the century. Outbursts of mass radical activity in these years, as in the 1790s, alarmed both the government and the propertied classes at a time when middle-class radicals remained quiescent [inactive].' (Wright 1988, p.64)

The main reasons for the revival and intensification of radical activity are summarised in Box 4.3, below.

Whilst there is broad agreement between historians over the identification of these factors, there is some debate about their relative importance in the revival and intensification of the activity which occurred.

1. The end of the Revolutionary and Napoleonic Wars

Between 1793 and 1815, the government had successfully linked domestic radicalism in Britain to both the 'anarchy' of the French Revolution and the subsequent threat of invasion posed by the French revolutionary government and then Napoleon (see Unit 2, Part 2). A flood of convincing conservative propaganda which tapped into deep-seated and militant popular loyalism had, therefore, played a major part in the suppression of radical organisations such as the London Corresponding Society which had emerged in the early 1790s. Victory against France in 1815, however, removed both the threat and the stigma of national treachery which had been skilfully associated with radical protest during wartime. Indirectly, therefore, the end of the long-term military conflict with France removed a significant obstacle to radical activity and was a factor in stimulating its revival in the period after 1815.

2. Economic distress

The part played by economic distress in the development of Luddism has already been discussed in Part 1 above and, for many historians, economic distress was also the chief catalyst in the revival of popular protest after 1815. Historians have argued that the following factors contributed to the economic distress of the period 1815-20.

a) The financing of wars

The historian John Plowright, commenting on the problems faced by Regency Britain, claims that:

'The French Revolutionary and Napoleonic Wars, which lasted from 1793 to 1815 were enormously costly and damaging. This was particularly so because of the "Continental System" - Napoleon's attempt to throttle British trade by means of a blockade which began in 1806. The Orders in Council of January, November and December 1807 were an attempt to break the blockade by restricting the scope for neutrals to trade with Napoleonic Europe. This not only induced [caused] recession but also contributed to the chronic deterioration in Anglo-American relations which ultimately led to the decision of the United States to declare war on Great Britain in June 1812, despite repeal of the Orders in Council in the same month. This war was to last until December 1814 and, in fact, continued into 1815 since it took time for the news of peace to reach the Americas. As a result of these conflicts, the National Debt increased from £238 million in 1793 to £902 million in 1816.' (Plowright 1996, p.10)

The financing of war was, therefore, a very costly business and the debts that had built up during the war limited the options of the post-war government.

b) Difficulties in adjusting to peace

If financing of the war was a cause of difficulties, so too was the adjustment to peacetime economic conditions. As the historian Eric Evans points out:

'With the coming of peace the government no longer needed armaments or so many uniforms...while the demobilisation of about 400,000 servicemen glutted an already depressed labour market.' (Evans 1989, p.15)

Wright (1988) points out that the end of the war meant that economic blockades were lifted and this, in turn, meant that Britain faced much greater foreign competition than it had faced during the war. In addition:

'Industries like iron and ship-building, which had expanded to meet wartime needs, now swiftly contracted. In Shropshire, for example, 7,000 ironworkers lost their jobs. Poor rates soared alarmingly. It seems likely that the real earnings of an average working-class family were lower between 1815 and 1819 than they had been in the 1780s.' (Wright 1988, pp.64-65)

c) The passage of the 1815 Corn Law

Most historians agree that the economic policies implemented by the Liverpool government in the period 1815-20 did little to reduce economic distress. In particular, the passage of the Corn Law in March 1815 did much to arouse political opposition.

The 1815 Corn Law prohibited the import of foreign corn until the domestic price reached 80 shillings a quarter. It was designed to ensure that the price of home-produced wheat remained high. This had a knock-on effect of guaranteeing landowners' rents and profits. Although laws of this type were not new, the emerging radical leadership and popular press (see below) rapidly targeted the Corn Law as the most glaring example of what was now termed 'class legislation' - legislation passed by an unrepresentative, landowning, elitist class to promote its own interests whilst cynically ignoring the needs of the country as a whole.

At the time, the Prime Minister, Lord Liverpool, defended the introduction of the law in the Commons on the grounds that it would benefit the nation as a whole:

'Liverpool soberly told the House of Lords that the purpose of the new law was to guarantee continued domestic production at a time of falling prices. This would not only stave off famine - a constant government worry at a time of population growth - but also help to stabilise prices.' (Evans 1989, p.14)

But there was widespread condemnation of the law from a broad cross-section of the population at large. For members of the working class, the Corn Law was to blame for higher bread prices during a period of already acute economic distress. Widespread rioting greeted its introduction during the spring and summer of 1815. For radical elements within the middle class, the legislation represented the most obvious example of the political strength of the landed elite which, despite industrialisation and the growth of commercial wealth, continued to dominate Parliament. By extension, the passage of the Corn Law was an obvious indication of the need for parliamentary reform.

The Corn Law can, therefore, be seen as particularly important in the development of a link between economic hardship and growing demands for political reform. This link was often made during the period 1815-21 by leading radicals and the rapidly expanding radical press (see below).

d) The abolition of income tax

The abolition of income tax in March 1816 is also seen as particularly damaging to the government's reputation with the working and middle classes. Income tax is a direct tax paid only by those earning above a certain amount. During the war against France it was paid only by a wealthy minority. Its abolition in 1816 meant that the government had to rely on indirect taxes, such as 'tariffs' (duties) on sugar, tea and beer, to raise money. Whereas income tax was only paid by a minority, indirect taxes were paid by everybody who bought, for example, sugar, tea and beer (in other words, most people). It is usually the case that indirect taxes hit the poor harder than the wealthy and this was the case in the period 1815-20. It has been estimated that the amount of revenue raised annually from indirect taxes rose from £16-17 million in the early 1790s to £50-60 million in the period after 1815.

It should be noted that some historians have defended the actions of the Liverpool government on the grounds that the government itself did want to retain income tax after the war, but a majority in the Commons voted against it:

'Liverpool and his colleagues planned to maintain the income tax into the peacetime years, at a reduced rate, in order that the complex tariff system might be simplified and reduced to encourage the growth of commerce. The two elements were interdependent for indirect taxation could only be cut if the administration could retain the income tax to meet necessary expenditure...Anxious consultations and estimates led the Cabinet to believe that it could carry the measure [to maintain income tax] by something like 40 votes in the Commons. It is an illuminating indication of the independence of MPs that, in the event, the crucial resolution was defeated by almost the same margin.' (McCord 1991, p.24)

3. Population growth and poverty

The revival of radicalism occurred against a background of massive population growth. In 1801, the first year in which a census was recorded, the population of Great Britain stood at 10.5 million. By 1811 this figure had risen to 12 million and in 1821 it stood at 14.1 million. Not only was the population expanding, but its age profile was also rapidly changing due to a combination of extremely high birth rates and a fall in the average age of marriage for women from 26.2 in the first half of the 18th century to 23.4 at the start of the 19th century (see Royle 1997). Historians now estimate that, in 1821, 48% of Britain's population were below the age of 15 and increasingly concentrated in the emerging industrial towns.

Although developments in agriculture meant that these demographic changes were not accompanied by mass starvation in Britain, it has been argued that population growth helped to trigger the revival of radicalism for the following reasons:

- Population growth contributed to rapid fluctuations in food prices as demand rapidly mounted. High food prices encouraged mass discontent.
- There was an increased burden on wage-earners since they had large numbers of dependants. This increased burden may have led to disillusion with the existing system.
- A larger population meant that there was a larger workforce. A larger workforce meant there was a greater chance of unemployment or wage cuts.
- Young people tend to find radicalism more appealing than old people and the population growth ensured that there were large numbers of teenagers and young adult males to provide the protest movements with their rank and file membership.
- Population growth was accompanied by urbanisation. Many of those to whom the

protest movements appealed were concentrated in the growing urban centres of the North and Midlands.

- Population growth ensured that there were high levels of seasonal unemployment in rural areas.
- Between 1775 and 1817, spending on poor relief rose from £2 million per year to almost £8 million per year since the growth in population led larger numbers to seek poor relief.

4. The impact of industrialisation

Historians such as Evans (1989) and Plowright (1996) suggest that the broader and longer-term significance of the onset of industrialisation should also be taken into account when explaining the revival of radicalism in the period 1815-20. Eric Evans argues:

'By the end of the war in 1815, parts of England which had either ignored or been lukewarm towards parliamentary reform in the 1790s were not only becoming receptive to the idea, but were also beginning to generate their own leaders and political consciousness. Liverpool's government after 1815, therefore, faced dual challenges which threatened to coalesce [come together] in a mighty engine of agitation which a landowner's Parliament would be powerless to resist. On the one hand, it was losing the support of the manufacturing interest [middle-class industrialists who did not have the vote], particularly in the North of England. On the other, working people, whose disaffection had previously been concentrated in places like London, Norwich and Sheffield - older urban centres occupied by literate and politically aware skilled men - were showing an increased tendency to challenge the government in the new industrial centres of Manchester, Stockport, Bolton and Leeds. The Industrial Revolution was making its first serious impact on the political life of the nation.' (Evans 1989, p.14)

5. The emergence of the radical press

Although the root cause of much of the discontent which arose in the period 1815-20 was economic, most of the demands made by the protest groups which were active during this period were political. Historians such as Dinwiddy (1986) have argued that an important reason for this was the growth of a new generation of cheap radical newspapers and journals. These newspapers and journals, it is argued, encouraged people to make the connection between economic distress, misgovernment and the need for political reform:

'From November 1816, when Cobbett began republishing the leading article from his *Weekly Political Register* as a separate twopenny pamphlet, the message that parliamentary reform was the key to an improvement in the condition of the people was being transmitted directly to a large working-class audience. Samuel Banford wrote later...that in the winter of 1816-17 Cobbett's writings were being read in nearly every cottage in south Lancashire and the East Midlands. "Their influence was speedily visible; he directed his readers to the true cause of their sufferings - misgovernment; and to its proper corrective - parliamentary reform. Riots soon became scarce and from that time they have never obtained their ancient vogue with the labourers of this country".' (Dinwiddy 1986, p.24)

Whilst William Cobbett's *Twopenny Trash* is generally regarded as the most influential radical newspaper at this time (see Box 4.4), a number of

BOX 4.4 William Cobbett 1762-1835

William Cobbett was born in 1762 in Farnham, Surrey. A self-taught ploughman's son, Cobbett first worked as a solicitor's clerk and then as a soldier, serving mainly in Canada. He returned to England in 1800 and, in January 1802, set up the *Weekly Political Register*. At first, the *Register* followed a Tory line and the profits from the paper soon allowed Cobbett to set himself up as a landowner. But, some time in 1804, Cobbett's thinking underwent a significant shift. His 'conversion' to radicalism was confirmed in 1810 when he was sentenced to a fine of £1,000 and two years imprisonment for criticising flogging in the armed forces. By then, the *Register* was also radical in its message, though, at a shilling a copy, it was too expensive for most workers. In 1816, however, Cobbett avoided paying Stamp Duty by publishing the editorial in a new single sheet format and sold the paper for two pence. As a result, circulation rose from 1,000 to 50,000 copies per issue. In 1817, Cobbett fled to the USA having allegedly rejected an offer of £10,000 from Sidmouth, the Home Secretary, to stop publishing and retire. Cobbett finally returned to Britain in 1819, bringing with him, as a symbolic act, the bones of Tom Paine. During the Queen Caroline Affair of 1820-21 (see Section 2.2 below), Cobbett acted as the Queen's unofficial adviser, hoping to discredit the Liverpool administration. During the 1820s, the *Register*'s emphasis on the need for parliamentary reform grew increasingly diluted by attacks on a wider range of issues such as currency policy and the 'bloated' Church of England. Cobbett was elected to Parliament as MP for Oldham in the first general election after the 1832 Reform Act. The *Register* ceased publication on his death in 1835.

Adapted from Gardiner & Wenborn 1995

other journals also had a wide circulation. These included:

- Edward Baines' *Leeds Mercury* (first published in 1815)
- Thomas Wooler's *Black Dwarf* (first published in 1817)
- William Sherwin's *Weekly Political Register* (first published in 1817).

Wright points out that:

'[People] made remarkable efforts to get at the news. They clubbed together to buy single copies; old newspapers circulated through entire streets; coffee houses and pubs provided papers for their customers. The "pothouse oracle" read aloud from the newspapers, commenting on what he had read. Access to newspapers could also be gained in Political Reading Societies, reading rooms attached to bookshops, hiring and lending arrangements and by hearing the newspapers read out at large public meetings.' (Wright 1988, p.66)

6. Hampden Clubs and Union Societies

The first Hampden Club was set up in London in 1812 by the veteran radical Major John Cartwright. The name of the club was taken from John Hampden, a Buckinghamshire squire who had opposed Charles I's imposition of Ship Money (a tax raised in various towns) in 1635. The club was designed to be an exclusive discussion group for gentlemen and middle-class reformers.

During the last years of the Napoleonic Wars, however, Cartwright organised a series of 'missionary' speaking tours through the industrial north. He met with regional radical leaders and urged them to set up local Hampden Clubs to educate workers and to campaign peacefully for universal suffrage through the organisation of mass petitions. Commenting on Cartwright's contribution to the development of radical activity in this period, the historian Frank O'Gorman concludes that:

'It is difficult to measure exactly the effectiveness of Cartwright's missionary tours, but the 1813 tour covered 900 miles in 29 days, visiting 34 towns and, ultimately, generating 130,000 signatures on 430 petitions. No immediate benefit to the radical cause was forthcoming, but it would be difficult to deny that Cartwright had laid some at least of the foundations for the wave of radical activity that flooded the country after the war.' (O'Gorman 1997, p.249)

The Hampden Clubs, and the so-called 'Union Societies' which began to succeed them after 1815, were responsible for organising many of the mass meetings and the petitioning of Parliament which were a feature of the post-war period. In January 1817, for example, a national conference of Hampden Club delegates was held at the Crown and

BOX 4.5 Major John Cartwright (1740-1824)

John Cartwright was born into an old Northamptonshire landowning family in 1740. After a distinguished career in the navy, he launched his political career in 1775 by making public his support of American independence. In the same year, he was appointed as major in the Nottinghamshire militia. In 1776 he wrote a pamphlet in favour of the radical reform of Parliament, including universal male suffrage, the secret ballot and annual Parliaments. For the next 48 years, Cartwright continued to campaign for radical reform. In the 1780s he was active in the Society for Constitutional Information. In 1812, he set up the first Hampden Club. In 1820 he was fined £100 for sedition. His respectable background, combined with radical views, ensured that he was viewed as a class traitor by some and as a persecuted champion of the oppressed by others. Cartwright died in 1824 but he left a legacy of roughly 80 political tracts and a string of about 150 Hampden Clubs. He was the brother of Edmund Cartwright, who invented the power loom, and he had shares in his brother's factory.

Adapted from Plowright 1996.

Anchor tavern in London, with 70 delegates attending. The intensified campaign of mass petitioning which resulted from this meeting has been described by one historian as representing:

'An outstanding success...the most spectacular radical mobilisation of public opinion for over two decades' (O'Gorman 1997 p.252).

7. Henry Hunt's public speaking

Just as William Cobbett's journalism was responsible for spreading support for parliamentary reform, so too was the oratory (public speaking) of Henry 'Orator' Hunt. Hunt, together with Cobbett, continues to be regarded by many historians as the most dynamic and influential of the radical leaders of this period. Hunt was born in 1773 in Wiltshire. Originally a wealthy gentleman farmer and member of the local yeomanry (the yeomanry was a volunteer cavalry force used to maintain order), he inherited over 3,000 acres of land in south-west England, including property in Bath and the estate of Glastonbury. Like Cobbett (who was, at first a Tory and then became a radical), Hunt's political views changed:

'An unthinking loyalist in his youth, Hunt...was converted to the reform cause during the protracted war against Napoleonic France when "Old Corruption" reached new levels of extortion and incompetence.' (Belchem 1985, p.22)

Many historians are scathing about Hunt's personality. Typical is the following description:

'Hunt was vain, fickle, unreliable and self-centred. He lacked Cartwright's honesty and integrity, but his demagogic [public speaking] talents were undeniable.' (Derry 1963, p.52)

Whereas radical leaders in the 1790s had failed to win mass support, Hunt gained a genuinely mass following. Belchem argues that:

'Hunt's great achievement in the post-war years was to transform [the] new political awareness into a powerful movement open to all...It was Hunt's platform campaigning which led to the mobilisation of the millions in the radical cause.' (Belchem 1985, p.22)

Organised mass meetings, with their own 'rituals' and banners, marshalled by demobilised ex-soldiers and addressed by Hunt in his trademark white top hat, became a characteristic feature of the period 1817-19. These were co-ordinated through the network of Union Societies (see above) and were designed to intimidate the authorities and to provoke the sort of violent response which Hunt hoped would ensure that the ruling elite lost any remaining public credibility. The tactic culminated in the Peterloo Massacre of August 1819 (see Section 2.2 below). Hunt was imprisoned for two and a half years for his role in the Peterloo meeting, during which time he began writing both his memoirs and a series of pamphlets which continued to promote constitutional radicalism. In 1830 he was elected to Parliament as an MP. He lost the seat in 1833 and died in 1835.

8. There was no alternative

Some historians, such as Dinwiddy (1986), have argued that members of the working class turned to more politicised forms of radical protest almost by default. In other words, they were forced into campaigning for parliamentary reform because their preferred means of directly protecting their economic interests and living standards through trade union activity was effectively blocked off to them. In part this was due to the continued operation of the Combination Laws of 1799-1800, which banned the formation of trade unions. However, the effectiveness of the Combination Acts is open to doubt and, besides, it has been suggested that a number of other factors contributed:

'The most important underlying factor was the almost permanent surplus of labour which existed in many areas as a result of the high rate of population growth. This was especially serious for outworkers in the textile industries. Being geographically scattered rather than concentrated in factories, and having skills which were not very hard to acquire, they had difficulty in organising effectively and controlling entry into their trades; and it was only in exceptional boom years that they could attempt strike action in the hope of retaining some of the ground lost at other times through wage reductions...There can be no doubt that many workers turned to parliamentary reform because of their weakness in the industrial sphere, and because they believed that state power was contributing to that weakness when it could be used to protect them. This was particularly true of handloom weavers in the North West...Handloom weavers were much involved in the Lancashire Hampden Clubs of 1816-17.' (Dinwiddy 1986, pp.26-27)

Dinwiddy also points out that the authorities' tough response to Luddism may have encouraged the discontented to turn to peaceful methods of protest.

9. The government's policies

Finally, the traditional view is that the policies of the Liverpool government were in themselves responsible for triggering the radical activity of this period - a view expressed at the time by the Romantic poet Percy Shelley, who famously described the administration as 'rulers who neither see, nor feel nor know'. Those historians who support the view that the early period of the Liverpool administration was characterised by 'reactionary Toryism' (for example, Brock 1941 - see Unit 3, Part 1) suggest that the government's economic policies were based on self interest (as noted above) and that the government's heavy-handed response to popular protest provoked resentment and actually contributed to further protest rather than providing an effective deterrent.

More recently, however, historians such as Gash (1984) and Plowright (1996) have revised this view (see Unit 3, Section 2.1). They argue that the Liverpool administration was not as reactionary as once claimed. In their view, the Liverpool government's response to the outbreak of popular protest was relatively moderate and well-judged - they did enough to ensure that the threat of revolution was never realised:

'Men like Liverpool and Castlereagh...were faced with problems that were unprecedented in their number, complexity and scope. Moreover, they had to deal with these problems, and particularly those relating to law enforcement, with few - if any - and often defective tools at their disposal. When all these facts are taken into account it can be seen that studied restraint and considered moderation rather than needless severity and reckless repression characterised the response of the Liverpool government to public unrest in the period 1812-21. Moreover, when conditions allowed - once the economy improved - Liverpool's government embarked upon reform or, to be more precise, continued along the path of economic reform upon which it had already embarked, with increasing vigour.' (Plowright 1996, p.38)

MAIN POINTS - Section 2.1

- There were nine main reasons why popular protest revived after 1815: (1) the end of the wars against France; (2) economic distress; (3) population growth and poverty; (4) the growth of industrialisation; (5) the radical press; (6) Hampden Clubs and Union; Societies; (7) Henry Hunt's public speaking; (8) the weakness of alternative means of protest; and (9) the nature of government policy.
- Propaganda played an important part. During the French Wars, the government had successfully linked radicalism with anarchy. After the end of the wars, the radical press strongly criticised the government.
- For many historians, economic distress was the chief catalyst in the revival of popular protest after 1815. Economic distress grew after 1815 because of - (1) debts arising from war, (2) difficulties of adjusting to peace, (3) the 1815 Corn Law, and (4) the abolition of income tax.
- Although the root cause of much of the discontent which arose in the period 1815-20 was economic, most of the demands made by the protest groups which were active during this period were political. This was due to a combination of - (1) the emergence of the radical press, (2) the growth of Hampden Clubs, (3) Henry Hunt's public speaking, (4) a lack of the means to improve economic conditions, (5) lessons learned from the recent suppression of Luddism, and (6) a dislike of the government and its policies.

Activity 4.2 William Cobbett and the radical press

ITEM 1 An example of Cobbett's journalism

As it is from the labour of those who toil which makes the country abound in resources, so it is the same class of men, who must, by their arms, secure its safety and uphold its fame. Titles and immense sums of money have been bestowed upon numerous Naval and Military Commanders. Without calling the justice of these in question, we may assert that the victories were obtained by you and your fathers and brothers and sons in cooperation with those commanders, who, with your aid, have done great and wonderful things. With this correct idea of your own worth in your minds, with what indignation must you hear yourselves called 'the Populace', 'the Rabble', 'the Mob', 'the Swinish Multitude'; and with what greater indignation, if possible, must you hear the projects of those cool and cruel and insolent men, who, now that you have been, without any fault of yours, brought to a state of misery propose to narrow the limits of parish relief, to prevent you from marrying in your youth, or to thrust you out to seek your bread in foreign lands, never more to behold your parents and friends. As to the cause of our present miseries, it is the enormous amount of the taxes, which the government compels us to pay for the support of its army, its placemen, its pensioners, etc. and for the payment of the interest on its debt...The remedy is what we have now to look to, and that remedy consists wholly and solely of such a reform of the Commons or People's House of Parliament, as shall give to every payer of direct taxes a vote at elections, and as shall cause the members to be elected annually.

From the Political Register, *2 November 1816.*

ITEM 2 An example of Wooler's journalism

France offers brandies to all the world, at less than three shillings a gallon; but an Englishman is not at liberty to drink it, unless he can pay six or seven and twenty shillings a gallon. And if the plenty of the world were to bring its superfluous corn to British shores, and offer it at twenty shillings a quarter, the masters of the freeborn Englishman would insist upon it that he should not have it at a price less than eighty. His salt costs him six times what it is worth, as salt...his tea pays a 100% duty; in short I am tired of enumerating all his privileges...the real and only freedom of an Englishman is money and money alone. If rich, what he can buy he may have. If great, what he can take is his; but your poor free-born Briton is one of the most miserable of human beings. He labours more, and earns less than any other labourer. His skill and enterprise are only equalled by his want and misery - his freedom, is the liberty of seeking his only refuge from calamity - the grave.

From T. J. Wooler's The Black Dwarf, *8 December 1819.*

ITEM 3 Historians' views

(i) William Cobbett typified all the virtues of the English yeoman. He had once been a patriotic anti-Jacobin. Now he was a no less patriotic radical, bringing home Tom Paine's ashes to be buried in English soil. But, for all his worth - his warm humanity, his compassion, his flashes of insight, Cobbett was blinded by prejudice. Because he hated the new urban industries, the new gentry, the new nobility and the new property classes, he idealised the England of his youth. His highly individual brand of Tory Democracy tells us more about his personality than the condition of England. He called for parliamentary reform because the existing Parliament had allowed old England to be exploited and destroyed. As a journalist he stirred his readers' feelings against the injustices of the age. But, for all his enthusiasm, Cobbett was the supporter of a vanished society, not the prophet of a new order. He could describe, with imagination, exaggeration and grief, the passing of the old way of life. He was incapable of pointing the way to new forms of social order.

Adapted from Derry 1963.

(ii) William Cobbett was the common man who had suddenly found his voice. Apart from a supreme gift of expression, he had nothing - no ideas, no policy, not even the ability to get on with others. Cobbett was a torrent of printed words. He began as a Tory and became a radical reformer, but both political descriptions are irrelevant to his real outlook. He hated the Establishment - the 'THING'. At first, he hoped to escape it by returning to an imaginary past. Later, he hoped to destroy it by an equally imaginary future. The *Political Register* was the first popular newspaper. Its secret was to express, clearly and forcefully, what every labouring man obscurely felt. Cobbett's political programme was simple. Government should cease to exist, and the THING along with it. The army should be disbanded and the civil service wound up. Then taxes could be ended and everyone would be prosperous. It will not do to turn Cobbett into a popular saint. Cobbett became a respected and admired character even in his own lifetime and he ended as an MP, put in by a wealthy radical mill owner.

Adapted from Taylor 1976.

Questions

1. a) Summarise the argument that is being made in Item 1.
   b) Is there any evidence in Item 1 to back the portrayal of Cobbett's personality in Item 3?
2. a) What do Items 1 and 2 tell us about the beliefs and tactics of radicals after 1815?
   b) Who were the newspapers aimed at? Explain how you know.
   c) 'The radical press played a crucial part in the revival of popular protest after 1815'. Give arguments for and against this statement.
3. a) Judging from Items 1 and 3, what was William Cobbett's political standpoint?
   b) Why do you think his newspaper was so successful?
   c) What do these items tell us about the nature of radicalism in the period 1815-21?

2.2 What were the main forms of protest in this period?

The debate

Those historians who believe that Britain came close to revolution during the period 1815-21 tend to emphasise the sheer volume of radical activity which occurred. Those, on the other hand, who argue that fears of revolution were exaggerated point to the lack of coordination between the individual instances of protest and the state's continued ability to respond decisively to it. The instances of radical activity which occurred in this period can be relatively easily identified. The key question facing historians is whether this protest was predominantly reformist or revolutionary in character.

1815-16: traditional protest

Most historians agree that the popular protest which characterised the immediate post-war period was essentially 'traditional' - non-political activity directly related to the immediate effects of economic distress. This activity took several forms:
- anti-Corn Law rioting in London
- a revival of Luddism in the East Midlands and West Yorkshire
- food rioting across the North and Midlands

● 'Bread or Blood' agricultural riots in East Anglia where crowds protested at high flour and bread prices, demanded higher wages and increased levels of poor relief, committed acts of arson and destroyed the threshing machines which threatened traditional patterns of winter employment.

It is the anti-Corn Law rioting which has attracted most attention from historians as this is sometimes interpreted as being indicative of the increasing politicisation of popular protest in this period. The historian John Stevenson, however, concludes that:

'The disturbances owed much to the 18th-century traditions of the London "mob" acting in collusion with its leaders in the City of London...The crowds which assembled outside Parliament and the mobs which went out to attack the premises of those associated with the Bill appear to have derived little impetus from the agencies of popular radicalism...The rioters in March 1815 showed the same discrimination and moderation in their attacks that had been seen many times before. No known radicals were arrested for taking part in the riots and the government found no suspicious background to those it seized, even at a time when it was inclined to do so. Instead, they dealt with the riots for what they were - a traditional display of opposition - in which protest ranged from the "respectable" elements in the House of Commons to the streets.' (Stevenson 1992, p.238)

The Spa Fields meetings

In 1816 a new phenomenon developed - the mass meeting:

'Although meetings of counties or corporations, officially convened to petition the king or Parliament, were a recognised feature of the constitution, the vast popular meetings which were held by radicals in places such as Spa Fields in London, Newhall Hill outside Birmingham and St Peter's Fields, Manchester were an innovation for which precedents could hardly be found, at least before the 1790s.' (Dinwiddy 1986, p.33)

During the period 1816-21, a series of mass meetings was organised by radical groups. Whilst historians agree that these meetings had the aim of both inspiring the public and intimidating the authorities, they are divided over the question as to whether the organisers hoped to use these meetings as the springboard for an uprising.

The first major meetings of this type were the three meetings held on Spa Fields in London on 15 November and 2 and 9 December 1816. These meetings were organised by the extreme Spencean group (see Box 4.6), though Henry Hunt (who was not a Spencean) was the main speaker. There is

BOX 4.6 The Spenceans

The Spenceans were a small, extremist revolutionary fringe group active in London in the period between 1815 and 1820. Their leaders were an ex-farmer, Arthur Thistlewood, the writer and thinker Thomas Evans, a shoemaker, Thomas Preston, and two doctors, a father and son both named James Watson. The Spenceans drew their ideas and inspiration from the revolutionary writings of a bookseller who lived in Newcastle, Thomas Spence (1750-1814). From the 1770s onwards Spence had argued for the establishment of a utopian society -'Spensonia' - in which all private property would be confiscated, the land nationalised and Britain transformed into a republic where everybody had equal rights. Before the clampdown of the mid-1790s (see Unit 2), Spence openly supported the use of violence to overthrow the political power of the landed elite. The Spenceans are generally regarded by historians as the most extreme of the protest movements which emerged in this period, with their actions culminating in the Cato Street Conspiracy of 1820 - an unsuccessful attempt to assassinate the entire Liverpool Cabinet.

Adapted from Evans 1996.

some debate about the aims of the Spenceans and the role of Hunt.

The aims of the Spenceans

It is well established that, in principle, the Spenceans supported revolution. What is less clear, however, is whether serious plans and preparations for revolution were being made at the time of the Spa Fields meetings or whether events at these meetings were spontaneous.

The first meeting was well attended (it has been estimated that 20,000 people attended) and mainly peaceful - most of the crowd dispersed peacefully, though a few did march through Westminster smashing windows in protest at high prices. Before Hunt arrived at the second meeting, however, leading Spenceans Dr Watson and his son stirred up the crowd and persuaded a group of about 200 to follow them on a march against the Tower of London:

'A considerable portion of the 2,000 or so people assembled in the fields clustered round the wagon where they were first addressed by the elder Watson and then by his son. Where the father had denounced the evils suffered by the nation, the younger Watson went further, declaiming: "If they will not give us what they want shall we not take it?" (answers of yes, yes). "Are you willing to take it?" (yes, yes). "If I jump amongst you will you follow me?". At that, he jumped from the wagon, seized the largest of the flags and set off towards the City followed by a crowd of around 200 - by far the greater part of the assembled throng remained to hear Hunt who had not yet arrived.' (Stevenson 1992, p.241)

The group following the Watsons marched towards the Tower of London, looting a gunshop on the way. On reaching the Tower, the crowd was dispersed by troops and the leading Spenceans arrested.

At the trial of the Spenceans in June 1817, witnesses (government spies) claimed that an uprising had been planned in advance. However, some historians discount this, arguing that the Spenceans were simply being opportunistic. Plowright (1996) even goes as far as suggesting that the episode was inspired more by drink and the desire for loot than serious desire for revolution.

The role of Hunt

There is also some debate over the role played by Henry Hunt. After the event, Hunt distanced himself from the action of the Spenceans, claiming that he knew nothing about any planned uprising. Most historians accept that Hunt acted as a restraint on the Spenceans. Wright (1988), for example, claims that, whilst the Spenceans were hoping at the first meeting to persuade the crowd to march to the Regent's house (which would have provoked a confrontation with the authorities), Hunt persuaded the main part of the crowd to disperse peacefully. Belchem asserts:

'Thanks to Hunt's commanding presence, the Spa Fields meetings were not sullied by criminal opportunism...by rioting...or by revolutionary putsch [uprising].' (Belchem 1996, p.41)

And Evans argues that Hunt's strategy was to intimidate the government into making concessions:

'The strategy adopted by Henry Hunt at the three meetings held in Spa Fields, London, was to show the authorities the force of public opinion and its latent [hidden] power if petitions for reform were denied. The largest such meeting was held in December 1816. It passed resolutions calling for annually elected Parliaments and universal suffrage.' (Evans 1989, p.17)

Stevenson, however, suggests that Hunt's part in the second meeting may not have been as straightforward as he later suggested:

'Suspicion remains that the full story was never told. A mysterious man on a white horse was seen directing the crowd in the Minories [where the gunshop was looted] at much the same time as Hunt had left the Spa Fields meeting on horseback, but it seems improbable that the government would have allowed Hunt to escape from prosecution had the slightest opportunity presented itself. Whether the incident was a semi-spontaneous insurrection [uprising] or a well laid plan which failed because of Hunt's caution will never be known for certain.' (Stevenson 1992, p.242)

The impact of the Spa Fields meetings

Most historians agree that, far from forcing the government to make concessions, the Spa Fields meetings alarmed the government and encouraged it to consider clamping down on protesters:

'Plans for repressive legislation were set in train as a result of the Spa Fields riots and the widespread disturbances in the country; although the government exaggerated the threat it faced, there was an element of genuine alarm.' (Stevenson 1992, p.243)

This alarm was intensified by an attack on the Prince Regent's coach at the state opening of Parliament in January 1817 (the Prince Regent was the future George IV, an acting monarch because of George III's illness). Crowds hissed at the Prince Regent and stones were thrown, breaking a window. This prompted the government to take action:

'The Spa Fields riots, reports of discontent in the country and the attack on the Prince Regent's coach...strengthened the Ministry's hand in calling for new repressive measures. As in 1795, Committees of Secrecy were formed to collect information on the state of the country. Although there was certainly some evidence of plotting...the report submitted to Parliament in mid-February was a lurid exaggeration both of the extent and organisation of subversive activity. All discontents in the country were seen as part of a gigantic plot to promote a revolution...As a result, Parliament sanctioned the suspension of Habeas Corpus and passed a Seditious Meetings Act.' (Stevenson 1992, p.277)

The March of the Blanketeers

In March 1817, William Benbow, a weaver from Lancashire, attempted to organise a hunger march from St Peter's Fields in Manchester to London. The marchers aimed to present a petition to the Prince Regent, asking him to relieve distress in the northern textile districts. Around 4,500 'Blanketeers' (so-called because they wore blankets strapped to their backs for bedding) gathered in Manchester on 10 March to set out in smaller groups on their protest march to London. Local magistrates, however, declared that the initial gathering was seditious and dispersed it. The leading figures were arrested and only about 300 'Blanketeers' set out. They had walked as far as Stockport, about seven miles south of Manchester, when they were turned back by the local yeomanry (an armed voluntary cavalry force used to maintain order). One Blanketeer was shot dead and several wounded.

The Pentrich Rebellion

The historian E.P. Thompson (1980) attaches great significance to the so-called 'Pentrich Rebellion'. He describes it as the first example of an attempt at revolution organised exclusively by members of the working class (see Box 4.7).

BOX 4.7 The Pentrich Rebellion

The Pentrich rising was one of the first attempts in history to mount a wholly working-class revolution, without any middle-class support. The attempt throws light upon the extreme isolation into which workers in the North and Midlands had been forced during the French Wars. Even without Oliver the Spy's obvious provocation, some kind of uprising would probably have been attempted, and perhaps with a greater measure of success. This offers a shred of justification for the actions of the government. Believing that some outbreak was inevitable, the government was determined to handle it by making it into an example of terror and punishment which would silence, once and for all, the rebellious nature of the 'lower orders'. But this is not to say that in any circumstances in 1817 a working-class uprising had any hope of success. Every detail of the story illustrates the weakness of the revolutionary organisation, and the lack of an experienced leadership.

Adapted from Thompson 1980.

According to those historians who accept Thompson's viewpoint that there was a widespread and genuine desire for revolution in 1817, small groups of radicals in the northern textile districts made plans for a series of simultaneous uprisings in major provincial centres during the summer of 1817. Having paralysed these towns and gained control in the North, the aim was then to organise a revolutionary march down to London to seize the capital itself. This conspiracy was discovered at its outset by the notorious government agent, W. J. Richards, known as 'Oliver the Spy', and he warned the authorities, allowing them to make preparations (for example, the leaders of a revolutionary cell in Sheffield were arrested in May 1817).

In the event, just two minor uprisings actually took place. The first, near Huddersfield on 6 June 1817, involved a few hundred men. It was stopped very quickly by a small detachment of troops with no loss of life. The second occurred at Pentrich in Derbyshire three days later. Here, Jeremiah Brandreth led an ill-armed group of 200 stocking-makers, ironworkers, quarrymen and general labourers in an abortive attempt to seize Nottingham Castle, from where a provisional people's government was to have been proclaimed in advance of a final assault on London. Before they

had even reached Nottingham, however, most of the 'revolutionaries' had melted away and the authorities, who had been kept informed of Brandreth's plans by Oliver, were easily able to round up those who remained. The leaders were arrested and charged with high treason. Three, including Brandreth, were executed and 30 transported.

Debate over the Pentrich Rebellion

The main difficulty with the Pentrich Rebellion is that a central figure was 'Oliver the Spy'. The question is whether he was simply a paid informer (merely reporting on the organisation which he saw) or whether he was an agent provocateur (actually playing a leading role in inciting the rebellion). The answer to this question is significant in that it has broader implications for how historians interpret the extent and nature of popular protest in this period. Was there a genuinely revolutionary impulse in the North at this time, or were men like Brandreth easily tricked into suicidal action by the wiles of the authorities? Whilst Thompson (1980) is convinced that there was a genuine revolutionary impulse, historians such as Plowright (1996, p.26) have argued that, on the contrary, all that the evidence shows is that there were a small number of 'gullible hotheads'.

The 'Peterloo Massacre'

According to Wright:

'The events of 1817 and anxiety about spies deeply divided the ranks of the reformers, persuading a majority of radicals to take the constitutional and legal path to reform, via petitioning and peaceful meetings. In 1817, there were 700 petitions from over 300 towns and over 1,500 the following year.' (Wright 1988, p.71)

Despite this, the authorities remained deeply suspicious of radical activity - as became clear in Manchester in August 1816.

The build-up to Peterloo

Following the restoration of Habeas Corpus and the release of a number of political prisoners in early 1818, Henry Hunt continued with his campaign for parliamentary reform. In January 1819 he spoke at St Peter's Fields, Manchester. According to Stevenson, this speech marked a change in tone and tactics:

'Setting a more aggressive tone than in the past, he advised people to leave off petitioning Parliament and instead to draw up a "Remonstrance" to the Prince Regent demanding universal suffrage and annual Parliaments.' (Stevenson 1992, p.281)

When it was announced that Hunt was to speak again at St Peter's Fields in August 1819, the Manchester magistrates were, historians agree, very nervous for the following reasons:

- Hunt was due to address the meeting (he was distrusted because of his association with the Spencean group, the events at Spa Fields in London in 1816, this apparent support of violence and the recent hardening of his line)
- recent strike activity had been broken by Manchester magistrates and this had created resentment and tension
- it was anticipated that very large numbers would attend
- spies had reported evidence of secret drilling and arming amongst local radical groups.

When the magistrates approached the Home Office for advice, a top civil servant, Henry Hobhouse, wrote to them as follows:

'Lord Sidmouth [the Home Secretary] is of the opinion that it will be the wisest course to abstain from any endeavour to disperse the mob.' (Part of a letter written on 1 August 1819)

Peterloo

There is little dispute between historians about what happened when a crowd of around 60,000 gathered at St Peter's Fields on 16 August 1819. Despite the Home Office guidelines, the magistrates sent in members of the Manchester yeomanry to arrest Hunt shortly after the meeting had begun. Not surprisingly in view of the size of the numbers involved, the yeomanry found it very difficult to move in on Hunt because he was standing on a wagon in the centre of the crowd. The magistrates then called in the regular forces of the 15th Hussars to rescue the engulfed yeomen and, in the panic and stampede which followed, 11 protesters were killed and 400-600 injured.

The incident entered popular folklore as the most potent symbol of ruthless repression, becoming labelled as the 'Peterloo Massacre' - an ironic reference to the Battle of Waterloo which had taken place just over four years earlier. The extent to which it can be seen as a turning point, however, is debatable (see Box 4.8).

The Cato Street Conspiracy

Organised by a number of the Spenceans who had been involved in the Spa Fields riots, the so-called 'Cato Street Conspiracy' of February 1820 is, arguably, the most extreme and potentially revolutionary action of the period. As with the Pentrich Rebellion, however, it should be noted that a government spy, George Edwards, was involved and the extent to which he acted as an agent provocateur is unclear.

The plan hatched by the Spenceans was to assassinate the whole of Liverpool's Cabinet as they gathered for a dinner party at Lord Harrowby's

---

BOX 4.8 The impact of Peterloo

(i) Peterloo provided the radical cause with martyrs. The press exploited the situation to maximum effect. Liverpool's government was obliged to defend the magistrates, but the defence had a hollow ring, as the Prime Minister himself privately admitted. Furthermore, Peterloo made reform a national cause. Political unions were formed in areas of the country such as Newcastle-upon-Tyne and the Black County area of Staffordshire where radicalism had previously been weak.
Adapted from Evans 1989.

(ii) The Peterloo Massacre inflamed radical spirits, aroused middle-class public opinion and unnerved the government, but the failure of the radicals to advance beyond the high point they had achieved after Peterloo reveals a crucial flaw in their constitutional strategy. At some point, leaders had to decide that the time had come when the downtrodden people should exercise their sovereign right to use physical resistance. It was this question of timing, this issue of judgement rather than any absolute commitment to 'moral force' or 'physical force' which divided radicals at critical moments like the post-Peterloo crisis. The refusal to resort to physical force proved self-defeating. As radicals agonised over what was constitutionally right, they lost their physical might. While they hesitated and debated, mass support dwindled, excitement was squandered and the initiative passed back to the relieved authorities.
Adapted from Belchem 1996.

---

house in Grosvenor Square on the evening of 22 February 1820. It appears that, as with the abortive Despard Conspiracy of 1802 (see Unit 2, Section 3.1), the rebels planned first to paralyse decision-making in the capital and then, in the ensuing chaos and confusion, to trigger a wave of subsequent risings throughout the country. The spy Edwards knew about the plan from its outset, however, and his information led to the arrest of Arthur Thistlewood and four other accomplices who had gathered in the loft of a coach house in Cato Street, off the Edgware Road. The men were rapidly tried and executed for high treason three months later. Five others implicated in the plot were transported.

The Cato Street Conspiracy has sometimes been interpreted as a wild, isolated and ultimately suicidal act of defiance by the most extreme members of an already extremist revolutionary fringe. According to Wright (1988), however, there is evidence to link the plotting of the London Spenceans with attempted uprisings near Glasgow and Barnsley in April 1820.

BOX 4.9 The Queen Caroline Affair

In 1795, Caroline of Brunswick married her first cousin, the future George IV. The marriage was a disaster from the start and the couple separated in 1796. Caroline's subsequent behaviour was unconventional and indiscreet - though a 'Delicate Investigation' found her not guilty of adultery in 1806. In 1814 she settled in Italy. When her husband succeeded to the throne as George IV in 1820, Caroline decided to return to England to claim her position as Queen. She landed in Dover in June, having refused to accept the government's offer of £50,000 a year if she stayed away. The next month, a Bill of Pains and Penalties was introduced by the government to divorce her and strip her of her queenship.

The unpopularity of George IV and the government's involvement on his behalf made Caroline an unlikely symbol for the radical cause. During the summer and autumn of 1820, huge crowds gathered in London to demonstrate their support. The abandonment of the Bill of Pains and Penalties in November was greeted with tremendous rejoicing, but there were no disturbances. This victory for Caroline, however, soon proved hollow. The government did not resign and, in January 1821, she lost a great deal of popularity when she agreed to accept a pension of £50,000.

The final confrontation came in July 1821 when she attempted to attend George's coronation. She marched to Westminster Abbey and, after banging on every door, was duly turned away - a rather embarrassing anti-climax. That evening, she was taken unwell. She died on 6 August. The government hoped to avoid further demonstrations by disposing of her body discreetly, but demonstrators blocked the funeral procession and forced it to take their preferred route. Two men were shot by troops during this showdown. It was the last mass demonstration before the Reform crisis of 1831-32.

Adapted from Stevenson 1992.

Neither of these attempted risings posed any real threat to the authorities (the numbers were small and the troops easily defeated them) but they do suggest that coordinated attempts at revolution may have been plotted by a determined minority.

The Queen Caroline Affair

The Queen Caroline Affair provides an instructive and illuminating contrast to the other threats faced by the government in this period. Whereas, before 1820, the radical threat had come from outside the Establishment, with the Queen Caroline Affair the threat came from within. The key details are provided in Box 4.9.

The character of the Queen Caroline Affair was quite different from the radical agitation that had preceded it. Wright suggests that the lesson of this was that:

'The Queen Caroline Affair demonstrated, as the Reform crisis was to do a decade later, that large numbers could only be moved to political activity in a context of general political excitement created by those in much more influential positions than were the radicals.' (Wright 1988, p.76)

Dinwiddy, on the other hand concludes that:

'The personalised, theatrical...nature of the affair meant that, although the agitation was larger in scale, it had less edge and substance than the working-class reform movement of the preceding years.' (Dinwiddy 1986, p.38)

How did the Liverpool government respond to the radical threat?

It has already been noted that, in 1817, Habeas Corpus was suspended (allowing the government to arrest political prisoners and to hold them without trial) and the Seditious Meetings Act was passed (making unauthorised meetings of 50 or more people illegal). Following Peterloo, the government then passed the 'Six Acts'. These six acts (all passed in December 1819) made the following provisions:

- The Seditious Meetings Prevention Act gave local magistrates extensive powers to restrict public meetings.
- The Seizure of Arms Act gave local magistrates powers to search for and to seize arms.
- The Blasphemous and Seditious Libels Act allowed local magistrates to conduct searches for and to seize blasphemous or seditious publications.
- The Training Prevention Act banned all unauthorised paramilitary drilling and training.
- The Newspaper and Stamp Duties Act introduced a four pence stamp duty on newspapers in an attempt to ensure that the price of radical newspapers was beyond the means of most members of the working class.
- The Misdemeanours Act simplified and speeded up procedures for bringing cases of treason to trial.

Traditional and revisionist views

The traditional view (see Unit 3, Part 1) is that the Liverpool government's response to radical activity in the period 1815-21 was repressive and reactionary. The government, it has been argued, outrageously overreacted to a virtually non-existent threat, using what limited evidence there was of politically motivated activity as an excuse to deny the masses their civil liberties. Recently, however, this line of argument has been challenged. A number of historians (such as Gash 1979, Derry 1990 and Plowright 1996) have argued that, rather than overreacting, the Liverpool government was, in fact, remarkably mild and tolerant in its response to the radicals:

'Liverpool's government acted with commendable restraint, so that it is misleading to label its maintenance of law and order as repressive...The government had no practicable alternatives to the policies which it pursued.' (Plowright 1997, p.14)

These historians have pointed out that the suspension of Habeas Corpus in March 1817 was limited to a period of only ten months. During this time only 44 people were arrested and 37 subsequently detained on suspicion of treason - a statistic which, they claim, supports the conclusion that the government used the measure as a deterrent rather than as the first step towards a reign of terror. Similarly, the Seditious Meetings Act was simply allowed to lapse in 1818. As for Peterloo, Plowright points out that the deaths resulted from misjudgements made by local magistrates, not by the government, and he argues that government had no choice but to back the actions of the magistrates (since it depended on the local magistracy to maintain law and order throughout the country). Failure to support the Manchester magistrates would have resulted in a dangerous crisis of confidence. And finally, the Six Acts have been reappraised. Derry, for example, claims that:

'[The Six Acts were] little more than gestures, a response to reassure backbench opinion in the House of Commons and conservative opinion in the country rather than a prelude to a sustained reign of terror....The Six Acts were never intended to effect any permanent or substantial change in the pattern of public life....All the Acts did was to strengthen the discretionary powers of magistrates....As gestures,...they seemed to work. The confidence of the country was restored. Magistrates felt that the government supported them. The propertied members of society believed that something had been done to secure order and to maintain public safety.' (Derry 1990, p.180)

The debate over the Six Acts

It should be noted, however, that whilst these revisionist historians are keen to emphasise that the measures taken by the government were never fully enforced, other historians claim that they made a marked impact on radical activity. The debate is summarised by Lee as follows:

'The effects of the Six Acts have been hotly debated. N. Gash, for instance, considers that they were never fully enforced, while J. Marlow (1969) argues that they were "a virtually watertight blanket over the radical activities". Either way, the government can be considered to have come out on top. If, as Gash believes, the powers allowed to the authorities went by default, the reason must have been the declining threat posed to them. Alternatively, as Marlow maintains, the Six Acts may have had a direct bearing on the bankruptcy of radicalism, reducing the movements from a peak in 1818 and 1819 to "next to nothing - a most spectacular collapse" ' (Lee 1994, pp.23-24)

How much did Liverpool owe to Pitt?

The historian Eric Evans argues that the Liverpool government's response to radical activity in the period 1815-21 was consciously modelled on Pitt's response to radical activity in the 1790s (see Unit 2, Section 2.1):

'Ministers' response to the growth of radical protest was entirely appropriate to men whose political apprenticeship had been worked against a background of Jacobin terror and excess in republican France. The establishment of committees of secrecy, followed by the suspension of Habeas Corpus and the granting of extra powers to magistrates for the control of public meetings, therefore, exactly mirrored in 1817 Pitt's response in 1794-95. The Six Acts (or "Whip with Six Strings")...concentrated on the use of force and, like Pitt in 1798, on the regulation of newspapers...Like Pitt also, though with rather more difficulty, Liverpool found it possible to forge a propertied alliance against the reformers.' (Evans 1996, p.197)

O'Gorman (1997) accepts that, like Pitt, Liverpool's aim was to maintain 'strong government' rather than to set up 'a legal tyranny', but argues that there were three important differences between the legislation passed in the 1790s and that passed in the period 1815-21:

'The first obviously is that the country was no longer at war and it follows that the tactic of labelling all reformers as traitors was no longer credible. The second is that, while conservative opinion was, of course, horrified at the mass rallies...there was nothing equivalent to the witch-hunting hysteria of, say, the winter of 1792-93. The Seditious Meetings Act of 1817 was not the action of a panic-stricken government...Third,

Liverpool had fewer resources with which to maintain law and order than Pitt had enjoyed. The armed forces and the Volunteer regiments had been hugely reduced. It was simply not in the power of central government to patrol the country.' (O'Gorman 1997, pp.263-64)

MAIN POINTS - Section 2.2

- Those historians who believe that Britain came close to revolution during the period 1815-21 emphasise the volume of radical activity. Those who argue that fears of revolution were exaggerated point to the lack of coordination between the individual instances of protest and the state's continued ability to respond decisively to it.
- Most historians agree that the popular protest in 1815-16 was essentially 'traditional' - non-political activity directly related to the immediate effects of economic distress.
- In 1816, a new phenomenon developed - the mass meeting. Between 1816 and 1821, a series of mass meetings was organised by radical groups. The most notable were those held at Spa Fields in London in late 1816 and at St Peter's Fields in Manchester in August 1819.
- Whilst historians agree that there were attempted uprisings during the second Spa Fields meeting, in 1817 (the Pentrich Rebellion), and in 1820 (the Cato Street Conspiracy), they are divided about whether a significant number of people had a revolutionary impulse.
- There were two other significant events - the march of the Blanketeers and the Queen Caroline Affair.
- Although the traditional view is that the Liverpool government's response to radical activity in the period 1815-21 was repressive and reactionary, this view has been revised. Some historians argue that the government acted with restraint and tolerance.

Activity 4.3 How serious was the threat of revolution?

ITEM 1 The Cato Street Conspiracy

This cartoon shows members of the Cabinet dancing around a Maypole upon which are impaled the heads of those executed for participating in the Cato Street Conspiracy. The music is being provided by George Edwards, the government spy who unmasked the conspiracy. The five conspirators were executed on 1 May 1820.

ITEM 2 The Spa Fields meeting of 2 December

This cartoon shows Orator Hunt addressing the crowd at the second Spa Fields meeting.

ITEM 3 The Pentrich Rebellion

Extract from a letter written by Lord Fitzwilliam, Lord Lieutenant of the West Riding of Yorkshire, to the Home Secretary, Lord Sidmouth.

17 June 1817

My Lord,

There prevails very generally in the country a strong and decided opinion that most of the events that have recently occurred in the country are to be attributed to the presence and agitation of Mr Oliver. He is considered the main spring from which every movement has taken its rise. All the mischievous in the country have considered themselves as subordinate members of a great leading body of revolutionists in London as cooperating with that body for one general purpose and in this view to be under its instructions and directions, communicated by some delegate appointed for the purpose. Had not then a person pretending to come from that body made his appearance in the country, it is not assuming too much to say that probably no movement whatever would have occurred…I am quite assured that the general opinion is that the mass of the people are sound, that the disaffected are few in number, and contemptible in description and consideration…

ITEM 4 Peterloo

Orator Hunt addressing the crowd at Peterloo.

ITEM 5 Historians' views

(i) The examination of successful revolutions suggests that for a revolution to succeed four processes must take place:

- the masses must lose of faith in the existing regime
- the revolutionary position must gain the approval of the masses
- the revolutionaries need to have built a force outside of the control of the state
- the loyalty of the state's forces must be very weak or non-existent.

If these four are accepted as the preconditions necessary for a revolution it is possible to say that the prospects for success during Liverpool's premiership were not good. The French Revolution clearly provided the means by which the masses would lose faith in the existing regime and by which the revolutionary position would gain the approval of the masses. Some radicals clearly tried to copy the tactics and borrow the symbols of their French counterparts. For example, the Spencean revolutionaries at Spa Fields in December 1816 spoke of setting up a Committee of Public Safety and they paraded the red, white and green tricolour of the future British Republic. But what is more remarkable is the way in which most radicals preferred to speak in traditional terms of the 'ancient constitution' and the rights due to a 'freeborn Englishman' rather than adopt the abstract philosophical language of the *Rights of Man* which had become common currency across the Channel. Moreover, when Britain emerged as the victor at the end of the wars with France this not only enhanced the prestige of the regime (despite the problems brought by peace), but also deprived potential revolutionaries of their only real chance of outside assistance in constructing a force outside state control. The threat of revolution in Britain, therefore, was greatly reduced by 1815. Last but not least, although there was much discontent among the demobilised, the armed forces remained loyal.

Adapted from Plowright 1996.

(ii) The five years following 1815 brought Britain nearer to the brink of revolution than at any other time in history. These were years of great unrest expressed in huge open-air rallies and occasional attempted uprisings. The radical voices which had been silenced during the French Wars resurfaced. In the new industrialised areas, working-men's associations - Hampden Clubs - sprang up. These were replaced just before 1820 by Political Unions which held open-air meetings and sent huge petitions to Parliament. At one of these meetings, on St Peter's Field, the local yeomanry dispersed the crowd and 11 people were killed, immediately billed as martyrs to the cause. Another group, of shoemakers and silk weavers plotted to blow up the Cabinet in what was known as the Cato Street Conspiracy. They failed, but all this was evidence that a revolutionary underground was clearly active. In 1819, after Peterloo, the government passed the Six Acts, designed to suppress any revolutionary movement. It was not long before the main troublemakers found themselves in jail. No revolution occurred. The radical groups were diverse and divided, but more significant was the fact that 1820 saw a sharp upturn in the economy.

Adapted from Strong 1996.

Questions

1. a) Look at Items 1-4 and write a paragraph putting each item into context.
   b) What does each item tell us about the way in which the authorities responded to protest in the period 1815-21?
   c) What are the difficulties with using sources like this?
2. Using Items 1-5, give arguments for and against the view that Britain came to the brink of revolution in the period 1815-21.

3. a) What does Item 5 tell us about the historical debate over the impact of radical protest in the period 1815-21?
   b) Write an account from the point of view of each author which explains the significance of (i) the Spa Fields meetings, (ii) the march of the Blanketeers, (iii) the Pentrich Rebellion, (iv) Peterloo, (v) the Cato Street Conspiracy, and (vi) the Queen Caroline Affair.

3 Unrest 1822-32

3.1 Radicalism in the 1820s

A lull in radical activity

Despite the continuation of economic distress and the survival of political unions in some parts of the country, the period 1822-30 saw a marked decline in the mass radical activity that had characterised the immediate post-war period. The decline in radical activity coincided with a general revival in trade and an economic boom. The relative prosperity of this period was underpinned by a run of good harvests which lasted until 1828. Most historians agree that the economic revival is an important factor in explaining the decline in mass radical activity, though Dinwiddy emphasises that it was not the only factor:

'After 1820 a number of factors combined to dampen radical agitation. One, probably the most important, was a markedly improved economic climate which lasted, apart from a sharp recession in 1826, until towards the end of the decade. Another was repression. The temporary immunity provided by the queen's affair did not interfere with the trials of leading radicals for alleged libels and acts of sedition committed in 1819...And even more efficacious [effective] than prison sentences in reducing the strength and influence of the radical press was the Publications Act of 1819 (one of the Six Acts) which imposed a stamp duty of four pence on all periodicals with any political content which were published more frequently than once a month and sold for less than six pence.' (Dinwiddy 1986, p.38)

Protest in the 1820s

Although the 1820s were, therefore, a relatively quiet decade in terms of popular radical activity, that does not mean that radical activity suddenly ceased altogether:

'Radicalism in the broad sense did not by any means die out in the 1820s, but it became rather disjointed, with a variety of lines being pursued by different people.' (Dinwiddy 1986, p.38)

Evans points out that:

'Developments in these years contributed to the maturity of later protests but they did not immediately threaten the government.' (Evans 1989, p.40)

As a result, the radical activity which did occur has not attracted a great deal of attention. Nevertheless it is possible to identify five strands of protest which run through this period.

1. The campaign for a free press

First, there was the defiant campaign for a free press, led by the republican thinker and writer, Richard Carlile. Carlile, a former tinsmith, spent six years in prison between 1819 and 1825 for publishing the works of Thomas Paine in the aftermath of the Peterloo Massacre. Thompson argues that:

'Carlile...rightly saw that the repression of 1819 made the rights of the press the fulcrum of [ie key issue for] the radical movement. But, unlike Cobbett and Wooler [the publisher of Black Dwarf], who modified their tone to meet the Six Acts in the hope of living to fight another day (and who lost circulation accordingly), Carlile hoisted the black ensign [flag] of unqualified defiance and...sailed straight into the middle of the combined fleets of the state and Church.' (Thompson 1980, p.791)

Wright (1988, p.77) argues, however, that Carlile's rather theoretical emphasis on abstract political rights rather than on the immediate economic grievances ensured that his message appealed to 'skilled artisans and small shopkeepers' rather than to unskilled or semi-skilled workers.

2. The development of anti-capitalist economics

Some historians (such as Wright 1988 and Belchem 1996) have argued that it was during the 1820s that key radical ideas were first developed. In particular, Wright and Belchem argue, it was in the 1820s that a new type of anti-capitalist economics began to be developed which blamed poverty and exploitation on the capitalist system rather than on government policies and corruption. These new ideas were promoted in cheap, unstamped newspapers such as the Crisis, the Pioneer and the Poor Man's Guardian.

3. The development of middle-class radicalism

Belchem claims that it was in the 1820s that middle-class radicalism first gained coherence:

'Previously swamped by mass agitation, middle-class radicals gained a hearing in the 1820s when liberalism...became a fashionable addition to the political vocabulary.' (Belchem 1996, p.56)

It was in the 1820s, Belchem argues, that the middle-class demand for greater representation was first voiced and the foundations of the mass campaign for the vote in the early 1830s was laid.

4. Isolated outbreaks of violence

Although there were fewer outbreaks of violence in the 1820s than there had been in the five years after the French Wars, there were some. These are described in Box 4.10.

BOX 4.10 | **Significant outbreaks of violence in the 1820s**

1821 - A group of 3,000 ironworkers and coal miners refused to disperse when the Riot Act was read and then fought against the yeomanry. Two miners were killed and several yeomen injured.

1822 - A worsted power loom was destroyed in Shipley.

1823-24 - When Scottish workers were brought in to replace striking ropemakers and sawyers in Liverpool, two were killed and there were several cases of arson.

1825-26 - A sharp depression in the cotton trade led to widespread unemployment in the North-West. In April a crowd destroyed power looms in a factory at Accrington and then destroyed every power loom within six miles of Blackburn. Over the next two days, more than 20 mills were attacked and over 1,000 looms smashed. In a confrontation with troops, seven machine-breakers were killed at Chadderton and two or three elsewhere. The disturbances spread to Manchester (where a crowd burned down a mill and some bread shops), Skipton (where looms were smashed in a mill) and Bradford (where two machine-breakers were shot trying to gain entry to a garrisoned mill). The disturbances were primarily a protest against distress and, except in Manchester, there is no evidence of radical involvement. The machine-breaking was a gesture of despair.

1829 - In April, several weavers were shot by soldiers guarding 16 men who had been placed in a lock-up in Rochdale after factory machinery had been destroyed. In May, four weaving shops in Manchester were attacked and over 150 power looms smashed and a factory set on fire.
Adapted from Stevenson 1992.

---

5. New forms of trade union activity

Stevenson (1992) suggests that one reason why there was a drop in violence during the 1820s may have been because of a growth in non-violent trade union activity. In particular, he claims, there was a growing use of the strike tactic:

'The post-war period was marked...by the increased growth of trade union activity, not only in the traditional craft trades but also in such diverse groups as cotton operatives, colliers, ironworkers and lead miners. Although often using clandestine [secret] or ad hoc [spur of the moment] organisation, many of these groups were beginning to use strikes rather than riots to obtain improvements in living standards or halt their erosion.' (Stevenson 1992, p.254)

When violence did occur, Stevenson claims, it was often because trade unionism was not strong in that area or because non-violent trade union tactics had failed. By the end of the 1820s, he claims, there was a clear trend towards non-violent tactics:

'The trend was clear. The first generation of notable trade union leaders...were, at least in public, opposed to violence, putting their trust in firm union organisation.' (Stevenson 1992, p.260)

3.2 What was the nature of the 'Swing Riots' of 1830-31?

What were the 'Swing Riots'?

The term 'Swing Riots' refers to the series of agricultural labourers' disturbances which broke out in Kent during the summer of 1830 and rapidly spread through the rural areas of southern and eastern England, continuing sporadically until the autumn of 1831.

Just as the Luddite disturbances of 1811-16 (see Part 1 above) drew their name from the mythical 'Ned Ludd', so the 'Swing Riots' were named after the mythical 'Captain Swing', whose name appeared at the bottom of threatening letters, and who was supposed to be the protesters' leader.

The multiformity of the protest

One of the most striking characteristics of these disturbances is what historians such as Hobsbawm and Rudé (1969) have termed their 'multiformity'. By this they mean the way in which the nature of protest - and its targets - varied from area to area. The forms which the Swing protests took included:

- sending threatening letters
- machine-breaking
- arson (especially the burning of hayricks)
- maiming pet or prize animals
- assaults on Poor Law overseers, parsons and landlords
- demands for a reduction in tithes (a tax on produce paid to the Church)
- demands for higher wages
- strikes
- attacks on Irish labourers.

Stevenson notes that the different forms of protest

varied from place to place:

> 'Although machine-breaking accounted for the largest single category of incidents, the disturbances had many different forms and targets. Demands for higher wages were particularly prevalent [common] in Essex and Suffolk. Tithes were a particular grievance in parts of East Anglia and Sussex...In East Sussex, workhouses were a principal target of the disturbances...In East Anglia, there were attacks on Irish labourers.. In Lincolnshire, arson attacks were the principal symptoms of "Swing" with virtually no other disturbances. In one or two areas, discontent took the form of strikes.' (Stevenson 1992, p.265)

The duration and spread of the Swing Riots is shown in Box 4.11.

BOX 4.11   The Swing Riots

This table shows the duration and spread of the Swing Riots county by county.

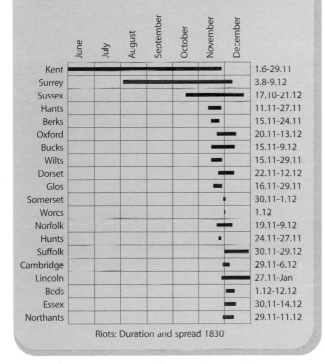

	June	July	August	September	October	November	December	
Kent								1.6-29.11
Surrey								3.8-9.12
Sussex								17.10-21.12
Hants								11.11-27.11
Berks								15.11-24.11
Oxford								20.11-13.12
Bucks								15.11-9.12
Wilts								15.11-29.11
Dorset								22.11-12.12
Glos								16.11-29.11
Somerset								30.11-1.12
Worcs								1.12
Norfolk								19.11-9.12
Hunts								24.11-27.11
Suffolk								30.11-29.12
Cambridge								29.11-6.12
Lincoln								27.11-Jan
Beds								1.12-12.12
Essex								30.11-14.12
Northants								29.11-11.12

Riots: Duration and spread 1830

Characteristics of the disturbances

Although the form taken by the Swing protests varied considerably, there were a number of characteristics which the protests had in common. Perhaps most notable was the discipline shown by the protesters. There were few reports of protesters carrying firearms or pikes and, despite the threats, nobody was actually killed. Like the Luddites, when they destroyed machines, they did not go on to attack other property or those who owned the machines (although the use of arson did cause the loss of a great deal of property).

A second common feature was the appointment of 'treasurers' and 'captains':

> 'In all village groups there was a recognised leader, either accepted as such for a single expedition or extending his authority over a longer period.' (Hobsbawm & Rudé 1969, p.207)

A third common feature was the pressing of locals into participating in disturbances. An example of this practice was described by Samuel White, a labourer in Berkshire who was pressed into service in November 1830:

> 'About three o'clock in the morning of yesterday week I was awakened by the blowing of a horn...I looked through the window. We have no upstairs. A great many persons came before the house and halloed to us to unlock the door or they would beat it open. I opened the door. Three or four came in. They said if we did not go with them they would draw us out. My brother and I went into the street...They would not let my brother stay indoors to do up his shoes.' (quoted in Hobsbawm & Rudé 1969, p.211)

And a fourth common feature is that, apart from a few isolated incidents, the disturbances appear to have been solely the work of local people. Despite accusations at the time, there is little evidence to support the view that outside agitators were responsible for the disturbances:

> '"Agitators" were widely blamed for stirring up the labourers and Cobbett was tried and acquitted for allegedly fermenting the movement, but there is little evidence that they played a crucial part...While there was considerable sympathy for the labourers' plight from radical groups in some of the small towns of southern England...where small groups of radicals existed and who certainly made some attempt to agitate both labourers and small farmers, they rarely did more than contribute to a movement which was derived from the hardships and grievances of the agricultural labourers.' (Stevenson 1992, p.269)

A typical Swing protest is described in Box 4.12.

Why did the Swing Riots break out?

'Swing' disturbances began in Kent in June 1830 and in the course of the next three months spread rapidly to over 20 counties. Not all of these counties were affected with the same intensity. Stevenson (1992) claims that Hampshire, Wiltshire, Berkshire, Kent, Sussex and Norfolk (in that order) were the areas which experienced the most concentrated bursts of activity. Elsewhere the disturbances were much more sporadic.

The following longer-term factors have been identified as playing a part in the outbreak of the Swing Riots.

1. Rural poverty in the South

Hobsbawm and Rudé show that, in the first decades

BOX 4.12 | A Swing protest at Horsham in Sussex

Early in the morning a large party assembled and strengthened their number by forcing work people of every description to join them, both from this and adjoining parishes, and at 3 o'clock they went in an immense body to the Church where they insisted on being met by Mr Simpson and the landowners...All these gentlemen were stationed at the altar to receive the demands of this lawless multitude who, I suppose, occupied every tenable place within the walls and by their shouts and threatening language [showed] their total disregard for the sanctity of the place...Mr Simpson in a very proper manner gave an account of the revenues of his living and after shewing that he did not clear more than £400 per annum promised to meet the gentlemen and farmers and to make such a reduction as they could reasonably expect. Mr Hurst held out so long that it was feared blood would be shed. The doors were shut till the demands were granted: no lights were allowed, the iron railing that surrounds the monuments torn up and the sacred boundary between the chancel and altar overleaped before he would yield; at last the three points were gained and happily without any personal injury. The Church is much disfigured. Money was afterwards demanded at different homes for refreshment and, if not obtained with ease, the windows were broken.

Part of a letter written by a local lady following events in Horsham on 18 November 1830 - quoted in Hobsbawm & Rudé 1969, pp.102-3.

of the 19th century, population growth in rural areas resulted in increased rural poverty and under- or unemployment. Living standards were generally lowest where farming was the only occupation, with little or no industry to compete for labour and push up wages. As May points out, these conditions were more acute in the cereal-growing southern counties than in the North:

> 'The standard of living of farm labourers was higher in the North. Cheap coal was more readily available which enabled labourers to keep their cottages warmer and allowed them to prepare more hot, cooked food...Improved diet made greater productivity possible...[Also] northern farmers tended to hire their labourers on an annual basis rather than from week to week.' (May 1996, pp.102-3)

Hobsbawm and Rud suggest that the shortening of the period of hire was particularly important in the southern counties where there was a labour surplus:

> 'There was a distinct tendency in counties with a labour surplus to hire...by the week, the day or even - in Suffolk - by the hour. In a word, the farmhand became essentially a casual labourer, hired and dismissed at will and lacking even the guarantee...that he would return home that night with any earnings at all.' (Hobsbawm & Rudé 1969, p.44)

2. The operation of the Old Poor Law

Hobsbawm and Rudé (1969) argue that the pattern of chronic rural poverty and unemployment in the South was reflected in growing expenditure on poor rates, with the largest rates recorded in Berkshire, Wiltshire and Sussex - the centres of the most intense 'Swing' activity in 1830-31. These rates rose markedly from the 1790s and reached a peak in the period 1815-20 when distress was heightened by the return of around 400,000 demobilised servicemen. Estimates suggest that in 1830 more than one in ten of the total population of the southern and eastern counties were receiving poor relief. This suggests that they were vulnerable to economic depression, technological change and high prices.

It has been suggested that this impoverishment of the southern agricultural labourer was made worse by the Speenhamland system - a system devised in 1795 to help the poor and prevent famine (a sliding scale of payments, funded from the poor rates, was made to poor people depending on the size of their family and on the price of bread). After 1795, variations on the Speenhamland system were adopted throughout southern England. The system of subsidising wages out of the poor rates, it is claimed, had the unforeseen consequence of exerting a downward pressure on rural wages. Although the system aimed to deal humanely with rural poverty, many farmers simply lowered wages, knowing that the impact of this reduction would be cushioned by the parish subsidy. This view has, however, recently been challenged by historians such as Rule (1986) and May (1996), who argue that heavy Poor Law expenditure was a consequence rather than a cause of low wages and unemployment.

It has also been suggested that the Law of Settlement (which stated that a labourer and his family could only obtain poor relief in a parish where they were settled) discouraged farm labourers in the South to migrate to the industrial North where there were more jobs. This view, however, has also been challenged:

> 'There were certainly many contemporary voices declaring the law to be a hindrance to migration. Once again, however, opinions have changed and it is now believed that the laws were never applied as severely as they might have been. The parochialism [local ties] of the average farm labourer no doubt proved a stronger obstacle to

mobility than any legal impediment.' (May 1996, p.105)

3. The breakdown of paternalism

Some historians (such as Hobsbawm & Rudé 1969 and Evans 1989) have argued that growing class conflict in the countryside led to a breakdown of the old system of 'paternalism'. The essence of the old system of paternalism was a strong acceptance of hierarchy and a willingness of those lower in the hierarchy to look up to and accept the authority of those higher up the hierarchy than them. According to Evans:

'The Swing Riots were a violent assertion that paternalism, which many MPs saw as the foundation of a social and political order dependent on hierarchy and reciprocal obligations, had broken down. Thus was a political message conveyed in sub-political ways.' (Evans 1989, p.83)

The evidence in support of this interpretation can be summarised as follows:

- The growing prosperity of farmers during the French Wars of 1793-1815 was not extended to farm labourers. This led to the polarisation of rural society. Farmers aspired to the status of the gentry while labourers sunk to unprecedented depths of poverty and demoralisation.
- In the southern and eastern counties, this widening social divide was reflected in a decline of the traditional practice of 'living in'. Before the French Wars, farm labourers had often lived in the farmer's own house. By 1815 this practice was rare. The end of the practice led to the development of a separate and more class-conscious community of labourers who shared a common sense of exploitation and resentment at the way in which agrarian capitalism had destroyed the old system of paternalism.
- Hobsbawm and Rudé point out that this process of social change was reflected in the gradual rise of 'covert' protest (usually referred to as 'social' or 'protest' crime) and, in particular, an increase in poaching, stealing of farm produce, arson and animal maiming in the period after 1815. On occasions, this covert protest could become 'overt' (open) - as in the East Anglian disturbances of 1816 (the first major protest by agricultural labourers in which, significantly, threshing machines were smashed).

The variety - and selectivity - of the Swing rioters' targets, it is argued, supports this hypothesis. Of the approximately 1,400 reported 'Swing' disturbances, there were many examples of what might be described as collective 'community' activity against influential local figures criticised for the failure to fulfil 'traditional' obligations. For example, clergymen who, in their function as local magistrates, convicted local poachers often received threatening letters, as did local Poor Law overseers who appeared particularly harsh or inquisitorial in their methods.

4. Conditions in 1828-30

Three consecutive poor harvests in 1828, 1829 and 1830 created what Hobsbawm and Rudé (1969) describe as a 'tense pessimism' in rural society as labourers prepared for another hard winter of shortage and unemployment:

'The harvest of 1828 was poor, though the winter was mild; the harvest of 1829 was worse...The labourers must have faced the spring of 1830 with the memory of cold, hunger and unemployment, and the reflection that another winter like the last was more than flesh and blood could bear. "Fear of the winter" was the cause given (together with low wages) for the riots in Marden (Kent) and we can be quite certain that the men of Marden were not alone in their sentiments.' (Hobsbawm & Rudé 1969, p.85)

5. Political upheaval in 1830

During the summer of 1830, 'tense pessimism' was combined with what Hobsbawm and Rudé describe as a 'vaguely stirred expectation' which resulted from the news of revolutions in France and Belgium and the end of the long period of Tory government in Britain (see Unit 5, Section 2.1). Hobsbawm and Rudé concede that these incidents were probably marginal to the concerns of most agricultural labourers and that there is little evidence of outside agitation. Nevertheless, they argue, a heightened sense of expectation (perhaps in the hope of Whig reforms) created, in a general way, the preconditions for more overt forms of protest. The actual protests, they claim, were then triggered by specific local grievances.

6. Trigger mechanisms - specific local grievances

A wide variety of local factors explain the precise timing and character of 'Swing' disturbances in each area. Examples include:

- the increased use of cheap Irish labour and the introduction of threshing machines in North and East Kent
- cuts in poor relief in the Sussex Weald
- demands for higher wages in Essex and Suffolk
- demands for a reduction in tithes in East Anglia and Sussex
- existing disputes over new drainage schemes and enclosure in Oxfordshire.

Who took part?

It might be expected that the majority of Swing rioters would be those who were the poorest - the unemployed or the lowest-paid labourers. Analysis of the occupation of those Swing rioters who were arrested and faced trial, however, shows that this was not the case:

'Generally, they appear to have earned above average wages and were not in any sense the poorest elements in the village community; although there were paupers among them, there were also some who were considered among the best paid...Many of those arrested were in their middle or late 20s, more than half were married. These were not the rootless young or the desperate poor, still less outside agitators, but a representative sample of the village community. One group who were under-represented were women: far fewer were involved than in many other disturbances.' (Stevenson 1992, p.268)

Was the outbreak revolutionary?

There is a consensus that, although the outbreak of Swing Riots was widespread and there was an underlying political message, the disturbances were conservative rather than revolutionary. This view is forcefully expressed by Stevenson:

'The striking feature of the men's demands was that they were almost entirely economic and backward-looking. They sought a restitution [restoration] of lost rights, of customary wages and levels of poor relief, and felt themselves to be resisting innovations such as the use of machinery. In that sense, the motivation of the labourers was deeply conservative. They posed no revolutionary threat to the government or to the local authorities, having neither the organisation nor the ideology to do so.' (Stevenson 1992, p.269)

How did the authorities respond?

Just as there was a 'multiformity' of disturbances, there was a great variety of responses from the authorities:

'To stop the riots, the authorities adopted a series of expedients [means] - some military, others judicial or political; some repressive, others conciliatory.' (Hobsbawm & Rudé 1969, p.253)

Hobsbawm and Rudé point out that the means of central government to deal with an outbreak of so many local disturbances at one time was limited and, at least at first, it left much of the responsibility of maintaining order to local authorities. Nevertheless, at the beginning of November 1830, the Home Secretary, Robert Peel, dispatched what troops were available to guard towns and to act as a deterrent. Peel's successor, Melbourne (who took office later in November 1830), adopted a more interventionist role. He offered a reward of £500 for

information leading to the conviction of rioters and sent a letter to local magistrates urging them to enrol special constables. Military officers were sent out to supervise military detachments and groups of volunteers. Stevenson argues:

'In practice, these measures were adequate because many of the disturbances lasted no more than a few days, the labourers and artisans involved being unable to stay away from work for much longer; merely providing a guard or nightly watch was often sufficient to deter further outbreaks.' (Stevenson 1992, p.268)

Punishing offenders

By December 1830, about 1,900 rioters had been arrested. Hobsbawm and Rudé argue that, because the government was concerned that these offenders might be treated leniently by magistrates, it appointed a special commission to try them. Stevenson reports that this special commission tried about 1,000 alleged offenders and other courts tried the remainder. The results were as follows:

'Of these prisoners, 252 were sentenced to death, 19 of whom were eventually executed, the rest being sentenced to transportation or terms of imprisonment. Nearly 500 were transported and over 600 imprisoned. While the number of executions was smaller than for the Luddites, the number of people transported was exceptional.' (Stevenson 1992, p.268)

Stevenson notes that one reason why a smaller number of Swing rioters was executed than Luddites was that Robert Peel had reduced the number of capital offences (see Unit 3, Section 2.2). The scale of punishment, he concludes was 'severe'. Hobsbawm and Rudé go further:

'In the South of England, there were whole communities that, for a generation, were stricken by the blow. From no other protest movement of the kind - from neither Luddites nor Chartists, nor trade unionists - was such a bitter price exacted.' (Hobsbawm & Rudé 1969, p.263)

Rural protest after 1831

Rural protest did not completely end with the severe repression of the Swing disturbances in 1830-31. Stevenson (1992) points out, for example, that there is evidence to suggest that covert protest - poaching, cattle and sheep stealing and animal maiming - continued through the 1830s and 1840s and was actually more vengeful after Swing than before it. Poor relief also remained a source of tension and resistance to the introduction of the New Poor Law was widespread in southern counties and East Anglia between 1834 and 1836 (see Unit 8). Arson became the most typical form of covert protest after Swing, and research on outbreaks of arson in East Anglia suggests that it was often pre-planned and, like Swing activity, preceded by a threatening letter. This may suggest a certain continuity. In some areas, Swing activity can be seen as the most intense phase in an ongoing tradition of rural protest. It should be emphasised, however, that Swing was an exceptional reaction in most areas and it was only the collision of a number of exceptional circumstances in 1830 that explains such widespread willingness to act.

MAIN POINTS - Part 3

- Between 1822 and 1830, there was a marked decline in the mass radical activity that had characterised the immediate post-war period.
- Radical activity, however, did not completely cease. There was (1) a campaign for a free press, (2) the development of anti-capitalist economics, (3) the development of middle-class radicalism, (4) isolated outbreaks of violence, and (5) new forms of trade union activity.
- The term 'Swing Riots' refers to the series of agricultural labourers' disturbances which broke out in Kent in mid-1830 and rapidly spread through rural areas, continuing sporadically until the autumn of 1831.
- One of the disturbances' most striking characteristics was the way in which the nature of protest - and its

- targets - varied from area to area. Nevertheless, the outbreaks had some common characteristics: (1) discipline, (2) the appointment of leaders, (3) the pressing of participants, (4) the lack of outside influence.
- Reasons for disturbances include: (1) rural poverty in the South, (2) the operation of the Old Poor Law, (3) the breakdown of paternalism, (4) the harvests of 1828-30, (5) political upheaval in Britain and Europe, and (6) individual trigger mechanisms in each affected area.
- Although some troops were dispatched, the government mainly relied on local authorities to maintain order. The punishment of rioters who were arrested was severe - 19 were executed, nearly 500 transported and over 600 imprisoned.

Activity 4.4 What were the causes of the 'Swing Riots'

ITEM 1 Distribution of Swing disturbances

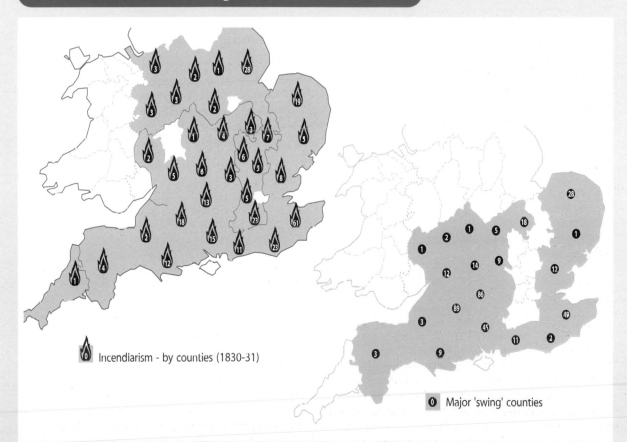

Incendiarism - by counties (1830-31)

Major 'swing' counties

ITEM 2 Wages c. 1750-1835

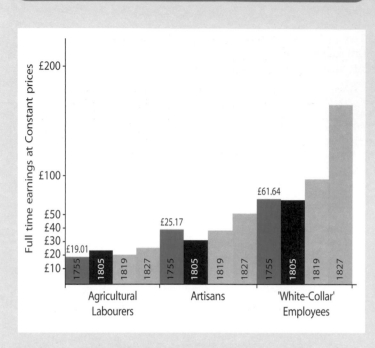

ITEM 3 The home of the rick burner

This cartoon was printed in Punch *magazine in 1830.*

ITEM 4 A contemporary account

On Monday last [the 15 November 1830], the labourers of Thatcham parish began to assemble at an early hour, for the purpose of inducing their employers to raise their wages. A sufficient number of them gathered together, they marched off (preceded by one of their company blowing a horn) to visit each of the farms, for the purpose of compelling the labourers to unite with them. By this means, their numbers increased and at noon they amounted to two or three hundred. They then marched into the churchyard and, the select vestry being convened, presented to the gentlemen assembled a verbal request that they might be provided with work, and have their wages advanced. To the former of these requests a favourable answer was returned, but no hope was held out of an improvement in the latter. Throughout the whole of these proceedings the men were quite peaceable, excepting forcing some who felt no inclination to join them.

Part of an article published in the Reading Mercury *on 22 November 1830. Later that week, the labourers destroyed local farmers' threshing machines.*

ITEM 5 A historian's view

The living conditions suffered by southern labourers were such that it required only some special stimulus to produce a very widespread movement. Admittedly, it would have to be an exceptionally powerful stimulus to overcome labourers' demoralised passivity. But the economic conditions of 1828-30 produced a situation which made their already bad situation worse. During these years, there was almost certainly an increase in rural unemployment, an attempt to reduce in some way or another the financial burden of poor relief on the rate payers, and an increase in the discontent of farmers and all those who depended upon agriculture. The combined effect of Continental revolution and British political crisis produced an atmosphere of expectation, of tension, of hope and potential action. These factors did not produce the actual spark. Rather, other local factors revived action in those villages where, for one reason or another, a tradition of resistance and action survived.

Adapted from Hobsbawm and Rudé 1969.

Questions

1. a) What do Items 1 and 2 tell us about the causes of the Swing Riots?
b) What do Items 1 and 2 tell us about the nature of the Swing Riots?
c) Explain the 'multiformity' of the Swing Riots.

2. a) Describe the context in which Item 3 was drawn.
b) What does Item 3 tell us about the causes of the Swing Riots?
c) 'Rural poverty was the cause of the Swing Riots.' How accurate is this statement? Explain your answer.

3. a) How typical was the event described in Item 4?
b) What does it tell us about the nature of the Swing Riots?

4. Look at Items 1-5.
a) Explain why the Swing Riots broke out.
b) Describe the character of the Swing Riots.
c) Would you say that the Swing Riots provided a greater threat to the authorities than the radical action of 1815-21? Explain your answer.

References

- **Belchem (1985)** Belchem, J., '"Orator" Hunt 1773-1835', *History Today*, March 1985.
- **Belchem (1996)** Belchem, J., *Popular Radicalism in Nineteenth-Century Britain*, Macmillan, 1996.
- **Brock (1941)** Brock, W.R., *Lord Liverpool and Liberal Toryism 1820-27* (2nd edn), Frank Cass, 1967.
- **Cole & Filson (1949)** Cole, G.D.H. & Filson, A.W., *British Working Class Movements: Select Documents 1789-1875*, Macmillan, 1949.
- **Derry (1963)** Derry J.W., *Reaction and Reform*, Blandford, 1963.
- **Derry (1990)** Derry J.W., *Politics in the Age of Fox, Pitt and Liverpool Continuity and Transformation*, Macmillan, 1990.
- **Dinwiddy (1986)** Dinwiddy, J.R., *From Luddism to the First Reform Bill*, Blackwell, 1986.
- **Downing (1988)** Downing, T., 'Television's Luddites', *History Today*, Vol.38, March 1988.
- **Evans (1989)** Evans, E.J. *Britain before the Reform Act: Politics and Society 1815-32*, Longman, 1989.
- **Evans (1996)** Evans, E., *The Forging of the Modern State: Early Industrial Britain 1783-1870*, Longman, 1996.
- **Gardiner & Wenborn (1995)** Gardiner, J. & Wenborn, N., *The Companion to British History*, Collins and Brown, 1995.
- **Gash (1979)** Gash, N., *Aristocracy and People*, Arnold, 1979.
- **Gash (1984)** Gash, N., *Lord Liverpool*, Weidenfeld, 1984.
- **Hargreaves (1995)** Hargreaves, J.A., 'Luddism', *Modern History Review*, Vol.7.1, September 1995.
- **Harrison (1984)** Harrison, J.F.C., *The Common People: a History from the Norman Conquest to the Present*, Flamingo, 1984.
- **Hobsbawm & Rudé (1969)** Hobsbawm, E.J. & Rudé, G. *Captain Swing*, Pimlico, 1969.

- **Lee (1994)** Lee, S.J., *British Political History 1815-1914*, Routledge, 1994.
- **Marlow (1969)** Marlow, J., *The Peterloo Massacre*, Rapp and W, 1969.
- **May (1996)** May, T. *An Economic and Social History of Britain 1760-1970* (2nd edn), Longman, 1996.
- **McCord (1991)** McCord, N., *British History 1815-1906*, Oxford University Press, 1991.
- **O'Gorman (1997)** O'Gorman F., *The Long Eighteenth Century British Political and Social History 1688-1832*, Arnold, 1997.
- **Plowright (1996)** Plowright, J., *Regency England: the Age of Liverpool*, Routledge, 1996.
- **Plowright (1997)** Plowright J., 'Lord Liverpool and the alternatives to "repression" in Regency England', *History Review*, No. 28, September 1997.
- **Royle (1997)** Royle, E., *Modern Britain: a Social History 1750-1997*, Arnold, 1997.
- **Rule (1986)** Rule, J., *The Labouring Classes in Early Industrial England 1700-1870*, Longman, 1986.
- **Stevenson (1992)** Stevenson J., *Popular Disturbances in England 1700-1870* (2nd edn), Longman, 1992.
- **Strong (1996)** Strong, R., *The Story of Britain*, Hutchinson, 1996.
- **Taylor (1976)** Taylor, A.J.P., *Essays in English History*, Pelican, 1976.
- **Thomis (1970)** Thomis, M.I., *The Luddites*, David and Charles, 1970.
- **Thomis & Holt (1977)** Thomis, M.I. & Holt, P., *Threats of Revolution in Britain 1789-1848*, Macmillan, 1977.
- **Thompson (1980)** Thompson, E.P., *The Making of the English Working Class*, Pelican, 1980 (first published in 1963).
- **Wright (1988)** Wright, D.G., *Popular Radicalism: the Working Class Experience 1780-1880*, Longman, 1988.

Introduction

The so-called 'Great' Reform Act has been interpreted as a turning point in modern British political history. Until its passage in 1832, the aristocratic ruling elite had successfully resisted all attempts to challenge its monopoly of political power. So, why did the equally aristocratic Whig government of Lord Grey launch a Reform Bill which, by extending the franchise (the right to

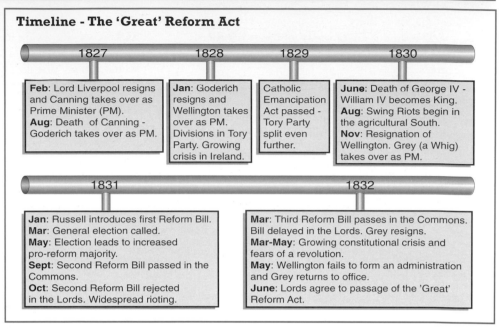

Timeline - The 'Great' Reform Act

1827
Feb: Lord Liverpool resigns and Canning takes over as Prime Minister (PM).
Aug: Death of Canning - Goderich takes over as PM.

1828
Jan: Goderich resigns and Wellington takes over as PM. Divisions in Tory Party. Growing crisis in Ireland.

1829
Catholic Emancipation Act passed - Tory Party split even further.

1830
June: Death of George IV - William IV becomes King.
Aug: Swing Riots begin in the agricultural South.
Nov: Resignation of Wellington. Grey (a Whig) takes over as PM.

1831
Jan: Russell introduces first Reform Bill.
Mar: General election called.
May: Election leads to increased pro-reform majority.
Sept: Second Reform Bill passed in the Commons.
Oct: Second Reform Bill rejected in the Lords. Widespread rioting.

1832
Mar: Third Reform Bill passes in the Commons. Bill delayed in the Lords. Grey resigns.
Mar-May: Growing constitutional crisis and fears of a revolution.
May: Wellington fails to form an administration and Grey returns to office.
June: Lords agree to passage of the 'Great' Reform Act.

vote), appeared to undermine the very basis of its authority? For a few historians, the answer lies simply in what they see as a genuine desire to begin a process of gradual but deliberate democratisation in British politics. Most historians, however, now reject this view, pointing out that the Reform Act must be interpreted against a background of mounting social, economic and political tension. In recent years, there have been two main debates. The first focuses on motivation. Some historians argue that the Whigs responded to events in the way that would gain them the greatest political advantage over their rivals. Others, however, disagree. They argue that the Whigs were not motivated exclusively by their own narrow party aims. Rather, they saw the Reform Act as a concession designed to unhinge what they saw as a growing radical alliance between the middle class and the working class. The extent to which such a threat actually existed in the early 1830s is itself a matter of controversy, but, according to this interpretation, even the perceived fear of unrest was sufficient to motivate the Whigs' actions. The second historical debate concerns the longer-term significance of the Reform Act. For some, it certainly represents a key moment in Britain's modern constitutional development. Whatever the Whigs' motives in introducing the legislation, they argue, it made further political reform inevitable and had major long-term repercussions in terms of the development of the party system and the balance of power between the Commons and the Lords. Others, however, suggest that there was, in fact, very little that was truly 'great' about the Act. They argue that the Act was deliberately designed to prevent further constitutional change and that the conscious exclusion of the working class was in itself a major reason for the emergence of the subsequent Chartist movement. This unit explores the different dimensions to the controversy surrounding the Act.

UNIT SUMMARY

Part 1 describes the key features of the unreformed system and considers the attitudes of the Whigs and Tories towards possible change.

Part 2 explores the background to the Reform Crisis of 1828-32 and outlines the passage of the three Reform Bills between 1831 and 1832. It also analyses the different interpretations of the Whigs' motives for introducing the Reform Bills

once they replaced the Tories in office.

Part 3 focuses on the extent of extra-parliamentary pressure for reform and examines whether there was ever a genuine threat of revolution.

Part 4 provides an overview of the consequences of the Reform Act and assesses both its short-term and long-term significance for the subsequent development of British politics.

1 The unreformed system: 'Old Corruption'

Key issues

1. What were the main features of the unreformed electoral system?

2. Why had this system survived so long?

3. How did the Tory and Whig parties differ over the question of reform?

1.1 The unreformed electoral system

'Old Corruption'

The electoral system which had survived unchanged throughout the 18th and early 19th centuries was termed 'Old Corruption' by the radical groups calling for its reform. Their description was not without foundation since bribery and corruption were, indeed, effectively institutionalised as the principal means of both securing and retaining power. This system had emerged out of the political upheavals of the 17th century when it had been established that government should be based on a relationship between the monarch and an aristocratic Parliament.

The two most striking features of the system were, first, the virtual monopoly of political power and influence held by the landed elite and, second, the lack of uniformity in the organisation of parliamentary constituencies and elections. There was, in reality, very little that was actually 'systematic' about the system and, together, these factors prevented the development of anything approaching democratic representation in early 19th-century Britain.

Historians estimate that under the unreformed electoral system less than 5% of the total population qualified to vote. The franchise and the right to stand for election were restricted to adult males and dependent upon property qualification. For the most part, this effectively limited the electorate to the country's wealthy landowners. In 1831, something like 400,000 men had the right to vote. The total population was 13.89 million people.

Growing pressure for reform was not due only to the limited and unrepresentative extent of the franchise. Inequality was just as evident in the organisation of constituencies and elections. Those who qualified to vote could vote in two types of constituency - counties and boroughs.

Counties

Whatever the size of its population, a county could send two MPs to Parliament. In this type of constituency, the franchise was standard across the country and depended upon the freehold occupation of land whose rental value was at least 40 shillings per annum. Although obviously restrictive and subject to variation due to regional differences in property values, this was as near to a standard franchise as existed in Britain before the 1832 Reform Act.

Boroughs

The situation in the other type of constituency - the boroughs - was much more confused (see Box 5.1). Boroughs were towns which had, at some point in their history, been granted a Royal Charter. Both the number of MPs returned to Parliament and the voting qualification varied greatly from borough to borough, depending upon local custom. Inequality and inconsistency were accentuated by the process of economic, social and demographic change associated with the Industrial Revolution. Many boroughs were settlements which had been important in medieval times, but had since decayed

BOX 5.1 Different types of borough constituency

1. Rotten boroughs
Ancient constituencies which had become so depopulated that MPs were selected and elected by a very small number of people - in some notorious cases, like Old Sarum, even by a single landowner.

2. Pocket boroughs
Constituencies in which a wealthy individual owned all the land and buildings which provided occupiers with the qualification to vote (the voters were therefore in the landowner's 'pocket') - the landowner could nominate candidates and use his power and influence to bribe or pressurise voters into voting for the candidate he favoured.

3. Scot and Lot constituencies
In these constituencies, all men who paid local taxes, such as the poor rate, could vote.

4. Potwalloper constituencies
Potwalloper constituencies were, perhaps, the most bizarre of the constituencies to the modern mind because, in these constituencies, men qualified to vote if they occupied a house which had a fireplace large enough to boil a pot.

5. Corporations
In these constituencies, only members of the local town council (known as the 'corporation') could vote.

6. Freeman constituencies
In these constituencies, all men who had acquired the title of 'freeman' through apprenticeship in a craft guild qualified to vote.

and declined. Some remained small villages. Some were almost completely depopulated. Despite this, as many as four MPs were returned to Parliament from each constituency. By way of contrast, the process of industrialisation created new and economically powerful urban centres with large populations. And yet, these areas remained totally unrepresented in Parliament. As the Whig politician Lord John Russell put it in a speech to the House of Commons on 1 March 1831:

> 'Allow me to imagine, for a moment, a stranger from some distant country, who should arrive in England to examine our institutions...He would have been told that the proudest boast of this celebrated country was its political freedom...What then would be his surprise, if he were taken by this guide...to a green mound and told that this green mound sent members to Parliament - or, to be taken to a stone wall with three niches in it, and to be told that these three niches sent two members to Parliament...But, his surprise would increase to astonishment if he were carried into the North of England, where he would see large flourishing towns, full of trade and activity... and were told that these places had no representatives in the Assembly which was said to represent the people.'

Historical debate over the unreformed system

Despite the confusion, historians have, until recently, agreed on three key features of the unreformed system. First, they agreed that, despite the large numbers and social diversity of the electorate in certain borough constituencies, the aristocracy and landed gentry controlled elections to their own advantage. Second, they agreed that the growing middle classes remained, for the most part, politically powerless and this created a potentially explosive mismatch between their mounting economic power and their increasingly frustrated political aspirations. And third, they agreed that the working class was excluded from the political nation altogether.

The revisionist view

A number of new surveys by revisionist historians such as Frank O'Gorman (1989), however, have argued that this assessment is too accepting of contemporary criticism of the unreformed system in the early 19th century and that Old Corruption was, in fact, far more representative and responsive to change than has previously been thought. In O'Gorman's view, modern historians have failed to appreciate the way in which the system worked. Although there was a high number of non-voters, he argues, local people could and did participate and express their views. Moreover, those who voted did

exercise some control over their vote. Elections were, he argues, a vital mechanism and the local elite had to work hard to maintain their power and influence within the community. Although there is scepticism about the range of evidence used by historians like O'Gorman, their work has begun to open up a new area of debate.

The organisation of elections

The organisation of elections themselves bore very little resemblance to anything we would recognise today. First, it has been estimated that around two thirds of elections were uncontested - nobody stood against the successful candidate. Second, elections were not, as they are today, concluded on a single day. The proceedings could take several weeks and the overall result (for the country as a whole) might not be known for up to two months. And third, in constituencies where contested elections did occur, there was no secret ballot. Voting took place publicly on a platform (called the 'Hustings') in an atmosphere which mixed drunken carnival with sometimes violent intimidation. The fact that people voted openly in public meant that corruption was widespread. 'Treating', where candidates would pay for their supporters' food, drink and accommodation during the election, was common practice as, more disturbingly, was the hiring of 'lambs' (gangs of armed thugs) and 'cooping' (the kidnapping of rivals' supporters until after the election).

1.2 Why did the unreformed system last so long?

Given the unrepresentative and increasingly outdated character of the electoral system, its survival into the 1830s may, at first, seem surprising. Most historians agree, however, that it lasted for so long for two reasons:

- the ruling elite remained united in defence of the status quo
- there was no genuinely revolutionary, or united, protest movement from below.

The French Revolution and the subsequent years of war with France in the 1790s helped to build a property-owning consensus against any change to the existing constitution. Indeed, the unity of both Tory and Whig politicians (who supported Prime Minister Pitt's desire to crush any form of popular radicalism) was bolstered by a wave of popular loyalism. This was stimulated by a mixture of patriotism at a time of war and fear that change in Britain might bring the violence and anarchy associated with the extreme Jacobin group which was in control of the revolutionary government in France. These factors, together with the absence of the sort of major economic dislocation or military disaster which, for example, was to bring down the rulers of Russia and

Germany in the First World War, combined to suppress the still relatively disunited radical groupings (see Unit 2). Once radicalism began to revive with the return of peace after 1815, the threat of reform was again effectively held in check by the Tory government of Lord Liverpool (see Unit 3). Liverpool's combination of repression (1815-22) and moderate but expedient economic reforms (1822-27) guaranteed the survival of almost exclusively aristocratic government in Britain until his resignation in 1827. Liverpool's resignation, however, ushered in a period of political division and confusion within the Tory Party. This provided new opportunities for political change - opportunities which the Whig government of 1830 became determined to exploit.

1.3 Political parties and reform

The influence of Edmund Burke

The first concerted attempts to justify and defend the unreformed electoral system appeared in the wake of the French Revolution. Initially, liberal Whig politicians, including the Whig leader Charles James Fox, welcomed the French Revolution (see Unit 2, Section 1.3). This initial enthusiasm was not shared by other Whig MPs, however, and it was in response to what he saw as the dangers of his party's flirtation with potentially revolutionary ideas that the young Whig politician Edmund Burke wrote *Reflections on the Revolution in France* (1790). In this essay, Burke attacked the idea of natural rights and defended Britain's existing constitution on the grounds that it had grown organically out of Britain's unique history. Moderate reform, Burke warned, would lead to violent revolution. Moderate reform, therefore, should be resisted. *Reflections on the Revolution in France* was a deeply conservative work and, consequently, it appealed to many in the Tory Party. Indeed, by the time that Lord Liverpool resigned from power in 1827, Burke's views had come to dominate thinking in the Tory Party.

Reform and the Tory Party

Whilst Lord Liverpool was Prime Minister, any attempt at reform was robustly resisted. In response to demands for reform, the Tory government developed a number of arguments in defence of the unreformed system (see Box 5.2). These arguments ensured that the path to reform remained blocked until the Tory government fell from power in 1830:

'Despite its eccentricities and imperfections, the system had very loyal and vocal support well into the 19th century from, among others...the Tory Prime Minister, Lord Liverpool, soldier-turned statesman, the Duke of Wellington, and individual MPs such as Sir Robert Inglis. These men stressed the openness and diversity of the system, its capacity for representing the major interest groups

BOX 5.2 Tory arguments in defence of the unreformed system

1. Reform would interfere with a system which had grown naturally and organically out of Britain's past. Arbitrary 'pruning' of the system would destroy rather than preserve the unique characteristics of Britain's constitutional development.

2. Once any reform - however modest - was passed, it would be impossible to resist further pressure for more extreme and dangerous change. As the future Conservative party leader and Prime Minister Robert Peel later put it: 'I was unwilling to open a door which I saw no prospect of being able to close.'

3. If the representation of the lower House (the Commons) was increased, the constitutional balance between the two Houses of Parliament and the monarch would be destroyed.

4. Reform would actually increase social tension by setting country against town, and land against industry. The interests of property as a whole would not be harmonised, leading to unnecessary conflict.

5. Reform would represent a surrender to extra-parliamentary pressure and, therefore, an abdication of an MP's traditional responsibility to act rationally on behalf of the nation. The governing classes should govern, not be dictated to.

6. MPs acted as representatives of the entire nation even if they were not elected by the whole population. All Britons were therefore 'virtually represented'.

7. Members of the aristocracy were the country's best and 'natural' rulers and should, therefore, continue to govern.

8. Britain continued to prosper under the existing system. It worked, so why tamper with it unnecessarily? When the French had experimented with 'liberty, equality and fraternity' the result had merely been Terror and military dictatorship.

9. Even where apparent flaws might be pointed out in the system, they were, in fact, strengths. For example, rotten boroughs enabled young politicians to find a seat in Parliament.

in society and its ability to evolve and adapt without the need for the sort of legislation being proposed in 1832. Though none (perhaps with the exception of Wellington) would have claimed that the system was without blemish, mostly they accepted its more unusual features as endearing quirks in a system which they believed - with some justification - had not only stood the test of time, but had produced balanced and stable government, underpinned military victory in the Napoleonic Wars and ensured unprecedented progress and prosperity. More fundamentally, it facilitated the continuing dominance of the landed aristocracy, which had no desire to travel the same road as the French Revolution had taken a generation earlier, by extending political rights and civil liberties to all citizens.' (Cole & Hartley 1997, pp.20-21)

The Whig position

Whilst the Tories were developing arguments against reform, the Whigs moved towards support for limited reform. It is important to realise, however, that the Whigs were not radical politicians calling for a revolution in the way in which Britain was governed. Nor were they democrats in any modern sense of the word. They were, rather, drawn from the same social class as the Tories in an age in which party politics lacked the element of ideological struggle we associate with it today. Nevertheless, after a generation in the political wilderness, the Whigs

had, by 1830, developed the following arguments in favour of a limited reform of the franchise:

1. The best means of protecting the constitution from sweeping revolutionary change was to make careful and controlled concessions to the middle class. If the landed elite could demonstrate their flexibility and responsiveness, they would also retain their right to govern.
2. Failure to introduce reform would strengthen a growing alliance between the middle and working classes. A concession to the middle class would draw its members into a broad, property-owning defence of the constitution whilst simultaneously unhinging the radical alliance.
3. Reform would end speculation over change and offer a permanent solution to the constitutional problem.
4. At the same time as preserving the key features of the old system, limited reform would bring the Whig party political advantage because it would mean reducing the number of rotten boroughs held by the Tories. It would also create a sense of gratitude towards the Whig Party from within the new middle-class electorate.

MAIN POINTS - Part 1

- Under the unreformed electoral system, historians estimate that less than 5% of the total population qualified to vote. Bribery and corruption were common means of securing and retaining power.
- Those who qualified to vote could vote in two types of constituency - counties and boroughs. Counties sent two MPs to Parliament. There were six types of borough constituency.
- Revisionist historians argue that the unreformed system was more sensitive to popular opinion than

traditional historians suggest.
- Historians agree that the unreformed system lasted for so long because the ruling elite was united in defence of the status quo and because there was no genuinely revolutionary, or united, protest movement from below.
- Until 1830, the Tories supported the Burkean view that reform was unnatural and should be opposed. By 1830, however, the Whigs had developed arguments in favour of limited reform.

Activity 5.1 Old Corruption

ITEM 1 Elections before 1832: the Appleby election of 1802

The fact is that yesterday morning, between eleven and twelve, I was unanimously elected by one elector to represent this ancient borough in Parliament. There was no other candidate, no opposition, no poll demanded, scrutiny or petition. So, I had nothing to do but thank the said elector for the unanimous voice by which I was chosen. On Friday morning I shall quit this triumphant scene with flying colours and a noble determination not to see it again in less than seven years.
Adapted from a letter written by Philip Francis in 1802.

Glossary
- **untractable** - unmanageable
- **hustings** - a wooden platform constructed for elections
- **veneration** - great respect
- **quintessence** - embodiment of
- **monied interest** - people with wealth

ITEM 2 Elections before 1832: a satirical account of an election in a pocket borough

The borough of Onevote stood in the middle of a heath and consisted of a solitary farm, of which the land was so poor and **untractable** that it would not have been worth the while of any human being to cultivate it, had not the Duke of Rottenburgh found it very well worth his while to pay his tenant for living there, for keeping the honourable borough in existence. The **hustings** were erected in proper form and immediately opposite them...was seated Mr Christopher Corporate [the single elector]...Mr Sarcastic stepped forward amidst the shouts of the assembled crowd and addressed Mr Christopher Corporate...'I stand forward an unworthy candidate...For, if the whole population is estimated at 11 millions, with what awe and **veneration** must I look on one who is, as it were, the abstract and **quintessence** of 33,636 people...The **monied interest**...for which you are as illustrious as the sun at noonday is the great interest between us. How high a value I set upon your voice, you may judge by the price I have paid for half of it.' The party on the hustings proceeded to business. Sir Oran Hautton, Baronet, and Simon Sarcastic, Esquire, were nominated in form. Mr Christopher Corporate held up both his hands...and the two candidates were pronounced duly elected as representatives of the ancient and honourable borough of Onevote.

Adapted from Peacock 1875.

ITEM 3 The unreformed system

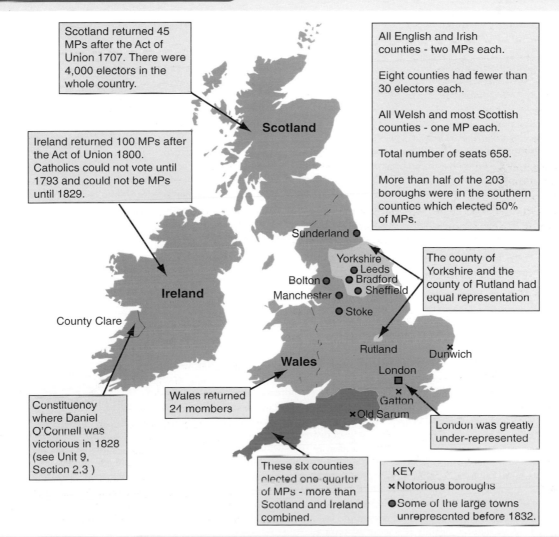

Scotland returned 45 MPs after the Act of Union 1707. There were 4,000 electors in the whole country.

Ireland returned 100 MPs after the Act of Union 1800. Catholics could not vote until 1793 and could not be MPs until 1829.

All English and Irish counties - two MPs each.

Eight counties had fewer than 30 electors each.

All Welsh and most Scottish counties - one MP each.

Total number of seats 658.

More than half of the 203 boroughs were in the southern counties which elected 50% of MPs.

The county of Yorkshire and the county of Rutland had equal representation

Constituency where Daniel O'Connell was victorious in 1828 (see Unit 9, Section 2.3)

Wales returned 24 members

These six counties elected one quarter of MPs - more than Scotland and Ireland combined.

London was greatly under-represented

KEY
× Notorious boroughs
● Some of the large towns unrepresented before 1832.

This map summarises the main features of the unreformed system.

ITEM 4 A historian's view

In about 20% of constituencies in 1715, the landowner enjoyed such unrestricted power that, in effect, they nominated the MP. The number of such boroughs reached around 30% by 1800. In a further 25% of seats, landowners made recommendations to the electors (which might not always, of course, be accepted). This figure rose to over one-third by 1800. Because it was considered to be a communal responsibility, voting remained public and so the disposal of the elector's votes could be (and often was) recorded and published. Electoral patronage was an inevitable fact of life because many electors were, to some extent, dependent upon their social superiors for employment, residence or purchase of goods and produce. The influence of electoral patrons, however, was rarely complete. Electioneering was expensive, insecure and enormously time-consuming. It was also a two-way affair. First, patrons and their servants had to respect and promote the needs of the constituency and its inhabitants. The results of elections were determined by the way that the patrons involved themselves in a long-term and often very expensive relationship with the community. Elections were opportunities for the non-voters as well as the voters to scrutinise their leaders, to criticise and to hold them to public account. We should not underestimate the enthusiasm with which people were prepared to use the system for their own purposes. Second, the elite's ultimate control of the electoral system depended on the work, loyalty and efficiency of thousands of canvassers, committee men, party workers and hundreds of people performing less elevated tasks. And third, the preoccupation of the elite with, and enormous investment in, the electoral system involved them in a permanent commitment to parliamentary politics and representative processes.

Adapted from O'Gorman 1997.

ITEM 5 Arguments for and against reform

(i) The Duke of Wellington
The Duke of Wellington was born Arthur Wellesley in Dublin in May 1769.
He played a leading role in the war against Napoleon and was the commander of the British forces in the decisive Battle of Waterloo. Wellesley was awarded his dukedom (and large estates) as a reward for his military services. He was elected MP in 1805 and served in the Cabinet from 1818. He became Prime Minister in 1828, but was forced to resign in November 1830. He remained leader of the Tory Party during the period when the Great Reform Act was debated and passed. The speech below was delivered in the House of Lords two weeks before Wellington was forced to resign as Prime Minister.

The Duke of Wellington said that he had never read or heard of any measure which could in any degree satisfy his mind that **the state of the representation** could be improved, or rendered more satisfactory to the country at large. He was fully convinced that the country possessed at the present moment a legislature which answered all the good purposes of legislation, and this to a greater degree than any **legislature** ever had answered in any country whatever. He would go further and say that the legislature and the system of representation possessed the full and entire confidence of the country. As far as he was concerned, as long as he held any station in the government of the country, he should always feel it his duty to resist such measures of reform when proposed by others.

Adapted from a report in Hansard, 2 November 1830.

(ii) Thomas Macaulay
Thomas Macaulay was born in Leicestershire in 1800. He made his reputation as a historian and is usually regarded as developing the so-called Whig view of history - a view which emphasises the idea that history is a matter of progress and it is inevitable that progress should be made as time goes on. He was elected as a Whig MP in 1830 and made a number of influential speeches in Parliament during the reform crisis.

If the **labourers** of England were in that state which I, from my soul, wish to see them, - if employment were always plentiful, wages always high, food always cheap, if a large family were considered not as an **encumbrance**, but as a blessing - the principal objections to **universal suffrage** would, I think, be removed. But, unhappily, the **lower orders** in England are occasionally in a state of great distress. This makes even wise men irritable, unreasonable, and **credulous**. They are eager for immediate relief and **heedless** of remote consequences. This state of distress blunts their judgement, it inflames their passions, it makes them prone to believe those who flatter them, and to distrust those who serve them. I oppose universal suffrage because I think that it would produce a destructive revolution. I support this measure [the Reform Bill] because I am sure that it is our best security against revolution. All history is full of revolutions produced by causes similar to those which are operating in England. **A portion of the community** which has been of no account expands and becomes strong. It demands a place in the system suited not to its former weaknesses, but to its present power. If this is refused, then comes the struggle between the young energy of one class and the ancient privileges of another. Such is the struggle which the middle classes in England are maintaining against an ancient aristocracy.

Part of a speech made in Parliament by Thomas Macaulay in March 1831.

- **the state of the representation** - the electoral system
- **legislature** - law-making body
- **labourers/lower orders** - members of the working class
- **encumbrance** - burden
- **credulous** - too ready to believe things one should not believe

- **universal suffrage** - the extension of the vote to everybody (like franchise, suffrage is another word for 'vote')
- **heedless** - take no notice of
- **a portion of the community** - ie the middle class

Questions

1. Look at Items 1 and 2.
   a) What do these items tell us about elections before 1832?
   b) How did elections in the early 19th century differ from elections today?
   c) What are the difficulties involved in using evidence of the type provided in Item 2?

2. Using Items 1-4, describe the advantages and disadvantages of the unreformed system.

3. Look at Item 5.
   a) What were the main points made in each passage?
   b) How did the view of Wellington differ from that of Macaulay?
   c) What other arguments could have been for and against the need for gradual reform?

4. Organise a debate on the motion that 'this house believes that the unreformed electoral system worked well and did not need to be changed'.

2 The development of the reform crisis 1828-32

Key issues

1. Why did a political crisis develop after Liverpool's resignation in 1827?

2. How far were the pressures for change different in this period from any earlier phase of radical activity?

3. What were the Whigs' motives in introducing a series of Reform Bills in 1831-32?

2.1 Key factors in the development of pressure for change

Why was the period 1828-30 so volatile?
When sustained pressure for political change revived after Lord Liverpool's resignation in 1827, the circumstances in which it developed were significantly different from those in either the 1790s or 1815-20. Historians have identified seven main factors to explain why the period 1828-30 was more volatile than any preceding phase of radical activity.

1. Pressure from the middle class
First, historians have pointed to a powerful middle-class element in the developing reform movement. This was significantly different from the 1790s or the period 1815-20, when the propertied classes had

BOX 5.3 **Jeremy Bentham and electoral reform**

Jeremy Bentham (1748-1832) was a philosopher whose ideas formed the basis of 'Utilitarianism'. He argued that the basis of morality was that an action should be judged to be right or wrong according to whether or not its consequences improved the general utility. In other words, actions are morally right if they lead to the greatest good for the greatest number of people and morally wrong if they do not. The logic of this argument led to demands for universal suffrage on the grounds that this was the only way to safeguard the greatest happiness for the greatest number against the selfish interests of the few. Followers of Bentham are known as Benthamites or Utilitarians. Bentham's ideas were particularly influential in the 1830s. It should be noted, however, that, although many members of the middle classes supported Bentham's critique of the existing electoral system, they called for an extension of the franchise, not universal suffrage.
Adapted from Royle 1997.

been relatively united in their opposition to the common threat posed by the emerging working class. However, middle-class support for political change was certainly not based upon any selfless support for an abstract idea of democracy or universal suffrage which might undermine the power of property and increase the influence of the working class. Instead, middle-class protesters desired more moderate changes which would enhance their own more narrow and specific class interests. In particular, they were critical of a system which radical philosophers (like Jeremy Bentham - see Box 5.3) attacked for its irrationality and they hoped that a Parliament more broadly representative of the developing business interest would legislate more effectively for free trade. Resentment at the landed elite's stranglehold on political power was focused on its most potent symbol - the 1815 Corn Laws - which many of those members of the middle class who were engaged in business saw as the fundamental cause of economic instability in this period (see Unit 7).

2. Working-class discontent
Second, historians have argued that it was not middle-class pressure alone which added a new ingredient to the political mix of the late 1820s. For some, the period represents a particularly acute crisis because discontent against the aristocracy developed in the working class as well as the middle class. The extent and effectiveness of an 'alliance' between the working and middle classes has been hotly debated (see Part 3 below), but it is certainly important to consider how far even a *perceived* collaboration between these classes might have spurred politicians into the belief that some form of response was necessary.

3. Political unions
Third, some historians have argued that, as well as being the main expression of this organised protest, the emergence of political unions (new extra-parliamentary pressure groups) was a further factor in the growing atmosphere of tension (see also Part 3). It is, however, important to note that these political unions were in fact very diverse in their character and aims. The best known group was the Birmingham Political Union (BPU) set up in 1830 by the banker Thomas Attwood (see Box 5.4).

Attwood described the BPU as 'a general political union between the lower and middle classes of the people'. If the BPU is compared to other groups which developed in this period, however, it is clear that it was not typical. In fact, Birmingham was, in many ways, exceptional in maintaining concerted pressure for reform from a combination of skilled workers, manufacturers and leading commercial figures. This was largely due to the structure of the city's many small workshops where employer and employee still met and worked closely together, with the result that social distinctions were blurred. In many other industrial areas, where social and economic divisions were more clearly defined (in the northern textile towns, for example), the reform movement tended to be more polarised, with

BOX 5.4 | Thomas Attwood
Thomas Attwood was a Birmingham banker whose family fortune had been made in the iron trade. By political inclination, Attwood was a Tory and he took no part in the 1815-20 reform movement because he was deeply opposed to universal suffrage. However, he attracted the support of men of his own class when he argued that the economy would continue to be unstable whilst the new industrial middle class was excluded from government. Attwood and many others who shared his views were inspired by the success of the Catholic Association in extracting Catholic emancipation from Wellington's government by the use of popular pressure. When Attwood set up the BPU in 1830, he modelled it closely on O'Connell's organisation. The problem with Parliament, he now argued, was the absence of men representing productive capital, that is men active in the world of commerce and industry (in fact, men like Attwood). He stressed the common interests of employers and employees who he saw as making up a single 'productive' class. 'The interests of masters and men', he said, 'are in fact one. If the masters flourish, the men flourish with them; and if the masters suffer difficulties, their difficulties must shortly affect the workers in threefold degree.' For Attwood, universal suffrage was not necessary. Given the common interests of employers and employees, in that both stood to gain if industry flourished, the needs of the labouring population would be fully catered for by the election of employers to Parliament.
Adapted from Behagg 1995.

middle-class and lower-middle-class political unions on the one hand and the so-called 'low' democratic unions exclusively representing the working class on the other. The National Union of the Working Class (NUWC) is usually seen as the best example of the latter type of political union. Nevertheless, despite these differences, the political unions' significance in shaping politicians' attitudes should not be overlooked. As the historian Eric Evans puts it:
'The cumulative effect of reform agitation via the political unions was more important than any differences of social composition and specific objective. They attracted huge crowds to political rallies; they were organised and generally disciplined; and, most important of all, they served notice on Westminster that the middle classes were prepared to labour mightily in the reformers' vineyard.' (Evans 1996, p.217)

4. The economic context
Fourth, most historians agree that it is important to understand the economic context and, more especially, the relationship between a series of bad

harvests and trade depression in 1829-30, and the wave of rural unrest in 1830-31 known as the 'Swing Riots' (see also Unit 4). These disturbances were named after the mythical Captain Swing, whose signature appeared at the bottom of threatening letters sent to landowners using new machinery on their farms. From the political elite's point of view the most worrying feature of the unrest (rick-burning, destruction of agricultural machinery, arson and the maiming of animals) was where it occurred. Swing rioting spread across the predominantly rural south and east of the country - regions which, unlike the growing industrial towns in the North or London, had never been regarded as centres of political consciousness or radical activity. It is probably the case that the Swing rioters, like the Luddites before them, were essentially a backward-looking movement, desperately trying to protect an older way of life which was threatened by the spread of technology into the countryside. If that is so, then they did not actually reflect a growing political awareness and motivation amongst the previously apathetic and largely apolitical agricultural workforce. On the other hand, the fact that landowners were often the target of their attacks was a cause of genuine concern to politicians. Some now feared that paternalism (the informal cornerstone of a rural society based on traditions of hierarchy and reciprocal obligations and respect) was beginning to break down. Whatever their actual motivation, the Swing Riots (at least indirectly) contributed to a growing feeling of insecurity and they conjured up a nightmare of simultaneous urban and rural unrest on a scale which might stretch the still rudimentary forces of law and order to breaking point.

5. Trade union activity

Fifth, some historians have suggested that an increase in the level of trade union activity contributed further to these fears. The repeal of the Combination Acts in 1824 (which made unions lawful for the first time) coincided with an economic boom and released a wave of union activity. Although many of the new unions did not survive the slump of 1825-26, their activities were sufficient to alarm MPs. MPs were also alarmed by the development of General Unionism in the late 1820s and early 1830s. Although this experiment was short-lived, it was perceived as being a threat at the time because general unionism had an ideological as well as an organisational dimension. This was expressed in the numerous pro-union journals which grew up - such as, Thomas Hodgskin's *Trades Newspaper*, which attacked capitalism, and John Doherty's *Voice of the People*, which called for political reform. Doherty was the leader of the Lancashire spinners and founder of the General Union of the Operative Spinners of Great Britain.

6. The international dimension

Sixth, some historians have emphasised that there

was also an international dimension to the growing pressure for reform. In July 1830, for example, France experienced another revolution which effectively increased the power of the middle classes at the expense of the older and clericalist ruling elite. Although the repercussions of this event were not as far-reaching as the Revolution of 1789, further uprisings took place in Belgium and across the multi-national Hapsburg Empire. Fears about what might happen in Britain if reform was refused consequently began to grow.

7. Instability in government

And seventh, some historians argue that the most important difference between this and preceding periods of radical activity was the extent of political instability at the heart of government. Between Liverpool's resignation in 1827 and the establishment of Grey's Whig administration in November 1830, a series of major political changes took place. Under Lord Liverpool there had been 15 years of stability. But, when he resigned, the Tory government imploded. After two very short-lived administrations headed by Canning and Goderich, the Duke of Wellington emerged as party leader and Prime Minister in 1828. During the next two years, he succeeded in splitting the party into three opposing factions.

First, he alienated the more liberal 'Canningite' wing of the party over his refusal to consider even a very moderate proposal for a limited redistribution of parliamentary seats. By refusing to consider the possibility of transferring the seats in two corrupt boroughs - Penryn and East Retford - to Manchester and Birmingham (Penryn was near Manchester, East Retford near Birmingham), he ensured the Canningite Tories' resignation from government. Then, and more surprisingly, given his personal views on the issue, Wellington estranged the very right-wing and staunchly Protestant 'Ultras' by supporting the passage of the Act of Catholic Emancipation in 1829 (which, for the first time, allowed Catholics to become MPs). This was regarded by the Ultras as an act of betrayal by Wellington - a spineless U-turn given his previously stated views on the issue. However, during 1828, the activities of Daniel O'Connell's Catholic Association in Ireland had convinced Wellington that further refusal to grant emancipation would lead to civil war (see Unit 9). He decided, therefore, that the Act of Catholic Emancipation was the lesser of two evils. The result was that, by early 1830, Wellington's position in Parliament was very unstable, with the Tory party split into three factions - the Canningites, the Ultras and the remaining supporters of Wellington. At the same time, outside Parliament, reformers were greatly heartened by the success of the campaign for Catholic emancipation.

O'Connell's Catholic Association had shown that extra-parliamentary pressure could lead to government action and this encouraged reformers to adopt similar tactics.

Developments, June-November 1830

Wellington's position was further weakened in June 1830 by the general election which followed the death of King George IV (see Box 5.5), himself a very pro-Tory opponent of reform. Although the results of the election were inconclusive and Wellington was able to struggle on as Prime Minister, he no longer had a majority. In November, the Whig leader Earl Grey was able to exploit this position to defeat Wellington's government. By announcing that a Whig government would introduce cautious reform, Grey was able to reach agreement with the two disaffected Tory factions who now, for very different reasons both supported the idea of electoral change. The Canningites' support for Grey's proposals is relatively easy to understand, given their previous commitment to moderate reform. The Ultras' apparent U-turn on the issue, however, was a direct result of their opposition to the Act of Catholic Emancipation. Although previously opposed to any form of constitutional change (whether in matters of Church or state), they now reasoned that a slightly broader electorate would give political expression to what they believed were deep-seated anti-Catholic prejudices in Britain. Any government elected by

BOX 5.5 | King George IV and King William IV

When King George IV died on 26 June 1830, his brother, William IV, succeeded him. Whilst both brothers had colourful personal lives, they differed in terms of politics. From the time when he became Prince Regent, George IV moved from supporting the Whigs (as George III had done) to supporting the Tories. He remained a staunch Tory until his death and was particularly opposed to both Catholic emancipation and parliamentary reform. William IV, on the other hand, supported the Whigs. Before becoming King, he introduced debates in the Lords on topics hostile to the Tories. It was William who invited Earl Grey, a Whig, to form a government In November 1830 and he then played an important part in the reform process by accepting Grey's request to dissolve Parliament after the first Reform Bill was requested against government wishes (the King had discretion to dissolve or not to dissolve Parliament). Although William refused Grey's request to create 50 extra Whig peers in May 1832 to force the third Reform Bill through Parliament, he did not refuse to give the Bill royal assent when it finally passed through the Lords.

Adapted from Rubinstein 1998.

such a franchise would, they concluded, be in a strong position to repeal the Act of Catholic Emancipation.

Having gained the support of these two Tory factions, Grey was able to set up a mainly Whig administration with himself as Prime Minister (the government included several Canningites and an Ultra Tory).

2.2 The passage of the Reform Act 1831-32

The three Bills

Three Reform Bills were introduced in Parliament before the final one became law in June 1832. The parliamentary and extra-parliamentary battle over its passage represents one of the most controversial episodes in modern British political history.

The first Reform Bill, March 1831

From December 1830, a committee of ministers worked on the drafting of the first Bill. This was introduced in the House of Commons in March 1831 by Lord John Russell (see Box 5.6). After one of the most dramatic debates in parliamentary history, it passed its second reading in the Commons by a single vote (302 to 301), but was subsequently amended at its committee stage against government wishes. Grey used the defeat during the committee stage to request a dissolution of Parliament and a general election in order to strengthen the pro-reform majority in the Commons.

The second Reform Bill, July 1831

The result was exactly what the pro-reformers hoped for. Supported by a majority of around 130, Grey's new administration introduced a second Reform Bill in July 1831. It comfortably passed through the Commons - this time with a majority of 136. In October, however, it was rejected by the House of Lords, which was dominated by Tory supporters. The Lords' decision triggered a wave of rioting across the country, with the most serious disturbances in Bristol, Derby and Nottingham (see Part 3 below).

The third Reform Bill, December 1831

A third Bill was then introduced with minor amendments in December. This followed the same pattern as the second. After an easy passage through the Commons, the Bill ran into a Tory wall of defiance in the Lords. In an attempt to break this apparent impasse and counteract Tory obstructionism, Grey asked William IV to create 50 new Whig peers. When William refused, Grey resigned in protest (in May 1832). Wellington was invited by the King to form a new administration in Grey's place. This triggered a period of acute tension now known as the 'Days of May'. Many historians have argued that this represents the point at which

BOX 5.6 | Lord John Russell

Lord John Russell was the third son of the Duke of Bedford and was, therefore, born into one of the wealthiest families in Britain. Since he was a younger son of a duke, he did not inherit a title (younger sons were given the title 'Lord' as a courtesy title) and was able to join the House of Commons as an MP in 1813. He remained in the Commons until 1861, when he was given an earldom and went to the Lords. After entering Parliament, Russell's first attempt at reform came in 1822 when, as Whig Leader in the Commons, he introduced a Bill to disfranchise 100 of the smallest and most corrupt boroughs. The Bill failed by a large majority. Because of his attempt at reform in 1822, he was invited to join the committee set up to draft the Whig Reform Bill in 1831. When this Bill was presented to the Commons on 1 March 1831, Russell introduced it. Russell also piloted the second Bill through the Commons in September 1831 and he presented the third Bill in mid-December 1831. While few contemporaries doubted Russell's capacity for hard work, some had doubts about his ability. Despite this, he served in the Cabinet between 1831 and 1839, was Foreign Secretary in 1852-53 and 1859-65 and was Prime Minister in 1846-52 and 1865-66. On a less serious (and possibly spurious) note, in 1814, Russell met Napoleon in exile on Elba. Various accounts survive of what was said, but, according to one, Russell talked at great length about the Russell family. Instead of replying, Napoleon 'went to the corner of the room and relieved himself'.
Adapted from Evans 1989 and Rubinstein 1998.

Britain came closest to experiencing revolution in its modern history. Not only was there the danger of an armed uprising from the more extreme political unions, but this danger was combined with the middle-class threat to trigger a major financial crisis by withdrawing gold coins from the banks. The atmosphere, however, calmed once it became clear that Wellington had failed in his attempt to raise the parliamentary support necessary to form a government. Grey subsequently returned as Prime Minister. The King, shaken by the events of May, now agreed to his request for new peers should the Lords continue to obstruct the passage of the Bill. This was not necessary. The 'Days of May' had been sufficient to convince most of the Lords, Wellington included, that further resistance might provoke an even greater calamity. The House of Lords, therefore, backed down and, in June, the Reform Act became law.

2.3 Interpreting the Whigs' motives

The debate

Historians have debated why, unlike in previous periods of intense radical protest (see Units 2 and 4), the Whigs chose to yield to pressure rather than simply to take measures to suppress it. In broad terms, it is possible to identify four lines of interpretation. Each offers a possible explanation for the Whigs' motives for introducing the Reform Bills of 1831-32. The theme of expediency - gaining some party political advantage by pursuing a practical though less than ideal path in difficult circumstances - figures in a number of these interpretations.

Interpretation 1 - The Whigs introduced the Reform Bills because their party stood to gain in electoral terms from a reform of the system.
The Whigs had been out of office for a political

generation. Although some aristocratic Whig families had a vested interest in the unreformed system, the period of Tory ascendancy under Lord Liverpool (see Unit 3) had made it increasingly obvious that their opponents had a much stronger hold of the pocket boroughs. Electoral reform, therefore, came to be seen as the Whig Party's best means of retaining power. By extending the borough franchise to £10 householders, leading Whig politicians were aware that they would be creating an electorate which, being composed largely of Nonconformists, shopkeepers and other lower-class townspeople, would be predominantly Whig in character. The effective collapse of the Tory Party over Catholic Emancipation presented the Whigs with an opportunity to push through a measure which would lead to a political advantage over their rivals.

Interpretation 2 - The Whigs introduced the Reform Bills in the hope of preventing revolution.
This interpretation also stresses political expediency, although here the Whigs' actions can be seen more broadly as a defence of the position of the ruling elite in general rather than an attempt to advance Whig interests in particular. According to this line of argument, the threat of revolution in 1831-32 forced the Whigs into making concessions to those who supported reform. In other words, the Whigs saw the Reform Act as a means of preventing, rather than introducing, fundamental changes in the constitution. In particular, so the argument goes, the Whigs were determined to unhinge what they saw as a growing radical alliance between the middle class and the working class. Their aim was to rejig the franchise and redistribute parliamentary seats in such a way that representation was given to the 'respectable' urban middle classes (roughly from

tradesmen and shopkeepers upwards). These groups would then come to have a vested interest in preserving the (only slightly modified) constitution. At the same time, this concession would be sufficient to prevent the middle class from making common cause with the unrepresented masses (which, if it happened, might lead to open revolt against the elite). According to this view, the Whigs believed that the masses would be powerless without middle-class leadership and support. The Reform Act, therefore, is seen as an essentially conservative measure - a means of avoiding radical reform. Box 5.7 shows that the Whig government certainly argued that its aim was to avoid revolution, though speeches like this should not necessarily be taken at face value.

BOX 5.7 Part of a speech made by Earl Grey

If any persons suppose that this reform will lead to ulterior measures, they are mistaken; for there is no-one more decided against annual Parliaments, universal suffrage and secret ballots than I am. My object is not to favour, but to put an end to such hopes and projects. The principle of my reform is to prevent the necessity for revolution - reforming to preserve and not to overthrow.

Part of a speech made in the House of Lords in November 1831.

Interpretation 3 - The Reform Bills represented a tactical manipulation of electoral boundaries, designed to eliminate the growing problem of competition between rural and urban interests.

This interpretation is associated with the historian D.C. Moore (1976). Moore's argument is based on the premise that the Whigs were not forced into reform, but instead made a conscious and deliberate attempt to 'oil' the existing system to the landed elite's advantage. This was achieved by two provisions in the Bill. The first provision, which stipulated that 40 shilling freeholders in the newly enfranchised towns forfeited the right to vote in county elections if they qualified for the borough franchise as £10 householders, was designed to prevent the 'seepage' of middle-class commercial influence into the county seats. The second provision, the Chandos Amendment, enfranchised tenant farmers - a particularly deferential group who were susceptible to the influence of their superiors, the great landowners.

Moore's interpretation, although ingenious, has been heavily criticised. It has been argued, for example, that the Whigs lacked the statistical evidence to make fine decisions about the relative balance of class influence and interest in different types of constituency. It has also been argued that Moore underplays the extent to which the Whigs were reacting to popular pressure and circumstances. In the perceived crisis of 1831-32, critics of Moore argue, what was important was that some measure of reform was carried. Exactly what, and who, were to be included or excluded was less important.

Interpretation 4 - The Whigs were motivated by a genuine and positive belief that reform was desirable for its own sake.

This interpretation suggests that leading Whig politicians (such as Lord John Russell, who introduced the Bill in 1831) saw ordered reform as both morally justifiable and necessary in order to prevent political structures becoming increasingly misaligned from the process of economic and social change in Britain.

MAIN POINTS - Part 2

- Pressure for reform grew up as a result of (1) middle-class agitation, (2) working-class agitation, (3) the work of political unions, (4) economic recession, (5) trade union activity, (6) political developments abroad and (7) instability at the heart of government.
- Earl Grey's Whig government introduced three Reform Bills. The first Bill was abandoned and a general election called. The second Bill was defeated in the Lords. The third Bill was passed after the Days of May persuaded a majority of Lords that there would be revolution if the Bill was not passed.
- The Whig scheme for limited reform contained two essential elements - (1) the redistribution of seats (143 seats were redistributed, mostly, to the English counties and to the new industrial towns) and (2) the remodelling and systematising of the franchise (a new, uniform property qualification was introduced in boroughs and the vote was extended in counties).
- There are four main interpretations of the Whig decision to support reform - (1) because the party stood to gain in electoral terms, (2) to prevent revolution, (3) to manipulate electoral boundaries in order to eliminate competition between rural and urban interests, and (4) because it was morally justifiable and necessary.

Activity 5.2 The struggle for reform

(i)

This cartoon shows, at the top, leading Whig politicians surrounding King William IV. The roar of reform from the lion in the middle is scaring Wellington and the Tories out of office. The mass of people (at the bottom) cheer as the lion roars and Britannia slays a dragon (which represents rotten boroughs).

(ii)

This cartoon shows reformers chopping down a tree full of rotten boroughs whilst anti-reform Tories crowd round trying to prop it up. Ordinary British people watch from the distance. Behind them, the sun is rising.

ITEM 3 A historian's account

The 1832 Reform Act can be seen as a hasty concession by the ruling elite to preserve authority at a time of unprecedented opposition and unrest. Put simply, the Reform Act was passed in 1832 and not before because those in authority did not fear for their position and authority any earlier. In the 1790s and between 1815 and 1820, reform could be avoided by government repression. In 1830-32, however, there were enough politicians who feared that further repression would lead to revolution to secure government majorities for reform. This explanation focuses on extra-parliamentary pressure, but it is possible that politicians at Westminster exaggerated the potential for revolution in 1831-32. Another way of looking at events is to examine the sudden weakening of the anti-reform majority in the Commons between 1827 and 1831. This weakening owes less to external pressure and more to the divisive effects of the religious question on the Tory Party. Even before Liverpool resigned, the Tory Party had been divided into two wings over Catholic emancipation. Few 'Protestants' would serve under Canning and his successor failed to unite the party. Then Wellington alienated the Ultras by supporting the Catholic Emancipation Act. The Tory majority in the Commons had been the sure safeguard against reform since the 1790s. Yet it was shattered by divisions over not political but religious reform. It can be argued, therefore, that reform was achieved more because the Tories, after a long period of effortless dominance, failed than because the Whigs succeeded. It should also be noted that the 1832 Reform Act was much more a matter of giving the vote to the lower middle class than to the middle class as a whole. It is too rarely noticed that the wealthier, commercial, industrial and professional figures already had the vote since they lived, or had property in, county constituencies. The Whigs knew that no section of society is more conservative and jealous of its property than those who have relatively little.

Adapted from Evans 1988.

Questions

1. a) Look at Item 1. Write a paragraph for each individual explaining the part they played in the reform crisis.
   b) 'Reform was inevitable, regardless of the views of the key players'. Give arguments for and against this view.

2. a) What points are the cartoonists making in Item 2?
   b) Do you think the cartoonists were pro- or anti-reform? Explain how you know.
   c) 'The cartoons underestimate the role played by extra-parliamentary forces.' Explain this statement using Item 3.

3. a) Judging from Item 3, why was the Reform Act passed in 1832?
   b) Do you agree with the views of the author of Item 3? Explain your answer.
   c) How far were the pressures for change between 1827 and 1832 different from those in earlier phases of radical activity?

4. a) Describe what Items 2 and 3 suggest about the Whigs' motives for supporting the Reform Act.
   b) Which of the four interpretations described in Section 2.3 above best fits with the views expressed in Items 2 and 3?

3 Extra-parliamentary pressure and threats of revolution

Key issues

1. What were the main features of extra-parliamentary protest?
2. How close did Britain come to revolution during the reform crisis?

3.1 Extra-parliamentary protest

The political unions

Whilst, as Section 2.3 above suggests, the Whigs may have initially considered the introduction of a Reform Bill partly for reasons of party advantage, extra-parliamentary protest ensured that the parliamentary campaign gained momentum. The emergence of the political unions as the principal form of extra-parliamentary protest has already been noted in Section 2.1. As the historian Frank O'Gorman observes:

'The demand for reform was exceptionally well organised and maintained...The organisational thrust of radicalism was provided by the political unions...There were slightly under 100 political unions, a third of them in the north, a third in the midlands, a sixth in the south west and the rest dispersed throughout the rest of England...Their objectives varied, but in general they campaigned for male universal suffrage, annual parliaments and the secret ballot. Their main functions were to politicise the public, to organise meetings and petition Parliament...The unions...preached the gospel of patriotic cooperation between the working and middle classes. Indeed, this was no mere fiction. Working-class individuals, including trade unionists, appeared on the lists of union councils and committees, bringing workers and their bosses under the same banner of collaboration.' (O'Gorman 1997, pp.362-63)

The pressure generated by the political unions is usually seen as being at its most acute during two distinct phases of the reform crisis:

- in October 1831, when a wave of violent riots occurred in cities such as Bristol and Nottingham after the Lords rejected the Second Reform Bill
- during the so-called 'Days of May' in 1832 whilst Wellington was attempting to form a regressive, anti-reform ministry.

The leading radicals

The issue of electoral reform was revived in the late 1820s by self-styled radicals like William Cobbett and Henry Hunt who had long argued for change (see Unit 4). The leading radicals, however, did not make up a single, coherent group or party. Different radicals had different views. Henry Hunt, for example, argued in favour of universal suffrage and, as a result, opposed the Bills proposed by the Whig government. Sir Francis Burdett, on the other hand, argued that universal suffrage was not necessary. Both men had large popular followings. It should be noted, however, that, although these leading radicals appealed to the working class, they did not belong to the working class and their interests were not necessarily working-class interests. Nevertheless, as the historian E.P. Thompson points out, it was traditional for members of the working class to look to aristocrats or 'gentlemen' to give them a lead.

'Only the gentlemen - Burdett, Cochrane, Hunt, Feargus O'Connor - knew the forms and language of high politics, could cut a brave figure on the hustings or belabour the ministers in their own tongue. The reform movement might use the language of equality, but many of the old responses of deference were still there even among the huzzaing [cheering] crowds. Whenever a working man appeared to be rising "above himself" even in the reform movement he quickly drew the jealousy of many of his own class.' (Thompson 1980, p.682)

Because there was no central organisation or party apparatus, the leading radicals often operated alone, using their own resources. Although some built up mass support - some editions of Cobbett's journals sold tens of thousands of copies, for example - the lack of coherence meant that their effectiveness was limited.

Working-class support for reform

Given that the three Reform Bills put before Parliament in 1831-32 completely excluded working-class representation, it is somewhat ironic that the working class should play such an important part in the reform campaign (the working-class support given to the political unions, for example, gave these organisations far greater authority than they would otherwise have had). So, why did the reform programme appeal to members of the working class? There are three main answers to this question. First, there was an economic incentive for political change. Pro-reformers argued that a reformed Parliament would mean lower taxes and greater economic prosperity (see Box 5.8). Second, Attwood's argument that the struggle for reform was a struggle between the 'productive' and 'unproductive' classes had support. And third, there was the hope that the Reform Act would pave the way to universal suffrage in the near future.

It is important to note that members of the working class turned up in large numbers to meetings supporting reform. The BPU regularly attracted 100,000 people to its outdoor meetings and a rally held in Birmingham during the Days of May attracted around 200,000 (mainly working-class) people. Given the size of the population and the difficulties of travelling compared to today, that

BOX 5.8   A cartoon in support of reform

This cartoon suggests that if John Bull (who symbolises Britain) takes the step of passing a Reform Act, there will be many benefits for ordinary people.

represents a huge turnout and testifies to the strength of feeling on the issue.

Riots - October 1831

There were fears of a total breakdown of public order in October 1831 when serious rioting broke out in a number of major urban centres. Nottingham Castle, the home of a notorious anti-reformer and Ultra Tory, the Duke of Newcastle, was burned during a violent riot in the city. Bristol was also the scene of particularly fierce protest. The city was controlled for three days by rioters who looted both public buildings and private houses, inflicting an enormous amount of damage. Order was finally restored by troops who killed 12 of the rioters and injured over 100 more. Four of the rioters were later executed. An eyewitness left the following account of the Bristol riot:

'About four o'clock we saw the new city and county gaol in flames; afterwards the Bridewell and another prison in the Gloucester Road, about a mile from Bristol. In the course of the evening, Queen's Square was fired and the Bishop's Palace...The cathedral was preserved, and is still standing, but was attempted. Other property to an immense amount is also destroyed. This morning an actual slaughter has taken place. It is supposed, though of course nothing precise can be known at present, that above 70 people have been killed, besides a large number who have been wounded. The military charged through some of the principal streets cutting right and left...May God preserve us and our guilty land! Our wretched ministers have raised a storm which, I fear, it will not be in their power to direct or control.' (from a letter written by the Reverend J.L. Jackson on 31 October 1831)

The Days of May

The other occasion on which extra-parliamentary protest appeared to be at its most threatening was in May 1832. Indeed, a number of historians conclude that this is the point at which Britain came closest to experiencing revolution. When the government was defeated on an amendment to the Reform Bill in May, Grey, having been refused 50 new Whig peers by the King, resigned (see Section 2.2 above). William IV subsequently asked Wellington to attempt to form a new Tory administration. The fear that such an administration would inevitably block reform and clamp down on the protest movement triggered the extra-parliamentary outcry known as the 'Days of May'. The tactics used in the Days of May are outlined in Box 5.9.

In the event, of course, Wellington failed in his attempt to form an administration, the Whigs returned, the Lords capitulated and the Reform Bill passed into law. However, there is still a major debate between historians over whether a revolution

---

BOX 5.9 Tactics used in the Days of May

1. Anti-Tory petitions flooded into Westminster.
2. Meetings were held between the leaders of the political unions to discuss tactics for coordinated protest across the country.
3. A plan was drawn up by Francis Place, the leading London radical, to encourage middle-class supporters of reform to withdraw private deposits from banks simultaneously in order to trigger a destabilising financial crisis. This gave rise to the famous slogan 'to stop the Duke, go for gold' ('the Duke' was the Duke of Wellington).
4. A further plan was drawn up to organise a tax strike by pro-reform property-owners.
5. Demonstrations were organised and civil disobedience threatened if Wellington succeeded in forming a government. Francis Place threatened: 'Let the Duke take office as Premier and we shall have a commotion in the nature of a civil war.'
6. Protest marches to London were organised from towns in the North and Midlands.

---

would have occurred if the crisis had lasted for longer or if Wellington had been able to form a government.

3.2 The threat of revolution reconsidered

A genuine threat of revolution?

At the time of the reform crisis, reformers themselves made much of the threat of revolution. By suggesting that Britain was on the brink of revolution, they put pressure on anti-reformers to back down. But was there a genuine threat of revolution or was talk of revolution exaggerated? This is a question that has exercised historians ever since.

The threat was genuine

Historians who believe that the threat of revolution was real in 1831-32 have pointed to a number of factors which, together, suggest that, unlike in previous periods of protest, there was a genuine threat of a national armed uprising if demands for reform were ignored. These are outlined in Box 5.10.

Supporters of the view that Britain was indeed on the brink of revolution in 1831-32 include the historian Eric Hobsbawm. He argues that:

'The Reform Act of 1832 corresponds to the July Revolution of 1830 in France, and had indeed been powerfully stimulated by the news from Paris. This period is probably the only one in modern history when political events in Britain ran parallel with those on the Continent, to the point where something not unlike a revolutionary

Historians argue that the following factors added up to a genuine threat of revolution:
- a background of economic distress, reflected in the Swing Riots of 1830-31, and exacerbated by the first cholera epidemic
- the example of a successful revolution in France in 1830, when Parisian workers had participated in the overthrow of King Charles X
- a period of confusion amongst the ruling elite following the fragmentation of the Tory Party under Wellington
- a well-organised protest movement, based on the political unions and involving both the middle and the working classes
- effective use of a range of radical tactics, including violent protest and the threat of a run on gold or a tax strike
- genuinely widespread support for the Reform Bill as a tangible objective of protest
- the difficulties which the government would have faced in maintaining law and order across the country during what might have become, for the first time, a genuinely national crisis.

situation might have developed in 1831-32 but for the restraint of both Whig and Tory parties. It is the only period in the 19th century when the analysis of British politics in such terms is not wholly artificial.' (Hobsbawm 1977, p.140)

Similarly, the historian Clive Behagg (1991) argues that, if Wellington had actually formed a government in May 1832, an armed uprising was a distinct possibility. In support of this argument, Behagg quotes part of a letter written by Frederick Hill, a Birmingham school teacher, to his brother in May 1832:

'The middle classes are, I think, rapidly prepared as a whole to refuse the payment of taxes. The general expectation is that the Duke will instantly resort to violent measures. An arrest of all of the members of the [BPU Political] Council is looked upon as a probable measure. I much fear that the people will not be able to restrain themselves in this case.'

Hamburger's thesis

There are, however, other historians who strongly argue against the idea that Britain was ever close to revolution. Perhaps the most interesting critique comes from the American historian Joseph Hamburger (1963), who argues that leading radicals such as Place and Attwood created a 'phoney' impression of revolution to undermine Wellington's attempts to form an administration and to persuade MPs to force the Reform Bill through Parliament quickly. According to Hamburger, leaders like Place

and Attwood deliberately exaggerated the strength and unity of the political unions to frighten the politicians. In other words, they were engaged in what was, in effect, an elaborate confidence trick.

The question of whether radicals such as Place and Attwood would have led a national revolution in May 1832 remains a matter of academic doubt. Hamburger contends that there was never any real threat of revolution - the object even of the radical leaders remained the limited one of exploiting the threat of unrest in the hope of pushing what was still essentially a moderate bill through Parliament. On the other hand, even if this was the object of the radical leaders, it can be argued that they were playing a particularly dangerous game and there was always the risk that they might unleash popular forces beyond their control.

No real threat of revolution

The main arguments in support of the view that there was no real threat of revolution in this period are as follows.

1. Little preparation

First, there is little evidence that Place or any of the other leading radicals (such as the Whig politician, Henry Brougham, and the editor of the *Leeds Mercury*, Edward Baines) made determined attempts to collect arms, infiltrate the armed forces or create a national revolutionary organisation. The majority of the activity in May 1832 was confined to London and centred on the threat of financial destabilisation.

2. Little class collaboration

Second, it is difficult to judge exactly how much class collaboration there really was, but, in reality, there probably was not a great deal. As noted above (Section 2.1), the Birmingham Political Union was highly unusual in maintaining class collaboration during the reform crisis. Also, E.P. Thompson (1980) has argued that there were middle-class members of the political unions who saw themselves as performing a dual function - to promote moderate reform whilst simultaneously controlling the volume of protest and protecting society from mob rule. As Thompson himself puts it:

'We can see why throughout these crisis months a revolution was in fact improbable. The reason is to be found in the very strength of the working-class radical movement; the skill with which the middle-class leaders, Brougham, *The Times*, the *Leeds Mercury* both used this threat of working-class force and negotiated a line of retreat acceptable to all but the most die-hard defenders of the *ancien regime*; and the awareness on the part of the Whigs and the least intransigent Tories that, while Brougham and Baines were only blackmailing them, nevertheless if a compromise was not come to, the middle-class reformers might no longer be able to hold in check the agitation at their backs. The industrial bourgeoisie desired, with heart and soul, that a revolution should not take place since they knew that, on the day of its commencement, there would be a dramatic process of radicalisation...these middle-class incendiaries carried in their knapsacks a special constable's baton.' (Thompson 1980, pp.889-91)

3. Divisions within the protest movement

Third, there is certainly evidence of divisions within the extra-parliamentary protest movement - both in terms of rivalries between the various political unions and differences of opinion between unions dominated by members of the middle class and those 'low' unions which claimed to represent more exclusively working-class interests. In London, for example, there were tensions between the National Political Union (NPU), led by Francis Place and calling for class collaboration, and the National Union of the Working Classes (NUWC), led by William Lovett, Henry Heatherington and John Cleave, and using: 'virulent class language which outraged middle-class reformers' (O'Gorman 1997 p.363). Place did all he could to exclude 'extremists' from the council of the NPU and the leaders of the NUWC branded him a traitor to his class (Place had originally been a tailor). It is interesting to speculate whether members would have responded willingly to the calls of men such as Place to risk their lives

for a bill which they regarded as conferring benefits on the property-owning middle class whilst offering working men very little. Probably, some would have responded and some would not since there were very different emphases within the NUWC itself. Some members took the view of the influential radical William Cobbett, who argued that the Reform Bill should be supported as the first stage in a process which might later lead to universal suffrage, while others dismissed it as a device to postpone indefinitely more sweeping change.

4. Local circumstances

Fourth, there were local circumstances which explain the intensity of protest at certain times and in certain places, and which suggest that violence was not indicative of a centrally organised revolutionary movement. For example, Bristol was in the diocese of the Bishop of Bath and Wells; the Duke of Newcastle's home was in Nottingham. Both men were outspoken in their opposition to reform. Local feeling against them explains, in part at least, why riots broke out in these towns.

5. Government strength

And fifth, there is no hard evidence to suggest that the government's commitment to maintain law and order would have crumbled. The ruthless manner in which the army cut down rioters in Bristol in October 1831 suggests that an armed uprising would have been stiffly opposed.

MAIN POINTS - Part 3

- The pressure generated by the political unions is usually seen as being at its most acute (1) in October 1831, when a wave of violent riots broke out after the Lords rejected the second Reform Bill, and (2) during the so-called 'Days of May'.
- Some historians argue that Britain was on the brink of revolution in 1831-32. Others argue that the threat of revolution was deliberately talked up by reformers to make anti-reformers back down.

- There are five main arguments in support of the view that Britain was not on the brink of revolution: (1) there was little preparation for revolution; (2) there was little class collaboration; (3) there were divisions within the protest movement; (4) outbreaks of violence depended on local circumstances; and (5) there is no evidence that soldiers could not have restored order.

Activity 5.3 The brink of revolution?

ITEM 1 A first-hand account

To attain our end, much was said that no-one really believed. Affairs never came to violence, though the danger was often threatened. In fact, often, when there was not danger, the cry of alarm was raised to keep the House of Lords and aristocracy generally in what was termed a state of wholesome terror. When some **recalcitrant** Tory attacked the Bill, when its provisions were threatened either with destruction or even mutilation, black clouds rose obedient to our call, as regularly as on the stage at the **scene-shifter**'s command. They who pulled the strings in this strange puppet show were cool-headed, determined men.

Extract from the memoirs of John Arthur Roebuck. Roebuck first published his memoirs anonymously in 1848.

Glossary
- **recalcitrant** - stubborn
- **scene-shifter** - person who moved the scenery on stage between scenes

ITEM 2 A contemporary cartoon

This cartoon was published in 1832. It shows (from the left), Earl Grey, the Duke of Wellington, Lord John Russell and William Cobbett.

ITEM 3 A historian's view (i)

Most 19th-century historians and some modern historians have argued that there was a revolutionary situation in 1831-32, and that timely concessions prevented the outbreak of revolutionary violence. But how realistic a view was this? Many historical interpretations have been greatly influenced by the rhetoric which was widely used in 1831-32. Yet, before 1832, the philosopher James Mill, writing about the tactics that should be used to achieve fundamental constitutional changes by peaceful means, had argued that concessions would only be made if the governing classes saw revolution as the only alternative to such concessions. The success of such tactics, then, depended upon the image of public feeling held by those in a position to make the concessions. Concessions would be granted, Mill said, from a fear of the consequences of withholding them. The crucial thing was to stimulate fear. When looking back at the events of 1831-32, leading radicals at least thought of themselves as having practised deception. There is John Arthur Roebuck writing in later years about the passage of the Reform Bill. He was, at the time, a close observer of the extra-parliamentary agitation in London, serving as a member of the Council of the National Political Union where he earned Place's commendation as one of the more clever, efficient and active workers. In an anonymous pamphlet published in 1848 Roebuck confessed that public feeling was often described, not as it was, but as it was meant to appear. Without denying the existence of genuine excitement, Roebuck does suggest that any belief that the people generally were in a revolutionary posture was the result of exaggeration and misinterpretation about the extent and intensity of public feelings.

Adapted from Hamburger 1963.

ITEM 4 A historian's view (ii)

Joseph Hamburger claims that the middle-class reformers were engaged in an extravagant form of bluff. They played up the extent of national support and exaggerated its violent potential in an effort to force the Bill through a reluctant Parliament. There never was a real threat of revolution - 'the professional reformer, like the public relations man,' Hamburger claims, 'dealt in images'. Other historians have found this a compelling analysis. D.G. Wright declares Hamburger's to be 'a brilliant book', but there are problems in accepting this view. As both government and reformers alike were aware, the popular movement always carried with it the threat of violent confrontation with the authorities. This had been the case in 1815-20 and, from this experience, working-class reformers knew what to expect from an anti-reform government under Wellington. Far from massaging images and manipulating figures of attendance at reform meetings, the middle-class leaders of the campaign were 'riding the tiger' in relation to their working-class rank and file. The working community possessed, by this time, a tradition of political activity and also a political programme far more radical than that envisaged by men like Place and Attwood. The crucial problem for the middle-class radicals was not the creation of false images to frighten the government, but rather retaining the leadership of a mass-based movement and directing it towards a moderate reform of Parliament. Riding the tiger is an exhilarating activity, but the rider is never totally in charge since the tiger has a mind of its own and can turn.

Adapted from Behagg 1991 and 1995.

ITEM 5 On the eve of revolution?

This picture shows the meeting of the Birmingham Political Union on Newhall Hill in May 1832.

Questions

1. a) Summarise in your own words the point being made by John Arthur Roebuck in Item 1.
   b) What does it tell us about the likelihood of revolution in 1831-32?

2. a) What point is being made by the cartoon in Item 2?
   b) Is it an accurate representation of the position taken by different shades of opinion? Explain your answer.

3. Comment on how Item 3 uses arguments given in Item 1.

4. In what ways does Behagg's interpretation of the Reform Crisis, in Item 4, differ from that put forward by Hamburger in 3?

5. Look at Item 5. Do you agree that Britain was on the verge of revolution in May 1832? Give reasons for your answer.

4 The consequences of the Great Reform Act

Key issues

1. To what extent did the Reform Act really change British politics?

2. What were the continuities between pre- and post-1832 politics?

3. How significant was the Great Reform Act?

4.1 The terms of the Reform Act 1832

The scheme
The Whig scheme for limited reform contained two essential elements:
- the redistribution of seats
- the remodelling and systematising of the franchise.

Both elements of reform accepted the principle that the franchise should still be based on a property qualification.

Redistribution
The 1832 Reform Act made the provisions outlined in Box 5.11.

BOX 5.11   Provisions of the 1832 Reform Act

The 1832 Reform Act made the following provisions:
- 56 boroughs (each of which had less than 2,000 inhabitants) were completely disenfranchised - they lost both MPs if they had previously sent two. This released 111 seats.
- 30 boroughs (each of which had less than 4,000 inhabitants) lost one of their MPs. This released 30 seats.
- The double borough of Weymouth and Melcombe Regis lost two of its four members.

This released 143 seats for redistribution. Mostly, these seats were assigned to the English counties and to the new industrial towns. They were assigned as follows:
- 62 seats were redistributed to English counties
- 22 new two-member boroughs were created
- 19 new single-member boroughs were created
- 5 new seats went to Wales
- 8 new seats went to Scotland
- 5 new seats went to Ireland.

Remodelling the franchise

a) Boroughs
In the boroughs, the older franchise systems were replaced by a new, uniform property qualification - the £10 householder franchise. This meant that every male over the age of 21 who occupied, either as owner or tenant, premises with an annual value of £10 was entitled to vote so long as he had been living in the property for at least one year, was up-to-date with any taxes on the property and had not received any poor relief during the previous year. Also, any man who had been entitled to vote before 1832 retained the right to vote if he lived within seven miles of the borough in which he voted.

b) Counties
The county franchise remained largely as it was. In other words, it was granted to freeholders whose property carried an annual value of 40 shillings. The 1832 Act also extended the vote to:
- certain copyholders and leaseholders of long residence
- any tenant who rented property worth at least £50 per year - the so-called 'Chandos Amendment' named after the Tory MP who proposed it as the Bill went through Parliament.

Other provisions in the Act
The 1832 Reform Act made two further important innovations. First, the Act required an official register of voters to be made and kept up-to-date. And second, polling was limited to two days.

4.2 What changes resulted from the passing of the Reform Act?

The historical debate
Just as historians have produced a number of different interpretations to explain why the 1832 Reform Act was passed, so too they have argued about the significance and extent of the changes which resulted from its passage. Many Whig historians writing later in the 19th century developed the view that the Act was an important step on the gradual road to democracy. It was, they argued, both a part and a reflection of Britain's progress towards becoming a politically stable and economically prosperous nation (it should be noted that these historians wrote with the knowledge that two further Reform Acts would be passed in 1867 and 1884).

Criticisms of the Whig interpretation
The Whig interpretation, however, has been

rejected by most recent historians. Few recent historians would agree, for example, that the 1832 Reform Act deserves the prefix 'Great'. Rather, they emphasise the powerful continuities between pre- and post-1832 politics, noting that, although there were modifications to the franchise and a redistribution of parliamentary seats, the 1832 Reform Act did little to address fundamental issues such as the degree of political control exercised by the aristocracy through managed elections and patronage. Indeed, in view of the Whigs' motives for passing the Bill (see Section 2.3 above), it is hardly surprising that many historians regard it as deliberately limited in scope - most notably in relation to the exclusion of the working class from the reformed franchise.

There is, however, little or no argument about the detail of immediate changes to the constitution introduced by the Act (these are summarised in Section 4.1 above). As the historian Robert Stewart puts it:

'The Reform Act effected certain mechanical changes in the electoral system, of which three stand out: (1) the size of the electorate was nearly doubled...and in most boroughs the new £10 householders constituted a majority; (2) there was established for the first time the principle of a uniform qualification for voters in all parts of the country, even though a distinction was made between rural and urban voters; and (3) the imbalance between southern and northern, also between urban and county, representation was partially redressed.' (Stewart 1989, pp.32-33)

The real debate, therefore, surrounds the broader significance of these changes in relation to the development of British politics in the 19th century.

4.3 Different interpretations of the 1832 Reform Act's impact

How important was the 1832 Act?

The recent debate between historians has centred on the extent to which limitations and continuities with the unreformed system mean that the Great Reform Act lacked real significance. The two lines of argument can be summarised as follows:

1. The limited change/important continuities argument

This interpretation suggests that the Great Reform Act 'tinkered' with the constitution and, in fact, changed little of fundamental importance. Continuities with the unreformed system are, therefore, emphasised, such as those outlined in Box 5.12.

BOX 5.12 Continuities after 1832

1. After 1832, overall control of the political system was still exercised essentially by the landed aristocracy and landowning influence in Parliament survived throughout the 19th century.
2. The continued power of the aristocracy can be explained by: (i) the continuation (and in some respects intensification) of electoral malpractice, (ii) the fact that there were still many quirks within the electoral system, and (iii) the costs of standing for election remained very high.
3. No Act could immediately destroy the forces of deference and family influence which had dominated the unreformed system - indeed, the Chandos Amendment, which enfranchised the tenant farmers, may have actually increased the importance of deference in determining voting behaviour.
4. Voting itself remained a public act and the continued absence of the secret ballot (until 1872) meant that bribery and intimidation could continue unchecked.
5. Sharp practice was equally evident in the new procedure of registering voters (see below).
6. There were also still significant discrepancies in the size of constituencies, and O'Gorman (1997) points out that 73 of the borough constituencies which survived the 1832 Reform Act had fewer than 500 electors and 31 possessed less than 300. This was largely because property rather than population had been the principal feature of electoral recalculation in 1832.
7. More generally, the South was still over-represented whilst the industrial North and Midlands were under-represented. The varying levels of rentals around the country also worked against the creation of what was in theory a uniform borough franchise. Where rentals were low - as in the many industrial centres - relatively few achieved the £10 qualification. For example, it is estimated that in Leeds only 5,000 people qualified to vote from a total population of 125,000 in 1832.
8. Despite the enfranchisement of urban middle-class voters, there was no sudden emergence of a new political class of industrialist MPs. Although there was a steady growth in the number of middle-class MPs from the 1840s onwards, they were not in a majority until the end of the century. Not surprisingly, this was also reflected in Cabinet positions, with one analysis by the historian Robert Stewart indicating that, of the 103 individuals who served in Cabinets between 1830 and 1866, only 14 could be said to be 'nouveaux riches'.
9. Despite changes in name, the same two political parties continued to contest power.
10. There had been no associated restructuring of the basic constitutional framework - the House of Lords and the monarchy's powers remained fully intact.

2. The significant change argument

Few historians would now challenge completely the view that there were major continuities between pre- and post- Reform Act politics. Some would, however, change the emphasis placed upon certain points and contend that, when viewed in context, the 1832 Reform Act should still be seen as a significant turning point in modern British political history. These historians point to factors like those outlined in Box 5.13.

The impact in the long term

In view of these rather static arguments perhaps the best approach to this issue is to consider any assessment of the impact of the Great Reform Act at a series of different levels. In this way, the significance of immediate changes in the franchise and distribution of parliamentary seats can, for example, be set against issues such as the Act's longer-term effects on the development of working-class political consciousness and the evolution of the British party system. In addition, it is worth distinguishing between what may be termed the intentional effects and the unintentional or indirect effects of the Reform Act. It seems clear, for example, that Grey and the other leading Whig politicians had no intention of setting Britain on a long-term road to democracy - they certainly could not predict that further reform acts would be passed and would probably have been appalled at the thought of a working-class electorate. Yet, with hindsight, it is difficult to argue against the view that the Act's passage did make resistance to subsequent reform more difficult. Equally, although the Reform Act appears to have been constructed to prevent working-class involvement in politics, its passage stimulated the development of a more coherent working-class political consciousness which was reflected in the Chartist movement of the late 1830s and 1840s (see Unit 6). It could be argued, therefore, that the real significance of the 1832 Reform Act lies in what it did not do, rather than what it did. Finally there is a case for assessing the 1832 Reform Act in the broadest possible context - something which the Victorian radical MP John Bright perhaps had in mind when he stated that 'it was not a good Bill, though it was a great Bill when it passed'. In other words, it is possible to argue that the actual terms of the Act were not as important as the simple fact and manner of its passing in the first place. The Act did create a precedent and its passage represented the first occasion when the aristocracy was forced into making political concessions as a result of extra-parliamentary pressure.

BOX 5.13 | **Significant change after 1832**

1. It was only in Westminster that the same social class held power and there is a danger of distorting the impact of the Reform Act by just considering it through the prism of parliamentary politics. After 1832, there were increased levels of political participation and activity in the localities - particularly in urban centres where key pressure group figures were often drawn from the socio-economic group enfranchised by the terms of the 1832 Act. The greater political vitality of the localities can be seen in the passage of the 1835 Municipal Corporations Act, which reformed local government, and the involvement of businessmen in initially regional and specialised extra-parliamentary protest groups such as the Anti-Corn Law League (see Unit 7). So there was both political change and changing political behaviour as a result of the Reform Act. It is a question of knowing where to locate it.
2. The increased size of the franchise - together with the new requirement for the registration of all electors - was a major stimulus to permanent party organisation at both a national and a local level. Electors often needed help in getting onto the register and soon local party agents were being appointed to provide this service. More formal party organisation and structure, both locally and nationally, led to increased party discipline and a decline in the number of independent MPs - an important feature of Britain's modern political system. In the long term, therefore, the 1832 Reform Act ensured that patronage effectively came through the political party rather than through the great families.
3. Although the Reform Act did nothing explicitly to reduce the power of the monarchy and the House of Lords, the limited role played by William IV in the crisis and the obstructionism of the House of Lords provided important lessons and bolstered arguments in favour of the primacy of the Commons.
4. The sheer fact that the Act had been passed despite fervent opposition within Parliament was in itself significant and weakened arguments in favour of resisting subsequent change on principle.

MAIN POINTS - Part 4

- The Whig scheme for limited reform contained two essential elements: (1) the redistribution of seats, and (2) the remodelling and systematising of the franchise. In addition, the Act required an official register of voters to be made and polling was limited to two days.
- Whig historians developed the view in the late 19th century that the 1832 Reform Act was an important step on the gradual road to democracy. Recent historians, however, emphasise that the Act did little to address the degree of political control exercised by the aristocracy through managed elections and patronage.
- The recent debate between historians has centred on the extent to which limitations and continuities with the unreformed system mean that the 'Great' Reform Act lacked real significance.

Activity 5.4 The significance of the 1832 Reform Act

ITEM 1 Changes introduced by the 1832 Reform Act

This chart shows how the 1832 Reform Act affected the British electoral system.

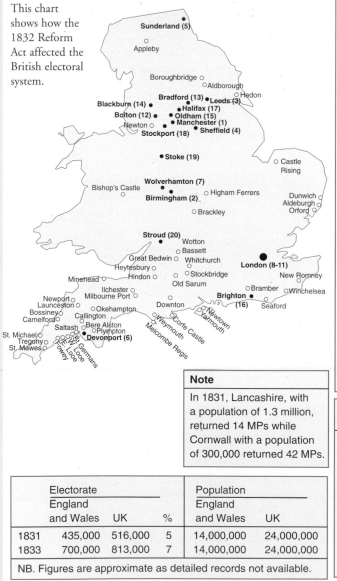

Key

New boroughs with 2 seats	Examples of new boroughs with 1 seat
1. Manchester	Ashton-under-Lyne
2. Birmingham	Bury
3. Leeds	Chatham
4. Sheffield	Cheltenham
5. Sunderland	Dudley
6. Devonport	Frome
7. Wolverhampton	Gateshead
8. Greenwich	Huddersfield
9. Finsbury	Kidderminster
10. Marylebone	Kendal
11. Lambeth	Rochdale
12. Bolton	Salford
13. Bradford	South Shields
14. Blackburn	Tynemouth
15. Oldham	Wakefield
16. Brighton	Walsall
17. Halifax	Warrington
18. Stockport	Whitby
19. Stoke-on-trent	Whitehaven
20. Stroud	Merthyr Tydfil

- Large towns with no MP before 1832 Act but two seats afterwards
- Examples of rotten boroughs which lost both seats after the Act was passed

Note

In 1831, Lancashire, with a population of 1.3 million, returned 14 MPs while Cornwall with a population of 300,000 returned 42 MPs.

Year	No. of contests	Constituencies	%
1818	93	243	38.27
1820	73	243	30.04
1826	88	243	36.21
1830	83	243	34.16
1831	75	243	30.86
1832	188	254	74.02
1835	153	254	60.24
1837	176	254	69.29
1841	138	254	54.33
1847	120	254	47.24

	Electorate				Population		
	England and Wales	UK	%		England and Wales	UK
1831	435,000	516,000	5		14,000,000	24,000,000
1833	700,000	813,000	7		14,000,000	24,000,000

NB. Figures are approximate as detailed records not available.

Adapted from Wright & Hill 1981 and Cook & Stevenson 1996.

ITEM 2 A historian's view (i)

Because it seemed to have been carried by quasi-revolutionary violence, it was easy to believe that the actual measure was revolutionary. The exaggerated hopes and fears which surrounded the Reform Bill owed much to the turbulence of its passage. Only gradually was it realised that the Act was not the subversive event it seemed in 1831. Its importance was largely psychological - it satisfied a pent-up demand for change - and the difficult obstacles that had to be overcome during the long struggle added to the sense of achievement. Divorced from its contemporary context and analysed dispassionately, the Reform Act represented no more than a clumsy but vigorous hacking at the old structure to make it a roughly more acceptable shape. Even so it was a great political achievement. A complete recasting of the electoral system would have been impossible in 1832. Inevitably, therefore, the characteristics of the old system persisted in the new. A lack of balance remained between North and South, county and borough. There were enormous differences in the size of constituencies. It is possible that, with the increased party activity and greater number of contested elections after 1832, bribery and corruption actually increased. In the smaller boroughs, family and personal control still sometimes decided the outcome of elections. Possibly only 300,000 new voters were added to the conjectural half a million of the old electorate in the United Kingdom as a whole. Of the total number of adult males no more than a seventh (a fifth in England and Wales) possessed the vote after 1832.

Adapted from Gash 1979.

ITEM 3 A historian's view (ii)

The 1832 Reform Act is legislation of prime importance and those who seek to minimise it by drawing attention to what did not change miss the point. The inescapable fact is that an unreformed Parliament willed its own downfall. The 1832 Act redrew the political map of Britain. The map was hurriedly and imperfectly redrawn, but the broad strategy was both clear and successful. Some Whigs believed a revolution to be imminent unless reform was immediately conceded. Others doubted this but agreed that the old system lacked the support necessary for government by consent. The Whigs made concessions to preserve the essentials of aristocratic government and were successful in achieving this. Those middle-class property owners whose loyalty had been in severe doubt in 1831 were detached from dangerous political entanglement with working class protest. Government based on property not only survived but was strengthened. Britain did not suffer the revolutionary upheavals which swept across Europe in the 1830s and 1840s. Chartism never had the remotest prospect of success once the middle classes had been given what they regarded as their rightful recognition by the legislature.

Adapted from Evans 1996.

ITEM 4 A historian's view (iii)

The basis of the political system had not been changed. The new House of Commons, elected in 1832, looked very much like the old one and acted in similar ways. But the urban middle class had been admitted to political life and their presence would be increasingly felt over the coming decades. This was really all that most middle-class reformers had wished to achieve - a recognition of the new middle-class 'interest' within a stable system built on the defence of property. Some, like Thomas Attwood expected a sudden change in the way the country was run. Elected MP for Birmingham in the reformed Parliament, he made no secret of his disappointment. For working people, there was only disappointment. The reforming Whigs were, after all, a party of traditional landowners. The actions of the reformed Parliament soon left those members of the working class who had campaigned for the 1832 Reform Act in no doubt that the Act had not been passed as a 'first instalment' of a wider reform of the system. The Reform Act left a legacy of bitterness. This sense of betrayal took working-class reformers back to their earlier political programme and this was now expressed in Chartism. Despite this, the Reform Bill campaign became the model which all later popular movements attempted to emulate.

Adapted from Behagg 1995.

Questions

1. a) Using Item 1, describe the changes made by the 1832 Reform Act.
   b) Is there any evidence to suggest that the system became more representative as a result of the passing of the Act?

2. Using Items 1-4, give arguments for and against the view that the passing of the 1832 Reform Bill was a significant landmark in the history of Britain.

3. a) How do the views of the three historians in Items 2-4 differ?
   b) Are there any points of agreement? Explain your answer.

References

- **Behagg (1991)** Behagg, C., *Labour and Radical Reform: Working Class Movements 1815-1914*, Hodder & Stoughton, 1991.

- **Behagg (1995)** Behagg, C., 'The government and people. Popular protest and government response 1815-32' in *Scott-Baumann (1995)*.

- **Cole & Hartley (1997)** Cole, M. & Hartley, D., '1832: an unseen advance for democracy?', *Modern History Review*, November 1997.

- **Cook & Stevenson (1996)** Cook, C. & Stevenson, J., *The Longman Handbook of Modern British History 1714-1995*, Longman, 1996.

- **Evans (1988)** Evans, E., 'The Great Reform Act reconsidered', *History Sixth*, October 1988.

- **Evans (1989)** Evans, E., *Britain before the Reform Act: Politics and Society 1815-1832*, Longman, 1989.

- **Evans (1996)** Evans, E., *The Forging of the Modern State: Early Industrial Britain 1783-1870*, Longman, 1996.

- **Gash (1979)** Gash, N., *Aristocracy and People: Britain 1815-65*, Edward Arnold, 1979.

- **Hamburger (1963)** Hamburger, J., *James Mill and the Art of Revolution*, Greenwood Press, 1963.

- **Hill & Wright (1981)** *British History 1815-1914*, Oxford University Press, 1981.

- **Hobsbawm (1977)** Hobsbawm, E., *The Age of Revolution*, Abacus, 1977.

- **Moore (1976)** Moore, D.C., *The Politics of Deference*, Hassocks, 1976.

- **O'Gorman (1989)** O'Gorman, F., *Voters, Patrons and Parties: the Unreformed Electorate of Hanoverian England, 1734-1832*, Oxford University Press, 1989.

- **O'Gorman (1997)** O'Gorman, F., *The Long Eighteenth Century: British Political and Social History 1688-1832*, Arnold, 1997.

- **Peacock (1875)** Peacock, T.L., *Melincourt*, 1875.

- **Royle (1997)** Royle, E., *Modern Britain: a Social History 1750-1997*, Arnold, 1997.

- **Rubinstein (1998)** Rubinstein, W.D., *Britain's Century: a Political and Social History 1815-1905*, Arnold, 1998.

- **Scott-Baumann (1995)** Scott-Baumann, M. (ed.), *Years of Expansion: Britain 1815-1914*, Hodder & Stoughton, 1995.

- **Stewart (1989)** Stewart, R., *Party and Politics, 1830-52*, Macmillan, 1989.

- **Thompson (1980)** Thompson, E.P., *The Making of the Working Class*, Penguin, 1980 (first published in 1963).

UNIT 6 Chartism

Timeline - Chartism

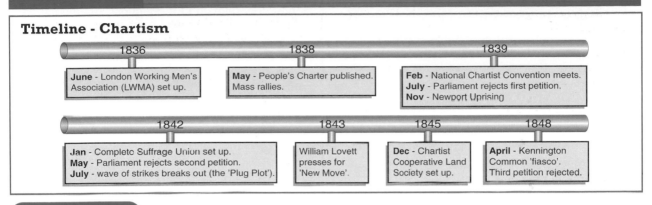

1836

June - London Working Men's Association (LWMA) set up.

1838

May - People's Charter published. Mass rallies.

1839

Feb - National Chartist Convention meets.
July - Parliament rejects first petition.
Nov - Newport Uprising

1842

Jan - Complete Suffrage Union set up.
May - Parliament rejects second petition.
July - wave of strikes breaks out (the 'Plug Plot').

1843

William Lovett presses for 'New Move'.

1845

Dec - Chartist Cooperative Land Society set up.

1848

April - Kennington Common 'fiasco'. Third petition rejected.

Introduction

Chartism - the movement which grew up in the late 1830s around the demands made in the six-point 'People's Charter' - has generated an enormous amount of historical literature and debate. Four areas are particularly controversial. First, there is the debate over the nature of the movement. Some historians argue that Chartism was a 'knife and fork question' - a movement which flared up in response to economic downturns - whilst others argue that the movement was essentially political - a movement which drew together, in a single organisation, the different strands of radical protest which had been developing in Britain since the middle of the 18th century. In essence, the focus of this debate is on whether or not there was anything fundamentally new about Chartism. To some historians, Chartism was the culmination of processes which had been taking place since the 1790s and which had resulted in the formation, for the first time, of a working-class political consciousness. Unlike the essentially localised and economically motivated bursts of popular protest which punctuated much of the period 1789-1832, those who supported Chartism in the late 1830s and 1840s did so because they recognised that it was only by uniting behind a coherent and nationally coordinated programme of political reform that working-class people would be able to exercise control over their lives. For other historians, however, this overstates the case. Chartism followed the pattern of earlier unrest, gaining support in times of economic crisis and falling away in times of economic prosperity.

Second, whilst there is no doubt that some Chartists supported 'moral force' tactics (non-violent direct action) and others supported 'physical force' tactics (direct action including the use of violence), there is a debate about how the tactics adopted influenced the effectiveness of the movement. In particular, historians are divided on how much influence physical force Chartists had and on the links between Chartists and radical protests such as the so-called 'Plug Plot'. Arguments over the role of Chartist leader Feargus O'Connor also feature in this debate. Third, whereas some historians claim that Chartism was a genuinely national movement, others dispute this, arguing that there was, in reality, a cluster of local movements which adopted the same banner but lacked any real unity. And fourth, there is a debate over the significance of the movement. Chartism failed in the short term, but most of its demands had been met by the end of the 19th century. Was this despite of or because of the agitation organised by Chartists in the late 1830s and 1840s?

UNIT SUMMARY

Part 1 starts by defining Chartism and then goes on to consider what led to the growth of the movement and how historians have explained its origins and nature.

Part 2 examines who supported Chartism and whether it was a national movement. It then looks at the tactics adopted by Chartists and how they changed over time. The final section focuses on the role of Feargus O'Connor. How important was he in the development of the movement?

Part 3 begins by exploring the reasons historians have put forward to explain Chartism's failure. It then goes on to consider what, if anything, Chartism achieved.

1 The origins and nature of Chartism

Key issues

1. What was 'Chartism'?

2. What led to the growth of the movement?

3. How have historians explained the origins and nature of Chartism?

1.1 What was 'Chartism'?

A definition

Put at its most simple, Chartism was the movement which grew up in the late 1830s around the demands made in the six-point 'People's Charter'. The 'People's Charter' was a document published in 1838 by leading members of the London Working Men's Association (a group set up in June 1836 to promote the interests of 'persons of good moral character among the industrious classes'). It made the demands outlined in Box 6.1.

BOX 6.1 **The People's Charter**

- Universal manhood suffrage - a vote for every man over the age of 21.
- A secret ballot - to protect the voter so that employers and landlords could no longer influence voting behaviour.
- Annual Parliaments - a general election every year to ensure that MPs kept in close touch with the needs and demands of their constituents.
- Abolition of property qualifications for MPs - to enable representatives from the working class to stand for election.
- Payment of MPs - to enable working men to give up their jobs in order to stand for election in the first place.
- Constituencies of equal size - to tackle the continued problem of the under-representation of industrial areas after the 1832 Reform Act.

Even the apparently simple task of defining Chartism, however, raises problems. Indeed, the definition offered above masks a complex debate between historians over what the movement actually represented and what it aimed to achieve. This is a debate which centres on the issue of whether Chartism is best seen as a social and economic movement which responded to economic hardship and deprivation, or as a political movement emerging from (and sustained by) the growing sense of working-class political consciousness after the disappointment of the 1832 Reform Act.

Origins of the debate

This debate can, in fact, be traced as far back as 1838, when a Tory Methodist and anti-Poor Law activist, the Reverend J.R. Stephens, claimed at an early Chartist meeting that the issue of electoral reform was 'a knife and fork question after all' (see Box 6.2).

BOX 6.2 **A speech made by the Revd J.R. Stephens**

Chartism was no political movement where the main question was getting the ballot...This question of universal suffrage was a knife and fork question after all; this question was a bread and cheese question and, if any man asked him what he meant by universal suffrage, he would answer that every working man in the land had the right to have a good coat to his back, a comfortable abode in which to shelter himself and his family, a good dinner on his table, and no more work than was necessary for keeping him in health, and as much wages for that life which a reasonable man could desire.

Report of a speech made by Revd J.R. Stephens to a Chartist meeting on Kersal Moor, near Manchester. The speech was reported in the Northern Star *newspaper on 29 September 1838. Stephens was a Methodist preacher and, although a leading figure in early northern Chartism, he was a supporter of the Tories. His involvement with Chartism developed initially from his opposition to the operation of the New Poor Law of 1834, which he regarded as inhumane.*

Stephens' assumption that socio-economic factors lay at the heart of Chartist protest was largely accepted by the first generation of historians to examine Chartism and then remained the orthodoxy for over a century until the work of historians such as E.P. Thompson (1980) opened up new perspectives on the ability of the working class to organise itself for political purposes. The work of Thompson and others means that there are now two main ways of interpreting the basic nature of Chartism. Each interpretation determines how questions on the origins, support, leadership, tactics and, ultimately, failure of Chartism are answered.

Two conflicting interpretations

The two conflicting interpretations are summarised below. Interpretation One represents a synthesis of the more traditional view that Chartism was indeed 'a knife and fork question' - a view first developed by R.G. Gammage (1854), writing in the mid-19th century, and subsequently developed by G.D.H. Cole (1941) and, most recently, Asa Briggs (1959). Interpretation Two is derived from the more recent work of historians such as E.P. Thompson (1980), Stedman Jones (1983), Dorothy Thompson (1984) and Royle (1996). It emphasises that Chartism was a fundamentally political movement which provided a national focus for increasingly coherent working-class protest.

Interpretation 1

According to this interpretation, Chartism only occasionally became a mass movement, and was certainly never a mass **political** movement. It was only at times when economic depression was at its most severe (in 1839, 1842 and 1848) that Chartism gained mass support. In other words, Chartism reflects 'hunger and hatred' rather than political or class consciousness.

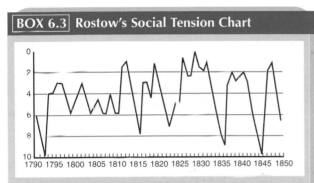

BOX 6.3 | Rostow's Social Tension Chart

In 1948 the historian W.W. Rostow developed a chart which traced the relationship between economic distress and the potential for protest. His so-called 'Social Tension Chart' used wheat prices and the trade cycle as a starting point for plotting moments of potentially high and low tension in society. On this scale, 0 represents a year of potentially very high tension when bread prices were at their highest and unemployment at its most severe, whereas 10 represents a year of potentially low tension when the opposite conditions applied. The Social Tension Chart for the period 1790-1850 is shown above.

Adapted from Rostow 1948.

Economic depression and Chartist activity

Economic factors also explain the distribution of Chartist support and the reasons for the movement's failure. Indeed, as Rostow's Social Tension Chart (see Box 6.3) demonstrates, the coincidence in the timing of economic depression and the peaks of Chartist activity are sufficiently obvious to highlight the existence of an important connection. Rostow pointed out that:

- many areas suffered during the economic depression which developed between 1837 and 1839 and it was during these years that Chartism first became a widespread movement
- similarly in 1842, the so-called 'Plug Plot' - a wave of strikes in favour of the People's Charter (see Section 2.2 below for details) - was sparked off by wage reductions resulting from the economic depression of that year and was

essentially apolitical (not political)
- the last great peak of Chartist activity, culminating in the Kennington Common 'fiasco' of April 1848 (see also Section 2.2 below) was also triggered by the economic dislocation which affected much of Europe in 1847-48.

Economic prosperity and the failure of Chartism

By way of contrast, in the more prosperous years of the mid-1840s, there was little mass support for the Charter and the movement itself lost much of its direction, fragmenting into a number of what were, in effect, regional splinter groups. Indeed, it can be argued that economic and social factors explain the geographical distribution of Chartist support and account for its regional and local diversity. Chartism was clearly at its strongest where economic hardship was at its greatest - in the decaying centres of the older handicraft industries or in some of the newer industrial towns which were dominated by a single industry (Stockport and Bolton, for example). Further, the collapse of the movement after 1848 can be said to confirm its true nature. The growth of prosperity effectively killed off Chartism by removing its essential ingredients of 'hunger and hatred'.

Interpretation 2

According to this interpretation, Chartism represents the first genuinely national political movement of the working class. In the late 1830s, it is argued, the various strands of popular protest which had been developing since the 1790s all came together and united behind a programme for political reform. Identification with the People's Charter then became, for many members of the working class, an essential ingredient of what may be described as a 'cultural experience' (Thompson 1984).

Admittedly, there was a close connection between the intensity of Chartism and economic distress, but the relationship was not as simple or mechanistic as the socio-economic interpretation (Interpretation One above) suggests. Rather, Chartism expressed the deep-seated radical belief that the economic grievances of the masses had political causes and, therefore, required political solutions - an idea, it is pointed out, which had been first advanced by Cobbett and other radical leaders after 1815 (see Unit 4). The process of working-class politicisation which had been developing since the 1790s was then completed by the exclusion of the working class from the reformed franchise in 1832 (see Unit 5). In other words, the origins of Chartism should not be sought primarily in worsening economic conditions after 1837, but in the passage of the 1832 Reform Act when the lines of political exclusion in Britain were decisively redrawn.

This view of Chartism as a fundamentally political movement can be supported in a number of different ways. Some of these are outlined in Box 6.4.

BOX 6.4 A political movement - arguments in favour

- Many Chartists had been radical campaigners before the People's Charter was drafted and remained politically active long after the final peak of Chartist protest in 1848. Chartism represented, therefore, a crucial stage in the long-term development of working-class political activity in Britain. It was certainly not the case that all Chartists were motivated by the immediate and short-term effects of economic depression.

- None of the six points were in themselves a new demand - indeed, most had been discussed at the end of the 18th century. What the Charter did was to draw together these long-standing radical demands into a single and coherent political programme. This programme can, therefore, hardly be seen as a knee-jerk reaction to immediate economic and social conditions.

- The 'hunger and hatred' view of Chartism fails to reflect the intellectual and ideological dimension of the movement. The original members of the London Working Men's Association (see Section 1.2 below) who played a key role in drafting and launching the Charter between 1836 and 1838 were not men suffering from distress but were, instead, radical and articulate artisans, convinced of the need for political reform on rational grounds.

- Although Chartism as a mass movement did disappear in the late-1840s as prosperity grew, it is too much to say that prosperity killed the movement outright, as not all Chartists abandoned the cause. In many parts of the country small groups of dedicated Chartists held together for many years after the final peak of mass activity in 1848 - some even playing a part in the parliamentary reform campaigns of the 1860s (see Section 3.2 below).

Why did historians lose sight of the political nature of Chartism?

There are three main reasons why historians lost sight of the political nature of Chartism. First, the conspicuous failure of Chartism's political strategy in 1839, 1842 and 1848 in itself did much to discredit the focus on political reform. Second, the Chartist contention that political change was an essential preliminary to meaningful social and economic change was shown to be increasingly irrelevant and unfounded. During the 1840s, a number of beneficial reforms were passed by the still unrepresentative Parliament - particularly under the Conservative administration of Sir Robert Peel between 1841 and 1846 (see Unit 7). The Mines

Act, the Ten Hours Acts, Corn Law repeal and even the dismantling of the hated Poor Law Commission were all implemented without the preliminary of a further extension of the franchise and accompanying political reforms. And third, the apparent success of the Anti-Corn Law League (see Unit 7, Section 3.2) pointed the way forward for single-issue pressure group campaigns.

Conclusion

Chartism, therefore, gave expression to a working-class political consciousness which had been growing for many years. Although it may have had economic and social undercurrents, Chartism was, from its beginning, a political movement, with political objectives, to be achieved by political means.

1.2 What led to the growth of the movement?

The birth of Chartism

Analysis of the reasons for Chartism's initial development is perhaps the area of investigation which is most closely related to the underlying debate about its character. As the historian Edward Royle puts it:

'Chartism was a product of the Industrial Revolution and, therefore, cannot be understood apart from the economic and social problems of Britain in the 1830s and 1840s, but it was also a political movement with a specific programme for radical reform. So, although economic and social circumstances must play an essential part the historian's understanding of...Chartist activity...[the historian] must also ask *why* the protest movement turned to politics.' (Royle 1996, p.6)

Five main factors have been isolated by historians in order to explain why Chartism first developed in the late 1830s. The emphasis a historian places on each factor, or group of factors, reflects their broader interpretation of the character of the movement as a whole. For example, those historians who regard Chartism as a primarily political protest movement are likely to emphasise Factors 1-4, as these suggest a clear link between the growing politicisation of the working classes after 1832 and the drafting of the People's Charter, whilst 'hunger and anger' historians are likely to emphasise Factor 5.

Factor 1. Disillusionment with the 1832 Reform Act

The 'Great' Reform Act of 1832 (see Unit 5) had conceded nothing to the working class - despite the initially widespread assumption that it would bring an end to political corruption and inequality. Some historians argue that the sense of alienation and exclusion from the political system which resulted from this created the impetus for the establishment of a more politically conscious - and exclusively working-class - protest movement. Chartism, they claim, emerged largely as a response to the 'Great Betrayal' of 1832. This was first reflected in the formation of the London Working Men's Association (LWMA) by William Lovett and others in 1836 (the LWMA was a group made up of London-based artisans who explicitly supported and decided to campaign for political representation for the working class). It was at a public meeting organised by the LWMA at the Crown and Anchor Inn in London in February 1837 that the decision was made to draw up a parliamentary Bill which, if implemented, would introduce radical electoral reform. This began the process which led to the drawing up of the People's Charter:

> 'Meetings on 31 May and 7 June between working men and the "liberal members of Parliament" led to a committee of six drawn from each group - and later, probably in December, limited to Lovett and J.A. Roebuck alone - which was then appointed to draw up a parliamentary Bill incorporating the Crown and Anchor petition. When Roebuck withdrew following his defeat at Bath in the 1837 election, it was Francis Place who did the drafting. The charter that emerged - a very moderate document that restated the traditional radical demand for universal suffrage - was essentially the work of Lovett and Place, although suggestions from the committee of twelve and from the LWMA led to revisions of the original document.' (Brown 1998, pp.51-52)

The LWMA's activities appear, in turn, to have stimulated the revival of Thomas Attwood's Birmingham Political Union (BPU) - perhaps the most prominent of the political unions involved in the agitation which preceded the passage of the Great Reform Act in 1832 (see Unit 5, Section 2.1).

Factor 2. Opposition to Whig reforms in the 1830s
Some historians argue that the working class's sense of betrayal at the hands of the middle class was heightened by the burst of legislation which followed the 1832 Reform Act (see also Unit 5). The 1833 Factory Act (which failed to secure the ten-hour working day desired by many working-class radicals) and the Poor Law Amendment Act of 1834, were interpreted as 'class legislation', clearly influenced by the interests of the newly enfranchised middle classes. The Poor Law Amendment Act, in particular, was criticised by working-class radicals because it abolished existing forms of relief and replaced them with prison-like workhouses. This, they argued, showed that the ruthless laissez-faire (anti-interventionist) approach of the commercial elite would damage rather than improve the living standards of those who remained disenfranchised. The Anti-Poor Law and Ten Hours movements which emerged in response to these laws (especially in many of the northern textile districts) provided the early 'building blocks' of Chartist activity in those regions.

Factor 3. The 'war of the unstamped'
Radical newspapers such as Cobbett's *Political Register* (the *Twopenny Trash*) and Wooler's *Black Dwarf* played a major role in the dissemination of radical ideas in the years of unrest after 1815 (see Unit 4). In response, the government introduced the Stamp Duty on Newspapers Act in 1819 which increased stamp duty on newspapers (it had first been imposed on newspapers in the 18th century) and made it compulsory for newspaper proprietors to deposit a large sum of money as security against fines. The aim of this Act was to push up the price of newspapers, making them too expensive for members of the working class to afford to them. During the 1820s, the Stamp Duty on Newspapers Act was simply ignored by a large network of publishers and printers who were, in turn, supported by thousands of street vendors, innkeepers and shopkeepers where the papers were sold. Between 1830 and 1836, however, the Whig government attempted to clamp down on the 'unstamped' press. The result was the so-called 'war of the unstamped'. Although over 700 sellers of radical journals were prosecuted, hundreds of illegal newspapers and journals were still distributed and, in 1836, the government relented, reducing the stamp duty by a penny. According to some historians the 'war of the unstamped' was important at a number of levels. First, it ensured the continued communication of radical political ideas. Second, it established local radical networks which were subsequently taken over by the Chartists. And third, it provided training for journalists and publishers in the techniques of radical communication and organisation. These techniques were later employed by Chartists. Indeed, the *Northern Star* newspaper became a vital organ of the Chartist movement and many of its journalists emerged as leading activists and speakers.

Factor 4. Attacks on trade unions
Alarmed at a wave of strikes in 1834, the Whig government decided to clamp down on trade union activity. In 1833, George Loveless, an agricultural labourer and lay Methodist preacher from Tolpuddle in Dorset, had set up a 'Friendly Society of Agricultural Labourers' to fight wage cuts. In 1834, a local JP (who had close contacts with the Home Secretary) had six of the leaders of the Friendly Society of Agricultural Labourers (including Loveless) arrested on the grounds that they had broken the 1797 Act against Unlawful Oaths. The six men were

put on trial and tried by a grand jury chaired by the Home Secretary's brother-in-law. They were convicted and sentenced to be transported to Australia for seven years (the maximum sentence). The immediate response was a wave of protest in support of the 'Tolpuddle Martyrs'. On 21 April 1834, at least 30,000 radicals and trade unionists marched through London in protest at the sentences. However, the case also sparked attempts to put a stop to trade union activity:

> 'The Oldham disturbances, which saw the impounding of trade union books and the arrest of two trade union leaders, attacks on police by the crowd, attacks upon mills and the shooting of James Bentley by those defending one of the mills, heightened tensions still further...Elsewhere, similar attempts were made to suppress trade union activity in Northamptonshire, Cheshire and Dublin.' (Laybourn 1992, p.29)

Some historians point out that this attempt to clamp down on trade union activity and the prosecution and transportation of trade union leaders during the Glasgow spinners' strike of 1837 further alienated the Whig government in the eyes of many workers.

Factor 5. The state of the economy

Historians agree that Chartism's emergence cannot be separated from worsening economic conditions after 1837. The strongest centres of early Chartist activity were those areas where distress and the impact of industrial and technological change were most acutely felt - notably Cheshire, Lancashire and the West Riding of Yorkshire. Hundreds of thousands of unemployed handloom weavers, displaced by the de-skilling effects of technological advances in the textile industry, were all too ready to join the growing bandwagon of Chartist protest in the late 1830s and 1840s.

MAIN POINTS - Part 1

- Chartism was the movement which grew up in the late 1830s around the demands made in the six-point 'People's Charter'.
- There is a debate between historians which centres on the issue of whether Chartism is best seen as a social and economic movement which responded to economic hardship and deprivation, or as a political movement emerging from (and sustained by) the growing sense of working-class political consciousness after the disappointment of the 1832 Reform Act.
- 'Hunger and hatred' historians emphasise the connection between periods of economic depression and Chartist activity. They claim that economic factors also explain the distribution of Chartist support and the reasons for the movement's failure.
- Other historians argue that Chartism gave expression to a working-class political consciousness which had been growing for many years. Although it may have had economic and social undercurrents, Chartism was, from its beginning, a political movement, with political objectives, to be achieved by political means.
- Five main factors have been isolated by historians to explain why Chartism first developed in the late1830s: (1) disillusionment with the 'Great' Reform Act, (2) opposition to Whig reforms in the 1830s, (3) the 'war of the unstamped', (4) attacks on trade unions, and (5) the state of the economy.

Activity 6.1 The origins and nature of Chartism

ITEM 1 The origins of Chartism (i)

The post-1832 Whig government resisted all demands for the more far-reaching democratic reforms supported by most radicals. Radical MPs like George Grote and Joseph Hume put forward motions for annually elected Parliaments and universal male suffrage, but the government opposed them and they attracted virtually no support in the Commons. By 1836, many radicals had become thoroughly disillusioned with the Whig government, despite its strong record of reform in many areas of government and administration. The radical MP J.A. Roebuck attacked the government as 'aristocratic in principle, democratic in pretence' and progressive members of the government such as Lord John Russell readily admitted that he and his colleagues could never fully satisfy the demands of the radical movement. As a result of this disillusionment (and, again, despite the government's notable record of reform in many areas), there emerged perhaps the best-known movement of political radicalism to be formed after the 1832 Reform Act, the Chartist movement or 'Chartism'.

Adapted from Rubinstein 1998.

ITEM 2 The origins of Chartism (ii)

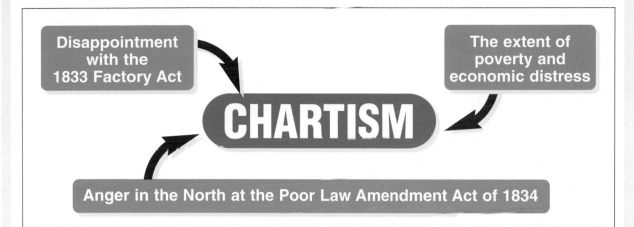

A school textbook published in 1987 claimed that the causes of the Chartist movement were those indicated above.
Adapted from Martin 1988.

ITEM 3 Historians' views on the nature of Chartism

(i) Gash's view

'Chartism' was a deceptively simple label. From small and identifiable origins, Chartism widened into a mass of activities. It floated, as it were, on a mass of working-class movements with different objectives, different philosophies, different grievances and different leaders. The Charter provided nothing new in the way of political thought. Regionalism, personality clashes, local and class rivalries were obvious weaknesses. Certainly there was much talk of fighting, but the more Chartism displayed the aggressive working-class nature of the movement, the more the middle classes doubted the fitness of the workers to exercise the parliamentary franchise. Though Chartism was, in one sense, only a continuation under another name of the old radical reform movement, what gave it contemporary importance was the great industrial depression of 1837-43. Hungry bellies filled the ranks of the Chartists. The return of economic prosperity after 1843 reduced their numbers.
Adapted from Gash 1979.

This picture shows Chartists carrying a petition to Parliament in 1842.

(ii) Evans's view

None of the Chartists' six points was new and all were political demands. Chartists wanted a say in how Britain was governed. They believed (like the radicals before them) that the cause of their distress was 'misgovernment'. The government was in the hands of an unelected (many members of the government sat in the House of Lords), unrepresentative land-owning elite. Chartists believed that landowners used powers to advance their own interests. Until 1832, the radical cause enjoyed considerable support among the middle classes. As a result of the 1832 Reform Act, however, working-class people were isolated. Overwhelmingly, Chartism was a movement of the working class and Chartists sought political solutions to their problems. They believed that a democratically elected government would not tax the poor, would not be corrupt and would not take the country to war. In part of the Revd Stephens' famous speech which is not often quoted, he shows how working people craved freedom and their just rights. Universal male suffrage was the means for a man to claim 'the right to have a good coat to his back, a comfortable abode to shelter himself and his family, a good dinner on the table and no more work than was necessary for keeping him in health'. Political struggle was the only route to material advancement.
Adapted from Evans 1999.

2 Tactics, supporters and leaders

Key issues

1. What tactics did the Chartists adopt?
2. How did the aims and tactics of the movement change over time?
3. Who were the Chartists?
4. Was Chartism a national movement?
5. How important was the role of Feargus O'Connor in the development of Chartism?

2.1 Chartist tactics - the first phase

Growing agitation in 1837

The People's Charter was not finally published until May 1838. The period between the LWMA's meeting at the Crown and Anchor Inn in February 1837 and the publication of the People's Charter saw two important developments.

First, the revival and activity of the Birmingham Political Union (BPU) was particularly significant. At first, the leader of the BPU, Thomas Attwood, refused to cooperate with the LWMA or to demand universal male suffrage. Instead, the tactic was to appeal directly to the Whig government for further limited electoral reform. A deputation from the BPU met the Prime Minister, Lord Melbourne, in June 1837 but nothing resulted from it. Support for the BPU declined after June, and in December the BPU publicly announced its conversion to universal male suffrage and its willingness to cooperate with other radical groups. According to Behagg:

'With Attwood's change of heart, working people flocked to join the BPU in the early months of 1838. Its Political Council, which still consisted entirely of middle-class men, came up with the idea of a national petition for parliamentary reform, rather than the series of local petitions that had been tried in earlier campaigns.' (Behagg

1991, p.48) And second, in November 1837, the militant Chartist leader, Feargus O'Connor (see Box 6.5), started to produce a radical newspaper, the *Northern Star*. In April 1838 he brought radical groups in northern England together in the Great Northern Union, an organisation based in Leeds.

BOX 6.5 Feargus O'Connor

Feargus O'Connor (1796-1855) was born in County Cork, Ireland. He trained as a lawyer and was a political activist from the early 1820s. He was elected as an Irish MP in 1832 and moved to London the following year. Unseated in 1835, he remained in England. He was a brilliant speaker and agitator who travelled thousands of miles speaking at hundreds of meetings. He inspired great loyalty and affection among the working class. In 1837, he founded the *Northern Star*, a radical newspaper which gained a mass readership and became a key means of spreading the Chartist message. O'Connor's approach alienated other Chartist leaders, especially William Lovett, but in 1841, after spending a year in prison, O'Connor became the undisputed leader of the Chartist movement. He was elected as MP for Nottingham in 1847, but Parliament's third rejection of the People's Charter in 1848 deeply affected him. In 1852, he was declared insane and he died three years later.
Adapted from Charlton 1997 and Brown 1998.

A national strategy

Following the publication of the People's Charter, a national strategy was agreed between the various groups pressing for reform (principally, the LWMA, the BPU and the Great Northern Union). A National Chartist Convention would be elected to pressurise the government into implementing the People's Charter and a national petition would be gathered to prove to the government just how widespread support was for the People's Charter.

The National Chartist Convention

The idea of a National Chartist Convention (an assembly made up of delegates elected from all parts of Britain) was not new. The term had revolutionary overtones (a 'National Convention' had proclaimed the establishment of the French Republic in September 1792) and a British National Convention had met briefly in 1793. As in 1793, views on the function of the National Chartist Convention were divided. Some Chartists saw the National Convention as an alternative Parliament whilst others saw it simply as a vehicle for pressurising Parliament into accepting the People's Charter.

The election of delegates

Delegates to the National Convention were elected at a series of mass meetings held around the country. Attendance at these meetings varied a great deal (see Box 6.6), but it should be noted that, since delegates were elected by those who attended the meetings and since many of these meetings were attended by many thousands of people, the delegates could claim to have the backing of the mass of the people. This was a challenge to the unrepresentative House of Commons. On the other hand, some regions were better represented than others. A quarter of all delegates, for example, lived in London. In addition, it was simply not practical for most working people to leave their jobs for several months whilst the work of the National Convention was carried out. As a result, most delegates were men of independent means (no women were elected) and not really representative of the mass of people:

'To leave work, travel from the provinces and sit for months in London, or Birmingham, was beyond the means of working men who formed the enormous mass meetings which elected delegates from many areas. Men of independent means, therefore, tended to be elected.

Consequently, only 24 out of the original membership of 53 were, in any sense, working men.' (Charlton 1997, p.19)

The Chartist Convention, February-May 1839

The Chartist Convention sat in London from February to May 1839 whilst the national petition was being collected (the petition was delivered to Parliament in June). During this period, important questions were raised about the status and role of the assembly. In addition to the debate over whether the National Convention should project itself as an alternative 'People's Parliament', there was the question of what tactics to adopt if Parliament rejected the People's Charter after the national petition had been presented to it. Disagreement amongst the delegates led to defections - some of the middle-class delegates (including seven of the eight members of the BPU who had been elected as delegates) went home and were replaced with more militant working-class delegates. Then, in May 1839, the National Convention agreed to move to Birmingham. In Birmingham, the National Convention issued a manifesto (see Box 6.7).

Having issued its manifesto, the National Convention called for local meetings to be held so that the rank and file could vote on the measures proposed. These meetings were to be held simultaneously in Whit week in late May. The National Convention itself adjourned until 1 July.

The rejection of the national petition

During the period when the National Convention was adjourned, the government stepped up its action against the Chartists. There were arrests in many areas and 6,000 troops were sent to the North under General Napier. Nevertheless, the government did not attempt to arrest the Chartist leadership as a whole nor did the authorities intervene to prevent

BOX 6.6 Electing delegates, 1838

From August 1838, a series of regional meetings was held to elect delegates to the National Chartist Convention that was scheduled to be held early in 1839 in London. The eight Birmingham delegates were elected at a meeting on 6 August, for example. The numbers attending fell somewhere between the 20,000 estimated by the conservative press and the inflated figure of 300,000 put forward by the *Northern Star*. The London meeting of 17 September was, by comparison, poorly attended, with a mere 15,000 in the audience. O'Connor held a meeting at Kersal Moor near Manchester, attended by 200,000, on 24 September (the meeting at which James Rayner Stephens spoke - see Box 6.2 above). At Liverpool the following day, only 5,000 people turned up. At the meeting on Hartshead Moor in the West Riding held on 15 October, an estimated 250,000 attended. The national pattern of meetings to elect delegates was patchy. In the Midlands, for example, neighbouring towns failed to send representatives to the Birmingham demonstration. Tory opponents prevented meetings at Kidderminster and Wolverhampton and rioting was narrowly avoided. Meetings at Coventry, Stratford-on-Avon and Nuneaton were poorly attended. When the Chartist Convention met in early 1839, the regions comprising Warwickshire outside Birmingham, Worcestershire and all of Staffordshire south of the Potteries contributed fewer than 20,000 signatures to the national petition.
Adapted from Brown 1998.

BOX 6.7 The Chartist manifesto of May 1839

The manifesto proposed a list of eight 'ulterior measures'. Chartists were encouraged to:
- withdraw funds from savings accounts
- convert paper money into gold
- join a 'sacred month' (ie to participate in a general strike lasting a month)
- defend their rights and constitutional privileges with arms
- elect Chartist candidates by a show of hands at the next election
- deal exclusively with Chartist tradespeople
- to struggle for nothing less than the People's Charter
- to obey all just and constitutional requests made by the National Convention.

Most of these points were purely rhetorical. Others, like the withdrawal of funds and conversion of currency, were irrelevant to the mass of Chartists who had no property and no bank accounts. The 'sacred month' was the one challenging idea. Here for the first time was a tactic relevant to the mass base of Chartism - the industrial working class.

Adapted from Charlton 1997.

BOX 6.8 The Bull Ring Riots, July 1839

On 4 July 1839 rioting broke out in the Bull Ring in Birmingham when the Mayor used a detachment of Metropolitan Police to break up a Chartist meeting. This was particularly unfortunate since the Mayor had been an early supporter of Chartism, though his enthusiasm had diminished upon his election to office. Other middle-class ex-delegates to the Convention were now local councillors and magistrates and were thus involved in the decision to use the police. Also, as local Chartists pointed out, the town's middle class had encouraged such meetings in the Bull Ring (a market place) during the Reform Bill campaign. The Convention, now sitting in Birmingham, condemned the attack in a placard composed by William Lovett, who was the Convention's Secretary, and published by its Chairman John Collins, a local tool fitter. Lovett and Collins were prosecuted for sedition and spent a year in prison for writing and publishing this placard. The rioting that followed the introduction of the hated London police lasted sporadically for a fortnight. The National Convention moved back to London.

Adapted from Behagg 1991.

the mass meetings being held during Whit week.

The National Convention reconvened on 1 July and immediately launched into a debate on whether to organise a 'sacred month' (general strike) if the petition was rejected. On 3 July a decision was reached to go ahead with a general strike, though a date was not to be set until Parliament responded to the national petition. The following day rioting broke out in the Bull Ring in Birmingham (see Box 6.8).

Parliament's response to the national petition came on 12 July when the Commons voted by 235 votes to 46 to reject the petition (more than half of the total number of MPs did not even bother to turn up to vote on the matter). This meant that it was up to the National Convention to take the initiative. At first, it decided to go ahead with a general strike in August, but a week later this decision was reversed and the initiative was lost:

'On 17 July, the Convention had voted by 13 to six to hold a "sacred month", despite letters from local associations questioning the wisdom of holding a general strike during a severe trade depression. On 24 July, however, following consultation with 63 Welsh, Scottish and English associations that only showed support from nine, and knowing of O'Connor's opposition, the Convention reversed the decision. This...left the movement without an effective strategy...and led to the dissolution of the Convention on 6 September. A truncated national holiday [general strike] was, in fact, held for three days during August 1839, but its importance mainly lay in the opportunity that it gave the government to arrest Chartist leaders in considerable numbers.' (Brown 1998, p.59)

'Moral force' v. 'Physical force' Chartism

When considering the tactics employed by the Chartists, historians have tended to follow the Victorian historian R.G. Gammage, who drew a basic distinction between what have been described as 'moral force' and 'physical force' strands within the movement. Each strand, in turn, has been associated with different leading Chartists.

The struggle between moral force and physical force Chartists first developed when the National Chartist Convention met in London between February and May 1839 (see above). As delegates debated what should happen if Parliament rejected the national petition, it became clear that there were two opposed viewpoints.

Moral force Chartism

Moral force Chartists emphasised the power of persuasion and rational debate. They supported non-violent forms of protest such as petitioning Parliament. They were willing to cooperate with the middle classes and they emphasised the importance of educating members of the working class (the idea being that, as a result of this education, members of the working class would prove themselves sufficiently responsible to be granted the right to vote). This strand is associated with leaders such as William Lovett, Thomas Attwood and Francis Place.

Physical force Chartism

'Physical force' Chartism was a term first used by Lovett to identify his opponents within the movement. Physical force Chartists argued that change could only be achieved through armed uprising. They also rejected the idea of cooperation with those who had higher social status. This strand is traditionally associated with Feargus O'Connor and George Julian Harney, but the position of O'Connor is the subject of debate. Recently, it has been suggested that it would be wrong to label him as a physical force Chartist (see Section 2.3 below).

Problems with these labels

There are three main problems with using these labels. First, the labels simplify what was, in reality, a complex picture. Whilst there clearly were important differences over the tactics that should be adopted, the position taken by some Chartist leaders varied over time or was ambiguous. Besides, it could be argued that there were many strands within the movement (see Section 2.4 below) not just two. Second, it can be argued that the labels themselves are inappropriate. It has been noted in Units 2-4 that radicals often used the threat of armed force to try to persuade the authorities to give in to their demands. Many physical force Chartists were not really calling for the use of physical force. Rather they were using fiery rhetoric to press their demands. The label, therefore, gives a false impression. And third, there is the danger of using the labels to make value judgements. In simple terms, moral force Chartists are sometimes seen as 'good' and physical force Chartists as 'bad'. By supporting the use of force, it is suggested, physical force Chartists ensured that the movement failed in the period 1838-48. This interpretation, however, is open to debate.

MAIN POINTS - Section 2.1

- Following the publication of the People's Charter, it was agreed to set up a National Chartist Convention and to collect a national petition.
- Some saw the National Chartist Convention as an alternative 'People's Parliament'. Others saw it as a vehicle for pressurising Parliament into accepting the People's Charter.
- Delegates to the Convention were elected at a series of mass meetings and, therefore, could claim to have the backing of the people. This was a challenge to the unrepresentative House of Commons.
- Between February and May 1839, important questions were raised about the status and role of the National Convention. In particular, there was a debate about what to do if Parliament rejected the petition.
- When Parliament did reject the petition, the National Convention drew back from confrontation with the government (it reversed the decision to organise a month-long general strike).
- When considering Chartist tactics, historians have tended to distinguish between moral force and physical force Chartists, but the use of these labels (1) oversimplifies a complex picture, (2) gives a false impression, and (3) reflects historians' own prejudices.

Activity 6.2 The National Convention, 1839

ITEM 1 The National Convention

This drawing shows delegates in London shortly after the National Chartist Convention first convened. By the summer of 1839, the number of delegates attending meetings of the National Convention had dropped considerably due to arrests and defections.

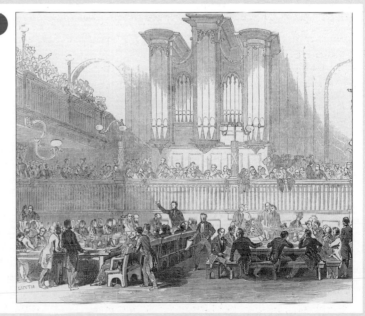

ITEM 2 Resolution of the National Chartist Convention (i)

The National Convention's resolution, 17 July 1839

That the House of Commons having refused to go into committee <u>on the prayer</u> of the national petition, it is vain to expect <u>redress</u> from the House; it is, therefore, the opinion of the National Convention that the people work no longer after the 12 August next, unless the power of voting for Members of Parliament to enable them to protect their labour and their rights is previously given and guaranteed to them.

Glossary

- **on the prayer of** - in response to the demands of
- **redress** - a favourable remedy
- **entail the bitterest privations** - result in the worst hardship

This resolution was passed by 13 votes to 6, with 5 abstentions, on 17 July 1839. The resolution was published in the Charter, a Chartist newspaper, on 21 July 1839. Note: an amendment that the general strike should start on 5 August was defeated by 20 votes to 5 (2 abstentions); an amendment that a committee be set up to examine the best time for starting the general strike was lost by the Chair's casting vote.

ITEM 3 Resolution of the National Chartist Convention (ii)

The National Convention's resolution, 24 July 1839

That this Convention continues to be unanimously of the opinion that nothing short of a general strike, or suspension of labour throughout the country, will ever suffice to re-establish the rights and liberties of the industrious classes, we nevertheless cannot take upon ourselves the responsibility of dictating the time or circumstances of such a strike...

- because our numbers have been greatly reduced by the desertion, absence and arbitrary arrest of a large portion of our members
- because great diversity of opinion prevails amongst the remaining members...
- because a similar diversity of opinion seems to prevail out of doors amongst our constituents and the working classes generally
- because, under these circumstances, it is more than doubtful whether an order from the Convention for a general holiday would be generally obeyed...
- because...a partial strike would only <u>entail the bitterest privations</u> and suffering on all parties who take part in it and...not improbably lead to confusion and anarchy...
- because...it is no part of our duty to create danger unnecessarily, either for ourselves or others...
- because we believe that the people themselves are the only fit judges of their right and readiness to strike work.

Part of a resolution carried on 24 July 1839 by 12 votes to 6 with 7 abstentions. The resolution was published in the Charter, a Chartist newspaper, on 28 July 1839.

Questions

1. What do Items 1-3 tell us about the nature of Chartism in 1839?
2. a) Using Items 1-3 and your own knowledge describe the tactics used by the Chartists in 1838-39.
   b) Why do you think these tactics were adopted?
3. Look at Items 2 and 3.
   a) Describe the events surrounding the two resolutions.
   b) Why do you think the National Chartist Convention changed its decision to organise a general strike?
   c) 'A failure of nerve on the part of the Chartist leadership'. Is that an accurate description of events in July-September 1839?

2.2 Chartist tactics - the later phases

A new phase
By September 1839, it had become clear that the tactics adopted in the first phase of Chartism had failed. Parliament had rejected the national petition and plans to organise a general strike to force Parliament to change its mind had fallen through. The tactics adopted by Chartists after September 1839 are usually divided into two categories - namely, confrontational tactics and constitutional tactics. It is significant that these two categories fit neatly with the division of the movement into two strands (ie the physical force strand and the moral force strand). In reality, however, the fit might not be as neat as it first appears.

A. Confrontational tactics
Despite all the talk of the use of force, there were only three occasions when there was the possibility that mass mobilisation might lead to a revolutionary uprising - during the Newport Rising of November 1839, during the so-called 'Plug Plot' of the summer of 1842 and at the time of the so-called Kennington Common 'fiasco' in 1848. Historians are divided about how each of these occasions should be interpreted.

The Newport Rising of November 1839
On the night of 3-4 November 1839, following weeks of careful preparation, several thousand armed ironworkers, miners from the South Wales coalfields and other workers marched in columns to the town of Newport (many thousands more waited in outlying villages for the order to advance). On their arrival, there was a delay. When they finally marched into the town, they headed for the Westgate Hotel, where they believed Chartist prisoners were being held. As they approached the hotel, soldiers read the Riot Act and then opened fire, killing more than 20 Chartists and wounding at least 50 others. An eyewitness reported:

> 'I did not see many with guns. I saw of this body two hundred or three hundred...They drew up in front of the Westgate...Then a rush was made. Then I heard firing...I could not say where the firing began...It is likely enough the firing began from the Westgate Inn.' (Part of the account given by Edward Patton at the trial of John Frost in December 1839)

This was the largest number of people to be killed in a single outbreak of civil unrest in the whole of the 19th century. The Chartists retreated in disarray and, over the next few days, many people were arrested, including the ringleaders John Frost (who had been a delegate on the National Convention), Zephaniah Williams and William Lloyd Jones. They were charged with treason and sentenced to death (their sentences were later commuted to transportation to Australia for life - to prevent them becoming Chartist martyrs).

Historians' interpretations
Historians have been divided over the significance of this action. Was it merely the expression of local grievances in a region which had experienced massive economic and social change as a result of industrialisation, or was it a trigger for what was intended to become a national uprising? Certainly, the local context was important. Three factors in particular should be mentioned. First, in April 1839, the authorities in the depressed linen manufacturing areas of mid-Wales had urged the Home Secretary to send troops to protect property. Three Metropolitan police officers were sent and, when they arrested three Chartists in Llanidloes, a crowd quickly gathered, attacked the hotel where the prisoners were held and freed them. Troops were then sent into the area and 32 arrests were made. This incident helped to polarise feelings. Second, Henry Vincent, a Chartist 'missionary' sent by the National Convention, was responsible for winning over many Welsh workers to the cause. By the autumn of 1839 there were over 25,000 paid-up Chartists in Wales, organised in over 100 lodges. Vincent's arrest in the summer of 1839 was extremely unpopular and some accounts suggest that the march on Newport was an attempt to free him (though other accounts point out that he was, in fact, being held prisoner in Monmouth). And third, it is clear that many Chartists in Wales were frustrated with the National Convention's decision not to go ahead with the general strike. Over 30,000 Chartists met at Dukestown on 12 August, the day when the 'sacred month' was supposed to start, for example, and there were many reports of drilling and the manufacture of weapons.

Historians have developed two main theories about the Newport rising. One theory is that Frost and the other leaders planned a mass demonstration in Newport rather than an armed uprising. The second is that the leaders hoped that, by taking control of Newport, they would be able to set up a Chartist republic in Wales and spark off copycat uprisings in other parts of Britain. There is evidence to support both theories (see Box 6.9). The trouble is that it is difficult to know which evidence to trust. Taking the two passages cited in Box 6.9, for example, it is clear from the first that Frost claimed in his trial that his aim was to organise a 'monster' demonstration rather than an armed uprising. However, that may have been the defence offered in the trial rather than his true motive. Similarly, although the eyewitness account reported in the Charter reveals that at least some participants thought they were participating in an armed uprising, their view may not have been representative and it may not have been shared by the leaders.

BOX 6.9 Motives for the Newport uprising

(i) The trial of John Frost

It is for you to say...whether it was an object with him [Frost] by the terror these armed men would inspire, by the force he carried with him, to seize the town of Newport and keep possession of it...The ground he takes is one of a much more moderate complexion. He says that all he intended to do was, **by showing the force of the men**, that they should be able to carry a measure of a more limited nature, the **amelioration** of **Vincent's treatment**.

An extract from the judge's summing up at the trial of John Frost in December 1839.

(ii) An eyewitness account

On Sunday night, 3 November, at about 11 o'clock, I saw Jenkin Morgan again. He came to my house and said he was captain of ten men and that I was appointed his man; he also said that Frost was on the hills and was coming down with thousands of men to attack the soldiers. He said he was coming down that night at 2 o'clock and that the Charter would be the law of the town of Newport on Monday morning...He also told me that there was to be a rising through the whole kingdom on the same night, and the same hour, and that the Charter would be the law of the land.

Part of an article published in The Chartist *on 17 November 1839.*

Glossary

- **by showing the force of the men** - ie by organising a mass demonstration
- **amelioration** - improvement
- **Vincent's treatment** - ie the way in which Henry Vincent was being treated in prison

The 'Plug Plot', 1842

The second occasion when there was the possibility that mass mobilisation might lead to a revolutionary uprising was in 1842. Significantly, like the Newport Rising, the Plug Plot followed the rejection of a national petition by Parliament. The second national Chartist petition was rejected by Parliament on 2 May 1842. A short time later, a wave of strikes swept through Britain:

'Up to 500,000 workers were involved in a series of strikes which swept across many of the industrial districts of the North and Midlands in July and August 1842. North Staffordshire coal-miners struck in July, followed by Lancashire textile-industry workers, in response to wage cuts. Mobs of strikers travelled through the country

enforcing a general stoppage by drawing out the plugs (hence the name "Plug Plot") of factory boilers, thus rendering them useless. Within weeks, the strikes had spread across the Pennines into Yorkshire and north into Scotland. By September, fifteen English and Welsh counties and eight Scottish counties were affected.' (Brown 1998, p.85)

It is the political demands made by the strikers which have interested historians. Chartists were certainly involved in the strikes and strikers adopted the People's Charter as one of their main aims (see Box 6.10). The extent and nature of Chartist involvement, however, has been the subject of considerable debate.

BOX 6.10 Extract from the memoirs of Thomas Cooper

The Plug Plot began in reductions of wages by the manufacturers....The people advanced at last, to a wild general strike, and drew the plugs so as to stop the works of the mills, and thus render labour impossible. The first meeting where the resolution was passed, 'that all labour should cease until the People's Charter became the law of the land', was held on Mottram Moor. In the course of a week, the resolution had been passed in nearly all the great towns of Lancashire.

From the memoirs of Thomas Cooper, a participant in the Plug Plot, published in 1877.

Historians' interpretations

On the one hand, some historians have argued that Chartist involvement in the Plug Plot was considerable. Max Beer, for example, claimed:

'The month of August 1842 will always be memorable in the annals of Chartism. It was the month in which the movement attained its zenith. It was the month of the general strike in the northern half of Great Britain and of the subordination of the trade unions to political Chartism...Chartist speakers were able at that time to declare without fear of contradiction or disapproval, in public meetings of trade unionists, that economic action had proven utterly ineffective and that the salvation of the people entirely depended on the passing of the Charter...A peaceful general strike was an impossibility, for the forces of government would make an attempt to suppress and to persecute the strikers, and this could only be countered by the armed opposition of the people.' (Beer 1929, pp.139, 147)

Armed opposition, Beer argues, could have brought the Chartists success, but the rank and file Chartists were let down by a lack of leadership nationally. According to this point of view, therefore, it was

Chartists who sparked the wave of strikes and the extent of Chartist involvement in the strikes was considerable. It should be noted that this view is close to that taken by Peel's government at the time. When the wave of strikes subsided at the end of August (following a good harvest and employers' agreement to cancel wage reductions), the government made it clear that it blamed Chartists for the unrest and arrested over 1,000 of them.

On the other hand, some historians have argued that Chartist involvement in the Plug Plot was opportunistic and not so significant. These historians argue that there is no clear evidence of a conscious change of Chartist tactics or a preconceived plan. Rather, the Chartists reacted to what was already happening:

'It was grassroots pressure, not Chartist "dictation", which transformed the wage disputes of 1842 into a general turnout for the Charter.' (Belchem 1996, p.85)

Historians who follow this line place emphasis on evidence that Chartist involvement in the strikes was patchy:

'Although there was some convergence of Chartist and trade union activity in Manchester, Glasgow and London, the extent to which Chartists were involved in the Plug Plot varied regionally. In Yorkshire, for example, where trade unions were weaker and less widespread than in Lancashire, local Chartists exercised strong influence over the strikers' tactics, but, generally, the Chartist leaders were too divided among themselves to take full advantage of the strike movement.' (Brown 1998, p.85)

If Chartist support was patchy and Chartist leaders were responding to events rather than initiating them, this suggests that they did not actually pose the threat the Peel government suggested they posed.

The Kennington Common 'fiasco', 1848

In 1847, Chartist leaders began organising a third petition and National Convention. This National Convention met in London in early April 1848 and planned a peaceful mass demonstration on Kennington Common for 10 April, followed by a procession to present the petition to Parliament. The National Convention also announced that, if the petition was rejected once more by Parliament, it would set itself up as an alternative 'National Assembly' and call on Queen Victoria to dissolve Parliament. The National Convention's threat provoked widespread concern among London property owners because they feared that the rally would spark revolutionary activity of the sort experienced earlier that year in Paris. The government responded rapidly by banning the planned procession (the meeting on Kennington Common was allowed, but the proposed march to

Westminster with the petition was banned), placing the Duke of Wellington in charge of the defence of the capital and swearing in thousands of special constables (see Box 6.11). When the meeting gathered, it was quickly and peacefully dispersed (largely because Chartist leaders made strong appeals to demonstrators not to defy the authorities). Although the pro-government press described this confrontation as a 'fiasco', it is clear that the government took the threat of revolution very seriously. Also, the fact that the meeting went ahead was, in some ways, a victory for the Chartists:

'O'Connor regarded the meeting as a decisive moral victory: he had insisted that the meeting went ahead and had ensured that it was peaceful; he had been able to call off the procession without any dissent...The constitutional right of assembly had been maintained and violence had been avoided.' (Brown 1998, p.109)

| BOX 6.11 | Preparations taken before the meeting at Kennington Common |

The measures of government, devised and personally worked by the Duke of Wellington were on a large and complete scale, though arranged so as not to **obtrude themselves needlessly on the view**. The Thames bridges were the main points of concentration - bodies of foot and horse police and assistant masses of special constables being posted on their approaches at either side. In the immediate neighbourhood of each of them, within call, a strong force of military was kept ready for instant movement... Two regiments of the line were kept in hand at Millbank Penitentiary; 1,200 infantry at Deptford Dockyards and 30 pieces of heavy **field ordnance** at the Tower, all ready for transport by hired steamers to any spot where serious business might threaten. At other places, also, bodies of troops were posted, out of sight, but within sudden command...and such places as the Bank of England were packed with troops and **artillery**, and strengthened with **sandbag parapets** on their walls, and timber barricading of their windows, each pierced with loop-holes for the fire of defensive **musketry**. In addition to the regular civil and military force, it is credibly estimated that at least 120,000 special constables were sworn and organised throughout the metropolis.

From the Annual Register, *an account of the year's key events, 1848.*

Glossary

- **obtrude themselves needlessly on the view** - be too obviously on show
- **field ordnance** - cannons
- **artillery** - large guns/cannons
- **sandbag parapets** - piles of sandbags placed on the top of walls
- **musketry** - rifles

Two days after the petition had arrived at Parliament, however, a select committee reported that, although the Chartists had claimed that it contained 5 million signatures, in fact only 2 million were genuine. Again, the pro-government press had a field day and Chartist credibility was severely dented. Following these events, plans for a rival National Assembly were abandoned, but there was a great deal of Chartist activity during the summer of 1848 (see Section 3.2 below).

Historians' interpretations

The traditional view of the meeting on Kennington Common in April 1848 was that it was a key confrontation which marked the end of Chartism as a significant force. Traditional accounts are highly critical of the Chartist leadership, particularly Feargus O'Connor, and suggest that the meeting effectively broke Chartism. Recent accounts, however, dispute such an interpretation. Whilst they accept that the government was determined to make the meeting on Kennington Common into a great set-piece confrontation, they do not accept that the event was a crucial turning point. Not only is there evidence that Chartist activity continued throughout the summer of 1848 (see Section 3.2 below), there is also evidence that people at the time did not think that the meeting was a turning point. The *Times* on 2 June 1848, for example, noted that:

'Chartism is neither dead nor sleeping. The snake was scotched not killed on the 10 April. The advancing spring has brought it warmth, vigour and renovation.'

Some recent accounts praise rather than condemn Chartist leaders for calming rather than inflaming passions at the meeting. Others suggest that the scale of government preparations ensured that the government was able to claim a great propaganda victory.

B. Constitutional tactics

1. The National Charter Association (NCA)

Following defeat in the first phase of Chartist activity, those who remained in the movement decided that what was needed was a permanent, central organisation which was financed by individual subscription, which encouraged as many working-class people to join as possible and which was organised along democratic lines:

'The survivors of this first phase of Chartism assessed their weaknesses, concluding that a much more efficient organisation was essential. It was in a climate of anxiety that proposals for a more structured national organisation were proffered. The outcome was the National Charter Association (NCA) inaugurated in Manchester in July 1840. Much more bureaucratic than its predecessor [ie the National Chartist

Convention], it started with a carefully drawn up 22-point constitution. In some respects, it was the first working-class political party in history. The model was a trade union one, drawn from the experience of its substantial working-class membership, with local sections (branches), standard subscription, an elected Executive Council with paid officials and the responsibility to take decisions.' (Charlton 1997, p.28)

Problems suffered by the NCA

The NCA suffered from three main problems. The first was financial. Many potential supporters could not afford to pay the subscription and some areas could not afford to send delegates to the Annual Delegate Convention - a gathering of delegates which was held each year to scrutinise the work of the Executive Council. As a result, members of the Executive Council were not paid properly and they did not always have the resources to do their job efficiently. The second was political. The NCA was dominated by Feargus O'Connor. Other leaders were reluctant to support O'Connor's lead - for example, William Lovett formed an alternative organisation (though in the long term it was by no means as popular as the NCA). And the third problem was legal. The Corresponding Societies Act of 1799 made it illegal for organisations to have branches. If local groups elected their own local officials and delegates, they would become branches and would, therefore, be illegal. During the early months of the NCA's existence, this was one of the reasons why supporters were reluctant to join (other reasons were fear of a loss of local independence and unwillingness to finance career politicians). At a meeting held in February 1841, however, a way was found round the Act. From then on, local groups elected members to a General Council. The General Council then appointed local officials and delegates. This solved the problem and membership increased rapidly from that point.

Membership

After February 1841, membership of the NCA grew rapidly and it became a genuinely mass movement:

'From February 1841 to the end of the year, the number of associations affiliated to the NCA grew from eight to nearly 300, with 20,000 members. By June 1842, there were over 400 local associations and 50,000 members, and by the autumn of 1842 when the NCA reached its peak in terms of numbers, some 70,000 membership cards had been issued.' (Brown 1998, p.81)

Although membership declined after the wave of strikes petered out in September 1842, the NCA continued to have a mass base throughout the 1840s and it remained the key national Chartist organisation.

2. National petitions

A second Chartist Convention met in London in April 1842 to present a second petition to Parliament. This was better organised than the first Convention as the election of delegates was coordinated by the National Charter Association (NCA). The petition was also better organised than in 1839, this time containing 3.3 million signatures. Once again, however, it was rejected by Parliament on 2 May 1842 - by 287 votes to 49. The organisation of a third national petition led to the Kennington Common 'fiasco' (see above) and a third rejection by Parliament. On this occasion, the petition lost credibility because Commons clerks discovered that, of the 5.7 million signatures supposedly collected, less than 2 million appeared to be genuine (see Box 6.12).

BOX 6.12 The third national petition

The hon. Member for Nottingham [Feargus O'Connor] stated, on presenting the petition, that 5,706,000 names were attached to it; but upon a most careful examination of the number of signatures in the committee room and at which examination 13 law-stationers' clerks were engaged upwards of 17 hours with the person ordinarily employed in counting the numbers appended to petitions, under the superintendence of the clerk of your committee, the number of signatures has been ascertained to be 1,975,496. It is further evident to your committee, that on numerous consecutive sheets the signatures are in one and the same handwriting. Your committee also observed the names of distinguished individuals attached to the petition, who can scarcely be supposed to **concur in its prayer**: among which occurs the name of Her Majesty, as Victoria Rex, April 1st, F.M. Duke of Wellington, Sir Robert Peel etc. etc. Your committee have also observed **in derogation of** the value of such petition, the insertion of numbers of names which are obviously fictitious, such as 'No Cheese', 'Pug Nose', 'Flat Nose'. There are others included, which your committee do not hazard offending the House and the decency of their own proceedings by reporting. It may be added that there are other signatures appended obviously belonging to the name of no human being.
From the report of the Select Committee on Public Petitions to the House of Commons on 13 April 1848.

Glossary
- **concur in its prayer** - agree with its terms
- **in derogation of** - undermining

3. The 'New Move'

The 'New Move' is the term used to describe the shift in strategy initially led by William Lovett and John Collins (see Box 6.13) after the failures of 1839 and, especially, 1842. The New Move placed an emphasis on four main areas:
- education (setting up schools for working-class children, mobile libraries and classes for adults)
- temperance (encouraging the avoidance of alcohol)
- Christianity (setting up Chartist churches and Sunday schools)
- a willingness to cooperate with members of the middle class.

BOX 6.13 Lovett, Collins and O'Connor - a historian's view

William Lovett and John Collins were both charged with sedition following the Bull Ring Riots (see Box 6.8) and sentenced to a year in prison. While in Warwick prison (a miserable experience which probably helped to shape their views), the two men wrote *Chartism: a New Organisation of the People*. Its stress on the need for education and organisation within the movement was nothing new. These had long been at the heart of radicalism. As soon as the book was published, however, it was strongly attacked in the *Northern Star* (whose editor was Feargus O'Connor). Lovett commented: 'Education was ridiculed, knowledge sneered at, facts were perverted, truth suppressed and the lowest passions and prejudices of the multitude was appealed to, to obtain a clamorous verdict against us.' Lovett's autobiography reveals that he did not understand the North. His schoolmasterly approach made little impact on Chartist supporters in the North because it had little to offer casualties of capitalism. O'Connor's public speaking, on the other hand, and his understanding of the misery and despair of industrial workers in the North allowed him to snatch the leadership of the Chartist movement out of Lovett's hands.
Adapted from Brown 1998.

In *Chartism: a New Organisation of the People*, Lovett and Collins argued that the working class could 'earn' the vote through 'respectable' behaviour. The idea was that better working-class education, meetings that took place away from the local alehouse and the founding of Chartist churches would convince the middle and upper classes that workers deserved the vote:

'Lovett and Collins argued that little had been achieved by 1840 because of working-class ignorance. What was needed was a grand scheme for moral and social reformation: self-supporting schools should be established and adult education - a particular interest of Lovett's -

would prevent the development of "vicious and intoxicating habits" and would result in self-improvement.' (Brown 1998, p.70)

In order to achieve their aims, Lovett and Brown set up the National Association of the United Kingdom for Promoting the Social and Political Improvement of the People (NAPIP) in the autumn of 1841 (it remained in existence until 1849). Membership was never higher than 500.

4. The Complete Suffrage Union (CSU)

The desire to form a radical alliance with the middle class was also the central theme of the Complete Suffrage Union (CSU). This was founded in Birmingham in January 1842 by Joseph Sturge, a Quaker corn merchant and free trader, who wished to encourage greater cooperation between Chartism and the Anti-Corn Law League (the ACLL - see Unit 7, Section 3.2). The CSU initially gained some support from middle-class dissenters who wanted greater religious equality, free trade and a more democratic franchise, but who were, at the same time, alienated by the militancy of Chartist leaders such as O'Connor. By April 1842, there were over 50 branches of the movement, and the CSU began organising its own petition to Parliament.

Collaboration between the Chartists and the largely middle-class Anti-Corn Law League, however, proved to be very difficult. This was largely because the Chartists were divided over the issue of the repeal of the Corn Laws. Some accepted the ACLL's argument that repeal would bring lower bread prices, promote exports and generally contribute to improved working-class living standards. Others suspected that lower food prices were only supported by employers as a 'back door' means of reducing costs. As soon as the Corn Laws were repealed, they argued, wages would be cut. As a result, these Chartists insisted that the repeal of the Corn Laws would only benefit workers if demands were made at the same time for further legislation to control wages and working conditions. Friction of this type and an attack on this movement by O'Connor (who argued that the CSU's approach diluted Chartism's original message) meant that the CSU did not survive beyond 1842.

5. The Land Plan

In order to hold the Chartist movement together during the difficult years of the mid-1840s, O'Connor came up with the so-called 'Land Plan' - a scheme to resettle industrial workers on smallholdings purchased by a Chartist land company. This, O'Connor argued, would tackle the problems of industrial unemployment and low wages as well as boosting individuals' self-respect. Like the ideas of Robert Owen (see Unit 8) from which the scheme was derived, O'Connor's Land Plan was designed as a means of restoring workers' independence and self-reliance.

Money for the scheme was raised by selling shares at three pence or more per week. The money raised was then used to buy land which was then divided into smallholdings. Shareholders, chosen by ballot, could then rent the land. The income received from rents would then be used to buy more land.

The scheme was organised through the Chartist Cooperative Land Society set up with NCA backing by O'Connor in December 1845. At first, it attracted considerable support and the first of five estates (later named O'Connorville, near Watford) was purchased in March 1846. However, although over £100,000 was collected from approximately 70,000 subscribers, only 250 people were ever actually settled on the two-acre allotments. This was largely due to the legal difficulties experienced by both the Society and the associated Land Bank after 1846:

'It was not a successful venture and had collapsed by 1851. It never had an administrative centre or accountancy procedures indispensable to efficient working. It was a financial disaster, with most of the participants left penniless and destitute. The scheme was subject to a parliamentary enquiry which cleared O'Connor of corruption. What neither most contemporary critics nor subsequent historians were aware of was that the government had attempted to sabotage the scheme from the start.' (Charlton 1997, p.54)

MAIN POINTS - Section 2.2

- The tactics adopted by Chartists after September 1839 are usually divided into two categories: (1) confrontational tactics, and (2) constitutional tactics. Although these categories correspond to the physical force strand and the moral force strand, in reality, the fit might not be as neat as it first appears.
- Confrontation with the authorities occurred on three occasions: (1) the Newport Rising of November 1839; (2) the Plug Plot of 1842; and (3) the

Kennington Common 'fiasco' in 1848. Historians are divided about how each of these occasions should be interpreted.
- Constitutional tactics included: (1) setting up a new permanent central organisation; (2) submitting national petitions; (3) placing an emphasis on education, temperance, Christianity and cooperation with the middle class; (4) working with the Anti-Corn Law League; and (5) organising the Land Plan.

Activity 6.3 Chartist tactics after 1839

ITEM 1 The Newport uprising

This drawing provides an artist's impression of the Newport Rising in November 1839.

ITEM 2 A physical force Chartist

This cartoon appeared in Punch *in 1848, just before the Kennington Common 'fiasco'.*

ITEM 3 William Lovett's address to the NAPIP in 1841

Our object [is] to form a general association for certain **explicit** purposes. These purposes being, first and foremost, to create and extend an **enlightened** public opinion in favour of the People's Charter among persons of all creeds, classes and opinions, by the means of missionaries, lecturers, circulating libraries, **tracts** etc. And in order to secure proper places of meeting for those purposes, we proposed a systematic and practical plan for the erecting of Public Halls for the People in every district of the kingdom, by which means our working-class brethren might be taken out of the contaminating influences of public houses and beer shops - places where many of their meetings are still held, in which their passions are inflamed, their reason drowned, their families **pauperised** and themselves **degraded** and politically enslaved. Seeing also that vast numbers of our infant population are the neglected victims of ignorance and vice...we urged on our brethren the necessity of remedying and averting those evils by adopting a Wise and General System of Education in connection with these Public Halls...As regards the best means of obtaining our Charter, we are of those who are opposed to everything in the shape of physical or violent revolution, believing that a victory would be a defeat to the just principles of democracy...We think that all that is necessary for the **carrying of the measure** is soberly and rationally to convince all classes of our population how far it is their interest to unite with us...But it is not the mere possession of the **franchise** that is to benefit our country...those who possess the power to elect must have knowledge, judgement and moral principles to direct them.

William Lovett made this speech in October 1841.

Glossary

- **explicit** - clear
- **enlightened** - informed
- **tracts** - ie the publication of pamphlets
- **pauperised** - made into paupers (ie made poor)
- **degraded** - brought low
- **carrying of the measure** - passing of the law
- **franchise** - the vote

ITEM 4 O'Connor on the New Movers

My **fustianed**, blistered and **unshorn** friends,

When a principle is once agreed upon, the safe, the sure and the speedy means of its accomplishment should be the one great and never abandoned object of its **advocates**; and, therefore, the labour which I have undertaken becomes narrowed to the simple consideration of the fact whether Church Chartism, Teetotal Chartism, Knowledge Chartism or **Household Chartism** are, each or all, or any of them, likely to be a safe, a sure and a speedy means towards the achievement of the Charter. I **contend for it** that, unless the four sections form of themselves, in the first instance, a quadruple alliance, that their four distinct and different means to an end, though that end be identical and the same, **constitute a prima facie case** against them and **is calculated to lead to sectional and party dispute**...Christian

Chartism, though apparently all-embracing, carries with it an exclusion of all other sects...I object to Teetotal Chartism because all who do not join in it, and I fear they are many, will be considered as unworthy their civil rights. I object to Knowledge Chartism because it **impliedly** acknowledges a standard of some sort of learning, education or information as a necessary qualification to entitle man to his political rights...I object to Household Chartism because it is not Chartism at all... I am anxious to see every Chartist a good Christian, a good neighbour and a good friend. I am desirous of seeing every Chartist sober, industrious and honest, full of knowledge and filling houses...But once make non-conformity grounds for exclusion and you establish sects and sections, instead of one universal **corps of regenerators**.

Part of a letter written to the Northern Star *by Feargus O'Connor on 3 April 1841.*

Glossary

- **fustianed** - 'fustian' is a type of cloth often worn by workers
- **unshorn** - bearded (many workers could not afford to shave)
- **advocates** - supporters
- **Household Chartism** - a group of Chartists who supported the vote for all householders rather than universal suffrage (ie they accepted the principle that the right to vote should be linked to ownership of property)
- **contend for it** - believe
- **constitute a prima facie case** - make an obvious case
- **is calculated to lead to sectional and party dispute** - will result in splits within the movement
- **impliedly** - by implication
- **corps of regenerators** - body of reformers

Questions

1. a) Using Items 1-4 and your own knowledge, make a list of the tactics used by the Chartists.
   b) Which tactics had the best chance of success and why?
   c) Why was the debate over tactics important?
2. a) How accurate is the portrayal of the Newport Rising shown in Item 1? Explain your answer.
   b) What does this tell us about the views of the artist?
3. Look at Item 2.
   a) Was the artist a supporter of Chartism? Explain your answer.
   b) 'Physical force Chartism was a figment of the imagination of opponents of Chartism'. To what extent do you agree with this view?
4. Look at Items 3 and 4.
   a) What are the main arguments being made in each passage?
   b) How do the views of the two men differ?
   c) What do the two passages tell us about the Chartist leadership in the early 1840s?

2.3 The role of Feargus O'Connor in the development of Chartism

O'Connor's early reputation

Until fairly recently, historians' verdicts on Feargus O'Connor were generally unfavourable. He was accused of being an egotistical and unprincipled flatterer of the masses whose refusal to work with rivals ultimately tore the movement apart. This hostile interpretation can be traced back to the writings of William Lovett, O'Connor's chief long-term rival for the overall leadership of the movement. In his memoirs, *The Life and Struggles of William Lovett*, published in 1876, Lovett blamed O'Connor for the failure of the movement in the period 1838-48, a view which was then adopted by R.G. Gammage, the first historian of the movement, who preferred the more moderate (but less popular) approach of Lovett (see Box 6.14).

O'Connor's recent reputation

Once this negative view of O'Connor had been established, it remained the standard view until the 1970s. Since 1980, however, there has been a

BOX 6.14 | Early criticisms of O'Connor

(i) William Lovett's view

I regard Fergus O'Connor as the chief **marplot** of our movement...a man who, by his personal conduct joined to his malignant influence in the *Northern Star*, has been the blight of democracy from the first moment he opened his mouth as its **professed advocate**...By his great professions, by trickery and deceit, he got the aid of the working class to establish an organ to spread their principles, which he soon converted into an instrument for destroying everything intellectual and moral in our movement...the *Northern Star*, a mere **reflex** of the nature of its master....By his constant appeals to selfishness, vanity and the mere **animal propensities** of man, he succeeded in calling up a spirit of hate, intolerance and brute feeling, previously unknown among reformers.
From Lovett 1876.

(ii) Gammage's view

To assert that he [O'Connor] possessed a mind solid and steady was to say too much, no man with an equal amount of intellect was ever more erratic. Had the solidity of his judgement been equal to his quickness of perception he would intellectually have been a great man, but this essential quality of greatness was lacked, hence his life presents a series of mistakes and contradictions...He never sought to raise the Chartist body by enlightening its members. He had no wish for that body to be anything more than a mob which should conclude every meeting with three cheers for Feargus O'Connor and the *Northern Star*.
From Gammage 1854.

Glossary

- **marplot** - troublemaker
- **professed advocate** - supposed supporter
- **reflex** - reflection
- **animal propensities** - instinctive feelings

significant reappraisal of the role of O'Connor by historians such as Thompson (1984), Saville (1990) and, in particular, Epstein (1982). These historians suggest that O'Connor was used as a scapegoat by leaders such as Lovett to cover up their own shortcomings. Without O'Connor's innovative leadership, organisational skills and oratory (public speaking), they argue, Chartism would never have developed as a genuinely national movement. Indeed, if anything, it is Lovett's conservative LWMA which should be criticised for failing to develop a more expansive strategy for the movement's development beyond the capital. Epstein argues that:

> 'As Chartism's most prominent national leader, O'Connor played a central role in maintaining the movement's radical challenge at least until 1848. He was able to unite the forces of Chartism behind his leadership. O'Connor's popularity was based on his unrivalled talents as an agitator, his brilliance as an orator, his indefatigable energy in the radical cause; but his standing within the ranks of Chartism was also founded upon the consistent and intelligent leadership which he had provided since the mid-1830s.' (Epstein 1982, pp.313-14)

The consensus among historians who agree with Epstein is that O'Connor possessed outstanding abilities as a radical leader, particularly in three areas:

- he was a powerful orator who had great skills on the radical 'platform'
- he was an innovative organiser
- he was a skilled propagandist.

1. Oratory and the radical 'platform'

O'Connor, who had trained as a lawyer in his native Ireland, first came to attention in radical circles in the early 1830s because of his flamboyant oratory. His speaking tours in the North of England in 1835 did much to mobilise widespread support for parliamentary reform. Most historians now agree that O'Connor emerged as the key successor to Henry Hunt (see Unit 4) on the radical 'platform'. Like Hunt, he adopted the almost ritualised strategy of powerfully addressing vast public meetings in a manner and tone designed to impress and intimidate the authorities. As with Hunt, this was really an elaborate form of bluff. Although O'Connor has often been described as a 'physical force' Chartist, most historians now accept that his aim was to 'mime' insurrection rather than to provoke actual violence, his hope being that the authorities would then be frightened into concession and reform.

2. Organisational innovation

Historians such as Epstein (1982) and Royle (1996) believe that O'Connor did far more than any other Chartist leader to develop the organisational structure of the movement. With hindsight, they claim, it is clear that O'Connor was the main architect of the first recognisably 'modern' pressure group. The NCA (see above, Section 2.2) was largely the work of O'Connor. Royle describes the NCA as the 'backbone' of Chartist organisation and, with its 400 branches and 50,000 members, it represented 'arguably the first national political organisation' (Cunningham 1994). The NCA was certainly dominated by O'Connor and, although Lovett set up the NAPIP (see Section 2.2 above), this had far fewer members than the NCA and had far less influence over the movement's activities.

As has already been suggested above, the Land Plan should also be mentioned in relation to

O'Connor's skills as an organiser because, despite its ultimate failure:

> 'This was O'Connor at his most visionary, and it is clear from the strength of the response over this issue that he had made contact with the aspirations of the world's first industrial working class, to an extraordinary extent.' (Behagg 1995, p.103)

3. Skills as a propagandist

The third quality O'Connor brought to the Chartist movement was his skilful use of the *Northern Star* newspaper both to spread Chartist ideas and to raise funds. O'Connor himself launched the *Northern Star* in Leeds in 1837 as an anti-Poor Law publication. It rapidly developed into the principal vehicle for the spreading of Chartist ideas across the country. At its peak it enjoyed a circulation of around 50,000 copies per issue (it was a weekly newspaper), but that figure does not show its true readership. Copies were frequently read aloud at local meetings so that even the non-literate could be kept informed of developments and ideas. Royle has no doubt about the paper's importance in the development of a national Chartist 'culture':

> 'The *Northern Star* is now regarded as probably the most important element in the Chartist organisation....it gave voice to the whole movement, reporting activities in obscure corners of the land, conveying the content of major speeches by national figures in a style intended for reading out aloud and providing a public forum for discussion of policy. Additionally, the *Star* was sufficiently profitable to fund the wider movement, enabling O'Connor to employ local reporters (often from among the unemployed or victimised) who could then, in effect, provide a semi-professional local leadership.' (Royle 1989, p.161)

O'Connor's leadership

There were three occasions when O'Connor's leadership of the Chartist movement was both crucial and controversial. His behaviour and the decisions he took on these occasions provided his opponents with ammunition they could use against him, therefore helping to shape his later reputation.

1. 1839 and the general strike

First, in the period after Parliament rejected the first national petition in 1839 (see above, Section 2.1), O'Connor's attitude towards the organisation of a general strike was crucial. Although O'Connor supported the idea of a general strike in theory, in practice he came to the conclusion that the time was not right because support was not solid enough. A general strike with only patchy support, he argued, would ruin the movement's reputation. As a result,

he opposed the organisation of a general strike in August 1839. His opposition to the general strike was enough for the National Convention to reverse its decision to go ahead with the general strike.

2. During the Plug Plot

Second, during the Plug Plot (see Section 2.2 above), O'Connor supported the strike action but he condemned those who talked of starting a revolution. On 17 August, there was a meeting of the NCA in Manchester at which a majority voted in favour of supporting the strike action:

> 'Feargus O'Connor equivocated [misled people about his true views]. Attending the Manchester meeting having opposed support for the strike, he said that he had no enthusiasm for it but voted in favour since it seemed to reflect the will of the majority. He left the Convention for London saying nothing further but subsequently repeating his charge that the strike had been fomented by Anti-Corn Law League factory masters.' (Charlton 1997, p.39)

3. Kennington Common, April 1848

Third, it was largely due to O'Connor that the meeting on Kennington Common in April 1848 remained a peaceful affair. In preparation for the meeting, the government had sworn in many thousands of special constables (the vast majority of whom were members of the middle class) as well as posting over 7,000 troops and 4,000 police officers in the area. The government accepted that a public meeting could be held, but announced that, if demonstrators attempted to march with the petition to Parliament, they would be stopped by force of arms. The Chartist leaders had a choice - to abide by the government's instructions (and risk being accused of backing down) or to ignore them (and provoke violence). O'Connor chose to abide by the government's instructions and, at the meeting, made a calming speech which did much to ensure that the crowd dispersed peacefully.

Different viewpoints

O'Connor's opponents used each of the three incidents described above as evidence of his failings. The two main charges made against him were that he was indecisive at crucial times and that he backed down whenever the government stood up to him. He was, in short, a weak leader and a hypocrite. Opponents also attacked him for being dictatorial and undemocratic.

Whilst it is possible to criticise O'Connor's leadership, it is also possible to provide arguments in support of his actions and decisions. First, concerning the general strike in 1839, O'Connor made a judgement based on consultation with local associations (see Section 2.1 above). In other words, he made a decision based on the actual circumstances prevailing at the time and there was nothing hypocritical about opposing the general strike. Far from being indecisive, his strong leadership was sufficient to ensure that the general strike was called off. Second, it is understandable that O'Connor should be ambiguous about the Plug Plot. This was not a Chartist initiative and, although the Chartists tried to exploit it, the movement was never within their control. Again, it could be argued, O'Connor took a pragmatic line and did the best he could to take advantage of circumstances beyond his control. And third, it is clear that the government was determined to have a showdown in April 1848. The fact that O'Connor was able to ensure that the meeting went ahead and did not end in violence meant that he was right to describe the day as a 'triumph'.

It should also be noted that, despite O'Connor's use of fiery rhetoric on occasion, he consistently opposed the actual use of force (further evidence that the distinction between physical force and moral force Chartists was misleading). For example, in January 1840, shortly after the Newport Rising, he wrote an editorial in the *Northern Star* making it clear that he opposed a national armed uprising. Similarly, during the Plug Plot, he opposed those who aimed to turn strike action into revolution. Thus it was consistent with past behaviour that O'Connor should choose to calm rather than inflame passions at the meeting on Kennington Common.

MAIN POINTS - Section 2.3

- Hostility towards O'Connor can be traced back to the writings of William Lovett, a rival for the Chartist leadership who blamed O'Connor for the failure of the movement. Since 1980, however, there has been a significant re-appraisal of the role of O'Connor.
- Some historians argue that O'Connor possessed outstanding abilities as a radical leader in three areas. He was (1) a powerful orator, (2) an innovative organiser, and (3) a skilled propagandist.

- There were three occasions when O'Connor's leadership of the Chartist movement was both crucial and controversial: (1) in 1839 when he opposed a general strike; (2) in 1842 when he was reluctant to become involved with the Plug Plot; and (3) in 1848 when he calmed rather than inflamed passions on Kennington Common.
- Despite O'Connor's use of fiery rhetoric on occasion, he consistently opposed the actual use of force.

Activity 6.4 Feargus O'Connor

ITEM 1 O'Connor's reputation before World War II

Feargus O'Connor was unquestionably the best-loved as well as the most-hated man in the Chartist movement. Not in one district alone, but all over England (much less, however, in either Wales or Scotland) he had an immense hold upon the people. Even amid the ruins of Chartism and the collapse of the Land Scheme in which many thousands lost their money, O'Connor kept his popularity. When, after several years in a madhouse, he died in 1855, thousands followed his body to the grave and there was mourning all over England for a lost leader. The judgment of historians has differed from the popular verdict. The vast majority of historians make it clear that they dislike O'Connor intensely. This is no doubt derived from the language used about him by colleagues such as William Lovett, whose hatred of O'Connor comes out plainly in almost every reference. It is indeed very clear that O'Connor was an impossible colleague. As an organiser and a leader he was ruined because he was unable to collaborate with others. He wanted to be boss, but he had no clear policy, especially at moments of crisis when he said first one thing and then another and always came down on what he felt likeliest to be the winning side. He was, in truth, a disastrous leader.
Adapted from Cole 1941.

ITEM 2 O'Connor's reputation today

(i) Of the importance of O'Connor as a national leader, there can be no question. He has been seen as the evil genius of the movement. In fact, so far from being the exploiter and distorter of the movement, O'Connor was so much the centre of it that, had the name Chartism not been coined, the radical movement between 1838 and 1848 must surely have been called O'Connorite radicalism. Remove him and his newspaper and the movement fragments, localises and loses its continuity. No other leader or would-be leader in those days had the energy, ability, physique or charisma of O'Connor. For good or ill, he was the main inspiration and guiding force of the movement.

Adapted from Thompson 1984.

(ii) No one matched O'Connor in the qualities demanded of a national leader. He was a superb platform speaker with a splendid presence, wonderfully racy and vivid in his language, and wildly funny both on the platform and in his writings. Many historians have seen only his boasting, the wild expression of prophecies and claims that could never be fulfilled. But much more important was the confidence that he generated among the poor and downtrodden. It was this crucial belief in the righteousness of the cause, and his ability to communicate it in unqualified terms, that allowed O'Connor to tower above his fellow Chartists.

Adapted from Saville 1990.

Feargus O'Connor

(iii) In the early history of Chartism, the central place given to the London Working Men's Association and the Birmingham Political Union is now being questioned. Instead, the LWMA is criticised for restricting the growth of Chartism in London by a policy of exclusiveness which was damaging to the development of a mass strategy in the capital. Far from having grabbed the leadership of the early movement, O'Connor is seen to have played a major role in creating it through his lecture tours in 1835 and the leading part he played in making the *Northern Star* newspaper the voice of Chartism across the county. The new picture of O'Connor which emerges is a more sympathetic one than that presented by most of his contemporaries. Through his oratory and his place on the NCA executive, and as proprietor of the *Northern Star*, he provided the Chartists with the leadership which the rank and file wanted, whatever the rival leaders may have thought.

Adapted from Royle 1989.

Questions

1. Using Items 1 and 2 describe Feargus O'Connor's strengths and weaknesses as a leader.
2. a) Describe the argument being made in Item 1.
   b) To what extent do you agree with the verdict? Explain your answer.
3. Look at Item 2.
   a) How has O'Connor's reputation changed since 1980?
   b) Did O'Connor make success for the Chartists more or less likely? Explain your answer.

2.4 Who were the Chartists?

A difficult question

There are a number of reasons why it is difficult to answer the question 'who were the Chartists?'. First, there are no membership lists or official records and so it is difficult to be sure who made up the rank and file of the movement. Second, the movement had peaks and troughs over the years and its membership was ever shifting. And third, support varied across the country as well as across time. The result is that it is even impossible to know exactly how many Chartists there were at any one time.

Despite the gaps in the record, historians have been able to build up a general picture of Chartist support. They have done this by focusing on two different but ultimately related and complementary angles:

- an occupational analysis of the groups supporting Chartism
- a geographical analysis of the distribution of Chartist support.

Drawbacks of such studies

These studies have the following drawbacks. First, the results tend to be tentative and provisional in character. Second, it is important to note that neither approach necessarily takes into account the issue of gender. Work by historians such as Dorothy Thompson (1984) suggests that women played a more prominent role in Chartist activity than previously thought:

'Their presence in the early years of the movement cannot be questioned. In opposition to the Poor Law, in the early demonstrations and processions and social organisations of all kinds they played a central part.' (Thompson 1984, p.129)

And third, these approaches do not capture the potential for what has been described as informal or fluid involvement with the movement through irregular or casual participation in mass meetings.

Occupational analysis

On three occasions (in 1839, 1842 and 1848), Chartists gathered mass petitions and presented them to Parliament in the hope that they would persuade the government to introduce legislation which adopted the People's Charter. On each occasion, the petition was considered and then rejected by the House of Commons. Parliamentary records show that the first petition had 1.2 million signatures, the second had 3 million signatures and the third had 5.5 million signatures (although a Commons committee concluded that it contained only 2 million genuine signatures). Given that the total adult population was 10 million in 1841, this shows that Chartism had mass support at these times. Other sources show that there were hundreds of thousands of active supporters during the peaks of Chartist popularity:

'From estimates of attendance at the great mass meetings in 1839 and 1848, we can safely assume hundreds of thousands of supporters. The peak sale of the *Northern Star* was registered at 50,000. Since many were sold on the streets and in the pubs, many readers were probably buying casually and not every time. Since we also know that copies were passed around many hands the readership may well have exceeded 200,000. For membership, since there are very few extant lists, we are reduced to intelligent guesswork.' (Charlton 1997, p.64)

Historians agree, however, that, despite the presence of shopkeepers, traders and small employers, Chartism was overwhelmingly a working-class movement, led by males but including a significant female membership. Whilst the evidence is still too patchy to present a systematic occupational analysis of Chartism, it is possible to draw out several broad conclusions.

With the exception of agricultural workers (21.7% of the workforce in 1841), virtually all trades appear to have been represented in Chartism - workers in the 'modern' occupations based in the factories as well as increasingly 'obsolescent' handworkers in the home-based textile industry. This point is developed in Box 6.15.

BOX 6.15 Trades which supported Chartism

Chartist support came from the home-based handloom weavers and the factory-based textile workers of South-East Lancashire and Lanarkshire in Scotland (cotton) and the West Riding of Yorkshire (wool). It also drew in the framework knitters of the East Midlands (Nottinghamshire, Derbyshire and Leicestershire) and the metal workers of Birmingham and the Black Country (the area around Wolverhampton). In all of these the typical work unit was the small workshop. Chartism was strong among the coal miners and iron workers in areas like South Wales and the North-East of England, among the pottery workers of Staffordshire and among the more traditional trades like tailoring, building and shoe-making. *Adapted from Behagg 1995.*

Textile workers - a key group

Textiles (with over 1 million workers in 1851) was Britain's largest industry and the second largest occupational sector after agriculture. Thus it is not surprising that textile workers appear to have formed the largest occupational grouping in the Chartist rank and file, with handloom weavers making up the largest group under the general heading of 'textile workers'. Both weavers and combers had experienced deteriorating living conditions as a result of the impact of technological changes and the de-skilling of their jobs had made it increasingly difficult for them to find any easy route back into the growth sectors of the economy in the later 1830s and in the 1840s.

At the same time, however, there is also evidence that considerable numbers of factory operatives - the newer occupational grouping within textiles - were a key element of the movement's support in some of the major Chartist centres such as Stockport.

Shoemakers and tailors

Shoemakers were a particularly prominent group - their control of the pace of work and lack of noise in the workplace being cited by historians as major factors in helping to promote political discussion. Tailors, like shoemakers, were members of a craft which was under severe pressure from dilution (the challenge to traditional skills through the introduction and increased use of machinery) and resultant wage cuts, and were consequently also prominent in Chartist activity.

A backward-looking movement?

The involvement of occupational groups such as handloom weavers and shoemakers has led some historians to conclude that Chartism was, in fact, essentially a backward-looking movement - its development and support being inevitably related to the last and increasingly desperate convulsions of a technologically displaced and dying breed of handcraft workers. This would fit with the argument that much of the Chartist rank and file was motivated by economic factors, above all declining living standards in the depressions of 1838-39, 1842 and 1847-48. For desperate groups like handloom weavers, the argument goes, Chartism was necessarily 'a knife and fork question'. However, the sheer diversity of occupations involved in Chartism can be used to support the view that the movement should not be seen simply as a reactive protest by deprived and decaying members of the pre- and proto-industrial workforce.

The importance of local context

Some historians have preferred to explain the nature and extent of Chartist support in terms of the specific traditions and structures of different local communities. In many places, it is argued, the intensity of support for Chartism depended on the presence of individuals and groups who had been involved in popular radical activity since the 1790s. These veteran campaigners were able to command allegiance and use their experience of previous campaigns to build support.

Geographical analysis

The historian Asa Briggs was the first to undertake a systematic analysis of Chartist support and activity region by region (Briggs 1959). He argued:

'A study of Chartism must begin with a proper appreciation of regional and local diversity. Some of the elements of diversity are measurable - rents, wages, prices, the incidence of unemployment, the degree of dependence on foreign markets. Some, however, cannot be measured quantitatively. Variations in local class structure, in the content of local grievances, in the traditions of political leadership and mass agitation, and in the adaptability and persistence of the Chartists and of their opponents require detailed investigation.' (Briggs 1959, p.2)

Briggs argued that Chartism had greater support in areas where the older systems of predominantly home-based work were located rather than in areas where the new factory system was based. However, research carried out since 1959 suggests that the size of community was more important than the system used:

'The real Chartist strongholds...were not the cities but surrounding towns and out-townships, the typical industrial communities of the manufacturing districts - the textile towns of Lancashire, Cheshire and the West Riding; the hosiery, lace and glove-making areas of the East Midlands; the depressed linen-weaving centres of Barnsley and Dundee; and the industrial villages of the mining and iron-working districts, the North East coalfield, the South Wales valleys and the Black Country.' (Belchem 1996, pp.75-76)

This point is reinforced in Box 6.16.

Was Chartism a national movement?

The apparent diversity of both the occupations and regions involved in Chartist activity has led some historians to question whether Chartism should be regarded as a national movement at all. Briggs, for example, argued that Chartism lacked any underlying sense of national unity and that it is best seen as a 'snowball' of local movements - in other words that it is better to talk about 'chartists' rather than 'Chartism'. Critics, however, have attempted to modify this view, arguing that, despite its local diversity, the national dimension to Chartism was indeed very significant. There is certainly something of a historiographical as well as historical issue here. As the historian James Epstein puts it:

'With the publication of Chartist Studies (1959), there has been a serious attempt to get back to the local roots of Chartist protest. Asa Briggs noted that a proliferation of local Chartist histories was a prerequisite to any new narrative history of Chartism. Since then, there has been such a proliferation. At its best, such local work

BOX 6.16 The geographical spread of Chartism

The real power base of Chartism lay in the three textile districts of the East Midlands, the West Riding of Yorkshire and in southern Lancashire. Within these areas, Chartism was stronger in industrial villages and medium-sized towns like Stockport and Bradford than in the major provincial centres of Manchester and Leeds. But there were other areas involved, like South Wales, the Black Country and parts of the South-West where there had been little organised radicalism before. In the first National Petition, 19,000 signatures came from London compared to 100,000 from the West Riding of Yorkshire. Mass support for Chartism in the cities only became significant in the 1840s. Support was limited in other areas. For example, Chartism's impact was limited in Ireland because of opposition from the Catholic Church and from other radical groups. Also, Chartism gained little support in areas where Wesleyan Methodism was strong. More generally, Chartism was weaker in rural areas where deference and traditional forms of protest remained strong - for example East Anglia. An exception was rural Wales, where rural workers were mainly non-conformists and, like urban workers, were opposed to English domination.

Adapted from Brown 1998.

has provided valuable insight into the character of rank and file Chartist activity; however, all too often, such studies have suffered from losing sight of a national framework to which to relate local protest. Without losing sight of the locality as the centre of activity for most Chartists, an understanding of Chartism must take into account the attempt to transcend local diversity, to create a sense of national class consciousness and to establish a national political party of the working class.' (Epstein 1982, p.2)

Many historians now share Epstein's view that there is a danger in too great an emphasis on the study of local movements and that focusing on local movements might distort the overall picture of Chartism which finally emerges. They emphasise that Chartist localities were bound together by the constant touring of national leaders, itinerant lecturers and central organisations such as the National Charter Association formed by Feargus O'Connor in 1840 (see Section 2.2 above). Also significant was the role of the Chartist press. O'Connor's *Northern Star* enjoyed a peak circulation of around 50,000 copies in 1839 and consequently did much to spread Chartist ideas and propaganda to a national audience. The view of those historians who support the idea that Chartism was a national movement can be summed up as follows:

'Diverse in composition and character, the localities were united in national protest by the press and the platform as Chartism extended the

techniques of mass agitation deployed by Hunt and the post-war radicals. Local and regional initiatives were accorded national significance through reports in the *Northern Star*, which quickly established itself as the comprehensive and definitive voice of the movement, a role which earlier radical papers had been unable to fulfil.' (Belchem 1996, p.76)

Women Chartists

Dorothy Thompson (1984) argued that there were three main reasons why women's participation in the Chartist movement has often been overlooked. First, many accounts examine Chartism as a national movement. Since no women played a leadership role at the national level, it is easy to overlook women in accounts of this sort. Second, as noted above, it is difficult to identify individual Chartists (whether male or female) and so it is easy to overlook women. And third, some historians have overlooked or downplayed the part played by women because it does not fit with their agenda. Women were particularly active in the social side of Chartism. They sewed banners and cooked food for tea parties, for example. This contribution is sometimes ignored by historians who want to portray Chartism as a serious political movement. Similarly, some feminist historians have downplayed women's contribution because the vast majority supported universal male suffrage and there is little evidence of demands for equal treatment for women.

Since the publication of Dorothy Thompson's work in 1984, more attention has been paid to female Chartists. Recent accounts have focused on three main areas:

- the role played by women
- the number of women involved
- the reaction to women's involvement.

The role played by women

There is some evidence to show that some women were involved in Chartist demonstrations:

'[Women] were reported to be in the front line against the soldiers' bayonets in the demonstration at Halifax in August 1842. There are also fleeting glimpses of women activists at Barnsley, Bradford, Sheffield, Aston, the Potteries and East London...Where action directly flowed from mass meetings, it is likely that women participated fully. This would be true of big turnouts like 1842 where young women formed a substantial part of the factory labour force in Lancashire and the Potteries...The *Northern Star* reported from Bradford in 1839: "The female radicals of the Bradford district, amounting to upward of 600, walked in procession through the principal streets headed by a band of music and banners".' (Charlton 1997, pp.67-68)

Despite this, it should be emphasised that, on the whole, the role played by women in the Chartist movement was a supportive one:

> 'As a general rule, women were much more involved in the social events than the political side of the movement. They sewed the banners and flags; they organised balls, dances and tea parties, for which they prepared food, put up displays, decorated halls and arranged speakers; they taught in Chartist chapels and Sunday schools; they raised funds by door-to-door collections and sold knitted handkerchiefs, books and other items; they acted as newsagents for the Chartist newspapers; they encouraged women to buy goods from sympathetic shopkeepers and to boycott those who were antagonistic to the Chartist cause.' (Bartley 1996, p.102)

Although around 80 female radical associations are known to have been set up in the early 1840s, there is little evidence that women demanded the vote themselves. Rather, it appears that they agreed with the national leadership that universal male suffrage should be the goal (there is some evidence that William Lovett wanted to include a demand for women's suffrage in the People's Charter but was persuaded to drop the demand on the grounds that including such a demand would delay the implementation of the whole charter). Bartley points out that:

> 'Most women who joined Female Chartists Associations were married women between the ages of 20 and 40 who had either been involved in other forms of working-class radical protest or whose husbands were engaged in Chartist activity. Many wives took an active role in furthering the Chartist movement.' (Bartley 1996, p.101)

It seems that many women supported the Chartist movement because they believed that gaining universal male suffrage would result in higher pay and better working conditions, which, in turn, would lead to better living standards. In other words, they were prepared to campaign for an extension to the male vote in the hope that the family as a whole would benefit.

The consequences of adopting such a role

June Hannam argues that the role adopted by working-class women in the Chartist movement had important long-term consequences. Following the decline of Chartist activity after 1848, working-class women were largely excluded from working-class political activity:

> 'With the failure of Chartism in the late 1840s and the increasing separation between work, family and community life, working-class women withdrew from political activism...The ideology of Chartism itself contributed to this withdrawal... Leading male Chartists encouraged and valued women's support, but the aim of the movement was to restore the traditional division of labour and sexual power between men and women in the family which, it was argued, had been disrupted by industrialisation. The ideal of a working-class family in which a male breadwinner supported his dependent wife and children, which subsequently became entrenched in the labour movement, was, therefore, encouraged by Chartism. Taylor (1983) suggests that this ideal of domesticity then hampered working-class women when new opportunities arose for them in the 1880s to take part in politics.' (Hannam 1995, p.219)

The number of women involved

It has often been suggested that, although women were active in the early years of Chartism, by the mid-1840s they were less involved:

> 'Women were prominent in early Chartism, the [consequence] of open-access protest on the streets. As the movement developed a more organised and structured form, however, women were marginalised, leaving the routine (and drink-assisted) organisational management...to the men...It was increasingly unusual for [women] to act as officers or committee members other than in specific female localities, which diminished in number in the early 1840s along with other purely female radical and democratic societies.' (Belchem 1996, p.89)

Brown (1998) points out that, as time went on, there were increasingly fewer references to women in the radical press and fewer women in the crowds. In particular, he refers to the famous photograph of the Chartist meeting on Kennington Common in April 1848 (see Box 6.17 below). This photograph, he argues, shows that the vast majority of the crowd was male (although it may be that women were congregated in a position away from the camera - after all, most of the crowd is a blur).

Bartley disagrees with the view that women became less involved in the Chartist movement in the mid-1840s. She argues:

> 'It used to be argued that as the Chartist movement became better organised and more highly structured, women became marginalised within working-class politics because they felt ill at ease in the hierarchical committees and delegations to an all-male Parliament which this entailed. However, this interpretation has been revised in recent years. After 1847, there was supposedly a revival in female Chartism and there were reports of large female attendances at Chartist rallies.' (Bartley 1996, p.102)

BOX 6.17 | The meeting on Kennington Common

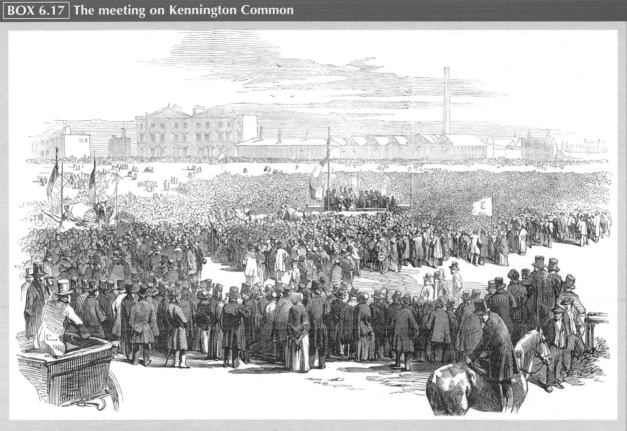

This illustration is taken from an early photograph by William Kilburn at the Chartist meeting on Kennington Common in April 1848, the only existing photograph of a Chartist meeting.

The reaction to women's involvement

Contemporary records show that the participation of women in the Chartist movement provoked a great deal of hostility from opponents. Newspapers such as the *Nottingham Mercury* and magazines such as *Punch* ridiculed women's participation in the movement and suggested that their participation somehow made the cause itself less credible. As Behagg put it:

'In the eyes of middle-class observers, women who were active in political movements were seen as particularly threatening. The presence of women in Chartism challenged accepted views of a woman's role and...singled them out for attack and ridicule.' (Behagg 1996, p.3)

MAIN POINTS - Section 2.4

- It is difficult to answer the question 'who were the Chartists?' because (1) there are no membership lists or official records, (2) membership was ever shifting and (3) support varied across the country as well as across time. There is evidence, however, that Chartism had mass support, thousands of active supporters (both men and women) and was predominantly a working-class movement.
- In terms of occupation there is evidence that, in addition to agricultural workers (21.7% of the workforce in 1841), virtually all trades appear to have been represented in Chartism.
- Support for Chartism varied from region to region. In general, the Chartist strongholds were not the cities but surrounding towns. Chartism was weak in Ireland and in rural areas (but not rural Wales).
- Most historians agree that, despite local variations, Chartism was a genuinely national movement whose activities were coordinated via the press and the public meetings called by the national leadership.
- Women generally played a supportive role, engaging in social rather than political activity. There is evidence that significant numbers were involved in the movement. Whether numbers declined in the mid-1840s is debated. The participation of women was ridiculed by opponents and used to discredit the movement.

Activity 6.5 Who were the Chartists?

ITEM 1 Delegates to the Chartist General Council, 1841

Weaver	130	Newsagent	9	Linen-weaver	5	Baker	3
Shoe-maker	97	Stonemason	9	Plasterer	5	Boot-closer	3
Tailor	58	Pitman	8	Schoolmaster	5	Bricklayer	3
Framework knitter	33	Smith	8	Twister	5	Brush-maker	3
Cordwainer	30	Silk-worker	7	Turner	5	Chair-maker	3
Labourer	19	Block-printer	7	Button-maker	4	Currier	3
Carpenter	18	Boot-maker	7	Carder	4	Engineer	3
Joiner	17	Flax-dresser	6	Cooper	4	Hairdresser	3
Wool-comber	17	Cabinet-maker	6	Fustian-cutter	4	Lace-maker	3
Boot & shoe-maker	13	Calico-printer	6	Gardener	4	Machine-maker	3
Mason	12	Cloth-dresser	6	Mechanic	4	Plumber	3
Hatter	12	Dyer	6	Moulder	4	Publican	3
Potter	11	Basket-maker	5	Nailer	4	Shipwright	3
Printer	10	Bookseller	5	Needle-finisher	4	Tinman	3
Painter	10	Grocer	5	Warper	4	Watch & clock-maker	3
Spinner	10	Glover	5	Watchmaker	4		

This table shows the occupations of those chosen to be delegates on the Chartist General Council in 1841. The Chartist General Council was a body set up because the Corresponding Societies Act of 1799 made it illegal for organisations to have branches. If local groups elected their own local officials and delegates, they would become branches and would, therefore, be illegal. To avoid this, local groups elected members to a General Council. The General Council then appointed local officials and delegates.
Adapted from Jones 1975.

ITEM 2 Centres of Chartist activity

NCA members in selected urban and manufacturing centres

Urban centres*	Population	NCA Members	Manufacturing centres**	Population	NCA Members
London	1.873m.	8,000	Merthyr	34,977	1,100
Liverpool	286,000	800	Newport (Mon.)	13,766	400
Manchester	242,983	2,800	Bilston	20,181	1,000
Birmingham	183,000	1,000-1,200	Oldham	42,595	700-900
Bristol	124,000	920	Halifax	28,000	450
Sheffield	111,090	2,000	Northampton	21,000	600
Newcastle	70,000	1,000	Loughborough	10,170	800
Bradford	67,000	1,500-1,900	Trowbridge	11,050	500
Nottingham	53,091	1,650	Aberdare	6,471	440
Leicester	53,000	3,100	Keighley	13,413	200

* Large cities (Pop. +50,000) with various industries.
** Smaller towns (Pop. -50,000) with a stronger community sense than the urban centres, one industry predominant.

The table above shows membership of the National Charter Association (NCA) in selected centres in 1842 (see Section 2.2 above for information on the NCA).
From Thompson (1984)

ITEM 3 *Punch* on female Chartists

This cartoon shows opponents of Chartism releasing rats and mice to disperse female chartists.

London is threatened with an **irruption** of female Chartists, and every man of experience is naturally alarmed, for he knows that the **VOX FEMINAE** is the **VOX DIABOLI** when it is set going...We have, however, something to propose that will easily meet the emergency. A heroine who could never run from a man would fly in dismay before an industrious flea or a burly black beetle. We only have to gather together a good supply of cockroaches with a fair sprinkling of rats, and a **muster** of mice, in order to disperse the largest and most ferocious crowd of females that was ever collected.

From Punch, 1848.

Glossary

- **irruption** eruption
- **VOX FEMINAE** - voice of women
- **VOX DIABOLI** - voice of devils
- **muster** - collection

ITEM 4 Chartism - a national movement?

(i) Harrison's view

In Birmingham the Chartist movement was at first closely allied with middle-class radicals and currency reformers. In Leeds, Owenite socialists (people who supported the views of Robert Owen - see Unit 8) combined with middle-class radicals and other militants to launch the Leeds Working Men's Association. And in other towns in the West Riding of Yorkshire and the industrial North and North-East, local movements and grievances provided a basis for Chartism. So, right from the start, Chartism was not a national movement with its headquarters in London, but a series of local and regional movements loosely federated together. This posed a problem of concerted action which was never solved. Attempts to build a national organisation repeatedly fell apart. The most effective link between Chartists was not their system of delegates to a National Convention, but the widely read newspaper the *Northern Star*. The point has been made that the British economy in the period 1830-50 was only partly industrialised. Machinery and factory organisation had been introduced unevenly. Wages, social relationships and working conditions varied. Chartism was directly related to these variations. Wherever there were large numbers of skilled artisans, organisation based on the moderate Working Men's Associations was to be expected (as in London and Birmingham). But, in areas with large numbers of distressed handloom workers (as in the West Riding), Chartism was fiercer. In Leicestershire, towns which were centres of the hosiery industry became Chartist strongholds, but in the eastern part of the county where there were practically no frames, Chartism did not develop.

Adapted from Harrison 1984.

(ii) Evans' view

Chartism had genuine national appeal. It is true that it had especially strong support in two types of community. It did well in rapidly growing industrial centres which were prone to violent swings of the economic pendulum. It has been estimated, for example, that almost half the population of Bolton was out of work in 1841. It was also strongly supported in smaller communities, especially where most handloom workers lived. In the early 19th century, handloom workers had been highly paid. From the 1830s, however, their skills were becoming redundant since mechanisation meant unskilled or semi-skilled labour could be used. Weavers were highly literate and politically aware. With shoemakers they made up the biggest occupational groups at the Chartist Convention of 1839 and in the General Council of 1841. Identifying areas of particular strength, however, does not mean that the movement was highly regionalised. The movement was never a series of loosely connected agitations. It cohered as a national whole. The leading Chartist paper, the *Northern Star*, never sold fewer than 10,000 copies per issue across the country in 1838-43, making it the highest-selling newspaper in the country. In 1839 it sold 36,000 copies per issue. The three great petitions delivered to Parliament in 1849, 1842 and 1848 were national petitions - petitions which had been gathered locally and brought together. Chartism prided itself on its organisation. For example, Chartist lecturers toured the country. In Lancashire between January and April 1841, for example, lectures were delivered by 17 different lecturers in 15 different venues. Chartism developed an effective political culture which encompassed not only the mass meeting and the packed lecture hall, but also social occasions which might involve the whole family.

Adapted from Evans 1999.

Questions

1. Who were the Chartists? Use Items 1-4 in your answer.
2. a) Judging from Items 1 and 4, why do you think Chartism was stronger in some areas than others?
   b) Give arguments for and against the view that Chartism was a national movement.
3. a) What evidence is there in Item 2 to suggest that Chartism was a predominantly working-class movement?
   b) What conclusions can be drawn from Item 2 about the type of people who joined the Chartist movement?
4. a) Who do you think the *Punch* article and cartoon in Item 3 were aimed at? Explain your answer.
   b) The date of Item 3 is important. Explain why.
   c) What are the problems with using sources like that in Item 3?
   d) Explain why Item 3 is a useful source.

3 Chartism's achievements and failures

Key issues

1. What reasons have historians put forward for Chartism's failure?

2. What, if anything, did Chartism achieve?

3.1 What reasons have historians put forward for Chartism's failure?

The debate

The debate over the reasons for Chartism's failure is, like that over its origins, central to answering the wider question of what, exactly, the nature of the movement really was. There is, therefore, a relationship between the way in which historians interpret the nature of the movement and the way in which they explain why it failed. Historians' views can be grouped together under three main headings in relation to this issue:

- Chartism failed because of economic factors - it was simply 'a knife and fork question'
- Chartism failed because of the inherent weakness of the movement and internal divisions within the movement
- Chartism did not really fail in the truest sense of the word - it was defeated by the state.

1. The 'economic factors' interpretation

Some historians (for example, Brown 1998) have argued that improving economic conditions ensured that the Chartist movement faded after 1848. The argument is as follows. Much as worsening economic conditions in the period after 1837 gave rise to the movement, so the alleged stability, growing prosperity and rising living standards of the period after 1848 removed the basis for widespread discontent. In a period of economic prosperity, Chartism could no longer be sustained.

In recent years, this interpretation of the movement's failure has been challenged. Economic historians have begun to question just how stable the British economy really was during the so-called 'Mid-Victorian Boom' of c.1850-73. Cunningham, for instance, points out that:

'Such a rise in living standards as occurred was concentrated almost exclusively in the late 1860s and early 1870s. The pattern of slump and boom continued, with particularly bad slumps in 1858 and 1866 providing a fertile breeding ground for such a movement as Chartism had been - but was no longer. In eight out of the 14 years between 1851 and 1864 real wages were at or below the level of 1850.' (Cunningham 1994, p.54)

At a more complex level, however, there is still a way of linking the fading of Chartism to economic circumstances. Rather than focusing on overall prosperity and linking that to the fading of the Chartist movement, it can be argued that a series of more subtle economic changes undermined the movement after 1848. Two changes are particularly important.

First, the development of the railways provided an important stimulus to industries such as iron, steel and coal. This meant, in turn, that economic growth was less narrowly based than in the period before 1850 when textiles had very much been the leading sector.

And second, the period after 1850 witnessed the first real impact of factory legislation - legislation which went some way towards redefining management practices and relationships in the workplace. For example, the 1850s and 1860s saw the development of a new and more moderate form of trade unionism - the so-called 'New Model Unions'. Some historians have claimed that these unions represented the interests of an emerging 'labour aristocracy' - the wealthiest 10-15% of the working class who now enjoyed superior wages and improved working conditions. Whereas this group might previously have provided the leadership for a working-class protest movement like Chartism, the increasingly favourable economic climate of the 1850s and 1860s prompted members of the group to work with employers to secure their position. Some historians have described this as the 'embourgoisement' of part of the working class (the process of adopting middle-class values). This embourgoisement, combined with the broadening of the economy, made the survival of a movement such as Chartism increasingly unlikely. Agitation (which was now organised by trade unions and Friendly Societies), now focused on gaining gradual improvements within the existing economic framework, rather than on a sweeping political victory which might change that system altogether.

2. The 'inherent weakness' interpretation

If it is accepted that Chartism was more than a 'knee-jerk' reaction to economic circumstances and that it did exhibit the characteristics of a political movement, then it is obviously difficult to explain its failure purely by looking at economic factors. A second interpretation of why Chartism faded focuses on the idea that the movement was riddled with inherent weaknesses. These included a divided leadership, regional differences and an underlying tactical naivety.

According to this interpretation, the bitter personal rivalry between O'Connor and Lovett made the divisions within the movement over strategy and tactics much worse. The basic split between the moral force and the physical force approaches could not be bridged and, after 1840, the movement fragmented into what were, in effect, a series of splinter groups. This fragmentation had a regional dimension: the North of England, where O'Connor was most influential, continued to favour physical force; in Scotland, Christian Chartism became increasingly popular; and in the Midlands there was backing for Sturge's Complete Suffrage Union. The physical force element was also significant in that it alienated any lasting middle-class support for the movement.

According to this interpretation, therefore, Chartism pushed itself into a tactical corner which was predominantly of its own making. Once the government had made it clear that it would not be intimidated by the tactics of either the mass platform or petitioning, the Chartist leadership really needed to define its approach more clearly in one direction or the other, but this did not happen. The moral force 'New Move' simply accelerated the growing diversification of the movement. Physical force Chartists, on the other hand, lacked both the will and the resources to organise a mass uprising. This was evident even at the 'height' of physical force activity. The fact that 30 troops in the Westgate Hotel in Newport could defeat thousands of armed protesters highlights the weakness of even the most militant and revolutionary Chartists.

3. The 'role of the state' interpretation

Rather than looking inside the movement to explain its failure, some historians have suggested that it is more instructive to look outwards and consider the ways in which the state dealt with the Chartist threat. Historians have identified two key strategies. First, there is the conventional idea that the state used what the historian John Saville (1990) describes as its 'coercive power' to suppress (put down) the movement. The argument here is that successive British governments dealt with the Chartists in the same repressive way in which they had responded to earlier waves of popular radical protest, most notably during the 1790s and in the period 1815-20. And second, there is the argument that the reforms introduced by Peel's Conservative government between 1841 and 1846 weakened Chartism. Taking these two strategies together, it can be argued that the Chartist movement did not simply fail. Rather, it was defeated by the government's combination of repression and reform.

Repression

Repression was certainly a recurrent theme. First, more than 20 Chartists were killed during the Newport rising of November 1839 and over 500 Chartists, including leading figures such as Lovett and O'Connor, were imprisoned for part or all of the period June 1839 to June 1840. Second, Peel's government ordered large numbers of troops and special constables to restore order during the Plug Plot:

'As early as the 14th [of August 1842] troops had fired on and killed four workers in Preston. The Home Secretary, Sir James Graham, congratulated the Mayor on his courage. Graham was the resolute organiser of the forces of the state. He had the foresight to see the importance of the trades conference and gave orders for its delegates to be arrested...Graham sent a Metropolitan magistrate to Manchester to stiffen the resolve of the local authorities. The conference was broken up and five delegates were arrested...By the time of these arrests, the NCA conference was in session. It too was broken up by the troops and in all 60 delegates were arrested. Meanwhile more and more troops were pouring into the North, including a regiment withdrawn from Ireland, 500 Grenadier Guards, 36 Royal Horse Artillerymen and their field pieces sent by rail from London. All were barracked in the centre of Manchester...Once organised, the state had enough power to deal with the strike and prevent escalation into insurrection.' (Charlton 1997, pp.46-47)

Following the end of the waves of strikes, over 1,500 workers were arrested, and imprison, and transportations followed. And third, in April 1848, those Chartists who gathered for the Kennington Common meeting were confronted by 7,000 troops, 4,000 regular police constables and many thousands of special constables sworn in specially to deal with any sign of disturbance. As this list suggests, the state was undoubtedly in a strong position to exercise its control in the period 1839-48. And, given the middle-class support gained as a result of the 1832 Reform Act, some historians would argue that the state's position was stronger than during any preceding phase of radical activity.

A further reason for the strength of the state during this period was the reforms that had been made in order to strengthen security. The Metropolitan Police Act of 1829 established a police force in London (the Metropolitan Police Force). The Municipal Corporations Act of 1835 required each borough to set up a watch committee and appoint constables. The 1839 County Police Act gave JPs the power to set up rural police forces:

> 'By 1842 there were perhaps 10,000 policemen in England and Wales, and the Home Secretary grew reluctant to employ metropolitan policemen outside their own area.' (Royle 1997, p.222)

The 'coercive power' of the state was further extended by the development of technology - the growth of a national railway network allowed troops to be moved from trouble spot to trouble spot with greater flexibility and speed and early telegraphy enabled information about potential threats to public order to be communicated more rapidly.

Reform

According to some historians, the state did not just rely on repression to counter Chartism. It has been argued that Robert Peel's Conservative administration of 1841-46 also undermined Chartism's appeal by adopting a high moral tone, distancing itself from 'Old Corruption' (see Section 1.1 in Unit 5) and passing legislation which made it increasingly difficult to sustain the movement's argument that beneficial reforms could never come from an unrepresentative political system. Cunningham, for example, argues that the Peel government's decision in the period 1841-46 to reduce tariffs, to introduce reforms such as the 1842 Mines Act and to repeal the Corn Laws (see Unit 7, Part 3) meant that:

> 'Chartism found it hard to operate in this new political climate. The language which it had inherited from the radical tradition had lost its relevance. By the late 1840s, those who talked about...the Englishman's right to bear arms seemed to belong to an age which had passed...Once the state had transformed itself by a combination of repression and reform, Chartism no longer had a role to play.' (Cunningham 1994, p.56)

This argument does, however, require qualification. First, it can be argued that, rather than being seen as a cause of Chartism's failure, the 'concessions' made between 1841 and 1846 can be seen as evidence of the Chartist movement's success in drawing the ruling elite's attention to economic and social problems. In other words, it could be argued that it was Chartist pressure which stimulated the government's interest in reform in the first place. And second, there is a problem of chronology and timing. Many historians point out that support for Chartism peaked and then dropped on three occasions - in 1839, 1842 and 1848. Since the first decline in support occurred in 1839, two years before Peel became Prime Minister, the reforms made by the Peel government were irrelevant and the argument does not apply. The fact that Chartism then revived in 1842 and 1847-48, however, goes against the idea that the reforms made by the Peel government affected support for Chartism. Why would Chartism revive in 1842, the very year in which important reforms were passed (for example, the Mines Act), if the passing of reforms had created a new climate which damaged Chartism's credibility? Similarly, by 1847, Peel was out of office and the Peel government's reforms had all been made. So, if the passing of reforms really had damaged Chartism's credibility, the revival of Chartism should not have occurred.

Conclusion

In view of the emerging consensus that Chartism was, on balance, a relatively sophisticated and effective protest movement, the argument that it failed due to inherent weaknesses becomes less compelling and the idea that defeat was due to the actions taken by the state all the more so.

Other explanations

It is, of course, possible to combine different elements of these interpretations. Dorothy Thompson (1984) for example, suggests that, whilst Chartism emerged as a political response to the process of industrial change, so, paradoxically, that very same process of change helped to kill it off. Chartism, she argues, was a 'cultural' or community-based experience and, as such, it needed small communities in which workers shared common experiences to survive. However, as larger cities began to develop, so working-class communities could be more easily divided, isolated and 'socially controlled' by police, teachers and the clergy. Consequently, the changing social context of everyday working life meant that new forms of working-class organisation replaced the old-style mass politics of the radical platform - trade unionism being the best example. Thompson sums up her argument as follows:

> 'Perhaps the ethos of Chartism could anyway not

have survived into the great urban centres of the later 19th century. It needed the small communities, the slack religious and moral supervision, the unpoliced public street and meeting place...As society in Britain became increasingly polarised between a depopulated countryside and large urban centres, the unifying influence of a common living area and shared institutions lessened...Organisation moved from the home, the inn and the street to the large workshop and the trades club.' (Thompson 1984, pp.338-39)

Chartism and the Anti-Corn Law League
The failure of Chartism is also sometimes contrasted with the apparent success of the Anti-Corn Law League (ACLL) - a predominantly middle-class pressure group which emerged at almost exactly the same time as Chartism (see Unit 7, Section 3.2). At least at first sight, the Anti-Corn Law League appeared to possess a number of advantages which the Chartists lacked:

- The ACLL represented the interests of the urban middle class whose influence had already been recognised in the passage of the Great Reform Act in 1832. Chartism, on the other hand, represented those who had been deliberately - indeed cynically - excluded from the franchise. Having ignored working-class demands for political reform in 1832, the ruling elite was unlikely to listen any more favourably only seven years later. According to many commentators, the 1832 Reform Act was, after all, designed to prevent the working class gaining the vote (see Unit 5).
- The ACLL's campaign drew on the commercial wealth of its middle-class supporters and, therefore, it did not lack resources. Chartism, representing the interests of poor, unemployed and increasingly deskilled workers, was under-resourced.
- The ACLL's objective was precise and limited - the repeal of the 1815 Corn Law. Chartism could also be said to have precise objectives in the form of the six points of the People's Charter, but implementation of these six points would mean a complete restructuring of the political structure of the state.
- By pressing for free trade, the ACLL supported a policy which many MPs already supported. Chartism, on the other hand, was regarded with fear and loathing by the vast majority of MPs and by 'respectable' society.

Using this comparison, it could be argued that Chartism demanded too much, too quickly, too soon.

3.2 What, if anything, did Chartism achieve?

The traditional view
When considering the question of whether Chartism should be considered to have been a complete failure, two relatively simple responses have, in the past, tended to predominate. The first response was that Chartism did not achieve anything because the national petitions were comprehensively rejected by Parliament on three separate occasions and, following the third of those occasions in April 1848, the movement effectively disappeared altogether. The second response was to suggest that Chartism cannot have been a complete failure because five out of the six points on the People's Charter eventually became law.

Most recent accounts, however, suggest that both of these responses are seriously flawed. The following arguments are used in support of this viewpoint.

Countering the first response
In the view of most recent historians, traditional accounts of the confused and confusing events surrounding the meeting on 10 April 1848 have misinterpreted what happened and its significance. The traditional view was that the meeting on Kennington Common was a turning point. At the meeting, the Chartist leader Feargus O'Connor lost his nerve and capitulated to the authorities by ensuring that, when the meeting gathered, it was quickly and peacefully dispersed (an interpretation which fitted with the view that O'Connor was a weak leader unable to stand up to pressure). This was a turning point because the apparent capitulation to the authorities disillusioned Chartist supporters and the movement then quickly faded away.

Recent accounts have revised this view. Royle, for example, argues that:
'The myth of the 'fiasco' of 10 April...is no longer accepted. What that day entailed was not folly and cowardice by the Chartists, but an enormous propaganda victory for the government...Far from the Chartists being discredited and disillusioned, they rallied and caused further problems in June, July and August.' (Royle 1989, p.168)
As in the period after the rejection of the first and second national petitions, it seems that Chartist attitudes hardened after Parliament rejected the third national petition. Whereas, in 1839, this led to the Newport Rising and, in 1842, this encouraged Chartist involvement in the Plug Plot, the authorities were able to prevent any serious outbreak of violence in 1848. The threat of violence in the spring and summer of 1848, however, was real (see Box 6.18). By the end of the year, however, the

authorities had managed to restore control and Chartism never re-emerged as a mass movement, although small groups of Chartists did continue to struggle for the People's Charter for another decade.

Countering the second response

Most historians now agree that the second response - that Chartism was not a complete failure because five of the six points eventually became law by 1918 - misses the point. There is a specific context which explains why and when each of these changes was introduced. None of these specific contexts is directly related to activities of the Chartists themselves. Rather, it is hindsight which encourages a link to be made:

'It is only hindsight, with its attendant dangers, which permits us to trace these links to the future. The five points were achieved not because the Chartists had voiced them: rather they were conceded by a state which had defeated Chartism with a mixture of stick and carrot, and which no longer felt threatened.' (Cunningham 1994, p.57)

As a result, historians such as Thompson (1984),

Royle (1989), Saville (1990) and Brown (1998) have developed an alternative perspective on the issue of Chartism's longer-term significance. They argue that the importance of Chartism is not to be found in any concrete achievement but, rather, in the psychological impact of its very existence. The fact that the movement had been created and had survived for so long in such difficult circumstances left a legacy of hope and confidence within working-class communities which was, in turn, to inspire further and ultimately more successful attempts at protest towards the end of the 19th century. Although, as has been suggested, this is a view which is characteristic of those writing in the 1980s and 1990s, it was, in fact, first developed as early as 1920 by the historian Julius West, who argued that

'The Chartist movement was the first organised effort to stir up class consciousness on a national scale. Judged by its crop of statutes and statues, Chartism was a failure. Judged by its essential and generally overlooked purpose, Chartism was a success. It achieved not the six points, but a state of mind.' (West 1920, pp.294-95)

BOX 6.18 Chartist activity after April 1848

The spring and summer of 1848 saw a great deal of activity - arrests, trials and several riots - being played out against the background of imminent revolution in Ireland. The most serious problems facing the government in late May and early June came from Bradford and Liverpool. The open drilling of men spread to Leeds and Halifax. Halifax Chartists attended meetings with 'glistening pikes flashing in the sun'. Matters came to a head on 29 May when the botched arrest of two local Chartist leaders led to street violence which the Bradford police eventually brought under control. In London the police broke up meetings in the East End on 4 June and a day of protest was called for 12 June. The government responded with a heavy display of force. The hostility of the press and the willingness of the courts to convict Chartists helped the government's repression of the movement. News from Ireland pushed some Chartists towards revolution. Government informers were pessimistic. They detected moves towards greater secrecy in Irish and Chartist circles and reported that northern England would rise if there was an uprising in Ireland. The August 'conspiracy' was the government's response - a government informer infiltrated local radical groups in London, as a result of which their leaders were arrested on charges of conspiracy. The events at Kennington Common were not seen as marking an end of the movement at the time, nor was it a decisive date. Perhaps the end of the year has a greater claim to that. By then, Chartist leaders were in prison, the Land Company was in difficulty and the year of revolutions in Europe had ended, not with the creation of democracy, but with the reassertion of traditional authority. As in 1838 and 1842, Chartism had been contained from without and critically weakened from within. As a mass movement, it was over.

Adapted from Brown 1998.

MAIN POINTS - Part 3

- Historians have provided three main explanations for Chartism's failure - (1) Chartism failed because of economic factors, (2) Chartism failed because of the inherent weakness of the movement, and (3) Chartism did not really fail in the truest sense of the word - it was defeated by the state.
- Thompson (1984) suggests that, whilst Chartism emerged as a political response to the process of industrial change, so, paradoxically, that very same process of change helped to kill it off.
- A comparison with the ACLL suggests that Chartism may have demanded too much, too quickly, too soon.
- When assessing Chartism's achievements, the traditional view was either (1) that Chartism failed to

make progress on three occasions and, following the third of those occasions in April 1848, the movement effectively disappeared altogether, or (2) that Chartism cannot have been a complete failure because five out of the six points on the People's Charter eventually became law.
- Most recent accounts suggest that the traditional view was seriously flawed. They also argue that the importance of Chartism was in the psychological impact of its very existence. It left a legacy of hope and confidence within working-class communities which inspired further and ultimately more successful attempts at protest.

Activity 6.6 Was Chartism a complete failure?

ITEM 1 The six points of the People's Charter

(i) The Charter

The Six Points
OF THE
PEOPLE'S
CHARTER.

1. A VOTE for every man twenty-one years of age, of sound mind, and not undergoing punishment for crime.

2. THE BALLOT.—To protect the elector in the exercise of his vote.

3. No PROPERTY QUALIFICATION for Members of Parliament —thus enabling the constituencies to return the man of their choice, be he rich or poor.

4. PAYMENT OF MEMBERS, thus enabling an honest tradesman, working man, or other person, to serve a constituency, when taken from his business to attend to the interests of the country.

5. EQUAL CONSTITUENCIES, securing the same amount of representation for the same number of electors, instead of allowing small constituencies to swamp the votes of large ones.

6. ANNUAL PARLIAMENTS, thus presenting the most effectual check to bribery and intimidation, since though a constituency might be bought once in seven years (even with the ballot), no purse could buy a constituency (under a system of universal suffrage) in each ensuing twelvemonth; and since members, when elected for a year only, would not be able to defy and betray their constituents as now.

Secret Ballot -1872

Payment for MPs -1911

Annual Parliaments -not achieved

Votes for all men over 21 -1918

No property qualifications for MPs -1858

Equal constituencies -1885

(ii) An evaluation

The quest for Chartist achievement has led sometimes to a listing of the Acts of the later 19th and 20th centuries by which many points of the Charter were granted. But such an approach is mistaken. Those Acts cannot even remotely be attributed to Chartist pressure, and the real spirit of democracy which lay behind the points of the Charter remains unrealised even in the later 20th century. The positive achievements of the Chartists are to be found not in legislation passed at the time or in the remoter future, but in the mobilisation of the considerable mental, spiritual and emotional capacities of the working men and women of early industrial Britain. The Chartists' greatest achievement was Chartism, a movement shot through not with despair but with hope.

Adapted from Royle 1996.

This diagram shows the dates when five of the six points of the People's Charter were achieved. The sixth point has never been achieved.

ITEM 2 A historian's account (ii)

The Chartists failed because the system against which they were fighting was too strong. Governments fell in Europe in 1848, as they fell in 1989-90, because they no longer believed in themselves. Conditions in Britain were quite different. The governing class in Britain was small, tightly knit and self-assured. The same aristocratic families controlled leading positions in government, Church and army. After 1832 they had the confidence of property owners, including the new urban middle classes. The army was small but professional. London was patrolled by a police force under the direct control of the Home Office. Above all, the governing aristocracy and its supporters controlled propaganda so effectively that they not only demoralised Chartists but have misled historians ever since. The one large-scale and almost successful attempt at armed revolt (the Newport Rising) was dismissed by a relieved government as a 'disturbance' so as not to admit the extent of disaffection. Similarly, in 1848, the meeting on Kennington Common was laughed off as a 'fiasco' - which it certainly did not seem at the time. The Chartists' inability to make an impression on government was a further cause of failure. It is difficult to sustain a mass protest over weeks or months. To sustain a mass protest over years is hardly possible and so mass support ebbed and flowed with the economic tide. The Chartist message that no reform could come without political reform sounded strange when the government began passing reforms. This undermined the Chartist message.

Adapted from Royle 1992.

ITEM 3 A historian's account (ii)

In one sense, Chartism was a resounding success. Throughout the country, but particularly in the industrial areas of Lancashire and Yorkshire, it became central to sustaining a distinctive political culture among working people which survived into the 20th century. This political culture had three main elements. First, there was scepticism and often hostility towards a state which united the interests of the propertied middle and upper classes against those of working people. Second, Chartism provided lessons in how to organise protests, how to organise, how to spread the message of dissent and how to sustain morale through dark times. And third, Chartism encouraged many of its followers to pursue their interests independently. Research on later movements designed to assert the rights and improve the conditions of working people shows how firmly embedded the Chartist tradition became - whether in education, temperance reform, trade unions, socialism or even the early development of Labour politics in the 1880s and 1890s. Chartism's legacy, therefore, was powerful and enriching. Chartism matters and deserves to be remembered for much more than its short-term failures.

Adapted from Evans 1999.

Questions

1. a) Using Items 1-3 give arguments for and against the view that Chartism was a failure.
   b) Write down any arguments not mentioned in Items 1-3 which might have been used to explain why Chartism was a failure.
2. 'Chartism did not fail. Rather, it suffered defeat.' Explain this statement using Item 2.
3. a) Judging from Item 3, what was Chartism's main achievement?
   b) Explain Chartism's importance in 19th-century Britain.

References

● **Bartley (1996)** Bartley, P., *The Changing Role of Women 1815-1914*, Hodder and Stoughton, 1996.

● **Beer (1929)** Beer, M., *A History of British Socialism*, Bell, 1929.

● **Behagg (1991)** Behagg, C., *Labour and Reform: Working-Class Movements 1815-1914*, Hodder and Stoughton, 1991.

● **Behagg (1995)** Behagg, C., 'The Chartist experience' in *Scott-Baumann (1995)*.

● **Behagg (1996)** Behagg, C., 'Taking Chartism seriously', *Modern History Review*, Vol.7.4, April 1996.

● **Belchem (1996)** Belchem, J., *Popular Radicalism in 19th century Britain*, Macmillan, 1996.

● **Briggs (1959)** Briggs, A. (ed.), *Chartist Studies*, Macmillan, 1959.

● **Brown (1998)** Brown, R., *Chartism*, Cambridge University Press, 1998.

● **Catterall (1994)** Catterall, P. (ed.), *Britain 1815-1867*, Heinemann, 1994.

● **Charlton (1997)** Charlton, J., *The Chartists: the First National Workers' Movement*, Pluto Press, 1997.

● **Cole (1941)** Cole, G.D.H., *Chartist Portraits*, Macmillan, 1941.

● **Cole & Filson (1951)** Cole, G.D.H. & Filson, A.W., *British Working Class Movements: Select Documents 1789-1875*, Macmillan, 1951.

● **Cunningham (1994)** Cunningham, H., 'The nature of Chartism' in *Catterall (1994)*.

● **Digby & Feinstein (1989)** Digby, A. & Feinstein, C. (eds.), *New Directions in Economic and Social History*, Macmillan, 1989.

● **Epstein (1982)** Epstein, J., *The Lion of Freedom: Fergus O'Connor and the Chartist Movement 1832-42*, Croom Helm, 1982.

● **Evans (1999)** Evans, E., 'Chartism revisited', *History Review*, No.33, March 1999.

● **Gammage (1854)** Gammage, R.G., *History of the Chartist Movement*, 1854.

● **Gash (1979)** Gash, N., *Aristocracy and People: Britain 1815-65*, Edward Arnold, 1979.

● **Hannam (1995)** Hannam, J., 'Women and Politics' in *Purvis (1995)*.

● **Harrison (1984)** Harrison, J.F.C., *The Common People: a History from the Norman Conquest to the Present*, Flamingo, 1984.

● **Jones (1975)** Jones, D., *Chartism and the Chartists*, Allen Lane, 1975.

● **Laybourn (1992)** Laybourn, K., *A History of British Trade Unionism, c.1770-1990*, Alan Sutton Publishing, 1992.

● **Martin (1988)** Martin, H., *Britain since 1700: the Rise of Industry*, Macmillan, 1988.

- **Purvis (1995)** Purvis, J. (ed.), *Women's History: Britain, 1850-1945*, UCL Press, 1995.

- **Rostow (1948)** Rostow, W., *British Economy of the Nineteenth Century*, Oxford University Press, 1948.

- **Royle (1989)** Royle, E., 'Chartism' in *Digby & Feinstein (1989)*.

- **Royle (1992)** Royle, E., *'The origins and nature of Chartism, History Review*, No.13, 1992.

- **Royle (1996)** Royle, E., *Chartism* (3rd edn), Longman Seminar Studies, 1996.

- **Royle (1997)** Royle, E., *Modern Britain: a Social History 1750-1997* (2nd edn), Arnold, 1997.

- **Rubinstein (1998)** Rubinstein, W.D., *Britain's Century: a Political and Social History 1815-1905*, Arnold, 1998.

- **Saville (1990)** Saville, J., *1848. British State and the Chartist Movement*, Cambridge University Press, 1990.

- **Scott-Baumann (1995)** Scott-Baumann, M., *Years of Expansion: Britain 1815-1914*, Hodder and Stoughton, 1995.

- **Stedman Jones (1983)** Stedman Jones, G., 'Rethinking Chartism' in *Stedman Jones (1983a)*.

- **Stedman Jones (1983a)** Stedman Jones, G., *Languages of Class: Studies in English Working Class History 1832-1982*, Cambridge University Press, 1983.

- **Taylor (1983)** Taylor, B., *Eve and the New Jerusalem: Socialism and Feminism in the Nineteenth Century*, Virago, 1983.

- **Thompson (1984)** Thompson, D., *The Chartists: Popular Politics in the Industrial Revolution*, Aldershot, 1984.

- **Thompson (1980)** Thompson, E.P., *The Making of the Working Class*, Penguin, 1980 (first published in 1963).

- **West (1920)** West, J., *A History of the Chartist Movement*, Constable, 1920.

UNIT 7 Political developments under Peel

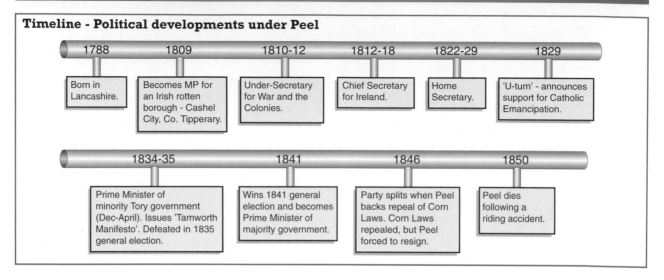

Timeline - Political developments under Peel

1788 Born in Lancashire.

1809 Becomes MP for an Irish rotten borough - Cashel City, Co. Tipperary.

1810-12 Under-Secretary for War and the Colonies.

1812-18 Chief Secretary for Ireland.

1822-29 Home Secretary.

1829 'U-turn' - announces support for Catholic Emancipation.

1834-35 Prime Minister of minority Tory government (Dec-April). Issues 'Tamworth Manifesto'. Defeated in 1835 general election.

1841 Wins 1841 general election and becomes Prime Minister of majority government.

1846 Party splits when Peel backs repeal of Corn Laws. Corn Laws repealed, but Peel forced to resign.

1850 Peel dies following a riding accident.

Introduction

Whilst Sir Robert Peel unquestionably remains one of the major political figures of the 19th century, historians have increasingly begun to challenge the assumption that he was also its greatest statesman. The view that Peel, Prime Minister between 1834 and 1835 and then again between 1841 and 1846, was the 'greatest statesman of his age' (Read 1987, p.1) is based, in part, on his decision to repeal the 1815 Corn Law. This decision, it is argued, showed great vision since it resulted in a period of free trade which allowed Britain to build its position as the unchallenged 'workshop of the world'. The fact that the decision also split the Conservative Party only shows how great Peel was because it demonstrated that he was prepared to place national above party interest - irrespective of the cost to his own political career. It was not just his actions as Prime Minister that have impressed historians, however. Peel is also credited with being the founder of the modern Conservative Party. It was Peel, his supporters argue, who broadened and modernised Conservatism, ensuring that the Tory Party became a national, rather than a narrowly (indeed dangerously narrowly) landed and Church of England party.

Whilst Peel continues to have his admirers, however, an increasing number of historians have begun to question his reputation. First, they point out that Peel made a number of startling U-turns on major policies. This leads to charges of inconsistency and even of betraying his party. Second, it has been suggested that Peel was dangerously isolated from backbench opinion and, as a result, lacked 'political sensitivity'. Third, it is argued that the split in 1846 shows that his so-called 'transformation' of the Tory Party during the 1830s was at best partial. And finally, it has been argued that Peel's achievements in his second administration, though not inconsiderable, were too narrowly focused on economic affairs. This unit outlines the main developments in the current historical debate.

UNIT SUMMARY

Part 1 examines Peel's background and early political career. Is it right to suggest that Peel was the founder of the modern Conservative Party? To what extent did the paradoxes and apparent contradictions of his later career take root in this period?

Part 2 explores the aims and policies of Peel's second administration of 1841-46. In particular, it considers the extent to which he regarded financial policy as the key to social improvement and political stability.

Part 3 focuses on the greatest controversy of Peel's career - his decision to repeal the Corn Laws. It concludes with an assessment of the arguments for and against the view that Peel was a 'great statesman'.

1 Peel's early political career and the development of the Conservative Party

Key issues

1. In what ways do Peel's background and early political career help to explain his later policies and actions as Prime Minister?

2. Why was the Tamworth Manifesto of December 1834 so important?

3. To what extent should Peel be regarded as the founder of the modern Conservative Party?

BOX 7.1 Peel's early career

Son of a northern cotton magnate and, therefore, always conscious of being something of an outsider in the landowning Parliament of the first third of the 19th century, Peel entered Parliament as a Tory in 1809 on the recommendation of Arthur Wellesley (who later became the Duke of Wellington). His early career combined administrative efficiency with political reaction. He moved from the backbenches to the frontbench in 1810 when the Prime Minister, Spencer Perceval, appointed him as Under-Secretary for War and the Colonies (the Secretary for War and Colonies - the senior minister in his department - was Lord Liverpool). When Liverpool became Prime Minister in 1812, Peel was appointed Chief Secretary for Ireland and he served there until 1818. Known as 'Orange Peel', he was fiercely anti-Catholic in policy and outlook. On his return from Ireland, he chaired an influential parliamentary committee on public finance. This established his reputation as an economic thinker. Between 1822 and Liverpool's death in 1827 and then between 1828 and 1830, he served as Home Secretary. During this time, he modified the criminal law and created the Metropolitan Police Force. Despite his anti-Catholic prejudices, he was persuaded to change his mind in 1829 and agreed to support Catholic emancipation. He became leader of the Tory Party in 1832.

Adapted from Gardiner & Wenborn 1995.

1.1 Peel's early career

Why is Peel's early career important?

Historians (and examiners!) often concentrate on Peel's policies and achievements during his one prolonged period in office as Prime Minister between 1841 and 1846. Since, however, Peel was at, or was near, the centre of political activity in Britain for almost 40 years (including a brief period as Prime Minister from December 1834 to April 1835), it is important to understand the long-term evolution of his political thinking and the way in which this was reflected in his policies and decisions (his early career is outlined in Box 7.1). There is a great paradox at the heart of Peel's political career - namely that a person whom some historians have described as the 'founder' of the modern Conservative Party can simultaneously be seen as having betrayed that party's interests over the key issues of Catholic emancipation, Ireland and the Corn Laws. Looking back at Peel's early career can help to explain why this paradox developed.

The first point to make is that Peel never had to compete in a genuinely popular election:

'Peel was in many ways a classic product of the unreformed electoral system. He entered Parliament as a member for Cashel City (in Ireland) in 1809 on the recommendation of Arthur Wellesley. He had never visited the constituency and Wellesley's letter commended a Mr Peele (spelt Peele), lamenting that he did not know Mr Peel's Christian name. Peel went on to sit for Oxford University and later for the family seat of Tamworth. As a result, he never once faced a genuinely popular election.' (Eastwood 1992, p.28)

Peel's roots

In the early part of the 19th century, there was a growing split amongst the wealthy between those whose wealth was based on land and those whose wealth was based on industry and commerce. It is sometimes suggested that, because Peel was the son of a wealthy cotton manufacturer who bought his way into the political establishment by purchasing land, he was somehow uniquely placed to heal this split since he straddled both the 'new' and the 'old'. As T.A. Jenkins puts it:

'The fact that Peel's family roots were in the Lancashire cotton industry, where his father had made a fortune, but that this manufacturing wealth enabled him to receive a conventional elite education at Harrow and Oxford, and proceed at once into a political career, suggested that he might be personally well equipped to broker a compromise between the social forces of land and industry.' (Jenkins 1999, p.3)

This suggests that there is a strong case for arguing that Peel's 'hybrid' background was an asset. Such a background ensured that he recognised that 'propertied interests' (the interests of all those with property regardless of whether that property came from land or commerce) should work in harmony to promote social and political stability.

An alternative viewpoint

Some historians, however, do not agree that Peel's 'hybrid' background was an asset. Rather, they argue that Peel's commercial roots were a problem for him because they ensured that he was never fully accepted by the landed, 'Ultra' Tory wing of the Party. A.J. Davies, for example, points out that:

'[Peel] was Northerner who always retained traces of his northern accent, for which he was ridiculed by some of his colleagues.' (Davies 1995, p.14)

Indeed, Davies goes on to suggest that this lack of understanding was mutual, and claims that:

'Having emerged from a commercial and industrial background himself, Peel felt no abiding loyalty to the landed aristocracy. Peel's background was, viewed from this angle, a source of potential conflict rather than consensus.' (Davies 1995, p.80)

It should be noted, however, that Hilton denies that opposition to Peel had social causes:

'Certainly there was good-natured banter about his accent ("Mr Peel did very well in seconding the address except that he *oped* too often and talked of the *ouse* as we Staffordshire men are apt to do," wrote Huskisson in a letter to his wife on 22 January 1819) but it would be anachronistic [not accurate at the time] to suppose that in Peel's day a regional accent carried any social stigma.' (Hilton 1979, p.590, slightly adapted)

Peel's outlook

Almost all of Peel's political experience before becoming Prime Minister was spent as a minister. He was appointed as a junior minister a year after becoming an MP and, between 1810 and 1834, spent only eight years out of office:

- August 1818 - January 1822, when Liverpool could find no suitable ministerial vacancy for him (ministers were not regularly reshuffled in the early 19th century and, generally, the Prime Minister had to wait until ministers died or resigned before making new appointments)
- April 1827 - January 1828, when Canning and Goderich, political rivals, were in power
- November 1830 - November 1834, when the Whigs were in office.

According to Evans (1991), it was because Peel spent so much time as a minister at such an early stage in his career that he became distanced from his backbench colleagues and lacked 'political sensitivity'. This lack of political sensitivity, it is alleged, was then reflected in the way in which he handled issues later in his career. Cooper agrees with this analysis, arguing:

'In at least one important sense, Peel's high-flying early career did not ideally equip him for his later responsibilities: it confined him to a restricted understanding of the business of politics. Hardly ever out of office between 1810 and 1830, he was never able to see the world from the perspective of the backbenches - a limitation which was to have dramatic consequences for Peel and the way in which he treated his own party in the 1840s.' (Cooper 1995, p.120)

Eastwood refines this argument by suggesting that Peel learned specific lessons from his experience of government under Lord Liverpool. In particular, it was important that the Liverpool administration survived for 15 years despite widespread popular protest (see Unit 3) and despite splits within the governing party over important issues such as Catholic emancipation (see Unit 9, Section 2.2):

'Peel's political apprenticeship under Liverpool did much to condition his later attitudes towards the party. He believed that his early career taught him two things. Firstly, that governments could survive major splits and important reverses; and, secondly that a broadly liberal Tory leadership could reasonably expect the loyalty of the more obviously High Tory backbenchers: parties ought to have the resilience to absorb the strains of internal political disruption, and ultimately it was the duty of ministers to lead and backbenchers to support.' (Eastwood 1992, p.28)

Gatrell (1994) and Jenkins (1999), on the other hand, argue that, whilst Peel's early political experience prepared him for the wide-ranging responsibilities of the premiership, it also reinforced personal characteristics of self-reliance and aloofness which were later to strain his relations with many other colleagues. Gatrell analyses Peel's personality as follows:

'Peel had his own personality to contend with. He was a reticent and formal man, remorselessly over-disciplined in boyhood by the upbringing which turned the son of a Lancashire calico-printer into the patrician leader his father intended him to be. He spoke with a Lancashire accent which he fought self-consciously to control. Rigorous parental pressure left its scars. It was always "easier for him to deal with problems than with people", Gash has written. O'Connell compared his smile to the glint of the silver plate on a coffin lid. Cold in manner, meticulous in matters of honour and duty, he managed "his elocution like his temper", Disraeli said, and "neither was originally good". Disraeli thought he lacked originality or imagination.' (Gatrell 1994, p.571)

Peel as Chief Secretary for Ireland

Peel served as Chief Secretary for Ireland between 1812 and 1818. Jenkins (1999) points out that his job was divided into two. On the one hand, Peel was the deputy of the Lord Lieutenant:

'When in Ireland, he was accountable to the King's representative, the Lord Lieutenant, who resided permanently in Dublin and performed the functions of an active constitutional monarch. The Chief Secretary was, in effect, the Lord Lieutenant's Prime Minister and he was, therefore, directly responsible for the whole range of governmental activities including finance, trade, law and order and defence.' (Jenkins 1999, p.9)

On the other hand, it was the job of the Chief Secretary to speak in Parliament on Irish affairs and to press the government to introduce legislation dealing with Irish matters. Peel, therefore, had to divide his time between Ireland and Westminster

Historians have suggested that Peel's term as Chief Secretary for Ireland was important in terms of his later career in five main ways.

1. Peel and Catholic emancipation

First, since Peel was Chief Secretary for Ireland, he was obliged to make it very clear where he stood on the question of Catholic emancipation (see also Unit 9, Section 2.2). In a number of speeches in the House of Commons in the period 1812-18, Peel declared himself utterly opposed to emancipation. By the time that he left Ireland, his reputation as a fierce opponent of emancipation was well established. This ensured that his later support of a Catholic Emancipation Bill in 1829 was extremely controversial.

2. Peel and O'Connell

It was while he was Chief Secretary for Ireland that Peel first clashed with Daniel O'Connell (see also Unit 9, Section 2.2). Peel's position on Catholic emancipation was bitterly resented by O'Connell, who regularly made personal attacks on Peel in speeches. The enmity which developed between the two men was so intense that in 1815 Peel even tried to arrange a duel with O'Connell on neutral soil in Belgium (O'Connell was prevented from leaving Ireland). This personal enmity was of particular significance later since O'Connell's Repeal campaign reached a peak after Peel became Prime Minister in 1841.

3. Peel's way of working

Jenkins (1999) points out that Peel was young (just 24) when appointed Chief Secretary for Ireland and, for six years, was almost single-handedly responsible for running the country. This heavy burden of responsibility, he argues, explains why, in later years,

Peel always found it difficult to delegate work to his colleagues properly.

4. Peel and law enforcement

It was while he was Chief Secretary for Ireland that Peel first experimented with the idea of a police force. In 1814 he set up the Peace Preservation Force (PPF) in Ireland - a group of police officers appointed by the government and under the command of a magistrate. The aim of the PPF was to combat rural unrest. Officers were sent to disturbed areas to keep the peace and local ratepayers were forced to pay for their upkeep whether they had requested them or not. Later, as Home Secretary, Peel was responsible for setting up the Metropolitan Police Force.

5. Peel's political principles

In a speech made in April 1816, Peel argued that Ireland's problems were too complex for the government to find any simple solution. Rather:

'Time alone, the prevalence of a kind and paternal system of government and the extension of education were the remedies which must chiefly be relied on.' (Part of a speech made in the House of Commons on 26 April 1816)

Whilst Peel was prepared to introduce reforms in Ireland (such as the PPF), he was hostile to over-reliance on aid from the state:

'Peel was exasperated, too, by what he considered to be the peculiarly Irish habit of looking to the government to do everything, including, apparently, clearing the snow. On one occasion he condemned the "monstrous impolicy" of maintaining a Foundling Hospital in Dublin at public expense: "Really to make the government of Ireland a nurse is painfully ridiculous...it is wrong, radically wrong, in principle".' (Jenkins 1999, p.16)

The political philosophy which emerges is not far from that later expressed in the Tamworth Manifesto (see Section 1.2 below).

Peel as Home Secretary

Apart from during an eight-month gap following the resignation of Lord Liverpool in April 1827, Peel served as Home Secretary between 1822 and 1830. His achievements during this period are the subject of a fierce historical debate. This debate is outlined in Unit 3, Section 2.2.

The question as to whether Peel can be described as a 'Liberal Tory' in the period 1822-27 has an important bearing on how his later behaviour is to be interpreted. Essentially there are two diametrically opposed views.

1. Peel the Liberal Tory

One view is that, during his term as Home Secretary,

Peel really was a Liberal Tory. He saw that the prison system and criminal law needed to be modernised and took steps to achieve this modernisation. Also, he supported the liberal economic policies of Huskisson and Robinson. Those historians who argue that Peel was a Liberal Tory in the 1820s tend to argue that he was consistent and principled throughout his career. Hilton (1979), for example, argues that Peel's views on economic policy did not change between the 1820s and the 1840s. Peel, he suggests, had a rather closed mind and refused to listen to those whose views did not fit his own. Another way of putting this is to argue that Peel had certain principles which he believed in strongly and he consistently tried to put these principles into practice. This explains why, as Prime Minister in 1841-46, he put national above party interest and sacrificed his own career for the good of the nation.

2. Peel the reactionary

The opposite point of view is that, in fact, Peel was not at all liberal during his term as Home Secretary. He introduced reforms because he wanted to make the existing power structure more secure, not because he wanted to change it in any fundamental way. At heart, he was a reactionary - a person who opposed change and wanted the old system to continue, but he was also a pragmatist. He knew that some change was necessary in order to preserve the fundamental structure of the old system. In other words, historians who deny that Peel was liberal tend to argue that he was a reluctant reformer. That explains why:

> 'On the criminal law, Peel tinkered, while Russell made drastic reforms.' (Beales 1974, p.880)

It also explains why, in 1829, Peel was prepared to change his mind over Catholic emancipation and why he opposed and then came to terms with the Great Reform Act of 1832. It also explains why, as Prime Minister, he refused to make concessions when faced by the Chartists (see Unit 6, Section 3.1) and when faced by Daniel O'Connell's Repeal campaign (see Unit 9, Section 2.5).

Peel and Catholic emancipation

Peel's decision to support a Catholic Emancipation Bill in 1829 was extremely controversial at the time and has remained so since. Looking back at Peel's career as a whole, some historians have identified three U-Turns - over Catholic emancipation, over the Great Reform Act and over the Corn Laws. This pattern of behaviour, they argue, shows that Peel was a pragmatic politician whose political judgement and realism earned him his later reputation as a great statesman. Other historians are less complimentary. Jenkins (1999), for example, argues that Peel took advantage of developments in Ireland in 1828-29 to relieve himself of Protestant baggage which he was finding increasingly burdensome. He also argues that Peel's support for Protestantism in the mid-1820s had more to do with his own ambitions to succeed Lord Liverpool than to his political principles.

When did Peel change his mind?

There is some dispute about when, exactly, Peel changed his mind over Catholic emancipation. The traditional view (see Eastwood 1992, for example) is that the turning point was the Clare by-election in 1828 when the Catholic Association's leader, Daniel O'Connell, was elected (see Unit 9, Section 2.2). This, it is argued, convinced Peel, like Wellington, that civil war would break out in Ireland if Catholic emancipation was not granted. Jenkins (1999), on the other hand, argues that Peel's opposition to Catholic emancipation had begun to cool well before the Clare by-election. He suggests that, in reality, Peel found that the anti-Catholic stance he had adopted as Chief Secretary for Ireland had become a burden by the mid-1820s. His argument is that, beneath the surface, there was a power struggle between Peel and Canning, both of whom aimed to succeed Liverpool as Prime Minister. Whilst the root of this power struggle was personal dislike and rivalry, the issue of Catholic emancipation became the battleground (Canning was the leading pro-emancipation member of the Cabinet). Peel continued to oppose any moves towards Catholic emancipation. For example, he spoke against Grattan's Catholic Emancipation Bill in 1825 and offered his resignation when it was passed by the Commons (the Bill was rejected by the Lords). But, Jenkins suggests, Peel's heart was no longer in the anti-Catholic cause:

> 'It is hard to avoid the conclusion that Peel's association with the "Protestant" wing of Toryism, dating back to his time as Irish Chief Secretary, had placed him in an increasingly artificial position...Privately, however, there were signs of fatalism in Peel's attitude towards the Irish question by 1826. His correspondence suggests that he realised that emancipation was going to be inevitable, eventually, and he even intimated that it might come as something of a relief to see the issue settled.' (Jenkins 1999, p.45)

If Jenkins is right, then the picture of Peel that emerges is very different from that which is painted by those who see him as the 'great statesman' who put country above party or personal ambition. By 1828, Canning was dead and, therefore, Peel's Protestant stance had less political capital. The Clare by-election and Catholic Association demonstrations which followed it provided Peel with the opportunity to shed his Protestant baggage whilst appearing to put country above self.

The consequences of the U-turn

As well as pointing out that Peel's U-turn alienated the Ultra Tories and created a legacy of suspicion and underlying mistrust which was to reassert itself forcefully during the Corn Law crisis of 1845-46, historians have argued that Peel's U-turn over Catholic emancipation had a number of other consequences. First, the passage of the Catholic Emancipation Bill was followed shortly afterwards by the fall of Wellington's government. Wellington's downfall was Peel's opportunity to gain the leadership of the Tory Party (see Section 1.2 below). Second, like Wellington, Peel made it clear that the strength of support for the Catholic Association was a major reason for changing his mind over Catholic emancipation. Jenkins (1999) points out that the Catholic Association's success encouraged other extra-parliamentary groups to press for change. In part, therefore, the U-turn in 1829 explains the growth of Chartism (see Unit 6, Section 1.2) and the growth of Daniel O'Connell's Repeal movement (see Unit 9, Section 2.5), both of which provided Peel with a challenge when he was Prime Minister in 1841-46. And third, Eastwood (1992) argues that the U-turn led to the damaging split in the Tory Party over the Maynooth Bill of 1845 (see Section 3.1 below).

MAIN POINTS - Section 1.1

- The paradox at the heart of Peel's career is that the 'founder' of the modern Conservative Party can at the same time be seen as betraying that party's interests. Looking at Peel's early career can help to explain why this paradox developed.
- Some historians have argued that Peel's 'hybrid' background was an asset. Others claim it was a hindrance. His personality and his later actions may have been shaped by the fact that he became a minister so young and spent so little time on the back benches.
- Peel's term as Chief Secretary for Ireland was important in terms of his later career because - (1) he made his opposition to Catholic emancipation very public, (2) he first clashed with O'Connell, (3) it helped to form his working habits, (4) he experimented with a police force and (5) his political philosophy developed.
- Those who argue Peel was a liberal Home Secretary tend to claim he was consistent and principled throughout his career. Those who argue he was an illiberal Home Secretary tend to argue that he was a reluctant reformer.
- Peel's decision to support a Catholic Emancipation Bill in 1829 was extremely controversial at the time and has remained so since. Some argue Peel was putting country above self. Others argue he was keen to rid himself of his Protestant baggage.

Activity 7.1 Peel and Catholic emancipation

ITEM 1 Peel's reaction to the Clare by-election

I have uniformly opposed what is called Catholic emancipation and have rested my opinion on broad and uncompromising grounds. I wish I could say that my views on the question were materially changed and that I now believed that full concessions to Roman Catholics could be made either exempt from the dangers which I have apprehended from them or productive of the full advantages which their advocates anticipate from the grant of them. But, whatever my opinions upon these points, I cannot deny that the state of Ireland under existing circumstances is most unsatisfactory; that it becomes necessary to make your choice between different kinds and different degrees of evil – to compare the actual danger resulting from the union and organisation of the Roman Catholic body and the incessant agitation in Ireland with prospective and apprehended dangers to the constitution or religion of the country, and maturely to consider whether it may not be better to encounter every eventual risk of concession than to submit to the certain continuance or rather perhaps the certain aggravation of existing evils.

> **Glossary**
> - **exempt from** - without
> - **apprehended** - anticipated
> - **productive of** - with
> - **advocates** - supporters
> - **Roman Catholic body** - the Catholic Association
> - **incessant agitation** - continuous unrest

Part of a letter written by Peel to the Duke of Wellington on 17 August 1828.

ITEM 2 A cartoon from 1829

This cartoon portrays Peel as a ratcatcher, suggesting that he had 'ratted' on his party.

ITEM 3 A historian's view (i)

Peel was extremely reluctant to agree to Wellington's desperate request that he take a leading role in piloting the Emancipation Bill through the Commons. He had himself in the past been the most persuasive defender of the Protestants' monopoly of power in Ireland. To throw his weight behind the Catholic cause would be to make an extraordinary U-turn. It would inevitably do grave damage to his reputation for political consistency and integrity and might well wreck his career. Peel was thus in an extraordinarily difficult position in 1828. In private he had been growing increasingly sceptical about anti-Catholic discrimination. But the Clare by-election gave the question a dreadful urgency. If Parliament rejected emancipation, many feared that rebellion would break out in Ireland. Peel felt that he had no choice. He actually introduced the Bill for emancipation to the Commons. This "betrayal" of the Protestant cause and the vilification that rained down on his head as a consequence was the price Peel believed he had to pay to prevent Ireland collapsing into bloody anarchy. His support for Wellington was instrumental in securing the passage of the Bill and perhaps saved Ireland from civil war. He showed cool judgement, great courage and a readiness to make considerable sacrifices for higher ends...Above all, it shows Peel's attachment to the executive tradition of government - his determination to serve what he saw as the national interest, regardless of the expectations of his fellow Tories.

Adapted from Cooper 1995.

ITEM 4 A historian's view (ii)

Although the growing momentum for a settlement of the Catholic question inevitably placed Peel in a predicament, any embarrassment he felt seems to have been outweighed by a sense of relief that events beyond his control were conspiring to remove an awkward political encumbrance from his back. In other words, he quietly welcomed the opportunity provided by the Clare by-election to release himself from his obligations to the Protestant cause. The big question was whether he could remain a member of the government. Eventually, he decided that it would be wrong to abandon the government for the sake of his personal consistency when, by doing so, he was likely to create a massive obstacle to a settlement which he agreed was necessary. Peel was surely right in thinking that Wellington's government, supported by the Whigs, was the only one capable of overcoming resistance in Parliament and from an unhappy monarch. He therefore concluded that he had no right to allow selfish considerations upset a legislative solution. He introduced the Bill on 5 March 1829, making a four and a half hour speech which some considered the finest he had ever made. By arguing that he was yielding to a 'moral necessity which I cannot control', he recognised that what had made the agitation in Ireland so formidable was its disciplined and orderly nature. The legitimate Catholic force which had been shown at the Clare by-election was far more difficult for the government to combat than an outbreak of violence. It was the long-term challenge posed to Britain's authority in Ireland that had caused Peel to change his mind about Catholic emancipation, not the fear of imminent civil war.

Adapted from Jenkins 1999.

Questions

1. a) What does Item 1 tell us about Peel's state of mind after the Clare by-election?
   b) Why do you think Peel did a U-turn on Catholic emancipation?
2. a) Place the cartoon in Item 2 in context.
   b) Is this an accurate view of Peel? Explain your answer.
3. a) How do the interpretations in Items 3 and 4 differ?
   b) Which is more acceptable? Explain your answer.
   c) From what you know of Peel's early career up to 1830 give arguments for and against the view that he was 'the greatest statesman of his age'.

1.2 Peel and the Conservative Party

The Whigs take over

By the time that the Catholic Emancipation Bill had been passed, the Prime Minister, the Duke of Wellington, had managed to alienate two wings of his party (see Unit 5, Section 2.1 for more details):

- the 'Canningites' (supporters of Canning, such as Huskisson and Palmerston), who had joined Wellington's government but resigned in May 1828 over Wellington's refusal to make concessions on electoral reform
- the 'Ultras', who broke with the Wellington government over emancipation.

Wellington's government limped through to November 1830 when it was defeated in a vote over the civil list. Wellington was then replaced by Earl Grey, whose administration went on to pass the 1832 Reform Act.

The term 'Conservative'

It is after the fall of the Wellington government in November 1830 that the term 'Conservative' first began to be used. Jenkins (1999) suggests that, in part, this was to avoid the term 'Tory', which had become discredited by recent events. In addition, he claims, it suggested a new emphasis:

'The distinction between "Tory" and "Conservative" was essentially one of methodology rather than of ultimate purpose: whereas the former title conveyed the idea of an uncompromising defence of the privileges and monopolies enjoyed by institutions connected to the Anglican landed elite, the latter allowed for the possibility of gradual, cautious change, designed to reconcile those attitudes with the prevailing attitudes in the modern world.' (Jenkins 1999, p.65)

Peel and the 1832 Reform Act

The second occasion on which Peel has been accused of making a U-turn was over the 1832 Reform Act. During the reform crisis, which began when the Whigs formed a government in November 1830 and lasted until the Reform Act was passed in June 1832 (see Unit 5), Peel remained an outspoken opponent of reform. Following the passage of the Reform Act, however, rather than campaigning to abolish the Act, he argued that Tories should work within the new system.

Peel and the reform crisis

Historians differ in their interpretations of Peel's behaviour during the reform crisis. A common argument (see Cooper 1995) is that, because Peel had made a U-turn over Catholic emancipation, he felt that his freedom of movement was severely restricted during the reform crisis. Once he had made his opposition to the Whigs' Reform Bill public, he could not then back down since that would have been seen as a second betrayal. The crunch point came in May 1832 when Grey resigned and Wellington tried to form a government. Peel, however, refused to join this government:

'[Wellington] believed that, with Peel's help, it might be possible to form a moderately reformist Tory ministry. But, this time, Peel turned down Wellington's - and the king's - appeals. By Peel's standards, this was a striking abdication of duty...But Peel believed that, in the debates over reform, his criticisms of the Whig proposals had been so strong as to make his joining any reform ministry - even one led by Wellington - look like another breathtaking U-turn. A second "betrayal" would have brought his political career to an end.' (Cooper 1995, pp.123-24)

Challenges to this view

This view, however, has been challenged in two ways. On the one hand, Eastwood (1992) argues that such an interpretation assumes that Peel was acting as a party leader during the reform crisis. In other words, it assumes that he was concerned about what his fellow Conservative MPs thought of him and tailored his actions to ensure that he retained the support of the majority of them. This, Eastwood argues, takes Peel's actions at face value and does not appreciate the direction in which he was moving. Rather than acting as a party leader, Eastwood argues, Peel was acting as a free agent:

'In fact, it is abundantly clear that Peel believed himself to be something of a free agent throughout the crisis...He was already moving away from considerations of party to considerations of good government...Party for Peel was always in imminent danger of descending into mere faction. Viewed like this, party is the enemy of government. For Peel, the greatest danger in 1831 was not that the Whig's reform Bill should pass, but that government should be undermined by party.' (Eastwood 1992, p.30)

For Eastwood, therefore, Peel acted out of principle during the reform crisis. Jenkins (1999), on the other hand, implies that Peel's motives were rather less pure. He suggests that whilst Peel's opposition to the Whig Reform Bill was genuine (Peel thought it was too radical), personal ambition is what motivated his behaviour. He argues that after the 1831 Reform Bill was defeated in committee in April (see Unit 5, Section 2.2), Peel hoped to become Prime Minister:

'Lord Ellenborough heard from Sir Henry Hardinge that Peel was "ready to undertake the government". If this report is correct, it is of interest for two reasons: first, because it shows that Peel expected the Whigs to respond to their defeat by resigning and, secondly, because it reveals his assumption that he, not Wellington, should be the one to form the replacement government.' (Jenkins 1999, p.59)

It could be, therefore, that personal ambition rather than principle explains Peel's refusal to serve in a government under Wellington in May 1832.

Peel in opposition 1832-34

Following the 1832 general election, the Conservative Party was at a very low ebb:

'[The Conservative Party was] a beleaguered minority amid the great tide of Whigs and radicals who swept into the House of Commons in the aftermath of reform.' (Adelman 1989, p.14)

It was out of the political wreckage of this period that Peel began to emerge as the new leader of the Conservative Party. Whilst Wellington remained the party's elder statesman, Peel was perceived as having the qualities necessary to lead the party:

'[The Conservative Party] possessed in Peel a man who in terms of intellect, experience and national influence stood head and shoulders above any other member of the party or of the House of Commons, as even his political opponents admitted. Whatever the reservations of some Tories, the party needed Peel.' (Adelman 1989, p.15)

Jenkins notes that relations between Wellington and Peel remained strained between 1832 and 1834:

'On a personal level the relations between the two men - respectful rather than cordial even in the 1820s - were frequently strained. This was a legacy of the mutual ill-feeling generated in May 1832 when Peel refused to serve in the projected Wellington Reform ministry.' (Jenkins 1999, p.70)

In May 1834, however, relations between the two men improved:

'In May 1834, with the Whig administration apparently on the verge of disintegration, it was necessary for Charles Arbuthnot and others to act as intermediaries in order to bring about an improved understanding between Wellington and Peel. As a result, the Duke let it be known that, in his opinion, the Prime Minister ought to sit in the House of Commons, thus acknowledging Peel's superior claims to the first place in a future Conservative government.' (Jenkins 1999, p.71)

Peel's strategy in opposition

A number of historians have argued that Peel's skilful approach to opposition following the general election of 1832 was crucial in redefining the character of Toryism and marked its transition to Conservatism. His approach has been described as follows:

'Peel's preferred strategy was, as far as possible,

to support rather than oppose the Whig ministers in Parliament...Peel was determined to resist the temptation to enter into opportunistic alliances with the radicals or Irish MPs merely for the pleasure of inflicting embarrassing defeats on the Whigs, choosing instead to shield ministers from the attacks launched by their own nominal supporters. In this way as Peel explained to his friend, John Wilson Croker, the Conservative opposition was "making the Reform Bill work"...Of course, the Conservatives were not precluded from criticising various aspects of the government's policy, nor from voting against it when a clear difference of principle existed, but there was to be no relentless opposition to everything the Whigs did.' (Jenkins 1999, p.67)

Historians suggest that the strategy that Peel adopted had six main aims. These are described in Box 7.2.

BOX 7.2 Peel in opposition

In opposition Peel's main aims were to:
- support rather than to oppose the Whig government wherever possible in order to prevent any relationship developing between the Whigs and the radicals
- encourage divisions to develop within the government in the hope that it would lose support
- win over moderate Whigs - to broaden the Tories' base
- gradually reabsorb the Ultras and create greater unity without having to depend on this more traditional wing of the party
- broaden the party's electoral fortunes by appealing to the middle classes without upsetting the Ultras or diluting the party with a large inflow of industrialists
- demonstrate the Tory Party's continued relevance in a rapidly changing society and in a new electoral system.

Why did Peel adopt this approach?

Historians have suggested three principal reasons for Peel adopting this approach. First, it is argued that Peel thought this would be the best way to prevent the radicals achieving their aims. Peel himself made this clear:

'I am adverse to any course of proceeding on our part which should justify the government in the eyes of the country in forming a cordial union with the radicals. That, I think, would be tantamount to positive destruction because it would be tantamount to the adoption of the views and principles of the radicals and their practical enforcement through the Crown and government.' (Extract from a letter written by Peel to J.C. Herries in early 1833)

Second, Jenkins suggests that Peel's personal ambitions may have played a part in the adoption of such an approach:

'Thomas Raikes, a Conservative diarist, suspected that a rational calculation lay behind Peel's display of statesmanlike forbearance toward the government: "He has declared himself to be of no party; but his object is insensibly to make one of which he shall himself be the centre and the chief. He is an ambitious man; and to this great object his endeavours will inevitably tend." In the reformed House of Commons, as Raikes noted, party connections were peculiarly weak and there were many MPs lacking firm allegiance to a leader - "loose Tories, loose Whigs, loose Conservatives and loose radicals" - who might well be persuaded "that Robert Peel is the fittest man to govern the country".' (Jenkins 1999, p.68)

And third, Eastwood (1992) and Cooper (1995) argue that Peel had a genuine fear of the 'mob' (ie the mass of people). They claim that he had been particularly afraid that anarchy might break out during the reform crisis and suggest that this explains why he was so keen to ensure that there was a stable government during this period.

Peel's first term in government

By the summer of 1834, Peel's strategy had paid off. In May 1834, four moderate Whig ministers resigned following a Cabinet split over policy towards Ireland. These defections appeared to justify Peel's strategy of constructive opposition and were a major source of encouragement. Then, later that year, King William IV dismissed the Prime Minister, Lord Melbourne - the last occasion on which a monarch dismissed a Prime Minister who had a majority in the Commons:

'William IV's belief that the Whigs were unsound on the Church was an important factor in his decision to dismiss Melbourne in November 1834 and install a Tory administration in its stead.' (Evans 1996, p.252)

The King invited the Duke of Wellington to form a caretaker government (which lasted for a month) and then asked Peel to form a minority government. Although Peel's first ministry lasted only for five months, it provided him with an opportunity to further consolidate party unity. For example, by appointing four Ultras to Cabinet posts, he improved relations with that wing of the party.

The Tamworth Manifesto

In the early 19th century, a Prime Minister who sat in the Commons was required, on appointment, to seek re-election at a by-election. This provided Peel with the platform to launch the second strand of his recovery strategy - the Tamworth Manifesto of December 1834 (see Box 7.3). Technically the manifesto was an address made to Peel's constituents

---

BOX 7.3 The Tamworth Manifesto

The main points in the Tamworth Manifesto were as follows:

- Peel appealed to 'that class which is much less interested in the contentions of party than in the maintenance of order and the cause of good government' - ie he appealed for the support of the newly enfranchised middle class
- Peel stated that he regarded the 1832 Reform Act as a final, irreversible settlement
- Peel accepted that there were circumstances in which moderate reform was necessary
- Peel rejected the idea that there should be further steps towards broader democracy
- Peel reassured traditional Tories about his commitment to protecting property and the interests of the Established Church.

---

in the Midlands town of Tamworth, but it was approved in advance by the Cabinet and was circulated to the national newspapers to ensure that it reached as wide an audience as possible. This was novel:

'For the first time a party leader was presenting a programme to a national electorate.' (Evans 1996, p.258)

According to Jenkins, Peel's aim in producing the Tamworth Manifesto was as follows:

'Peel's object was to reassure the country as to the intentions of his government by providing "a frank exposition of general principles and views". He was anxious above all else to emphasise that he accepted the Reform Act of 1832 as "a final and irrevocable settlement of a great constitutional question". There would be no attempt, in other words, to reverse the changes already made by the Whigs. Indeed, Peel claimed that the administration of which he was the head had its own moderate reforming intentions. No one in the 1830s would have expected the Prime Minister to produce a detailed programme of policies and Peel's main aim was to show that he was willing to give dispassionate consideration to all practical suggestions for the improvement of laws and institutions and all legitimate demands for the removal of proven abuses.' (Jenkins 1999, pp.73-74)

The traditional (positive) view is that the Tamworth Manifesto was a turning point in the history of the Conservative Party. By accepting modest reform and by appealing to middle-class voters, it is argued, Peel was attempting to broaden the electoral appeal of the party. Eastwood (1992), however, takes issue with this view, arguing that the document was less a party manifesto and more a personal manifesto:

'It is wrong to think of Tamworth as a party document, still less as a party manifesto. This was not a party leader rallying the faithful: this was the Prime Minister (albeit of a minority government) speaking to the people.' (Eastwood 1992, p.31)

Was Peel the founder of the modern Conservative Party?

The Tamworth Manifesto is seen by the historian Norman Gash (1986) as the key document in the formation of the modern Conservative Party because the commitment to gradual change and moderate reform has been a characteristic of British Conservatism ever since. According to Gash, therefore:

'The events of November-December 1834 marked the birth of the modern Conservative Party; and the Tamworth Manifesto was designed to assist its delivery...Its significance was not in its form but in its content...With politics still in the fluid state in which they had been since 1827, it redefined party lines in a manner which could never have been anticipated only two years earlier. The general expectation after the passage of the Reform Act was that the battle of the future would be between an aristocratic party led by the Whigs and a Radical Party pressing for fundamental changes. This never happened.' (Gash 1986, pp.105 and 106-7)

This view has some support. For example:

'Robert Peel's great achievement was to develop a political party which could represent the interests of all people of wealth whether that wealth was derived from property or land, industry or the professions. He managed to create this new voting alliance by advancing a new political creed - conservatism. Peel argued that social, economic and political change should not automatically be opposed. It should be welcomed, but only if it occurred slowly and if it built upon established institutions rather than sweeping them away. By encouraging change, Peel appealed to entrepreneurs and all those who had become wealthy through the changes brought about by the industrial revolution. By emphasising respect for established institutions such as the monarchy and the Church, Peel appealed to the ancient traditions of the landed aristocracy.' (Roberts 1999, p.254)

Gash's view, however, has not won universal support. In fact, a significant historical debate has developed over whether Peel has a rightful claim to be regarded as the founder of modern Conservatism in Britain. In part, this debate reflects different views about the significance of Peel's background, his political apprenticeship under Lord Liverpool, and the possible conflict between his perception of the role of the party leader and that of the executive Prime Minister.

Hilton's view

Unlike Gash, Hilton (1979) argues that Peel was a dogmatically inflexible politician. On certain key matters (especially economic matters) his mind was fixed by the 1820s and it remained fixed for the rest of his career. In particular, Peel remained committed to laissez-faire, free-market solutions to the political and social problems of his age. Since commitment to such solutions was to become a hallmark of Gladstonian Liberalism, if Peel is to be seen as the founder of any political party, it is of the Liberal Party.

Other criticisms of Gash's view

Historians such as Evans (1991, 1994), Stewart (1995) and Newbould (1983) have used evidence from the 1830s and the 1841 general election to suggest that the Conservative victory was based not on any new Peelite vision of 'middle of the road' conservatism but rather on the loyalty of 'traditional' and protectionist Tory supporters in rural England. Evans points out:

'During the debates which preceded the 1841 general election, Peel was careful to give absolutely no hint to his supporters that he was anything other than a convinced protectionist... Peel's backbench supporters were given no reason in 1841 to think that their leader would do other than continue to defend the Corn Laws.' (Evans 1994, p.29)

As a result, Gash's claims about the significance of the Tamworth Manifesto must be significantly tempered. Newbould goes furthest, arguing that Peel's problems in the 1840s were largely due to his failure to transform the Tory Party in the 1830s. He argues that many of Peel's policies were designed to outmanoeuvre his Ultra rivals and to strengthen his own position in the party. In other words, he was using the party as a vehicle to gain power for himself and he cared little about it other than that. Like Evans and Stewart, Newbould believes that the election result in 1841 was a victory for traditional Tory values, not for the new values promoted by Peel.

The two interpretations

The two interpretations below summarise the cases for and against the view that Peel should be regarded as the founder of the modern Conservative Party in Britain.

Interpretation 1 - the case for

The first interpretation starts from the premise that, after the passage of the 1832 Reform Act, there was a very real chance that the Tory Party would be unable to adapt to the new political climate and a very real danger, therefore, that it would collapse. That this did not happen, so the argument goes, was due to Peel's foresight and ability. By redefining conservatism and broadening its appeal, Peel revived the fortunes of the Conservative Party. Peel himself had opposed the passage of the 1832 Reform Act on the grounds that it would 'open a door which we may never close again'. Faced with the political reality of a reformed parliament, however, Peel's pragmatism enabled him to transform the party into a truly national entity capable of appealing to the new middle-class electorate. The aim of the Tamworth Manifesto was to reposition the party, and it succeeded because Peel cleverly combined a commitment to consider further reform (which appealed to the new middle-class voters) with reassurances to the traditional wing of the party. The 1841 general election result was the perfect vindication of Peel's strategy and reveals the extent to which his new vision of Conservatism had been accepted by the British electorate. Peel's subsequent leadership continued the trend, with the repeal of the Corn Laws in 1846 being the culmination of a process designed to confirm the Conservative Party's relevance to the industrial age. Thus Peel guaranteed the survival of Conservatism as a political force in modern Britain and did more than any other leader to shape its development over the next century.

Interpretation 2 - the case against

According to interpretation 2, there are three principal reasons why Peel does not have an exclusive claim to be the founder of modern Conservatism in Britain.

a) The organisation of the party

First, it is questionable how much Peel himself did to reconstruct the party's organisation in the 1830s and, therefore, how effective his attempts to convert his party to his views really were in practice. The Tamworth Manifesto may have made some impact in the short term, but it was not in itself sufficient either to transform the party or to win over substantial sections of the new middle-class electorate in the long term. At a national level, the party's new electoral organisation - a response to the new political climate created by the 1832 Reform Act - was developed not by Peel, but largely through the work of F.R. Bonham. It was Bonham, for example, who set the Carlton Club up as the party's headquarters - a base from which all aspects of electoral performance, including the registration of voters, selection of candidates, canvassing, press relations and finance, could be coordinated. At the

local level, Bonham's work (he was, in effect, Party Chairman) was supplemented by the emergence of new Conservative Associations in towns throughout the country. These set out to mobilise - and maximise - Conservative support by ensuring the registration of voters. They were, however, not set up as a result of some central directive from Peel. Rather, they were the work of 'traditional' Tories attempting to rebuild their local power bases following the difficulties of the period 1828-34. As a result, these new Conservative Associations tended to support traditional Tory policies which had little in common with those proposed in the Tamworth Manifesto. These Conservative Associations fought the 1841 general election campaign, for example, on the basis that the party was committed to agricultural protectionism (Peel himself kept quiet about the future of the Corn Laws). This explains the growing (if temporarily concealed) divide between Peel and his backbenchers. Peel may have been a Conservative Prime Minister, but he was leading an essentially Tory Party.

b) Data from the general election of 1841

Second, data from the general election of 1841 confirms these doubts about the extent to which the policies and character of the Conservative Party were fundamentally changed as a result of Peel's leadership. Some historians argue that the Conservative victory in 1841 was the result not of a spectacularly successful Conservative campaign which won over newly enfranchised middle-class voters in the industrial towns and cities, but rather the result of traditional Tories winning back their former strongholds in the English counties.

c) Peel's legacy

And third, Peel's legacy is not as clear-cut as Gash has claimed. As noted above, it has been suggested that Peel was the founder of the Gladstonian Liberal Party rather than the modern Conservative Party. This argument is based on the emphasis that Peel placed both on laissez-faire, free-market solutions to social and political problems and on the 'moral energy' of executive government - a combination which was also at the heart of Gladstonian Liberalism thirty years later. Many other influences, particularly the Disraelian strand of 'one nation Toryism' in the 1870s shaped the Conservative Party in the second half of the 19th century and the impact of Peelite thinking should therefore be set in its proper context.

MAIN POINTS - Section 1.2

- The second occasion on which Peel has been accused of making a U-turn was over the 1832 Reform Act. He was one of the most outspoken critics of the Bill and yet, once it was passed, he did not campaign to abolish it.
- The traditional view is that Peel felt that his hands were tied during the reform crisis because of his U-turn over Catholic emancipation. Eastwood, however, argues that he acted on principle, whilst Jenkins suggests that ambition explains his actions.
- It was in 1832-34 that Peel emerged as Conservative leader. Wellington conceded the leadership to Peel in May 1834 when he made it known that, in his opinion, the Prime Minister should sit in the Commons.
- In opposition, Peel's strategy was to support the Whig government wherever possible. Historians suggest there were three reasons for this: (1) to ensure that the Whigs were not driven towards the radicals; (2) personal ambition; and (3) fear of the 'mob'.
- Peel's strategy paid off in 1834 when Melbourne was dismissed and he became head of a minority government. Although it lasted only five months, Peel consolidated party unity and, via the Tamworth Manifesto, publicised his political vision.
- Gash argues that Peel was the founder of the modern Conservative Party. Hilton, however, argues that Peel founded the Gladstonian Liberal Party. Other historians have questioned Gash's view that the Tamworth Manifesto explains the Conservative victory in 1841.

Activity 7.2 The Tamworth Manifesto and the 1841 general election

ITEM 1 Extracts from the Tamworth Manifesto

Glossary

- **contentions of party** - party rivalry
- **irrevocable** - unalterable/irreversible
- **insidious** - craftily underhand
- **vortex** - whirlpool
- **agitation** - protest
- **in public estimation** - in the eyes of the public
- **impression** - belief
- **redress** - remedy
- **deference to** - willingness to obey
- **prescriptive authority** - traditional authority
- **ecclesiastical** - concerning the Church

To the electors of Tamworth

I...appeal...to that class which is much less interested in the **contentions of party**, than in the maintenance of order and the cause of good government...With respect to the Reform Bill itself, I will repeat now the declaration which I made when I entered the House of Commons as a member of the reformed Parliament, that I consider the Reform Bill as a final and **irrevocable** settlement of a great constitutional question - a settlement which no friend to the peace and welfare of this country would attempt to disturb, either by direct or **insidious** means...If by adopting the spirit of the Reform Bill it be meant that we are to live in a perpetual **vortex** of **agitation**; that public men can only support themselves **in public estimation** by adopting every popular **impression** of the day, by promising the instant **redress** of anything which anybody may call an abuse, by abandoning altogether that great aid of government, more powerful than either law or reason - the respect for ancient rights and the **deference to prescriptive authority**; if this be the spirit of the Reform Bill, I will not undertake to adopt it. But if the spirit of the Reform Bill implies merely a careful review of institutions, civil and **ecclesiastical**, undertaken in a friendly temper, combining with the firm maintenance of established rights, the correction of proved abuses and the **redress** of real grievances - in that case, I can for myself and colleagues undertake to act in such a spirit and with such intentions.

Part of the Tamworth Manifesto.

ITEM 2 The 1841 internal general election (i)

(i) General election results 1832-41

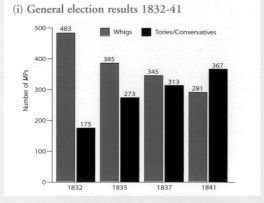

(ii) The general election of 1841

Party	Total votes	%	Unopposed	Elected
Conservative	306,314	50.9	212	367
Whigs/Liberal	273,902	46.9	113	271
Chartist	692	0.1	0	0
Irish Repealer	1§2,537	2.1	12	20

ITEM 3 What is Conservatism?

Glossary
- **subversion** - overthrow
- **encroachment** - spread
- **innovation** - new and original ideas
- **illiberal and contracted** - bigoted and narrow minded
- **peerage** - aristocracy

'What is a Conservative - what does the word mean?' I think I can give a short and clear definition. A Conservative is a man attached on principle to the English constitution, to the Established Church, to our mixed institutions. Well, so is, or at least so was, a Whig of the old school. There is another characteristic - a Conservative is one who, having this loyalty to the constitution, believes that it is threatened with **subversion** by the **encroachment** of democracy and is prepared to defend it against that danger. The Conservative Party, therefore, includes all those shades and degrees of political opinion...who agree in these two points - attachment to king, Lords, Commons, Church and state, and a belief that there is a pressing weight of these institutions being overthrown by the weight of democracy...The Conservative Party is not identical to the Tory Party - it includes, indeed, the Tories, but it is a more comprehensive term and the basis of a wider one...[The definition of a Conservative given above] does not necessarily suppose an abstract horror of all **innovation**, or an **illiberal and contracted** view of politics. On the contrary, the opinions and feelings of the great body of Conservatives in this country are liberal, candid and generous...With regard to its numbers and social position, the Conservative Party does not consist alone of the **peerage**...it embraces a vast proportion of the numerical amount of the population. It extends to every quarter of the Empire and every class of the community...I claim for the Conservatives the rank of a national party, comprising a vast section of the people.

From Chapters of Contemporary History, *written in 1836 by Sir John Benn Walsh, Conservative MP 1830-34 and 1838-68 and a supporter of Peel.*

ITEM 4 A contemporary view

February 18th 1838

I know no more of Peel's opinions and designs than what I can gather from his conduct and what he is likely to entertain under present circumstances; but it must be his object to delay coming into office till he can do so as a powerful minister and till it is made manifest to Parliament and the country that he is demanded by a great public exigency and is not marching in as the result of party triumph. If the resignation of the present government should take place under any circumstances which admitted of reunion of the Whigs and radicals, and of the whole reunited party being held together in opposition to a Conservative government, Peel would be little more secure, and not more able to act with efficiency and independence than he was in 1835 and this he will never submit to...His interest, therefore, (and consequently, I suppose, his design) is to restrain the impatience of his followers; to let the government lose ground in public estimation gently and considerately, not violently and rancorously...so that his return to power may be more in appearance the act of the Whig ministry than any act of his own.

Extract from The Greville Memoirs, *the diary of Charles Greville, a Whig who worked as clerk to the Privy Council.*

Glossary
- **exigency** - urgent demand
- **in public estimation** - in the eyes of the public
- **rancorously** - bitterly

ITEM 5 A historian's view (i)

At first sight, an analysis of the election according to type of seat seems to support the conclusion that Peel had broadened the Tory base. Conservatives won almost as many seats as the Whigs/Liberals in the English and Welsh boroughs. For a 'party of the land' this was a notable achievement. Yet an examination of these boroughs shows that only 44 seats were won in places with electorates of 1,000 voters or more. In the 58 largest boroughs, the Whigs/Liberals won three times as many seats. These large boroughs were concentrated in the Midlands and the North - precisely where Peel was seeking to broaden the party's electoral base. But, in general, the Conservatives did best in boroughs least changed by the 1832 Reform Act. In many of these, actual contests were a rarity, and it is not often mentioned that there were actual contests in 1841 in only 47% of constituencies. The Conservative majority of 1841, therefore, was based in the smaller boroughs and, especially, in the counties of England. The Conservatives hardly made any showing in Scottish boroughs. They won in 1841 because they had majority support where the seats were thickest on the ground, not where electorates were most numerous or most changed by recent developments. It was the party of rural England and its small market towns - deferential, Church-loving, intolerant of other religious views and keener to preserve the past than to look to the future. Despite Peel's efforts, his party remained dominated by old-style Tory opinion. The reformist elements so prominent in the Tamworth Manifesto of 1834 hardly featured in the election literature of 1841. The 1841 general election was properly a victory for Protectionist Toryism, not Peelite Conservatism.

Adapted from Evans 1991.

ITEM 6 A historian's view (ii)

The Melbourne government's proposals in 1841 to lower tariffs on timber and foreign (not colonial) sugar and to introduce a fixed duty on wheat led to its downfall. The opposition decided to attack the government over the sugar duties and won the vote by 317 to 281. In the no-confidence vote which was then proposed, the government lost by a single vote and Parliament was dissolved. The Melbourne government's decision to introduce a fixed duty on wheat provided Conservative candidates at the general election with an ideal war cry. Agricultural protection, an issue which united the interests of landowners and farmers, naturally dominated the county contests. But in many small and medium-sized boroughs, too, the maintenance of the Corn Laws was of paramount concern. In Essex, for example, all ten borough and county seats were won by supporters of protectionism. Meanwhile, in certain northern industrial towns, such as Blackburn, the Conservatives were arguing that the ruination of British agriculture, arising from the loss of protective tariffs, would lead to the urban labour markets being flooded with unemployed farm labourers whose competition for jobs would force down wage rates.

Adapted from Jenkins 1999.

ITEM 7 A historian's view (iii)

It was, without question, Peel who reunited the Tory Party and he did so in a way that nobody else in the 1830s could have done. The Ultras, who had defected to the Whigs after Catholic emancipation now returned to the fold. If anything, it was the Whigs who began to fragment. During the 1830s, Peel experienced less embarrassment from his backbenchers than Melbourne did from his frontbenchers. Although it was brief, Peel's first administration was important because it provided experience of office and helped to boost the Tory vote in the 1935 election. Peel's priority in the late 1830s appeared not to bring down the Whigs but, on occasion, actually to keep them in office. This could certainly be seen as a desire to uphold the integrity of a reforming government and maintain respect for the constitution. Gash argues that Peel was guided by the 'governmental ethic' in which the main duty of the parliamentary party was to sustain a government, not to try to remove it. There was also an element of political wisdom here. If Peel had combined with the radicals to unseat the Tories, the Tories could easily have been portrayed as the party which had undermined reform. Peel realised that the Conservatives had to develop an image as a government in waiting. This restraint of the 19th century is difficult to appreciate in the light of the more aggressive style of leadership in the 20th century.

Adapted from Lee 1994.

Questions

1. a) Judging from Item 1, who was the Tamworth Manifesto aimed at?
   b) What does Item 1 tell us about Peel's political stance at the time of his first administration?
   c) Why do you think historians have claimed that the Tamworth Manifesto is a key historical document?
2. a) Judging from Items 1 and 3, what was the difference between Toryism and Conservatism in the 1830s?
   b) What do these items tell us about the way in which Peel attempted to transform his party?
3. a) Judging from Items 2 and 4, did Peel succeed in transforming his party?
   b) Would you agree that the Tamworth Manifesto is a key to explaining the 1841 general election result? Give reasons for your answer.
4. Using evidence in Items 1-7 give arguments for and against the view that Peel was the founder of the modern Conservative Party.

2 Peel in power 1841-46

Key issues

1. What sort of Prime Minister was Peel?
2. To what extent was financial policy at the heart of Peel's approach to government?
3. To what extent did Peel's financial and Irish policies foreshadow the problems caused by the Corn Law crisis?

2.1 What were the aims of Peel's second administration?

Peel's record

Peel's second administration of 1841-46 has been widely regarded as amongst the most significant governments of the 19th century - perhaps *the* most significant. The administration's reputation is largely based on the breadth and intensity of its policy-making. This has led historians such as Donald Read to conclude that:

'Peel was arguably the best peace-time Prime

Minister in British history.' (Read 1987, p.ix)

A controversial administration

Whatever its successes, Peel's second administration was also a very controversial one - in that his policies have also been interpreted by many historians (see, for example, Lee 1994) as setting up a fundamental conflict between 'Peel the Prime Minister' and 'Peel the party leader'. It is often argued that, by acting in what he interpreted as the national interest, Peel betrayed the interests of his party - over tariff reform, income tax, Ireland, and ultimately (and, as it turned out, also fatally), the repeal of the Corn Laws. In other words, whilst Peel spent the 1830s rebuilding the Conservative Party, his approach to the premiership in 1841-46 seemed to be consciously designed to destroy it. Discussing the Corn Law crisis which led to the downfall of Peel's government, for example, Eastwood argues :

> 'Peel had quite deliberately isolated himself and, in so doing he had destroyed his party, or at any rate driven an immovable wedge between Peelism and Toryism. The destruction of the party was not an unfortunate, unintended consequence of the Corn Law crisis - it was, rather, quite deliberately engineered by Peel.' (Eastwood 1992, p.33)

Peel's statements

Those historians who argue that the second administration witnessed a betrayal of Conservative interests focus on Peel's own statements in which he describes the role of the Prime Minister as being 'above' party. When he came to power in 1841, Peel wrote of the role of Prime Minister that:

> 'I am told that in the exercise of power...I must be the instrument of maintaining the opinions and feeling which I myself am disposed to repudiate. With my views of government, the obligations which it imposes, the duties which it entails, the sacrifices it involves - I am not disposed to add to these sacrifices, by accepting it with a degrading and dishonourable condition...If I exercise power, it shall be upon my conception - perhaps imperfect, perhaps mistaken - but my sincere conception of public duty.'

Comments like this are often used to suggest that Peel believed that party had a completely subordinate function. It is suggested that his belief was that the Prime Minister should do his public duty on behalf of the monarch (who, from 1837, was Queen Victoria) and in the national interest, and that it was also part of his responsibility to interpret what the national interest was. Jenkins (1999), for example, describes this as 'Peel's instinctively 'executive' approach to high office and goes on to argue that the eventual split in the party over the Corn Laws was largely the result of Peel's reluctance to take into account the interests and prejudices of

the Conservative backbenchers, even though he owed his position as Prime Minister to their support. Evans puts it like this:

> 'He was the Queen's minister and he answered first to her and through her to the nation. Party considerations ranked low on his list of priorities. He saw the Corn Law crisis as essentially a conflict between the interests of the nation and the interests of a section of his party. He was arrogant enough to believe, furthermore, that even this section was misleading itself...He thought that he was saving Tory backbenchers from their ignorance and folly. He would not stoop to saving his party by compromising his policy.' (Evans 1994, p.30)

The composition of Peel's Cabinet

Some historians have argued that the composition of Peel's Cabinet (see Box 7.4) was insensitive. For example, Adelman argues:

> 'As a whole...Peel's government was an exceptionally strong one in terms of personality, experience and administrative ability...Politically, however, its outlook was blunter. Even before the final crisis of 1846 (over the repeal of the Corn Laws), ministers failed to gauge accurately the temper of the House of Commons over a number of key issues....the government was essentially "Peel's Ministry"...but...that very domination produced its own problems for the Conservative Party.' (Adelman 1989, pp.27-28)

BOX 7.4 Key posts in Peel's first Cabinet

- **Prime Minister** - Robert Peel
- **Minister without Portfolio** - the Duke of Wellington
- **Lord Chancellor** - Lord Lyndhurst (he had served in this position in Peel's first administration and was an Ultra)
- **Chancellor of the Exchequer** - Henry Goulburn (the only untitled member of the Cabinet - though he did have aristocratic connections through his mother and wife)
- **Home Secretary** - Sir James Graham (one of the Whigs who had left Melbourne's government and joined Peel's front bench)
- **Foreign Secretary** - Lord Aberdeen (he had been Secretary for War and the Colonies in Peel's first administration)
- **Secretary for War and the Colonies** - Viscount Stanley (another of the Whigs who had left Melbourne's government and joined Peel's front bench)
- **President of the Board of Trade** - Lord Ripon (formerly Lord Goderich and, before that, Frederick Robinson - the man who had served as Chancellor under Lord Liverpool during the so-called 'Liberal' Tory phase)

It should be noted, however, that this view is disputed. Jenkins, for example, argues:

'The composition of Peel's Cabinet inevitably reflected his need to achieve a balance between the various sections of the Conservative Party...Taking an overall view of Peel's Cabinet team, the most striking fact is that it was an almost entirely aristocratic body.' (Jenkins 1999, p.96)

Arguments against the view that Peel betrayed his party

There are two main arguments against the view that Peel betrayed his party. First, some historians have suggested that the conflict between 'Peel the Prime Minister' and 'Peel the party leader' was actually less of a conflict than has sometimes been suggested. It is argued that, in reality, the two positions were, at least in Peel's mind, complementary. Besides, Gash (1976) argues, national leadership is often more effective than party leadership.

And second, there is the theory that, by acting in the national interest rather than in the narrow party interest, Peel believed he could best demonstrate the continued relevance of the Conservative Party in an ever-changing industrial nation. In other words, there was no conflict between 'Peel the Prime Minister' and 'Peel the party leader'. By doing what he thought was in the national interest, Peel was doing what he thought was in the Conservative Party's interest - even if this was not a view shared by many of his own backbenchers.

Peel's leadership style

It was noted above in the section on Peel's period as Chief Secretary for Ireland that he found it difficult to delegate tasks to his colleagues. As Prime Minister, Peel was something of what today would be called a 'control freak':

'Although his colleagues were an unusually able group of men, Peel wished to be fully informed about every aspect of policy. As far as he was concerned, responsibility ultimately lay with him and so he took on a burden of work which was quite exceptional. He even introduced his own Budgets and Gladstone [a junior minister until being promoted to the Cabinet in 1843] noted that government was not so much conducted by Cabinet, as by heads of department in individual consultation with the Prime Minister.' (Watts 1994, p.58)

Peel's supervision of his colleagues meant that, on occasion, he interfered in the way in which they ran their department. This was particularly the case when it came to foreign policy:

'In the field of foreign policy, Peel exercised a close scrutiny over Lord Aberdeen's work, often amending the drafts of despatches before they were sent to British ambassadors abroad. Indeed, Peel sometimes found it necessary to counter the pacific and conciliatory disposition of his Foreign Secretary, believing as he did in a more robust assertion of Britain's interests - especially in any dealings with France.' (Jenkins 1999, p.99)

2.2 Economic policy

Peel and economic policy

Most historians agree that the main focus of the Peel administration was on economic reform and economic recovery because, Peel believed, economic recovery would lead to greater social harmony. This view is summarised by Eric Evans as follows:

'[Peel's] first task, like Pitt's, was the reconstruction of the economy. Peel had come to power during an economic crisis. Chartism flourished and briefly threatened the social order. The government's deficit had been mounting steadily since 1837 and stood at £7.5 million early in 1842. Peel perceived the short-term crisis but was more concerned with the damage which depression did to social harmony. He needed to reduce the financial disabilities under which working people laboured.' (Evans 1996, p.262)

In support of this view, it is often noted that Peel himself said in 1841:

'We must make this a cheap country for living in.'

The standard view, therefore, is that Peel was keen to improve the lives of ordinary people and that he believed that the best way to achieve this was by introducing economic reforms. In other words, his thinking was as follows:

- The only means of achieving social and political stability was through economic growth.
- The only means of achieving economic growth was through sound financial planning and balanced budgets.
- The only means of achieving balanced budgets was to keep government cheap and to ensure that the country's principal wealth generators within the commercial classes remained productive.
- If wealth generators continued to expand their activities, this would generate greater revenue, create greater employment opportunities and improve the living conditions for the people as a whole.

Not all historians accept that Peel's main aim was to improve the lives of ordinary people, however. Beales (1974), for example, argues that Peel's reformism has been exaggerated. Hilton (1979) suggests that Peel was ideologically motivated - he had fixed views on economic management and his policies were determined by these fixed views. Watts (1994) claims that Peel's main concern was the maintenance of public order.

The 1842 'Free Trade' Budget

The 1842 Budget was an important turning point in terms of economic management. It marked a significant shift away from protectionism and towards free trade. For some historians (such as Hilton 1979), this is confirmation that Peel had long been a convinced free trader. For others (such as Gash 1976), it is evidence of Peel's vision and flexibility - Peel saw what was in the national interest and devised policies accordingly.
Peel introduced the Budget himself in March 1842 in a speech lasting over four hours. In his speech, he argued that there was a major economic crisis. To solve this crisis, he said, two key measures were necessary.

First, income tax (which had been abolished in 1816) was to be reintroduced at seven pence in the pound on all incomes greater than £150 per year. This was the first time that income tax had been imposed in peacetime. By excluding incomes less than £150 per year, Peel ensured that the measure left poorer sections of the population unaffected. The new tax was to be a temporary measure - initially imposed for three years.

And second, export duty was to be abolished altogether on manufactured goods, whilst the level of import duty was to be reduced on 750 out of the 1,200 products which charged duty. In general, imported raw materials would be taxed at no more than 5%, imported partly manufactured goods at no more than 12% and imported manufactured goods at no more than 20%. In addition, a new sliding scale of duties was to be charged on imported corn. The aim of this measure was to stimulate a trade revival which would allow the government to balance its books (since a significantly greater volume of trade would provide a greater amount of government revenue even though the amount of government revenue collected on each item would be less than in previous years).

A controversial Budget

The 1842 Budget was controversial, but by no means a complete break with the past:
'It should be noted that Peel was reverting to ideas which he had advocated as a member of Wellington's government early in 1830 and which were inspired by Huskisson's "liberal" tariff reforms of the mid-1820s. But while the policy prescription was not new, the introduction of an income tax in peacetime remained politically controversial and was something that the Whigs had never dared to propose.' (Jenkins 1999, p.106)

The political context at the time of the Budget may also help to explain why Peel was prepared to be controversial:
'Peel asked the wealthier classes to make an additional contribution, in the form of income tax, during an economic crisis so that the "labouring classes of society" might not be further burdened. As this appeal was made near the time of substantial disturbances by the Chartists...it is not surprising that the middle and the upper classes might consider their self-interest better served by a small additional tax burden than by resisting the income tax and risking popular disturbances.' (Evans 1991, p.51)

The impact of the Budget

The measures put into place by the 1842 Budget did not work instantly:
'The Free Trade Budget of 1842 did not produce instant results in terms of reviving trade and improved employment prospects .This explains the otherwise surprising impression recorded by Charles Greville in August 1843 that the government seemed to be in the doldrums [ie very unpopular] and Peel's own prestige on the wane.' (Jenkins 1999, p.109)
Nevertheless, by 1845, it was clear that the 1842 Budget had contributed to a general economic recovery. Income tax revenue and the general stimulus to consumption provided by the reduction of tariffs offset the lower tariff returns on individual items, ensuring that government income grew overall. In 1845, Peel was able to predict that there would be a 'Budget surplus' (a surplus of government revenue) in 1845-46 - for the first time since 1836.

In addition, according to Peel's admirers, the 1842 Budget made a longer-term impact:
'Peel's Budget was not just a masterly exercise in fiscal management [the management of public revenue] and free trade principles. It marked a decisive shift in the way 19th century politicians thought about the economy and presented economic policy to the nation. It was the first time that government fiscal policy had been conceived as a remedy for poverty and unrest. And, in its immediate political impact, it opened an era in which Budget Day became an event of national significance that could capture the imagination of Westminster and the world beyond. Gladstone, for one, was to take both these lessons to heart.' (Cooper 1995, p.133)

Tariff reductions 1842-45

Between the 1842 Budget and that of 1845, the government introduced three Bills designed to reduce import tariffs on individual items unaffected by the 1842 Budget. In 1842, import duty on cattle was lowered. In 1843 a Canada Corn Bill was passed, allowing corn from Canada to be imported with a very low tariff. And then, in 1844, a Bill was introduced which was designed to lower the tariff on imports of foreign (ie non-colonial) sugar. Whilst a group of 85 Conservative backbenchers voted against the lower import duty on cattle and 60 Conservative backbenchers voted against the Canada Corn Bill, the opposition of 62 Conservative MPs in the vote on an amendment to the Sugar Bill was enough to ensure that the government was defeated. Peel's response was to call a meeting of Conservative MPs and to threaten to resign unless the decision was reversed. When a second vote was taken on the amendment a short time later, the government won a majority.

The debate over the Sugar Crisis of 1844

The 'Sugar Crisis' of 1844 has been the subject of debate. Whilst Stewart (1969 and 1971) argues that this crisis was the point at which Peel alienated a substantial number of backbenchers, making his eventual defeat over the Corn Laws inevitable, Fisher (1975) argues that, in fact, Peel patched up relations with his backbenchers after the crisis and there is no evidence of any sustained or organised backbench opposition before 1846.

The 1845 Budget

Since Peel was able to predict a Budget surplus for 1845-46, he could have chosen to end income tax after its initial three-year term. Instead, however, the 1845 Budget imposed income tax for a further three-year period so that the forthcoming Budget surplus could be used to cut tariffs further. All surviving export duties (ie those on raw materials and on partly manufactured products) were abolished in the 1845 Budget and import duties were further reduced and, in some cases, abolished altogether. Most controversially, import duties on sugar were further reduced and those on cotton (and many other raw materials) abolished altogether.

Most historians would agree that the net result of these changes was that:

'In all, between 1842 and 1846, the work of transforming Britain into a free-trade country was largely accomplished, leaving only a remnant to be done by Gladstone in 1853 and 1860.' (Gash 1979, p.234)

Other economic reforms

The Peel government introduced two other important economic reforms designed to foster a more stable economic climate in which business activity might readily flourish - the Bank Charter Act and the Companies Act, both passed in 1844.

The Bank Charter Act

The Bank Charter Act was designed to regulate the banking system and restore business confidence by stabilising the currency. Its main features are outlined in Box 7.5.

BOX 7.5 **The Bank Charter Act 1844**

The Bank Charter Act's main provisions were as follows:

- The Bank of England was to be the central issuer of banknotes.
- Other existing banks were restricted to issuing the average number of notes they had issued in the three months prior to the passing of the Act.
- Banks which amalgamated were prohibited from issuing banknotes.
- New banks were prevented from issuing banknotes.
- The Bank of England could issue banknotes up to £14 million, but any paper money issued above that figure had to be covered by the Bank's gold bullion reserves.

The Act has generally been praised by historians on three grounds. First, it is suggested that it introduced a period of financial stability. Second, it is argued that it made a psychological impact, creating a climate of business confidence because people were no longer worried that banks would collapse. And third, it put into place a system which remained the foundation of the British banking system until the First World War. Jenkins, however, notes that:

'If Peel's measure had operated according to his intentions, the effects would have been deflationary, limiting the scope for banks to finance economic growth and diversification. But for the new gold discoveries from the late 1840s onwards (a substantial proportion of which found their way into the Bank of England reserves, enabling money supply to be increased), and the development of alternative forms of "money", such as cheques and Bills of Exchange, the expansionary economic conditions of the 1850s and 1860s, which Peel is usually credited with fostering, could not have occurred.' (Jenkins 1999, p.111)

The Companies Act 1844

Like the Bank Charter Act, the Companies Act was designed to encourage public and business confidence and, as a result, to stimulate greater investment activity. The Act made it compulsory for all companies to be officially registered and it required them to issue prospectuses and to publish their accounts annually. This element of greater scrutiny gave investors added confidence that their investments in company stocks and shares would be safe. Prior to the Act, a 'company' could advertise for funds without any form of supervision and many individual investors had, as a result, lost their money to bogus companies or dishonest individuals who had published misleading advertisements inviting investment.

2.3 Peel and social reform

Peel had no 'social policy'
Even those historians who look back at Peel's administration with admiration tend to accept that he did not have a 'social policy'. Indeed, they argue that he did not need one because he was convinced that economic growth would lead to social improvements. It would create jobs and provide people with more money to spend. This would then lead to improved working and living conditions. Many historians point out that this is consistent with Peel's attitude towards state intervention. Peel, they suggest, regarded state intervention as potentially counter-productive and far less efficient than free-market solutions to social problems.

Peel was a genuine reformer
Even if Peel had no 'social policy', a number of important social reforms were introduced during his premiership. For some historians (such as Gash 1976), this shows that Peel was a genuine reformer who accepted that change was necessary but understood that the best way to maintain stability was to take small steps forward over time. There are two main arguments in support of the view that Peel was a genuine reformer.

First, in many of his speeches in support of the imposition of income tax in 1842 and its renewal in 1845, Peel emphasised that economic growth would be beneficial to the whole population, including members of the working class. The fact that income tax was imposed only on those earning over £150 per year shows that he was sensitive to the needs of poorer people. Although Peel appeared to be against reform in that he opposed the reduction of daily working hours in textile mills from 10 to 12 hours (by rejecting the Ashley amendment - see Box 7.6), in fact he was being consistent. He was concerned that the loss of two hours' production would lead to a drop in output and therefore to a loss of earnings for the workers - what he described as 'an income tax on the poor man'. Such sentiments show that he was genuinely concerned with the welfare of the poor - as does the fact that he set up a commission to examine

BOX 7.6

(i) The Mines Act 1842
In 1840 the MP Lord Ashley (he became the Earl of Shaftesbury in 1851) managed to persuade the government to set up a Committee of Inquiry into the working of the 1833 Factory Act and into child employment in industries not covered by the Act. The committee's first report on coal mining was published in May 1842 and led to the 1842 Mines Act. The report so shocked Parliament that the 1842 Mines Bill passed its first and second readings in June and, despite some opposition from mine-owning lords, became law in July. The main provisions of the law were as follows:
- girls, women and boys under the age of 10 were prevented from working underground in mines
- an inspector was appointed to enforce the regulations.

Although Ashley originally proposed that boys under the age of 13 should be prevented from working underground and although the appointment of a single inspector was clearly inadequate, this Act was significant because it was the first time that adult women had been protected and because it accepted the principle that the industry needed to be regulated.

(ii) The Factory Act 1844
Following pressure from the Ten Hour Movement and, in particular from Lord Ashley in the

Commons, the Home Secretary, James Graham, introduced the Factory Bill in 1843. This Bill, however, had to be withdrawn by the government after protests from Nonconformists (Graham's Bill had proposed that factory schools should be set up and run by committees chaired by local Anglican priests). Despite this setback, a Factory Act, also introduced by Graham, was passed in 1844. The Factory Act 1844 (which applied only to textile mills) contained the following provisions:
- children aged 8-13 could work a maximum of 6.5 hours per day
- girls and women over the age of 13 could work a maximum of 12 hours a day
- dangerous machinery should be fenced
- meals were to be eaten in a place away from the work area.

Although the Act was an advance on the 1833 Factory Act (see Unit 8), it did not go as far as those who supported the Ten Hour movement wanted. When Lord Ashley proposed an amendment to the Bill which would have reduced the maximum hours worked in a day by women to ten hours, the amendment was initially passed by the Commons with a majority of nine. But, as with the Sugar Crisis which broke out a short time later, Peel threatened to resign if the amendment was not defeated. When a second vote was taken on it, it was defeated by 138 votes.

Adapted from Royle 1997 and Jenkins 1999.

the state of public health in towns and cities.

And second, Peel accepted the need for some regulation of working conditions. After all, the government could have blocked the Mines Act of 1842 and the Factory Act of 1844 (see Box 7.6), but it did not do so. This shows that Peel accepted that gradual reform and a degree of regulation was necessary and acceptable.

Peel was a reluctant reformer

Other historians (such as Beales 1974) have argued that Peel was a reluctant reformer who would have preferred no change at all but was forced to make small concessions in the hope that more radical reform could be avoided. Five main pieces of evidence can be cited in support of this theory.

First, Peel resisted pressure from backbench Conservative MPs to change the Poor Law Amendment Act, arguing that the system was right in principle and generous and generally fair. A genuinely reforming Prime Minister would have used the pressure to change the Act as an opportunity to introduce reform.

Second, although the 1842 Mines Act was an important advance, it was obviously inadequate (especially the clause providing for just a single inspector). One interpretation is that the mood of Parliament following the publication of the report on mines was one of such shock that Peel and his government realised that they would have to make some kind of concession. The fact that the final Act was inadequate, it could be argued, reveals that Peel and his colleagues were only prepared to make the minimum concession acceptable to Parliament in the circumstances.

Third, Peel resisted Ashley's amendment reducing women's maximum daily working hours to ten and he even threatened to resign over the issue. Peel claimed that there were good economic reasons for objecting to the amendment (he argued that mills would lose two hours' production and, since the export of textiles made up 80% of exports as a whole, Britain's economic position would be undermined). The fact that he put economic growth above humane working conditions, it could be said, shows that he was not really interested in people's welfare. In September 1842, Lord Ashley suggested as much when he said:

'Imports and exports, here is Peel's philosophy! There it begins and there it ends.'

Certainly, there is an argument that Peel's refusal to accept the Ashley amendment is evidence that he was reluctant to accept reform and concerned to ensure that any reforms that were passed resulted in minimal change.

Fourth, although Peel set up a commission to examine the state of public health in towns and cities, he produced no legislation to combat the serious problems which the commission exposed. Again, this suggests that he was reluctant to introduce reforms.

And fifth, many historians have pointed out that, by the time that Peel became Prime Minister, the political climate was changing. The series of parliamentary reports commissioned by the Whigs in the late 1830s and the extra-parliamentary agitation for a range of humanitarian causes supported by radical politicians and evangelical Tories like Lord Ashley had begun to change the public mood. The exposure of cruel and degrading working practices and horrendous living conditions suggested that there might be cases in which it was right for the government to intervene. If this was the case, then it is significant that the impetus for the 1842 Mines Act and the 1844 Factory Act came from Lord Ashley and the Ten Hour movement rather than from the government. Far from being an enthusiastic reformer, Peel can be seen as a reluctant reformer, desperately trying to keep the new enthusiasm for government intervention at bay.

MAIN POINTS - Part 2

- Some historians argue that, by acting in what he saw as the national interest, Prime Minister Peel betrayed his party. Other historians deny this because (1) there was no real conflict between his role as Prime Minister and as party leader or (2) Peel's actions were designed to demonstrate the continued relevance of the Conservative Party.

- Peel found it difficult to delegate tasks to his colleagues and closely monitored their work. On occasion, he interfered in the way in which they ran their departments.

- Most historians agree that the main focus of the Peel administration was on economic reform and economic recovery because, Peel believed, economic recovery would lead to greater social harmony.

- The 1842 Budget was an important turning point in terms of economic management. It marked a significant shift away from protectionism and towards free trade (a shift which continued in 1842-45).

- Two other important economic reforms were the 1844 Bank Charter Act and the 1844 Companies Act.

- Most historians accept that Peel did not have a 'social policy': he did not need one because he was convinced that economic growth would lead to greater social harmony. Nevertheless, two important social reforms were passed - the 1842 Mines Act and the 1844 Factory Act.

- Some historians argue that Peel was a genuine reformer. Others argue that he was a reluctant reformer.

Activity 7.3 Peel's second ministry

ITEM 1 The reintroduction of income tax

THE QUEEN'S "SEVENPENCE."

Among the great benefits of direct taxation is its far greater economy in three ways. In the first place the people would save half the whole amount now spent on the levy of customs and excise - supposing customs to be altogether abolished - therefore by this amount would taxation be decreased. But there would be another and far larger gain, not always borne in mind. The consumers of indirectly taxed articles pay much more in addition to the value of the article than the actual duty, the price of the goods being always augmented by more than the tax...There is a third advantage and that is the diminution, if not removal, of the present irresistible inducement to adulterate taxed goods which the duties create. To the all important interest of the working man in his scheme of an income tax, Sir Robert Peel showed that he was fully alive. He said in one of his speeches: 'I do think myself warranted in saying that I have done all that could be accomplished for the working man.'

From Sir Robert Peel, As a Type of Statesmanship, Jelinger Symons (1856).

This cartoon from 1842 shows Robert Peel collecting sevenpence from Queen Victoria. Sevenpence was the amount in the pound that those who earned more than £150 per year had to pay in income tax.

ITEM 2 Peel and the Ashley amendment

Peel's objection to the Ashley amendment (which proposed that women workers' should work for no more than ten hours a day) was not just based on his economic principles (ie that there should be a free market). He also argued that the amendment would harm the interests of those it was supposed to protect. Always the master of plausible arguments, he managed to disguise his distaste for over-enthusiastic state intervention behind a wall of practical difficulties and concerns. It was clear to all that the amendment would effectively have also restricted male workers to a ten-hour day, because women and children made up a majority of the workforce in mills. In Peel's view, this was going beyond the legitimate scope of state intervention. He warned that a shorter working day would lead to loss of production, and therefore to a loss of earnings for the workers. It would also lead to a reduction in the competitiveness of British exports in overseas markets at a time when textiles made up around 80% of total exports and provided employment for nearly half a million people.

Peel's judgement was that the dangers posed to the success of the textile industry and the livelihoods of those who depended on it far exceeded any benefits to society derived from women working shorter hours, however desirable that might be in principle. Whilst it would be inaccurate to describe his attitude as being purely based on a belief in a laissez-faire approach (he had already accepted a degree of government intervention), it is obvious that he wished restrictive legislation to be minimised. In addition, there is a strong suspicion that his stance was taken, in part, out of annoyance at the way in which the House of Commons was trying to dictate the details of his government's legislation.

Adapted from Jenkins 1999.

ITEM 3 Peel and social reform

In terms of social reform, Peel did little, and what he did do was in response to public pressure or the campaigning of committed individuals. The Mines Act of 1842, for example, was carried after the report of the Royal Commission had shocked public opinion. That Act and the 1844 Factory Act were very much the work of Lord Ashley, who drew attention to the issues and provided the impetus for improvement. Both Peel and his Home Secretary, Graham, were sceptical about the value of direct measures of social reform. They believed that, at best, they tackled the symptoms and not the cause and, at worst, they were a serious limitation on the freedom of manufacturers to run their businesses as efficiently as possible. They believed that it was not the state's role to produce legislation to tackle social discontent. It was more important to ensure that there was plenty of employment and cheap bread available. Only by improving the purchasing power of the masses could the condition of the people be transformed. Whilst, therefore, Peel could claim in his speeches that his policies were designed to help the poorer sections of society, Ashley could equally claim, with frustration, that 'all Peel's affinities [sympathy] are towards wealth and capital. What has he ever proposed for the working class?' When Peel was not forced to act, he did not - for example, he set up a commission to examine problems in towns and cities but took no action when it reported.

Adapted from Lee 1994.

Questions

1. Look at Item 1.
   a) Why did Peel reintroduce income tax?
   b) How did his approach to economics differ from that of previous administrations?
   c) 'Peel's economic reforms were his main achievement.' Explain this statement.
2. Using Items 1-3, give arguments for and against the view that Peel had the interests of the working class at heart.
3. a) What does Item 2 tell us about (i) Peel's beliefs and (ii) his political skills?
   b) Why exactly did Peel oppose Ashley's ten-hour amendment?
   c) What does Peel's behaviour tell us about his leadership style?
4. Using Item 3, give arguments for and against the view that Peel was a reluctant reformer.

3 Peel and the repeal of the Corn Laws

Key issues

1. What led to the crisis over the Corn Laws?
2. Why did Peel decide to repeal the Corn Laws?
3. Did Peel betray his party over the Corn Law issue?
4. What were the consequences of the repeal of the Corn Laws for both Peel and the Conservative Party?

3.1 Peel, Ireland and the Corn Laws

Had Peel lost the support of backbenchers before 1845?

It was noted in Part 2 above that there is a debate over the extent to which Peel's actions in the period 1841-44 (particularly his threats to resign over the

Sugar Crisis and Ashley's ten-hour amendment) alienated him from his backbenchers. Some historians (notably Stewart 1969 and 1971, Adelman 1989 and Evans 1991) argue that, by the time the crisis over the Corn Laws arose, Peel had already alienated a large number of backbenchers. The abolition of the Corn Laws was, in other words, simply the last straw. Others (notably Fisher 1975 and Gash 1976) argue that only a small group of Conservative backbenchers consistently voted against the government in the period 1841-46 and that it is wrong to assume that an anti-Peel faction had developed with the intention of overthrowing him when the opportunity presented itself. Although Peel faced backbench revolts in the period 1841-45, he was always able to patch up relations with most of those who had rebelled.

In addition to the Sugar Crisis and to Peel's stance over the ten-hour amendment in 1844, the Maynooth Grant Crisis of 1845 has been cited as severely denting Peel's reputation with his backbenchers.

Background to the Maynooth Grant Crisis of 1845

Peel's rise to power coincided with the resurgence of Daniel O'Connell's Repeal movement (see Unit 9, Sections 2.4-2.5). The way in which Peel dealt with the threat posed by the Repeal movement in the period 1841-43 was similar to the way in which he responded to the threat posed by the Chartists in 1842 (see Unit 6, Section 3.1). He refused to make any concessions and took a tough stand against the leadership.

When, in October 1843, the government banned a Monster Meeting of the Repeal movement at Clontarf, O'Connell backed down (by calling the meeting off) and, a week later, he was arrested and imprisoned. This effectively ended the threat posed by the Repeal movement - in the short term at least.

Whilst Peel took a tough stance against the Repeal movement, many historians have pointed out that there is good evidence to suggest that he realised that coercion and the temporary removal of O'Connell would not provide a lasting solution to the problems faced by Ireland, where some 80% of the population was Catholic. As a result, Peel's longer term strategy was to persuade moderate Catholic property owners to support the Act of Union. If such people could be persuaded to support the Act of Union, this would undermine O'Connell's Repeal Movement at its foundations. The main measures taken by Peel after October 1843 are summarised in Box 7.7.

Peel's strategy after October 1843

Some historians suggest that, whilst these measures were enlightened for the time, they made little impact in Ireland and they enraged Conservative backbenchers. According to the historian David Cooper, for example.

'This package of measures constituted a brave and far-sighted departure in the policy of British governments towards Ireland. It is one of the tragedies of Peel's career, however, that their actual impact on the Irish problem was, in fact, minimal, while their impact on British politics was disastrous....Peel was attempting something like a programme of what the 20th century would call 'social engineering'. If his visionary plans had come to fruition, he believed that the whole of Irish society would have been set on the path to stability, liberalism and "modernisation".' (Cooper 1995, pp.139 and 141)

Cooper argues that Peel believed that, once Catholic emancipation had been conceded, the Act of Union could best be maintained if the British government worked to develop an effective relationship with the Catholic Church. If there could be seen to be equality of treatment for both the Catholic and Protestant citizens of Ireland, there was a much

BOX 7.7 Peel's Irish policy after October 1843

Peel took the following steps to persuade moderate Catholic property owners to support the Act of Union:

● In 1844, Peel appointed Lord Heytesbury to replace Lord de Grey as Lord Lieutenant of Ireland (the monarch's official representative in Ireland). De Grey had been a hardline upholder of the Protestant ascendancy, whereas Heytesbury was prepared to recruit Catholics as magistrates and civil servants.

● In 1844, Peel appointed Lord Devon, a progressive landowner, to chair a commission to investigate how the question of land tenure, rural poverty and landlord-tenant relations could be improved in Ireland.

● In 1844, the Charitable Bequests Act made it easier for individuals to make private endowments of land or money to the Catholic Church in their wills.

● In 1845, Peel's Maynooth Bill made a one-off grant of £30,000 to develop the Catholic Seminary (training college for priests) at Maynooth and virtually trebled its annual grant from the government to £26,000.

● In 1845, the Irish Colleges Bill set up three new higher education colleges in Belfast, Cork and Galway aimed at preparing middle-class Catholics to compete for careers in the legal profession and civil service.

greater chance that Catholics would develop a genuine recognition of - and allegiance to - the Act of Union. As Peel himself put it, the key to his approach was:

'To detach (if it be possible) from the ranks of repeal, agitation and disaffection, a considerable portion of the respectable and influential classes of the Roman Catholic population'.

Central to this strategy, Cooper argues, was the targeting of the Catholic priesthood, whose influence over the peasantry as opinion formers and educators was enormous. Jenkins agrees that this was central, arguing that:

'Ideally the solution would have been for the state to pay salaries to the priests and thus gain some political leverage over them, but such a policy was [opposed by both Anglicans and Nonconformists]. The best alternative, in Peel's judgement, was to strengthen the link between members of the gentry and their Church by [allowing grants to be made to improve Catholic property]. In this way, theoretically, the Catholic priesthood might be induced to behave responsibly, if their interests were more closely tied to those of the landowning class, and they would certainly be less inclined to stoke up inflammatory thoughts in the minds of their peasant flocks.' (Jenkins 1999, p.121)

The Maynooth Bill

Maynooth College was a training college in Ireland for Catholic priests. According to Jenkins:
> 'Its poor standards had the tendency of deterring entrants from respectable gentry families. Instead, it was young men from the lower ranks of Irish society who were taking holy orders and this merely served to reinforce the connection between Catholic priests and nationalist agitators.' (Jenkins 1999, p.122)

The Maynooth Bill proposed making a grant of £30,000 for building improvements and almost tripling the college's annual state grant.

Opposition to the Maynooth Bill

According to Eric Evans:
> 'Peel had anticipated trouble with his party over Maynooth, but not the ferocity of the opposition it engendered [created]. For loyal Anglicans bent on the defence of the Protestant constitution in Church and state, it was yet another Peelite betrayal. To the original perfidy [treachery] of emancipation was now to be added a policy of Catholic appeasement.' (Evans 1991, p.59)

Whilst Peel had experienced backbench rebellions before 1845, the rebellion over the Maynooth Bill was particularly large. In the crucial vote at the third reading of the Bill, the Conservatives were split down the middle with 148 MPs voting for the Bill and 149 voting against. The Bill was passed, however, because sufficient members of the opposition voted for it. According to Adelman:
> 'From a party point of view Peel seemed to have behaved over Maynooth even more stubbornly and impetuously than he had done...in 1844...As far as Ireland was concerned the results of the Maynooth Act were not very dramatic, although it did do something to enhance Peel's policy of conciliation and slightly improve his popularity there. In English politics, on the other hand, the consequences were profound. Maynooth proved to be an important turning point in the relations between Peel and his party.' (Adelman 1989, p.48)

3.2 Why did Peel decide to repeal the Corn Laws?

Why were the Corn Laws so important?

To make a contemporary parallel, the issue of Corn Law reform aroused the same sort of passions within the Conservative Party in the 1840s that the issue of a single European currency aroused within the party in the late 1990s. For many Conservative backbenchers in the 1840s, the Corn Laws (like the

pound in the 1990s) had immense practical and symbolic significance. These MPs could just about stomach the relaxation of tariffs on the import of industrial goods like coal or cotton, but the protection of agricultural interests remained a matter of fundamental principle. An explanation of why the Corn Laws had become so important to these MPs is given in Box 7.8.

BOX 7.8 Why were the Corn Laws so important?

The famous Corn Law of 1815 had been passed to ensure that, with food prices across Europe dropping sharply at the end of the Napoleonic wars, British producers (ie aristocratic landowners) would have some protection against the dumping of large quantities of grain at rock bottom prices. Opponents to this Act argued that it was class legislation which protected the landed interest whilst ensuring that the price of bread remained artificially high. For Conservatives who believed in free trade, the Corn Laws produced a dilemma. On the one hand, they were an obvious obstacle to the freeing of trade restrictions which, they believed, would lead to greater economic growth and prosperity. On the other hand, they were strongly supported by the landed interest which made up the great bulk of Tory support. Protectionist Tories (ie those who opposed the repeal of the Corn Laws) criticised Huskisson's and Peel's reduction of duty in their separate Corn Law amendments of 1828 and 1842. Abolition of the Corn Laws would be considered by many of Peel's supporters as the ultimate betrayal. On the other side, failure to remove agricultural protection was increasingly regarded as a crime against the productive classes. As Britain industrialised, so its population increased, virtually doubling between 1801 and 1851, and these extra mouths had to be fed. It became increasingly difficult to argue that the Corn Laws protected a sector of the economy whose contribution to the economy as a whole was less by the year whilst imposing a heavy burden (ie expensive bread) on those who were contributing to economic growth. Employers complained that agriculture was receiving unfair and unnecessary, protection to preserve the high levels of rent on which landowners lived. Rent, furthermore, was unearned income. Manufacturers had to work hard and take risks if they were to make profits and provide work for their employees. The fact that those employees had to pay artificially high prices for their bread was intolerable.
Adapted from Evans 1991.

Peel's dilemma

As Box 7.8 indicates, Peel was faced with a dilemma. On the one hand, the repeal of the Corn Laws was the natural extension of his government's policy of moving towards free trade. Indeed, Evans argues that:

'The repeal of the Corn Laws was the natural extension of the policy of trade liberalisation begun by William Pitt in the 1780s, continued by Robinson and Huskisson in the 1820s and accelerated by Peel's own Budgets of 1842 and 1845.' (Evans 1991, p.63)

On the other hand, Peel had already been accused of betraying his party (over emancipation). He had already experienced backbench rebellions (over sugar, the ten-hour amendment and the Maynooth Grant Bill, for example). Also, it was well known that many Conservative MPs who won county seats had campaigned in support of agricultural protection in 1841 and that there was strong support for the Corn Laws amongst the Conservative backbenchers. A number of interpretations have developed to explain why Peel decided to repeal the Corn Laws.

Interpretation 1. A response to the Irish Famine

One view is that Peel's decision to repeal the Corn Laws was a snap decision in response to the outbreak of famine in Ireland in October 1845. Peel himself placed a great deal of emphasis on the connection between the growing difficulties in Ireland and his decision to repeal the Corn Laws:

'Faced with the prospect of an imminent famine crisis in Ireland, Peel urged upon his Cabinet colleagues the policy of throwing open United Kingdom ports immediately, admitting foreign grain and all other foodstuffs without importation duties. Rather than proposing a temporary solution to a (hopefully) short-term emergency, however, Peel was adamant that there must be "a total and absolute repeal forever of all duties on all articles of subsistence". Once the Corn Laws and other tariffs on foodstuffs were removed, he argued, it would be impossible to reconcile public opinion to their reimposition at a future date.' (Jenkins 1999, p.124)

Most historians now reject the view that the Irish Famine stimulated Peel's decision to repeal the Corn Laws. Rather, they argue that the outbreak of famine helps to explain the timing of the announcement of a decision which had already been reached:

'It is almost certain that the official reason given by the government - that repeal was necessary to cope with the consequences of the Irish potato famine - was not the real one. It is true that the failure of the Irish potato crop in 1845 and the imminent prospect of widespread famine presented Peel with a humanitarian crisis on a massive scale...But immediate repeal would not enable sufficient supplies of food to be transferred to Ireland...We should conclude that the Irish

potato famine was the occasion, rather than the cause, of Corn Law repeal.' (Evans 1991, pp.63-64)

Interpretation 2. Peel's long-term goal

The second interpretation suggests that, far from being a snap decision made in response to a particular crisis, Peel had long planned the repeal of the Corn Laws. This is the argument proposed by Boyd Hilton (1979). He claims that Peel had become convinced that the Corn Laws would have to be repealed as early as the mid-1820s:

'Peel probably knew as early as 1828 that, unless something happened to stop population growth, repeal of the Corn Laws was only a matter of time.' (Hilton 1979, p.601)

Once in power, Hilton argues, Peel waited for the right political opportunity to act. As it turned out, he

BOX 7.9 The Anti-Corn Law League (ACLL)

In 1838 the worst harvest for 30 years and the onset of economic depression stirred up opposition to the Corn Laws. In September a group of manufacturers and businessmen in Manchester decided to set up an organisation for their repeal. The idea caught on and a number of associations were set up in northern towns. When Parliament refused to hear delegates' arguments, the repealers decided that only a massive demonstration of public support would achieve their aim. They set up the Anti-Corn Law League (ACLL) with its headquarters in Manchester to organise and coordinate the activities of local associations. The most prominent members were Richard Cobden and John Bright. The ACLL's propaganda campaign's basic message was that the free importation of corn would bring down the price of food. It would also encourage the expansion of trade in general and increase the demand for British products abroad - which would in turn increase employment and cause wages to rise.

The message was spread via a fortnightly newspaper (later weekly), other sympathetic newspapers and individuals. Huge meetings were held and lecturers employed. At the height of the campaign, 300 people were producing propaganda at the ACLL's headquarters. At first, many workers (and employers) were unreceptive. The ACLL was perceived as (and indeed was) a middle-class movement. Offers of a 'cheap loaf' were dismissed by many workers as a device to cut wages. The turning point was Peel's 1842 'Free-Trade' Budget. Cobden, who had just entered Parliament, pushed tirelessly at the door Peel cautiously opened. The apparent success of the ACLL in 1846 ensured that it became a model for later pressure groups.

Adapted from Hinde 1998.

calculated that the combination of the outbreak of famine in Ireland and the growing pressure of the Anti-Corn Law League (see Box 7.9 below) in late 1845 provided the right political opportunity. If, however, these circumstances had not arisen, Hilton suggests, Peel's preferred tactic was to play on the evidence of the success of the free-trade Budgets of 1842 and 1845 and to make repeal of the Corn Laws in the early 1850s the centrepiece of an 1848 general election campaign:

'He could say nothing before the 1841 election because he was rebuilding his bridges with a Tory Party which...regarded him as its natural leader. Even so, he tried to avoid committing himself to protection at the polls...At this stage, he was probably contemplating reductions of the Corn Law in 1842 and (say) 1845, so that in the election due in 1848 he could carefully displedge himself from protection, claiming meanwhile that the two downward revisions had done no harm to agriculture. Final repeal might come in 1851 or 1852.' (Hilton 1979, p.604)

Interpretation 3. A response to the success of the 1842 Budget

The third interpretation (see, for example, Eastwood 1996 and Jenkins 1999) is that, whilst Peel may have agreed in theory that there might be a case for repealing the Corn Laws before 1841, it was only when the tariff reforms of 1842 (and afterwards) began to prove successful that Peel decided that repeal should and could actually be implemented:

'A plausible suggestion might be that his silent shift away from the sliding scale and towards the alternative policy of repeal, was connected to the early signs that his wider free-trade measures, introduced in the Budget of 1842, were yielding positive results. In other words, as soon as it became apparent that the reduction in tariff levels was having a beneficial effect on the economy, stimulating production and increasing employment, Peel was finally satisfied that he could safely dispense with protection without doing any great harm to British agriculture.' (Jenkins 1999, p.126)

Eastwood (1996) argues that Hilton's idea that Peel was intending to repeal the Corn Laws before 1841 is wrong. He argues:

'It is much more persuasive to see Peel in 1842 as a tariff reformer, committed to dramatic lowering of duties to encourage economic recovery. The logic of this policy of tariff reform might well be an eventual abandonment of substantial agricultural protection and Peel was intimating [hinting at] this to close colleagues by late 1843. Nevertheless, the 1842 Budget was an experiment and there is no evidence at all to suggest that, even as late as 1844, Peel was

intending to repeal the Corn Laws in the present Parliament.' (Eastwood 1996, p.9)

Some earlier historians (see Kitson Clark 1929 and Ramsay 1971) argue that Peel changed his mind over the Corn Laws during the period 1842-45. In other words, they start from the premise that Peel did not believe in repeal when he came to power in 1841, but was persuaded to change his mind once the success of his free-trade reforms became apparent.

Interpretation 4. Peel was pressurised into repeal by the ACLL

Some historians have argued that it was pressure from the Anti-Corn Law League which persuaded Peel to make the decision to repeal the Corn Laws. Trevelyan, for example, argues that:

'The Anti-Corn Law League was almost as formidable in industrial England as O'Connell's Catholic League had been in rural Ireland. Peel, who had surrendered to the one in 1829, surrendered to the other in 1846.' (Trevelyan 1945, p.644)

Historians like Trevelyan are impressed by the fact that the ACLL was a predominantly middle-class organisation which succeeded in achieving a number of significant election and by-election results. For example, when J.B Smith stood as a free-trade candidate in the Walsall by-election of 1841,

---

BOX 7.10   The impact of the ACLL

There is a strong case for arguing that the ACLL increased support for repeal within Parliament by raising the temperature of debate and by publicising all the arguments in favour. It may even have helped Peel come to a decision, although it is unlikely that it converted him completely. On the other hand, it might have taken Peel a lot longer to make the decision to repeal the Corn Laws if pressure had not been applied by the ACLL. It is true that the main pressure came from the Whigs, who had come out in favour of repeal in 1845, but their conversion had been accelerated by the arguments of the League - especially through Bright's speeches in Parliament. The free-trade MPs made a direct impact on Peel himself. This explains the incident in the Commons on 13 March 1845 when Peel, on hearing Cobden's speech, did not reply, crumpled his notes and said to his colleague Sidney Herbert, 'You must answer this, for I cannot.' It could also be argued that the ACLL helped create throughout the country the sort of tension and passion which persuaded the House of Lords (mindful of the threat of violence in 1832) to pass the Bill repealing the Corn Laws.

Adapted from Lee 1994.

the Whig candidate (a protectionist) withdrew, leaving Smith to fight the Tory candidate. With a clear run, the Tory won, but only by 27 votes. In the general election which followed, Richard Cobden was elected as MP for Stockport. Then, in a by-election in 1843, John Bright was elected.

Other historians argue that the impact made by the ACLL on Peel has been exaggerated. Norman McCord (1968) goes as far as describing the idea that the ACLL pressurised Peel into making the decision to repeal the Corn Laws as a 'legend'. This view has recently been revised by Lee - see Box 7.10.

Interpretation 5. A strategic retreat

The fifth interpretation (see, for example, Chambers & Mingay 1966) suggests that Peel's main motive in repealing the Corn Laws was his desire to protect the interests of the landed elite and of the Conservative Party. According to this view, Peel had three main reasons for believing that the repeal of the Corn Laws was the best way to preserve the interests of the landed elite and of the Conservative Party.

1. It would be economically beneficial

First, Peel was a genuine free trader and he simply did not believe that free trade would damage the interests of the landed elite. He saw no good economic reason, therefore, why the Corn Laws should not be repealed. As it turned out, Peel was right and Britain was by no means swamped with cheap foreign corn after the Corn Laws had been repealed (something which the diehards had feared would happen).

2. It would benefit the Conservative Party

Second, from a party political point of view, Peel was trying to do in 1846 what he had also attempted to achieve with the Tamworth Manifesto of 1834. In other words, by repealing the Corn Laws, he hoped to persuade the Conservative Party to adapt to a changing economic and social environment. By doing so, he believed that he would save the party from self-destruction. To put this the other way

round, Peel believed that, if the Conservative Party continued to stick dogmatically to its support for the Corn Laws, it would alienate sufficient numbers of voters to condemn it to the political wilderness. Far from betraying his party, therefore, Peel was acting in its best interests.

3. It would protect the interests of the elite

And third, Peel believed that the forthcoming struggle between free traders and diehard supporters of the Corn Laws had the potential to develop into a major crisis and he aimed to avoid a repetition of the sort of turmoil which surrounded the passage of the 1832 Reform Act. This explains Peel's timing of his announcement on repeal. In late 1845 the combination of the ACLL's agitation and the diehards' short-sightedness seemed to be setting up a dangerous - but ultimately avoidable - conflict between the new commercial elite and the traditional landed elite. The beneficiaries of such a conflict could only be radical groups like the Chartists who would go on to exploit any power vacuum that was created. Peel recognised that the defenders of the Corn Law would have to retreat, but wanted to ensure that this retreat was strategic and well planned. In order to protect the interests of the aristocracy, the retreat had to be orderly, statesmanlike and, above all, controlled step by step by an executive Prime Minister within Parliament. By taking the initiative, Peel would have the advantage of simultaneously neutralising both the ACLL and the Chartists. So, far from signalling a defeat for the landed interest, Peel's decision to repeal the Corn Laws completed a process begun by Grey in 1832. Just as Grey had hoped that the 1832 Reform Act would strengthen the aristocracy's hold on power, so too Peel hoped that this would be the outcome of repeal of the Corn Laws. As Chambers and Mingay put it:

> 'Repeal was a strategic retreat, the sacrifice of the bastion of the Corn Laws to keep intact the main stronghold of aristocratic power.' (Chambers & Mingay 1966, p.157)

MAIN POINTS - Sections 3.1-3.2

- Some historians argue that, by the time the crisis over the Corn Laws arose, Peel had already alienated a large number of backbenchers. Others argue that, although Peel faced backbench revolts in the period 1841-45, he was always able to patch up relations with most of those who had rebelled.
- Peel refused to make any concessions to O'Connell's Repeal movement and, in October 1843, forced O'Connell to back down. After October 1843, Peel's Irish policy was to try to win the support of moderate Catholics. The Maynooth Bill of 1845, however, resulted in a big Conservative backbench rebellion.
- For many Conservative backbenchers in the 1840s,

the Corn Laws had immense practical and symbolic significance. In addition, Peel had already been accused of betraying his party over emancipation. Backbenchers had already rebelled over several issues. And Conservative MPs had campaigned for agricultural protection in 1841.
- In order to explain why Peel decided to repeal the Corn Laws, five main interpretations have developed: (1) it was a snap response to the outbreak of famine in Ireland; (2) it had been Peel's long-term goal since the 1820s; (3) it was a response to the success of the 1842 Budget; (4) Peel was pressured into repeal by the ACLL; and (5) it was a strategic retreat.

Activity 7.4 The Corn Laws

ITEM 1 A cartoon from *Punch* magazine

PAPA COBDEN TAKING MASTER ROBERT A FREE TRADE WALK.

PAPA COBDEN.—" Come along, MASTER ROBERT, do step out."
MASTER ROBERT.—" That's all very well, but you know I cannot go so fast as you do."

This cartoon shows Richard Cobden leading Peel towards repeal of the Corn Laws.

ITEM 2 The view of an Ultra Tory

For all my affection to him, I cannot excuse this latest **tergiversation** and, above all, the deception of endeavouring to attribute it to the potato famine in Ireland...What the real cause of the change of opinion was I cannot possibly assert...There was, perhaps, some original **disposition** to idealise free trade and the advancement of the manufacturing interest, and some **latent** hatred of the 'proud aristocracy'. But the main and immediate cause was terror, cowardice - terror of the League.

Part of a letter written by the leading Ultra Tory MP J.W. Croker to Sir Henry Hardinge, the Governor-General of India, on 24 April 1846.

Glossary

- **tergiversation** - U-turn
- **disposition** - inclination
- **latent** - underlying

ITEM 3 Prince Albert's assessment

He [Peel] said he had been determined not to go to a general election with the fetters the last election had imposed upon him and he had meant at the end of the next session to call the whole Conservative Party together and to declare this to them, that he could not meet another Parliament pledged to the maintenance of the Corn Laws, which could be maintained no longer and that he would make a public declaration to this effect before another general election came on. This had been defeated by events coming too suddenly upon him and he had no alternative but to deal with the Corn Laws before a national calamity would force it on. The League had made immense progress and had enormous means at their disposal. If he had resigned in November, Lord Stanley and the protectionists would have been prepared to form a government and a revolution might have been the consequence of it. Now they felt that it was too late. Sir Robert has an immense scheme in view; he thinks he shall be able to remove the contest entirely from the dangerous ground upon which it has got - that of a war between the manufacturers, the hungry and the poor against the landed proprietors, the aristocracy, which can only end in the ruin of the latter...He will adopt the principle of the League, that of removing all protection and abolishing all monopoly, but not in favour of one class and as a triumph over another, but to the benefit of the nation, farmers as well as manufacturers...The experiments he had made in 1842 and 1845 with boldness but with caution had borne out the correctness of the principle: the wool duty was taken off and wool sold higher than ever; foreign cattle were let in and the cattle of England stood better in the market than ever. He would not ask for compensation to the land, but wherever he could give it, and at the same time promote social development, there he would do it.
Memorandum written by Prince Albert on 25 December 1845.

ITEM 4 Peel speaks to the Commons

I think you could have continued this law [the Corn Law]...for a short time longer; but I believe that the interval of its maintenance would have been but short and that there would have been, during the period of its continuance, a desperate conflict between different classes of society...It was the foresight of these consequences - it was the belief that you were about to enter into a bitter and, ultimately, an unsuccessful struggle that has induced me to think that for the benefit of all classes, for the benefit of the agricultural class itself, it was desirable to come to a permanent and equitable settlement of this question. These are the motives on which I acted. I know the penalty to which I must be subject for having so acted; but I declare, even after the continuance of these debates that I am only the more impressed with the conviction that the policy we advise is correct...Sir, I do not rest my support for this Bill merely upon the temporary ground of scarcity in Ireland. I do not rest my support of the Bill on that temporary scarcity, but I believe that scarcity left no alternative to us but to undertake the consideration of this question; and that consideration being necessary, I think that a permanent adjustment of the question is not only imperative, but the best policy for all concerned...The mere interest of the landlords - the mere interests of the occupying tenants, important though they are, are subordinate to the great question - what is calculated to increase the comforts, to improve the condition and elevate the social character of the millions who subsist by manual labour, whether they are engaged in manufactures or agriculture?

Part of a speech made by Peel in the House of Commons on 15 May 1846. The speech was frequently interrupted by Benjamin Disraeli, Peel's principal Conservative opponent in the Commons.

Questions

1. Look at Item 1.
   a) Write a paragraph explaining the background to this cartoon.
   b) What point is being made by the cartoon and how accurate is it?
2. a) Take each of Items 1-4 and say which of the five interpretations described in Section 3.2 above fits with the evidence in the item.

b) Why is it so difficult to be sure why Peel made the decision to repeal the Corn Laws?
3. a) How accurate is Item 2's suggestion that Peel betrayed the Conservative Party over the repeal of the Corn Laws?
   b) Using Items 3 and 4 suggest arguments Peel might have used to combat the charge that he betrayed his party.

3.3 Peel's downfall

Peel's resignation in December 1845

When, in December 1845, Peel announced his decision to introduce legislation to repeal the Corn Laws, two members of the Cabinet (Viscount Stanley and the Duke of Buccleuch) resigned. This led Peel himself to offer his resignation in the hope, most historians agree, that Lord John Russell would be able to form a government which would then go on to repeal the Corn Laws:

'[Peel] knew that Lord John Russell, the leader of the Whig-Liberals, had recently publicly announced his conversion to repeal and his calculation was that, if he allowed the Whigs to pass the measure, albeit with a substantial minority of Conservatives supporting it, he might just keep his own party together.' (Evans 1991, p.68)

Russell, however, was unable to form a government and Peel was therefore invited to resume as Prime Minister:

'The fact was that, with both party leaders committed to repeal, this solution looked to be politically inevitable, and the Whigs' failure to provide an alternative ministry placed executive-minded Conservatives such as Wellington under a moral obligation to serve again with Peel for the sake of carrying on the Queen's government.' (Jenkins 1999, p.128)

In January 1846, Peel introduced his Free Trade Budget. Whilst this had the support of the Conservative front bench and most of the Whigs, it was strongly opposed by a majority of Conservative backbenchers.

The Anti League

One important reason for the strength of opposition on the backbenches was the pressure put on backbenchers by the so-called 'Anti League' - the Central Agricultural Protection Society. The Anti League, an alliance of farmers and landowners, was set up in February 1844 to defend protection. Although, at first, it made little impact in Parliament, in the winter of 1845-46 it put great pressure on MPs:

'By the end of the year [1845], worried by the rumours of Peel's intentions over the Corn Laws, the farmers were impatient for action. After the Prime Minister's resignation and return to office in December, they began to organise meetings and petitions on a wide scale, throughout the southern counties especially, in defence of protection...The farmers began to tighten the screw on their more cautious representatives in the House of Commons to ensure that they continued the parliamentary struggle against repeal and ultimately voted as their constituents expected. It was a pressure most of the agriculturalist MPs found difficult to resist.' (Adelman 1989, p.74)

Then, in March 1846, protectionist Conservative backbenchers formed a committee chaired by Lord George Bentinck. Bentinck, together with Benjamin Disraeli, led the attacks on repeal (see Box 7.11).

Peel's final resignation

The final vote on the repeal of the Corn Laws was taken in the House of Commons on 15 May 1846. The government won a majority of 98 but, according to Adelman (1989) and Jenkins (1999), only 106 Conservatives voted with the government whilst 222 voted against it (Evans (1991) and Watts (1994) say that 112 voted for and 241 against). The Bill was approved by the Lords and given royal assent in June.

Although, therefore, Peel managed to get the measure through Parliament, it was only at great cost to his own position:

'Fatally, Peel had lost his hold over the hearts and minds of the agrarian interest which still constituted the bedrock of support for Conservatism.' (Jenkins 1999, p.132)

Whether or not a significant number of backbenchers had lost faith in Peel before 1846 (there is a debate over this - see Section 3.1 above), a significant number certainly did lose faith in him in 1846. In the early hours of 26 June 1846, a few hours after the Lords had taken their final vote on the repeal of the Corn Laws, the Commons voted on a Bill designed to combat growing violence in Ireland. In that vote, 116 of those Conservatives who had voted against the government over the repeal of the Corn Laws switched to support the government, but 74 voted against and 51 did not vote. The result was that the government was defeated by 73 votes. On 29 June, Peel resigned.

Peel after his resignation

Peel died in 1850, following a riding accident. In the period 1846-50, however, he was in an unusual political position. Adelman (1989) describes Peel as standing 'virtually above politics'. Other historians

have concluded that his approach was ambiguous - perhaps even inconsistent:

'For the last four years of his life, Peel's determination to occupy an independent position, free from party associations and obligations, did more than anything else to perpetuate the incoherence of the political scene at Westminster. Some contemporaries indeed felt that he was guilty of inconsistency in the way he behaved. On the one hand, Peel repeatedly asserted to his friends that he had no wish to

---

BOX 7.11 Parliamentary opposition to repeal

(i) During the debates on the repeal of the Corn Laws in the first half of 1846, Peel took the high ground of national interest, arguing that repeal of the Corn Laws would end the threat of class conflict because it would benefit all classes - including those who did not have the vote. Peel's concern for those without votes cut no ice with either Disraeli or Bentinck. Bentinck angrily condemned Peel's inconsistencies and lack of loyalty to party and colleagues alike. He accused him of harassing Canning to death in 1827, of 'base and dishonest conduct...inconsistent with the duty of a minister to his sovereign' and of deserting his followers. Disraeli composed numerous variations, both witty and vulgar, on the theme of abandoning principles. He accused Peel of causing all 'confidence in public men' to be lost by his underhand and faithless dealings with his supporters. His most positive contribution was to assert that Peel had betrayed more than his party, he had bent the constitution. Other backbenchers were not slow to weigh in. Colonel Sibthorp, for example, regretted that 'the Treasury benches [were] so infested with the noxious animals called rats'.
Adapted from Evans 1991.

(ii) Last week the debate in the House of Commons came to a close at last, wound up by a speech of Disraeli's, very clever, in which he hacked and mangled Peel with the most unsparing severity, and positively tortured his victim. It was a miserable and degrading spectacle. The whole mass of protectionists cheered him with vociferous [loud] delight, making the roof ring again; and when Peel spoke, they screamed and hooted at him in the most brutal manner. When he vindicated [justified] himself and talked of honour and conscience, they assailed him with shouts of derision and gestures of contempt. Such treatment in a House of Commons where for years he had been an object of deference and respect, nearly overcame him.
Entry made by Charles Greville, the Whig diarist for 21 May 1846.

return to office, and yet, on the other hand, he evidently had no intention of retiring from public life, as he retained his seat in the House of Commons and regularly attended and spoke in the debates.' (Jenkins 1999, p.135)

Despite this view, however, there is a consensus that Peel's behaviour in the period 1846-50 was consistent in four areas:

- his absolute opposition to a return to agricultural protection
- his willingness to support the Whig government
- his refusal to organise his followers, the 'Peelites', into a proper third party
- his repeated claim that he had no desire to return to office.

According to Adelman (1989), Peel's absolute opposition to a return to agricultural protection explains his support for the Whig government:

'Peel's main aim now was to ensure that no attempt was made by his successors to return to a policy of agricultural protection; and he was prepared, therefore, to go to almost any lengths to maintain the Whig government in power and keep it on the right Peelite path. This meant supporting it against the protectionists and, when necessary, its own radical wing.' (Adelman 1989, p.78)

The Peelites

During the struggle over the repeal of the Corn Laws, an important debate emerged on the role of political parties. Whilst Peel's main opponent, Disraeli, argued that party loyalty should be the government's main consideration, Peel claimed that there were circumstances where the government should act in the national interest even if that meant going against the wishes of the government's party.

Following Peel's resignation in 1846, most of those Conservatives who had supported him over the repeal of the Corn Laws - the so-called 'Peelites' - joined him on the backbenches. Peel, however, refused to make any attempt to organise his supporters into a party:

'When his whip, Sir John Young, sent a circular to 240 possible supporters at the beginning of the 1847 session, Peel refused to endorse his action...It was an impossible and unsatisfactory situation. Peel would neither lead a party nor allow others to lead it. His attitude was an anachronism [out of date] in an age of increasing party domination. "The position of Sir Robert Peel in the last four years of his life was a thoroughly false position," wrote Gladstone.' (Blake 1985, p.69)

Although the number of Peelites was maintained after the 1847 general election, the lack of leadership began to bite:

'What is clear is that the Peelites suffered after the 1847 general election from their lack of leadership and cohesion. As Gladstone observed despondently in 1849: "We have no party, no organisation, no whipper-in; and, under these circumstances, we cannot exercise any considerable degree of permanent influence as a body." This was reflected in a continuous decline in their numbers and divisions within the hard core of Peelites who remained over tactics and policy.' (Adelman 1989, p.80)

Nevertheless, the split within the Conservative Party remained, despite a number of attempts to reunite the party. This split helps to explain why the Conservatives were unable to win an overall majority throughout the period 1846-74:

'The Corn Law crisis left the Conservatives divided into two irreconcilable wings...and two decades were to pass before the highly defined two-party system of the years 1832-46 made its return. Three times in the 1850s and 1860s, the Conservatives formed a government; but the split in the party meant that they were never able to gain a majority and each of the administrations was short-lived.' (Stewart 1995, p.21)

What were Peel's long-term aims?

There is some debate between historians over whether Peel might have returned to office if he had not suffered his riding accident. Jenkins, for example, points out that:

'It is easily forgotten that [Peel] was four years younger than both Lord Aberdeen who headed the Peelite-Whig coalition government of 1852-55 and Lord Palmerston who dominated the political scene in the decade after 1855. Despite his consistent avowal that he had no ambition to return to office, it is not inconceivable that his view might have changed if the Russell ministry had collapsed...and the only choice was between leading a free trade coalition government or allowing the protectionists into power.' (Jenkins 1999, p.149)

Unlike some political leaders whose fall from power is followed by obscurity, Peel remained a political heavyweight right up to the time of his death. The Chancellor of the Exchequer in the period 1846-50, Charles Wood, frequently met with Peel to ask for his advice on commercial and financial matters, for example. As a result, there was speculation amongst his contemporaries that he would, at some point, return to power:

'Out of office, without an organised party behind him, he was still regarded by the majority of the press and the public as the greatest statesman of the day whose eventual return to office was among the certainties of politics. The disruption of 1846 in an age which attached less importance to party ties and party fortunes than was common later in the century, seemed to them a matter of little concern compared with his record of national achievement.' (Gash 1979, p.248)

3.4 Was Peel the 'greatest statesman of his age'?

Reactions to Peel's death
News of Peel's riding accident and death three days later led to a great outpouring of public grief. Tributes came from all sections of society. Parliament and local authorities used public funds to build statues in memorial to Peel whilst the radical MP Joseph Hume set up the 'Poor Man's Testimonial to Sir Robert Peel' - a fund into which working people paid one pence (the fund raised £1,736, the equivalent of nearly 417,000 donations and was used to set up a scheme to promote working-class education). The initial response to Peel's death, was, therefore, to set his achievements in a positive light:

'In the hearts and minds of the mid-Victorian public, Peel's reputation was now secure. He was the wise statesman who had risen above the selfish interests of classes and parties to deliver cheap food and prosperity to the whole of the British people. The sudden and shocking manner of his death lent added poignancy to the belief that here was a man who had willingly sacrificed his career for the good of others.' (Jenkins 1999, pp.141-42)

The view of Peel's contemporary admirers
It was noted in the introduction to this unit that, for some contemporary historians, Peel remains a 'great statesman'. Admirers such as Gash (1976) and Read (1987) argue that he made a number of outstanding contributions:
- he was the architect of the era of mid-Victorian stability and prosperity
- he restored confidence in the political system
- he was a progressive reformer
- he was a man of principle who, by putting nation above party, acted as a true statesman.

The viewpoint of Peel's admirers is summarised in Box 7.12.

Critical views of Peel
As has been emphasised throughout this unit, however, the way in which Peel's actions have been interpreted by his admirers has been questioned by more critical historians. Beales (1974) and Gatrell (1994), for example, reject the view that Peel was an enlightened and progressive reformer when he was

BOX 7.12 The view of Peel's admirers

Peel tends to be remembered as the man who sacrificed his career for the good of the nation, as a gifted administrator who put national above party interests and who provided decisive and gifted leadership through a period of massive change and considerable political and social crisis. His enlightened policies are said to have given working people cheap bread, stimulated industry and laid the foundations of mid-Victorian prosperity. Peel, the wealthy landowner from an industrial background, was uniquely placed to reconcile the divergent interests of aristocracy and commerce for the benefit of the nation as a whole. His leadership of the Conservative Party broadened its base. It was on this base that Disraeli was able to build a national, patriotic party in the 1860s and 1870s. Peel was the founder of modern Conservatism and the chief architect of the age of stability. By the time he died, he had become a hero both of the propertied middle classes and the propertyless workers. He had extraordinary ability and was a superb parliamentarian. His second administration was the most able in the 19th century.
Adapted from Evans 1991.

Home Secretary. Hilton (1979) argues that Peel was blinkered because of his inflexible belief in free-market economics. Newbould (1983) downplays Peel's role in reviving the Conservative Party in the 1830s. Coleman (1988) argues that, far from being concerned with the interests of the nation as a whole, Peel's main concern was to protect the interests of the ruling elite and to stem change rather than to encourage it.

Central to any analysis of Peel's career is his relationship with his party. In recent years, a number of accounts have been highly critical of the way in which Peel treated members of his party. The main criticisms are outlined in Box 7.13.

The problem that historians face when making judgements about Peel's actions is that they have to make assumptions about what his motives were and, to do this, they have to give the impression that they know Peel so well that they understand how his mind worked. But the only way of understanding how Peel's mind worked is to read what survives of his writing and what survives of what others wrote about him - written material which is open to more than one interpretation. To some extent, whether Peel is judged to be a 'great statesman' or not depends on whether the starting point is that adopted by Gladstone or that adopted by Disraeli:

'[Gladstone's] view was that Peel was so far convinced that the national interest demanded

BOX 7.13 Peel and his party

In the late 1830s, Peel needed protectionist support to cement Conservative recovery and, arguably, he deceived both the electorate and the protectionists about his real feelings on free trade during the 1841 election campaign. He certainly took backbench support for granted when in office. Because he despised his backbenchers' lack of experience, relevant political education and, as he saw it, lack of vision, he underestimated the extent to which they were attached to established institutions and their sense of grievance against him. Peel's ideas on the role of party can be criticised as being both narrow and selfish. In the 1830s, he had seen more clearly than most that political reorganisation in the constituencies was needed as a result of the 1832 Reform Act. What he had not seen, or had chosen to ignore, was that party was becoming a dynamic factor whose importance in government would inevitably grow. The backbench case in 1846 that Peel deserved his fate is reasonable. Between 1841 and 1845 Peel either ignored backbench opinions or battered the backbenchers into submission. He proved himself untrue to their Tory principles on Ireland, on religion, on commerce and, finally and fatally, on the English landed interest itself.

Adapted from Evans 1991.

repeal that he alone could be entrusted with seeing it through. Gladstone said in later life: "From the language he held to me in December 1845, I think he expected to carry the repeal of the Corn Laws without breaking up his party. But meant at all hazards to carry it"...Disraeli had a different perspective. He always felt that what motivated Peel was personal arrogance rather than high principle. As he said in December 1845, Peel "is so vain that he wants to figure in history as the settler of all great questions, but a parliamentary constitution is not favourable to such ambitions: things must be done by parties, not by persons using parties as tools".' (Lee 1994, pp.87-88)

MAIN POINTS - Sections 3.3-3.4

- Peel resigned in December 1845, but resumed office when Russell could not form a government. He then immediately began the process repealing the Corn Laws.
- In part, the opposition to repeal in Parliament was the work of the Anti League. The speeches made by Bentinck and Disraeli were particularly hostile towards Peel.
- Peel resigned on 29 June 1846 after a Bill designed to combat growing violence in Ireland was defeated. He remained in Parliament until his death following a riding accident in 1850.
- Between 1846 and 1850, Peel's behaviour was characterised by (1) his absolute opposition to a return to agricultural protection, (2) his willingness to support the Whig government, (3) his refusal to organise the Peelites' into a proper party, and (4) his repeated claim that he had no desire to return to office.
- The split in the Conservative Party continued after Peel's death. This split helps to explain why the Conservatives were unable to win an overall majority throughout the period 1846-74.
- Historians are divided as to whether Peel was a 'great statesman'.

Activity 7.5 Was Peel a 'great statesman'?

ITEM 1 *Punch*'s tribute to Peel

PUNCH'S MONUMENT TO PEEL.

This cartoon was printed in Punch magazine just after Peel died.

ITEM 2 A historian's verdict (i)

To be described as a 'great statesman', a politician must have several attributes: administrative skill, capacity for work, personal integrity, high standards, and a sense of duty. Peel had all these. The combination of intellectual ability and wide government experience put Peel during the last 20 years of his life in a class by himself. In terms of mental capacity alone he was one of the ablest Prime Ministers in British history. The main quality which Peel exhibited after 1841 was his desire to reunite the country. He based his power on party but his policy was neither sectional nor partisan. The events of 1846 were only a supreme example of an attitude which underlay his whole conduct as a minister. By 1845 the Corn Law had been elevated in the public mind to a test of governmental integrity. Peel's response and the sacrifice that resulted did more than anything else to restore public confidence in the good faith of a system which was still essentially aristocratic. By 1850 the larger problems of his age had been met and solved. The age of revolt was giving way to the age of stability; and of that age Peel had been the chief architect. This, in the last analysis, is the basis on which Peel's claims to greatness must be judged. His allegiance was to an older concept than party loyalty. It was to the service of the state.

Adapted from Gash 1976.

ITEM 3 A historian's verdict (ii)

Peel's Irish policy ended in failure. Even the connection between his tax and tariff reforms and Britain's economic recovery is open to doubt. Some economic historians believe that the cycle of boom and slump which characterised the early 19th century economy went on regardless of government policy. Peel overreacted to the threat posed by the Chartists in 1842. He may well have overreacted to the threat posed by the Anti-Corn Law League too. But, above all, the focus on Peel as the all-conquering hero of these years belittles the important contribution that the Whigs made in the difficult transition to mid-Victorian stability. Peel's inflexible laissez-faire beliefs left little room for factory reform. His dogged resistance to the Whigs' Bill for Parliamentary Reform highlighted the negative, authoritarian streak in Peelite Conservatism. In late 1848, Peel reflected on why, unlike on the Continent, Britain had not suffered revolution. His answer, with an element of self-congratulation, was that the repeal of the Corn Law demonstrated to the British working class that an aristocratic Parliament could respond to their needs, even at the cost of sacrificing its own material interests. But Peel should also have asked himself what the Great Reform Act had contributed to the survival of the established order. Grey's bold extension of the franchise - the scale of which had amazed and outraged Peel - had successfully recruited enough of the forces of 'property and respectability' to the side of the aristocracy to see the British state through the crisis of the 1840s. There was no one architect of the prosperity and stability of mid-Victorian Britain. Peel achieved much, but perhaps the Whigs achieved more.

Adapted from Cooper 1995.

Questions

1. a) Judging from Item 1, for what did *Punch* magazine think Peel should be remembered?
    b) Is this a fitting memorial to Peel?
    c) Write your own obituary of Peel outlining his achievements and failures.
2. a) Using your own knowledge give arguments for and against the view that Peel had the qualities mentioned in Item 2.
    b) Would you agree with the verdict that Peel was a 'great statesman'? Explain your answer.
3. a) Compare and contrast the views of Peel in Items 2 and 3.
    b) Which argument is more convincing? Explain why.
    c) 'A controversial figure both in his own lifetime and afterwards'. How accurate is this description of Peel?

References

- **Adelman (1989)** Adelman, P., *Peel and the Conservative Party 1830-50*, Longman, 1989.

- **Beales (1974)** Beales, D., 'Peel, Russell and reform', *Historical Journal*, Vol.17, 1974.

- **Blake (1985)** Blake, R., *The Conservative Party from Peel to Thatcher* (2nd edn.), Fontana Press, 1985.

- **Chambers & Mingay (1966)** Chambers, J.D. & Mingay, G.E., *The Agricultural Revolution*, Batsford, 1966.

- **Coleman (1988)** Coleman, B., *Conservatism and the Conservative Party in 19th Century Britain*, Edward Arnold, 1988.

- **Cooper (1995)** Cooper, D., 'Peel and the Conservative Party' in *Scott-Baumann* (1995).

- **Davies (1995)** Davies, A.J., *We, the Nation: the Conservative Party and the Pursuit of Power*, Little Brown, 1995.

- **Eastwood (1992)** Eastwood, D., 'Peel and the Tory Party Reconsidered', *History Today*, March 1992.

- **Eastwood (1992)** Eastwood, D., 'Corn Laws and their repeal: realities behind the myths', *History Review*, Number 25, September 1996.

- **Evans (1991)** Evans, E., *Sir Robert Peel: Statesmanship, Power and Party*, Routledge, 1991.

- **Evans (1994)** Evans, E., 'Sir Robert Peel: a suitable case for reassessment?', *History Review*, Issue 18, March 1994.

- **Evans (1996)** Evans, E., *The Forging of the Modern State: Early Industrial Britain 1783-1870*, Longman, 1996.

- **Fisher (1975)** Fisher, D.R., 'Peel and the Conservative Party: the Sugar Crisis of 1844 reconsidered', *Historical Journal*, Vol.18, 1975.

- **Gardiner & Wenborn (1995)** Gardiner, J. & Wenborn, N., *The Companion to British History*, Collins and Brown, 1995.

- **Gash (1976)** Gash, N., *Peel*, Longman, 1976.

- **Gash (1979)** Gash, N., *Aristocracy and People*, Arnold, 1979.

- **Gash (1986)** Gash, N., *Pillars of Government*, Arnold, 1986.

- **Gatrell (1994)** Gatrell, V.A.C., *The Hanging Tree: Execution and the English People 1770-1868*, Oxford University Press, 1994.

- **Hilton (1979)** Hilton, A.J.B., 'Peel: a reappraisal', *Historical Journal*, Vol.22, 1979.

- **Hinde (1998)** Hinde, W., 'The Corn Laws" protection versus free trade', *Modern History Review*, Vol.10.2, November 1998.

- **Jenkins (1999)** Jenkins, T.A., *Sir Robert Peel*, Macmillan Press Ltd, 1999.

- **Kitson Clark (1964)** Kitson Clark, G., *Peel and the Conservative Party* (2nd edn), Frank Cass, 1964 (first published in 1929).

- **Lee (1994)** Lee, S.J., *British Political History 1815-1914* Routledge, 1994.

- **McCord (1968)** McCord, N., *The Anti-Corn Law League* (2nd edn), Unwin, 1968 (first published in 1958).

- **Newbould (1983)** Newbould, I., 'Sir Robert Peel and the Conservative Party', *English Historical Review*, Vol.98, 1983.

- **Ramsay (1971)** Ramsay, A.A.W., *Sir Robert Peel*, Constable, 1971 (first published in 1928).

- **Read (1987)** Read, D., *Peel and the Victorians*, Blackwell, 1987.

- **Roberts (1999)** Roberts, D. (ed.), *British History in Focus*, Causeway Press, 1999.

- **Royle (1997)** Royle, E., *Modern Britain: a Social History 1750-1997* (2nd edn), Arnold, 1997.

- **Scott-Baumann (1995)** Scott-Baumann, M. (ed.), *Years of Expansion: Britain 1815-1914*, Hodder and Stoughton, 1995.

- **Stewart (1969)** Stewart, R., 'The Ten Hours and Sugar Crises of 1844: government and the House of Commons in the Age of Reform', *Historical Journal*, Vol.12.1, 1969.

- **Stewart (1971)** Stewart, R., *The Politics of Protection*, Cambridge University Press, 1971

- **Stewart (1995)** Stewart, R., 'Party in the Age of Peel and Palmerston', *History Review*, Issue 21, March 1995.

- **Trevelyan (1945)** Trevelyan, G.M., *History of England*, Longman, 1945.

- **Watts (1994)** Watts, D., *Tories, Conservatives and Unionists 1815-1914*, Hodder and Stoughton, 1994.

UNIT 8 Poverty and reform

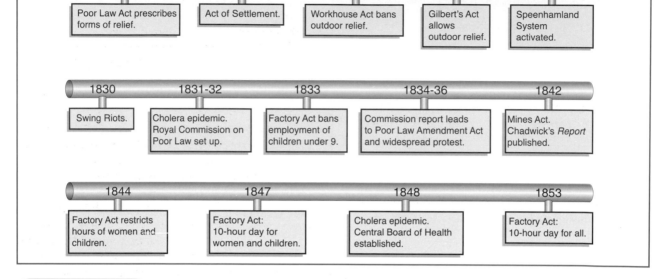

Timeline - Poverty and reform

1601	1662	1722	1782	1795
Poor Law Act prescribes forms of relief.	Act of Settlement.	Workhouse Act bans outdoor relief.	Gilbert's Act allows outdoor relief.	Speenhamland System activated.

1830	1831-32	1833	1834-36	1842
Swing Riots.	Cholera epidemic. Royal Commission on Poor Law set up.	Factory Act bans employment of children under 9.	Commission report leads to Poor Law Amendment Act and widespread protest.	Mines Act. Chadwick's *Report* published.

1844	1847	1848	1853
Factory Act restricts hours of women and children.	Factory Act: 10-hour day for women and children.	Cholera epidemic. Central Board of Health established.	Factory Act: 10-hour day for all.

Introduction

The social and environmental impact of the Industrial Revolution posed a series of searching questions which required early 19th-century governments to reassess both their role and areas of responsibility in relation to the living standards and conditions of the people. This unit deals with both the challenges and the nature of the state's response to the unprecedented pressures in three key areas of social change: (1) factory employment and its impact on children and the family unit; (2) the nature and relief of poverty; and (3) public health - the combination of medical and environmental issues arising from the process of urbanisation which accompanied that of rapid economic change. Various approaches to the resolution of these problems emerged. These ranged from the paternal - based on traditional notions of social responsibility and the relationship between rich and poor, to the Benthamite - emerging from a newly defined concept of efficiency and 'the greatest happiness of the greatest number'.

UNIT SUMMARY

Part 1 considers the effect of the Factory Acts of 1833-53 on children and the family, how child labour became the central focus of reform and was gradually restricted, and the provision of education during working hours. It also traces the campaign for a 10-hour day and employers' attempts to evade legislation.

Part 2 considers the origins of the unreformed Poor Law and how it operated in the early 19th century, and why opposition to it grew after 1815. It considers the debate over the Speenhamland System, and looks at the role of the Poor Law Commission of 1832-34.

Part 3 focuses on the Poor Law Amendment Act and its ending of outdoor relief in favour of workhouses, looks at why the Anti-Poor Law movement arose, and how far the Act was actually put into effect. It also considers how effective the New Poor Law was.

Part 4 examines the impact of industrialisation on public health, including the problems created by urbanisation. It looks at the main obstacles to progress on public health – both technical and political, at the main pressures for reform, and at what improvements were achieved, especially as a result of the work of Chadwick.

1 Children and the Factory Acts

Key issues

1. How did the Factory Acts passed between 1833 and 1853 affect children and the family?

2. What was the importance of child labour in the movement for the reform of factory conditions?

3. What education was provided for the children of the poor?

1.1 How the 1833-53 Factory Acts affected children and the family

The 1833 Factory Act – origins, enforcement and evasion

By 1830, although there had been several attempts, very little significant factory reform had been achieved despite the fact that many of the terms of reference for future legislation had been established. The picture was to change when, in 1833, a government bill introduced by Lord Althorp became law.

The background to the Act

In 1830, Richard Oastler and John Fielden had launched the Ten Hour Movement (see Box 8.3). Oastler was a Tory land agent of estates near Huddersfield and Leeds, and Fielden a radical mill owner from Todmorden in Lancashire. They were supported by a politically diverse group that included: John Wood, an enlightened mill owner; Michael Sadler, Tory MP for Leeds; Joseph Rayner Stephens, an ex-Tory Methodist minister; and Lord Ashley, Tory MP for Dorset. Their work complemented that of the Short Time Committees and they looked for an early opportunity to introduce a Ten Hour Bill. The reform movement drew support from various sections of the political community. Indeed as Hopkins points out, 'Factory reform was never a party matter' (Hopkins 1979, p.57).

Sadler's Ten Hour Bill of 1831 was referred to a Parliamentary Committee of Enquiry which, despite the reservations and suspicions of the reformers, reported unfavourably on factory conditions. In 1833, Ashley reintroduced the bill, which this time was made the subject of a Royal Commission. The commissioners' modifications led Ashley to withdraw his proposals. They were replaced by Althorpe's government bill, which became the 1833 Factory Act (see Box 8.1).

Opposition and evasion

Enforcement was widely acknowledged as the key to the success of the Act. The role of the Inspectors would be crucial. Jones rightly observes:

'The fact that they were appointed at all makes the 1833 Act a landmark in 19th-century legislation. No longer were Acts of Parliament to be words on paper: they were to be enforced.' (Jones 1971, p.96)

Perhaps out of anger that the central agenda of the Ten Hour Movement had been ignored, the Act, surprisingly, was vehemently opposed by the reformers.

It was clear that many mill owners would seek to counter and minimise the impact of the new legislation, which was seen by many as a threat to productivity and profits. They rejected the principle and the details. They were opposed – ironically, given later developments - for instance, to the 'relays', recommended by the commissioners, preferring the traditional system with children and adults working the same hours. The commissioners had suggested using two shifts or 'relays' of children under 13, one working in the morning and one in the afternoon, leaving the adults free to work 12 hours or more a day. Workers who favoured a 10-hour day also rejected the suggestion and the new regulations for children up to 13 threatened the overall family income (see Section 1.2). Such a climate of opposition from the very people whom the Act was meant to benefit was likely to create a situation in which workers put up with their employers' failure to comply with legislation, or actively encouraged their attempts at evasion.

The work of the inspectors

The appointment of a paid inspectorate was recognised at the time as significant but few reformers had much confidence in it. Four inspectors – Saunders, Rickards, Howell and Horner – were appointed to cover the whole country. Rickards alone was responsible for covering 2,700 factories with about a quarter of a million workers. Unsurprisingly, in 1836 he died from excessive workload and worry. Inspectors were assisted by superintendents and numbers of both inspectors and superintendents were later increased. The inspectors were committed, diligent and independent and their persistence and tenacity, while widely constrained and frustrated, established the new regulatory procedures on a firm footing. It would be foolish, however, to overestimate their impact in the years that immediately followed the passing of the Act.

The challenge to the inspectors through evasion and non-compliance took a variety of forms. Mill owners were only allowed to employ children who could produce certificates verifying their age or health:

'Some doctors were rather less than scrupulous in issuing certificates, and they were often appealed to by parents to accept their word that the child was of lawful age.' (Finlayson 1969, p.48)

The qualifications of many doctors were suspect, substitution of one child for another was frequently practised, and fraud was common. Measures taken by the inspectors to counter such practices - guidance for doctors on age-related health and appearance criteria such as height and condition of teeth - reflected the detailed concerns of the inspectors but could not guarantee results. Doctors' certificates had to be countersigned by magistrates, who were not infrequently willing to be involved in attempts to deceive and confuse. Even baptismal certificates were open to abuse. The introduction of the compulsory registration of births in 1836 addressed this situation effectively. At a more spontaneous day-to-day level, children too young to work legally were simply hidden if an inspection was imminent.

BOX 8.1   The terms of the 1833 Factory Act

- The employment of all children under 9 years old was prohibited.
- The working day for children aged 9-13 was reduced to 9 hours, with a weekly maximum of 48 hours.
- For children aged 9-13, two hours' education a day had to be provided by the factory owner.
- For young persons aged 13-18, the daily and weekly maximums were 12 and 69 hours respectively.
- There was to be no night work for anyone under 18.
- Factory owners were instructed to keep a register of all the children and young persons that they employed.
- A break of 1 1/2 hours was to be provided for meals during the day.
- Factory owners were obliged to whitewash their premises at least once a year.
- Four full-time paid inspectors were appointed to enforce the Act.

Penalties and their effect

The Act introduced fines for those who broke the law. Inspectors regularly complained that the magistrates, often factory owners themselves, applied these fines too leniently for them to work as a deterrent. The historian Fraser has suggested that fines were never primarily intended to work in this way:

'The level of fines was of course limited by what Parliament laid down, intended more to educate than to punish offenders.' (Fraser 1973, p.24)

While fines per offence might appear small, their cumulative effect on a factory owner could prove significant. Obviously, when such levels compromised profits, there was a strong incentive to obey the law.

It was clear at the time that it would be difficult to implement the Act. The work of the inspectors was compromised by the terms of reference within which they operated and deliberate attempts to frustrate and mislead them. Their reports do, however, indicate that their work was fruitful. By the end of the 1830s, fewer mill owners were breaking the law. Horner, who had replaced Rickards in 1836, was ready to offer a positive judgement on the impact of the legislation when he commented to the review commission in 1840:

'The chief evils that formerly existed have been remedied to a great extent, and therefore...the Act has been productive of much good.' (See Activity 8.1, Item 3.)

Legislation of the working environment 1833-53

There were several strands to further progress for the reformers in the twenty years that followed the passing of the 1833 Factory Act. Consequently the protection of the interests of children, young people and women as 'unfree agents' in a safer working environment became increasingly secure. More difficult was the continuing struggle to achieve the aims of the Ten Hour Movement.

The 1842 Mines Act

Unsuccessful factory bills introduced by Ashley in 1838, 1839 and 1840 all contained Ten Hour clauses. In 1840 Ashley chaired a committee looking at the working of the 1833 Act. Its report endorsed the principle of government intervention in factories (as opposed to a *laissez-faire* – non-interventionist – approach) and highlighted the need for further reforms. Robert Peel, newly installed Tory Prime Minister in 1841, dampened any optimism by declaring that the government was opposed to a Ten Hour Bill. The impetus towards further reform was revived in 1842 with the publication of the report of the Royal Commission on children at work, including mines. Public opinion was horrified by the graphic, often vividly illustrated, accounts of conditions for children in the mines (see Activity 8.1, Item 2). The subsequent Mines Act of 1842 banned the underground employment of children under 10 and women. The reformers were encouraged by the extension of the interventionist principle to another area of the economy beyond that of textile manufacturing.

The 1844 Factory Act

In 1843 the Home Secretary, Sir James Graham, had unsuccessfully introduced a bill further regulating children's working hours but designed primarily to improve the provision of education for factory children (see Section 1.3). In the following year a modified bill, shorn of its educational clauses, became law as the 1844 Factory Act. The Act brought considerable progress in several areas but saw no advance towards the 10-hour day. Peel even chose to make the 12-hour day an issue of confidence. Nevertheless the Act is a significant one. Children were allowed to start work younger, at the age of 8, but were to work half-time and not more than $6^{1}/_{2}$ hours daily. Young persons aged 13-18, and women, importantly, were to work a maximum of 12 hours a day. Night work for women was forbidden. More inspectors were appointed. Safety was improved by rules to fence off dangerous machinery, and to prohibit machines from being cleaned when in motion. In 1845 the scope of the Factory Acts was extended to include calico printing works.

The 1847 Factory Act

Fielden became the standard-bearer for the Ten Hour Movement when Ashley resigned his seat to support Peel over the Corn Laws in 1846. It is his name that is associated with the legislation that became instrumental in achieving the 10-hour day. This was the 1847 Factory Act. For women and young persons the working day was limited to 10 hours. Nothing was said about the hours of adult males but the economic slow-down of the period had created a situation in which many factories, unprompted by the law, had reduced daily hours to 10 anyway. Factory owners, however, did not concede. By arranging relays and managing lunch breaks they were able to sustain the 12-hour day.

When the legality of relays was taken to the courts by Horner, Baron Parke, the presiding judge, supported the factory owners. In 1850 hasty and ill drafted legislation was introduced to make relays for young persons and women illegal. As a concession their working day was increased to $10^{1}/_{2}$ hours.

The issue was finally resolved in the 1853 Factory Act carefully drafted by Horner for Palmerston to introduce. The working day for all factory workers was normally restricted to the period between 6 a.m. and 6 p.m. Children were not allowed to work their $6^{1}/_{2}$ hours outside these hours. Young people and women were restricted to a $10^{1}/_{2}$-hour day. Since women and children were an essential part of the workforce, this in effect restricted adult male hours to a similar length. The 22-year campaign of the Ten Hour Movement was over.

The impact on the family

There can be no doubt that the Factory Acts affected the working lives of all members of working-class families to whom they applied. It must be remembered, however, that the vast majority of working people were employed in workshops where the legislation did not apply.

The impact on children

It is easier to assess the impact that the legislation had on children, young people, mothers and fathers as individuals within the family than to make judgements about any overall impact on the family as a unit. It is now generally agreed that the classic Industrial Revolution family unit was nuclear (consisting of two parents and their children) rather than extended (including grandparents, uncles, aunts, etc.) and had become so before the breakdown of the domestic system. Smelser (1959) has argued that from about 1820 the family as an identifiable unit within the factory workplace began to be dismantled by technological change. Factory legislation, as it became effective between 1833 and 1853, would have served to accentuate this process by reducing the hours during which the family could be together in the factory. Furthermore, the relay systems, introduced by the owners to preserve at least a 12-hour day for adults, meant that authority over children and young persons was being exercised by people other than their fathers. These views have been widely challenged by historians such as Rule, who consider that Smelser was inaccurate in his analysis and too sweeping in his conclusions. Rule prefers evidence suggesting that, even in the early factory period before 1820, relatively few children worked in direct contact with other family members as a working group (Rule, 1986, p.174).

The economic impact on the family

What must be accepted is that working-class families operated at a variety of levels. Sentiment did not play a major part in the way they were managed. Times were too hard for that and hard-nosed attitudes applied, particularly to children (see Section 1.2). Vincent identifies for parents, 'the fundamentally insoluble problem of how to simultaneously nurture their children and exploit them economically' (Vincent 1982, p.85).

Factories initially increased the earning capacity of the average family and factory legislation obviously threatened this situation. Any resultant financial hardship would hit all the family. More threatening perhaps were the uncertainties of the market and the economic cycle. Children spent longer at home and some might benefit from elementary education (see Section 1.3). New regulations sought to protect their health and safety at work. Many women stayed at home as mothers to bring up the family. It is estimated that in Lancashire, in 1851, only about 30% of wives went out to work. Not all children would therefore be out on the streets as some claimed. Some fathers found the new environment different and difficult but it would be wrong to suggest that a fundamental, and in some way harmful, change had taken place in the chemistry of family relationships.

MAIN POINTS - Section 1.1

- The Factory Acts passed between 1833 and 1853 firmly established the right of the government to legislate within a key manufacturing sector of the economy. This was a victory for Benthamism and a defeat for *laissez-faire*.
- Factory inspectors were overworked and often met with attempts at evasion. But by 1853 the influence of a professional and independent inspectorate was becoming increasingly important in securing compliance with the law. Inspection procedures could be applied in other legislative areas.
- The working conditions of children, young persons and women were undeniably improved and a meaningful restriction on the hours worked by adult males had been achieved.
- Reformist legislation still applied only to a minority of working-class occupations. It would be wrong to claim that substantial benefits had been achieved for the poor.

Activity 8.1 Early legislation and its implementation

ITEM 1 An interview with a former flax mill child worker

Do you consider doffing a laborious employment? Yes.
Explain what it is you had to do. When the frames are full, they have to stop the frames, and take the flyers off, and take the full bobbins off, and carry them to the roller; and then put empty ones on, and set the frame going again.
Does that keep you constantly on your feet? Yes, there are so many frames, and they run so quick.
Your labour is very excessive? Yes; you have not time for anything.
Suppose you flagged a little, or were too late, what would they do? Strap us.
Are they in the habit of strapping those who are last in doffing? Yes.
Constantly? Yes.
Severely? Yes.
Is the strap used so as to hurt you excessively? Yes, it is.

From the Report on Child Labour, 1832.

ITEM 2 The 1842 Mines Act

Children were often used for work in restricted spaces. The 1842 Mines Act banned the underground employment of children under 10 and women.

ITEM 3 The work of Leonard Horner

(i) I now see that it is impossible for my superintendents to visit 700 factories each, twice in a year, taking into account the time they are occupied by prosecutions, in keeping their books, in making their monthly reports, and in their correspondence; and your Lordship will probably agree with me that each factory ought to be visited by a superintendent at least twice a year, in addition to the visits of the Inspector.

Letter from Horner to the Home Secretary, Lord John Russell, 1837.

(ii) Parliament must tell the factory owners that they will just have to get used to the new arrangements for employing children as well as they can. The interests of children now quite rightly have the backing of the law and this situation meets the best interests of the economy.

Adapted from Horner's address to the Committee enquiring into the working of the 1833 Factory Act, 1840.

(iii) Horner found that clever operators would always evade the legislators' intentions. He pursued the issue through the courts so that the illegality of working shifts could be confirmed, or so he thought. When a test case went to court in February 1850, shift working was found to be legal.

Adapted from Fraser 1973.

Questions

1. From Items 1 and 2, and your own knowledge, describe the conditions under which children and young people worked in the first half of the 19th century.
2. Refer to Item 2.
   a) Why were children useful in mines and why was this work difficult for inspectors to regulate?
   b) How did the situation of girls like the one pictured influence public opinion?
3. Using Item 3 and your own knowledge, what difficulties were encountered in implementing the 1833 Factory Act?

1.2 The importance of child labour in the factory reform movement

The importance of children for the legislation

Children, the major but not exclusive beneficiaries of factory legislation during this period, played an important part in furthering the cause of the Short Time Committees and the Ten Hour Movement. Legislation before 1833, unsurprisingly, reflected a preoccupation with improving the lot of children, and began to establish the idea of children as 'unfree agents'. Subsequent legislation built on this principle and narrowed the range of those that could be classified as 'free agents' until only adult males fell into this category. In the process, they too found that their working day had been shaped by interventionist legislation.

For the reformers, be they Benthamite Whig radicals or Tory philanthropists, it seemed sensible to begin by establishing the statutory protection of factory children, however flawed the enforcement regime might be. They knew that formal review and reporting procedures would generate a stream of evidence to sustain their own campaigning momentum and keep a continuing focus on factory conditions in general. They reasoned that the working environment achieved for children was bound to affect that of adults, which indeed proved to be the case.

Not all factory owners were barbarous and greedy, nor were they disciples of Robert Owen (see Box 8.2). What they all shared was a desire to maintain levels of productivity and remain profitably competitive. They saw the 1833 legislation as an unwelcome management challenge rather than a commercial catastrophe. As legislation evolved, they experimented with relays and upgraded technology to account for the changing profile of the workforce. It could be argued that the abolition of child labour stimulated the imaginative and organisational ingenuity of the mill owners and their managers.

By 1853 it was clear that there could be no return to child labour and that regulatory legislation, be it Whig or Tory, had arrived to stay in a key laissez-faire stronghold. What was also clear was that the textile manufacturing base could survive such uninvited intrusion.

Working conditions for children in the factories

Child labour was not invented by the Industrial Revolution. It had been a natural and essential part of working life in the pre-industrial agricultural community. It was also an important part of the domestic system within manufacturing. Children were familiar with hard work and long hours. There was little challenge to child labour.

Conditions for children who found themselves working in the factories deteriorated. Children had always worked from an early age but now hours were long and certain, regulated by the factory bell rather than tiredness and the seasons. Harsh discipline, often marked by violent ill treatment, enforced the rules. Working conditions were dangerous and injurious to health. Children were ideal for working in cramped conditions amidst dangerously moving machinery. Such work was vital to making full use of the new technology in the mills. More generally, children suffered from the unhealthy working environment of the factory, where damp, hot, dusty and poorly ventilated conditions were the norm. There were moral dangers too, which were important in drawing the attention of the reformers to the need to protect children:

> 'Factories...were corrupting influences upon young children, who soon adopted the...morals of their adult colleagues. Children in factories were clearly at risk physically and morally.'
> (Fraser 1973, p.12)

Many people found such conditions appalling and unacceptable and decided to do something about it.

What motivated the 'reformers'?

One of the strengths of the reform movement was that it cut across political, sectional and class boundaries. Those involved could be Whigs or Tories, Anglicans or Dissenters, enlightened industrialists or members of the landed aristocracy. The cause of improving conditions for factory children achieved a degree of consensus, and it would be true to say that its supporters embraced it with real fervour. The protection of children was an emotive issue and it was not difficult to find compelling evidence that something needed to be done. The appointment of a Parliamentary or Royal Commission of Enquiry into factory conditions, as in 1833 and 1842, always provided an opportunity to argue a compelling moral case, however contested it might be.

The importance of legislation before 1833

The 1802 Factory Act was the work of two men: Robert Owen, whose mill at New Lanark reflected his progressive social ideas, and Sir Robert Peel, factory owner and father of the future Prime Minister. It was primarily designed to check abuses in the recruitment of pauper apprentices but also dealt with hours, education and night work for all children. The 1819 Factory Act tried to go further by prohibiting work for children under the age of 9, and limiting the working day for children aged 9-16 to 12 hours. The Act was generally ignored. No inspectors were appointed. Informers were to be rewarded for informing on factory owners who broke the law. Compliance with the law was therefore essentially voluntary. The 1802 Act was important because, however modestly, it challenged laissez-faire in the textile factories. The 1819 Act was important in that it tried to regulate the hours of significantly greater numbers of children. The absence of effective inspection arrangements was not lost on those who framed future legislation.

BOX 8.2 Robert Owen

Robert Owen

Owen was a mill owner, and the focus of his attention was on solving the problems which faced him as an employer. He wanted to create an efficient labour force in his factories, but he was also concerned about the curse of unemployment and poverty. His factory was the largest cotton mill in Britain. Wages were relatively low, but were offset by above-average welfare benefits. Owen provided housing at reasonable rent, and a contributory sickness and pension fund, free medical services, and a remarkably enlightened school for children. All of these and other facilities sprang from Owen's belief that character was shaped by environment. Yet these measures were in no sense charity, for there could be no mistaking that New Lanark was, first and foremost, a commercial enterprise. While this aspect of his work made him popular with the government and some of his fellow factory owners, his interest in welfare for the community and decent conditions for the workforce meant that he quickly came to be seen as a dangerous influence.

Adapted from May 1987.

The Ten Hour Movement

The Ten Hour Movement spearheaded the campaign to improve working conditions in the factories. Richard Oastler, whose letter to the *Leeds Mercury* had galvanised supporters of reform, had originally seen himself as an individual - if not lone - voice in the cause of decent conditions for children. In the decisive 'Fixby Hall Compact', however, he was persuaded to make common cause with the leaders of the recently formed Short Time Committees. Oastler now discovered a talent as a popular orator, and under his leadership the Ten Hour Movement became a mass movement that organised meetings, demonstrations, petitions and pamphlets in favour of factory reform. The objective was a ten-hour day for all factory workers but Oastler came to realise that it would not be readily conceded. Improving conditions for children and women was then vigorously pursued as a more accessible means to the more contentious end.

There was widespread opposition to the idea of a ten-hour day. Many potential sympathisers were influenced by the views of those whose job it was to manage the factories, 'practical men' familiar with industry. In effect practical men came to mean the employers themselves, who were hardly an unbiased authority. It may be assumed that almost all of the arguments put forward by factory owners to defend the status quo were motivated by self-interest. Less dishonest and unworthy was the widely held and publicised view that a substantial reduction in hours would have serious economic repercussions. Much was made of foreign competition, of economist Nassau Senior's belief that profits were made in the last hour of the day, and of the threat of reduced output and increased unemployment.

Other, somewhat stronger, arguments were marshalled to undermine the case for the ten-hour day. Both factory owners and reformers agreed that to reduce children's hours would inevitably reduce adult hours as well and that this would in turn reduce wages. Even Oastler admitted that there could be no justice in demanding 12 hours' wages for 10 hours' work.

Adapted from Fraser 1973.

1.3 What education was provided for the children of the poor?

The children of the poor

As late as 1860 a government document defined elementary education as that 'suited to the condition of workmen and servants'. Despite significant developments which gathered pace in the period that followed the first government intervention of 1833, it remained true, in crude terms, that elementary education was being provided by the upper and middle classes for the lower classes on terms that favoured the former. As May has suggested, elementary education was provided as training in 'followership' in a world in which 'attention, docility, submissiveness and reasonableness were seen as qualities desirable in the poor' (May 1987, p.157).

Need and provision

The need to preserve the social order therefore largely inspired those whose work marked the first provision of elementary education for the poor (see Box 8.4). The right sort of education could avoid the kind of social and political upheaval that had occurred in France during the Revolutionary period. It could also help the working classes to come to terms with the unpleasant realities of industrialisation. Those best placed to provide it were the upper and middle classes and the churches, whose members, were educated and who also had most to lose. As in other areas of national life, it was not initially thought necessary or appropriate for the government to become involved.

Elementary schools were provided by religious charities. In 1811 the Church of England set up the National Society for the Education of the Poor to continue the long-established work of the Society for the Promotion of Christian Knowledge (SPCK). In response, in 1814 the Nonconformists set up the British and Foreign Schools Society. From then on 'National' and 'British' schools almost exclusively provided what elementary education was available for the poor. Andrew Bell and Joseph Lancaster were as much personal rivals as were the 'National' and 'Foreign' societies which they respectively led. Most historians would agree with May that 'rivalry between denominations...held up the state provision of elementary schools for generations' (May 1987, p.155).

Predictably, the curriculum offered was narrow. Reading, almost exclusively from the Bible, came first, followed by writing, not considered a priority for the children of the poor. Arithmetic came a poor third and consisted of the four basic rules. At first the monitorial system was used to address the inadequate numbers of teachers. Older and more competent pupils taught pre-learnt material to smaller groups of younger children while the teacher supervised the class as a whole. When it became clear that attendance during the working week was difficult for children working in the factories, Sunday Schools were set up.

The government gets involved

The 1833 Factory Act made the provision of education during the working day a legal requirement for factory children aged 9-13. Some factory owners set up schools within their factories. Some children left the factory and attended local schools, where they often arrived tired, dirty and smelly. In some towns special schools were set up for the factory children. Legislation also introduced schooling to prisons and workhouses.

More importantly, in 1833 the government made a grant of £20,000, split equally between the 'British' and 'Foreign' societies to assist with the building of schools. The grant was renewed annually until 1838, when it was reviewed. From 1839, further grants were to be administered directly by the state and inspection procedures were introduced.

Positive proposals to improve teacher training were opposed in 1839 and 1840 by the Church of England, and educational clauses in the 1843 Factory Bill were challenged by the Nonconformists and subsequently dropped from the 1844 Factory Act. However, during this period the work of James Kay-Shuttleworth did much to improve the quality of government inspectors and establish the acceptance of state-sponsored teacher-training colleges. Compulsory state elementary education was not introduced until 1870, but by the middle of the century the right of the state to be centrally involved in the monitoring and regulation of education for the poor was largely uncontested.

BOX 8.4 Educational changes in perspective

By the 1850s it was clear that significant progress was being made in educating working-class children. The religious charities had achieved much and the monitorial system was proving effective in meeting the growing demand for teaching. The beginnings of state aid to the societies was obviously of great importance, as was the introduction of the pupil-teacher system. Indeed, by the late 1840s there was a much wider acceptance of the idea that government should encourage the development of schools for the working class. *The Edinburgh* Review, for example, expressed the opinion that 'The state has a right to see that children are so brought up that they are able to fulfil their social obligations towards their fellow citizens.' The

Not all schools were as enlightened as Robert Owen's, where the curriculum included dancing (shown here).

Quarterly Review agreed with this point of view, declaring: 'Sooner or later, popular education must be an affair of the State.' Nevertheless, the strength of these views must not be exaggerated. An uneasy partnership existed between the state and the church societies from 1833 onwards, with the societies being very much the senior partner. They succeeded in maintaining their control for another twenty or so years. It must also be recognised that, by today's standards, working-class education in 1850 still had a long way to go. The idea persisted that education should consist of the minimum amount of instruction to keep the working classes contented and ready to accept their humble position in society.

Adapted from Hopkins 1979.

MAIN POINTS - Sections 1.2-1.3

- Improving conditions for factory children was an important part of the process of reforming conditions for all factory workers. This is why the Ten Hour Movement supported attempts to improve children's conditions.
- There was a real need to improve factory conditions, especially for children. New machine technology created a highly dangerous and unhealthy working environment.
- The reformist campaign, in and beyond Parliament, was motivated by a crusading zeal and brought together a cross-section of society, appalled by factory conditions.
- Early Factory Acts in 1802 and 1819 proved ineffective because there were no inspection

procedures. Their regulations would have made a significant difference had they been observed.
- Educating poor children was seen as important for social and political stability, not to prepare them for employment or to enable their personal development.
- Much good work was done by religious charities to provide education for the poor. Rivalry between Anglicans and Nonconformists, however, inhibited its progress.
- By 1853 the government's right to be involved in the provision of elementary education had been established, although it was not expected to be a direct provider.

Activity 8.2 Children and reform

ITEM 1 A 'reformist view'

It is well known to the public that I have for some years rather prominently advocated the necessity of Parliamentary interference for the protection of all children and young persons working in factories, and that I agreed with Mr Sadler and Lord Ashley in their opinion that 'ten working hours per day' was the maximum that the law should allow such persons to work. It is also well known to the public that these two gentlemen's labours were not successful and that they were defeated in their attempts to achieve better conditions for factory workers. Public excitement throughout the country, arising from knowledge of the firm evidence presented to the Parliamentary Committee and the Royal Commission indicating strongly that government legislation was necessary, had forced the government to act. Mr Sadler and Lord Ashley were, however, disappointed by the terms of the new regulations. May I say that I stand by all the evidence that I have produced to illustrate the cruelty of the appalling conditions that exist in the factories. I believe that my arguments have been based on the best interests of the country and reflect a Christian approach to the issue.

Adapted from Richard Oastler, 'A Well Seasoned Christmas Pie', 1834.

ITEM 2 An alternative view of government intervention

In my opinion, and I hope to see the day when such a feeling is universal, no child ought to be put to work in a cotton mill at all so early as the age of 13 years; and after that the hours should be moderate, and the labour light, until such time as the human frame is rendered by nature capable of enduring the fatigues of adult labour...I am aware that many of the advocates of the cause of factory children are in favour of a Ten Hours Bill for children and young persons that would, in effect, limit the hours worked by all factory workers...It has always, however, appeared to me that those who are in favour of this policy lose sight of the very important consequences which are involved in such a principle. Have they considered that it would be the first example of the legislature of a free country interfering with the freedom of adult labour?...Have they taken into account that if workers in the textile industry are to be protected by the law then justice will demand that the same should apply to the thousands of workers in other parts of the economy?...It appears to me that if we allow the government to regulate adult working hours then we will be going back to the days of the feudal system.

Adapted from Richard Cobden in a letter to Hunt, 1836.

ITEM 3 A 19th-century cartoon by Robert Cruikshank

Harsh treatment for child mill workers.

ITEM 4 Numbers of children under 15 employed in various occupations in Britain, 1851

Boys Occupation	%	Girls Occupation	%
Agriculture	28.4	Textiles	41.3
Textiles	19.4	Domestic Service	30.0
Navigation/Docks	10.9	Dress	13.5
Mines	8.7	Agriculture	7.2
Metal workers	6.1	Metal workers	1.7
Other trades	26.5	Other trades	6.3

Based on C. Booth, 'Occupations of the people of the United Kingdom 1801-1881', Journal of the Royal Statistical Society, 1886.

Questions

1. Using Item 1 and your own knowledge:
   a) Explain why Oastler, Sadler and Ashley were campaigning to regulate the hours worked by children and young persons in factories.
   b) What arguments did the 'reformists' use to support their case?
2. Study Items 1 and 2.
   a) Outline Cobden's argument in your own words.
   b) How might Oastler have reacted to Cobden's views?
3. Using Items 1-3 and your own knowledge, suggest how (a) the 'reformists' and (b) Cobden might have reacted to Cruikshank's cartoon.
4. Using Item 4 and your own knowledge, how far would you agree that, by the middle of the 19th century, significant progress had been made in securing better working conditions for children?

2 The unreformed Poor Law

Key issues

1. What were the origins of the Old Poor Law?
2. How did the unreformed Poor Law operate in the early 19th century?
3. Why did opposition to the unreformed Poor Law grow after 1815?
4. What was the role of the Poor Law Commission of 1832-34 in bringing about change?

2.1 The origins of the Old Poor Law

Until 1834, relief of poverty was largely based on legislation from the Tudor and Stuart age which had been subsequently shaped and developed through local variation and practice. The keystones of the approach to relieving the poor were the Elizabethan Act of 1601, which codified a range of earlier Tudor legislation, and the Act of Settlement of 1662. The emphasis was on local responsibility and, as the historian John Rule puts it, 'the local base of the Poor Law meant that it operated in a face-to-face world where people and their problems were known'. (Rule 1992, p.120)

The Elizabethan Act of 1601

The Elizabethan Poor Law was shaped by a combination of Tudor paternalism and the fear that the problem of unchecked poverty and vagrancy would have political consequences in the form of widespread social unrest. The Elizabethan Act of 1601 abandoned earlier repressive Tudor legislation in favour of a more logical and soundly administered 'system'. The key was what was later referred to as 'classification' - finding appropriate remedies for particular groups of people. Essentially, the Elizabethan Poor Law identified three main groups to be dealt with:

1. The impotent poor (the aged, chronically sick, blind or lunatic), who required institutional relief and were therefore to be accommodated in 'poorhouses' or 'almshouses'.
2. The able-bodied poor, who needed to be provided with work, sometimes in a non-residential workhouse. Pauper children were to be apprenticed to a trade so that they would become useful, self-supporting citizens.
3. The able-bodied idler, who needed to be disciplined in a 'house of correction'.

The administration of the scheme was based at local, parish level, with Vestries or local JPs in each of the 15,000 parishes in England annually appointing unpaid 'overseers of the poor'. These overseers were empowered to levy a poor rate on property owners, which was enforced by magistrates. The poor rate income was then used by the overseer to care for the impotent poor, set up work for the able-bodied, and for taking punitive action against the idle and disorderly. By far the most common form of poor relief was a small pension to the aged or infirm poor. It was also a frequent practice for overseers to make occasional grants of food, clothing or medicine when needed. In some areas, overseers developed formal 'scales' for the supplementation of inadequate wages by cash payments from the poor rates. These forms of relief were usually referred to as 'outdoor relief', as they were not administered in any special institution or building. In 1662 the Act of Settlement attempted to clarify the responsibility of parishes and clamp down on what was seen as a long-standing problem of vagrancy by making parish overseers responsible only for those paupers 'settled in their parish by birth, marriage or apprenticeship' and ordering that outsiders be returned to their own parishes for relief.

The 1662 Act of Settlement

The Act of Settlement has been criticised for bringing a new brutality and harshness to the operation of relief - particularly with regard to pregnant women, who were likely to be victimised as the bearers of a future drain on parish resources. Indeed, some historians have discerned in this Puritanical attitude towards poverty the beginnings of the sorts of ideas which were to shape the development of the New Poor Law in the early 1830s (see Part 3, below). However, it is possible to exaggerate the importance of the Act of Settlement. It was never strictly enforced everywhere, owing to the often haphazard system of unpaid overseers. At any rate, internal migration (the moving of families and individuals from one part of the country to another), which led to the growth of the towns in the 18th century, was clearly significantly reduced.

Eighteenth-century developments

By 1700 there was a growing feeling that the able-bodied poor - sometimes now referred to as the 'undeserving' - should only be granted relief in specifically designed workhouses, as several parishes were in fact doing already. The 1722 Workhouse Act (also known as Knatchbull's Act) allowed all parishes to build workhouses without the need for a special Act of Parliament. Under this Act, those who refused to enter a workhouse forfeited their right to relief. As a result, there was, in theory at least, no more outdoor relief, and the principle of deterrence was clearly introduced into the operation of relief. Workhouses were farmed out to contractors who set the inmates to work and made what profits they could. In practice, however, local outdoor relief continued and, in 1782, Gilbert's Act, motivated by

concern for the plight of the agricultural labourer affected by enclosure and the loss of common rights, once again allowed parish overseers to give the able-bodied destitute employment outside of the workhouse near their homes, and, when this was impossible, to grant other forms of outdoor relief. A common practice arising from the Act was to hire out impoverished able-bodied labourers to local tradesmen and farmers at a very cheap rate and to make up wages to a bare subsistence level from the parish rates. This sometimes became known as the 'Roundsmen System'.

2.2 How did the Old Poor Law operate in the early 19th century?

General characteristics of the Old Poor Law

By its very localised nature, it is difficult to draw together the general characteristics of the Old Poor Law - indeed in this respect it may be misleading to talk of the operation of any 'system' as such. There is still no real consensus between historians about the nature of its operation and effectiveness. Many criticisms of the Old Poor Law by the Royal Commission of 1832-34 have now been seriously questioned. For example, the historian J.D. Marshall concludes:

'The ultimate result of the Old Poor Law was the creation of a vast but rather inefficient system of social welfare, based on the close relationships of the village and hamlet, and roughly adapted to the requirements of English rural society between 1601 and about 1750.' (Marshall 1985)

This view is mirrored by Henriques in his claim that poor relief provided 'a personal service in which the pauper was relieved in familiar surroundings...The small parish provided for its poor without frills; but it provided on the basis of personal knowledge of immediate needs' (Henriques 1979). At the other extreme, the historian Blaug's description of the Old Poor Law as 'a welfare state in miniature, combining elements of wage escalation, family allowances, unemployment compensation and public works' is equally difficult to sustain.

Although no other country in Europe had an organised system of public poor relief, the Old Poor Law was essentially a supplement to existing private charity. The underlying governmental motive was the promotion of social stability by alleviating immediate discontent and preventing food riots - bursts of legislation tended to follow periods of extreme hardship when charitable resources were scare and the threat of unrest at its greatest. If any general characteristics of the operation of the old 'system' can in fact be identified they are:

- The parish remained the most important unit

of administration. This could of course mean either that the 'face to face' relationships of the village or small parish would lead to greater humanity in the relief of poverty, or that the overseer might rule as a petty tyrant over his small territory.

- Paradoxically, variety of practice was a recurrent theme: the operation of the Poor Law became a hotchpotch of diverse measures and customs which varied from parish to parish according to local circumstances. For example, some parishes set up a single workhouse in which all the local poor were set to work, while other parishes built separate institutions for the aged and infirm. Elsewhere there were no separate buildings at all and all paupers received 'outdoor relief'.

- It could also be argued that, in the period from 1600, a feature of the Old Poor Law's operation had been its considerable adaptability in relation to social needs. However, by the last quarter of the 18th century even the resourcefulness of this 'system' had been stretched to its limits by a combination of population growth increased social mobility, industrialisation and economic fluctuations.

2.3 Why did opposition to the unreformed Poor Law grow after 1815?

There is a direct link between the Poor Law Amendment Act of 1834, which established the so-called New Poor Law (see Part 3 below) and the report of the Royal Commission on the Poor Law (1832-34) which was set up to investigate the workings of the increasingly criticised old system.

Contemporary criticisms of the Old Poor Law

The increasing cost of poor relief had been generally accepted during the period 1793-1815 as a necessary consequence of the war with France. After 1815, however, there was increasing dissatisfaction with the escalating costs and operation of the Old Poor Law, with allowance schemes like the Speenhamland System becoming the focal point of the criticism. It was argued that:

- The system was inefficiently administered and had become much too costly. Cost-cutting expediency was therefore at the centre of many of the recommendations.

- Many able-bodied workers had been made dependent upon the public charity of schemes like the Speenhamland System, with its allowances in supplementation of

wages, and were thus reduced to degradation. The system depressed low wages, contributed to the immobility of labour, acted as a disincentive to work and encouraged unsupportable population growth through the supplement provided to larger families. It therefore created an artificial situation that was in fact a heavy burden on everyone concerned at a time when the demands of industry for labour matched the surplus rural population.

Further impetus for reform came in 1830 with the Swing Riots (see Unit 4, Section 3.2) - spontaneous outbreaks of rick-burning, rioting and machine-smashing - which were largely confined to those southern counties where the Speenhamland System was most established. This agricultural unrest was interpreted as evidence of the system's inadequacy in the face of continued economic stress.

The Speenhamland System

The form of outdoor relief (allowances in aid of wages) which attracted most contemporary attention was the so-called Speenhamland System, set up in 1795 as a spontaneous local response to the distress and disturbances caused by a series of bad harvests combined with a rise in prices (due to the war with Revolutionary France) by a group of Berkshire JPs at the village of Speenhamland in Berkshire. These JPs decided to supplement local wages from the poor rates on a sliding scale in accordance with the price of bread and the size of the family concerned. The higher the price of bread, and the larger the family, the more relief would be given. It was the costs associated with this system, which combined traditional paternalism with a pragmatic response to fears about the heightened dangers of unrest in the 1790s (see Unit 2), that were at the centre of mounting criticism of the Old Poor Law, and hence the pressure for reforms which reached a head in 1832. Poor relief, which cost less than £2 million per annum in 1780, had by 1803 risen to more than £4 million.

The Speenhamland System, and the many variants of it which rapidly spread to the counties of southern and eastern England, provided a stop-gap measure which prevented mass destitution and starvation during the period of abnormally high prices through to the end of the war with France in 1815. However, the system came in for a barrage of increasing contemporary criticism about the development of a costly, damaging and ultimately counter-productive dependency culture which in fact increased the problem it set out to resolve. The operation of the system was attacked at a number of different levels:

- It was argued that the measure was as much a system of relief to the employers as labourers as it artificially kept down wages and enabled farmers to employ on a casual basis.

- It tied the workers even more to the land at a time when there was redundancy in rural trades and a growing need for industrial labour.
- Malthusians (see Activity 8.3, Item 3) claimed that the system encouraged the poor to produce large families, leading to population growth which would outstrip the means of subsistence.
- Finally, the system encouraged idleness, as labourers would do the minimum amount of work in the knowledge that they would have their wages subsidised by the parish. Conversely, the honest, conscientious labourer was degraded by the system. No matter how hard he worked he would still have to rely on the parish for at least part of his earnings, and his independence was thus taken away from him.

MAIN POINTS - Sections 2.1-2.3

- The Old Poor Law prescribed relief and correction of the poor according to their circumstances. The poor could only receive relief in their own parish. The 1722 Workhouse Act allowed all parishes to build workhouses without a special Act of Parliament and theoretically abolished outdoor relief. Gilbert's Act (1782) introduced the hiring out of the poor at cheap rates.
- The local basis of poor relief meant that at best it was administered with some personal sympathy, and at worst it could be subject to a petty tyrant. There was no uniformity of practice.
- The unreformed system was criticised for being inefficient and costly, and for making able-bodied workers dependent on charity and depressing wages. The Speenhamland System, which supplemented low wages according to a sliding scale, was particularly criticised for tying rural workers to the land, and for encouraging idleness and large families.

Activity 8.3 The Speenhamland System

ITEM 1 The operation of the Speenhamland System

The magistrates will provide for those who try to support themselves; when the gallon [1.8 kilo] loaf shall cost 1 shilling, then every poor and industrious man shall have for his own support 3 shillings, either produced by his own or his family's labour or an allowance from the poor rates; and for the support of his wife and every other of his family, 1 shilling 6 pence. When the gallon loaf shall cost one and fourpence, then every poor and industrious man shall have 4 shillings weekly for his own and 1 shilling and 10 pence for the support of his family, and so in proportion as the cost of the loaf rises.

Statement by Berkshire Magistrates at the Pelican Inn, Speenhamland, May 1795.

ITEM 2 Expenditure on Poor relief 1750-1832

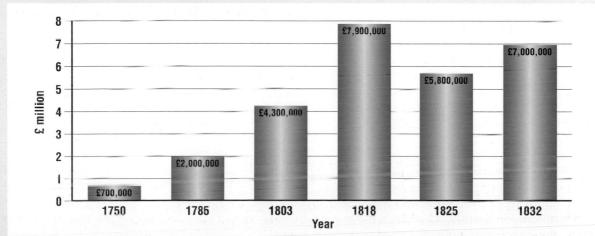

ITEM 3 Malthus' views

I say that the power of the population to reproduce is infinitely greater than the power of the earth to produce subsistence for man. By that law of nature which makes food necessary to the life of man, the effects of these two unequal powers must be kept equal. This implies a strong and constantly operating check on population from the difficulties of subsistence. No fancied equality, no agrarian regulations in their utmost extent can remove the pressure even for a single century. The poor laws of England tend to depress the general condition of the poor in two general ways: a poor man may marry with little or no prospect of being able to support a family in independence. They may be said in some measure to create the poor which they maintain. Secondly, the quantity of provisions consumed in a workhouse upon a part of society, that cannot be considered as the most valuable part, diminishes the share that would otherwise belong to the more industrious, and more worthy members.

Reverend Thomas Malthus

Extract from Essay on Population, 1798, Reverend Thomas Malthus.

ITEM 4 A historian's view

Did the poor relief paid to able-bodied workers create a dependency culture by reducing the incentive to work and encouraging early marriage and childbirth? It has been suggested that farmers tended to discriminate in favour of married labourers, since they would otherwise have been a greater burden on the parish rate - which was largely paid by farmers. This may have been so, but it is unlikely to have become significant until after the end of the war, in 1815, when a depression in cereal prices, the flood of demobilised soldiers onto the labour market, and the accumulating impact of the rising birth rate all began to take effect. Allowances under the Berkshire scale of 1795 began with a 'gallon loaf' at 1 shilling and increased with each penny rise up to 2 shillings. A single man was guaranteed 3 shillings a week, and a married one an extra 1 shilling and 6 pence for each dependant. Thus in cheap years a family with three children was guaranteed 9 shillings, while the doubling of the bread allowance in more expensive ones would bring the figure up to 12 shillings.

In 1795 a single labourer in the Midland and southern arable regions could, with supplements in kind, earn the equivalent of 10 shillings per week. If unemployed, the scale would have given him 5 shillings per week. A married man and his wife who could between them earn 15 shillings per week and had one child would, if unemployed, have received 10 shillings. If, however, a married man had children young enough to keep his wife at home, then during the high price years his income would not have supported his family unless supplemented. But it was an allowance on top of wages: he was expected to earn as much as he could. The Berkshire JPs had made it clear that the scale was payable to 'every poor and industrious man'. In the small world of the agricultural village, the character of each claimant was known. The existence of the bread scale was to guarantee subsistence at a very low level. It seems likely that with parishes concentrating on basic food needs, the other kinds of discretionary payments, which had been a feature of life for the 18th-century poor, were made less often and with declining generosity. It may also have been the case that magistrates were less willing to overturn the appeals of disappointed claimants, since they knew that the increasing burden of relief was being thrown onto a decreasing number of shoulders as the proportion of the village population either needing assistance or no longer able to pay poor rates increased. In general, the move towards wage supplementation in the rural South and East just about enabled the Old Poor Law to cope with the problem of feeding the poor in a period when bread prices were higher than they had ever been before.

Adapted from Rule 1992.

Questions

1. Using Item 1, describe in your own words the way in which the Speenhamland System was designed to operate.
2. Using Items 1 and 2 and your own knowledge, to what extent can the pattern of poor expenditure identified in Item 2 be explained by the operation of the Speenhamland System?
3. Summarise in your own words the arguments put forward by Malthus in Item 3.
4. What parts of the argument put forward by Malthus in Item 3 relate specifically to the operation of the Speenhamland System? Is the attack justified? Explain your answer with reference to Items 1 and 3.
5. Using Items 1-4 and your own knowledge, list the arguments for and against the view that the operation of the Speenhamland System contributed to the development of a 'dependency culture'.

2.4 The role of the Poor Law Commission of 1832-34

The composition and aims of the Commission

Promoted by both this wave of critical opinion and renewed unrest in the early 1830s (see Unit 4), in February 1832 the new Whig government of Earl Grey launched a full-scale inquiry into the operation of the Poor Law in the form of a Royal Commission. This was carried out by 26 Assistant Commissioners working through the 15,000 parishes and reporting to a nine-man Commission dominated by Nassau Senior, Professor of Political Economy at Oxford University, and Edwin Chadwick (see Box 8.9) - both leading advocates of the ideas of economic individualism associated with the Classical Economists and so-called Benthamites (those who followed the ideas of the thinker Jeremy Bentham) or Utilitarian thinkers (see Box 8.5). Therefore, whilst the work of the Commission was intended to be free from any political bias or preconceptions about the nature of the problem it was in practice heavily shaped and influenced by the social and economic ideas of the Classical Economists and Utilitarians as developed by Senior and Chadwick. Its final report also reflected the underlying objective of cutting what was now seen as the excessive and unjustifiable cost of poor relief under the old system.

The Commission's ideology and conduct

The conduct of the Commission has been a cause of considerable controversy amongst historians. Blaug, for example, describes the approach adopted as 'wildly unstatistical' (Blaug 1963). In particular, Senior and Chadwick have been criticised for deciding on - and actually writing - the essentially ideologically driven conclusions of the report even before the evidence had been fully collected. This evidence was gathered through a combination of the use of questionnaires and personal visits to parishes to undertake interviews with overseers and others involved in the administration of the old 'system'. There was, however, no compulsion to reply to the questionnaire and only about 10% of parishes submitted a return. Similarly, as the historian Eric Evans puts it, 'witnesses were led down prepared Benthamite paths' (Evans 1996, p.232) so that the report became 'propaganda for a predetermined case' (Fraser 1973, p.40). The report was therefore written on the basis of limited and selected evidence which fitted a preconceived conclusion - namely, that allowance systems undermined individualism amongst the able-bodied rural poor and depressed wages.

BOX 8.5 | The ideas of the Classical Economists and Benthamite Utilitarians

In the first three-quarters of the century (1800-75), British public life was strongly influenced by the complementary ideologies of the Classical Economists and the Benthamite Utilitarians, who both preached the virtues of economic individualism. Their ideas fitted the needs and aspirations of the rising middle classes and powerfully influenced government policy.

Jeremy Bentham began with the proposition that human existence is guided by the pursuit of pleasure and the avoidance of pain. He argued that if everyone were left free to pursue pleasure, then the sum of all such successful hunts would be happiness for the greatest possible number. This view had much to recommend it to 19th-century politicians and businessmen, sickened as they were by 18th-century political corruption and inhibited in the world of commerce by rigid tariffs and embargoes. Bentham examined every institution and rule, asking simply 'What is its use?'. That is, to what extent does it aid or hamper the human search for happiness? Some commentators have suggested that Benthamism has the same defect as Marxism - namely, that it attempts to combine two incompatible elements, a mechanistic explanation and a moral end. If all actions are essentially selfish, who can be moral and unselfish enough to be concerned for everyone's happiness? Be that as it may, the yardstick of utility made a definite appeal to the hard-headed rationalism of the Victorian industrialist and entrepreneur.

Benthamism split into two main groups. One group supported complete and unadulterated self-help, believing that self-interest would produce a 'natural harmony of interests'. The other felt that too many obstacles existed for man to be able to act freely. It considered that the state should therefore play a positive role in eliminating such obstacles, so that mankind would be at liberty to pursue individual pleasures. This was the idea of the tutelary state, which guided its members towards self-help and sought to facilitate their fulfilment. The idea of the tutelary state was the branch most directly concerned with social reform. Its most dedicated champion, in both theory and practice, was Edwin Chadwick.
Adapted from Taylor 1972 and Midwinter 1968.

The influence of the Classical Economists

In terms of the ideas of the Classical Economists, the report contained clear reflections of the work of the 'St Paul' (Taylor 1972, p.19) of the movement, David Ricardo. In his *Principles of Political Economy*, written in 1817, Ricardo developed the concept of a 'wages fund', according to which a set proportion of the national wealth was available as wages.

Therefore, the more that was paid in poor relief, the less there remained for actual wages. The Poor Law was consequently counter-productive and a cause of the problem it was trying to solve: the old system sucked more people into pauperism all the time as wages were being constantly forced down.

The influence of Benthamism

The influence of Benthamism was even more evident. The central idea of Jeremy Bentham's utilitarian philosophy was the utility principle that everyone should always act to achieve 'the greatest good of the greatest number', and that this test was applied to all institutions to see whether they achieved the required end. From Chadwick's Benthamite perspective, the Old Poor Law seemed to be clearly lacking in this respect - in fact since paupers still constituted a minority of the population it followed that the needs of the majority were being sacrificed as a result of the disproportionate amount of the country's resources being used for the benefit of a lazy minority, encouraged in their apathetic approach as long as the old system continued. Bentham had also argued that in certain circumstances the individual would benefit from government guidance. He, and therefore Chadwick, were in favour of state intervention in matters of poor relief as a degree of central policy was necessary to control and counter the inefficiencies caused by local practice. Paradoxically, Benthamites such as Chadwick consequently argued that some state intervention was necessary to defend individualism, which the operation of poor relief tended to undermine. Benthamism therefore explains two of the key features of the New Poor Law: first, the controversial concept of 'Less eligibility' (see below) - a deterrent element to relief so that only those most in need would apply for relief; and second, the need for a central body to control the operation of the poor laws.

The Report's recommendations

The Commission's 8,000-page long report of 1834 contained four major recommendations which in turn directly shaped the 1834 Poor Law Amendment Act. These were as follows:

1. The establishment of a 'workhouse test' so that no outdoor relief should be given to the able-bodied poor. The Speenhamland System would therefore be abolished. In order to claim relief, the applicant must enter the workhouse.

2. The concept of 'Less eligibility' - the deterrent principle that conditions of relief within a workhouse must be such that the position of the pauper was worse (less eligible) than that of the poorest labourer in work outside. In this way deterrence was also built into the system as no one who could work was likely to opt for relief in a workhouse and there was no attempt to distinguish between the deserving and undeserving poor. In this way the Report may also be said to include a measure of 'social engineering' to encourage self-help and transform those seen as idle and apathetic into useful members of society.

3. The segregation of sexes so that even if married, the sexes should be kept apart in the workhouse. This would once again act as a deterrent and keep down the numbers of potential paupers.

4. An emphasis on centralisation: to establish unity in pauper relief throughout the country, local administration of the workhouses should be transferred to Poor Law Unions formed by groups of parishes. The unions would elect Poor Law Guardians and appoint full-time parish officers, who should function under central supervision. A Central Board of three Poor Law Commissioners would provide this supervision, with assistants to serve as inspectors. This system was to be financed by local poor rates, although overall expenditure was expected to fall since less people were likely to seek relief.

MAIN POINTS - Section 2.4

- In 1832 the new Whig government launched a Royal Commission to report on the Poor Law. It was led by Senior and Chadwick, both Benthamite Utilitarians. Their philosophy favoured self-help as the prime means of achieving happiness for the greatest possible number.
- The Report was driven by the belief that allowance systems of poor relief undermined individualism among the rural poor and depressed wages – as well as being unnecessarily costly.
- The ideas of Classical Economics suggested that the more that was paid in poor relief, the less money

remained for wages – and so poor relief created more poverty.
- The Commission's report of 1834 made four recommendations: (1) abolition of the Speenhamland System and other forms of outdoor relief; (2) 'Less eligibility' – conditions in the workhouse should always be worse than those of the poorest labourer outside; (3) segregation of the sexes within the workhouse; (4) centralisation – parish responsibilities were to pass to Poor Law Unions formed by groups of parishes, which would elect Poor Law Guardians.

Activity 8.4 The Poor Law Commission

ITEM 1 The Poor Law Report 1834 (i)

It appears from all our returns, especially from replies to the rural queries, that in every district, the discontent of the labouring classes is proportioned to the money dispensed in poor rates, in voluntary charities. The violence of the mobs seems to have arisen from an idea that all their privations arose from the **cupidity** or fraud of those entrusted with the management of the fund provided for the poor. Whatever addition is made to allowances under these circumstances excites the expectation of still further allowances, increases **the conception of the extent of the right**, and ensures proportionate disappointment and hatred if that expectation is not fulfilled.

The Poor Law Report, 1834.

> ### Glossary
> - **cupidity** - greed
> - **the conception of the extent of the right** - the poor's belief that they are justified in expecting more

ITEM 2 The Poor Law Report 1834 (ii)

It may be assumed that in the administration of relief, the public is warranted in imposing such conditions on the individual relieved, as are conducive to the benefit either of the individual himself, or of the country at large, at whose expense he is to be relieved.

The first and most essential of all conditions, a principle which we find universally admitted, even by those whose practice is at variance with it, is that his situation on the whole shall not be made really or apparently so eligible as the situation of the independent labourer of the lowest class. Throughout the evidence it is shown, that in proportion as

Segregation of the sexes was just one of the hardships of the workhouse.

the condition of any pauper is elevated above the condition of independent labourers, the condition of the independent class is depressed, their industry is impaired, their employment becomes unsteady, and its remuneration in wages is diminished. Such persons, therefore, are under the strongest inducements to quit the less eligible class of labourers and enter the more eligible class of paupers. The converse is the effect when the pauper class is placed in its proper position, below the condition of the independent labourer. Every penny bestowed, that tends to render the condition of the paupers more eligible than that of the independent labourer, is a bounty on **indolence and vice**. We have found, that as the poor's rates are at present administered, they operate as bounties of this description to the amount of several millions annually.

We recommend, therefore, the appointment of a Central Board to control the administration of the Poor Laws, with such assistant Commissioners as may be found **requisite**, and that the Commissioners be empowered and directed to frame and enforce regulations for the government or workhouses, and as to the nature and amount of relief to be given and the labour to be exacted in them, and that such regulations shall, as far as may be practicable, be uniform throughout the country.

To effect these purposes we recommend that the Central Board be empowered to cause any number of parishes which they may think convenient to be incorporated for the purpose of workhouse management, and for providing new workhouses where necessary.

The Poor Law Report, 1834, pp. 228, 291, 314.

> ### Glossary
> - **indolence and vice** - laziness and sin
> - **requisite** - necessary

ITEM 3 The Poor Law Commission Report – summary

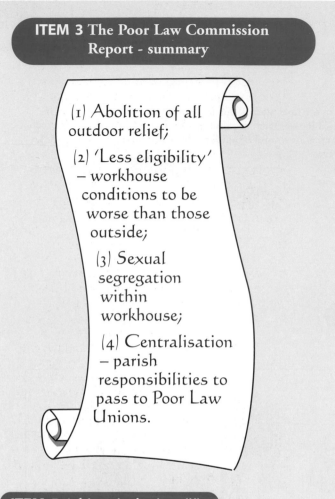

(1) Abolition of all outdoor relief;

(2) 'Less eligibility' – workhouse conditions to be worse than those outside;

(3) Sexual segregation within workhouse;

(4) Centralisation – parish responsibilities to pass to Poor Law Unions.

ITEM 4 A historian's view (i)

The Old Poor Law, with its use of outdoor relief for the underpaid, was essentially a means of tackling the problem of surplus labour in the lagging rural sector of a fast-growing but still underdeveloped economy. Given the quality of social administration at the time, it was by no means unenlightened. However, the Poor Law Commissioners of 1834 thought otherwise and deliberately sought to undermine the existing administration. What evidence they did present consisted of little more than colourful tales of inefficient administration. Even the detailed questionnaire which they circulated amongst the parishes was never analysed or summarised. No attempt was made to make a census of the poor. The 1834 Report presents a lengthy recital of ills from the mouths of squires, magistrates, overseers and clergymen, but as evidence of a social problem it has little value.

Adapted from Blaug 1963.

ITEM 5 A historian's view (ii)

Whatever the shortcomings of the report, no one can deny its great influence, since the Poor Law Amendment Act was based on it. If we are to understand the social policy in this period, we must understand the motivation and philosophy of the report itself, however misguided the report might appear to be. What the Commissioners believed may not have been true, but the resulting legislation was based on the belief that what people thought was happening was, in social policy terms, more important than what was really happening. All this is quite distinct from the question of whether the Commissioners were accurate in their assessment of the Old Poor Law. It may eventually be shown that the report was based on inaccurate data and poor evaluation, but this would not make it any less important in social policy. In other words the debate over the Poor Law Report is about whether the report is a reliable historical source on the early 19th century Poor Law. Its reputation as a description of the Old Poor Law may lose credibility, but its significance for the New Poor Law can never be diminished. The main accusation that has been made is that either the Assistant Commissioners were very selective in their coverage and fed back to London the sort of evidence they knew would be well received, or that Chadwick and Senior were highly selective in extracting material from the local reports which supported their preconceptions.

Adapted from Fraser 1973.

Questions

1. In what ways does Item 1 suggest that the operation of the Old Poor Law is to blame for unrest?
2. Explain in your own words the recommendations that are being put forward in Item 2.
3. Study Items 3-5.
   (a) How can the methodology adopted by the Commission be criticised?
   (b) What evidence is there in Items 1 and 2 to support these criticisms?
4. Study Item 5. Why does Fraser regard the Royal Commission as being so important?

3 The 1834 Poor Law Amendment Act

Key issues

1. What were the main features of the 'New' Poor Law?
2. Why was there so much opposition to the operation of the New Poor Law?
3. How far were the 'principles of 1834' actually put into effect?
4. How effectively did the New Poor Law tackle the problem of poverty in early industial Britain?

3.1 What were the main features of the 'New' Poor Law?

The proposals contained in the 1834 Report were immediately accepted by the Whig government and, with a series of political concessions such as a fudging of the recommendation for a definite banning of outdoor relief for the able-bodied within two years, provided the basis for Poor Law Amendment Act which was passed in August 1834. The combination of unintended continuities with the old system and opposition (see below) meant that in practice there was actually far less that was 'new' about the New Poor Law than Chadwick and the other architects of the 1834 had originally intended.

3.2 Opposition to the operation of the New Poor Law

The range of opposition

Opposition to the New Poor Law came from a wide range of sources and areas, for an equally wide variety of reasons and was certainly not simply limited to the potential recipients of relief amongst the most disadvantaged sections of the working class. Four broad sources of protest can be identified:

1. **Propertied Tory paternalists.** Individuals such as Richard Oastler (see Box 8.3) attacked the New Poor Law because they believed that it destroyed what they perceived as a traditional understanding and relationship between the rich and poor. The New Poor Law was a rejection of the rich's first obligation to relieve the poor - an obligation which was, in turn, a basis of social and political stability. As Oastler himself argued in 1834 'It [the 1834 Poor Law Amendment Act] lays the axe to the root of the social compact; it must break up society and make England a wilderness.'

2. **Working-class radical groups.** These saw the New Poor Law as part of a wider pattern of the

---

| BOX 8.6 | The main features of the New Poor Law |

The Poor Law Amendment Act resembled the Royal Commission's recommendations, but with some differences. The Commission favoured a complete ban on outdoor relief for the able-bodied, effective from a given date, but the Act gave the new administrative Poor Law Commission power to regulate this. The powers given to the three-man central Poor Law Commission in relation to the new local Poor Law Unions were, in accord with a continuing belief in local responsibility, far weaker than Chadwick and his associates wanted. In reality the 'New Poor Law' was an amalgam of old and new. The new Poor Law unions were federations of existing parishes and towns rather than a complete re-drawing of the administrative map of England and Wales. The parishes elected their own representatives to the union's board of guardians. More importantly, until the 1860s each parish remained responsible for the cost of caring for its own poor, even if the work was now done by union officials. This was a serious weakness. It often happened that one or two parishes within a union were especially poor, but until 1865 the other parishes in the union were not obliged to share the costs of the poorest parishes. The local magistrates lost most of their old supervisory powers, but remained members of the local board of guardians. Most of the board members were now elected by the ratepayers, voting rights being graduated by the rateable value of voters' property. In addition, an owner-occupier could vote in both capacities and therefore have 12 votes. The new central Poor Law Commission found it difficult or impossible to enforce its policies in the face of recalcitrant local boards of guardians. The Poor Law Amendment Act did not transform patterns of local influence, and the New Poor Law was effectively controlled locally by the same men who had controlled the Old Poor Law. The cost of the Poor Law continued to be met from local rates, which strengthened the position of local authorities. The central Poor Law Commission was partly an attempt to take the Poor Law out of politics. The new Commission was a kind of extra-parliamentary corporation to administer the Poor Law in England and Wales, deriving its powers entirely from the 1834 Act. Edwin Chadwick was its Secretary. In addition, a small team of Assistant Poor Law Commissioners acted as a link between the London-based Commission and the local unions.
Adapted from McCord 1991.

Whigs government's contempt for the working class, which included the 1832 Reform Bill (see Unit 5), the 1833 Factory Act and persecution of the Tolpuddle Martyrs. As the later Chartist leader, Bronterre O'Brien put it, 'The New Poor Law was passed...to place the whole of the labouring population at the utter mercy and disposal of the moneyed and property-owning classes.'

3. **JPs and overseers.** This group objected to the Act's centralising tendencies, its imposition of control by outsiders, its inherent criticism of their previous administration of the system and the obvious unsuitability of indoor relief in some areas.

4. **The working-class poor.** Some were terrified into action by rumours of the privations associated with the new 'Bastilles', as the workhouses became known. (The Bastille was an infamous 18th-century Paris prison, stormed during the French Revolution.)

The pattern of protest

The Poor Law Commissioners' attempts to apply the new system - particularly in the North and Midlands - provoked a wave of popular resentment and led to the growth of Anti-Poor Law Associations. These grew out of the Short Time Committees which had already developed in Lancashire and Yorkshire in the early 1830s to demand factory reform and were eventually to feed into the Chartist movement (see Unit 6).

The North and Midlands

Opposition to the introduction of the new system (which came into effect in 1837) in the North was particularly strong, well organised and effective because of a number of factors:

- **Previous Reform of the Poor Law.** Under pressure from urban population growth, many towns in industrial regions had already set about reforming their own Poor Law systems, with key changes including the appointment of salaried assistants to help overseers. In many areas these changes had led to a significant reduction in Poor Law expenditure and those responsible for local administration had assumed that, since the criticisms of the Old Poor Law no longer applied to them, the New Poor Law would not be introduced in their areas. Thus northern opposition came not just from potential paupers, but also from what Alfred Power (one of the first Assistant Commissioners whose job it was to manage the introduction of the system in the North) described as 'a considerable number of respectable and influential persons'. The introduction of the New Poor Law therefore stimulated a temporary and localised alliance of middle-class and working-class protest, with the participation of the former

helping to explain the well-organised character of the Anti-Poor Law Movement in the North.

- **Criticisms of inappropriateness in industrial areas.** Resentment was intensified by the 1834 Act's apparent failure to take into account the nature and causes of poverty in the new industrial areas. In these areas, patterns of employment (and hence also unemployment) were cyclical - being dependent on fluctuating patterns of trade - rather than seasonal, as tended to be the case in rural areas. It was therefore seen as both absurd and unjust to insist that there should only be punitive indoor relief for men in temporary and short-term need of relief.

- **Resentment of centralisation.** Opposition to central control was often organised or actively promoted by local JPs and manufacturers - influential individuals such as W.B. Ferrand in Bingley, John Fielden in Todmorden, and Matthew Thompson and J.G. Paley in Bradford. These individuals interpreted the New Poor Law as part of a wider Whig plot to control local affairs through creeping centralisation.

- **Bad timing.** The New Poor Law was introduced in the North between late 1836 and early 1837 - just as the trade cycle moved into a down-swing, and this intensified fears about the treatment of poor families that were already acute due to rumours from the South.

The character of protest in the North and Midlands

Opposition was characterised by a high level of organisation. A close relationship developed between the Anti-Poor Law and Factory Movements (see Part 1, above), with the former taking over the existing infrastructure of protest provided by the Short Time Committees. Thus in 1837 delegates from a number of towns in the West Riding of Yorkshire met to discuss both a Ten Hour Bill and Anti-Poor Law demonstrations. Activities were coordinated by the West Riding Anti-Poor Law Committee (chaired by William Stokes of the Ten Hour Movement) and the Lancashire Anti-Poor Law Association (chaired by P. J. Richardson, a later Chartist). By 1838 the Movement also had 38 local committees in Lancashire towns. The movement employed a variety of methods:

- **Public meetings.** These were usually chaired by local clergymen or dignitaries. Petitions were often drawn up at these meetings and presented to Parliament by radical MPs such as John Fielden and John Walter.

- **Mass meetings.** These were often called to

coincide with the arrival of commissioners to organise the implementation of the new scheme with local officials. Although these could be stormy and intimidating, such as those at Keighley, Bury and Bradford, 'on the whole the leaders of the movement preferred to maintain control over followers and direct the campaign in a peaceful direction without causing outright violence' (Stevenson 1979, pp.249-50). The largest of these meetings occurred at Hartshead Moor in Yorkshire on Whit Tuesday in 1837, when a crowd estimated at anything between 100,000 and 250,000 was addressed by a range of leading orators including Parson Bull, Richard Oastler and Joseph Rayner Stephens (who later became a Chartist).

- **A press campaign.** In most northern towns newspapers hostile to the New Poor Law such as the *Leeds Intelligencer, Bolton Chronicle, Sheffield Iris, Northern Liberator* and *Northern Star* (see also Unit 4) gave extensive coverage to Anti-Poor Law activities.
- **Local obstructionism.** In some towns local overseers simply refused to cooperate with commissioners in implementing the new system. Their obstructionism was often backed by locally orchestrated popular disturbances and, in Huddersfield in June, an attack on the workhouse itself. Action of this type led to implementation of the New Poor Law having to be deferred (see below), with the Commissioner Alfred Power observing in 1839 that 'The difficulties to be feared from almost any degree of popular excitement are not so great as those to be encountered from an adverse and factious Board of Guardians.'

These methods achieved a number of notable successes. In Huddersfield and Barnsley implementation of the Act had to be deferred until 1838, and in Rochdale until 1845. Elsewhere only administrative changes were made and new Guardians were ordered only to administer the Poor Law according to the Elizabethan Act, with no mention of less eligibility or the workhouse test. Outdoor relief therefore effectively continued in industrial districts, with an outdoor labour test officially and generally authorised in 1841.

The South
Southern opposition to the New Poor Law was more sporadic and far less organised than that in the North. This may partly be explained by two good harvests in 1835 and 1836 and a growing demand for labour in the mines and for railway construction. Also in the North the Short Time Committees provided a ready-made framework for protest which was missing in the South. Nevertheless, there were protests from a number of local clergy who organised meetings and regularly wrote to *The Times* newspaper, ratepayers in London parishes who were opposed to central interference, and individuals such as Earl Stanhope, who attempted to set up a Metropolitan Anti-Poor Law Association in 1838. There were also a range of popular disturbances in response to the Act's implementation from 1835 onwards, including the 'Bread or blood' demonstration at Ampthill, Bedfordshire, in May 1835, a week of disturbances in villages around Ipswich in Suffolk in December 1835 which required troops and police from London to be called in, and a series of disturbances in Devon and Cornwall throughout 1836 and 1837.

The extent of protest
Although protest against the New Poor Law continued throughout the 19th century, serious agitation was in fact very short-lived and by 1838 had virtually died out completely. This can be put down to a number of reasons. First, radical activity and effort became focused on the developing Chartist movement (see Unit 6). Many Poor Law agitators such as O'Connor, Stephens, Richardson, and Vincent became prominent Chartists, turning to the demand for all-embracing parliamentary reform because the Anti-Poor Law Petition was rejected in the House of Commons. Second, divisions began to appear within the movement. Popular resentment of some of the wealthy, paternalistic leaders led to the formation of splinter groups following the Chartist lead and demanding universal suffrage instead. This in turn led to the alienation of Tory leaders such as Bull and Oastler. Finally, and paradoxically, the very success of the movement in the North in resisting the full implementation of the Act undermined its *raison d'être*. In Lancashire and the West Riding of Yorkshire poor relief was administered much as before, with considerable local autonomy in practice. Ongoing motivation for a prolonged and intensive campaign was therefore lacking.

MAIN POINTS - Sections 3.1-3.2

- The 1834 Poor Law was a compromise. It fell short of a complete ban on outdoor relief, giving the Poor Law Commission powers to regulate this. However, the Commissioners had less power than was recommended by the Report. Poor Law Unions amalgamated existing parishes, but individual parishes had to fund their own poor relief.
- Boards of guardians were elected by ratepayers, whose voting rights were graded according to their property.
- The New Poor Law was criticised on four main grounds: (1) Tory paternalists believed that it destroyed a traditional understanding between the rich and poor; (2) working-class radicals saw it as an attempt to subjugate the working class; (3) JPs and

overseers objected to centralisation; (4) the poor themselves were terrified of the workhouses.
- Anti-Poor Law Associations grew out of the Short Time Committees which had already developed to demand factory reform. Protest was especially strong in the Midlands and the North. The new system was seen as particularly inappropriate in the industrial towns. There were public meetings, mass meetings, a press campaign and local attempts at obstruction. Protest in the South was less organised.
- The Anti-Poor Law movement had declined by 1838 because (1) some of its members became Chartists, (2) there were divisions in the movement, (3) the success of the movement in undermining the system in the North removed its reason for existence.

Activity 8.5 The Anti-Poor Law movement

ITEM 1 An Anti-Poor Law poster

This illustration for an 1837 Anti-Poor Law poster depicts a workhouse in which emaciated, shaven-headed inmates work at hard, repetitive tasks such as unpicking old rope and beating the fibres. Some are chained to the wall or suspended from the ceiling. Other starving labourers are turned away. The handwritten poster heading reads: 'The New Poor Law, with a description of the new workhouses. Look at the picture. See.'

ITEM 2 The principle of deterrence in action

It is not by means of labour alone that the principle [of deterring the able poor from applying to the workhouse] is applicable, nor does it imply that the food or comforts of the pauper should approach the lowest point at which existence may be maintained. Although the workhouse food be more ample in quantity and better in quality than that of which the labourer's family partakes, and the house in other respects superior to the cottage, yet the strict discipline of well-regulated workhouses, and in particular the restrictions to which the inmates are subject in respect to the use of acknowledged luxuries, such as fermented liquors and tobacco, are intolerable to the indolent and disorderly, while to the aged, the feeble and other proper objects of relief, the regularity and discipline render the workhouse a place of comparative comfort.

From the Poor Law Report, 1834.

ITEM 3 A report of an Anti-Poor Law speech

And if this damnable law, which violated all the laws of God, was continued, and all means of peaceably putting an end to it had been made in vain, then, in the words of their banner, 'for children and wife we'll war to the knife'. If the people who produce all wealth could not be allowed, according to God's word, to have the kindly fruits of the earth which they had...raised by the sweat of their brow, then war to the knife with their enemies who were the enemies of God.

From the Northern Star *(6 January 1838), reporting an attack on the Poor Law launched by Revd J.R. Stephens, a Chartist.*

ITEM 4 A historian's view

By 1839 the Anti-Poor Law campaign had begun to fall apart as working-class resentment was reduced by the continued use of outdoor relief and as rivalries between middle-class and working-class elements began to emerge. Increasingly, the more radical campaigners were attracted to the Chartist movement, whose wider political objectives included repeal of the New Poor Law as one of the results expected from the granting of universal suffrage. Indeed, one of the most prominent Chartist leaders, Feargus O'Connor, emerged out of the Anti-Poor Law agitation. His *Northern Star* newspaper campaigned against the New Poor Law, but after 1838 it increasingly gave its support to the Chartist cause. Middle-class Anti-Poor Law campaigners were increasingly alienated by the growing Chartist influence and concentrated their efforts on softening the law's operation through the local boards of guardians. Thus the Anti-Poor Law movement in the North represented a short-term alliance between the working and middle classes against what was widely seen as an unjust and intrusive measure. In a sense it was a local reaction against centralisation which cut across class lines. Eventually the differences in emphasis and ideology between Tory radicals such as Oastler and the emerging Chartist leaders ruptured this alliance. In tactics, the movement was transitional. The disturbances were only a small part of a well-organised campaign in which the threat of popular violence was far more important than its reality. The Tory radicals were using the 'language of menace' in much the same way as the parliamentary reformers in the reform crisis. Their major effort was directed towards exerting pressure through the press, pamphlets and meetings.

Adapted from Stevenson 1979.

Questions

1. What criticisms of the Poor Law are implied by Item 1?
2. How does the view of workhouses given in Item 2 differ from that of Item 1?
3. a) How far does Item 3 represent the kind of opposition encountered by the Poor Law?
   b) Referring to Items 1, 3 and 4, summarise the forms and extent of protest against the Poor Law.
4. Using Items 3, 4 and your own knowledge, explain why the Anti-Poor Law movement ended.

3.3 How far were the 'principles of 1834' actually put into effect?

As the sections above suggest, it is important to distinguish between the theory and practice of poor relief under the provisions of the 1834 Act and question exactly how far the ideas of men such as Senior and Chadwick were actually implemented. In one sense the Poor Law Amendment Act may be said to have achieved its objective as in the ten years following 1834 poor rates fell nationally between £4 million and £5 million per annum, suggesting that the new administrative structure was more cost-effective than the old and that the philosophy of deterrence did have real effect. But closer examination suggests that the practice of 1834

proved very different from the theory. Most ironically, perhaps, variation and diversity of local practice remained as much a feature of the New Poor Law as of the old 'system' which it replaced. Diversity rather than uniformity was particularly marked when it came to the abolition of outdoor relief for the able-bodied. The issue of divergence from the objectives of the reform can be explored at a number of levels and it is particularly important to adopt a longer-term perspective on the extent of change.

The continuation of outdoor relief for the able-bodied

Local resistance to centralisation in the North (see Section 3.2 above) made it practically impossible to enforce the principle of less eligibility and the workhouse test. Consequently, relief for the able-bodied continued outside the workhouse. Of the 4-5% of the population receiving poor relief in the 1850s and 1860s, more than four-fifths were relieved outside the workhouse. For one thing there was simply not enough space in workhouses to cope with the volume of unemployed labourers who applied for relief in the northern towns during trade depressions, and in such circumstances the only sensible reaction from the Commissioners was to compromise. No workhouse was built anywhere in Yorkshire during the 1840s, and a considerable measure of local discretion remained. Indeed, the inappropriateness of the New Poor Law when forced to deal with large-scale industrial unemployment was effectively recognised by the Poor Law Board itself during the so-called Lancashire 'Cotton Famine' of 1863 when the needs of factory workers were acknowledged by an order to local boards of guardians to be flexible with regard to outdoor relief for the able-bodied.

Administrative change: the Poor Law Board (1847) and the Local Government Board (1871)

Many contemporary critics of the New Poor Law blamed cruelty on an uncaring shift towards centralisation as enshrined in the 1834 Act. However, criticisms of the Poor Law Commission can in this respect be overplayed. First, the powers of the Poor Law Commissioners were in fact far more limited than opponents of the Act claimed. For example, the 'General Orders' by which the Commissioners administered the Act could be challenged in Parliament and although Poor Law guardians were elected in each union, many existing JPs became guardians by virtue of their existing authority and continued to make key day-to-day decisions on the administration of local relief. Moreover, as part of the backlash to the Andover Workhouse scandal (see below), the Poor Law Commission was actually replaced in 1847 by the Poor Law Board, with its President being a member of the government. As a result the Poor Law system came under much closer parliamentary supervision. The Poor Law Board was itself replaced in 1871 with the Local Government Board, which in 1919 became the Ministry of Health.

The growth of associated and specialist services within the Poor Law framework

Continued local variation allowed flexibility and the adaptation of the New Poor Law as demands for greater specialisation of treatment began to develop later in the century. Moreover, as the Poor Law provided one of the few ready-made administrative structures in mid-19th-century Britain, this meant

that associated general public services relating to education and health were increasingly grafted onto the framework - although each addition clearly compromised the idea of less eligibility. Specialised services developed for children as the Poor Law Inspector Dr J.P. Kay increasingly pushed for boards of guardians to provide education in their workhouses. At the same time, the appointment of Dr Edward Smith as a Medical Inspector with special responsibility for supervising the relief of the sick poor created an administrative momentum which led to the provision of a wider public service. The role 'gradually became a sort of general practitioner for the poor at large' (Fraser 1973, p.83) - a development which was also encouraged by changes in relation to the administration of the new process of vaccination. The implementation of the Vaccination Act of 1840 for the whole population became his responsibility as the Poor Law provided the only available administrative network and the Medical Officer the only available vaccinator. In this way, a general medical service was being provided under the auspices of the Poor Law for everyone. The Poor Law's further development as 'an embryo state medical authority' (Fraser 1973, p.87) was largely a result of the Metropolitan Poor Act of 1841. This provided for the establishment of separate asylums for the sick, infirm, insane poor in London and the setting up of dispensaries to administer outdoor medical relief.

3.4 How effectively did the New Poor Law tackle poverty?

Criticisms of the New Poor Law

It can be strongly argued that the New Poor Law was seriously flawed and, being formulated on an oversimplified and outmoded view of poverty, therefore also ineffective in dealing with the problems of a developing industrial society. The Report of the Royal Commission on which the 1834 Act was based failed to draw any distinction between the old problems of rural poverty (caused by underemployment) and the new and often temporary problems of urban poverty resulting from involuntary cyclical unemployment. The deterrent workhouse test and less eligibility were therefore inappropriate instruments of 'social control' in a society where poverty was not the result of an individual weakness of character, but rather the fluctuations of the trade cycle. Cruelty may therefore be said to have resulted from this mistaken assumption about the changing causes and nature of poverty in such a society. Less eligibility was extremely difficult to apply and as a result led to the psychological cruelty associated with life in a 'total institution'. In order to deter the able-bodied poor from applying for relief, the conditions in the workhouse would be worse than the worst conditions endured outside the workhouse by those in employment. However, given the already dreadful living conditions in the towns, it was impossible for worse conditions to be created whilst still meeting the paupers' basic survival needs. In practice, less eligibility therefore had to be achieved, not through cutting food, but rather by a series of psychological devices designed to degrade and stigmatise the individual. For example, workhouse inmates were forced to wear prison-style uniforms, families were divided, and silence was enforced at meal times.

Deliberate cruelty

However, the issue of deliberate physical cruelty is slightly different, and must be qualified. Many contemporary claims of inhumanity focused on a number of high-profile workhouse scandals, which were seen as symptomatic of an insensitive and centralised administration. But whilst there were a number of workhouse scandals, the most infamous of which was in 1845 at Andover, where starving

paupers were discovered to be eating marrow from the bones supplied to the workhouse for crushing, these were usually the responsibility of sadistic individual workhouse masters, rather than part of central policy directives. Cruelty of the Andover type was therefore the exception rather than the rule. If a longer-term perspective is taken, it is also possible to see how the continuance of local diversity (see above) in practice took the edge off the reformers' original intentions.

Contradictory aims

Above all the New Poor Law was perhaps most fatally flawed by the fact that it attempted to combine the contradictory aims of deterrent and relief within the same system. As the historian Fraser puts it:

'The Poor Law was saddled with the paradoxical aim of alienating its clientele and the stigma of pauperism induced a reluctance to seek official relief which became firmly rooted in popular culture.' (Fraser 1973)

MAIN POINTS - Sections 3.3-3.4

- In one sense the Poor Law Amendment Act achieved its objective as in 1834-44 poor rates fell nationally between £4 million and £5 million per annum.
- Much diversity of application of the Poor Law remained, especially in terms of outdoor relief.
- There was considerable continuity between the old and new systems. The Poor Law Commission was replaced in 1847 by the Poor Law Board, which eventually led to the Ministry of Health in 1919.
- General public services relating to education and health were increasingly grafted onto the framework of the Poor Law. Dr Edward Smith was appointed Medical Inspector with special responsibility for supervising relief of the sick poor.
- The 1841 Metropolitan Poor Act established asylums for the sick, infirm and insane poor in London and

dispensaries to administer outdoor medical relief.
- Arguably, the 1834 Act failed to distinguish between rural underemployment and urban cyclical unemployment, and wrongly blamed poverty on the individual. It also tried to combine relief and deterrence within the same system.
- Workhouses often degraded and deprived inmates in their efforts to apply the 'less eligibility' principle, which demanded that conditions be worse in the workhouse than for the poorest labourer outside.
- Some historians argue that the system paid too much attention to the able-bodied poor, as opposed to those pauperised by ill health, old age or being orphaned, although these accounted for the largest proportion of those on relief.

Activity 8.6 The effectiveness of the New Poor Law

ITEM 1 A historian's view (i)

The report of the Royal Commission on the Poor Laws, and the resulting Act, were flawed in ways which severely limited their usefulness in dealing with poverty, or even with pauperism (the condition of those incapable of earning a living), in the second half of the 19th century. First, the Royal Commission had concentrated too much of its attention on the problem of the able-bodied unemployed, particularly in rural areas, fearing that they were being demoralised by grants of outdoor relief. It paid too little attention to the problem of those who were pauperised because of physical or mental ill health, old age or being orphaned, although these accounted for by far the largest proportion of those on relief. The important and complex problem of settlement received inadequate treatment in the Report and was only modified in a few minor details by the Act, and the vital question of rating and the finance of poor relief was dealt with in a similar fashion. These were questions, which were to be a problem for poor law administrators and social reformers for the next 100 years. Second, the reformers focused their attention upon rural poverty, and produced the administrative framework to deal with it. Yet the problem of the future was to be the far more difficult one of urban industrial poverty. The Poor Law thus was increasingly ignored as a vehicle for social reform.

Adapted from Rose 1972.

ITEM 2 A historian's view (ii)

Once established, the basic philosophy of the poor relief system formulated in the 1830s and 1840s persisted almost until the end of the 19th century. From an early stage, the poor were encouraged to regard pauperism as a terrible disgrace, and only those who could manage in no other way resorted to Poor Law assistance. So while the 1834 Act may have fostered self-dependence – it boosted membership of self-help 'friendly' societies, for example – it failed to recognise the genuine needs of the poor.

Adapted from Horn 1980.

ITEM 3 A historian's view (ii)

The doctrine of discipline and restraint was more important than that of material 'less eligibility'. The most inventive state would have found it hard to create institutions in which conditions were worse than those of Dorset labourers, framework-knitters and nailers. Systematic starvation was replaced by psychological deterrence. One Assistant Commissioner said: 'Our intention is to make the workhouses as like prisons as possible.' Another aimed to establish 'a discipline so severe and repulsive as to make them a terror to the poor and prevent them from entering.'

Adapted from E.P. Thompson 1980.

ITEM 4 An Anti-Poor Law poster

This detail from an 1837 Anti-Poor Law poster shows able-bodied claimants being turned away.

Questions

1. Using Items 1-3, explain in your own words what the main faults of the New Poor Law were.
2. From Items 1-4 and your own knowledge, how effective was the New Poor Law in dealing with poverty
   (a) from the point of view of the authorities, and
   (b) from that of the poor?
3. Item 4 shows claimants being refused relief in the workhouse.
   (a) In what ways did the fate of such claimants vary from one locality to another?
   (b) Account for the local inconsistencies in the application of the Act.

4 Public health

Key issues

1. What was the impact of industrialisation on public health?

2. What were the main obstacles to progress on the public health issue?

3. What were the main pressures for reform?

4.1 The impact of industrialisation on public health

The rapid process of urbanisation which accompanied industrial development intensified the environmental and public health problems of the early 19th century. The process of urban growth that had begun in the 18th century accelerated in the first half of the 19th. The population in urban areas grew much faster than that of Britain as a whole, increasing by an average of 27% every decade between 1801 and 1851. The process reached its peak between 1841 and 1851, and was accentuated further by Irish immigration. Towns with populations over 2,500 absorbed 67% of the total increase of England's population between 1801 and 1841. The historian Herman Finer has described the acute overcrowding which resulted from this interplay of social and economic factors as 'congregation' (Finer 1950) - a concept which lies at the heart of the public health issue.

The increasing pace of urbanisation created a series of issues which together posed the public health problem. Such was the growth of the urban population that proper amenities like drainage, sanitation and water supply were not developed, and housing accommodation was 'jerry-built'. Diseases were rife and death rates alarmingly high. Public health was a multi-dimensional issue.

Housing
The standard of housing in the towns was extremely poor. Builders were unscrupulous and set out to capitalise on the unprecedented conditions by making huge profits. As housing was in such great demand, small areas of land were given over to high-density houses, which were built as quickly as possible. As the historian Fraser explains:

'Such rapid growth posed enormous housing problems for urban communities, which first filled unused spaces such as cellars and attics and then embarked on providing private-enterprise cheap housing for the new industrial workers. In the absence of personal transport, houses and factories had to be in close proximity, and so began that process of residential zoning which characterised industrial cities, with workers living in the smoke and middle classes beyond it. The style of housing varied: sometimes the terraces of small cottages, which had been a feature of industrial villages; sometimes the classic creation of the Industrial Revolution, the back-to-backs which dominated northern cities such as Leeds; sometimes the enclosed courtyard which was typical of Birmingham; and sometimes the great tenements which housed Glasgow's teeming population.' (Fraser 1973, p.51)

The absence of local government and the provision of amenities
Despite general issues regarding lack of light and poor ventilation, the physical construction of working-class housing was less of a problem than the lack of amenities and services - drainage, sewerage and water supply. The problem was exacerbated by the fact that the growth of towns had not been accompanied by a simultaneous and planned growth of local government, and there was certainly no equivalent of modern local authorities. Existing urban government did not possess the administrative machinery necessary to exercise effective control over building and town planning, or for disposing of sewage and piping purified water. Some older towns did have corporations, but these were often self-electing and corrupt oligarchies which did not have to account for the way they spent the rates. Most significantly, newer cities, without corporations, were still governed under the parochial arrangements that pre-dated industrial development. Though the 1835 Municipal Corporations Act did bring a greater degree of both uniformity and middle-class control, its immediate impact on the urban public health problem was minimal. The key issues related to the impact of sanitation, street pollution, water supply and the regulation of burials and graveyards on the spread of disease and life expectancy.

Sanitation and street pollution
Most towns had totally inadequate systems of drainage and sewage disposal. Where sewers did exist, they were built of porous brick and were consequently incapable of dealing with the large volume of effluent. The water closets of the wealthy were generally not connected by pipe to the sewer and the waste was instead fed into the nearest river or ditch; the outside privies shared by most working people usually drained into a cesspit or an open ditch. In addition, slaughterhouses filled the open sewers with offal and blood, whilst the factories pumped in waste products. Chadwick, in his 1842

Report (see Section 4.3), stated that of 687 streets inspected in Manchester, 248 were unpaved, 112 were ill ventilated, and 252 had such health risks as stagnant pools or heaps of rubbish.

Water supply

Fresh running water in the towns was at a premium - only available to the wealthier classes. Most urban workers obtained their water from standpipes in the streets or wells. Private joint stock companies, who competed fiercely with each other, supplied the water. Hence the taps were only turned on for a limited period during the day, and families would have to 'recycle' their water. London's water came from the Thames, which is also where the city's sewage was deposited.

Burials and graveyards

As towns expanded, churchyards and burial grounds simply could not cope with the dead. The thousands who died during the cholera epidemics accentuated the problem. Not surprisingly, susceptibility to disease was increased by a combination of poor diet and environmental conditions. Diphtheria and scarlet fever struck young people in the cities, and typhus claimed about 4,000 victims a year. Dysentery, typhoid and smallpox, whooping-cough and measles were also a threat. There were four major outbreaks of typhoid from 1830 to 1836. It was Asiatic cholera, however, which caused the greatest fear. Appearing first in India in 1818, the disease gradually spread north-westwards through Europe, reaching Britain in October 1831. It spread rapidly and by the summer of 1832 had killed 52,000 people. Further cholera epidemics struck Britain in 1848-49 (70,000 deaths), 1853-54 (30,000 deaths) and 1866 (18,000). Moreover, medical understanding of the causes of disease was very limited, being based on Miasma theories (see below). In 1842, Chadwick's *Report on the Sanitary Condition of the Labouring Population of Great Britain* (see Section 4.3 below and Activity 8.8) demonstrated that city-dwellers had a much lower life expectancy than those living in rural areas. Furthermore, social class was suggested as a factor determining how long a person would live. Chadwick also highlighted a high rate of infant mortality in the cities: 'It is an appalling fact that of all who are born of the labouring classes in Manchester, more than 57% die before they attain five years of age.'

4.2 The main obstacles to progress on the public health issue

There are four overlapping factors which help to explain why progress on public health issues was so slow and urban conditions were not significantly improved until after 1850 - technical, financial, ideological and political.

Technical problems

Technical problems were in fact of two types: those relating to medical understanding of the spread of disease and those concerned with the development of the civil engineering skills and technology necessary to effect change.

Lack of medical knowledge

Much emphasis is usually placed on misdirected miasma theories as a delaying factor. Chadwick and most doctors believed that refuse and decomposing matter resulted in the air becoming contaminated by a poisonous gas or 'miasma', and that this transmitted disease. As Chadwick put it, 'all smell is disease'. Consequently, no one as yet understood the bacteriological cause of disease, and particularly the importance of water-borne bacteria. However, it is possible to argue that limited medical knowledge was not a crucial delaying factor since the right action could be taken for the wrong medical reasons. It was not strictly necessary for people to know how cesspools and soil heaps caused disease, providing they were identified as causes and removed.

Civil engineering

Arguably, civil engineering problems were a much more significant technical obstacle than the lack of medical knowledge, particularly in relation to the interlinked questions of plentiful supplies of water and water-driven sewage. New sciences such as civil engineering were in their infancy, and new techniques had to be invented before they could be tried and tested. Chadwick himself recommended the arterial system, which was an integrated scheme for water supply and the removal of filth: sewage should be flushed away in narrow earthenware pipes to be used as agricultural manure on farmers' fields. However, projects such as that suggested by Chadwick posed the greatest civil engineering challenges of the age, and could not be implemented immediately.

Financial and ideological factors

Because of the unprecedented dimensions of the public health problem, the financial cost of resolving it was certain to prove a major obstacle. Local resources for social improvements were scarce, and both self-interest and contemporary ideology meant that, except during epidemics, pressure for improvement was very limited. Apart from the issue of overall cost, the financing of improvements illustrates a series of debilitating paradoxes: wealthy local property owners, having paid for their own private water supply and sanitary needs, were reluctant to pay again - via increased rates - for those of the labouring classes. If the localities were either unable or unwilling to finance public health reforms, the only alternative could be central government. However, this presupposed national taxation and, in any case, any increase in the power of central government was generally interpreted as an attack upon individual liberty and private property rights (see below). The financial question therefore raised a series of related, and central, ideological questions about the importance of individualism and laissez-faire thinking (see Activity 8.7, Item 4).

The early Victorian approach to the issue of change was fundamentally negative. In the age of laissez-faire, central government did not attempt to set the pace but rather to provide the powers which others might, if they wished, use. This point is best illustrated by the 1848 Public Health Act (see Box 8.10), which was a permissive rather than an obligatory Act: except where the death rate was higher than 23 per 1,000 the Act merely empowered but did not compel local health boards to pursue public health reforms. Most importantly, as long as decision makers placed individual property rights above almost anything else, then it was impossible to overcome the forces of inertia. For example, building regulations enforcing sewerage involved infringements of individual liberty which many contemporaries regarded as unacceptable on ideological grounds. As the historian Fraser puts it:

'Individual liberty was reinforced by self-interest, for those who were loudest in the defence of property rights were often the owners of the property which needed sanitary improvement. Deference to an individualist ideology was therefore sometimes a rationalisation of economic self-interest and an excuse for inaction.' (Fraser 1973, p.62)

Political factors
Ideological debates about acceptable levels of local environmental control were very closely linked to political issues. Political obstacles to greater public health progress were of essentially two types. First, there were local political squabbles over who should exercise power within the local community, arising in turn from vested administrative and commercial interests in the maintenance of the status quo. This was essentially an administrative or structural problem. Second, there was a much broader debate about centralisation and the legitimate extent of state intervention.

Local political rivalries
In terms of the structure of local politics, this obstacle was at one level a product of administrative inefficiency and the inadequacies of local government control. In the absence of a proper

administrative organisation to take overall control of the functions which, today, would be exercised by one local authority, such public health provision as had been secured between 1700 and 1830 had been the work of bodies formed for specific local purposes and deriving their power from Local Improvement Acts.

Such an Act allowed for the establishment of Improvement Commissions which initiated the lighting, paving and cleansing of streets. These were run by groups of men - Improvement Commissioners - appointed for life, with specific functions. They could either hire labour or contract the work out and could levy a local rate to meet the expense. However, an inherent weakness of this 'system' was the way in which people living in those areas which could afford to pay the highest rates received the greatest attention whilst the poorer and generally most needy districts remained virtually untouched.

Furthermore, the commissions often competed with each other and indulged in nuisance tactics in order to prevent a rival body from gaining an advantage. For example, the two drainage commissions in Lancaster refused to integrate the drainage system for the town as a whole. London typified the confusion. By 1830 there were nearly

| BOX 8.7 | The role of Improvement Commissions - a historian's view |

Such limited services as did exist in the form of private joint-stock waterworks companies could not hope to meet the needs of the expanding cities. Modern society tackles these problems by environmental control and the provision of public services, but there were no administrative organisations to take over these functions effectively, to regulate building, to provide sewers, to pipe water to homes. Some of the older towns had corporations, but these were self-elected, often corrupt, and lacked powers to exercise real local control. Many of the newer cities, such as Manchester and Birmingham, had no corporation at all, still being governed under parochial arrangements dating from their village days. In any case, in both sorts of towns what public health provisions existed usually stemmed from bodies deriving their powers from Local Improvement Acts. These were called Improvement Commissioners and it was they rather than other local government bodies which organised the lighting, watching and cleaning of streets. Since those who paid the most improvement rates expected the best service, it was the better-class streets and thoroughfares which were paved, lit, drained and scavenged at public expense rather than the unsanitary areas with the greater needs.
Adapted from Fraser 1973.

300 different improvement commissions operating under 250 local Acts. Such chaos obviously militated against reform: the whole system needed rationalising, but vested interests were so strongly entrenched that change was difficult to achieve.

Local politics revolves around the pursuit and exercise of parochial power. Water Commissioners, Commissioners for Sewers, Highway Surveyors, Poor Law Guardians, Street Commissioners and so on, all had vested political (as well as administrative and commercial) interests in resisting change. Any enlargement of the administrative functions of local government to deal with public health problems inevitably meant a diminution of the influence of such private bodies, and was therefore resisted. The situation in Birmingham clearly illustrates the inertia caused by such local private battles, where it took 14 years to amalgamate the various commissioners into the council.

From a related point of view, the extension of municipal power was also sometimes resisted because of fears about a changing balance of local political power. For example, in Leeds in the 1830s many Tories who had previously favoured a public scheme for water supply reverted back to the advocacy of private provision by a joint-stock company when they realised that a public scheme might increase the power of their Whig opponents to control local affairs. In this way the local political situation could hinder or prevent improvement.

The broader ideological debate

The rivalries over who should exercise power within the local community were, however, subsumed in the broader debate over fears about the extent and desirability of centralisation - and in particular the proposal to remove local control completely and establish a central administrative organisation, as advocated by the most influential reformer of the period, Edwin Chadwick (see Box 8.9). Chadwick was basically suggesting the same approach to public health reform as he had already established for the Poor Law. He believed that the environmental controls necessary to prevent disease would require much more than the remodelling of existing corporations and thus necessitated a centralised and uniform administrative structure along the lines of the Poor Law Commission (see Section 2.4, and Activity 8.4, above). However, public health reform differed in one important respect from that of the Poor Law. In the latter case, the Parish provided a ready-made local administrative unit capable of reorganisation. However, as has been suggested, public health provision was a jungle of vested private and public interests. Many local communities therefore feared a scenario in which impersonal bureaucrats could enforce changes from London and incur expenditure over which there would be no local control. In this respect, the spate of local Acts in the 1840s obtained by cities such as Leeds (1842), Manchester (1844) and Liverpool (1846) to deal with their own circumstances is in fact best seen as a reaction against growing pressure for national action on public health issues.

Paradoxically, the Liverpool Sanitary Act of 1846 can be regarded as the first comprehensive health legislation passed in England. The Act effectively made the corporation a health authority and empowered it to appoint an engineer, and Inspector of Nuisances and, most importantly, a Medical Officer of Health. W.H. Duncan was the country's first permanently appointed Medical Officer and worked to tackle the problems of what was seen by contemporaries as 'the unhealthiest town in England'. A further Act of 1847 then enabled the city to purchase the two private water companies trading in Liverpool.

MAIN POINTS - Sections 4.1-4.2

- Industrialisation and rapid urban growth, accentuated by Irish immigration, created new environmental and public health problems. Cramped conditions and a lack of sanitary amenities encouraged the spread of disease.
- New urban housing tended to be low-standard and high-density.
- Local government was not equipped to provide amenities. Town corporations were often corrupt and self-serving.
- Effluent mostly drained into cesspits, ditches or rivers – which in some cases supplied drinking water for the poor. Only the wealthy could afford fresh running water.
- The mortality rate was high, especially in cities. Graveyards could not cope with the dead. Diphtheria, scarlet fever and typhus were common.

- Dysentery, typhoid, smallpox, whooping-cough and measles were also a threat, though Asiatic cholera caused the greatest fear.
- Obstacles to public health reform fell into four categories: (1) technical - lack of medical knowledge and engineering expertise; (2) financial - the wealthy were reluctant to pay for public facilities, and Improvement Commissions focused on the wealthier districts; (3) ideological - politicians believing in laissez-faire were reluctant to make health provision compulsory; and (4) political - provision of amenities was marred by the rivalry of different bodies.
- Chadwick proposed centralising the provision of amenities to make it more efficient.
- The Liverpool Sanitary Act of 1846 was the first comprehensive health legislation passed in England.

Activity 8.7 The nature and causes of public health problems

ITEM 1 Industrialisation, urbanisation and public health - a historian's view

In many ways, despite occasional epidemics of bubonic plague, there was no real public health problem in pre-industrial England. London and the centres of some of the provincial market or cathedral towns contained cramped houses, but the bulk of the population was spread thinly over the rural areas. It was the Industrial Revolution, accompanied by a huge shift in population from rural to urban areas, which created a public health problem. As with so many other social problems, it was the very concentration of people which caused the difficulty. It was only urbanisation that necessitated that essential combination of preventive medicine, civil engineering and community administrative and legal resources known collectively as 'public health'.

Adapted from Fraser 1973.

ITEM 2 The causes of disease (i)

FATHER THAMES INTRODUCING HIS OFFSPRING TO THE FAIR CITY OF LONDON
(A Design for a Fresco in the New Houses of Parliament.)

An 1858 cartoon links polluted water and disease: Father Thames introduces his children - diphtheria, scrofula and cholera.

ITEM 3 The causes of disease (ii)

Filthiness, foul smells, and all lodgements of nastiness in Houses, Courts, Alleys, and especially in confined situations, tend to produce Disease. If you wish to preserve your own health, or the healthiness of your city, be cleanly in your persons and premises. Do not let any sort of filth gather in drains and gutters, especially when they run through narrow courts, and in the midst of a thickly peopled neighbourhood. If the pump be handy, clean out your gutters, morning and evening, by pumping; if the pump be not handy, throw down buckets of water. Nothing is more likely to spread Disease than the foul smells coming from stagnation of filth.

Advice from Revd Vaughan Thomas, 1835.

ITEM 4 Laissez-faire - a historian's definition

The French origins of the term *laissez-faire* lie deep in the 18th century and it was mentioned by Lord Liverpool in the House of Commons as early as 1812. However, like many terms familiar to historians, it was used more by later generations than in the period to which it most closely refers. There are some who would appear to equate it with anarchy. Others, notably Carlyle and Spencer, have identified it with 'anarchy and the constable' or the 'negatively regulatory' state. At the other extreme are those who use it to mean no more than a preference for private rather than public enterprise. More frequently, laissez-faire has been used as a convenient shorthand for the general prescriptions of the Classical Economists and in particular for the efficacy of a free-market economy. While some restrict its use to economic questions, others place equal emphasis on social policy or extend their use of the term to embrace the entire field of governmental action.

Adapted from Taylor 1972.

Questions

1. Using Items 1-2 and your own knowledge, summarise the main causes of growing public health problems in the first half of 19th-century Britain.
2. Using Items 3-4 and your own knowledge, explain the main obstacles to progress in public health.
3. Using Item 4 and your own knowledge, explain how the ideological debate influenced developments in public health. (See also Box 8.5 regarding Benthamism.)

4.3 What were the main pressures for reform?

It is possible to identify a series of levers for change, operating from the mid-1830s onwards. The major pressures came from the impact of epidemic diseases, and in particular cholera, more focused medical opinion, the commitment of individual reformers, most notably Edwin Chadwick, and the effects of resultant legislation, although the potential of the 1848 Act to effect substantial change has been seriously questioned.

Disease
Paradoxically, epidemic diseases such as cholera were one of the major catalysts of reform - although it is worth emphasising that the impetus dissipated once the immediate danger receded. Significantly, however, political opposition to the 1848 Public Health Act (see below) was temporarily muted by the cholera epidemic of 1848-49 (see Box 8.8). In this respect, it may be better to argue that rather than a factor working positively for change, the impact of epidemic diseases such as cholera operated as a means of breaking down some of the opposition against change.

Medical opinion
During the late 18th and early 19th centuries, individual surveys by doctors were building up evidence about the connection between environmental conditions, disease and life expectancy. The most important of these was James

Kay's survey of Manchester in 1832 - *The Moral and Physical Condition of the Working Class.* However, the efforts of a collection of individual doctors working largely independently on their own local problems was not sufficient to focus popular attention on the public health issue, and it really needed a national figure to provide such a focus for the hitherto diffuse pressures for change. This was to be the role fulfilled by Edwin Chadwick.

The role of the individual: Edwin Chadwick
Chadwick's involvement in the public health issue developed out of his utilitarian background (see Box 8.5) and role in the reform of the Poor Law. In the Report of the Poor Law Commission, Chadwick had assumed that the main problem was the able-bodied poor, and that the deterrent principle of less eligibility (see p.230) would facilitate reductions in poor relief expenditure. However, Chadwick's first years as Secretary to the Poor Law Commission revealed to him that a large proportion of expenditure was in fact taken up with widows and orphans of those killed by disease. Chadwick therefore came to realise that disease and poverty were closely linked. As Chadwick himself put it in 1838:

'In general all epidemics and all infectious diseases are attended with charges, immediate and ultimate, on the Poor Rates. Labourers are suddenly thrown by infectious disease into a state of destitution, for which immediate relief must be given. In the case of death the widow and the children are thrown as paupers on the parish. The

BOX 8.8 | The impact of cholera - a historian's view

As far as the government was concerned, only a major epidemic could mobilise state action. A short-lived Board of Health had been established under the privy Council in 1805-6 under the threat of yellow fever ('Gibraltar sickness'). Far more serious was the cholera epidemic of 1831-32, repeated in 1848-49, 1854 and 1866-67. Being a water-borne disease, cholera attacked all, notably the middle classes with their better water supplies, and terrified governors, both local and national. This galvanised the state into forming a Central Board of Health in June 1831, and eventually 1,200 local boards created by Orders in Council. In addition, the so-called Cholera Act of 1832 empowered local boards to finance anti-cholera provisions out of poor rates. However, since doctors disagreed on the causes of cholera or on the best treatment to be used, preventive measures such as lime-washing achieved very little. Since the first epidemic

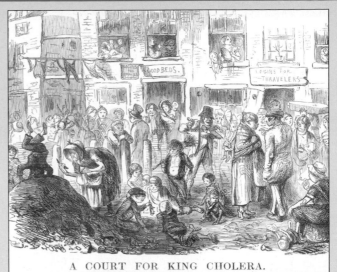

A COURT FOR KING CHOLERA.

This cartoon 'The Court of King Cholera' shows the kind of unsanitary conditions that Chadwick identified as spreading disease.

coincided with the Reform Bill crisis, it added to the tension of those years and there were many anti-medical riots, as people became anxious about the dissection of infected corpses. It is sometimes assumed that public health provision was simply a response to cholera epidemics. In reality, many doctors working on 'fevers' in the public health field found cholera a distraction as much as a catalyst. Cholera was an epidemic rather than an endemic disease (appearing in sudden waves and then dying down). Thus it was dramatically newsworthy but not, overall, a great contributor to death rates. Hence while the first cholera epidemic killed 22,000 people, domestic fevers were killing over 50,000 annually in England and Wales. Cholera, by virtue of its novelty and middle-class impact, created far more of a stir than the much more deadly and common diseases which were the bane of the poor. Accepted by virtue of their familiarity, these diseases swelled the death rate in early 19th-century cities. Typhus fever was both widely endemic and more frequently epidemic in the 19th century. It was closely associated with cramped unsanitary housing conditions and was a classic environmentally caused disease. Hence it was almost exclusively a poor man's disease. Hence, too, though doctors became increasingly aware of its nature, little was done to control it. This was even truer of tuberculosis or pulmonary consumption, which was so common as to be deemed a natural hazard about which nothing could be done. This disease caused more deaths (perhaps one-third of all deaths) than any other in the first half of the 19th century. It thrived on a favourable environment: a smoky atmosphere, squalid houses and bodies weakened by malnutrition.

Adapted from Fraser 1973.

amount of burthens [burdens] thus produced is frequently so great as to render it good economy on the part of the administrators of the Poor Laws to incur the charges for preventing the evils where, they are ascribable.'

Basically, Chadwick was arguing that taking preventive action with regard to the environmental conditions of the cities could, in the long-term, reduce expenditure on poor relief. It was as a result of this growing awareness of the economic cost of disease that his sanitary report of 1842 developed. Chadwick's concern with public health must therefore be seen in terms of two related aims: (1) to cut the costs of poor relief, and (2) to create a tutelary state - one whose administrative agencies attempt to remove any obstacle which might stand in the way of the individual's self-help and self-improvement.

Chadwick's approach to the problems of poverty and public health was therefore very similar. In Chadwick's mind, all social evils impeded the individual's contribution to the greatest happiness (which he regarded as synonymous with the gross national product) and consequently undermined liberty. In the case of public health, preventable deaths and unnecessary illness reduced economic efficiency, and meant that poor rates were being used to provide medical care for paupers. The solution to these problems in the form of preventive administrative agencies was therefore also similar. There were three basic administrative suggestions:

1. Traditional institutions should be challenged and, where necessary, abolished and replaced by locally elected committees with knowledge and understanding of the issues under their control. Hence the advocacy of the

BOX 8.9 | Edwin Chadwick - a historian's view

Edwin Chadwick was a civil servant, not an MP, but he may have had more influence on people's lives for good or ill than all the Victorian parliamentarians put together. His friend J.S. Mill called him 'one of the organising and contriving minds of the age', and he had a hand in many of the major Victorian social and administrative reforms. He was the principal author of the 1842 report on *The Sanitary Condition of the Labouring Population* that spurred on improvements in sanitation, drainage, water supply and refuse disposal in towns and cities. He took a leading part in this initiative as one of the four Board of Health commissioners appointed in 1848. Chadwick was not an easy man to work with. Impatient if crossed, he had a driving energy, a coldly logical intellect and an inability to suffer fools gladly. Dogmatic and convinced of his own wisdom, he was a workaholic and his enthusiasm for improving public health and administration seems to have been inspired by an intolerance of inefficiency rather than by any humanitarian impulse. A prime mover in putting Benthamite ideas into practice, he played a heroic role in making British towns safer places to live.

Chadwick was born in Lancashire in 1800, the son of a radical journalist who had him educated at home. He started his career as a lawyer, but soon attracted the attention of Bentham and became his secretary. In 1832 he was employed by the Royal Commission on the Poor Laws and he and Nassau Senior, a leading economist, wrote the Commission's report, which led to the Act of Parliament of 1834, though Chadwick was dissatisfied because he wanted a system operated by officials responsible to a central authority instead of local boards of guardians. Chadwick was a lifelong advocate of centralisation and the employment of trained expert officials. 'Sir,' he once magisterially observed, 'the Devil was expelled from heaven because he objected to centralisation and all those who object to centralisation oppose it on devilish grounds.' He had no confidence in local self-government and was contemptuous of democracy and public opinion. At the Board of Health he was attacked as 'the autocrat, pope, grand lama of sanitary reform'. He made so many enemies that Lord Palmerston pensioned him off in 1854.

Adapted from Cavendish 2000.

establishment of the Boards of Health and Poor Law unions (see Section 2.4 above).

2. That professional, salaried administrators should replace unpaid amateurs such as the Inspector of Nuisances or Poor Law Relieving Officer.
3. A central body should be created, with well-developed advisory and financial powers, to control each service and subject it to inspection and, hence, accountability. In the case of public health this meant the Central Board of Health, and, in relation to poverty, the Poor Law Commission (see Section 2.4 and Activity 8.4).

Chadwick's 1842 Report

The opportunity for Chadwick to undertake a wide-ranging sanitary inquiry was created by developments in 1838 when, following official questioning of Poor Law expenditure in the East End of London, the Poor Law Commission inaugurated a 'pilot study' on the connection between environmental factors and disease in the worst areas of the capital. Three doctors - James Kay, Neil Arnott and Southwood Smith - conducted the survey, and their reports were the first to receive any form of official sanction by being included as appendices in the Poor Law Commission's annual report. As a follow-up to it the House of Lords ordered in 1839 that a nationwide inquiry into the sanitary condition of the labouring class was now needed and Chadwick was appointed to undertake the survey.

The inquiry was nominally under the auspices of the Poor Law Commission and Chadwick made use of a wide range of evidence, including questionnaires and interviews with Poor Law Assistant Commissioners, Boards of Guardians, Relieving Officers, Poor Law Medical Officers, prison officers, employers and doctors, together with his own personal visits to major towns. The resulting 1842 *Report on the Sanitary Condition of the Labouring Population of Great Britain* had three main themes:

1. A detailed statistical analysis designed to prove beyond doubt the link between environmental conditions and disease.
2. Preventive and technical recommendations with regard to the civil engineering problem of sewage disposal - in particular an advocacy of the arterial system of water-borne sewage disposal via narrow glazed pipes.
3. Recommendations for a centralised and uniform administrative structure that would replace the numerous bodies and assume overall responsibility for drainage, paving, water supply and street-cleansing. (These recommendations were, for Chadwick, uncharacteristically vague.)

Perhaps the most significant impact of the report was the way in which, by extension, it challenged contemporary social theory: by emphasising the social evils caused by unsanitary living conditions, and identifying sociological and geographical variation in life expectancy, Chadwick's report clearly suggested that low moral standards were the result of domestic physical environment, and not, as previously held, vice versa (Activity 8.4, Item 2).

Chadwick's Report on Intra-Mural Internments, 1843

As a follow-up to the 1842 Report Chadwick went on to recommend the opening of public cemeteries on the outskirts of towns in a subsequent 1843 report and in 1844-45 unofficially directed the work of the Health of Towns Commission - a body set up by Peel's government to monitor the findings of the 1842 Report itself.

The Health of Towns Association

Chadwick's Report had unprecedented sales for an official publication - possibly approaching 100,000 copies. The momentum created for subsequent legislative action was sustained after 1844 not only by Chadwick but also the Health of Towns Association. This was a pressure group organised by Southwood Smith and grew rapidly, establishing branches throughout Britain. Each disseminated information about the urgent need for legislation and campaigned for such reform.

Legislation - the 1848 Public Health Act

It is also interesting and instructive to compare and contrast Chadwick's impact on Poor Law and public health reform. Within months of the heavily Chadwick-influenced 1834 Report the Poor Law Amendment Act was passed largely in its direct image; it took six years for any public health legislation to be passed following Chadwick's 1842 Report, and this was only a very partial reflection of the sort of reform he advocated. Historians have advanced two principal explanations for this contrast. First, that in 1834 he was essentially preaching to the converted: his recommendations chimed with assumptions of the ruling elite in relation to the causes and preferred treatment of poverty, whereas in 1842 Chadwick was radical and original in his approach - as suggested above. Second, the sheer complexities of issues raised by public health reform (see Section 4.2) delayed an effectively coordinated response.

The obstacles to public health reform also help to explain the partial nature of the one piece of major improving legislation passed in this period - the 1848 Public Health Act. The centralisation debate reached a peak in 1847-48 when Lord Morpeth, a minister in Russell's Whig government, introduced a Public Health Bill. Although defeated in 1847, the return of cholera in the following year allowed it to be passed as the 1848 Public Health Act. Although often regarded as a watershed in social reform, its permissive character largely undermined its effectiveness.

The slow progress of sanitary reform before 1850 can be explained by a combination of the sheer size of the problem, the extent of opposition, the complexity of the issues and the power and extent of

BOX 8.10 The 1848 Public Health Act - a summary

- The Central Board of Health set up in London was essentially a coordinating and advisory body - not an executive policy-maker.
- The Central Board's life was limited to five years - effectively a probationary period. Enthusiasm for it soon evaporated and although granted a year's extension because of the third cholera epidemic (1853-54), the Central Board was abolished in August 1854.
- Chadwick himself had perhaps hastened the Board's demise through his dogmatic and abrasive approach. Opponents of centralisation were able to personalise the issue, caricaturing Chadwick as someone who wished to 'bully' the country into cleanliness. The Act was therefore presented as an attack on personal liberties and the principle of representation.
- Except where the death rate was higher than 23 per 1000, the Act empowered but did not compel local health boards to undertake reforms.
- A local board of health could be set up if a tenth of the ratepayers petitioned for it, but most larger towns did not bother with the Act and bypassed it by continuing with the old system of obtaining a private Act of Parliament to carry out local improvements. This had the advantage of keeping matters on a local level and avoiding centralised interference.
- By 1854 only 182 local boards had been set up, and only 13 of those had established waterworks and sewerage schemes.
- The Act was based entirely on preventive measures. As such, it was very narrow in its focus.
- The Act did not legislate for London, which remained an administrative nightmare.

the vested interest affected. Paradoxically, Chadwick's own approach to the issue could also be cited as a factor, since this often had an alienating effect. (See Box 8.9 and Activity 8.8, Item 4).

From a longer-term perspective, progress towards a public health system in Britain was contained in two phases. First, the gradual provision of a clean living environment by efficient sanitation - essentially preventive measures. Second, an attack on the causes of individual diseases, which developed with the science of bacteriology from about 1865 onwards - essentially curative measures. During the period up to 1850, only the preventive approach was cautiously established.

MAIN POINTS - Section 4.3

- Disease epidemics provided leverage in the campaign for public health reform. The first cholera epidemic led to the creation of a Central Board of Health in 1831, and eventually to 1,200 local boards. The so-called Cholera Act of 1832 empowered local boards to finance anti-cholera provisions out of poor rates.
- Doctors disagreed on the causes and treatment of cholera, so preventive measures achieved little. Moreover, other less dramatic diseases, such as typhus and tuberculosis, were actually bigger killers.
- Chadwick came to believe that preventive measures to control disease would reduce the cost of poor relief and contribute to the economy. His 1842 report on sanitation set out to prove the link between environment and disease; it made recommendations for a system of water-borne sewage disposal and for centralised provision of drainage, paving, water supply and street-cleaning.
- In 1843 Chadwick went on to recommend the opening of public cemeteries on the outskirts of towns.
- The 1848 Public Health Act was only a piecemeal enactment of Chadwick's recommendations. The Central Board of Health set up was only a coordinating and advisory body. It empowered but did not compel local health boards to undertake reforms. By 1854 only 13 local boards had established waterworks and sewerage schemes.

Activity 8.8 The role of Edwin Chadwick

ITEM 1 Chadwick's approach to social reform

'Locally elected committees should supervise a natural ambit [extent] of control.'

'A central body to control each service and subject it to itinerant inspection.'

Edwin Chadwick

'Expertise should replace the amateur bunglings of archaic authorities.'

Extracts from Midwinter 1968, p.23.

ITEM 2 Chadwick's view - the 1842 Report

That the various forms of epidemic, endemic and other disease caused or **aggravated or propagated** chiefly amongst the labouring classes by atmospheric impurities produced by decomposing animal and vegetable substances by damp and filth and close and overcrowded dwellings prevail amongst the population in every part of the kingdom whether dwelling in separate houses in rural villages, in small towns or in the larger towns - as they have been found to prevail in the lowest districts of the metropolis.

...That the population so exposed is less **susceptible of** moral influences and the effects of education are more transient than with a healthy population. That these above circumstances tend to produce an adult population short-lived, **improvident**, reckless and **intemperate** and with habitual **avidity** for sensual gratifications.

That these habits lead to the abandonment of all conveniences and decencies of life and especially lead to the overcrowding of their homes which is destructive to the morality as well as the health of large classes of both sexes.

That defective town cleansing fosters habits of the most abject degradation and tends to the demoralisation of large numbers of human beings who subsist by means of what they find amidst the noxious filth accumulated in neglected streets and by-places.

That the expenses of local public works are in general unequally and unfairly assessed, oppressively and uneconomically collected, by separate collections, wastefully expended in separate and inefficient operations by unskilled and practically irresponsible officers.

That the existing law for the protection of the public health and the constitutional machinery for reclaiming its execution, such as the Courts Leet, have fallen into **desuetude**, and are in the state indicated by the prevalence of the evils they were intended to prevent.

Edwin Chadwick, Report on the Sanitary Condition of the Labouring Population, *1842, Conclusions.*

Glossary

- **aggravated or propagated** - made worse or caused
- **susceptible of** - open to
- **improvident** - not providing for the future
- **intemperate** - given to excesses – especially alcoholic
- **avidity** - greed
- **desuetude** - disuse

ITEM 3 Contemporary views of Chadwick's impact

The first and undoubtedly greatest objection to the Board of Health is the deserved unpopularity of two of its members; the second, the vice of its constitution by which those members are empowered to carry out their perverse will, their petty intrigues and their wrong-headed dogmatism without restraint and without responsibility. Mr Chadwick and Dr Southwood Smith are just such men as always arise when a dynasty, a Ministry, or a Board is accumulating those elements of destruction of which it alone is unconscious. Possessing faculties by no means miraculously comprehensive, engaged upon, and brought in contact with many honest prejudices and much not unreasonable scepticism, these men seem heated with all the zeal of propagandists and all the intolerance of inquisitors. Firmly persuaded of their own infallibility, intolerant of all opposition, utterly careless of the feelings and wishes of the local bodies with whom they are brought in contact, determined not only to have their own way, and using the powers delegated to them to exercise influence over matters which Parliament has placed beyond their control, these gentlemen have **contrived to overwhelm a good object with obloquy** and hatred and to make the cholera itself scarcely a more dreaded visitation than their own. We prefer to take our chance of cholera and the rest than be bullied into health.

There is nothing a man so hates as being cleansed against his will, or having his floors swept, his walls whitewashed, his pet dung heaps cleared away, or his thatch forced to save way to slate, all at the command of a sort of sanitary **bombaliff**. It is a positive fact that many have died of a good washing. All this shows the extreme tenderness with which the work of purification should advance. Not so, thought Mr Chadwick. New mops wash clean, thought he, and he set to work, everywhere washing and splashing, and twirling and rinsing, and sponging and sopping, and soaping and mopping, till mankind began to fear a deluge of soap and water. It was a perpetual Saturday night, and Master John Bull was scrubbed, and rubbed, and small-tooth-combed, till the tears came into his eyes, and his teeth chattered, and his fists clinched themselves with worry and pain. The truth is, Mr Chadwick has very great powers, but it is not so easy to say what they can be applied to. Perhaps a retiring pension, with nothing to do, will be a less exceptionable mode of rewarding this gentleman, than what is called an active sphere.

Extracts from The Times *11 July 1854.*

> **Glossary**
> - **contrived to overwhelm a good object with obloquy** - managed to make people regard a worthy project (i.e. public health) with scorn
> - **bombaliff** - debt collector

ITEM 4 A historian's view (i)

Having conceived the 'sanitary idea' and worked so hard for the cause of sanitary reform, Chadwick's legislative and practical achievements seem slight. This was partly due to the size of the task, the force of opposition and the combination of factors associated with the sanitary issue. At the same time his own egoism, arrogance and impatience marred his effectiveness. The image was always one of a one-man band.

Adapted from Fraser 1973.

ITEM 5 A historian's view (ii)

What cannot be doubted is the huge importance of Chadwick's initiative and influence in the critical period 1838-54. Even where there was a strong local tradition, Chadwick's drive made all the difference. It might be argued that his bad temper, difficult manner and narrow-mindedness nearly ruined the cause of public health, but it is certain that without his enterprise, ideas, genius and determined courage a national health policy would not have come as soon and as effectively as it did. Yet one should remember that he had intelligent allies without whose help he would probably not have succeeded. They supplied him with trained observers, with expert witnesses to appear before Parliamentary committees and Royal Commissions, and with skilled assistants. They also probably helped to stir up and guide public opinion. No doubt much of the interest was generated by Chadwick's reports, particularly the report of 1842, which was a bestseller. But in Liverpool, Manchester and elsewhere there were men who had already addressed themselves to these problems, and that must have contributed to the speed and effectiveness with which public opinion was mobilised. No doubt Chadwick's personal force was behind all this, but this achievement would have been impossible without public opinion, local leaders, and a tradition prepared to stimulate action. Local medical men were important, as was the tradition of public service to a man's own town or neighbourhood, particularly among the Unitarians. Liverpool and Manchester had not waited for the general Act to be passed in 1848. By that time Manchester had already started to build sewers; by its Police Act of 1844 it had started to control housing and in 1845 it followed these things up with a Sanitary Improvement Act. In 1846 and 1847 Liverpool had obtained a Sanitary Act, and in 1847 had appointed the first borough engineer in the country, Mr Newlands, and the first medical officer of health, Dr Duncan, who had played a considerable part in the agitating for public health in Liverpool. The importance of independent local action does not negate Chadwick's influence. On the contrary, the stimulus of his activities was very great, even in communities which preferred to act on their own. But it does mean that there were men who were still prepared to take the initiative when he was driven from the scene in 1854.

Adapted from Kitson Clark 1962.

Questions

1. Using Items 1 and 2, and your own knowledge, to what extent was Chadwick's general approach to social reform specifically reflected in his approach to the public health issue?
2. In what ways did the content of Item 2, Chadwick's 1842 Report, represent a significant challenge to contemporary social thinking?
3. Use Item 4 and your own knowledge to explain the view of Chadwick and public health reform expressed in Item 3.
4. Using Items 1-5 and your own knowledge, list the arguments for and against the view that Chadwick's role was crucial to the development of public health reform in the period up to 1854.

References

- **Blaug (1963)** Blaug, M., 'The Myth of the Old Poor Law and the Making of the New', *Journal of Economic History* 23, 1963.
- **Cavendish (2000)** Cavendish, R., 'Birth of Sir Edwin Chadwick', *History Today* website Jan. 2000.
- **Evans (1996)** *The Forging of the Modern State Early Industrial Britain 1783-1870* 2nd edition, Longman, 1996.
- **Finer (1950)** Finer, H., *The Theory and Practice of Modern Government*, Methuen, 1950.
- **Finlayson (1969)** Finlayson, G., *England in the 1830s – Decade of Reform*, Arnold, 1969.
- **Fraser (1973)** Fraser, D., *The Evolution of the British Welfare State*, Macmillan, 1973.
- **Henriques (1979)** Henriques, U.R.Q., *Before the Welfare State*, Longman, 1979.
- **Hopkins (1979)** Hopkins, E., *A Social History of the English Working Classes*, 1815-1945, Arnold, 1979.
- **Horn (1980)** Horn, P., *The Rural World 1780-1850*, Hutchinson, 1980.
- **Jones (1971)** Jones, R.B., *Economic and Social History of England, 1770-1977*, Longman, 1971.
- **Kitson Clark (1962)** Kitson Clark, G., *The Making of Victorian England*, Methuen, 1962.
- **Marshall (1985)** Marshall, J.D., *The Old Poor Law 1795-1834*, Macmillan, 1985.
- **May (1987)** May, T., *An Economic and Social History of Britain, 1760-1990*, Longman, 1987.
- **McCord (1991)** McCord, N., *British History 1815-1906*, Oxford University Press, 1991.
- **Midwinter (1968)** Midwinter, E.C., *Victorian Social Reform*, Longman, 1968.
- **Rose (1972)** Rose, M.E., *The Relief of Poverty 1834-1914*, Macmillan, 1972.
- **Rule (1986)** Rule, J., *The Labouring Classes in Early Industrial England, 1750-1850*, Longman, 1986.
- **Rule (1992)** Rule, J., *Albion's People: English Society 1714-1815*, Longman, 1992.
- **Smelser (1959)** Smelser, N.J., *Social Change in the Industrial Revolution. An application of theory to the Lancashire cotton industry, 1770-1840*, Routledge and Kegan Paul, 1959.
- **Stevenson (1979)** Stevenson, J., *Popular Disturbances in England 1700-1870*, Longman, 1979.
- **Taylor (1972)** Taylor, A. J., *Laissez-faire and State Intervention in 19th-Century Britain*, Macmillan, 1972.
- **Thompson (1980)** Thompson, E.P., *The Making of the English Working Class*, Pelican, 1980 (first published in 1963).
- **Vincent (1982)** Vincent, D., *Bread, Knowledge and Freedom: A study of 19th-Century Working-Class Autobiography*, Methuen, 1982.

Timeline - Ireland to the mid 19th century

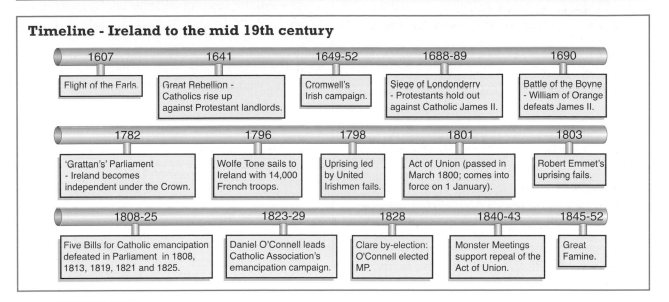

1607	1641	1649-52	1688-89	1690
Flight of the Earls.	Great Rebellion - Catholics rise up against Protestant landlords.	Cromwell's Irish campaign.	Siege of Londonderry - Protestants hold out against Catholic James II.	Battle of the Boyne - William of Orange defeats James II.

1782	1796	1798	1801	1803
'Grattan's' Parliament - Ireland becomes independent under the Crown.	Wolfe Tone sails to Ireland with 14,000 French troops.	Uprising led by United Irishmen fails.	Act of Union (passed in March 1800; comes into force on 1 January).	Robert Emmet's uprising fails.

1808-25	1823-29	1828	1840-43	1845-52
Five Bills for Catholic emancipation defeated in Parliament in 1808, 1813, 1819, 1821 and 1825.	Daniel O'Connell leads Catholic Association's emancipation campaign.	Clare by-election: O'Connell elected MP.	Monster Meetings support repeal of the Act of Union.	Great Famine.

Introduction

Since 1970, two distinct approaches towards Irish history have been battling for supremacy. On the one hand, there are the 'traditionalists' - historians who believe that many of the problems facing Irish people in the late 18th and 19th centuries stemmed from British misrule and exploitation. And, on the other hand, there are the 'revisionists' - historians who are less willing to blame the British and who are eager to reappraise what they see as the mythology that has developed around many key historical events. As a result of this battle, what used to be taken for granted is now a matter of keen debate. Take the 'Great Famine' of 1845-52 for example. Since the 1860s, most historians have taken the traditionalist line that the policies of the British government (and, in particular, the government's obsession with free-market economics) were primarily responsible for the huge loss of life.

Recently, however, revisionists have attacked this interpretation. Although, they admit, the British government did make mistakes, these mistakes were generally due to the time taken to implement policies, not to the policies themselves. This shifts the blame from the politicians (who decide policy) to the machinery of government and, at the same time, avoids criticism of free-market economics. At heart, therefore, this is not just a debate about the Great Famine. It is also a debate about the merits (or otherwise) of free-market economics. As is often the case with history (and with Irish history in particular), historical debate reflects contemporary concerns. This unit explores the ways in which historical developments in Ireland in the late 18th and early 19th centuries shaped questions which are still being addressed today.

UNIT SUMMARY

Part 1 traces the links between Britain and Ireland from the 12th century to the Act of Union in 1801. In particular, it looks at why an Act of Union was passed.

Part 2 examines the consequences of the passage of the Act of Union and focuses on two campaigns, both led by Daniel O'Connell - the campaign for Catholic emancipation and the campaign for repeal of the Act of Union.

Part 3 explores the causes and course of the Great Famine. It also outlines the arguments for and against the view that the Famine was inevitable.

Part 4 looks at how Irish history has been written. It considers how the writing of Irish history has developed over recent years and analyses the traditionalist and revisionist approaches.

1 What led to the Act of Union?

Key issues

1. What were the long-term reasons for the passing of an Act of Union?

2. What were the short-term reasons for the passing of an Act of Union?

3. What were the aims and provisions of the Act of Union?

1.1 Early ties between Britain and Ireland

Early contact
To understand why the Act of Union was passed at the start of the 19th century, it is necessary to examine the long and involved ties that had been formed between Ireland and Britain before then. These ties went back as far as the 12th century when, in 1170, a group of English knights (invited over by an Irish king) used their superior weaponry to conquer South-East Ireland. From that time onwards, the history of Ireland and England was intertwined.

Henry VIII and Elizabeth tighten the ties
At first, the ties between Ireland and Britain were loose. From the reign of Henry VIII (1509-47), however, they began to tighten. Two developments were important in Henry VIII's reign. First, Henry rejected Catholicism and embraced Protestantism. This sowed the seeds of what became a growing divide between Protestantism, which flourished on the British mainland, and Catholicism, which remained the predominant faith in Ireland. And second, in 1534, Henry issued a declaration that all lands in Ireland were to be surrendered to the Crown and re-granted.

This was not so important for the 'Old English' (English settlers who, over the years had seized Irish land) as they had recognised the British monarch as their overlord (in theory at least) all along. It was, however, a particularly important development for the Gaelic (native Irish) chieftains since it meant conceding that their position relied on the goodwill of the British monarch. To make his point, in 1541, Henry was granted the title 'King of Ireland'.

Although Henry made no attempt to conquer Ireland (the title was sufficient), Elizabeth I (ruled 1559-1603) did. She sent English generals with English troops over to Ireland on a mission to impose loyalty to the Crown and to civilise the 'rude and barbarous nation'. The Elizabethan conquest of Ireland was only achieved with a great deal of bloodshed. Kee (1980) suggests that this had two consequences. First, it marked the beginning of 'traditional Irish hatred for governing Englishmen'.

BOX 9.1 | **The Battle of Yellow Ford and the Munster plantation**

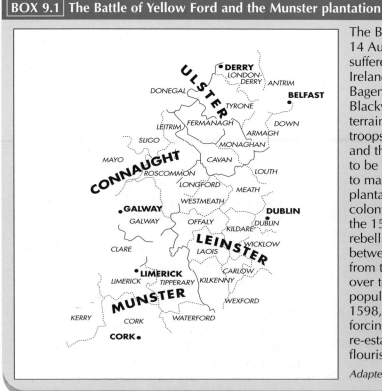

The Battle of Yellow Ford, which took place on 14 August 1598, was the greatest single defeat suffered by English forces in 16th-century Ireland. The Queen's army under Henry Bagenal, taking supplies to the beleaguered Blackwater Fort, was ambushed in difficult terrain north of Armagh by Hugh O'Neill's troops. Bagenal and 800 of his men were killed and the Blackwater and Armagh garrisons had to be abandoned. As a result, O'Neill was able to march south and overthrow the Munster plantation. The Munster plantation was a colony of English settlers originally set up in the 1560s. Following the second 'Desmond rebellion' of 1579-83, a large arc of land between Cork and Limerick was confiscated from the rebels and English colonists were sent over to occupy it (the plantation had a population of 3,030 in 1592). In October 1598, O'Neill's troops overran the plantation, forcing the colonists to flee. The plantation was re-established in 1601 and eventually flourished.

Adapted from Connolly 1998.

And second, closer ties between the Old English and the Gaelic Irish (against the common British enemy) can be seen as 'early faint traces of a modern Irish nation'.

A further development of importance during the Elizabethan period was the intervention of foreign forces on the side of those fighting against the English. During Elizabeth's reign there were four serious rebellions against English rule. The first, led by Shane O'Neill, sought help from Rome and France (no help materialised). The fourth and most serious was led by Hugh O'Neill, the Gaelic Earl of Tyrone. In 1598, O'Neill's forces won the Battle of Yellow Ford - the only major defeat for the English in Ireland during this period (see Box 9.1).

O'Neill's rebels were supported by the Spanish, and in 1601 a Spanish fleet arrived in the Irish port of Kinsale to help them. The rebels were defeated in a battle just outside Kinsale, but the lesson for the English was clear. In times of war, Ireland might provide a useful base for England's enemies. This was an added incentive to ensure that the island remained under English control.

The Flight of the Earls, 1607
The rebellion led by Hugh O'Neill dragged on after the Battle of Kinsale until the rebels were finally defeated on their home turf in Ulster in 1603. O'Neill surrendered and was pardoned by King James I (1603-25) who had succeeded Elizabeth after her death. On 4 September 1607, however, O'Neill and his allies, Rory O'Donnell (who was Earl of Tyrconnell) and Cuconnacht Maguire (Lord of Fermanagh), sailed away from Ireland into voluntary exile. This event, the 'Flight of the Earls', was important for two reasons. First:

'It is generally taken as signalling the death of the old Gaelic order, though in fact that order lingered on, rallying occasionally, for nearly a century more. But it had been a very hard hit by Mountjoy [the English commander who had put down the rebellion], and it was never again to look as near ultimate success and secure survival as it had done immediately after O'Neill's victory at the Yellow Ford.' (O'Brien & O'Brien 1985, p.61)

And second, the self-exile of the earls was declared treacherous by the British government and the land they owned (six of the nine counties in Ulster) was confiscated and plans were made to settle (or 'plant') Protestants from England and Scotland there (see Box 9.2).

The Ulster plantation
Other plantations had been set up in Ireland in the 16th century, but only the Munster plantation (referred to in Box 9.1) was of a similar scale to the Ulster plantation. The setting up of this plantation

BOX 9.2 Plantation
'Plantation' (another word for 'colonisation') became the predominant policy under James I. Policy-makers thought that colonies of mainland British settlers in Ireland would:
- be models of civilisation and religion for the 'barbarous' natives
- stimulate economic growth
- provide protection against foreign invasion
- be centres of command and control
- provide land for the younger sons of English and Scottish nobles
- provide outlets for surplus population in mainland Britain.

In government-organised plantations such as that in Ulster, high-ranking English or Scottish settlers (nobles or members of the gentry) were granted large parcels of land. This land was then divided up into smaller tenant farms occupied either by settlers from mainland Britain or by native Irish farmers. By 1641, 22,000 English had settled in Munster and 15,000 English and Scots in Ulster, but there was immigration from mainland Britain to Ireland into all parts of the country and some native Irish landlords brought in settlers. Having encouraged settlement in Ireland, the government was faced with the problem of defending colonists who often did not take basic precautions against attack. Also, natives who had been dispossessed, exiled or made redundant became a threat.

Adapted from Connolly 1998.

was of great long-term significance. Since the plantation did not involve the wholesale ejection of the native population (many locals were retained as labourers or tenant farmers), the population of Ulster became divided into a landowning, English-speaking Protestant overclass (the settlers from England and Scotland) and a Gaelic-speaking, Catholic underclass (the native population). By 1622, around 13,000 settlers had come over to Ulster, many of them Scottish Presbyterians. As Robert Kee points out:

'This was an age in which religion determined political thinking. With the Protestant plantations, a cleavage between two sections of the Irish population was established which - though it was to make no distinction between who was an Irishman and who was not, set a pattern for the social and political development of Ireland for many centuries.' (Kee 1972, p.13)

The Rising of 1641
The next major event to shape future developments in Ireland was the Rising of 1641. In that year, Catholic labourers and tenants rose up in arms against the Protestant landowners, killing several thousand in the early stages of the rebellion. This rebellion had three main consequences. First, it

increased Irish Protestants' hatred of Catholicism and provided them with martyrs and stories of atrocities that could be cited in justification of future action. Second, it strengthened ties between the Gaelic Irish and 'Old English'. (The Old English were the descendants of English settlers who had seized land in the period between the 12th and 16th centuries. They were, therefore, landowners, but they were also Catholics.) In 1641 the Old English joined the rebellion against the Protestant settlers, and so cemented the religious divide in Ireland. And third, the rebellion paved the way to Oliver Cromwell's Irish campaign in 1649-52. Indeed, Cromwell claimed that revenge for the atrocities committed in 1641 was an important motive in his coming to Ireland.

Cromwell's Irish campaign

Cromwell's campaign was notable for two reasons. First, it was a campaign of the utmost cruelty against Catholics. After capturing the towns of Drogheda and Wexford, for example, Cromwell's soldiers went on the rampage massacring both soldiers and civilians. Cromwell himself admitted that just 30 survived the massacre at Drogheda out of a population of 3,000. And second, Cromwell began a process of confiscating land from Catholics. Those who had taken part in the rebellion of 1641 were dispossessed and those who could prove that they were not involved in the rebellion were resettled in the (infertile) west. The result was that:

> 'The percentage of the land of Ireland owned by Catholics, which had shrunk by the time of the great rebellion [of 1641] to 59%, was reduced by the Cromwellian land settlement to a mere 22%. After further Catholic humiliation in great events to come, it was to shrink by 1695 to 14% and by 1714 still further to 7%.' (Kee 1980, p.48)

The land that was seized was used to settle Protestants, in what was by now a familiar way. Downing concludes:

> 'Cromwell had completed the conquest of Ireland and his settlement had created a Protestant English upper class in a country of Catholics. Ireland, now, was an English colony.' (Downing 1980, p.20)

Events leading to the Battle of the Boyne

The next crisis in Ireland had both a religious and a political dimension. James II, who became king in 1685, was a Catholic. Determined to restore Catholicism in Britain, he pursued pro-Catholic policies and appointed Catholics to key positions (such as Viceroy of Ireland). In 1688, however, leading British politicians executed a bloodless coup which placed the Protestant William of Orange on the throne and forced James into exile in France. At the end of 1688, James sent a small (Catholic) garrison to relieve the garrison in Londonderry. News of this divided the (mainly Protestant) population. Some were ready to open the gates to the new garrison (since James was still the legitimate king). Others argued that Protestants would be massacred as they had been in 1641. The matter was settled when a group of 13 apprentice boys seized the keys of the city (on 7 December) and locked the gates. The following spring, James brought a small force (mainly of French troops) into Ireland in the hope of winning back the Crown. His attempt to capture Londonderry failed after a siege was unsuccessful (the town was relieved by an English fleet on 28 July 1689) and then his army was defeated by William of Orange's troops on 1 July 1690 at the Battle of the Boyne. As Downing notes:

> 'If Londonderry represents fortitude and the spirit of "no surrender", then the Battle of the Boyne in July 1690...represents Protestant triumph... William's victory set the final seal on the Protestant ascendancy, and the English dominance of Irish affairs that lasted 200 years. The Irish had been defeated three times in a century. This time it was decisive.' (Downing 1980, p.20)

MAIN POINTS - Section 1.1

- Ties between Britain and Ireland go back as far as the 12th century. In the late 16th century, Elizabeth I used military force to impose British rule on Ireland. Then, shortly after her death, the Flight of the Earls led to the setting up of the Ulster plantation and the settlement of a large number of English and Scottish colonists.

- The Rising of 1641 was followed by Cromwell's brutal campaign - which resulted in Catholics losing more land. The struggle between the Catholic King James II and Protestant William of Orange led to the Battle of the Boyne and Protestant victory in 1690.

Activity 9.1 Ireland before 1800

ITEM 1 The Flight of the Earls

This 20th-century painting by Thomas Ryan RHA depicts a priest blessing Hugh O'Neill and Rory O'Donnell as they left Ireland on 4 September 1607.

ITEM 2 The Great Rebellion of 1641

Driuinge Men women & children by hund: reds vpon Briges & casting them into Riuers, who drowned not were killed with poles & shot with muskets.

This picture shows Catholic rebels throwing Protestants from a bridge at Portadown in Ulster. Around 100 Protestant men, women and children were drowned, shot or clubbed to death in November 1641 during the Great Rebellion. The rebels proclaimed their loyalty to the Crown but demanded their land back.

ITEM 3 The Battle of the Boyne

This 17th-century painting depicts William of Orange at the head of his troops. William arrived in Ireland on 14 June 1690 and defeated James' forces on 1 July. This victory is celebrated every year when the members of the Orange Order march in Northern Ireland.

Questions

1. Look at Items 1-3 and write a paragraph explaining what is happening in each picture and why this had long-term significance.
2. a) Using your own knowledge and Items 2 and 3, explain how religious divisions led to political divisions.
   b) Why was the Battle of the Boyne important (a) in the short term and (b) in the long term?
3. a) Take any of Items 1-3 and suggest why an artist might choose to create a picture like that.
   b) How might the picture affect our view of the past?

1.2 Ireland in the 18th century

The Penal Laws

The 'Protestant triumph' in 1690 led to a period in which the ruling Protestant minority attempted to stamp out the Catholic faith of the majority. In the early part of the 18th century, a series of laws was passed by the Irish Parliament which penalised Catholics. Collectively, these laws are known as the 'Penal Laws'. The laws made the provisions outlined in Box 9.3. It should also be noted that Presbyterians, as well as Catholics, were barred from civil and military employment.

BOX 9.3 The Penal Laws

- It became illegal for Catholics to hold public office, stand for Parliament, vote, join the armed forces or work in the legal profession.
- It became illegal for Catholics to buy land or to hold land on a lease for more than 31 years.
- On a Catholic landowner's death, the land had to be divided equally between all children.
- Catholic parish priests were allowed to work only if they registered with the authorities.
- Members of the Catholic clergy other than parish priests were banned from the country and liable to be hanged if they returned (a reward of £5 was offered to anyone who caught them).
- All forms of Catholic education were illegal.
- If a Catholic was caught with a horse worth more than £5, it could be confiscated.

In practice, many of the Penal Laws were not enforced. Foster argues that:

'Support for such measures was always more vehement among the MPs at Dublin than the government in Whitehall, or in Dublin Castle [where the Irish Viceroy and staff were based]. It was certainly true that, whatever some zealots [enthusiastic promoters of the laws] may have hoped, the imposition of the penal laws as a unified code never achieved a very high standard of efficiency, and small-minded restrictions like forbidding a Catholic to own a horse worth more than £5, or to bear arms, rapidly fell into desuetude [disuse].' (Foster 1991, p.165)

Catholics in the 18th century

Even though many of the Penal Laws were not enforced, Catholics remained second-class citizens throughout the 18th century. It is true that some Catholics prospered (Catholics were not banned from trading), but most lived in poverty. Since they were excluded from public life, many turned to non-political, clandestine organisations. Out of necessity, for example, Catholic mass had to be held in secret in many places. In addition, numerous secret societies emerged, becoming known collectively as the 'Whiteboy movement'. The first of these groups appeared in 1711:

'Bands of armed men, with blackened faces and wearing white shirts over their clothes for easier mutual recognition at night, started to roam the countryside mutilating cattle and carrying out other reprisals for the tyranny and rapacity [greed] of harsh landlords or the subservience of those who played along with them.' (Kee 1972, p.24)

Groups like this sprang up all over Ireland, especially after 1760. Robert Kee argues that the activity of these groups was:

'wholly unpolitical or politically very crude. Even when, as happened from time to time, attempts were made to enlist it for political purposes, it tended to remain most stubbornly what it had always been: the simplest form of war that the poor can wage against the rich or those who play the rich man's game.' (Kee 1972, p.26)

Protestants in the 18th century

The Catholic majority may have lacked political direction in the 18th century, but that was certainly not the case for the ruling Protestant minority. As O'Brien and O'Brien point out:

'The active politics of Ireland during this period were Protestant politics.' (O'Brien & O'Brien 1985, p.80)

Protestant politics in the 18th century, however, were complex. An Irish Parliament had been in existence since the Middle Ages, but two Acts ensured that it had little power:

- Poynings Law of 1494 prevented the Irish Parliament from meeting without royal licence and provided that all draft bills should first be approved by the British monarch and Parliament.
- the Declaratory Act of 1720 asserted the right of the British Parliament to pass legislation binding on Ireland.

In the 18th century the Irish Parliament was dominated by a rich elite - the 'Ascendancy'. As Box 9.4 shows, members of the Ascendancy had a great deal in common.

The development of 'Patriotism'

Despite the common interests outlined in Box 9.4, however, different political positions emerged during the course of the 18th century. The heart of the matter was a debate about the relationship between the British government and the Irish Parliament. In

The Ascendancy

Members of the Ascendancy shared the following characteristics:
- they were all wealthy landowners
- they lived in relative luxury
- they were members of the established (Protestant) Church of Ireland
- they mixed socially and shared similar tastes
- most were recent settlers
- despite their position of dominance, most lived with a degree of insecurity (the memories of the Catholic revival in 1685, when the Catholic James II became king, remained fresh, as did memories of the Great Rebellion of 1641)
- in general terms, their main priority was to maintain their privileged position.

the second half of the 18th century, some members of the Ascendancy began to argue that Ireland should have independence under the Crown. Irish Protestants, they argued, should remain loyal to the British monarch, but the Irish Parliament should be the supreme law-making body in Ireland. In short, a kind of Protestant nationalism emerged. This nationalism was termed 'Patriotism'.

By no means all or even a majority of the Ascendancy supported Patriotism. Many accepted that the British Parliament was supreme and that it was right to cooperate with British officials. It was only after the American Declaration of Independence (1776) and the War of Independence which followed (ending in 1783) that support for the Patriot position gained strength. In 1780, the leading Patriot MP, Henry Grattan, called on the Irish Parliament to vote on an Irish Declaration of Independence. On this occasion, he was unsuccessful. His attempt, however, was a sign of what was to come.

Growing pressure on the British government
There were a number of reasons why the American War of Independence made such an impact in Ireland. First, there were obvious parallels between the two countries. Both had strong and close ties with Britain. When America proved itself able to break these ties and gain its independence, it showed the Irish what could be achieved. Second, many Irish people had emigrated to America and so there were very real ties between Ireland and America. And third, the war had repercussions in Ireland - British troops were withdrawn, for example, and there were threats that France and Spain would invade Britain through Ireland.

During the American War of Independence, the last thing that the British government wanted was further imperial trouble on its doorstep. In 1778, when British troops were withdrawn to fight in

America, Irish Protestants began setting up armed groups to guard Ireland against a French attack. By the end of 1781, the number of Volunteers had risen to around 80,000. When delegates from the Volunteers met early in 1782 and drew up a Declaration of Independence, this coincided with a change of government in Britain (the Whigs took up office). The Whigs had promised concessions to the Irish Patriots whilst in opposition. These promises and the implied threats of the Volunteers were sufficient to persuade the British government to repeal Poynings Law and the Declaratory Act. Britain and Ireland were now 'two sovereign independent kingdoms linked by the inalienable identity of the Irish Crown with that of Britain' (Kee 1980, p.59).

Grattan's Parliament, 1782-1801
The new arrangement later became known as 'Grattan's Parliament' because Grattan had played a leading role in pressing for British concessions. Grattan, however, was no radical. He liaised between the Volunteers and the Irish Parliament, but rejected all talk of armed uprising. The nature of the settlement reflected his cautious approach. Independence was more apparent than real, owing mainly to corruption, patronage and British interference behind the scenes.

The debate over parliamentary reform
The 19 years of Grattan's Parliament were dominated by a single issue - parliamentary reform. It soon became clear that an unreformed Parliament meant a continuation of domination by Britain, but there was not the same support for parliamentary reform as there had been on the issue of independence. One reason was that many MPs had a vested interest in opposing reform (they received money and posts from the British). A second reason was that, unlike in 1782, there was no military pressure on the Irish Parliament and therefore no incentive to introduce reforms. The Volunteers dispersed after the defeat of a Reform Bill (introduced by a radical Patriot, Henry Flood) in 1783. And third, reform necessarily involved broadening the electorate. As in Britain (see Unit 5), this was a can of worms that the political elite was reluctant to open. Besides, in Ireland there was the further complication that the political elite was Protestant. Broadening the electorate would mean either allowing some Catholics the vote or openly discriminating against them.

Calls for Catholic emancipation
By the end of the 18th century, the issue of Catholic emancipation had moved up the political agenda. Protestant attitudes towards Catholics at the end of the 18th century were complex. Although there were still hardliners opposed to Catholics having any political rights, there were also signs of greater

tolerance. Before Grattan's Parliament was set up, an important concession had been made to Catholics. In 1778, the first Catholic Relief Bill was passed, allowing Catholics to buy property again. Once independence had been achieved, the issue of Catholic emancipation could no longer be ignored. Indeed, it became the issue which dominated Irish politics.

The Rebellion of 1798

Ireland - like most European countries - was deeply affected by the French Revolution of 1789:

'The ideals of the French Revolution gave great sustenance to radicals everywhere; in the Irish context "liberty" implied that the Irish should have their own government, while "fraternity" and "equality" would mean the end of Catholic and Presbyterian disabilities.' (Downing 1980, p.32)

The French Revolution showed that the old order could be overthrown by force and a new, republican order put in its place. This was a lesson which radicals active in Ireland in the 1790s learned and tried to copy. The result was bungled attempted uprisings in 1796 and 1798 followed by the reassertion of British power and the Act of Union.

The Society of United Irishmen

The Society of United Irishmen, a group founded in 1791, enthusiastically supported the French Revolution and set out to win, from all sections of the community, support for an independent Irish republic (see also Unit 2, Section 3.1). Although most of its leading figures were Protestants, some Catholics and Presbyterians joined and the group established centres of support in Belfast, Dublin, Antrim and Down. In its early years, the group remained small, predominantly middle-class and lacking in political clout.

The second Catholic Relief Act

In 1793 war broke out between Britain and France and the British government pressurised the Irish Parliament into passing a second Catholic Relief Act which allowed Catholics who met the necessary property qualification to vote (though not to stand for Parliament). Britain may have hoped that this was sufficient to ensure that calm would prevail until the war with France was over. By 1796, however, two developments had ensured that, although the Society of United Irishmen remained a small group, it was able to spark a major crisis.

First, the Catholic Relief Act of 1793 raised and frustrated hopes for full emancipation and sparked increasing unrest amongst the Catholic peasants in the countryside. Many of these peasants joined a secret society called the Defenders. From 1793, attempts were made by the (mainly middle- and

upper-class) United Irishmen to established links with the Defenders in the hope that unrest in the countryside could be channelled into revolutionary activity.

And second, leading United Irishmen - notably Wolfe Tone (see Box 9.5) - went to France to try to persuade the government to send troops to help in an uprising against British rule. In December 1796 the French did indeed send a force of 14,000 troops to Ireland with Wolfe Tone on board. Although, Tone remarked, they sailed so close to the shore of Bantry Bay that you could toss a biscuit onto it, they were prevented from landing by the weather and, after 10 days, were forced back to France.

Even before December 1796, the British government had taken measures to combat the threat to security posed by the Irish radicals - the Society of United Irishmen was outlawed in May 1794 and the Insurrection Act of 1796 increased magistrates' powers to seize arms and arrest suspects. After December 1796 the British government pursued a policy of military repression. General Lake was sent against the United Irishmen in Belfast and by March 1797 most of Ulster was under martial law. The United Irishmen's response to this repression was to plan an uprising for May 1798.

A sporadic uprising

By 1798 the Society of United Irishmen was riddled with informers and many of its leading members (including Wolfe Tone) were in exile. Most of those who remained were rounded up and arrested on 12 March 1798. Then, on 19 May - a few days before the uprising was due to take place, Lord Edward Fitzgerald (the United Irishmen's military leader) was arrested and fatally wounded (see Box 9.6). The uprising went ahead, but it was sporadic and uncoordinated and only effective in Antrim, Down and Wexford (where the rebels held out for several weeks). A month after the final defeat of the rebels (at the Battle of Vinegar Hill on 21 June), another French fleet arrived with 1,000 troops. By then, enthusiasm for rebellion had waned and, despite a notable success against the British, the French army was forced to surrender in September, just as further French ships were on their way to Ireland. These ships were captured and amongst the prisoners was Wolfe Tone. He was condemned to death but died in prison (either he cut his own throat or his gaolers cut it). For later generations of republicans, Wolfe Tone was a hero and a martyr. His main legacy was the idea that only unity between Catholics and Protestants would bring about the Irish republic that was his main goal.

It is estimated that in the months after the uprising as many as 30,000 people were killed by the victorious British troops and the loyalist militia (mainly members of the Orange societies) which

BOX 9.5 | Wolfe Tone (1763-98)

Wolfe Tone

Born in Dublin, the son of a prosperous Protestant coach-builder who went bankrupt, Tone was educated at Trinity College and qualified as a barrister. Initially he supported the Irish Whigs, but he soon became disillusioned with their moderation. In 1791 he published *An Argument on Behalf of the Catholics of Ireland*, which insisted that Protestants and Catholics had common political interests. This attracted much attention and, later in the year, he was invited to the meeting at which the Society of United Irishmen was set up (with the aim of parliamentary reform and the removal of English control of Irish affairs). Initially the society stopped short of separatism or republicanism, though some members had begun to work towards an armed uprising which would break all ties with Britain before the government banned the society in May 1794. The society's most distinctive commitment was to a union of Irishmen of all denominations - though some Protestant members were uneasy at the prospect of Catholic emancipation.

Tone was a great admirer of the French Revolution and, according to Roy Foster, 'his most important quality was his ability to become a dedicated and ruthless revolutionary'. By 1794 he was sending memoranda to French agents, arguing that Ireland was ripe for revolution (see Item 2 in Activity 9.2 below). When information about this 'treasonable' activity was leaked to a government spy, he was forced into exile in the USA. From there, he travelled to France in February 1796 and, claiming to be the national representative of a foreign power, he managed to persuade the French government to support an Irish uprising. He travelled with the two French fleets which sailed to Ireland in 1796 and 1798. His aim, it seems, was to bring about a revolution which would unite Protestants and Catholics as one Irish nation in an Irish Republic which had broken all its connections with Britain.

Adapted from Connolly 1998 and Foster 1988.

supported them. As a result, the uprising became a major landmark in republican history.

It was not just government troops who committed atrocities, however. During the uprising the old religious divides reappeared, with Catholics massacring Protestants (during the rebellion in Wexford, for example) and vice versa.

BOX 9.6 | The arrest of Lord Edward Fitzgerald

Fitzgerald was the younger son of the Duke of Leinster, born in 1763. In 1799 he served as a soldier in America. In 1781 and 1790 he was elected to serve as an MP. He supported the French Revolution and, in 1792, visited Paris and stayed with Thomas Paine. On his return he was discharged from the army for toasting the abolition of hereditary titles. Although a supporter of the United Irishmen from the early 1790s, he joined only in 1796. From 1797 he was chief organiser of the United Irishmen's military efforts. He escaped arrest in March 1798 but was betrayed by an informer a few weeks later and was shot in the shoulder resisting arrest (during the arrest he stabbed one officer to death). Although his wound at first did not appear serious, he died in prison six weeks later.

Adapted from Connolly 1998.

The Act of Union

The attempted French invasion in 1796 and the 1798 uprising shook the British government to the core, not only because they were inspired by revolutionary republicanism but also because they took place at a time when Britain was at war and was therefore vulnerable. The government's response was to remove all trappings of independence and to incorporate Ireland into the UK. The thinking behind this was:

'Never again: the back door to England must be shut and firmly locked. The solution of the English Prime Minister William Pitt, was the Act of Union: Direct Rule.' (Downing 1980, p.33)

Pitt's decision to propose an Act of Union reveals how much the political landscape had changed since Grattan's Parliament was established. Pitt proposed full Catholic emancipation with the Act of Union, a proposal which brought support for Union from the majority of Catholics. This measure was rejected by King George III (as well as by many members of the Ascendancy), however, and was dropped - a move which angered Catholics, intensified opposition to the Act of Union and forced Pitt and his supporters to resign (see Unit 1, Section 1.3).

The terms of the Act of Union

The terms of the Act of Union were eventually agreed by both Houses of the Irish Parliament on 28 March 1800 (after a great deal of debate, pressure and the exercise of patronage). The Act came into force on 1 January 1801. The terms were as follows:

- The United Kingdom of Great Britain and Ireland was established.
- The Irish Parliament was abolished. Instead, Ireland was to be incorporated into the British parliamentary system, sending 100 MPs, four bishops and 28 life peers to Westminster.
- The Church of Ireland was to be united with the Church of England.
- Free trade was to be established between the two countries.
- Ireland was to contribute two-seventeenths to the expenditure of the UK whilst Britain was to contribute fifteen-seventeenths.
- The legal systems and financial systems of the two countries were to remain unchanged.
- The Viceroy and staff would remain in place.

MAIN POINTS - Section 1.2

- The 'Protestant triumph' in 1690 led to a period in which the ruling Protestant minority attempted to stamp out the Catholic faith of the majority. Catholics became second-class citizens and Protestants controlled the political process.
- In the second half of the 18th century, some Protestants ('Patriots') began to demand independence under the Crown. This was granted in 1782. Grattan's Parliament (1782-1801) was dominated by the debate over parliamentary reform.
- The French Revolution brought a new political climate. The United Irishmen called on all sections of Irish society to rebel against British rule. The Rebellion of 1798 failed, but it provoked the British government to take action - an Act of Union was passed, making Ireland an integral part of the UK.

Activity 9.2 The Rebellion of 1798

ITEM 1 The United Irishmen

(i) In the present great era of reform when unjust governments are falling in every quarter of Europe, we think it our duty as Irishmen to come forward and state what we feel to be our heavy grievance and what we feel to be its effectual remedy. We have no national government. We are ruled by Englishmen and the servants of Englishmen whose object is the interest of another country, whose instrument is corruption, whose strength is the weakness of Ireland. These men have the whole power and patronage of the country as a means to subdue the honesty and the spirit of her representatives in the **legislature**.

Part of the Dublin Society of United Irishmen's Declaration, written by Napper Tandy for its inaugural meeting on 9 November 1791.

Napper Tandy

(ii) I, in the presence of God, do pledge myself to my country that I will use all my abilities and influence in the attainment of an adequate and impartial representation of the Irish nation in Parliament, and as a means of absolute and immediate necessity in the attainment of this chief good of Ireland, I will endeavour as much as lies in my ability to forward a brotherhood of affection, an identity of interests, a communion of rights and a union of power among Irishmen of all religious persuasions.

The affirmation which all members of the United Irish Society were called upon to make, 1791.

Glossary

- **legislature** - ie the Irish Parliament.

ITEM 2 Wolfe Tone's memorandum to French agents

In Ireland, a conquered and oppressed and insulted country, the name of England and her power is universally **odious**, save with those who have an interest in maintaining it, such as the government and its connections, the Church and its dependencies, the great landed property and so on. But since the power of these people is founded on property, the first convulsion would level it with the dust. It seems idle to suppose that the prejudices of England against France spring merely from the **republicanism** of the French. These prejudices proceed rather from a spirit of rivalry, encouraged by continued wars. In Ireland, the **Dissenters** are enemies to the English power from reason and reflection. The Catholics are enemies from hatred to the English name. In a word, the prejudices of the one country are directly favourable and those of the other directly adverse to an invasion. The government of Ireland is to be looked on as a government of force. The moment a superior force appears it would tumble at once as being neither founded in the interests nor in the affections of the people. Indeed the great bulk of the Irish people would throw off the yoke, if they saw any force in the country sufficiently strong to resort to for defence.

> ### Glossary
> - **odious** - hateful
> - **republicanism** - rule without a monarch
> - **Dissenters** - Protestants not belonging to the established Church (ie the Church of England or the Church of Ireland)

A memorandum written by Wolfe Tone in April 1794 in order to brief French agents about the situation in Ireland

ITEM 3 The rebellion of 1798

The County of Wexford was not one in which anyone was expecting rebellion in 1798. Branches of the Defenders had long existed there, but in 1797 an official report had claimed that they were inactive. As a result, few soldiers were stationed here. When the government found a note from Fitzgerald naming the port of Wexford as a possible site for a French landing, officials gave the job of searching for information to the local Protestant yeomanry who were to be assisted by the North Cork militia. As soon as the militia arrived, floggings started, even though, by official proclamation, people had 14 days grace in which to surrender arms. The outbreak of rebellion seems to have resulted from a panicky determination not to submit to the torture which was spreading through the county. Father John Murphy took charge of the peasantry in that incident and became a key figure in the rebellion - which was more an indignant peasants' revolt in Wexford than a national rebellion.

An execution at the rebel camp on Vinegar Hill.

The rebels won an important early victory and then gathered on Vinegar Hill. There, a dozen Protestant captives were lined up in front of a windmill and clumsily put to death with pikes. A few days later, a barn holding Protestant men, women and children was set on fire and those not burned alive were shot or piked to death. The number of dead may have been 200. Such atrocities did the rebels no good. They were a particularly bad advertisement for a cause which was theoretically meant to be uniting Catholics and Protestants as fellow Irishmen. A member of the United Irishmen, Bagenal Harvey, took charge and prevented further atrocities. But the rebels' lack of strategy caught up with them. Less than a month after taking the field, they were driven from their main encampment in a decisive battle on Vinegar Hill itself. A vicious slaughter of scattered rebels by government troops continued for some time. The rebellion was over.

Adapted from Kee 1980.

A suspected rebel is flogged.

The wooden triangle on which victims were spreadeagled and flogged was first set up in Athy, County Kildare at the headquarters of the Ninth Dragoons in the spring of 1798. Standard army sentences of the day for their own men consisted of 500-999 lashes - though usually only 200-400 were administered. So, it is not difficult to imagine how they treated people they thought might be rebels. There is an account of a man who, while his flesh was being torn to shreds, begged to be shot. And there are many descriptions of flesh torn off in lumps and the baring of bones. This torture had an undoubtedly successful effect in extracting information. Thousands of arrests were made and thousands of hidden arms were recovered. The United Irish organisation in the midlands was in such confusion by the time the signal to rise was given that, though the rebels had a few temporary successes, the whole thing went off half-cock with great slaughter of the peasantry.

Adapted from Kee 1980.

Questions

1. Why was the Act of Union passed in 1800? Use your own knowledge and Items 1-3 in your answer and include both short-term and long-term causes.
2. a) Judging from Items 1 and 2, what were the aims of the United Irishmen?
   b) Describe the main characteristics of the group.
3. a) What does Item 2 tell us about the political views and aims of Wolfe Tone in 1794?
   b) How did Tone attempt to achieve these aims?
   c) Would you agree that Tone was 'a significant figure in Irish history'? Explain your answer.
4. a) What do Items 3 and 4 tell us about the causes and the nature of the rebellion?
   b) 'The uprising of 1798 was a fiasco but it was a turning point in Irish history'. Explain this statement using your own knowledge and Items 3 and 4.

2 The consequences of the Act of Union

Key issues

1. Did the Act of Union lead to significant change in Ireland after 1801?
2. What impact did Daniel O'Connell make on Irish affairs in the 1820s?
3. What were the consequences in Ireland of the passing of the Catholic Emancipation Act in 1829?
4. Why did the Repeal movement fail whilst the emancipation campaign succeeded?

2.1 Did the Act of Union lead to significant change?

The impact of the Act of Union

Most historians agree that, in some ways, the impact of the Act of Union was limited. Kee (1972) and Foster (1988), for example, give very different interpretations of many events and yet they both

agree on this. Kee argues that:

'If the Union were to be a political success, it had to bring about some definite change in Irish life. Its justification lay in ushering in a new era. The one thing it could not afford to be in everyday terms was meaningless. Yet, for the vast majority of Irishmen clinging with unceasing precariousness to their smallholdings of land, the Union made no practical difference at all; if anything, by making them more remote from government, it made things worse.' (Kee 1972, p.170)

Similarly, Foster asserts that:

'Apart from the absence of the College Green Assembly [the Irish Parliament], changes were ostensibly minimal - which may be a reflection of the limited nature of that Assembly itself. The government of Ireland, far from being integrated with that of Britain, remained a special case.' (Foster 1988, p.289)

When Kee and Foster claim that there was little change after the passage of the Act of Union, they are thinking mainly in terms of mainstream politics. The Viceroy (the monarch's representative) remained in place as did the Chief Secretary (the British government's representative - who was normally a member of the Cabinet). The British continued to administer Irish affairs from Dublin Castle and members of the Ascendancy continued to control Irish affairs at local level. It should be noted, however, that the Irish Parliament ceased to exist. Those Irishmen who were qualified to vote, voted to elect MPs to Parliament in Westminster.

Constitutional significance

There may not have been a great deal of concrete change in terms of mainstream politics after the Act of Union was passed, but that does not mean that the passing of the Act was of little importance. On the contrary, not only did the Act have great symbolic importance, it also framed the terms of political debate that took place in the 19th century and determined the political stance taken by the main political protagonists and their supporters. As Macdonagh points out, the Act was of great constitutional significance. It meant a fundamental change to the British constitution and was, therefore, not a law to be put aside lightly:

'The Act of Union possessed for many the solemnity of fundamental law, far beyond the pretensions of ordinary legislation. With the finality of a vast constitutional rearrangement, it fenced in the range of the politically possible in the 19th century.' (Macdonagh 1977, p.13)

In legal terms at least, the Act meant that Ireland was an integral part of the United Kingdom on an equal footing to Wales or Scotland. As such, it had a very different status from colonies such as India or, later, Rhodesia. As attitudes on both sides of the political divide began to harden later in the 19th century, the Act of Union became the focus of attention.

The Act and Catholic emancipation

The Act of Union also had great significance because of what it failed to deliver - namely, Catholic emancipation. Pitt made the mistake of raising expectations (by promising emancipation) and then failing to keep his promise. By resigning rather than challenging the stance of both anti-emancipation politicians in Ireland and Westminster and of George III (who argued that he would break his coronation oath in which he swore to defend the Church of England if he agreed to emancipation), Pitt sowed seeds which would result in the re-emergence of sectarian divisions (ie hostility between Catholics and Protestants - 'sectarian' means being divided because of religion or beliefs). The Act of Union was supposed to solve the Catholic 'problem' (Catholics, who were a majority in Ireland, would become a minority group in the UK and so Protestant domination in Ireland would no longer be a matter of a minority oppressing the majority). Instead, the passage of the Act made the problem worse.

The economic impact

In addition, the Act of Union failed to bring economic benefits. British industry outperformed Irish industry in almost every sphere (linen produced in Ulster was an exception) and so free trade worked to Britain's advantage not Ireland's. British investors were reluctant to invest in Irish industry - which consequently fell further behind. Although the Act of Union was not necessarily to blame for the economic imbalance between the two islands, it was easy for those who were disaffected to blame it. Economic discontent was made worse because of population growth (the population doubled between 1800 and 1841) and the 'land question'.

The land question

The problem posed by the 'land question' was summed up as early as 1796 by a Frenchman called Jacques de Latocnaye who had toured Ireland:

'A rich man, unwilling to be at any trouble, lets a large tract of country to one man who does not intend to cultivate it himself, but to let it out to three or four others. Those who have large shares farm them out to about a score who again let them to about 100 comfortably situated peasants who give them at an exorbitant price to about a thousand poor land labourers - whom necessity obliges to take their scanty portion at a price far beyond its real value.' (Latocnaye quoted in Kee 1972, p.171)

The result of such a system was that those at the bottom of the chain found it difficult to survive and had no capital to invest in new equipment or techniques whilst those higher up the chain had no incentive to make improvements. Whilst prices remained high (during the French Wars), even those at the bottom of the chain had enough to eat. But when the post-war boom ended, subsistence became a struggle. Insecurity was heightened by the threat of eviction which, in most parts of Ireland, faced those who failed to pay their rent.

A permanent British military presence

A further consequence of the passing of the Act of Union was the permanent British military presence in Ireland. Barracks were built on the outskirts of many Irish towns and the presence of British troops was a constant reminder of British rule. Significantly, before introducing a police force on the mainland, Robert Peel (Chief Secretary for Ireland between 1812 - when he was aged just 24 - and 1818) had tried out the idea in Ireland first (the success of the pilot scheme in Ireland led to the development of a nationwide police force in mainland Britain). The British government's attitude towards Ireland in the early part of the 19th century was summed up by Arthur Wellesley (who later became the Duke of Wellington) when he was Chief Secretary in 1807:

'We have no strength here but our army...Ireland,

in a view to military operations, must be considered to be enemy's country.'

Robert Emmet's uprising

Another short-term consequence of the passing of the Act of Union was a further attempt at rebellion. Robert Emmet, a Protestant and a United Irishman, planned an uprising in Dublin in 1803 in the hope of reviving the enthusiasm for republicanism that had briefly surfaced at the end of the 18th century. Emmett and his co-conspirators planned to take control of Dublin Castle and declare an Irish Republic in the hope that this would lead to a general uprising throughout Ireland. Whatever the merits of the plan, its execution was totally inefficient. On 16 July 1803, a house containing hidden arms accidentally exploded, arousing the authorities' suspicions and panicking the conspirators into action. Although preparations were by no means complete, the 'uprising' went ahead on 23 July as planned. Poor communications, however, meant that, whereas Emmett expected a force of 2,000, just 80 turned up. The march on Dublin Castle became a farce. Emmett went into hiding. There was no sign of an uprising elsewhere in Ireland - not least because nobody had prepared for one. A month later Emmett was arrested. He was tried and executed and it was through his trial and execution that his reputation was sealed. He is reputed to have said in his trial:

'Let no man write my epitaph...When my country takes her place among the nations of the earth, then and not till then let my epitaph be written.'

Whether or not he actually did say this, his uprising became shrouded in myth and, to republicans, Emmet became one of Ireland's noblest heroes.

MAIN POINTS - Section 2.1

- Most historians agree that the impact of the Act of Union was limited: the political machinery did not change a great deal after 1801.
- That, however, does not mean that the passing of the Act was of little importance. Not only did the Act have great symbolic importance, it also framed the terms of political debate that took place in the 19th century and determined the political stance taken by the main political protagonists and their supporters.

- The consequences of the passing of the Act of Union were as follows: (1) in legal terms Ireland now had a very different status from other colonies; (2) the issue of Catholic emancipation remained unresolved; (3) Ireland continued to suffer economically; (4) the land question remained unresolved; (5) the presence of British troops was a constant reminder of British rule; (6) Robert Emmet's failed uprising provided a new martyr.

Activity 9.3 Robert Emmet's uprising of 1803

ITEM 1 Robert Emmet at the time of his trial: two views

ITEM 2 Robert Emmett's execution

There is said to have been a curious delay at the scaffold. Emmet, who was allowed by the hangman to give the signal for his own drop by letting go of a handkerchief, continually replied 'Not yet' to the hangman's repeated question: 'Are you ready, sir?' Finally, the hangman lost his patience and tipped him into eternity mid-sentence. The incident gave rise to some speculation as to whether or not Emmet was hoping for some last-minute rescue by some of Dwyer's men from Wicklow. But no rescue could have achieved the dramatic effect of the execution itself. After hanging for half an hour, his unconscious body was cut down and, in accordance with the judicial custom of the day, his head was cut off with a butcher's knife. It was exhibited by the hangman, who strode about the scaffold crying: 'This is the head of Robert Emmet, a traitor.'

The reason why the Emmet debacle should have become transformed into a myth of such powerful emotive force is not immediately easy to see. His failure could hardly have been more complete. It is true that the myth gained colour from Emmet's romantic attachment to Sarah Curran. Letters compromising her were found on Emmett at the time of his arrest and there is a story of her waiting in a closed carriage and waving a last farewell to him as he proceeded to the scaffold. But why was it Robert Emmet's portrait above all others that was to go up along with the crucifix in countless small homes in Ireland for over a century and may even be seen there still? The proximity of the crucifix may provide a clue. The success of the Emmett myth lay in the very need to ennoble failure. For tragic failure was to become part of Ireland's identity.

Adapted from Kee 1972.

Questions

1. Describe what views of Robert Emmet are presented by the two artists in Item 1 and how these images of his character might be historically significant.
2. Look at Item 2.
    a) Which elements surrounding Emmet's execution may have been myth and which fact?
    b) Write an account of Robert Emmet's execution from the viewpoint of a member of the British government.
    c) What was the long-term importance of Robert Emmet's uprising?

2.2 Why was the Roman Catholic Emancipation Act passed in 1829?

The struggle for Catholic emancipation 1800-23

In the early 19th century, prejudice against Catholics was widespread in mainland Britain:

'Though the old idea that Catholics were actively plotting to overthrow the Hanoverian dynasty had faded, most members of the political classes believed that it would be unwise to give full political rights to Roman Catholics when their loyalties were divided between allegiance to the British Crown and support for the spiritual supremacy of the pope at Rome, especially as the latter still ruled as an independent sovereign in the papal territories.' (Adelman 1996, pp.35-36)

To some extent, prejudice against Catholics was institutionalised. Although Catholics living in Britain had not been subjected to Penal Laws like those imposed on Irish Catholics, they were still barred from holding public office. Before entry to the House of Commons, for example, every MP had to swear that:

'The invocation or adoration of the Virgin Mary or any other saint and the sacrifice of the mass, as they are now used in the Church of Rome, are superstitious and idolatrous.'

Whilst it was not actually illegal for a Catholic to stand for Parliament, this oath ensured that, in practice, Catholics could not become MPs.

Historians writing about the mass movement in favour of Catholic emancipation that developed in Ireland in the 1820s have often remarked on the apparent irony that Catholic emancipation was an issue that affected only a small elite, since Parliament remained unreformed and the majority of Catholics would not qualify to vote, never mind being able to afford to stand for or take up public office. Yet, in Ireland in the 1820s, emancipation became the focus of a mass movement. One reason for this was that Catholic emancipation came to have a symbolic importance:

'The Irish peasant saw himself as the victim of injustice in almost all the relations of life: the landlord and the parson oppressed him; the magistrate refused him justice; his Protestant neighbour, simply as a Protestant, had the advantage of him at every turn...Emancipation was to put an end to all these grievances and to give the Irish Roman Catholic the freedom, and the equality of opportunity, hitherto denied him.' (Beckett 1981, p.300)

As noted in Section 2.1 above, the expectations of Irish Catholics were raised during the passage of the Act of Union and then dashed in 1801 when Pitt resigned. Until 1823, however, there was no organisation capable of channelling the frustration and desire for change desired by ordinary Irish Catholics.

Developments before 1824

Some historians argue that little progress was made before 1824:

> 'There was at this time a kind of vacuum in Irish politics. There was no national party in Parliament and no revolutionary movement in the country, though there was material for both. The demand for Catholic emancipation, which might have provided a programme and a rallying cry, was but feebly and timorously raised.' (Beckett 1981, p.285)

This view, however, underestimates the groundwork that was prepared in the period 1800-24. It is true that no breakthrough was made, but, when emancipation was finally conceded by the government (in 1829), Robert Peel made it clear that those responsible for pushing for emancipation in Parliament in the early part of the century had paved the way:

> '[Peel] traced the record of division in British governments since 1794: in every ministry there had been a division [a vote] on the issue; four of the five Houses of Commons elected since 1807 had pronounced, in some form or other, in favour of a settlement and the fifth only voted against by a margin of two votes. This reflected the divisions in the country.' (O'Ferrall 1985, p.247)

The Veto

The campaign for Catholic emancipation suffered during the first two decades of the 19th century because its supporters were divided. Some - including Henry Grattan, who led the campaign for emancipation in Parliament (he was elected MP in 1804) - supported 'safeguards' which, it was hoped, would ease Protestant fears:

> 'The proposed safeguards centred on two main conditions:
> 1. that the state should have some form of control over the appointment of Catholic bishops and possibly of parish priests;
> 2. that some state provision should be made for the payment of Catholic clergy.
>
> The reasons underlying both these conditions are easily appreciated - they indicate a desire...to institutionalise in some way the state's claims on the loyalty of the Catholic clergy.' (O'Tuathaigh 1990, p.50)

Other campaigners for Catholic emancipation, however, opposed compromise and argued strongly against the acceptance of the proposed safeguards - which were also known as the 'Veto' because they aimed to allow the British government to veto appointments. A strong opponent of the Veto was Daniel O'Connell (see Box 9.7). O'Connell and his supporters argued that the Veto would drive a wedge between the Catholic Church and the people (the freedom of the Catholic Church was seen as the last remnant of Irish independence).

BOX 9.7 | Daniel O'Connell

Daniel O'Connell was born in County Kerry in 1775, the nephew (and eventually the heir) of a Catholic landowner. He studied in France briefly, but fled to escape the developing extremism of the French Revolution. He then trained as a barrister in London in 1794-96 and, after that, worked in Dublin. In November 1797 he was forced to leave Dublin when it was alleged that he supported the United Irishmen. But he appears to have been genuinely horrified by the Rebellion of 1798. His first political appearance was in 1800 when he was one of the minority of Catholics openly hostile to the proposed Act of Union. From 1805 he was prominent in a succession of movements in support of Catholic emancipation. His strong opposition to the Veto, along with his rising fame as a barrister, established him as a Catholic champion.

Adapted from Connolly 1998.

Emancipation Bills 1808-21

In May 1808, Grattan introduced an Emancipation Bill in the House of Commons. The Bill included the proposed Veto but was defeated by 281 votes to 128. During the debate, Grattan claimed that he had been authorised to make his proposals by Irish Catholics - a claim that was angrily disputed by opponents of the Veto. The extent of opposition to the Veto became clear three months later when Irish Catholic bishops decided by an overwhelming majority to reject it.

Between 1808 and 1821, three further Emancipation Bills (all containing the Veto) were introduced in the House of Commons. The first was defeated in committee (1813). The second was defeated in the Commons by two votes (1819). The third (introduced by William Plunkett in 1821 and actually two bills - one for emancipation and one for the Veto) was passed by the Commons but defeated in the Lords. The defeat of Plunkett's Bill was a turning point:

> '1821 was the last occasion when quarrels over the Veto played a prominent part in the struggle; "unqualified emancipation" now became the slogan.' (O'Ferrall 1985, pp.8-9)

This was a victory, in particular for Daniel O'Connell, who had been a prominent campaigner for unqualified emancipation throughout the period. But it was only after the setting up of the Catholic Association in May 1823 that O'Connell was able to build a campaign which had the capacity to pressurise the government into making concessions.

The campaign for Catholic emancipation 1824-29

Historians agree that the key to the Catholic Association's eventual success was the decision made in January 1824 to reduce its membership fee from one guinea a year to one penny a month:

'This enabled poorer Catholics to join and identify closely with what might otherwise have seemed a remote cause. This, added to better organisation and a more energetic leadership, allowed the Catholic Association to found its emancipation claim not only on grounds of abstract justice...but also on mass support and mass pressure.' (Boyce 1992, pp.12-13)

The consequences of the decision to lower the membership fee were startling. Within months, the Catholic Association had become a truly mass movement. By the autumn of 1824, for example, the 'rent', as the one penny per month subscription became known, was averaging £300 per month, and by March 1825 over £19,000 had been collected. Not only did this provide the Catholic Association with a large political fighting fund, it also provided it with the mass backing to press its case. Over the next five years the Catholic Association used this mass support in two main ways.

1. Mass meetings

First, it organised a series of huge, outdoor public meetings, usually featuring Daniel O'Connell as the keynote speaker. O'Connell was a highly regarded barrister and, by all accounts, an effective orator. However, it is important to note that, although his rhetoric could be inflammatory, he had absolutely no time for violence or revolution. It was his clear and consistent belief that the only way in which the campaign would succeed was by acting within the law, and fighting a 'constitutional' campaign. The mass meetings were a way both of maintaining morale and of making a public display of strength.

2. Targeting forty-shilling voters

The second tactic cannot be credited to O'Connell, although he eventually benefited from it. In 1825, O'Connell was convinced that the extra-parliamentary pressure being exerted by the Catholic Association would bring victory and he supported an Emancipation Bill which contained two important clauses: a clause allowing state funding of Catholic priests' salaries, and a clause abolishing the forty-shilling franchise (most forty-shilling voters were Catholic tenant farmers who traditionally voted

according to the wishes of their landlord). O'Connell accepted these clauses on the grounds that:

- state payment would not interfere with priests' independence
- landlords prevented forty-shilling voters from voting independently (by threatening to evict tenants if they did not vote as they were directed).

The Emancipation Bill was defeated, but some members of the Catholic Association set out to prove O'Connell wrong about the forty-shilling voters. In the general election of 1826 the Association called upon forty-shilling voters in selected places (Waterford, Louth, Monaghan and Westmeath) to assert their independence by voting for pro-emancipation candidates. The backing of the Association and of the many local priests who supported it gave these voters the confidence to assert their independence at the ballot (money from the 'rent' as available to compensate any voter who was evicted by a spiteful landlord). The constituencies targeted by the Association were transformed. Green flags, sashes and banners (the colour of the Association) dominated proceedings and, with members of the Association patrolling the streets to keep order, there was (unlike previously) little drunkenness and no rioting. As a result of these tactics (see Box 9.8), four pro-emancipation candidates were elected, including the candidate in Waterford, where the local Tory landlord's family, the Beresfords, had controlled the seat for several generations.

The Clare by-election

The climax to this campaign came in May 1828 when a by-election was held in County Clare. Until this point the Catholic Association had supported Protestant candidates who had expressed their support for emancipation. In Clare, however, Daniel O'Connell himself (a Catholic) was persuaded to stand for election:

'O'Connell's candidature at County Clare faced the government with an intolerable dilemma. Since O'Connell was a Roman Catholic, he would be unable to take his seat in the House of Commons if elected - without a change in the law - in effect Catholic emancipation. To oppose his right to enter the Commons, however, would run the risk of widespread disorder and violence in Ireland with the unenviable prospect of further Catholic candidacies at elections in the future.' (Adelman 1996, p.40)

Once again, the Association's election campaign was characterised by great discipline.

'The discipline of the crowds was uncanny for an Irish election. Drunkenness was actually made a subject for mob punishment, offenders being thrown into the river where they were kept for

BOX 9.8 | The Louth election, 1826

I entered the contest with upwards of five-sixths of the votes promised to me...A systematic organisation was immediately developed. A lay committee was formed in every parish to **levy forced subscriptions**, to collect the people, to **harangue** them, and make them drunk. The priests preached in all their chapels the most violent sermons and visited every Catholic who had a vote. The eternal salvation of the voter being at stake, was distinctly the **proposition insisted on with the tenantry**...I was stated to be the enemy of the Church - the enemy of Christ...A personal fury almost **demoniacal** was thus raised against me, and soon became directed against all my supporters. Very many Protestants were forced to vote against me by the threats of assassination or having their houses burned. My voters were waylaid by large mobs along every line of road, and severely beaten, not merely in coming but in returning...When the poll commenced, all the priests of the county were collected and distributed through the different booths, where they stood with glaring eyes directly opposite to the voters of their respective **flocks** as they were severally brought up...The result of these proceedings was a very general **defection** of the tenants from their landlords as to their first votes, and one almost universal as to their second. Dawson's **legitimate force** was less than 120 votes; he polled 862, and all the difference proceeded from piracy. Lord Roden's **interest** was about 250 votes, he gave it to me heartily. Out of it I obtained about ten, and Dawson all the rest. There are two cousins of mine...From one of their estates I obtained about six votes and from the other literally but one.

Extract from a letter written by Leslie Foster to the Home Secretary, Robert Peel, on 8 July 1826.

Glossary

- **levy forced subscriptions** - force people to pay a fee
- **harangue** - give a good talking to
- **proposition insisted on with the tenantry** - message put to tenants
- **demoniacal** - devil-like
- **flocks** - ie congregations
- **defection** - falling away of support
- **legitimate force** - ie the votes he would have gained without intimidation
- **interest** - ie the number of tenants with votes

two hours and subjected to repeated duckings. The commander of the troops described how the people marched in regular columns under officers who gave orders to "keep in step" and "right shoulders forward" which were immediately obeyed.' (Kee 1972, p.185)

Once again, the campaign was a success. When the poll had been open for five days, William Vesey-

Fitzgerald (O'Connell's opponent) bowed to the inevitable and withdrew from the contest. O'Connell was elected by 2,057 votes to 982.

'The triumph of O'Connell convinced the Roman Catholics of their strength. In every part of the country there were great demonstrations of a semi-military character; and though they were peacefully conducted, the determination and confidence which inspired them could not fail to alarm the government.' (Beckett 1981, p.303)

The government's response

Lord Liverpool's resignation in February 1827 was followed by a period of instability in which the governing Tory Party split into factions (see Unit 5, Section 2.1). At the time of the Clare by-election, the Duke of Wellington was Prime Minister. The Duke of Wellington was an arch opponent of Catholic emancipation, but O'Connell's triumph and the demonstrations which followed it were enough to convince both Wellington and the Home Secretary, Robert Peel (also an arch opponent of Catholic emancipation), that a concession would have to be made to the Catholics. There were serious concerns that the situation in Ireland might deteriorate into civil war. Also, members of the government realised that, if other Catholics stood for Parliament, there was a real chance that they would be elected and simply gather together in an unofficial Catholic Parliament (which would challenge the legitimacy of the British Parliament). As a result of the conversion of Wellington and Peel, the Cabinet was able to persuade George IV of the necessity to act and the King's Speech in February 1829 duly announced that an Emancipation Bill would be introduced. This Bill was rushed through and became law in April 1829. It allowed Catholics to hold all public offices, but banned the Catholic Association and changed the electoral laws in Ireland, disenfranchising the forty-shilling voters and raising the property qualification to £10.

2.3 What were the lessons of the campaign?

The lessons of the campaign

According to the historian Robert Kee, the key to the success of the campaign for Catholic emancipation was the 'menacingly disciplined display of Irish opinion':

'It was this rather than the Emancipation Act which soon followed which was O'Connell's real victory. He made Irish popular opinion a force in British politics for the first time.' (Kee 1980, p.74)

A model for future campaigns

The consequences of this were far-reaching and not

just confined to Ireland. The success of the Catholic Association campaign revealed, for the first time, that it was possible for an extra-parliamentary group to exert so much pressure on a government (even a government in an unreformed Parliament) that the government was forced to take action. This pressure was all the more effective because constitutional methods were used - though the threat of violence (even revolution) was never far from the surface. This was a lesson which was soon learnt by other organisations:

'The modus operandi [way the operation worked] of the Catholic agitation served as a model for many subsequent pressure groups in British politics, most notably the Birmingham Reform Union and, later on, the anti-Corn Law League.' (O'Tuathaigh 1990, p.76)

There were also three other lessons which were to have a bearing on future campaigns - not that all were immediately apparent to contemporaries.

Parliamentary support was vital

First, an important reason for the campaign's success was that the groundwork was prepared. By 1823 there was a majority of MPs in favour of Catholic emancipation in the House of Commons. The presence of so many pro-emancipation MPs was an important source of pressure on the government. It is significant that, in the period 1838-48, Chartism - which, like the campaign for Catholic emancipation, was a genuinely mass movement - had hardly any support in Parliament and was, consequently, unable to achieve its goals (see Unit 6).

Fears of revolution were important

Second, there were genuine fears of a revolution in Ireland in 1828-30. When revolution broke out in France and Belgium in 1830, the Lord Lieutenant of Ireland, the Duke of Northumberland, was convinced that the passing of the Emancipation Act was the reason why Ireland had not followed suit:

'It is my clear conviction, if that law [the Emancipation Act] had not passed, that Ireland would have been at this moment in arms.' (Letter from Northumberland to Wellington, 2 October 1830)

The fact that the pro-emancipation campaign played on these fears of revolution was important. Its success suggested that Britain would make concessions only under the threat of revolution.

The campaign gained support from the 'other side'

And third, although the pro-emancipation campaign gained the mass support of Catholics, it did not just rely on its core supporters. It also carried along a substantial number of Protestants (for example, MPs were Protestants and yet there was strong support for emancipation in the Commons). It is true that there was anti-Orange rhetoric, but the campaign was by no means sectarian.

MAIN POINTS - Sections 2.2-2.3

- In the early 19th century, prejudice against Catholics was widespread in mainland Britain. Although Catholics living in Britain had not been subjected to Penal Laws, they were still barred from holding public office.
- Although no breakthrough was made before 1824, when emancipation was finally conceded by the government (in 1829) Robert Peel made it clear that earlier campaigning paved the way.
- The turning point came in January 1824 when the Catholic Association lowered its subscription to a penny a month. Within months a mass movement had developed.
- The Catholic Association used two main tactics to put pressure on the government. First, it held mass meetings. And second, it targeted seats and showed that it could manipulate the election result in favour of the Catholics.
- In May 1828, Daniel O'Connell won the Clare by-election. This presented the government with a dilemma - either allow O'Connell to enter the Commons (ie pass legislation) or prepare for violence and further Catholic candidacies. The government decided to legislate.
- The success of the emancipation campaign showed that (1) an extra-parliamentary mass movement using constitutional means could pressurise the government into action, (2) it was important to have support in Parliament, (3) threats of violence added pressure, and (4) it was important to gain support from the 'other side'.

Activity 9.4 Daniel O'Connell and the Clare by-election

ITEM 1 Daniel O'Connell

(i) Daniel O'Connell's family, though Catholic, had survived as landlords. His world was to a considerable extent still a Gaelic world and it is clear that he had a shrewd insight into the minds and ways of the people. His political principles and methods owed a great deal to British parliamentary conventions. The French Revolution was quite alien to his ways. He was deeply conservative on some issues - for example he opposed a French invasion in 1796. He wanted a Kingdom of Ireland with its own Parliament suitably reformed and opened to Catholics. The link with the Crown was an essential part of such thinking. In political terms, O'Connell's two great objectives were the repeal of the Act of Union and the winning of status for Irish Catholics. Even before the Act of Union was passed he declared his opposition to it. But the question of repeal did not have the same appeal as the demand for emancipation and he shaped his plans accordingly.

Adapted from Nowland 1984.

Daniel O'Connell

(ii) O'Connell was 25 at the time of the Union. He was, by then, a promising lawyer from County Kerry in south-west Ireland. Like many better-off Catholics in the 18th century, he had been educated in France - he left on the day of Louis XVI's execution. Appalled by the bloodshed in 1798, he was by the time of Emmet's fiasco a member of the loyalist Lawyers Artillery Corps. But although O'Connell rejected the United Irishmen's ideas of a separatist nationalism, he had a very strong emotive Irish consciousness and he successfully took over much of the United Irishmen's rhetorical thunder and converted it to his own uses. Indeed, his language was often indistinguishable from that of the separatist nationalists. For O'Connell, however, the British connection and acceptance of the Crown was never questioned. When George IV visited Ireland in 1821, he presented the king with a laurel crown on bended knee. The sort of nationality and Irish independence he supported was an extension to all people of Ireland on the very sort of independence within the Empire which Protestant Irishmen had so proudly insisted on for themselves in the 18th century.

Adapted from Kee 1972.

(iii) In the early 1820s, O'Connell was already a legendary figure because of his exploits in law and politics. The big, handsome man, with the head of copper curls and the bright blue eyes, had enormous energy and his cocky swagger inspired lowly Catholics with a confidence previously out of their experience. Political activity among Catholics had, up to then, centred on the country houses of aristocrats or the drawing rooms of wealthy merchants or lawyers in Dublin. O'Connell, as the 'man of the people' was conscious of the vast numbers of Irish Catholics and of his ability to make their numbers count. He was not a man to be crossed - his popular oratory was capable of bitter sarcasm - and his self-assured manner was often resented. To ordinary Catholics, however, who faced armed Orangemen swaggering at local fairs, who were burdened with rents, rates and tithes (a tax paid to the Church of Ireland), who went in fear of magistrates and who often faced despair and famine, O'Connell loomed as a great hero - the 'Counsellor' who could stand up against the Ascendancy and win against the odds.

Adapted from O'Ferrall 1985.

(iv) By 1826, O'Connell was the focal figure in Irish politics. Perhaps most importantly, his background blended Gaelic clansman and local Catholic gentry. Ignorant of Ulster, having rarely been north, his roots were deep in the family home in Kerry where he was reared. Fostered out to a local family, his first language was Irish, but he was not the 'man of the people' his European admirers often supposed. He dismissed the Irish language as a drawback in the modern world. This earned him the disapproval of later nationalists. It also gave him a genuine feeling for popular politics and an ability to identify with the people. His self-presentation in his letters bears examination. He was grandiose and self-mocking at once. He loved organisations, bands, public show, emotion, uniforms. He was, above all, a Catholic leader, playing the Catholic card. His victory at County Clare was a vast demonstration of populist political organisation and clerical power. Priestly influence had managed to dent that of the landlords. And it provided the possibility of a break-away Parliament of elected but unlawful Catholic MPs returned by well-drilled Catholic tenants.

Adapted from Foster 1988.

ITEM 2 The Catholic Association

Apart from its innovative ways of raising money, its organisational work and its great public meetings, the Catholic Association also used the press and even public posters to build up support. In many ways its work was pioneering. It was, in effect, the first major mass pressure group. Geographically its main area of support was in the South. In the North, O'Connell was seen by the large Protestant community as a Catholic rabble-rouser. Three main Catholic groups provided organisational support for the Association: (1) the urban middle classes (particularly lawyers), who hoped to gain most economically from emancipation; (2) the rural middle classes, whose links with the peasants were particularly important; and (3) the parish priests who did most to promote the Association at local level. The rapid growth of the Catholic Association and O'Connell's strong language at public meetings alarmed the authorities. He was arrested in 1824 on a charge of incitement to rebellion, but the prosecution failed. In 1825 the government, using the recently passed Unlawful Societies Act, banned the Association, but it was soon reorganised by O'Connell as the New Catholic Association. This remained within the letter of the law by confining its formal proceedings to issues of religion and public welfare, leaving direct airing of Catholic grievances to public meetings.

Adapted from Adelman 1996 and Connolly 1998.

ITEM 3 The Clare by-election

(i) In this cartoon a forty-shilling voter is being lobbied by a Catholic priest and a landlord. Many Catholic priests were involved in the campaign for emancipation.

Catholic electors of Clare

follow the great and glorious example of the forty-shilling freeholders of Waterford, Louth, Westmeath and other counties of Ireland. The Catholic Association have protected such of them as have been persecuted by their landlords for voting in favour of their religion and their country. The Catholic Rent and the Catholic Association will also protect the Catholics of Clare if they vote honestly and nobly for Daniel O'Connell.

(ii) *From the 'Address to the Independent Electors of Clare', written by O'Connell's agent Richard Scott and published on 28 June 1828.*

(iii) Everything is perfectly quiet! Thousands and thousands of people were marched into town this morning by Priests and returned to their bivouacs this evening in the same good order in which they entered it. No army can be better disciplined than they are. No drunkenness or any irregularity is allowed. O'Connell is called the Irish equivalent of George Washington. People instead of saying 'God be with you' say 'O'Connell be with you'. The children in the street sing 'Green is my livery' and the 'Liberty tree'.

From a report written by Baron Tuyll, the Lord Lieutenant's aide-de-camp, in June 1828.

(iv) I confess that what has moved me has been the Monaghan, the Louth, the Waterford and the Clare elections. I see clearly that we shall have to suffer from all the consequences of a practical democratic reform in Parliament if we do not do something to remedy the evil; and if I could believe that the Irish nobility and gentry would recover their lost influence, the just influence of property, without making these concessions, I would not stir.

Letter to Robert Peel from the Duke of Wellington 12 September 1828.

Questions

1. a) What does Item 1 tell us about (i) the character and (ii) the beliefs of Daniel O'Connell?
   b) Using Item 2 and your own knowledge, describe the nature of the Catholic Association.
   c) 'Without O'Connell, Catholic emancipation would not have been conceded in 1829'. Using Items 1 and 2, give arguments for and against this view.
2. Look at Item 3.
   a) What point is the cartoonist making in Item 3(i)?
   b) What do you think Richard Scott hoped to achieve by publishing the electoral address given in Item 3(ii)?
   c) What was the significance of the Clare by-election?
3. Using Items 1-3 and your own knowledge, explain how the Catholic Association managed to win its campaign in support of Catholic emancipation.

2.4 The origins of the Repeal movement 1829-35

The aftermath of the emancipation campaign

Since the Emancipation Act was not retrospective, Daniel O'Connell had to stand for re-election. Once the Act had gained royal assent and become law, he returned to County Clare and was duly re-elected, unopposed.

The Tithe War, 1830-33

The passage of the Emancipation Act was followed by a period of unrest in Ireland. Between 1830 and 1833, much of southern Ireland was engaged in the 'Tithe War' - a campaign against the payment of tithes (tithes were a tax on agricultural produce which went to the Church of Ireland). An agricultural depression, combined with raised expectations following the passage of the Emancipation Act, encouraged peasants and large landowners alike to refuse to pay their tithes, on the grounds that, as Catholics, they should not have to subsidise the Protestant Church of Ireland:

> 'By 1833, there were 22 counties in which half or more of tithes owed were unpaid. The campaign differed from contemporary agrarian protest in having the active support of large farmers who had been particularly affected by the return of tithes on pasture land under the Tithe Composition Act 1823 [between 1735 and 1823 tithes did not have to be paid on land under pasture]. It was openly supported by Archbishop MacHale, Bishop Doyle and many of the Catholic parish clergy as well as by local O'Connellite activists, although O'Connell himself kept his distance.' (O'Connolly 1998, p.543)

The campaign resulted in a breakdown in law and order and escalating violence as the authorities attempted to seize tithes from those refusing to pay them. Two particularly violent outbreaks occurred in 1831. In July, yeomen killed 14 campaigners in Newtownbarry in County Wexford and, in December, 12 police officers were killed by protesters. It was as a result of this unrest that the 1833 Coercion Law for Ireland was passed (see Box 9.9 below).

Origins of the Repeal movement

Throughout the campaign for Catholic emancipation, Daniel O'Connell had made no secret of his ultimate goal - the repeal of the Act of Union (usually shortened to 'Repeal'), a measure which had little support in Parliament. The dilemma O'Connell and his allies faced in the 1830s was between reform and Repeal. To what extent should they work with governments in the hope of bringing about reform and to what extent should they push towards the ultimate goal of Repeal (see Box 9.9)?

Barriers against Repeal

Although O'Connell and his allies attempted to channel the popular support for emancipation into a campaign for Repeal in the period 1829-35, they faced a number of problems. First, although the emancipation campaign had not been sectarian, there was something of a sectarian backlash following the passing of the Emancipation Act. Protestants - especially Tory 'Ultras' - felt that too much ground had been conceded to Catholics and opposed any measure which might provide them with further benefits. Second, Repeal lacked support in a Parliament dominated by MPs and peers from mainland Britain. O'Connell and his allies even made up a minority of Irish MPs - 39 pro-Repealers out of a total of 105 Irish MPs. Unlike the emancipation issue, which had gained momentum in Parliament, the idea of Repeal came up against a parliamentary brick wall. Third, there was some opposition to Repeal and a lack of enthusiasm amongst the Catholic middle classes, an attitude shared by most Catholic bishops (though not by the

BOX 9.9 | O'Connell after 1829

After the success of the emancipation campaign, O'Connell was able to give up the law and devote his whole time to politics, as he received a gift of £20,000 from Irish Catholics in recognition of his great services, and further regular payments afterwards, known as the 'O'Connell Tribute'. Since he was now both Irish national leader and a British parliamentary politician he had to decide what role to adopt. Should he concentrate on a policy of Repeal of the Act of Union and rely on another campaign in Ireland to ensure its success? Or should he use his new position in the House of Commons to press for immediate reforms in Ireland? In practice, O'Connell was never prepared to come down firmly on the side of Repeal or reform and veered from one to the other as circumstances dictated.

In the 1830 general election, 30 O'Connellite MPs were elected. Their support for Earl Grey, the Whig Prime Minister, was important in getting the 'Great' Reform Bill through Parliament in 1831-32. But the terms of the Act were disappointing to the Irish (the vote was not restored to the forty-shilling tenants and Ireland only obtained five new MPs). In the post-reform election, the O'Connellites emerged with 39 MPs, the largest bloc of Irish MPs in the Commons. But O'Connell was not prepared to cooperate fully with the Whigs - an attitude which seemed justified when they passed a new Coercion Law for Ireland in 1833, to last for just one year. This was one of the toughest pieces of legislation to affect Ireland in the 19th century. It gave the authorities wide powers of arbitrary arrest and imprisonment and control of public meetings.

Adapted from Adelman 1996.

majority of the lower clergy who supported Repeal):

'Many reforms, social and political, were obviously and urgently necessary; and it might seem more sensible to work for these, by pressure in Parliament, than to plunge the whole country into a fresh agitation. Moreover, many of these reforms, though by no means all, could command support not only among middle-class Roman Catholics but also among moderate Protestants in Ireland and Whigs and Radicals in Britain.' (Beckett 1981, p.307)

And fourth, there was some confusion over what exactly O'Connell hoped to achieve if the Act of Union actually was repealed:

'"Repeal" in theory meant the unqualified restoration of the pre-1800 Irish Parliament. In practice, O'Connell must have recognised that no British government would return to a definition of the Anglo-Irish connection as loose and undefined as the constitution of 1782. Instead, "Repeal" was at the same time an effective

slogan, the focus at popular level of extravagant... expectations, and an opening bid in a process of negotiation that might lead to some form of limited self-government.' (Connolly 1998, p.481)

The Lichfield House compact

The dilemma between Repeal and reform came to a head in 1834. In April, O'Connell brought a motion supporting Repeal before the House of Commons. The motion was comprehensively defeated by 523 votes to 38 (with just one non-Irish MP voting for Repeal).

1834 - the year of four Prime Ministers

Three months after the rejection of Repeal by the Commons, the Prime Minister, Earl Grey, resigned. O'Connell had found it increasingly difficult to support Grey's government, partly because the property qualification for voting had not been lowered in Ireland despite the support given to parliamentary reform by O'Connell and his allies, and partly because the Grey administration had passed the repressive Coercion Act of 1833. Grey's resignation, therefore, raised the possibility that a government more sympathetic to the O'Connellite MPs' demands might be formed. In other words, in 1834 the pendulum began to swing towards reform rather than Repeal.

In July 1834 another Whig, Viscount Melbourne, formed a government, but this collapsed in November after Viscount Althorp, the Chancellor of the Exchequer and Leader of the Commons, inherited his father's title and moved to the Lords. The Duke of Wellington took over as caretaker Prime Minister for a month and then Robert Peel formed a minority government.

An agreement is negotiated

In March 1835, Whigs, radical MPs and O'Connellites met and made an informal agreement to cooperate (the Lichfield House compact). By joining forces, they were able to overthrow Peel's minority government. The O'Connellites then agreed to support a minority Whig government led by Melbourne - in exchange for promises that the government would introduce reforms which benefited Irish Catholics. For five years, the issue of Repeal remained on the back burner as O'Connell and his allies supported Melbourne's government (see Box 9.10).

2.5 The revival of the Repeal campaign after 1840

Why did O'Connell's tactics change in 1841?

At the time when the Lichfield House compact was agreed, O'Connell asserted:

'The people of Ireland are ready to become a

276 The consequences of the Act of Union

BOX 9.10 The Whig reforms 1835-41

From the O'Connellites' point of view, the decision to support the Melbourne government produced mixed results. The Tithe Rentcharge Act (1838) went some way to ending popular discontent with the tithe system (the tithe now became a fixed additional rent charge, payable by the landlord). The 1840 Corporations Act attempted to apply to Ireland the main features of the 1835 Act which had applied to England, but opposition in the House of Lords ensured that its terms were narrower - it was based on a £10 household suffrage (in England the suffrage was wider) and the powers of the new elected Irish councils were more limited than in England (control of the police was excluded, for example).

The 1840 Act, however, did offer some opportunities to Catholics. The O'Connellites won control of ten councils, for example, and O'Connell himself became the first Catholic Lord Mayor of Dublin since the reign of James II (1685-88). The real gains, however, were in the day-to-day administration of Ireland. The new Lord Lieutenant, Chief Secretary and Under-Secretary ensured that 30-40% of appointments (of magistrates, for example) went to Catholics and many others to liberal Protestants. Law enforcement became more impartial (a new national police force was established and Catholics encouraged to join). The extremist Protestant Orange Order (a Protestant political society set up to defend Protestants against Catholics) voluntarily disbanded after a parliamentary committee set up by the Whig government published a highly critical report in which it accused the Orange Order of infiltrating the yeomanry and the army.

In real terms, however, Irish Catholics gained little of real substance, mainly because measures had to pass through the Tory-dominated House of Lords. Ireland was still treated differently from Britain and the power of the Protestant Ascendancy remained unbroken.

Adapted from Adelman 1996 and Connolly 1998.

portion of the Empire, provided they be made so in reality and not in name alone; they are ready to become a kind of West Britons if made so in benefits and in justice; but if not, we are Irishmen again.'

As the historian James Beckett points out (1981, p.318), the crucial phrase here is 'but if not, we are Irishmen again'. The point O'Connell was clearly making was that he was prepared to give the government time to implement significant reform - to show that Ireland really was to be treated as an equal partner in the United Kingdom, but, if after sufficient time had elapsed little of significance had been achieved, then he would resort to more populist tactics.

The traditional view of the period of cooperation (see Box 9.10) is that Irish Catholics gained little of real substance. In other words, the alliance was one-sided. The government gained what it wanted (Irish parliamentary support), but O'Connell was forced to compromise time and time again. Although some historians dispute this view (Foster 1991, p.188, for example), there is no doubt that, when the Whigs lost office in November 1841, O'Connell and his allies changed their tactics radically - from pursuing the parliamentary route to reform, to rebuilding a mass campaign in support of Repeal.

Reasons for the change in tactics

On one level, this change in tactics was purely a response to political circumstances. O'Connell and his allies knew that the limited reforms achieved under the Whigs were unlikely to be furthered by the new Tory government which came into power under Robert Peel in 1841. On another level, there was a clash of personalities. Enmity between O'Connell and Peel went back to the period when Peel served in Ireland as Chief Secretary (1812-18). O'Connell assumed that his opinions would carry little weight with the new regime. On a third level, the change in tactics was a response to falling popular support and a discontent amongst supporters:

'Already in 1838, [O'Connell] had founded the Precursor Society, which was to be a prelude to a new Repeal initiative if "full and prompt justice for Ireland" were not forthcoming soon. In founding this society, he was responding to the deep dissatisfaction of a section of his supporters with the inadequacy of Whig legislation, and also to the fact that the cessation of skirmishing between the government and the "movement" had caused a considerable falling off in popular interest in O'Connellite politics.' (O'Tuathaigh 1990, p.185)

Developments in 1841

At first there was little sign that a mass movement in support of Repeal could be built. A Repeal Association was set up in 1841 along the same lines as the Catholic Association (with a penny-a-month subscription which became known as 'Repeal rent'), but the 1841 general election returned just 18 pro-Repeal MPs. Then, in November 1841, O'Connell was elected Lord Mayor of Dublin (the first Catholic elected to this post since 1688). On taking up office, he made a pledge of strict political impartiality for his year in office - a pledge which, on the whole, he kept. As a result, the pro-Repeal movement lacked his formidable presence for a year.

Developments in 1842

In 1842, however, a combination of factors led to a

change in the political climate in Ireland. These are outlined in Box 9.11.

BOX 9.11 **A changing political climate in Ireland in 1842**

The following factors combined to ensure that the political climate changed in Ireland in 1842:

- A bad harvest in 1842 resulted in widespread distress and discontent.
- The influential Catholic Archbishop MacHale of Tuam publicly declared his support for Repeal, a lead quickly followed by many bishops and the majority of the lower clergy.
- Propaganda produced by a new nationalist group ('Young Ireland') began to make an impact via the group's new newspaper *The Nation* (which was launched in October 1842 and had a readership estimated at over a quarter of a million by the beginning of 1843).
- Momentum - towards the end of 1842, the structure of the Repeal Association had begun to resemble that of the Catholic Association at its height with local branches springing up throughout the country and subscriptions rising significantly.
- Throughout 1842 and 1843, Daniel O'Connell remained in Ireland concentrating on the Repeal campaign rather than on his parliamentary duties.

Monster Meetings in 1843

The main tactic used to press for Repeal in 1843 was the organisation of what *The Times* in London described as 'Monster Meetings' - huge public meetings at which O'Connell and other speakers put forward the case for Repeal. As in the campaign for emancipation, these meetings were huge but disciplined. As in the campaign for emancipation, O'Connell backed up his demands with an implied threat that, unless they were met, the masses would rise up in arms.

Why was the campaign unsuccessful?

In 1828-29 the threat that, unless concessions were made, the masses would rise up in arms had been enough to ensure government action. In 1843, however, it was not - for a number of reasons.

Peel's position

First, in 1828-29 the Tory government under Wellington lacked the solid majority that the Tory government under Peel enjoyed in 1843. Peel could be certain of carrying the Commons with him on the question of Repeal whereas Wellington could not on the question of emancipation. This essential difference became evident over the question of civil war. Whilst Wellington reluctantly made a U-turn and conceded emancipation because he was

genuinely concerned that civil war would break out, in May 1843, Peel made a speech in the House of Commons in which he said:

> 'Deprecating [disliking] as I do all war, but, above all, civil war, yet there is no alternative which I do not think preferable to the dismemberment of this Empire.'

This attitude did not only reflect Peel's position of strength in Parliament, it also reflects his confidence that public opinion - in Britain at least - was behind him (unlike in 1828-29 when there was a groundswell of support for emancipation).

A lack of democratic legitimacy

Second, a crucial difference between the two campaigns was that the emancipation campaign gathered momentum with a run of successes at the polls, culminating in the Clare by-election. By disenfranchising the forty-shilling voters who had done so much to put pressure on the government to pass the Emancipation Act, however, Earl Grey's Whig government had ensured that the majority of Irish MPs elected after 1830 were Whigs or Tories, and were therefore wholeheartedly opposed to Repeal. When the Whig regime came to an end in 1841, the number of pro-Repealers in the Commons had dwindled to 18 (partly because O'Connell and his allies had supported the Whig government and had therefore suffered from its loss of popularity). So, whereas success at the polls had bolstered the extra-parliamentary campaign in 1826-28, O'Connell and his allies resorted to an extra-parliamentary campaign after 1841 because of their failure at the polls. As a result, the later campaign lacked the democratic legitimacy of the earlier campaigns.

The meeting at Clontarf, October 1843

Third, a reason for the success of the emancipation campaign had been its novelty. O'Connell had called the government's bluff and won. In 1843, however, the tables were turned. Peel called O'Connell's bluff and won. When the Repeal Association announced that a Monster Meeting was to be held at Clontarf in the outskirts of Dublin on 8 October, crowds began to converge there from all over the country. But on 7 October the government declared the meeting illegal (on the grounds that the notices summoning the meeting implied that it was to have a military character) and sent troops to enforce the decision. The leadership of the Repeal Association immediately backed down. Messages were sent out cancelling the meeting and those on their way were turned back (without any disturbance of the peace). This was a turning point. Although O'Connell had always argued that the campaign should be constitutional, backing down like this disappointed rank and file members of the Repeal movement. As a result:

'[O'Connell] never again enjoyed the completely dominant position that he had held on the eve of the Clontarf meeting.' (Beckett 1981, p.327)

O'Connell becomes a spent force

A week later O'Connell and his close associates were arrested and charged with conspiracy. In February 1844, O'Connell was fined and jailed and, although the prison governor received those convicted as guests in his house and although the House of Lords overturned the verdict in September 1844, there is a consensus among historians that:

'The spell in prison, though every comfort was given him, had taken its toll of [O'Connell's] mental and physical resources.' (O'Tuathaigh 1990, p.192)

MAIN POINTS - Sections 2.4-2.5

- Although O'Connell and his allies attempted to channel the popular support for emancipation into a campaign for Repeal in the period 1829-35, they faced (1) a sectarian backlash, (2) lack of support in Parliament, (3) lack of support amongst the Catholic middle classes, and (4) confusion over what would happen after Repeal.
- Following Parliament's overwhelming rejection of Repeal and Grey's resignation, the O'Connellites agreed to support a Whig government in the hope of achieving reforms. The struggle for Repeal was temporarily halted.
- In 1841, the O'Connellites' tactics changed for three main reasons: (1) political circumstances had changed - a Tory government had been elected; (2) O'Connell realised that Peel, an old enemy, was unlikely to listen to his demands; and (3) O'Connell's support was declining.
- A Repeal Association was set up in 1841, but it was only in 1842 that it began to grow into a mass movement due to (1) a bad harvest, (2) support from the Catholic Church, (3) propaganda from Young Ireland, (4) momentum, and (5) O'Connell's presence in Ireland.
- The Repeal Association failed because (1) Peel's position was much stronger than Wellington's in 1828-29, (2) the movement lacked democratic legitimacy, (3) on being confronted by the authorities in October 1843, O'Connell backed down, and (4) O'Connell's spell in prison exhausted him.

Activity 9.5 Daniel O'Connell and Repeal

ITEM 1 Notice issued on 7 October 1843 at 3pm

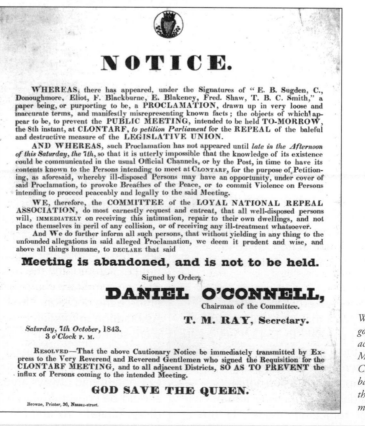

When faced with government military action to prevent a Monster Meeting at Clontarf, O'Connell backed down and issued this notice cancelling the meeting.

ITEM 2 Monster Meetings

(i) I came here to recruit. I want you to enlist with me; and reversing the old method of enlisting, where they gave the recruit a shilling, I want you to enlist by giving a shilling to me...I am one who would give the last drop of his life's blood and smile to see it flow to do any good for Ireland. I would wish to have life to make Ireland free, to get that without which she can never be prosperous or happy, to get Ireland for the Irish and the Irish for Ireland.

Extract from O'Connell's speech at the Monster Meeting in Trim, reported in the Nation *on 25 March 1843.*

(ii) They tell us there will be civil war if we attempt to get the repeal - bah! We will put them in the wrong, and, if a civil war should break out, it must be of their making. And I will tell you what, if they attack us then, who will be the coward? We will put them in the wrong, and if they attack us, then in your name I set them at defiance.

Extract from O'Connell's speech at the Monster Meeting at Longford, reported in the Nation *on 3 June 1843.*

(iii) We are at Tara of the Kings, emphatically the spot from which emanated then the social power - the legal authority - the right to dominion over the furthest extremes of this island...The strength and majority of the national movement was never exhibited so imposingly as at this great meeting. The numbers exceed any that ever before congregated in Ireland in peace or war. It is a sight not grand alone, but appalling - not exciting merely pride but fear. Such an army - for you have the steadiness and order of trained men - no free state would willingly see in its bosom, if it were not composed of its choicest citizens. The great review of the Volunteers was the precursor of Ireland's independence - the repealers of Tara outnumber as three to one the citizen army of 1782. Step by step we are approaching the great goal itself; but it is at length with the strides of a giant.

Extract from O'Connell's speech at the Monster Meeting at Tara, reported in the Nation *on 19 August 1843.*

KING O'CONNELL AT TARA.

This Punch *cartoon portrays O'Connell as King of the Irish, enthroned at Tara, the ancient royal seat of Ireland. Peasants prostrate themselves and bring gifts. O'Connell uses the British Constitution as a footstool, and rests his elbow on a pair of scales labelled 'Justice to Ireland'. A lurking devil rests one hand on a document headed 'Dan's allowance' which tilts the scales.*

ITEM 3 O'Connell and Repeal

During the debate held in Parliament on the question of repeal (in April 1834), O'Connell stated clearly the exact constitutional position he was aiming at. Ireland, he said, should be regarded 'not as a subordinate province, but as a limb of the Empire - as another and distinct country, subject to the same King, but having a legislature totally independent of the legislature of Great Britain'. He put this forward as a simple call to restore Ireland to the station it occupied 'when I was born'. But it was, of course, naive to pretend that what he sought was no different from the old Protestant Ascendancy's idea of national sovereignty. Political circumstances had changed out of all recognition since 1782. Catholic emancipation and the Reform Act had altered the whole balance of power in Ireland. Irish national sovereignty under the Crown now meant, not a nation ruled by a small elite, but an increasingly democratic nation. O'Connell also argued that repeal would not lead to separation. This was to remain the central point of debate for the rest of the century. The arguments would apply whether the issue at stake was Repeal (a wholly independent Irish government under the Crown) or, as later, Home Rule (an Irish government with limited powers under the Crown). Opponents of Repeal or Home Rule always argued that concession would lead to further Irish national demands and eventually to total separation. Repealers and Home Rulers, however, argued that the only danger of separation arose from a refusal to grant Irish demands since this would play into the hands of the small minority of separatists.

Adapted from Kee 1972.

Questions

1. Why did O'Connell's campaign for emancipation succeed but his campaign for Repeal fail? Use Items 1-3 in your answer.
2. a) What do Items 1 and 2 tell us about (i) the nature of the Monster meetings held in 1843 and (ii) O'Connell's leadership style?
   b) What criticism is suggested in the cartoon, and why might the English cartoonist want to portray O'Connell in this way?
   c) Why did these meetings fail to persuade the authorities to meet the Repeal Association's demands?
3. a) Read Item 3 and then write the arguments which you would expect (i) Daniel O'Connell and (ii) an opponent of Repeal to use in the debate over Repeal which was held in the Commons in April 1834.
   b) Using Item 3, explain how Irish nationalism changed during the period 1780-1845.

3 The Great Famine

Key issues

1. What factors led to the Great Famine?
2. What policies did the British government pursue?
3. Was the Great Famine inevitable?

3.1 What factors led to the Great Famine?

The extent of the Great Famine

In the autumn of 1845, the potato crop failed in Ireland - as it did in several other European countries, notably Belgium and Holland. Although people did not know it at the time, the potato plants which suffered from 'blight' in 1845 and the years which followed were attacked by *Phytophthora infestans*, a fungus which thrives in damp conditions destroying first the leaves and stalk of the potato plant and then the potato tubers. This was a new disease (no treatment was discovered until the 1880s) and in Ireland its impact over the next seven years was devastating. Whilst the 1841 census shows that Ireland had a population of 8.17 million people, the next census (taken in 1851 as the 'Great Famine' neared its end) showed that the population had dropped to 6.55 million. Although this decline can be explained in part by the large-scale emigration of the late 1840s, there is a consensus amongst historians that around one million Irish people lost their lives as a result of the Great Famine.

Dependence on potatoes in the 1840s

To understand why the disaster was on such a large scale, it is necessary to understand the role played by potatoes in Ireland in the 1840s:

'The poorer classes, who ate them exclusively, consumed potatoes in large amounts: an average male would have eaten approximately 12 pounds [5.4 kilos] per day throughout most of the year, less during the so-called "hungry months" of June, July and August.' (Kinealy 1995, p.19)

The 'average male' mentioned above and his family ate potatoes and little or nothing else. Most did not even eat bread because they did not have any cash to buy it. Each year, they grew potatoes on the land they rented, stored them and gradually ate their way through them. Excess potatoes (and peelings) might be fed to a pig or chickens - so that their owners could sell them to pay the rent. By June, the store of potatoes would be low and the family would have to miss meals. By August, the family would be genuinely hungry. If the crop failed, it is easy to see how a crisis would quickly develop.

Total dependence and the 'land question'

In most parts of Ireland it was in the second half of the 18th century that this total dependence on the potato had developed. In 1802, for example, William Tighe, a landowner from Kilkenny recorded:

'Before [the introduction of the apple potato], the cottagers frequently sowed beans...and had little plots like a small kitchen garden...but the apple potato has superseded everything of this sort.' (Tighe 1802, pp.479-80)

This dependence on the potato was bound up in the so-called 'land question' (see Section 2.1 above). It is just about possible to live off potatoes with little or no dietary supplements (medical records from the late 18th century suggest that the Irish poor were healthier than the British poor because they subsisted mainly on potatoes rather than bread). Since enough potatoes for a year could be grown on a small patch of land, larger tenants could sub-let small patches of land:

'On the eve of the famine, 45% of the tenancies in Ireland were for land of between one and five acres. In some areas in the west of Ireland, the figure was as high as 70%...Of a population of 8.25 million people, two-thirds lived off the land and one-third was wholly dependent on the potato.' (Downing 1980, p.39)

The problem was that there was no slack in the system. If the crop failed or was lower than usual, families simply could not manage. This had been demonstrated on a number of occasions before 1845. The potato crop had failed in 1817-19, 1822 and 1831-32. When it failed in 1817-19, an estimated 50,000 people died (Kinealy 1995, p.19).

Population growth

A further factor adding strain to the system was growth in population. Although some historians argue that growth was slowing by the 1840s, there had been a significant increase. Whilst the population of Ireland in 1800 was around 4.5 million, it had grown to 8 million by the time of the official census in 1841. As a result, land was further subdivided and more people subsisted on potatoes.

The course of the Great Famine

Potato blight was first found in Ireland in September 1845. By the late autumn it had spread to 17 counties and around one-third of the crop was lost. This caused some hardship, but the effect was by no means catastrophic. The real problems began when the blight struck again in August 1846. The crop of 1846 was a total failure:

'By late 1846, famine conditions were widespread. Nature played another cruel trick with the hopes of those dependent on the potato in 1847. Because of the scarcity of seed and the signals given by the failures of 1845 and 1846, the acreage planted in 1847 was small. Yields per acres turned out to be generous, however, encouraging people to revert to planting a bigger acreage in 1848. But, in 1848, the crop failed disastrously once more.' (O'Grada 1993, p.103)

The blight peaked with the failure of the crop in 1848, but it did not end in that year. In 1849-51 it struck again in some areas, though its impact on Ireland as a whole was less severe. It was only in 1852 that the potato crop was almost totally free from blight and even after that year the blight reappeared from time to time.

The first deaths from starvation occurred in October 1846, but, as in most famines, it was disease rather than starvation which claimed most of the victims. Contagious diseases such as typhus (in 1847) and cholera (in 1848) reached epidemic proportions and other diseases associated with malnutrition, such as scurvy, accounted for many other deaths. Lack of adequate medical facilities ensured that many who contracted these diseases died:

'The provision of medical facilities in Ireland had been amongst the best in Europe - a network of hospitals and dispensaries existed by 1845. But this provision was often rudimentary and ill-distributed, and was overwhelmed as the Famine passed into its second year.' (Gray 1995, p.57)

3.2 What measures did the government take to relieve the Famine?

Peel's government

In autumn 1845, the British Prime Minister was Robert Peel. He had served as Chief Secretary in Ireland (1812-18) and had experienced the food crisis of 1817-19 first hand. Peel's government acted swiftly, making three important decisions. First, in November 1845 a large supply of maize was shipped from the USA to Ireland for sale at a low price:

'It was not Peel's intention that the government should undertake responsibility for feeding the people; but he believed that by selling this grain cheaply it would be possible to keep down the general price of food.' (Beckett 1981, p.337)

Second, a Relief Commission was set up to organise local relief committees. These committees were to sell cheap food to the poor and to begin public works programmes which, by providing employment for the poor, would enable them to afford the cheap food. Over 650 committees were set up by January 1846.

And third, Peel repealed the Corn Laws (see Unit 7, Section 3.2). This ensured that grain prices (and therefore bread prices) fell - not that this helped the poor in Ireland as they could not afford bread anyway. The repeal of the Corn Laws split the Tories and resulted in the downfall of Peel's government in July 1846.

Some historians have praised Peel's actions. O'Tuathaigh, for example, describes the measures as 'prompt', energetic and imaginative' (1990, p.208). But Peel had resigned by the time that food shortages in Ireland had really begun to bite. Besides, the measures he introduced were not in themselves enough to prevent widespread starvation and disease from 1847 onwards.

Russell's government

The new Whig government, headed by Lord John Russell, had clear ideas about how to deal with food shortages in Ireland:

'The state role in alleviating Irish distress ought to be confined to providing employment on public works which, ideally, ought to be of a non-productive nature; the provision of food ought to be left to private enterprise, except in isolated areas where a very limited degree of state intervention seemed unavoidable; the cost of relieving Irish distress should, in the final analysis, fall on Irish shoulders.' (O'Tuathaigh 1990, p.212)

As a result, the government at first refused to purchase corn (as Peel had done), arguing that food imports should be left to market forces.

Whig policy towards the Famine passed through three distinct phases.

Phase 1 - a new programme of public work

At first, the government relied on a new programme of public work overseen by a central Board of Works but organised and financed on a local basis (through local rates). Wages were deliberately set at a level barely sufficient to prevent starvation to discourage scrounging. The programme, however, was not a success. First, red tape delayed the launch of the schemes and prevented some wages being paid on time or even at all. And second, the schemes were unable to cater for the huge numbers who needed relief. Between October 1846 and spring 1847 the number employed on public works increased from 250,000 to 720,000.

Phase 2 - outdoor relief

The second phase began in January 1847, when the decision was made to wind up the public works and to resort to an emergency scheme of outdoor relief (in other words, to set up soup kitchens to feed the needy who were not in workhouses). Although this decision was taken in January, it was only in March that the relief works were wound down and, in some places, soup kitchens only began distributing food in June. For many, this delay was fatal. Nevertheless, by July more than 3 million people were receiving rations from soup kitchens. The result was a sharp decline in deaths.

Phase 3 - The Poor Law Extension Act, June 1847

The emergency scheme of outdoor relief was always intended to be a temporary measure, and in June 1847 government policy entered its third phase. Campaigners argued that soup kitchens were an extravagant burden on British taxpayers and that an extension of the Poor Law should place responsibility for looking after the poor on localities. The result was the Poor Law Extension Act (of June 1847) which allowed relief to be given to those outside workhouses as well as to those inside. The cost of this relief was to be found by raising local rates (with the government advancing a loan, repayable with interest, to set the scheme up). As a concession to Irish landowners, the government agreed to the 'Gregory clause', which stipulated that anybody with more than a quarter of an acre of land was to be excluded from relief. This meant that those with small farms had to abandon them and go to the workhouse if they wanted relief.

From mid-August the soup kitchens were phased out. By October the workhouses were full. The existing system was designed to provide relief for 100,000 people, but in the winter of 1847-48 over 1.5 million people needed relief. Outdoor relief was provided to cope with this demand and by June 1848 over 800,000 people were receiving outdoor relief in the form of food rations (in return for doing jobs such as breaking stones). The system simply could not cope and mortality rates grew rapidly again. Further aid from the government, however, was not forthcoming.

Rate-in-aid

By May 1849 it was clear that, in the areas where the Famine was biting hardest, local rates could not meet the demands placed on them. As a result, the government introduced a 'rate-in-aid', which taxed the eastern and northern parts of Ireland, providing funds for workhouses in the west. This was not only greatly resented in the north and east (especially in Ulster), it also showed (again) that the government was unwilling to step in to provide relief.

Voluntary groups and the Famine

From the start of the Famine, charities and other voluntary groups took independent action to provide relief. From November 1846, for example, the Quaker Central Relief Committee began to organise soup kitchens. Quakers also did a great deal of useful work collecting and disseminating accurate information.

In addition, aid came from British charities (such as the British Association, which collected over £400,000) and from the USA, where funds and foodstuffs were collected and shipped across the Atlantic (over 100 ships reached Ireland in 1847).

As time went on, however, 'famine fatigue' set in - especially after the summer of 1847, when reports in Britain suggested that, because of the 'success' of the harvest, the Famine was over. Also, some Protestant voluntary bodies made relief dependent on conversion to Protestantism - a condition which produced a great deal of ill will. In addition:

'Severe economic recession in Great Britain itself during 1847 further limited sympathy for Ireland's problems, as did the apparent ingratitude for help given displayed in the return of 36 Repeal MPs in the general election of 1847 and the Young Ireland rebellion of 1848.' (Connolly 1998, p.228)

The Young Ireland rebellion is discussed in Box 9.12. By the end of 1848, private charity had dried up and in June 1849 the Quakers abandoned their work, arguing that the government should supply aid.

BOX 9.12 | The Young Ireland rebellion of 1848

Young Ireland was a romantic nationalist group, active in the years 1842-48. The group was mainly made up of middle-class graduates from both Protestant and Catholic backgrounds. It aimed to promote a non-sectarian sense of national identity and believed it necessary to promote a national literature and to revive the Irish language. The group was involved in the Repeal movement, but clashed with O'Connell in 1844-45. Young Ireland first gave serious thought to an uprising after the Paris revolution of February 1848, but failed to win the support of the French revolutionary government or to cooperate effectively with the Chartists. After the conviction of John Mitchel (a leading member of Young Ireland) in May, a conspiracy was formed for a rising after the harvest, and a war council was elected. The government, fully informed by its spy network, responded quickly by swamping Dublin with troops and announcing the suspension of Habeas Corpus (on 21 July). Members of the war council abandoned Dublin and tried to raise forces in the south. Crowds of poorly armed peasants assembled to hear the leaders, but dispersed rapidly in the face of clerical opposition and the failure to distribute food. A last stand was made in Ballingarry, County Tipperary, when 100 rebels confronted a party of police. The police refused calls to surrender and killed two of the rebels. The remaining rebels dispersed as military reinforcements arrived. The rising collapsed and the leaders either fled to the USA or were arrested. Those arrested were transported.

Adapted from Connolly 1998.

Was the Great Famine inevitable?

Historians are divided about who or what was responsible for the Great Famine and whether or not a disaster on this scale was somehow inevitable. The main arguments can be summarised as follows.

The traditional view

The traditional view focuses on three key areas.

1. The policy of the British government

First, the traditional view is that, whilst pre-Famine economic developments (especially over-dependence on the potato) meant that a severe food shortage was inevitable if the potato crop failed (especially if it failed for more than one year), the scale of the actual disaster was increased dramatically by British government inaction. In other words, it was the policies pursued by the British government which ensured that a crisis escalated into a major disaster. In particular, supporters of this viewpoint criticise the British government's ideological obsession with laissez-faire economics.

Reliance on market forces, they argue, was an entirely inappropriate response, as was the premise that local rate-payers (rather than central government) should finance relief.

2. The role of Charles Trevelyan

Second, some historians have criticised the role of the senior civil servant Charles Trevelyan, the permanent Head of the Treasury, who was entrusted with implementing the policies initiated by Peel and who remained in charge of relief measures under Russell. Trevelyan, it is argued, was a dogmatic free marketeer who shaped the government's policy towards Ireland during the Famine. Trevelyan (like many of his contemporaries) also believed that the Famine was nature's way (or God's way) of dealing with overpopulation in Ireland. The logic of this argument was not only that the Famine was somehow inevitable, but also that it would be 'unnatural' to intervene.

3. The question of exports

And third, there is the question of exports. Throughout the Famine, Ireland continued to export a great deal of foodstuff to Britain and elsewhere. Kinealy calculates, for example that:

> 'On the eve of the Famine, sufficient corn was being exported to Britain to feed an estimated two million people.' (Kinealy 1995, p.19)

Some historians have argued that if this food had been used to feed people in Ireland rather than being exported, the distress caused by the Famine would have been mitigated.

The revisionist view

Each of the viewpoints outlined above has been challenged by revisionist historians.

1. The machinery of government

First, there is the argument that it was not the British government's ideological commitments that were to blame, but the machinery of government. The government did make mistakes, but generally these mistakes were due to the time taken to implement policies, not to the policies themselves:

> 'No British government wanted the Irish people to starve...Much of the failure of the government's measures was because of its slowness to grasp the scale of disaster (and, even more important, to anticipate its recurrence) and the difficulty of administering relief in the more remote areas which had poor communications.' (Boyce 1992, p.33)

2. The pre-famine economy

Second, some historians have examined the pre-famine economy and noted that it was more diverse and less poverty-stricken than once thought. As a result:

'The pre-famine economy, for all its problems and injustices, did not contain the seeds of its own inevitable destruction by famine.' (O'Grada 1993, p.40)

3. The role of Charles Trevelyan

Third, there is the argument that, although Trevelyan was in a powerful position, blame should not be attached to him personally. He was a civil servant and his personal views on policy only prevailed because they fitted with the views held by members of the Cabinet.

4. The question of exports

And fourth, there is scepticism about the idea that the food exported from Ireland during the Famine could somehow be used to feed people in distress:

'More than twice as much food came into Ireland as left it in 1846-47. Imported maize and rice were cheaper than the grain sent to Britain, and both merchants and landowners insisted that any ban on exports would destroy the confidence required to support these shipments, while creating a disincentive for farmers to plant for the following year.' (Gray 1995, pp.46-47)

MAIN POINTS - Part 3

- The Great Famine began after blight affected the potato crop in 1845. Blight continued to affect the potato crop until 1852. Around one million Irish people lost their lives as a result of the Great Famine. The famine was on such a wide scale because many people were totally dependent on the potato crop.
- The first deaths from starvation occurred in October 1846, but, as in most famines, it was disease rather than starvation which claimed most of the victims.
- The Peel government imported maize, set up a Relief Commission and, by repealing the Corn Laws, ensured that the price of grain was low.
- The Russell government's response was in three

phases: (1) a programme of public works; (2) government-organised outdoor relief; and (3) outdoor relief provided by local authorities (Poor Law Extension Act, June 1847).
- British voluntary groups provided aid, but by 1847 'famine fatigue' had begun to set in.
- The traditional view is that (1) government inaction increased the scale of the disaster, (2) Charles Trevelyan's attitude ensured that the government did not provide sufficient aid, and (3) food exported from Ireland during the famine could have been used to alleviate the suffering. Revisionists argue against all three points.

Activity 9.6 The Great Famine

ITEM 1 Living conditions before the Famine

An Irish cabin is like a little ark since husband, wife and children, cow and calf, pigs, poultry, dog and frequently cat repose under the same roof. In 87 cabins inspected in Wicklow County, there were 127 full-grown pigs and 47 dogs. The family live upon potatoes and butter milk six days a week. The Sabbath is generally celebrated by bacon and greens. Insufficiency of provision which operates so powerfully against marriage in England is not cared about it Ireland. Lover lingers only until he can find out a dry bank, pick a few sticks, collect some fern, knead a little mud with straw and raise a hut about six feet high, with a door to let in the light and let out the smoke. The happy pair, united by their priest, enter the dwelling and a rapid race of chubby children soon proves by what scanty means life can be sustained. Upon average a man, his wife and four children will eat 37 pounds (16.78 kilos) of potatoes per day.

Adapted from an account by John Carr, an English travel writer, 1806.

An Irish family, with its potato store and livestock, before the Famine.

ITEM 2 Living conditions during the Famine (i)

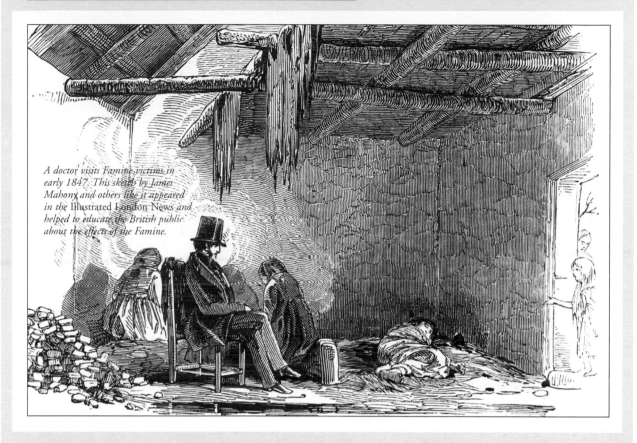

A doctor visits Famine victims in early 1847. This sketch by James Mahony and others like it appeared in the Illustrated London News and helped to educate the British public about the effects of the Famine.

ITEM 3 Living conditions during the Famine (ii)

My hand trembles as I write. The scenes of human misery and degradation we witnessed will haunt my imagination. We entered a cabin. Stretched in one dark corner scarcely visible from the smoke and rags which covered them were three children huddled together. Lying there because they were too weak to rise, pale and ghastly, their little limbs - on removing a portion of the covering - perfectly emaciated. Crouched over the turf embers was another form, wild and all but naked. It stirred not, nor noticed us. On some sodden straw was a shrivelled old woman, imploring us to give her something. Above her on a ledge was a young woman with sunken cheeks who scarcely raised her eyes to answer our enquiries. Many cases were widows whose husbands had recently been taken off by the fever and thus their only pittance, obtained from the public works, entirely cut off. We entered upward of 50 of these cabins. The scene was one and invariable, differing in little but the numbers of sufferers.

Adapted from an account written by William Bennett, an English Quaker who visited Erris in County Mayo to distribute seed in March 1847.

ITEM 4 A senior civil servant's view

Using public money to provide free relief is a false principle which eats into the moral health and prosperity of the people. People conceal their advantages, exaggerate their difficulties and relax their exertions. There is only one way in which the relief of the destitute ever has been or ever will be conducted consistently with the general welfare and that is by making it a local charge. Those who know how to discriminate between the different claims for relief are then motivated to use that knowledge. They are spending their own money. The struggle now is to keep the poor off the rates and, if their labour only replaces the cost of their food, it is cheaper than having to maintain them in perfect idleness.

Adapted from the 'Irish Crisis' by Charles Trevelyan, the senior civil servant who was largely responsible for shaping the British government's policy towards Ireland during the Famine, 1848.

ITEM 5 Statistics on deaths during the Famine

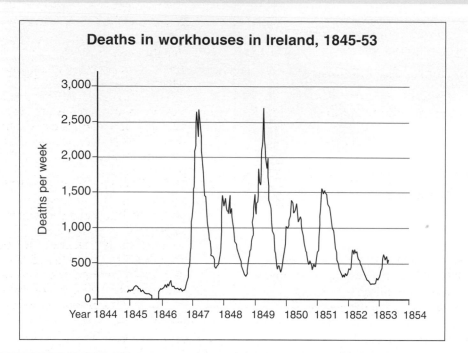

Deaths in workhouses in Ireland, 1845-53

Excess deaths during Famine years, by age and sex (in 1,000s)

	Males				Females			
Age groups	Excess deaths		Av. number in population		Excess deaths		Av. number in population	
		%		%		%		%
0-4	146	(29)	508	(14)	139	(29)	491	(13)
6-9	95	(18)	471	(12)	92	(20)	455	(12)
10-59	204	(40)	2,526	(68)	191	(40)	2,659	(69)
60+	66	(13)	211	(6)	52	(11)	234	(6)
Total	511	(100)	3,716	(100)	474	(100)	3,839	(100)

Source: O'Grada 1993. 'Excess deaths' refers to the number of deaths for each age group in excess of that to be expected in a normal year before the Famine.

Questions

1. Was the Great Famine inevitable? Use Items 1, 2, 3 and 5 in your answer.
2. Explain how and why the scene described in Item 1 was transformed into that pictured in Item 2 and described in Item 3.
3. a) What does Item 5 tell us about the nature and extent of the Famine?
   b) Why was the famine on such a large scale?
4. a) How might a historian use Item 4 to explain the British government's approach during the Great Famine?
   b) To what extent was the British government responsible for the scale of the Great Famine? Use Items 4 and 5 in your answer.

4 The writing of Irish history

Key issues
1. How has the writing of Irish history developed over recent years?
2. What characterises the traditionalist approach?
3. What characterises the revisionist approach?

4.1 What are the main trends in recent historical research?

The historical debate
It can be argued that:
- all historical interpretations are determined to some extent by what is happening at the time when the historian is writing
- all historians write from an ideological perspective.

A study of recent historical research into developments in Ireland in the late 18th century and early 19th century confirms that both these conclusions are valid. Since the 1970s, two very distinct approaches to Irish history have been fighting for supremacy. Each approach is derived from and reflects a particular view of contemporary Ireland and each has a distinct ideological stance. The two approaches can best be termed the 'traditionalist' approach and the 'revisionist' approach.

The traditionalist approach
In simple terms, historians who subscribe to the traditionalist approach are sympathetic to a 'nationalist' interpretation of Irish history. What is meant by the 'nationalist' viewpoint was outlined by Peter Berresford Ellis in a lecture delivered in 1989:

'The "nationalist" historian starts from a basic moral premise - the premise that no nation has any defensible right to invade, conquer and seek to destroy the political, economic, social or cultural fabric of another country. Having assumed this view - that imperialism is wrong in all its forms - the historian can commence to interpret Irish history.' (Ellis 1989, p.9)

In general terms, this approach has the three main elements outlined in Box 9.13. Taken together, these might be said to produce the following view of Irish history:

'For the nationalist community, England's and Britain's involvement in Ireland is an unending story of misrule, from which part of the island escaped only with the establishment of an independent Irish state. Each generation of Irish

BOX 9.13 The traditionalist approach

The traditionalist approach is based on the following three main beliefs:
1. That the British government and British interests dominated Ireland in the late 18th century and early 19th century. Ireland was, in effect, a colony and any decisions of any importance were made by the British. The Irish (especially the Catholics who made up the majority of the population) had no real say.
2. That 18th-century and early 19th-century Ireland was an economically underdeveloped and desperately poor society.
3. That there was a bitter conflict between a ruling landowning elite and the desperately poor peasants - a conflict fuelled by a long history of seizure of land, economic oppression and religious persecution.

Adapted from Connolly 1996.

people produced heroes who fought and usually died to achieve this freedom. Time and again their efforts were betrayed by compromisers who tried to find an accommodation with the English. The continuing British presence in Northern Ireland is the last relic of this misrule.' (Hughes 1994, p.2)

The development of the traditionalist approach
The traditionalist approach itself has a long history stretching back to the 1930s - the period just after southern Ireland gained independence from Britain. The gaining of independence and subsequent developments help to explain the appeal of this historical approach. It helped the new state come to terms with its past and to develop its own, independent identity. At the same time, it had a clear, political (and ideological) goal, as Ellis points out:

'In the context used in Ireland, "nationalism" simply means a policy of securing national rights, the claim of Ireland to be an independent nation...It is a moral stance and one, in my opinion, which goes hand in hand with a socialist view of history.' (Ellis 1989, p.9)

Since the 1970s, however, there has been something of a backlash against this sort of approach to Irish history. Those responsible for this backlash have sometimes been described as 'revisionists'.

The revisionist approach
Although it is difficult to describe exactly what the term 'revisionism' means (see Boyce & O'Day 1996, pp.1-14), it can be characterised as follows:

- revisionists claim to write value-free or objective Irish history
- revisionism is a deliberate reaction against the traditionalist approach
- the starting point of the revisionist approach is the premise that many conclusions reached using the traditionalist approach are simplistic and misleading.

There were attempts to write value-free Irish history in the 1930s (the journal *Irish Historical Studies* was founded in 1938 for this very purpose), but it is only since the 1970s that a concerted effort has been made to substantially alter the view of Irish history put forward by the traditionalists. Since then, the approach has gained so much support that, by 1982, one prominent historian (Roy Foster) could claim: 'We are all revisionists now.'

Ideology and the revisionist approach

Whilst, at first sight, the growth of revisionist Irish history might seem to counter the claim made above that both approaches to Irish history have a distinct ideological stance, in fact the claim remains valid on two grounds.

First, even if revisionists did write value-free history, then their ideological stance (ie that they had no ideology) would be very different from that of traditionalists who admit to writing history from a distinct ideological perspective.

And second, there are good grounds for denying that revisionists actually do write value-free history. Peter Ellis (1989) argues that, in fact, the revisionists do have a political agenda and do bring their values to their work. He argues that the starting point for revisionists is 'the acceptance, overt or implied, that England's invasion and conquest of Ireland is not a matter for moral judgement'. Starting from this point, revisionists arrive at judgements about the past that are very different from traditionalist interpretations, but they are by no means 'value-free'. Take, for example, some of the phrases used by the revisionist Marianne Elliot in her book on Wolfe Tone, one of the leaders of the 1798 rebellion (see Section 1.2). She claims that Wolfe Tone was:

- a negligent husband and father
- no great initiator of ideas
- prickly and self-righteous
- temporarily unhinged in his mind
- not an original thinker.

Whatever the truth behind these statements, they have one thing in common - they are all value judgements. And Marianne Elliot is not the only revisionist to use language like this. In other words, it is misleading to claim that revisionism is value-free. It would be more accurate to say that it has different values from those expressed using the traditionalist approach.

Development of the revisionist approach

As with the traditionalist approach, there is an argument that the development of revisionism reflects the changing political climate in Britain and Ireland. First, there was a sustained attack on socialism and socialist ideas in Britain during the 1980s and, at the end of the decade, Communism collapsed in Eastern Europe raising questions about the accuracy and effectiveness of Marxist (socialist) analysis. This undoubtedly made an impact on historical scholarship. And second, there has been a shift in the Irish government's attitude towards Britain since Ireland joined the EU (in 1973) and especially since the mid-1980s when the Irish and British governments began to work together in the hope of finding a solution to the problems in Northern Ireland. Given these developments, it is no surprise that new interpretations of history which are less hostile towards British rule in Ireland should gain currency.

The impact of the debate

It is necessary to be aware of the debate between the traditionalists and revisionists because that debate has a bearing on any question which is asked of Ireland's past. This unit has attempted to provide the context within which the debate has raged. As space is short, the account is necessarily selective. One task for the reader is to consider how the events described above might be used by either a traditionalist or a revisionist to further their cause.

MAIN POINTS - Part 4

- Since the 1970s, two very distinct approaches to Irish history - the traditionalist and revisionist - have been fighting for supremacy.
- The traditionalist approach is sympathetic to a 'nationalist' interpretation of Irish history and has three core beliefs: (1) that Ireland was treated as a British colony in the period 1700-1900; (2) that Ireland was an economically underdeveloped society during this period; and (3) that, during this period, there was a bitter conflict between a ruling landowning elite and the desperately poor peasants.
- After partition, the traditionalist approach helped the new Irish state come to terms with its past and to develop its own, independent identity.
- Revisionism can be characterised as follows: (1) it is value-free or objective; (2) it is a deliberate reaction against the traditionalist approach; and (3) it assumes that many conclusions reached using the traditionalist approach are simplistic and misleading.
- Revisionism is not actually value-free. Rather, it has different values from those expressed using the traditionalist approach.
- Revisionism gained ground as relations between Ireland and Britain improved and as Marxist ideas came under attack following the collapse of Communism.

Activity 9.7 Traditionalist and revisionist accounts

ITEM 1 A scene from the Uprising of 1798

This cartoon by Cruikshank shows rebels destroying a house and its furniture during the 1798 uprising.

ITEM 2 Interpretation 1

I see the Great Famine as the tragic outcome of three factors: an ecological accident that could not have been predicted, an ideology ill-geared to saving lives and, of course, mass poverty. The role of sheer luck is important. Ireland's ability to cope with a potato failure would have been far greater a few decades later, and the political will - and the political pressure - to spend more money to save lives greater too. Food availability was a problem; nobody wanted the destruction of the Irish as a race.

Adapted from O'Grada 1993.

ITEM 3 Interpretation 2

Unbelievable as it must now seem, English ministers had already done all they were ever going to do to deal with the Irish Famine. Throwing responsibility for relief onto the rates and the Poor Law Unions was the last major positive step the government was to take. Some of those Poor Law Unions, particularly in the west, were already bankrupt. All were going to be strained far beyond their resources by the pressure of the starving thrown upon them. Quite prosperous farmers, ruined by the high rates themselves, sometimes had to become inmates of the workhouses which the rates were levied to sustain. These cruel realities were all too easily lost sight of from Westminster beneath a growing conviction that all that could possibly have been done for Ireland had been done and that Ireland must be left to what Trevelyan in a terrifying phrase described as the 'operation of natural causes'.

Adapted from Kee 1980.

Questions

1. Using Item 1, write (a) a traditionalist account and (b) a revisionist account of the uprising of 1798.
2. Look at Items 2 and 3. Say whether each is a revisionist or a traditionalist account. Explain how you know.
3. Look back through this unit and try to work out whether the author supports a traditionalist or revisionist approach. Provide evidence to support your viewpoint.

References

- **Adelman (1996)** Adelman, P., *Great Britain and the Irish Question 1800-1922*, Hodder and Stoughton, 1996.

- **Beckett (1981)** Beckett, J.C., *The Making of Modern Ireland 1603-1923*, Faber and Faber, 1981.

- **Boyce (1992)** Boyce, D.G., *Ireland 1828-1923*, Historical Association Studies, Blackwell, 1992.

- **Boyce & O'Day (1996)** Boyce, D.G. & O'Day, A. (eds.), *The Making of Modern Irish History: Revisionism and the Revisionist Controversy*, Routledge, 1996.

- **Connolly (1996)** Connolly, S.J., 'Eighteenth-Century Ireland' in *Boyce & O'Day (1996)*.

- **Connolly (1998)** Connolly, S.J., *The Oxford Companion to Irish History*, Oxford University Press, 1998.

- **Downing (1980)** Downing, T. (ed.), *The Troubles*, Thames Macdonald, 1980.

- **Ellis (1989)** Ellis, P.B., *The New Anti-Nationalist School of Historians*, text of a lecture delivered in 1989 from website: www.etect.org/Politics/INAC/historical.revisionism

- **Foster (1988)** Foster, R.F., *Modern Ireland 1600-1972*, Penguin, 1988.

- **Foster (1991)** Foster, R.F., *The Oxford Illustrated History of Ireland*, Oxford University Press, 1991.

- **Gray (1995)** Gray, P., *The Irish Famine*, Thames and Hudson, 1995.

- **Hughes (1994)** Hughes, M., *Ireland Divided: the Roots of the Modern Irish Problem*, University of Wales Press, 1994.

- **Kee (1972)** Kee, R., *The Green Flag Volume 1: The Most Distressful Country*, Penguin, 1972.

- **Kee (1980)** Kee, R., *Ireland: a History*, Abacus, 1980.

- **Kinealy (1995)** Kinealy, C., 'The Famine 1845-52: how England failed Ireland'. *Modern History Review*, Vol.7.1, September 1995.

- **Macdonagh (1977)** Macdonagh, O., *Ireland: the Union and its Aftermath*, Allen and Unwin, 1977.

- **Moody & Martin (1967)** Moody, T.W. & Martin, F.X. (eds.), *The Course of Irish History*, Mercier, 1967.

- **Nowland (1984)** Nowland, K.B., 'O'Connell and Irish nationalism' in *Nowland & O'Connell (1984)*.

- **Nowland & O'Connell (1984)** Nowland, K.B. & O'Connell, M.R. (eds.), *Daniel O'Connell: Portrait of a Radical*, Appletree Press, 1984.

- **O'Brien & O'Brien (1985)** O'Brien C.C. & O'Brien, M., *Ireland: a Concise History*, Thames and Hudson, 1985.

- **O'Ferrall (1985)** O'Ferrall, F., *Catholic Emancipation: Daniel O'Connell and the Birth of Irish Democracy*, Gill and Macmillan, 1985.

- **O'Grada (1993)** O'Grada, C., *Ireland before and after the Famine: Explorations in Economic History 1800-1925*, Manchester University Press, 1993.

- **O'Tuathaigh (1990)** O'Tuathaigh, G., *Ireland before the Famine 1798-1848*, Gill and Macmillan, 1990.

- **Tighe (1802)** Tighe, W., *Statistical Survey of County Kilkenny*, Dublin, 1802.

- **Whyte (1967)** Whyte, J.H., 'The age of Daniel O'Connell' in *Moody & Martin (1967)*.

Index

Aberdeen, Lord 193, 194
Act of Union
    background 254-64
    Catholic emancipation, and 265
    consequences 264-79
    immediate reasons for 261
    impact 264-67
    Irish support for 262
    Repeal movement 183, 201, 274-80
    terms 262
Administration of Justice Act (1774) 8
agriculture
    capitalist 58
    Chartism, and 163
    economy, and 64
    employment in 106
    paternalism 107
    poor relief for labourers 225
    protection 192, 202, 207-8
    riots 94, 104 10
Albert, Prince 206
Althorp, Viscount 215, 217
Amending Act (1825) 68
America, Britain at war with (1812-15) 58, 87
American Non-Intercourse Act (1811) 81
American War of Independence
    British defeat 7
    causes 7, 8
    European nations join 7
    impact on Britain 7-8, 14, 18, 33
    impact on Ireland 259
Amiens, Treaty of 27, 54
Andover Workhouse scandal 238, 239
Anti League 207-8
Anti-Corn Law movement
    businessmen in 135
    Chartism, and 142, 156, 173
    class base 204
    founding 203
    riots 94
    strength 204-6
Anti-Poor Law campaign 234-37, 143
    aristocracy
    concessions 135
    governing 113, 116, 134, 175, 212
    middle class, and 37, 118, 120, 124
    paternalism 107, 233
    support for 44
    working class, and 120, 124, 127, 233
Arnott, Dr Neil 248
Ashley, Lord 197, 198, 199, 200, 215
Association for Preserving Liberty and Property (APLP) 46
Attwood, Thomas 120, 127, 129, 146, 148

Baines, Edward 90, 129
ballot, secret 31, 35, 126, 140
Bank Charter Act (1844) 196
Bell, Andrew 221
Benbow, William 95
Benthamism 229, 230
Bentinck, Lord George 208
Birmingham Political Union 120, 127-28, 129, 132, 146, 162
Black Lamp conspiracy 48, 50-51, 53
Blanketeers 59, 95
Blasphemous and Seditious Libels

Act (1817) 98
bonded warehouses 18-19
Bonham, F.R. 189
Boston Port Act (1774) 8
Boston Tea Party 7, 8
Boyne, Battle of 256, 257
Brandreth, Jeremiah 96
Bright, John 203, 205
Brougham, Henry 129
Burdett, Sir Francis 67, 68, 127
Burke, Edmund 9-10, 37, 115
Bute, Earl of 32, 34

cabinets
    class composition 134
    solidarity of 6, 61, 72, 75
Campo Formio, Treaty of 26
Canada 7, 196
Canada Corn Bill (1843) 196
Canning, George
    appointment by Liverpool 63-64, 70, 74
    career 64
    Disraeli, and 64
    duel with Castlereagh 64
    liberalism 62, 69, 70
    Peel, and 182, 208
    popularity 69
capital punishment 64-65, 66-67
capitalism
    agricultural 58
    opposition to 103
Carlile, Richard 103
Carlton Club 189
Caroline, Queen 63, 64, 75, 89, 98
Cartwright, Edmund 33, 90
Cartwright, Major John 31, 33, 35, 90
Cartwright, William (mill owner) 82, 84
Castlereagh, Viscount
    duel with Canning 64
    Grand Alliance 72
    Irish rebellion, and 61
    reactionary 62
    suicide 63
Catholic Association
    banned 270
    Clare by-election, and 182, 269-70, 273
    formation 68
    success 183, 269-71, 273
    support 273
Catholic Church
    bequests to 201
    discrimination against members 258, 267
    Peel, and 201-2
    priesthood, influence on peasantry 201
    Repeal, and 277
Catholic emancipation
    Act of Union, and 265
    Bills (1825, 1829) 181, 182, 184
    conceded 68, 120, 121-22
    early calls for in Ireland 259-60
    Liverpool, and 61, 60-69, 72-73
    opposition to 34, 121
    Peel, and 68, 179, 181, 182-84, 201-2

    Pitt, and 14, 16, 17, 29
    Roman Catholic Emancipation Act (1829) 267-73
    Tories split by 121, 126
    Wellington supported 121
Catholic Relief Acts 260
Cato Street Conspiracy 97-98, 100, 102
Chadwick, Edwin
    career and achievements 248, 251
    centralisation, advocated by 244, 240, 249
    ideology 229, 230, 246
    medical theories 242, 246-48
    personality 248, 249, 251
    Poor Law Amendment Act (1834), and 249
    Poor Law Commission, and 233, 246
    Report on Intra-Mural Internments 249
    Sanitation Report 242, 247-48, 250
Charitable Bequests Act 201
Chartism
    achievements 173-74, 176
    Anti-Corn Law League, and 142, 156, 173
    Charter, People's 140, 145, 174, 175
    delegates to Convention 147, 154, 155
    economic factors 141, 145, 164, 170
    education 155-56
    failure 170-73, 174-76
    growth 140, 142-45
    Kennington Common 153-54, 155, 160, 167, 172, 173
    Land Plan 156, 159-60
    meetings 147
    membership 163-69
    middle class, and 137, 148, 237, 155-56
    moral and physical force 51, 139, 148-49, 151, 171, 173-74
    National Charter Association 154, 165
    National Conventions 146-48, 149-50, 153
    nature of 139-42, 145, 164-65, 169, 172
    Peel, and 171, 172, 205
    petitions rejected 147-48, 150, 154, 155, 163, 173
    Plug Plot 141, 151, 152-53, 160, 161, 171
    police, and 172, 175
    Reform Act, and 142-43
    regional variations 164-65, 168, 169, 171
    roots 135, 137, 183, 234, 235, 237
    social tension, and 141
    strike tactic 148, 150, 152-53, 160-61, 171
    tactics 146-58
    women members 165-67
    working class, and 139, 141-42, 145, 155-56, 163, 166
    see also Newport Uprising; O'Connor, Feargus
child labour
    conditions 210, 220, 223

education, and 217, 221-22
Factory Acts, and 215-21
hours 216, 217, 221, 223
Mines Act (1842) 216
occupations 224
cholera 242, 246-47, 249
Church
clergymen as magistrates 107
education, and 221
English and Irish united 262
protection of 45
repression by 103
tithes 104, 107, 274
Church and King clubs 45-46, 47-48
Clare by-election 68, 117, 182, 183,
269-70
class, radicalism, and
18th-century 36-37, 38
Poor Law, and 234, 237
Reform Act, and 120, 123-24, 127,
129, 132
Classical Economists 229-30, 246
Clontarf Monster Meeting 201, 277-78
clubs, political 31-32, 33, 37-38, 90, 91,
189
Cobbett, William 89-90, 92, 93, 127, 130
Cobden, Richard 203, 205
Coercion Act (1833) 275
Coercive (Intolerable) Acts (1774) 8
Collins, John 155
Combination Acts (1799, 1800, 1824)
43, 67-68, 70, 91
Commutation Act (1784) 14, 18
Companies Act (1844) 196-97
Complete Suffrage Union 150
conservatism, popular 33-34, 36, 44-48,
87, 114
Conservative Party, development
188-92, 210
Consolidated Fund Act (1787) 19, 20-21
constituencies
boundaries 124
sizes 134, 140
unreformed system 113-14, 117
Constitutional Information, Society for
33, 35, 38, 91
Constitutional Society 43
Corn Laws
Anti-Corn Law League 156, 173,
203-6
cause of economic instability 120
landords benefited from 59, 87
radicalism, and 87-88, 94
Repeal 178, 189, 193, 200, 202-8
sliding scale 58, 67, 195, 204
see also Anti-Corn Law movement
corporation constituencies 113
Corporations Act 276
County Police Act (1839) 172
Crewe, Francis Anne 12
Crewe, John 12
Cromwell, Oliver 16, 256
crowds, behaviour 44-45
Crown see monarchy

Days of May 127-28
Declaratory Act (1720) 258, 259
Defenders (Irish secret society) 260
Devon, Lord 201
Despard conspiracy 48, 50, 51
Disraeli, Benjamin 64, 189, 208

dissenters, religious 45
Duncan, Dr W.H. 244, 251

Earls, Flight of 255, 257
East India Company 8, 11-12, 22
economy
1820s 64, 71, 72
1840s 194
Irish 283-84
radicalism, and 87-88, 107
Eden Treaty 21
Edwards, George (spy) 97, 100
education
Chartism, and 155-56
factories, in 221-22
workhouses, in 238
Eldon, Lord 60, 61, 69
elections
1784 12, 13
1818 63
1830 122
1841 189, 190, 191-92, 204
1847 209
demand for annual 38, 126, 140
Louth (1826) 270
pre-reform 114, 116-18
Elizabeth I, Ireland, and 254-55
Emmet, Robert 51, 266-67
Erskine, Thomas 43
Evans, Thomas 94

Factory Acts
(1802) 220
(1819) 220
(1833) 143, 197, 215-16
(1844) 197, 198, 200, 217
(1847) 217
Chartism, and 170
education, and 221-22
evasion 215-16, 219
families, and 217-18
inspectors 215-16, 219
women, and 216
see also child labour;
Ten Hour movement
Famine, Great Irish
'Gregory Clause' 282
causes 280-81, 283-84, 285
conditions 284-85
course 281
deaths 280, 286
government measures 281-84
outdoor relief 282
Poor Law Extension Act (1847) 282
public works 282
Rate-in-aid 282
voluntary groups, and 282-83
Fielden, John 215, 217, 234
Fitzgerald, Lord Edward 260, 261
Fox, Charles James 10, 11, 13, 15, 37, 115
Fox-North coalition 8, 9, 10
France
1830 revolution 121, 128, 129
trade treaty with 21
war with Revolutionary government
26-27, 46, 51, 57
franchise
18th-century 31, 32, 35, 38
19th-century 113, 120, 123-24, 126,
33-34, 140
free trade

Budgets 195-96, 203, 204, 207
liberalism, and 67
Liverpool, and 67, 69, 77
Peel, and 188, 189, 195-96, 202-7
freeman constituencies 113
Friends of the People, Society of 37
Frost, John 151

Gaols Act (1823) 65
George I 13
George II 9
George III
anti-constitutional 9, 33
Catholic emancipation, and
14, 16, 17
character and ideas 8-9, 16
illness 15
opposed Fox-North coalition 9, 11-12
popularity 34
George IV
King 61, 64, 72, 75, 98
Caroline, and 98
death 122
Prince Regent 10, 58, 95
Gladstone, William 28, 188, 189, 194
Glorious Revolution (1688) 32
Goderich, Lord see Robinson, Frederick
Gordon, Lord George, Protestant
Association 34
Gordon Riots 34
Goulburn Henry 193
Graham, Sir James 193, 197, 200
Grattan, Henry 182, 259, 268
Grattan's Parliament 259-60
Grenville, Lord 75
Grey, Earl
Reform Act, and 122-23
resignation 128, 275

Habeas Corpus, Act
restored 97
rights conferred 43
suspended 43 59, 60, 95, 98, 99
Hampden Clubs 90, 91, 102
Hanoverians 8 see also under George III
Hardy, Thomas (radical) 37, 38, 41, 43
Harney, George Julian 149
Harrowby, Earl 69
Health, Ministry of, origins 238
health, public
burials and graveyards 242, 249
centralisation 244
civil engineering, and 242-44
disease 242, 245, 246-47, 249, 250
housing, and 241
Improvement Commissions 243
industrialisation, and 241-42, 245
local government, and 241
Liverpool 244, 251
London 241, 245, 249
Manchester 251
medical knowledge, and 242, 246,
249
obstacles to progress 242, 249
political rivalries, and 243-44
Poor Law, and 238
population growth, and 241
Public Health Act (1848) 243, 246,
249
reform pressures 246-51
sanitation 241, 244, 245

water supply 242, 244, 245, 249
Health of Towns Association 249
Henry VIII, Ireland, and 254
Henson, Gravener 82
Heytesbury, Lord 201
Hobhouse, Henry 64
Home Office, expansion 43
Horner, Leonard 215, 219
Horsfall, William, assassination 82, 84
hours, working 197, 198, 215-16, 217, 223
Hovering Act (1780) 18
Howe, Admiral 26
Hume, Joseph 67-68, 210
Hunt, Henry 90-91, 94, 95, 97, 101, 127
Huskisson, William 62, 64, 67, 69, 70, 182

income tax
    abolished after war 58, 59, 88
    Peel reintroduces 195, 196, 199
    Pitt introduces 26
India 21-22
India Act (1784) 22
India Bill (Fox's) 11
industrialisation
    Chartism, and 142, 144, 172-73
    constituencies, and 113-14
    economic effects 51, 53, 64
    family unit, and 166, 217
    health, public, and 241-42, 245
    Poor Law, and 238
    radicalism, and 89
    social effects 58, 89, 202
    urbanisation 241
Irish Colleges Bill 201
Irish Famine 203
Irish history, writing of 287-89
Irish labour 104, 107

Jacobinism 25, 30, 37, 41, 99, 114
James II 256

Kay, Dr J.P. 238, 246, 248
Kay-Shuttleworth, James 222
Kennington Common 'fiasco' 141, 153-54, 167, 172, 173

laissez-faire 67, 243, 246
Lancaster, Joseph 221
Liberal Party 188, 189
liberalism
    defined 63
    free trade, and 67
Licensing Act (Charles II) 32
Lichfield House compact 275
Liverpool, Lord
    achievements 71-73, 77
    Cabinet 62, 63
    Canning, and 63-64, 70, 74
    Catholic emancipation, and 61, 68-69, 74
    character 76-77
    Corn Law (1815), and 88
    Disraeli on 56
    early career 57
    elitism 59
    failings 73-74, 76
    ideology 75
    imagination, lack of 74
    longevity 73, 74-75
    luck 74-75

monarchy, and 72
Peel, and 179, 180
Pitt, and 28, 29, 61, 69, 99-100
problems faced 57-58
reforms 60, 64
repression under 59, 72, 74, 91, 98-100, 115
reputation 76-77
skill, political 75
toleration 60, 72
Liverpool Sanitary Act (1846) 244, 251
Lloyd Jones, William 151
Locke, John 63
London Corresponding Society
    agenda 38, 39, 40
    founding 37
    leaders prosecuted 43, 87
    membership 38, 41
    revolutionary survivors 48, 49
    spies infiltrating 43, 49
    structure 38
    threat, seen as 30, 41, 43
    working-class 31
London Working Men's Association 143, 162
Louis XVI, execution 37
Loveless, George 143
Lovett, William 143, 148, 155, 157, 158, 171
loyalism, popular see conservatism, popular
Luddism
    attacks 82-84
    causes 57, 81-82
    croppers 82
    government response 83-86, 91
    machine-breaking 80, 82, 104
    nature of 80-83, 85-86
    post-war 93
    regional variations 80, 81-83, 85
    roots 37, 48, 51, 80
    trade unions, and 80
Lyndhurst, Lord 193

Macaulay, Thomas 118
MacHale of Tuam, Archbishop 277
Madison, US President 58
magistrates
    clergymen 107
    factory owners 216
    Poor Law, and 225, 233, 238
    prison inspectors 65
    role in curbing radicalism 42-43, 45
Maguire, Cuconnacht 255
Malthus, Revd Thomas 228
Marxist history 288
Maynooth Act 183, 200-2
Mealmaker, George 49
Melbourne, Lord 108, 146, 187, 192, 275
merchants, interests and influence 14, 16, 18, 19, 31
Metropolitan Police Act (1829) 172
Metropolitan Poor Act (1841) 238
Michel, John 283
Mill, James 131
Mines Act 1842 197, 198, 200, 216, 218
Misdemeanours Act (1819) 98
monarchy
    decline in power 72
    power 6, 7, 8, 10-11, 134, 187
    support for 34, 44

Monster Meetings 201, 277-79
Morpeth, Lord 249
Muir, Thomas 40, 43
Municipal Corporations Act (1835) 135, 172, 241
Munster plantation 255

Napoleon I 57, 72, 81
national debt 18, 19-20, 26, 58
National Political Union 130
National Union of the Working Class 120
Navigation Acts (1650), relaxation of 67
Navy
    funding 20
    mutinies 48, 49-50, 52-53, 54
    successes in war against France 26
Newcastle, Duke of 128
Newport Uprising 151-52, 157, 171, 173, 175
Newspaper and Stamp Duties Act (1819) 98, 103
Nonconformists, education, and 221-22
North, Lord 7-8, 33
North Briton 32
Northumberland, Lord 271

Oastler, Richard 215, 221, 223, 233, 235
O'Connell, Daniel
    aims 275, 279
    career 268, 272, 275, 276
    Catholic Association, and 68, 121-22
    Clare by-election, and 182, 269-70, 272
    imprisoned 278
    Mayor of Dublin 276
    Melbourne government, and 275
    oratory 269
    Peel, and 181, 201, 276
    personality 272
    Repeal movement, and 201, 274-79
    Veto, and 268
O'Connor, Feargus
    Anti Poor Law campaign, and 237
    career 146
    contribution to Chartism 158-59, 162
    criticisms 154, 158, 160-61, 173
    education, views on 155, 158
    gentleman 127
    Kennington Common, and 160
    Land Plan 156, 159-60
    leadership 160
    Lovett, and 171
    militancy 149, 154, 156, 159, 161
    Northern Star 146, 155, 160, 162, 163, 169
    oratory 159, 161, 162
    personality 146, 158
    Plug Plot 160, 161
    propagandist 160
    strike action, and 148, 160-61
O'Donnell, Rory 255
O'Neill, Hugh 254-55
Old Corruption 113-19
Oliver the Spy 96
Oracle 44
Orange Order 49
Orders in Council (1807) 57, 58, 87
Owen, Robert 220

Paine, Thomas 38, 39, 40, 47, 93, 103
Palmer, Revd Thomas 43

Palmerston, Viscount 217
Parke, Baron 217
Parker, Richard 54
Parliament
    Houses 7, 134, 135, 186
    Irish 258, 259, 264
    Members 134, 140, 275
    reform 34, 35, 36, 38, 63, 74
      (*see also* radicalism; Reform Act)
    role 6
    unreformed 113-15
parties, political, development of 7, 15,
    58, 209
paternalism, breakdown of 107, 233
patriotism
    English 36, 44, 114
    Irish Protestant 258-59
patronage 7, 20, 21, 31, 33, 135
Peace Preservation Force (PPF) 181
Peel, Robert
    aims of second ministry 192-94
    backbenchers, and 193, 200, 208, 211
    background 179-80, 220
    Cabinet 193, 194, 207
    Canning, and 69, 182, 208
    Catholic emancipation, and 68, 179,
      181, 182-84, 201-2
    Chartism, and 172
    Chief Secretary for Ireland 64, 181-84
    Clare by-election, and 183
    Corn Laws, and 178, 193, 202-8,
      212, 281
    death 208, 210
    early career 179-84
    economic policy 194-97
    evaluation 210-12
    Famine, Great Irish, and 281
    free trade 188, 189, 195-96, 202-7
    legacy 189
    legal and prison reforms 64-67, 108,
      179, 181
    liberal 62, 180, 181-82
    minority government (1834) 187
    O'Connell, and 181, 276
    opposition, policy in 186-87
    personality 180, 182, 188, 194, 210-11
    Pitt, and 28
    reactionary 182
    Reform Act (1832), and 182, 189
    Repeal of the Act of Union, and 277
    resignation and period after 208-10
    second administration 192-207
    social policy 142, 197-98, 199-200,
      217
    Swing Riots, and 108
    Tamworth Manifesto 181, 187-88
    Tory Party, and 185, 188-92, 193,
      205, 209, 210-11
    Ultras, and 183, 187, 188, 192, 193,
      206
    Wellington, and 184, 186, 193
Penal Laws 258
penal reform 64-67, 72
Peninsular War 72
Pentrich Rebellion 96, 101
Perceval, Spencer 57, 179
Peterloo Massacre 59-60, 61, 63, 91,
    96-97, 99
Pitt, William, the Younger
    Chancellor of the Exchequer,
     appointed 11

commercial policy 21
free trade, and 21
French Revolution, and 25
George III, and 16
legacy 28-29
luck 13-14
political skill 14-15, 25
pragmatism 21
repression 42-48
retention of power 13-15
Tory Party, and 15
wartime coalition 15
wartime leader 25-27
Catholic emancipation, and 14, 16,
    17, 262
reforms 14, 17-21
'Reign of Terror' 15, 17, 25
national revival, and 18, 21-22, 23-24
consolidation of power base 12-13
PM, appointed 6-12, 16
Place, Francis 67-68, 128, 129, 130,
    131, 148
plantations 255
Plug Plot 141, 151, 152-53, 171, 173
Plunkett, William 268
pocket boroughs 113, 123
police force
    Chartism, and 172, 175
    Irish (PPF) 181, 265
    Metropolitan 65, 172, 179
    planned 65
political unions 102, 120, 126-27, 146
Poor Law, Old
    Act of Settlement (1662) 225
    criticisms of 226, 230-31
    Elizabethan Act (1601) 224-25
    Gilbert's Act 225
    operation 225-26
    Speenhamland System 106, 226-28,
      230
    Workhouse Act (1722) 225
Poor Law Amendment Act (1834)
    Chadwick, and 249
    Chartism, and 143
    continuities with old system 233,
      237-38
    effectiveness 238-40
    features 233
    operation 235, 237-38
    opposition to 143, 233-37
    Peel, and 198
Poor Law Board 238
Poor Law Commission
    administrative 233
    composition 229
    ideology and conduct 229-30
    Report 230-31, 232, 248
Poor Law Extension Act (1847) 282
Poor Law Unions 233, 235
poor relief
    health, public, and 246-47
    spending 89, 106, 225, 237, 246-47
population growth
    Corns Laws, and 202
    health, public, and 241, 245
    Irish Famine, and 281
    radicalism, and 88-89
Portland, Duke of 11, 15
potwalloper constituencies 113
Poynings Law (1494) 258, 259
Preston, Thomas 94

press
    freedom 103
    influence 32, 39, 89-90, 235
    North Briton 32
    Northern Star 146, 155, 160, 162,
      163, 169
    Oracle 44
    stamp duty, and 143
    Sun 44
    True Briton 44
Price, Richard 19-20, 35
Prime minister, role of 6-7
prison reform 65
Protestants, Irish 258-59, 268, 271
Public Health Act (1848) 243, 246, 249
Publications Act (1819) *see* Newspaper
    and Stamp Duties Act (1819)

Quartering Act (1774) 8

radicalism
    1820s 103-4
    aims 36, 38, 39
    class, and 36-37, 103-4, 119-20,
      132, 137
    clubs 31, 33, 35, 37-38
    defined 31
    economy, and 87-88, 102, 103, 104,
      120-21
    French Revolution, and 36-42, 44, 87
    ideology 39, 40, 93
    industrialisation, and 89, 93
    leadership 32-33, 34, 37, 39, 103
    National Convention 39-40
    opposition to 33-34, 37, 42-48, 98-99
    population growth, and 88-89
    press 39 89-90, 92, 143, 235
    revival after Napoleonic War
      58, 87, 93
    tactics 38-39, 129, 130
    taxes, and 88, 129
    unemployment, and 87, 88, 89, 91,
      104, 169
    urbanisation, and 31, 88-89
    violence, real or threatened 104, 130,
      131-32
railways 170
Rebellion of 1798 (Irish) 260, 261,
    262-63, 289
Reciprocity of Duties Act (1823) 67
Reeves, John 46
Reeves Associations 45, 46
Reform Act (1832)
    Chandos Amendment 124, 133, 134
    Chartism, and 142-43
    conservatism 124
    impact 134-37
    Irish MPs, and 275
    middle class, and 119-20, 124
    motives behind 112, 123-26
    need for 113-14, 116-19
    passage 122
    Peel, and 185-86
    Pitt anticipated 28, 29
    terms 133
    Tory arguments against 115
    working class, and 127, 135, 141
Regency Crisis 15, 17
republicanism 39, 40, 49
Revenue Act (1767) 8
revolution

fear of 115, 121, 131
requirements for 102
threat of 48-54, 95-98, 102, 123,
128-32, 151
Revolution, French (1789)
Britain, impact on 30, 36-54,
57, 81-82
conservative reaction to 114
extremism 37, 115
Ireland, impact on 260
masses approved 102
welcomed in Britain 36
Ricardo, David 229-30
Richards, W.J. *see* Oliver the Spy
riots
'Bread or Blood' 94, 235
anti-Corn Law 93
Birmingham 45-46, 148
Bristol 122, 127, 128, 130
Church and King 45-46, 50
Derby 122
food 36, 39, 50, 93
Gordon (1780) 34
Manchester 45-46
nature of 44-45
Newport 151-52
Nottingham 122, 127, 128, 130
Poor Law, and 235
Swing 105-9, 121
Rising of 1641 (Irish) 255-56
Robinson, Frederick (Lord Goderich, then Ripon) 62, 64, 67, 69, 70, 182, 193
Rockingham Whigs
see Whigs, Rockingham group
Rockingham, Marquess of 10-11
Roebuck, Arthur 131, 143, 144
Roman Catholic Relief Bill (1778) 34
rotten boroughs 16, 22, 33, 38, 113, 115, 116, 133
Russell, Lord John 66, 74, 122, 123, 207, 281-82

Sadler, Michael 215
Scot and Lot constituencies 113
Seditious Meetings Act (1795) 43, 44, 59, 60, 98
Seditious Meetings Prevention Act (1819) 98
Seizure of Arms Act (1819) 98
Senior, Nassau 229, 248
Septennial Act (1716) 13
Settlement, Law of 106-7
Sheffield Society for Constitutional Information 38
Shelburne, Earl of 10, 11
Shelley, Percy 91
Sherwin, William 90
Short Time Committees 219, 221, 234
Sidmouth, Lord 59, 62, 69, 89
sinecures 14, 20
Sinking Fund 14, 18, 19-20
Six Acts 59, 98, 99
Smith, Adam 21, 63
Smith, Dr Edward 238
Smith, Dr Southwood 248, 251
smuggling 18
Spa Fields meetings 61, 94-95
Speenhamland System
see under Poor Law, Old
Spenceans 94-95, 97-98
spies, government 43, 49, 54, 63, 83-84,

96, 97
Supporters of the Bill of Rights, Society of 33
Stamp Act (1767) 8
Stamp Duty on Newspapers Act (1819) 143
Stanley, Viscount 193
Stationery Office 20
Stephens, Joseph Rayner 140, 215, 235
Sturge, Joseph 156
suffrage *see* franchise
Sugar Crisis (1844) 196, 197
Sun 44
Swing Riots
aftermath 108-9
causes 105-7, 110, 121, 129
characteristics 105
conservative nature 108
distribution 105-6, 109, 121
duration 105
forms of protest 104-5
government response 108
machine-breaking 105
participants 108

Tamworth Manifesto 181, 187-88, 190
Tara Monster Meeting 279
tariffs, trade 67, 70, 88, 92, 195-96
taxes
radicalism, and 88, 129
shop 19
tea 7, 8, 18
tobacco 18, 19
window 19
wines and spirits 18, 19
see also income tax
Temple, Earl 12
Ten Hour movement 197, 198, 215, 217, 219, 221, 223
Thistlewood, Arthur 94, 97
Thompson, Baron, Judge 84
Tithe Rentcharge Act (1838) 276
Tolpuddle Martyrs 143-44, 233
Tone, Wolfe 260, 261, 263, 288
Tooke, John Horne 43
Toryism
defined 59
development of modern 178, 188-92
Liberal 56, 62, 63, 69-71, 180, 181-82
party organisation 189
Reactionary 58-59, 62, 63
split 121, 123, 178
Ultras 69, 121
Townsend, Charles 8
trade unions
Chartism, and 170-71
Combination Laws, and 43, 67-68, 91, 121
Luddism, and 80
radicals failed to cooperate with 39
Reform Act, and 121
strikes 67, 68, 91, 104, 144
Whig attacks on 143-44
Toulon, British forces landed at 26
Training Prevention Act (1819) 98
Treasonable and Seditious Practices Act (1795) 43
Trevelyan, Charles 283, 284
True Briton 44
'Two Acts' 43, 44, 54

Ulster plantation 255
unemployment 87, 88, 89, 91, 104, 106, 144, 169, 234, 238
United Irishmen 49, 50, 260
United Scotsmen, Society of 49
United Societies 37, 48, 49, 90
Unlawful Oaths Act (1797) 143
Utilitarianism 229, 230, 246-48

Vaccination Act (1840) 238
Vansittart, Nicholas 62
Vincent, Henry 151
Vinegar Hill, Battle of 260, 263
Volunteers, loyalist 46

Walker, Benjamin 84
Wallace, Thomas 67
Walpole, Sir Robert 18, 19
Walsall by-election 204-5
Watson, James (father and son) 94-95
Wellington, Duke of (Arthur Wellesley)
Canning, opposed to 69
caretaker government (1834) 187, 275
Catholic emancipation, and 121, 184-85, 270
Chartists, and 153
conservatism 115, 118
failed to form ministry 122-23, 127, 128
fall of government 183
Peel, and 179, 184, 186, 193
William IV, and 122-23
West Indies 22, 26
Whigs
Catholic emancipation favoured by 75
Chartism, and 143
divided 75
families 7
French Republic, and 37
landowning 8-9, 123
legal reforms 66
Liverpool, and 72
reform, and 116, 123-26, 143
Rockingham group 8-10, 11
working class, and 233
Whiteboy movement 258
Wilkes, John 31-33, 34
William IV
Melbourne, dismisses 187
Reform Act (1832), and 122
William of Orange 256, 257
Williams, Zephaniah 151
Wood, Charles 209
Wood, John 215
Wooler, Thomas 90, 92
workhouses
conditions 236, 238-40
inadequate 238
'less eligibility' concept 230, 231, 236, 237-40
scandals 238
Workhouse Act (1722) 225
working-class fear of 234
Wynn, Charles 69
Wyvill, Revd Christopher 33, 35

Yellow Ford, Battle of 254, 255
Yorkshire Association 33, 34
Yorktown, Battle of 7
Young Ireland group 277, 283

ACKNOWLEDGEMENTS

Dedication

To Jackie, Jane, Sarah, Ruth, Lisa, Maisie, Esme, Daisy and James

Acknowledgements

Cover design	Caroline Waring-Collins (Waring Collins Ltd)
Page design	Caroline Waring-Collins (Waring Collins Ltd)
Graphic origination	Derek Baker (Waring Collins Ltd)
Graphics	Tim Button (Waring Collins Ltd)
Reader	Wendy Janes

Unit 8, Part 1, written by John Pickford.

Picture Credits

Mary Evans Picture Library 8, 9, 10, 11, 23, 28 (all), 34, 39, 52, 61, 70 (both), 77, 85, 86, 93, 98, 101 (bottom), 149, 157 (both), 167, 169, 206, 212, 218, 220, 222, 223, 228, 231, 245, 247, 250, 257 (bottom), 261 (right), 262, 263, 266 (right), 272, 284, 289

National Portrait Gallery 16

TopFoto.co.uk 17, 27, 40, 41, 47, 100, 101 (top), 110, 145, 162, 175, 184, 199, 236, 240, 257 (top right), 261 (left), 264, 266 (left), 273, 278, 279, 285

Bridgeman Art Library 24

Thomas Ryan RHA 257 (top left)

Cover pictures

All Mary Evans Picture Library (clockwise from top-left: Chartist petition delivered, Pitt, Peterloo, pauper).

Every effort has been made to locate the copyright owners of materials used in this book. Any omissions are regretted and, if brought to the attention of the publisher, will be credited in subsequent printings.

British Library in Publication Data. A catalogue record of this book is available from the British Library.

ISBN 1-902796-19-5

Causeway Press Limited, PO Box 13, Ormskirk, Lancs, L39 5HP

© Derek Peaple, Tony Lancaster
First impression 2003

Printed and bound by Scotprint